C0-AYQ-396

Contemporary Authors

Autobiography Series

ISSN 0748-0636

Contemporary

Authors

Autobiography Series

Mark Zadrozny

Editor

volume **8**

Gale Research Inc. • Book Tower • Detroit, Michigan 48226

Contents

Preface

Each volume in the *Contemporary Authors Autobiography Series (CAAS)* presents an original collection of autobiographical essays written especially for the series by noted writers. *CAAS* has grown out of the aggregate of Gale's long-standing interest in author biography, bibliography, and criticism, as well as its successful publications in those areas, like the *Dictionary of Literary Biography, Contemporary Literary Criticism, Something about the Author, Author Biographies Master Index,* and particularly the bio-bibliographical series *Contemporary Authors (CA),* to which this *Autobiography Series* is a companion.

As a result of their ongoing communication with authors in compiling *CA* and other books, Gale editors recognized that these wordsmiths frequently had more to say—willingly, even eagerly—than the format of existing Gale publications could accommodate. Personal comments from authors in the "Sidelights" section of *CA* entries, for example, often indicated the intriguing tip of an iceberg. Inviting authors to write about themselves at essay-length was the almost-inexorable next step. Added to that was the fact that the collected autobiographies of current writers were virtually nonexistent. Like metal to magnet, Gale customarily responds to an information gap—and met this one with *CAAS*.

Purpose

This series is designed to be a congenial meeting place for writers and readers—a place where writers can present themselves, on their own terms, to their audience; and a place where general readers, students of contemporary literature, teachers and librarians, even aspiring writers can become better acquainted with familiar authors and make the first acquaintance of others. Here is an opportunity for writers who may never write a full-length autobiography (and some shudder at the thought) to let their readers know how they see themselves and their work, what carefully laid plans or turns of luck brought them to this time and place, what objects of their passion and pity arouse them enough to tell us. Even for those authors who have already published full-length autobiographies there is the opportunity in *CAAS* to bring their readers "up to date" or perhaps to take a different approach in the essay format. At the very least, these essays can help quench a reader's inevitable curiosity about the people who speak to their imagination and seem themselves to inhabit a plane somewhere between reality and fiction. But the essays in this series have a further potential: singly, they can illuminate the reader's understanding of a writer's work; collectively, they are lessons in the creative process and in the discovery of its roots.

CAAS makes no attempt to give an observer's-eye view of authors and their works. That outlook is already well represented in biographies, reviews, and critiques published in a wide variety of sources, including *Contemporary Authors, Contemporary Literary Criticism,* and the *Dictionary of Literary Biography.* Instead, *CAAS* complements that perspective and presents what no other source does: the view of contemporary writers that is reflected in their own mirrors, shaped by their own choice of materials and their own manner of storytelling.

CAAS is still in its youth, but its major accomplishments may already be projected. The series fills a significant information gap—in itself a sufficient test of a worthy reference work. And thanks to the exceptional talents of its contributors, each volume in this series is a unique anthology of some of the best and most varied contemporary writing.

Scope

Like its parent series, *Contemporary Authors,* the *CA Autobiography Series* aims to be broad-based. It sets out to meet the needs and interests of the full spectrum of readers by providing in each volume twenty to thirty essays by writers in all genres whose work is being read today. We deem it a minor publishing event that more than twenty busy authors are able to interrupt their existing writing, teaching, speaking, traveling, and other schedules to converge on a given deadline for any one volume. So it is not always possible that all genres can be equally and uniformly represented from volume to volume. Of the nineteen writers in Volume 8, about half are poets, with the other half made up of novelists. Like most categories, these oversimplify. Only a few writers specialize in a single area. The range of writings by authors in this volume also includes books of nonfiction as well as quite different work in music and the plastic arts.

Format

Authors who contribute to *CAAS* are invited to write a "mini-autobiography" of approximately 10,000 words. In order to give the writer's imagination free rein, we suggest no guidelines or pattern for the essay. The only injunction is that each writer tell his or her own story in the manner and to the extent that each finds most natural and appropriate. In addition, writers are asked to supply a selection of personal photographs, showing themselves at various ages, as well as important people and special moments in their lives. Barring unfortunate circumstances like the loss or destruction of early photographs, our contributors have responded graciously and generously, sharing with us some of their most treasured mementoes, as this volume readily attests. This special wedding of text and photographs makes *CAAS* the kind of reference book that even browsers will find seductive.

A bibliography appears at the end of each essay, listing the author's book-length works in chronological order of publication. If more than one book has been published in a given year, the titles are listed in alphabetic order. Each entry in the bibliography includes the publication information for the book's first printing in the United States and Great Britain. Generally, the bibliography does not include later reprintings, new editions, or foreign translations. Also omitted from this bibliography are articles, reviews, and other contributions to magazines and journals. The bibliographies in this volume were compiled by members of the *CAAS* editorial staff from their research and the lists of writings provided by many of the authors. Each of the bibliographies has been submitted to the author for review. When the list of primary works is extensive, the author may prefer to present a "Selected Bibliography." Readers may consult the author's entry in *CA* for a more complete list of writings in these cases.

Each volume of *CAAS* includes a cumulative index that cites all the essayists in the series as well as the subjects presented in the essays: personal names, titles of works, geographical names, schools of writing, etc. The index format is designed to make these cumulating references as helpful and easy to use as possible. For every reference that appears *in more than one essay,* the name of the essayist is given before the volume and page number(s). For example, W.H. Auden is mentioned by several essayists in the series. The index format allows the user to identify the essay writers by name:

Auden, W.H.
  Abse **1:**24, 31
  Allen **6:**18, 24
  Ashby **6:**36, 39, 43
  Belitt **4:**60, 65
  Bourjaily **1:**68
  Bowles **1:**86

For references that appear *in only one essay,* the volume and page number(s) are given but the name of the essayist is omitted. For example:

CAAS is something more than the sum of its individual essays. At many points the essays touch common ground, and from these intersections emerge new mosaics of information and impressions. *CAAS* therefore becomes an expanding chronicle of the last half-century—an already useful research tool that can only increase in usefulness as the series grows. And the index here, for all its pedestrian appearance, is an increasingly important guide to the interconnections of this chronicle.

Looking Ahead

All of the writers in this volume begin with a common goal—telling the tale of their lives. Yet each of these essays has a special character and point of view that set it apart from its companions. Perhaps a small sampler of anecdotes and musings from the essays ahead can hint at the unique flavor of these life stories.

Gabriel Josipovici, commenting on the problems of the form: "Autobiography and memoirs can never make manifest their own limitations. They always give the illusion (to their authors as well as to their readers) that they are adequate to the task in hand. Only fiction can point to its own limits, can remind us that not everything has been said or can be said. Autobiography fosters the illusion that our lives are stories and as such can be told. It thus does nothing to appease the deep sense we all have that this is not so."

H. R. F. Keating, defining what can and should be told: "So I find I can commit this self-description only by looking at myself from afar, by pondering what influences made me the writer that I am, by asking myself what contributions came from ever more distant ancestors. My life in terms of the events that have occurred has been no different from thousands, from millions, of others. It is worth no particular record. But the books that it has come to me to write are, perhaps, perhaps, worth considering. An account of how they came to come to be must constitute my life story."

Raymond Federman, reflecting on the link between the time of his youth and his art: "In retrospect, the first twenty-five years of my life certainly contained enough drama, enough adventures, misadventures, and misfortunes to inspire several novels. I lived those years oblivious to myself and to the sordid affairs of the world around me, unaware that the experiences I was living, or I should say enduring, would someday make a writer of me. My life began in incoherence and discontinuity, and my work has undoubtedly been marked by this. Perhaps that is why it has been called experimental."

Edwin Honig, considering the challenge of life: "Somewhere in the night back then—possibly later too, there came to me, and still occasionally comes, something unspoken but seen, heard, or simply felt: a sense of the fascination of new beginnings, the beginnings that invite us to be free. They tell that simply by living we are visited by the possibility of freedom each day without knowing how to take it. The moment tells us that we are not merely locksteppers in a constant duty drill but free agents able to erase time for an hour, a day, a year, erase time with full consciousness of who we are. And however locked in we are, or determined to be so, a quick flash of recognition continues to invite us to seize the freedom we abjure. The recognition may come unannounced in an ordinary glimpse—say, while driving by in a car—of a girl in her early twenties walking, bent, or squatting on the street. And the girl is suddenly transformed into another me, starting out again, desperately wanting things with the ravenous need that will last a lifetime. She becomes some opposite young me in whom I embrace again the lost vision of the burden that comes with freedom—wishing for it and wanting to avoid it, both."

These brief examples can only suggest what lies ahead in this volume. The essays will speak differently to different readers; but they are certain to speak best, and most eloquently, for themselves.

Acknowledgments

A special word of thanks to all the writers whose essays appear in this volume. They have given as generously of their enthusiasm and good humor as of their talent. We are indebted.

Authors Forthcoming in *CAAS*

Mulk Raj Anand (novelist, short-story writer, nonfiction writer, critic)—As an eminent guide to the culture and life of India, Anand has increased the world's understanding of the great Asian subcontinent through such powerful books as *Untouchable* and *Confession of a Lover.*

Robert Creeley (poet, novelist, short-story writer, essayist, editor)—In such major collections of poems as *For Love, Words,* and *Pieces,* Creeley uses wit and his subtle feeling for measure to give unique definition to the dilemmas of identity and human relationships.

Etheridge Knight (poet, short-story writer, essayist, editor)—The author of *Poems from Prison, Born of a Woman,* and *Belly Song,* Knight employs traditional oral and musical forms found in jazz and the blues to produce his colloquial verse.

Tadeusz Konwicki (novelist, short-story writer, filmmaker, journalist)—Konwicki's artistic vision, as seen in his satiric novels *A Dreambook of Our Time* and *The Polish Complex,* has been shaped by the idealism and tragic events that mark both his life and his country's history.

Jessica Mitford (essayist, journalist)—Her *American Way of Death* and *Kind and Unusual Punishment* are muckraking masterpieces. Equally renowned for her autobiographies, Mitford is a writer of wonderful humor, profoundly concerned with civil liberties.

Sławomir Mrożek (dramatist, short-story writer, cartoonist)—Penetrating critiques of modern society in the idiom of the absurd, Mrożek's plays—*Tango* in particular—enjoy great popularity with his fellow Poles, though not always with the authorities.

Harry Mark Petrakis (novelist, short-story writer, screenwriter, educator)—In such novels as *Nick the Greek, A Dream of Kings,* and the award-winning *Odyssey of Kostas Volakis,* Petrakis combines an enthusiasm for life with elements of classical tragedy in exploring the lives of Greek immigrants in America.

Gregory Rabassa (translator, writer, educator)—Rabassa's award-winning English translations have introduced the modern classics of Cortázar, García Márquez, and Vargas Llosa to new readers everywhere.

Khushwant Singh (novelist, short-story writer, historian, journalist, editor)—Singh integrates humor and stark realism in his novels dealing with the conflicts of contemporary Indian life. *Train to Pakistan* and *I Shall Not Hear the Nightingale* have established him as an eloquent, sardonic observer of a turbulent world.

Bernard Slade (playwright, screenwriter)—First an actor and then a successful writer for television, Slade later returned to the theater and became well known as the author of the hit *Same Time, Next Year*, which, like many of his plays, is a lighthearted, poignant look at love and marriage in modern times.

Wallace Stegner (novelist, short-story writer, editor, critic)—Well known for his Pulitzer Prize–winning novel *Angle of Repose*, Stegner adds a dimension to the problems of human ethics and the quest for identity by exploring them against the backdrop of the rugged, rootless American West.

Anne Stevenson (poet)—A unique blend of objectivity and emotion, traditional and modern poetic forms, Stevenson's verse explores love, loss, solitude, and family history. Her collections include *Living in America, Enough of Green,* and *Correspondences: A Family History in Letters.*

Contemporary Authors

Autobiography Series

John Brunner

1934-

A SHORT AUTOBIOGRAPHY

John Brunner: "Showing off with my awards and some of my output"

Have you ever met your *Doppelgänger*? If not, I wish you never may. I've undergone the experience and can assure you that it's most unpleasant.

I began to suspect the existence of my going-double in December 1969, when during its meeting at Denver, Colorado, the Modern Language Association devoted its annual symposium on science fiction to a single book that happened to be one of mine: *Stand on Zanzibar.* Full confirmation followed in 1975. A genial guy called Joseph Wayne DeBolt from Central Michigan University had been using that novel to provoke discussion among his sociology students. Pleased with the results, he decided to compile a book about my work. He visited my home in Somerset, originally for a weekend, and in the upshot stayed more like ten days. The fruit of his endeavours was called *The*

Happening Worlds of John Brunner, published by Kennikat Press. It contained a biography, a bibliography, various critical studies, and a response by myself.

My friends were puzzled to know why I didn't feel over the moon. After all, wasn't it a signal honour, immensely flattering? Especially since I had barely passed forty!

All that was true enough. But, you see, this was when I met my *Doppelgänger* face to face. I had to confront the alarming truth that there are two John Brunners in the world: the person I think of as the Real Me, and Another, constructed by readers, critics, and academics on the basis of my published output.

The latter is larger than me, louder than me, better known than me—and over his actions I have absolutely no control. I'll do my best to keep him from intruding into what follows.

But I dare not offer any guarantee.

*"With my mother, Felicity, at the age of,
I suppose, about two"*

At least, though, I can start by setting forth some facts into which he can't poke his nose because they relate to a time before he existed.

I was born into the unsettled world of the 1930s. Like all the best people I'm a mongrel. I'm mostly English, but with a lot of Celtic—Scots-Irish and Manx—and even a dash of Russian on my mother's side, while my family name, which is Swiss, traces back to a long line of Protestant pastors in Canton Zürich. One of them, a namesake, moved to Britain in 1832 to work as a teacher near Liverpool. His son, another John, became half of Brunner Mond (eventually part of ICI) and immensely rich. So was my father, his grandson, until the Wall Street Crash. He was in China at the time, out of reach, and lost his fortune. He used to grouse endlessly about not being able to give his children the "advantages" he had enjoyed. But I stopped worrying about that when I heard him and his sister arguing about whether they had had twenty-five or twenty-nine servants. Not my scene!

My mother, Amy Whittaker, was the daughter of a strange and secretive man about whom even his children knew almost nothing except that he played bass and wrote arrangements for the leading London dance bands. Tall and slim with long dark hair, she became a model and adopted the name Felicity, by which she has been known ever since. She and my father had something in common even before they met, for he too had changed his name. His parents had had the bad taste to baptise him Egbert, but he managed to survive at school by creating the vague impression that his *E* stood for Ebenezer. In his teens he acquired the nickname Tony—stylish, fashionable—and at twenty-one he converted it officially to Anthony. Who could blame him?

When I was born, they were living at a house in Oxfordshire, near the Thames. I picture it less from actual memory than from the watercolour paintings of its magnificent gardens that hang in my mother's present home, for we left it when I was about three. The RAF had decided to build a new base nearby, and if there was to be a war—as seemed increasingly probable—airfields would be high on the list for enemy attack.

Followed, for a year, a rented house near Oxford, and after that a Georgian manor at Towersey, near Thame, site nowadays of a famous folk festival that I must get around to attending. It was there, towards the end of 1938, that my father gave me what he always swore was my one and only reading lesson. Sitting with him in a chintz-covered armchair, in the drawing-room which was often so cold that frost-flowers formed on the windows, I was led through a story in *Chicks' Own Annual*. It concerned a little girl who grew tired of her doll and golliwog and left them on a sand castle to be washed away by the tide. Just in time she changed her mind, and a helpful grown-up rescued them.

Oddly, the little girl was called Marjorie.

With the outbreak of war Towersey Manor was sold to the Hays Wharf Company. We moved again, this time to Brimfield, near Ludlow. There I was taken to a metalworking shop and saw what weapons were being improvised for the Home Guard against the threat of invasion: pikes and daggers and drainpipes converted into launchers for homemade rockets.

My father was turned down for military service owing to a back injury—he'd fallen off a polo pony—and decided to run a farm as his contribution to the war effort. The one he bought was near Droitwich in Worcestershire, and it became my favourite childhood home. It was a half-timbered Elizabethan manor with Jacobean additions. A canal ran behind it, with a swing bridge where I loved to sit and watch the water, and nearby grew one of the many rivals to the Boscobel Oak as the tree up which King Charles had to hide after losing the Battle of Worcester.

There, when I was six going on seven, certain things of major importance happened to me.

I woke one morning to discover pus leaking out of my ear and staining my pillow. Later I was told that I'd come within the ace of cerebrospinal meningitis. They managed to cure me with sulfa drugs—hard to come by at the time, being mainly reserved for the forces.

As a result, I lost the use of the semicircular canals on that side, and along with it part of my sense of balance. I did learn to ride a bicycle, but I could never mount one on the move, and to this day I find it risky to climb even a short ladder.

This was far from the first of my illnesses. When I went for my RAF medical at eighteen, the doctor looked at my medical history and inquired, "Were you a sickly child?" I'd never thought of myself as such, but it is true that whatever was going around I seemed to catch. It was at the same house, for instance, that I went down with scarlet fever, which to my fury prevented me from seeing the film of Rafael Sabatini's *Black Swan*. I was looking forward to it because it was in Technicolor.

And it was also on that farm that I fell from a haystack on to a brick threshing floor and tore all the ligaments in my right ankle, leaving me with another weakness from which I have never recovered. Once, in London, I had to wear a high heel for six months. I grew very bored with that pair of shoes.

Of the events that were ultimately to affect me most deeply, however, one had already taken place, only I didn't find out until years afterward. The other . . .

I have often said that the best thing my parents ever did for me was raise me in a house full of books, for as soon as I learned to read by myself, I preferred it over any other pastime. But these books, as a result of our frequent moves, weren't properly sorted or shelved, and one which wound up by mistake in my nursery "printed" me as permanently as one of Konrad Lorenz's geese. It was *The War of the Worlds*.

Precisely why it should have been that book, rather than any of the others I was devouring (*Robinson Crusoe*, Agatha Christie, Kipling, *The Old Curiosity Shop*, regardless of whether or not I understood them), which had so determinative an effect, I can only guess. Perhaps it was our wartime awareness that victory would go to the side with more and superior machines. At all events, I realised that this was my favourite kind of reading and yearned for more.

A cupboard in an outbuilding yielded *The Time Machine*. Verne's *Clipper of the Clouds* was a birthday present. A visit to a shop where wastepaper was being salvaged was my first introduction to the D. C. Thomson comics, for some of them featured a serial about Earthmen roaming from planet to planet in a spaceship based on Cavor's, and I begged to read them before they were pulped. By now we had Land Girls helping with the farm work, and it was thanks to the boyfriend of one of them that I encountered my first real science fiction magazine. The lead story concerned a robot who became so like a human that he fell in love . . .

All this, though, still left me unsatisfied. When I was nine, having run out of stories to read, I attempted one of my own. I remember only two things about it: it featured a Martian called Gloop (not, on reflection, an ideal choice); and I couldn't figure out how to put an ending on it.

But that was a real landmark. From that day on I knew what I was going to be when I grew up—not a pilot, not an explorer, not a racing-driver, but a writer.

My education was more than somewhat haphazard owing to our frequent moves. I was sent to school, I had governesses, I shared a governess with friends of my parents, I was sent to other schools, and we moved again as the war drew to its close, this time back to Oxfordshire, near a town with the improbable name of Nettlebed. From that house my parents dispatched me to boarding school.

I had never bitten my nails before. I did so for the next six years.

Looking back later, I worked out that this was because my subconscious mind interpreted being sent away while my sisters were allowed to remain at home as being rejected by my parents in their favour.

I have, or rather had, two sisters. Verena, three years my junior, took a late degree at Edinburgh, where she met and married a nice guy called Arthur Thornton, who designs electronic testing gear for Hewlett-Packard. They have two bright little girls—whom I must soon stop calling little, come to think of it. My sister Jennifer, five years my junior, married one John Marchant, bore him two children, and died of cancer at forty. Young Anthony went into the furniture trade; young Verena—we tend to have a limited repertoire of names, we Brunners, as you may have noticed—graduated in law and, I am glad to say, is doing well.

In passing: I remember how amused I was when I learned, from James Cleugh's *Love Locked Out*, that Verena is the patron saint of prostitutes, and her image hangs in Swiss brothels.

I was not amused to find out, much later, about

the third major event of my early life, which I referred to above. I should have had another sister. But she died.

Oddly enough, though, when I was finally told, I was relieved. To explain why, I'd have to take a long detour into the future, so for the moment I'll revert to chronological order, more or less. Where was I? Oh, yes: biting my nails.

At that time I was a conceited but desperately insecure little boy, proud of my knowledge gained from reading but terrified of my own age-group, whom I always seemed to meet as strangers, thanks to living in six homes by the time I was ten. As a result I was forever striving to make an impression, to disguise an underlying pathological shyness. Not long before, I'd been invited to a party held for the children of a neighbour. I knew them, I played with them sometimes, but the prospect of having to attend their party made me physically sick. I recovered as soon as I was told I didn't have to go after all.

But there was no choice when it came to Saint Andrew's, Pangbourne. Nor when I went off to it at the start of one term and came back at the end to yet another strange house.

Oh, there were worse schools, I'm sure, even though about the first thing they did to me there was ruin Dickens for me. I'd read one of his novels for fun; they forced me to study and answer questions about a child's abridgment of *David Copperfield,* and that was that. To this day I've never managed to finish another book of his, not even *The Pickwick Papers.*

Saint Andrew's is not, by the way, the prep school portrayed in *A Perfect Spy,* although John le Carré was there for part of my time. I knew him as Cornwell D., older and taller than me, with a sweep of fair hair and a magisterial manner. He and his chums poked fun at me occasionally, but they weren't among the real bullies, who tormented anyone who would rather read a book than turn out for cricket or soccer, especially those with physical handicaps. (Mine was petty: flat feet. But I couldn't run to save my life and had to do remedial exercises in the gym each morning.)

Towards the end of my stay things improved. There were three of us in the sixth form who regularly came top in everything except maths, where we regularly came bottom. Then a marvellous teacher joined the staff, a Canadian called John Turner. He loved mathematics, and he had the fire in his belly

"In Twelfth Night *at my prep school in 1947, the summer before my thirteenth birthday": Mark Douglass as Sir Andrew Aguecheek, Tim Eastwood as Feste, John Brunner as Malvolio, Nick Byam Shaw as Sir Toby Belch, and Christopher Thornton as Maria*

which I was later to encounter in J. D. Bernal. Within six weeks he had the three of us studying trigonometry in our rest periods.

Life was suddenly not so bad. My parents hadn't moved again—indeed they stayed at that house until my father died—and I dared to believe in security and stability. For a while. My parents didn't move again, but I did. I had to start anew at the bottom of the totem pole when I was sent to Cheltenham College at thirteen.

It was around then that I began to suffer a series of nightmares that have haunted me ever since. First I dreamed of arriving back at my prep school in midterm, with no desk in the classroom and no seat at the meal table. During National Service the nightmares concerned my public school, and in turn, after my discharge, my Air Force station. Gradually, however, they overtook the present, and now they're about places I have not yet visited. Once, I recall, I was at a science fiction convention in a foreign country. I took out my folder of travel cheques to pay a bill, and it held nothing but blank paper. Quite recently I found myself on the moon, with no recollection of how I'd got there and terrified at the prospect of being shot back to Earth in a rocket.

Such dreams are as disturbing as my *Doppelgänger.* When they are paralleled in reality, of course, it's even worse. At the end of one Christmas term my parents left me shivering for hours on Reading station, lacking even the money for a phone call, because they hadn't bothered to check what day I was due home from Cheltenham.

Another factor which made life at Saint Andrew's bearable was that I was good at telling stories after lights-out. I created a superman called Flash the Terrible, the heroic pilot Squadron-Leader Neil McClachan, and a boy called Stone who got away with most appalling mischief. I also made up science fiction yarns. Some I wrote down.

During one Easter holiday I was at a newsagent's with my father, wondering how to spend my pocket money, when he pointed at a magazine and said, "That looks like fun."

He was right. It was the April 1947 British edition of *Astounding Science Fiction.* The lead story was Hal Clement's *Cold Front,* supported by Philip Latham's *The Blindness,* A. E. van Vogt's *Film Library,* Murray Leinster's *Rain Check* . . . I must have read it twenty times. I collected my first rejection slip when I sent a manuscript to its London publishers and was told they merely reprinted from the American edition.

Six years later a story of mine was featured on *aSF*'s cover. But much had happened in the interim.

Boys confined with only other boys can be incredibly cruel. The fact that I remained more-or-less sane from thirteen to seventeen I owe to luck, a ruse, and a book.

The luck lay in the fact that I have a memory like a flypaper; I never know what's going to stick, but something always does. Not only did this free much of my study time for reading what I wanted to read rather than what I was ordered to; it also enabled me to pass examinations by presenting the sum total of my knowledge as though it were a mere fraction, because as well as the set texts I'd found time to read commentaries on them. Sometimes I even added footnotes to my answers.

The ruse consisted in exploiting the fact that those who were the worst bullies in my house were often those doing least well with their studies. I recall how smug I felt the first time that one of the dimwits who thought it amusing to throw me and others like me fully dressed under a shower, so as to make us late for class or chapel and incur punishment accordingly, shyly requested help with a difficult assignment. After that I managed pretty well.

As to the book . . .

I wish I could remember who lent it to me, for it had a more profound impact than anything since *The War of the Worlds,* and I can think of few books that affected me more deeply later. It was *Really the Blues,* the autobiography—written up by Bernard Wolfe—of the jazz clarinetist Mezz Mezzrow. He was and is the only person I have ever heard of who decided he, born white, would rather pass for black.

All of a sudden my horizons opened. There *was* a world outside the one I had been raised to. There *was* something beyond the failed gentility of my home. More important still in the long run, people existed who were as obsessed with music as I was by books. I won't say literature, for by that stage I'd been conditioned into regarding that as something not to enjoy but to be examined about. (I still haven't entirely recovered.)

By and large I had been raised in a house without music, except when someone turned on the radio. My first term at Saint Andrew's our music teacher attempted to inculcate the rudiments of musical notation in the new intake and wrote a tune on the blackboard. Everybody else recognised it and crossed the classroom until I was left alone. When they chorused, "Three Blind Mice!" I had to say, "I didn't know it had a tune!" The teacher looked at me with melting eyes and said, "You poor child!"

I resented that. Until I read *Really the Blues*.

Instantly I wanted to hear the music that had shaped the course of Mezzrow's life. He'd been in jail, he'd been an opium addict, he'd been a down-and-out, and something had hauled him back and back, and back again . . .

Luckily there were already jazz fans at the school. We founded a band—in which I played atrociously bad clarinet—and spent our pocket money on what are now rare and precious 78s. I still have the first Muddy Waters record ever released in Britain, the one from which the Rolling Stones took their name. And the first by John Lee Hooker, and Baby Dodds's *Drum Improvisation #1* on a pirated French label, and forgotten items by Tampa Red and—never mind. But 'Barts Arnold, who played trumpet with us, not long afterwards rescued the Humphrey Lyttelton band one New Year's Eve when Humph had bent his elbow once too often, and was hired by Cy Laurie as a result, while Guy Playfair, who doubled piano and trombone—and with whom I collaborated on a best-forgotten novel about murder in a Dixieland band—later showed me the part of Rio that tourists seldom see and went on to write books about the paranormal, such as *The Flying Cow*.

All of a sudden I was enjoying myself. I longed to thank Mezz Mezzrow, but the only time we met he was too busy to do anything except sign the copy of his book that I had bought. Eventually I wrote to *Jazz Journal* to ask what became of him and learned that he survived past seventy and died in Paris, a city that he loved because jazz was popular and there was no colour bar. I hope I do as well.

Back then I worried a lot. I still do. When I was thirteen I developed a blinding headache that lasted two days. The matron ordered me back to class even though I literally couldn't see. I didn't know my condition was called migraine until long after, but it plagued me for years. (Curiously, it stopped about the time I started to have regular sex. I think there's a connection.) I used to get double vision, and that scared me, too.

My first term at Cheltenham I caught mumps. I'd already had measles and rubella and chicken pox and tonsillitis and ringworm and conjunctivitis and goodness knows what else. Mumps, though, turned out to be the worst. I lay in bed with one testicle swollen to the size of a tennis ball and hurting so badly I could scarcely move. As I recovered, it more or less disappeared. I'd been developing normally up to then, but at that point I stopped. I have no hair on my chest, pubic hair in the female delta rather than the male lozenge, a tendency to eunuchoid fatness,

and bald patches on my cheeks so that I can never grow a full beard. And there were other consequences that ambushed me in later life.

By the age of seventeen I wanted out of school. I'd passed my exams, usually with high marks, and I wanted *out* for a while before yet another enforced move, this time to be conscripted. Though I was inclined towards pacifism I'd grown disillusioned with the Christianity that was force-fed to pupils at my schools (I was reading widely in Oriental religions) and had no firm convictions that would have entitled me to status as a conscientious objector. Besides, when I was told that if I wanted to be exempted from the Cadet Force I'd have to give up playing saxophone in the school band, my new-found fondness for music prevailed.

(Early jazz was a great route into music, incidentally. Being polyphonic, it led me to composers like Josquin des Prés when they were almost unknown, and via madrigals and Elizabethan keyboard music I eventually found my way to the full repertoire. I wish I'd come to it sooner, for by then it was too late. I'm not tone-deaf, but I'm tone-dumb, and cannot sing in tune. Blast it!)

But among the reasons I was so desperate to escape from school was that I had realised I'm a depressive, and I wanted to know whether it was solely due to being constantly prevented from doing what I actually enjoyed. As it turned out, it wasn't. At the risk of getting ahead of myself: I eventually discovered why.

Remember I should have had another sister, but

"At work in my parents' garden, 1952; I was probably writing the story that became my first American sale"

Peter A. West

"A jazz and folk-song session during one of my earliest SF conventions, in the George Hotel, Kettering. This would have been in the middle fifties. The time, I see, was 4:00 A.M., and the guitarist was my fellow author Dan Morgan." (Brunner is at lower right.)

she died at birth? Our house must have been full of mourning when I was scarcely of an age to talk. Only a few years ago I read in *New Scientist* about an American study of chronic depressives. It had shown that a recurrent factor was a death in the family at a preverbal stage. My life, I realised at last, has been shadowed by misery that no analysis could ever bring to light, for when it struck I possessed no words to express it. I wish I'd known that sooner! When I did find out, it was like a curtain being drawn aside, a shutter being folded back. I wasn't cured, but I had an explanation, like the one that saved me when—

No, that hasn't happened yet. I'm not even in the RAF.

During my last term at school I wrote and sold a short SF novel. It paid me enough to buy a typewriter of my own. Thus encouraged, while waiting to be called up I wrote several more stories. Two sold. One, *Thou Good and Faithful*, was the aforementioned lead novelette in *aSF* the following March. The other, a short novel, went to *Two Complete Science Adventure Books*. I'd made over a thousand dollars from my first year's sales, and I was only just eighteen. I celebrated

by attending a meeting of the London Science Fiction Circle and met Arthur Clarke and William Temple and Charles Eric Maine and John Christopher and came away with a sense of something right having happened, for they had treated me, a brash novice, with tolerance and courtesy. More than ever I felt I'd been well advised to drop out of school, for I was beginning to suspect the extent not just of my ignorance but of my incompetence. That suspicion was borne out, over and over, during the next two or three years.

I shall skate lightly over my time in the RAF, except to observe that it was the most completely wasted period of my life. The only benefit I derived from it was the chance to discover how shallow, ignorant, and lacking in compassion are those into whose hands we have delivered power sufficient to destroy us all. I tried to go on writing, but in two years I managed to sell only one story. I did meet someone who remains a good friend, but that was by chance.

I should, though, say that while I was at recruit camp I received a letter from my father's younger brother. I had a state scholarship and a place at Oxford awaiting me, and the letter stated that ICI would pay for me to go through university provided I read the subjects they chose. I considered the idea for at least a minute. The next day I wrote politely to my uncle, and the Ministry of Education, saying they should offer this chance, and my scholarship, to someone who wanted it. I was sick of being told what I ought to know instead of what I wanted to know.

I have never regretted my decision. I am still mortaring up the gaps in what passed for my education, still discovering how many lies I was told. Out of the scores of teachers that I had, one was incontestably first-rate, and that I think puts me among the lucky few.

After the RAF I went home to my parents for a while. 'Barts Arnold had a bedsitter in Saint John's Wood. Visiting him, I asked his landlady to let me know if the adjacent room fell vacant. It did, and with thirty-three pounds in my bank account, saved from my pre–Air Force sales, I moved to London under the mistaken impression that I was already a writer. I worked hard enough to surprise the landlady, divorced wife of an artist who worked an hour or two a day, but my main market was the Nova magazines, *New Worlds* and *Science Fantasy,* and their rates were less than generous. I was paying two guineas a week rent and earning about four pounds. I learned an awful lot of ways of cooking potatoes.

Curiously enough, I called characters in three of the stories I wrote at this time Marjorie, Margery, and Marjory.

One morning the phone rang. Sam Youd (aka John Christopher) was looking for someone to take over his job at the Industrial Diamond Information Bureau while he did the boss's work because the latter was in hospital. They hired me, and my weekly income soared to the munificent sum of eleven pounds. Six months later, when the boss returned, I became an editor with the Books for Pleasure group, working under John F. Burke, whom I knew from the SF Circle, where I was now a regular attender. I stayed two years, learning to prepare scripts for printing and read and correct proofs. During that time occurred the most important event of my life.

As well as the SF Circle I was going to jazz, and later skiffle, clubs ('Barts had left to get married and the next occupant of his room was trumpeter Al Fairweather). But I was dissatisfied with my circle of acquaintances; above all I wasn't meeting any girls to speak of, and when I did I kept finding that my boarding-school education had left me a hopeless social cripple. Who introduced me to the *London*

Peter A. West

"With Marjorie at the World SF Convention in London, 1957. We went as Krishnans (with green hair and antennae) from L. Sprague de Camp's "Viagens Interplanetarias" series. It took ages to wash the Leichner makeup out of our hair—but we were interviewed for BBC television by Alan Whicker!"

Weekly Advertiser, I don't remember; perhaps I just chanced on it. At all events I plucked up courage and, towards the end of 1956, inserted an advertisement. One of the people who answered invited me to her birthday party at Swiss Cottage, within walking distance. I went. The hostess was a slender, dark-haired woman, fourteen years older than me, with a wonderfully mobile face and ready smile. Her name was Marjorie. She came to a party I held in January. Soon we were spending more time together than apart. I invited her to Paris at Easter and she accepted. The day before our departure I moved in with her. At the end of the summer we enjoyed a premature honeymoon in Nice, and in July 1958 we took a three-year lease on a flat in West Hampstead and got married. Much to the annoyance of my parents.

Marjorie wasn't in the least what I was looking for but she was exactly what I wanted. Later I was to say of her, "I won't call her my right arm. She's more like my right leg, for if I try and do anything without her I'm liable to fall flat on my face."

We had many tastes in common—although she

Edward Sterndale Exclusive Photography, London

"Our wedding day," 12 July 1958

was a Beethoven and Wagner type and I'm more Bach and Mozart, we'd both been enjoying skiffle clubs, albeit different ones—but most importantly she was a fully adult person, whereas I was dreadfully immature, and it was thanks to her that I at last grew up.

In addition she not only held but acted on the kind of views I was groping towards. It was she who persuaded me to the inaugural meeting of the Campaign for Nuclear Disarmament—CND; it was in her flat that skifflers and others met to organise a singing group for the first of the famous Aldermaston marches; and it was for them I wrote the song that later came to be called "the national anthem of the British peace movement," "The H-Bombs' Thunder."

That, naturally, wasn't all that I was writing.

In November, while recovering from an appendicectomy, I learned that a serial I had sold to *New Worlds* had been accepted by Ace Books in New York. I resigned my job—somewhat to Marjorie's alarm—and became a free-lance writer again, which is what I still am.

It hasn't always been easy.

Initially Ace paid me $1,000 for a novel of 45,000-plus words, or $750 for a 30,000-worder to make up the second half of a Doublebook. Doublebooks were a splendid way to launch a new author. At first I rode the backs of established writers like Poul Anderson, van Vogt, and Philip K. Dick; then came a turnover point, and within a few years I was the one

supporting newcomers. (The one I'm proudest of is Samuel R. Delany.)

But at that time $1,000 equated to £357, and it wasn't long before it dawned on me that writing as much as I could, though it might earn me a living, entailed the risk of being regarded as—or even becoming—a hack. (One year I wrote eight novels and sold six.) Accordingly I undertook a series of self-imposed exercises, which consisted essentially in choosing a stock science fiction theme and seeing what I could do with it that would be unique to *me*. The first such task I selected was the conversion of a chess game, move for move, into a novel. I worked at it on and off for eighteen months and eventually finished it in May 1960. I knew it was the finest thing I'd so far done, and I felt I had rather a good title, too: *The Squares of the City.*

It bounced for five years in America, and it didn't see print in Britain for nine.

When in the end Ballantine Books did issue it, it became the first original SF paperback ever to be accorded the *New York Times* daily book review. The notice was a rave. And it went on to make the short list for the Hugo Award.

If only it had appeared in 1961 . . . ! (It wouldn't have won that year, either, being up against *Stranger in a Strange Land,* but it could have been rather useful to my career if I'd reached the finals, so to speak, four years sooner.)

That was my first taste of a bitter lesson which I have been taught over and over: whenever I set out to write as well as I know how, I must expect to be disappointed and even punished for my temerity.

In 1959 a frequent argument raised against supporters of nuclear disarmament was to the effect that people in the West knew all about the H-bomb—why weren't we preaching to the communists? Hampstead CND, to which we belonged, had prepared an exhibition about Hiroshima and Nagasaki called "No Place to Hide." Marjorie and I decided to try and show it in Eastern Europe and wrote to various embassies accordingly. Weeks dragged by, and the advance I'd received for *The Brink,* which I was relying on to fund the trip, was leaking away.

Unexpectedly, we received an invitation to put it on in Stockholm, where it would be opened by Dr. Linus Pauling. We wrote letters the same day to Sweden and Poland, deciding that whoever replied first would get the exhibition. *Aktionsgruppen mot Svensk Atombomb*—AMSA—responded by return of post, and we translated the captions into four languages and set forth on a tour that also took us to Denmark, West Germany, France, Switzerland, Belgium and Holland. Living night and day for four months with images of horror and destruction left a permanent impression on my work. My future worlds tend to be unified and pacified not so much from political conviction as because, writing as I do mainly about the future, I have a vested interest in there being a future worth writing about.

I remember Erich Kästner, author of *Emil and the Detectives,* saying, when he visited the exhibition in Munich, "I didn't know pictures like these existed!" And in the same city we also met Hans Hellmut Kirst, the title of whose nuclear-war novel had been borrowed by the German organisers for their publicity: *Keiner kommt davon.*

But the person I recall most vividly was a young Spaniard who chanced across the exhibition in Lausanne and sat down to copy out the captions because, as he explained, "In Spain we don't know anything about all this."

In 1960 an old friend of Marjorie's, named Rita, wrote to say she had found a job at the British School of Archeology in Athens. We both felt the need for a holiday; our tour with the exhibition had exhausted us. On the spur of the moment I said, "Let's go and call on Rita." Which we did, and instantly—as she had done—fell in love with Greece. I'd been hunting for some time for the right setting for a novel I had in mind about a young man afflicted with impotence. (It was those damned mumps. I'd gone through considerable hell until Marjorie put me in touch with a psychiatrist she knew. The first question that guy asked me was, "Has anybody ever run a urinalysis on you?" No one had . . . He arranged it, and the report came from the lab: chronic deficiency of male hormone. Being told that my trouble was due to a physical, not a psychological, cause was like a miracle. I realised it was something I'd just have to live with, like colour blindness, which my father suffered from, or my own inability to sing in tune.)

The emotional impact Greece had on me was precisely what I needed, and the result was *The Crutch of Memory.* The *Daily Telegraph* reviewer said, "Very few authors have had the courage to write a novel about impotence," called it "a work of great insight and sensitivity," and added that I had succeeded where Stendhal failed and Hemingway chickened out. To be told I had outdone such giants at the age of twenty-nine was giddying! But all the novel earned me was a hundred-pound advance, less commission to my agent.

I could tell plenty of horror stories about agents. I'd better not. There wouldn't be room. A few about

publishers, however, I must cram in.

I wrote another non-SF book about this time. I was the only working writer to go right through CND from local-group level to its National Executive Council, and I wound up as a contributing editor to its monthly journal, *Sanity.* Out of my experiences I distilled a novel about the kind of people who were sweating their butts off for the cause. I knew it to be both good and relevant. But it bounced, and bounced . . . In the end a well-known left-wing publisher agreed to issue it in time for the following Easter—when the last-ever Aldermaston march was to be held—provided I abridged the text somewhat. I promised to do it in two weeks: just tell me what to cut and where!

He never did. By November, when I enlisted the help of the Society of Authors to reclaim the script, its topicality had been destroyed. It will finally appear at Easter 1988, to coincide with the thirtieth anniversary of the first March to Aldermaston. Twenty-five years from writing to publication . . . That's my record, so far. May it stand.

The title, by the way, is *The Days of March.*[1]

The middle and late 1960s were a terrific time to live in London. Never had I dreamed that our drab old town would become the fashion capital of the world, or the place where "good Americans go before they die"—rather than Paris, after. I was never much involved in the Swinging London that centred on Carnaby Street and King's Road, but it was impossible to avoid the sheer excitement that pervaded the air. And I'd been sensitised to the remarkable social changes that were occurring, not only in Britain but elsewhere too, by a decision I took even though I couldn't really afford it—to explain which, I ought to say something about science fiction conventions.

We SF writers are blessed with extraordinary support from the readership. Since the 1930s our fans have banded together and organised, with volunteer labour and donated funds, meetings where the professionals can have their egos stroked (a most comforting sensation) and find out what the people who buy their books are really interested in. I first attended a con when I was seventeen; I've been going to them ever since, because I know that (a) I shall enjoy unexpected and fascinating conversations, and (b) I shall benefit from direct feedback. Many writers

---

[1] After writing the above, I received a letter from my agent saying that the publishers have not, so far, sent back the countersigned copy of the contract . . . Not *again!*

seldom or never have a chance to meet their readers in person. We in SF can.

The biggest of such events is the World Science Fiction Convention, which like the baseball World Series is primarily American. But as early as 1957 one was held in London—I was on the committee—and in 1964 I decided I *must* go to America, to see my publishers and agents who previously had been mere signatures on letters, attend a con, and meet colleagues who were only names on the covers of books. I stayed in New York with a trades-union organiser whom I'd met through CND and explored every street of Greenwich Village. I went to California for a convention of fifteen hundred fans, at a time when in Britain we attracted one or two hundred. I fell in love with the Bay Area. I met Poul Anderson, who had shared my first Ace Double, and my idol Philip K. Dick, and—and—and—!

I came back determined to repeat the experience as often as possible.

In 1965 the Worldcon returned to London, and as a direct result my then agent secured me a marvellous deal. For fifteen hundred pounds, payable quarterly, Penguin Books asked me to produce two novels. In high delight I said, "Now's my chance to write as well as I know how!" I submitted three ideas; they chose the two I hoped they would; and I proceeded to write them. The first was *Quicksand*. The second, into which I poured everything I knew and felt and sensed about the changes taking place in the world around me, was *Stand on Zanzibar*.

Penguin turned them both down.

Oh, all was not lost—thanks to the fact that I went back to America in 1966. I walked into Larry Ashmead's office at Doubleday to find that he had *Quicksand* on his desk and was about to sign a rejection letter. I sat him down and talked at him very hard. By the time he left to keep a lunch date, he had torn up the letter, offered me the biggest advance he could without applying to higher authority, and the same again, sight unseen, for *SoZ* of which at the time I literally had not written one word.

Quicksand became an SF Book Club selection and went twice to American paperback. It sold twice in Britain and has been translated into three languages.

Stand on Zanzibar—eleven English-language editions and seven translations—was the first book by a non-American to win the Hugo for best novel.

But two years to the day after I started work on it, all I had to show for the effort I'd invested was the Doubleday advance: net of commission, $1,350. Marjorie, who had by then quit her full-time job, wound up tending our friends' gardens at 50p an hour to

make ends meet. See what I mean about being punished for writing at the top of my bent?

By the way: around this time there was a case reported in the papers concerning the widow of a writer who for two years was forbidden to touch her husband's estate because the Inland Revenue were attempting to have his unsold copyrights included in its valuation and thereby make them taxable. (They lost, I'm pleased to say.)

I didn't want that to happen to Marjorie. But I was planning to return to the States, and aircraft have been known to fall off the sky . . . So I asked my accountant what to do, and he said, "Form a company. Companies don't die when their directors die."

Accordingly, in 1966, we set up Brunner Fact & Fiction Limited. But it was two years before I could persuade Marjorie to change the profession in her passport from "housewife" to the correct—and well-deserved—"company director."

She earned every penny of her salary, and more.

Throughout this period we were constantly on the move. In that respect my adult life felt like a continuation of my childhood. Marjorie and I had had to quit the house where she was living when we met—it belonged to an old lady who died, and it was sold. The house we lived in when we got married belonged to an old lady downstairs, who died, and it was sold. We found a bigger flat, with a marvellous garden that in spring was like a Kentish bluebell wood, and might have stayed, except that the house belonged to an old lady, who died. When we tried to buy it we were outbidden by a firm of developers who wanted to build over the garden. At that point we grew sick of upping sticks every four years and bought a long lease on a flat in Frognal. After four years . . .

No, this house didn't belong to an old lady, but there was an old lady involved: Marjorie's mother, whom I dearly loved. She'd been widowed and was suffering from abdominal cancer, and we decided it would be best for her to spend her last days with us rather than in an anonymous hospital. Besides, we had befriended a single mother with a charming little girl who rolled her eyes at me and said, "I want you to be my daddy!"

Gulp.

So I took a very deep breath, and the plunge. Thirteen years after moving to London, I found I'd parlayed my thirty-three-pound savings into a four-storey house on the edge of Hampstead Heath.

No, I wasn't rich. It was done by ruses like the ones I'd exploited at school.

You see, long before, I'd bought a secondhand

car on hire purchase. (I still have never been able to afford a brand-new car, but this was the first with four wheels.) When after twelve months I paid my final weekly instalment of £2, I received a letter saying, "We hereby pass the title of the vehicle to you, and would take this opportunity of thanking you for your prompt and regular payments." I showed it to Marjorie and said, "We've got it made!"

I still have that letter. *Very* useful.

Something else that helped . . . Once I went to call on my bank manager and was kept waiting. At last the door of his office opened and out came an elderly man in a long black cape and wide-brimmed hat, helped along by his wife. The manager saw them to the door and came back to me saying, "So sorry to have kept you! But do you know who just went out? John Dickson Carr! Penguin have published two million of his books in paperback!"

"Really?" I said—then being about thirty. "I suppose my two-millionth paperback must have sold some time last year."

And it was true. Ace had published over twenty of my books, and even though they printed fewer than 100,000 of each, many had been sold for translation, especially into German.

After that the manager treated me with more respect than my financial soundness warranted.

Within a regrettably short time of buying our house in Nassington Road, we discovered why the single mother was one. (She took to treating us as built-in baby-sitters while she went out on the town.) So the setup didn't last, and thereafter we shared our home with various friends. One was Tom Paley, the American banjoist. He asked if we could put him up for two weeks while he looked for a new flat, and stayed two years. He was a fine lodger but for his habit of beating time with his foot while practising in the room above the one we slept in.

Another was Michael Kenward, one-time editor of the British SF Association's journal, *Vector*. He went on to become editor of *New Scientist*. I went on to become Chairman of the BSFA and served four years in that capacity. I've done a lot of odd things like that—Joint President of the European SF Association, where my opposite number was a Russian; Advisory Vice-President of the Science Fiction Foundation, the first formal academic institution of its kind, which is based at the North-East London Polytechnic; and even though after the 1957 Worldcon I swore I'd never serve on a convention committee again, I did that too—for the Oxford SF con in 1969 (after which I again swore off); *and* when I was persuaded to recruit a committee and bring the European Science

Fiction Convention, Eurocon, to Britain for the first time in 1984. I think it must have something to do with sunspots.

Eurocon . . . My Italian publisher and good friend, GianFranco Viviani, recounted his first meeting with me and Marjorie at one of those. I was supposed to declare the convention open, but that day happened to be our wedding anniversary, so before I did so I called Marjorie on stage and presented her with a bunch of roses. (The trouble I had making sure she didn't know what was coming!) We had been married fourteen years.

I'd never bought her an engagement ring. I couldn't afford to. Our wedding rings were second-hand, from a shop that specialised in unredeemed pawnbroker's pledges. It became a standing joke between us. I was very proud when, at the party we held to celebrate our twentieth anniversary, I was able in front of our assembled guests to offer her a ring I felt she would prefer. I handed her a ticket for an all-in trip to see Wagner's Ring, at Bayreuth.

Keeping *that* a surprise was really tough!

Looking back, I find it hard to believe, but notwithstanding my various successes—including an assortment of prizes and awards: the British Fantasy Award, the British SF Award (twice), the French *Prix Apollo* and *Grand Prix du Festival de l'Insolite*, the Italian *Cometa d'Argento* (twice), the *Premio Italia* and sundry others, and also being invited as Guest of Honour at various conventions, up to and including the Worldcon in Baltimore, 1983—I was still, as they say, scuffling. It was as though events like those were happening not to me but to my *Doppelgänger*. I'd never achieved my ambition to stop living from year to year on what I earned in each respective year. I dreamed of making enough from a single book to be able to decide, partway into a doubtful project, that I'd do better to scrap it and try another, without feeling the pinch. I hadn't managed it, and I still haven't. I think I must spend too much time writing to become businesslike.

I'm not a greedy person. I don't like four-star hotels—Marjorie and I always travelled across France, for example, following the *Routiers* (truckers) guide, as we did when we went to Greece in 1960. I prefer it that way.

But I was driven out of that fine house I was so proud of. The crisis point occurred not long after we moved in. We'd been nursing Marjorie's mother through her cancer, waking in the small hours to administer her painkilling injections, and a short time before she departed this world my father suffered a cerebral aneurysm, and it killed him. I was wiped out.

Brunner (far left) with other recipients of the "Europa Special" award at the European SF Convention in Stresa, Italy, May 1980. In the back row at far right is Dutch artist Karel Thole, and in the front row (left to right) are publisher GianFranco Viviani, Ion Hobana (Romania), Ernesto Vegetti, and Waldemar Kumming (West Germany).

When it came to my father's funeral I literally could not feel sad.

My doctor diagnosed "a classic case of acute nervous exhaustion," put me on tranquillisers, and ordered me not even to think about writing for at least a week. I complied, and after a dreadful period when I simply made black marks on white paper, looked at them, and threw them away, I did begin to write again.

However, this could not continue indefinitely. It was costing me a book a year to keep the roof over our heads, plus another one to live on, and my imagination was becoming bruised and battered. Much though we both loved Hampstead, by 1973 I felt I couldn't stand the pressure. I hated the idea of moving yet again, but our mortgage was linked to inflation, and the interest charges had been raised twice within a year, so we were in a rat race. While I was in America on business Marjorie consulted an estate agent she knew and found out that we could sell the house for enough to buy another outright, in the country. Instead of taking a holiday on my return, we went house hunting, and in November we moved to a village we'd never heard of called South Petherton. If you want an idea of its location, visualise

England with London to the east and Land's End to the southwest and draw a line between the two. South Petherton is almost exactly halfway.

What we acquired was one wing of a substantial Victorian mansion built of eighteen-inch sandstone blocks, ideal for two people both working at home, with a garage and a garden and a barn. And it was *ours.*

Unfortunately our troubles were far from at an end. It didn't help matters when, a few months after leaving London, I discovered that the new owners of Ace Books had sold British rights to one of my novels without the precaution of buying them from me first, and without even sending me my half-share of the advance. Investigation proved this was not the only way I had been cheated. I raised considerable hell. When the overdue money eventually arrived, it turned out that it would have sufficed to cover another year's mortgage payments, so we hadn't actually had to move . . .

Small wonder, then, that not long afterwards I developed high blood pressure. My new doctor prescribed Aldomet (methyldopa). It did appalling things to me. It wiped out my imagination, so that for a year I was incapable of writing. It also affected my short-term memory, so that the period I spent on it is largely a blank. Worst of all, it altered my personality. It made me violent and irrational, and people who first met me at the time can't believe I'm the same person. I became unbearable to the point where Marjorie once packed her bags to take a bus to Greece and get the hell out of earshot.

So deranged was I by the drug that I never suspected it could be the cause. I was convinced this must be my real self emerging at long last, because of my childhood, and I was indescribably and horribly ashamed . . .

Eventually, because we were planning a trip abroad, I asked my doctor whether now might be a safe time to stop. He said okay. Within six weeks I was writing again and life was back to normal. Later, at a French SF con, I met a friend of one of my colleagues, a pharmacist, and told her I had been on Aldomet. Without prompting, she asked whether it had done this to me, that, and the other—three questions that bracketed my suffering. *She* knew!

Now I distrust synthetic drugs and take only herbal medicines unless it's unavoidable.

At the Science Fiction Shop on Eighth Avenue in New York, with its founder, Baird Searles, 1983

One event lightened that miserable year. Back in London we'd become acquainted with Martin Walker, later to become the *Guardian*'s correspondent in Moscow. He needed a refuge to concentrate on a book about the National Front. We provided it. I lent him the typewriter on which I'd written *Stand on Zanzibar,* and he liked it so much that at the end of his stay he bought it and took it home.

I desperately needed to tackle something utterly different from anything I had attempted before. Casting around, I decided it would be a novel about a steamboat race on the Mississippi. I estimated it would take me two years, including time for research. On that basis I obtained a twenty-thousand-dollar advance—twice the best I had previously commanded—and in 1976 I spent the Bicentennial weekend riding the towboat *John D. Geary* from New Orleans to Memphis—a rare privilege! The captain said he'd been on the river twenty-seven years and never shipped a passenger before.

To my dying day I shall never understand why *The Great Steamboat Race* took more like five years than two. (I had to break off twice and write quick books for ready cash, but that didn't account for it.) Perhaps it was that I became too much of a perfectionist, agonising for days over a single line for fear of perpetrating an anachronism. At all events, I was unprecedentedly late in delivering it, and when it did

appear my New York publishers accorded it (so testifies my good friend Samuel "Chip" Delany) Monday-to-Friday display. Chip saw it in a Manhattan bookstore on Monday and felt pleased that my work was being properly promoted. When he returned on Saturday to buy a copy he was told they were all being sent back to the warehouse.

My fault, I suppose.

In other ways, though, life was turning out to be rather pleasant. Not only did many friends visit us— we'd held open house in London on the final Friday of each month, and in Petherton switched to the first Saturday so people travelling long distances could stay the night—but Marjorie got us very much involved in the community.

There had been a folk festival nearby at East Coker (yes, the Eliot one—he's buried there). When it was discontinued she started saying, "Wouldn't Petherton be a great venue for a folk festival?" Eventually she said it to the right people, and lo! It happened! Now it's a landmark in the village year. For the whole of a weekend every June the place is full of singers, dancers, and musicians, and it's wonderful.

Partly as a result, two television programmes were made about me. The morning after the first was broadcast, I discovered how tremendous is the influence of the Box when two urchins yelled at me from a hedge as I walked past with my dogs, "Hey, mister! Weren't you on the telly?"

I still wonder what they were doing up at that late hour . . . But it led to an embarrassing consequence. Hundreds of people in the area—whom I don't know from Adam and Eve!—recognise me and greet me when we pass.

I'm catching up gradually. Recently I learned the name of someone who's been calling me John for about five years.

On the fourteenth of April 1986 Marjorie didn't wake up.

She had suffered a deep stroke that left her paralysed on her right side and virtually incapable of speech. She fought back valiantly, and indeed at one stage the staff at her hospital—where she was accorded marvellous care—were hoping she might be transferred to the Wolfson Foundation in London, where they specialise in rehabilitating cases like hers. But two months later she had a second stroke and after that it was only a matter of time. She died in August, and with her went half of my heart.

I've been alone now for almost two years, except for my dogs, who have preserved my sanity, more or less. I had a cat as well, but Puck developed cancer of the pancreas. He wasn't even nine years old. If we are doing that to our pets, what are we doing to ourselves? I think a lot about *The Sheep Look Up*. I didn't want it to be prophetic—on the contrary I hoped it wouldn't be—but that vision of a poisoned world will not stop haunting me, as my nightmares do not.

Now I'm scuffling again, as usual. I had to abandon what would have been my best-paid novel. I'd invested six months in it and it was about three months from completion. The day after Marjorie was taken to hospital, after I'd been to visit her, I switched on the machine and looked at my text and said to the air, "I've lost this book."

Because, you see, for the foreseeable future it could not be in the forefront of my mind. She must. She still is.

At least, though, I've paid off what I owed my publishers, by turning in a different book. They say it's pretty good. It may well be on sale before this piece appears. I think the title's quite a striking one. It's *Children of the Thunder*.

And there's another in the works. Money must be earned, somehow. Life must go on. I still get around—not long ago, for example, I attended the first conference of SF writers to be held in the Soviet

"*My favorite picture of Marjorie and me together, at a restaurant called Le Sabra during one of the Metz Science Fiction Festivals in France—1976, I think*"

Union. But it's no fun any more. It used to be. It isn't now the light's gone out.

When I proposed to Marjorie I warned her there would always be one thing more important in my life than she was: my writing. She accepted me on that basis.

I was wrong.

Copyright © Brunner Fact & Fiction Ltd., 1989

BIBLIOGRAPHY

Fiction:

The Brink. London: Gollancz, 1959.

Echo in the Skull (bound with *Rocket to Limbo*, by Alan E. Nourse). New York: Ace Books, 1959; also published separately in a revised edition as *Give Warning to the World*. New York: DAW Books, 1974; London: Dobson, 1981.

The Hundredth Millennium (bound with *Edge of Time*, by David Grinnell). New York: Ace Books, 1959.

Threshold of Eternity (bound with *The War of Two Worlds*, by Poul Anderson). New York: Ace Books, 1959.

The World Swappers (bound with *Siege of the Unseen*, by A. E. van Vogt). New York: Ace Books, 1959.

The Atlantic Abomination (bound with *The Martian Missile*, by David Grinnell). New York: Ace Books, 1960.

Sanctuary in the Sky (bound with *The Secret Martians*, by Jack Sharkey). New York: Ace Books, 1960.

The Skynappers (bound with *Vulcan's Hammer*, by Philip K. Dick). New York: Ace Books, 1960.

Slavers of Space (bound with *Dr. Futurity*, by Philip K. Dick). New York: Ace Books, 1960; also published separately in a revised edition as *Into the Slave Nebula*. New York: Lancer Books, 1968; London: Millington, 1980.

Meeting at Infinity (bound with *Beyond the Silver Sky*, by Kenneth Bulmer). New York: Ace Books, 1961.

No Future in It, and Other Science Fiction Stories. London: Gollancz, 1962; New York: Doubleday, 1964.

Secret Agent of Terra (bound with *The Rim of Space*, by A. B. Chandler). New York: Ace Books, 1962; also published separately in a revised edition as *The Avengers of Carrig*. New York: Dell, 1969.

The Super Barbarians. New York: Ace Books, 1962.

Times without Number (bound with *Destiny's Orbit*, by David Grinnell). New York: Ace Books, 1962; revised and expanded edition. Leeds, England: Elmfield Press, 1974.

The Astronauts Must Not Land [and] *The Space-Time Juggler*. New York: Ace Books, 1963; *The Astronauts Must Not Land* also published separately in a revised edition as *More Things in Heaven*. New York: Dell, 1973; London: Hamlyn, 1983.

Castaways' World [and] *The Rites of Ohe*. New York: Ace Books, 1963; *Castaways' World* also published separately in a revised edition as *Polymath*. New York: DAW Books, 1974.

The Dreaming Earth. New York: Pyramid Books, 1963; London: Sidgwick & Jackson, 1972.

Listen! The Stars! (bound with *The Rebellers*, by Jane Roberts). New York: Ace Books, 1963; also published separately in a revised edition as *The Stardroppers*. New York: DAW Books, 1972; London: Hamlyn, 1982.

To Conquer Chaos. New York: Ace Books, 1964.·

Endless Shadow (bound with *The Arsenal of Miracles*, by Gardner F. Fox). New York: Ace Books, 1964.

The Crutch of Memory. London: Barrie & Rockliff, 1964.

The Whole Man. New York: Ballantine, 1964; also published as *Telepathist*. London: Faber, 1965.

The Altar on Asconel (bound with *Android Avenger*, by Ted White). New York: Ace Books, 1965.

The Day of the Star Cities. New York: Ace Books, 1965.

Enigma from Tantalus [and] *The Repairmen of Cyclops*. New York: Ace Books, 1965.

The Long Result. London: Faber, 1965; New York: Ballantine, 1966.

Now Then: Three Stories. London: Mayflower, 1965; New York: Avon, 1968.

The Squares of the City. New York: Ballantine, 1965; Harmondsworth, England: Penguin, 1969.

Wear the Butchers' Medal. New York: Pocket Books, 1965.

No Other Gods but Me. London: Compact, 1966.

A Planet of Your Own (bound with *The Beasts of Kohl*, by John Rackham). New York: Ace Books, 1966.

Born under Mars. New York: Ace Books, 1967.

Out of My Mind. New York: Ballantine, 1967.

The Productions of Time. Harmondsworth, England: Penguin, 1970; New York: DAW Books, 1977.

Quicksand. Garden City, N.Y.: Doubleday, 1967; London: Sidgwick & Jackson, 1969.

Bedlam Planet. New York: Ace Books, 1968; London: Sidgwick & Jackson, 1973.

Catch a Falling Star. New York: Ace Books, 1968.

Father of Lies (bound with *Mirror Image*, by Bruce Duncan). New York: Belmont Books, 1968.

Not before Time. London: New English Library, 1968.

Out of My Mind. London: New English Library, 1968.

Stand on Zanzibar. Garden City, N.Y.: Doubleday, 1968; London: Macdonald, 1969.

Black Is the Color. New York: Pyramid Books, 1969.

Double, Double. New York: Ballantine, 1969; London: Sidgwick & Jackson, 1971.

The Evil That Men Do (bound with *The Purloined Planet*, by Lin Carter). New York: Belmont Books, 1969.

The Jagged Orbit. New York: Ace Books, 1969; London: Sidgwick & Jackson, 1970.

A Plague on Both Your Causes. London: Hodder & Stoughton, 1969; also published as *Blacklash*. New York: Pyramid Books, 1969.

Timescoop. New York: Dell, 1969; London: Sidgwick & Jackson, 1972.

The Devil's Work. New York: Norton, 1970.

The Gaudy Shadows. London: Constable, 1970; New York: Beagle Books, 1971.

Good Men Do Nothing. London: Hodder & Stoughton, 1970; New York: Pyramid Books, 1971.

Honky in the Woodpile: A Max Curfew Thriller. London: Constable, 1971.

The Traveler in Black (short stories). New York: Ace Books, 1971; London: Severn House, 1979.

From This Day Forward. Garden City, N.Y.: Doubleday, 1972.

The Dramaturges of Yan. New York: Ace Books, 1972; London: New English Library, 1974.

Entry to Elsewhen. New York: DAW Books, 1972.

The Sheep Look Up. New York: Harper, 1972; London: Dent, 1974.

Age of Miracles. London: Sidgwick & Jackson, 1973; New York: Ace Books, 1973.

The Stone That Never Came Down. Garden City, N.Y.: Doubleday, 1973; London: New English Library, 1976.

Time Jump. New York: Dell, 1973.

Total Eclipse. Garden City, N.Y.: Doubleday, 1974; London: Weidenfeld & Nicolson, 1975.

Web of Everywhere. New York: Bantam, 1974; London: New English Library, 1977; also published as *The Webs of Everywhere.* New York: Del Rey, 1983.

The Shockwave Rider. New York: Harper, 1975; London: Dent, 1975.

Interstellar Empire. New York: DAW Books, 1976.

The Book of John Brunner. New York: DAW Books, 1976.

Foreign Constellations: The Fantastic Worlds of John Brunner. New York: Everest House, 1980.

The Infinitive of Go. New York: Ballantine, 1980.

Players at the Game of People. New York: Ballantine, 1980.

Manshape. New York: DAW Books, 1982.

The Crucible of Time. New York: Ballantine, 1983; London: Arrow, 1984.

The Great Steamboat Race. New York: Ballantine, 1983.

The Tides of Time. New York: Ballantine, 1984; Harmondsworth, England: Penguin, 1986.

The Compleat Traveller in Black (short stories). New York: Bluejay, 1986; London: Methuen, 1987.

The Shift Key. London: Methuen, 1987.

Under pseudonym Keith Woodcott:

I Speak for Earth (bound with *Wandl the Invader*, by Ray Cummings). New York: Ace Books, 1961.

The Ladder in the Sky (bound with *The Darkness before Tomorrow*, by Robert Moore Williams). New York: Ace Books, 1962.

The Psionic Menace (bound with *Captives of the Flame*, by Samuel R. Delany). New York: Ace Books, 1963.

The Martian Sphinx. New York: Ace Books, 1965.

Poetry:

Life in a Explosive Forming Press. London: Poet's Trust, 1970.

Trip: A Sequence of Poems through the U.S.A. (illustrated by Paul Piech). Richmond, England: Keepsake Press, 1971.

A Hastily Thrown-Together Bit of Zork. South Petherton, England: Square House Books, 1974.

Tomorrow May Be Even Worse. Cambridge, Mass.: New England Science Fiction Association, 1978.

While There's Hope (illustrated by P. Piech). Richmond, England: Keepsake Press, 1982.

A New Settlement of Old Scores (songs). Cambridge, Mass.: New England Science Fiction Association, 1983.

Editor of:

The Best of Philip K. Dick. New York: Ballantine, 1977.

Translator of:

The Overlords of War, by Gérard Klein. Garden City, N.Y.: Doubleday, 1973.

Screenplay:

The Terrornauts. London: Amicus Productions, 1967.

Barbara Cartland

1901-

LIVING AND LOVING

M y father, Captain Bertram Cartland of the Worcestershire Yeomanry Militia, married my mother, Mary Hamilton Scobell, in 1900.

The Cartlands are reported in ancient chronicles as being in Lanarkshire, Scotland, before A.D. 1200. There was a village called after them and there are the *Cartland Crags* which are still a beauty spot.

The name could possibly be of Norman origin and belongs to the eleventh century or even earlier.

One of the first references to the name in literature occurs in the minstrel poem of "Blind Harry" who lived between 1470 and 1495. His poem covers eleven books and contains some eleven thousand lines.

In Book VI Harry writes of how Wallace, one of Scotland's heroes, fought against the English.

Harry recounts that as a young man, after an affray with the English garrison in Lanark, Wallace fled to the "Cartland Crags."

His wife delayed the English pursuers by a trick and, when they discovered that Wallace had escaped, they killed her. Later, in the nineteenth century, there was a town called Cartland in Lanarkshire.

Some of the Cartlands moved south from Scotland and my great-grandfather had an estate in Worcestershire.

During the Industrial Revolution, in about 1840, he moved nearer to Birmingham and started a brass factory which made him very rich. He had a large family and his second son, James Cartland, my grandfather, became a great financier.

He helped build up the City of Birmingham, and was twice offered a baronetcy and a knighthood, which he refused. He fell in love with a Scottish girl who was on the verge of marrying a peer.

Flora Falkner was beautiful and a direct descendent of Robert the Bruce, King of Scotland. She was swept off her feet by James Cartland.

Their only son, James Bertram Falkner Cartland—my father—was very handsome, tall, and intelligent. He fell in love when he was twenty-three with Mary Hamilton Scobell—my mother—when he

Barbara Cartland

walked into a ballroom and saw her dancing.

"That is the woman I am going to marry!" he said.

He had some difficulty, as Mary, who was always called Polly, was pursued by a large number of young men.

The Scobell family was one of the oldest Saxon families in existence—an ancestor was Sheriff of Devon in 1022.

My maternal grandfather, Colonel George Treweeke Scobell, was a great traveller. He was one of the first men to climb Mont Blanc and received a diploma for doing so.

He was at the opening of the Suez Canal and he and my grandmother went round the world three times in sailing ships. They were also among the first passengers on the Trans-Siberian Railway.

After my father and mother were married they moved into a large, attractive house in Worcestershire where they hunted. My mother was exceptionally good on a horse—and my father was a first-class game-shot. They entertained a great number of their friends with tennis, billiards, and punting on the river which was at the bottom of the garden.

In 1902 there was a national financial crisis and my grandfather had just financed the building of the Fishguard Railway. The banks called in their loans and there was no limited liability in those days. He would have had to live on his dividends of about six thousand pounds a year, with income tax at only eleven pence in the pound, until the situation improved.

He was, however, in ill health and he shot himself.

Everything he possessed was sold, and my father was left with only the furniture which had been a wedding present. Their house was in my grandfather's name.

They rented from an old friend, the Earl of Coventry, a much smaller house in Pershore, called Amerie Court.

I had been born in 1901 and christened Mary Barbara Hamilton. This was after Mary Ann Hamilton, my mother's grandmother, and my great-grandmother, who came from Philadelphia and was an heiress.

Her great-great-grandfather Andrew Hamilton was a relative of the Duke of Hamilton who left Scotland under a cloud after he had killed someone of importance in a duel. He was an exceedingly clever and astute lawyer. He became Governor of the Jerseys and defender of Zenger in Pennsylvania and he showed the State how to secede from the Crown of England.

He had two sons, one who became Lieutenant-Governor of Pennsylvania in 1748, the other who was the great-grandfather of Mary Ann Hamilton.

She came to England on her father's death and married Captain Septemus Palairet, member of an old Huguenot family who had settled in England after the troubles in France.

She was tiny, with feet smaller than Queen Victoria's and she had six children—the sixth being my grandmother Edith, and died with her seventh when she was twenty-seven.

In 1910 there was a General Election and my father, as a Knight of the Primrose League for five counties, organised the Parliamentary Seat of South Worcestershire for Mr. Eyres Monsell—later Viscount Monsell, First Lord of the Admiralty.

They became great friends and my father worked with him politically, he himself intended to stand later on as a Member of Parliament.

In 1914 civil war was expected in Ireland and at the request of the Duchess of Abercorn my father was organising the evacuation of all the women and children from Ulster.

On 4 August war was declared and my father was "called up," having been in the Militia. He joined his Regiment and very shortly left for France. After four terrible years in the trenches, he was killed in action in the Germans' last push towards Paris before they were defeated.

My mother was heartbroken. She was left with me aged seventeen and my two brothers who were at an expensive public school.

As we had very little money she asked me where I would like to live. I said, "London," and we moved there. I found it a thrilling and exciting experience as I wrote in my book *We Danced All Night.*

I published my first novel in 1923 and after that began to write seriously to make money.

I had forty-nine proposals of marriage before in 1927 I accepted Alexander McCorquodale, formerly of the Argyll and Sutherland Highlanders.

He had served in the First Army in France, which was commanded by his uncle, Lord Horne of Stirkoke.

We had a large wedding at Saint Margaret's, Westminster, with pipers escorting us from the church.

In August 1927 we went to Scotland to stay at Saluscraggie in the Strath of Kildonan, with my husband's uncle and aunt, Mr. and Mrs. Harold McCorquodale.

I had been to Scotland several times before, but it was the first time I had been so far north.

I was entranced by the beauty of the Strath and when I was taken out fishing the first day after I had arrived, I caught my first salmon of fourteen pounds in the Surfaceman's Pool. Also three other fish the same day. Naturally as I had never fished before, I lost quite a number.

The total bag was twenty-three salmon and I thought at the time that salmon fishing was very easy. I did not know then how many hours I would spend either fishing myself or watching other fishermen catch nothing.

The McCorquodales were a fief to the Campbells whose Chieftain is the Duke of Argyll. One of their ancestors, Duncan McCorquodale, recorded ensigns armorial in the Public Register of Arms on or about the year 1672.

The Chief of the Clan was known as Baron of the Phantilands but they diminished somewhat after they had been invaded near Loch Awe by the McClouds and a great many were killed.

For some reason they did not wear their own tartan and after I had been married for some years, with the help of the Lord Lyon I took it out of abeyance. It was a very attractive tartan that had not been woven for over a hundred years.

Alexander and I had one daughter, Raine, who was married first to the ninth Earl of Dartmouth and later to the eighth Earl Spencer, father of the Princess of Wales.

Alexander's father had rented Kildonan Lodge for many years but had grown too old to come to Scotland and had taken to yachting.

My marriage, however, was not successful and in 1933 I divorced Alexander and in 1936 married his first cousin, Hugh McCorquodale.

Hugh had been in the Queen's Own Cameron Highlanders and very badly wounded at the Battle of Passchendaele where he received the Military Cross for gallantry.

After I was married to Hugh, as his father and mother lived at Saluscraggie, we went there every year and I became really proficient at salmon fishing.

My mother-in-law had been a Granville, one of the most famous families in the country.

It started with Rollo, the first Duke of Normandy, who died in 932 and who was a Norseman and a pagan. He invaded Normandy where he became a Christian.

He had a large family and his great-granddaughter Emma married two of the English kings, Ethelred the Unready and King Canute, and was the mother of two others, Hardicanute and Edward the Confessor.

His great-great-great-grandson was William the Conqueror in 1066.

His granddaughter, Geraldine, married the third Earl of Corbeil and their son became the fourth Earl of Corbeil and also Earl Granville.

He was the founder of the Granville family who, during the years, became related to many of the most famous families in England, including the Earls of Devon, Bath, Edgemont, and Rochester, the Marquess of Worcester, and the Dukes of Rutland and

The author with her late husband Hugh McCorquodale and sons Ian and Glen
in the Highlands of Scotland

Sutherland.

Lady Georgiana Caroline Granville married the Honourable John Spencer in 1734 and their son became the first Earl Spencer.

This means that my sons, Ian and Glen, are connected to the daughter of the eighth Earl Spencer, Lady Diana Spencer, now the Princess of Wales.

Late in the war we made the somewhat arduous journey to Scotland on holiday. It was safe for my two small sons as there were no bombs on Helmsdale.

There was also no petrol and we stayed at Torrish Lodge and my husband and I could only fish the piece of river outside it.

My sons Ian and Glen adored Scotland and became as attached to it as their father had always been.

When my father-in-law died he left the estate between his four sons. Now they are dead and their sons have inherited it so that Ian and Glen have a third part divided between them.

It is the greatest joy of their lives to come to Scotland and I would not miss my yearly visit for anything in the world.

Inevitably I write a novel with a Scottish background after I have left.

One of the best-looking men I have ever seen, the Duke of Sutherland becomes the hero for many of my Scottish novels. Just as Dunrobin Castle, Dunbeath, Stirkoke, or the Castle of May creep into the story, so does the loch at the top of the river and the people of Helmsdale.

I travel all over the world. I am thrilled by the exotic beauty of the East and the vital virility of the West.

But as I turn for home "My Heart's in the Highlands."

I was asked recently to write how, when I die, I would like to be remembered. After eighty-seven years of life, this was quite an undertaking because so many things have happened during those years.

I have been ecstatically happy, very miserable, and deeply saddened, especially when I lost first my father in the 1914–18 War, then both my brothers at Dunkirk.

Since then, many of my closest friends who meant a great deal in my life have died.

I have been shown great kindness, I have endured a certain amount of teasing and sometimes ridicule by the press. At the same time, they have helped and supported wholeheartedly my often very controversial "crusades."

For example, at the moment I have fought for a year that women who make marriage and having

children "a career" and stay at home should be paid the national wage. This March the former French Prime Minister Jacques Chirac brought this in.

I am fighting, as President Reagan is doing, to bring back prayers into the state schools. It is horrifying that the nation is divided in that only children who go to private schools are allowed to learn of the necessity and wonder of prayer.

No. 1. I would like to be remembered for my books, especially for my novels, through which I have tried to give Beauty and Love to the world.

I have written 475 books all together and have sold approximately 500 million. The *Guinness Book of World Records* says that I am the "best-selling author in the world" and it delights me to think that I am now published in every country, except China.

I may actually be in China, as I am in several other countries that do not pay, but who simply because they like my books have committed piracy and translated them into their own languages.

When I was in Indonesia two years ago to see the Buddhist temples, I found that every publisher was bringing out my latest books without paying a penny, using my covers, but with the text going sideways, as it does in Japan.

What really matters however is that I do bring happiness to people, for the simple reason that my heroines are the sweet, loving, genuine women who were first portrayed by Shakespeare, with *Romeo and Juliet,* and whose example has been copied by all classical authors.

It is they who evoke in a man the real love that is both spiritual and physical, and it is the woman in a marriage who stands for Morality, Compassion, Sympathy, and Love.

This is the message I have tried to impart to the world, and when people tell me or write to say that I have made them happy, that is the greatest compliment I can have.

I would add that I have written every other sort of book besides three autobiographies of myself, the biographies of my mother and my brother, and sixteen historical works.

I have had books published on health, sociology, cookery, philosophy, cartoons, and a children's pop-up book, also a book of poems.

I have had two stage plays performed and one play on the radio. In 1987 my book *A Hazard of Hearts* was made into a film and shown on television in the U.S.A. receiving a "No. 1 Rating."

It has now been sold to a number of other countries including Britain, Australia, New Zealand, Germany, etc., etc.

No. 2. In 1931 I and two young Air Force officers thought of the idea of an aeroplane-towed glider.

It was then a commercial action owing to the financial recession, but we thought that an aeroplane could set off with a number of gliders towed behind it, using only one tankful of petrol.

Gliders were, at that time, very cheap, so to prove our point I started to build my own glider.

Before it was finished, the *Daily Mail* heard that something was afoot and said they would give one thousand pounds to the first person who could "glider" the Channel.

They had no idea how it was to be done, but the man who was making my glider wanted to enter the competition and we had only one towrope.

He therefore set off first and when he had gone to the starting point I said to the Air Force men:

"It is no use us trying to win the contest. We will take the first aeroplane-towed air-mail glider to Reading."

This we did and were met by the Mayor.

Everybody was very impressed by what had been achieved, but a German had crossed the Channel before dawn.

Soon afterwards the Air Ministry banned aeroplane-towed gliders because they said it was too dangerous.

The Germans however went on with the experiment and used them in large quantities for their invasion of Crete.

We, as a country, did not use aeroplane-towed gliders again until D Day.

No one recognised our idea until in 1984 the Americans realised what had been achieved and I went to Kennedy Airport to receive the Bishop Wright Air Industry Award for my "contribution to aviation."

This is a very important award in America because Bishop Wright was the father of the Wright brothers who made the first chronicled powered flight in 1903.

No. 3. In 1941 I was gazetted Honorary Junior Commander (Captain), ATS.

I would like to be remembered for being the only lady welfare officer in Bedfordshire.

I was gazetted an Honorary (unpaid) Captain (Junior Commander) in the Auxiliary Territorial Service and looked after twenty thousand troops; a great many in secret Air Force stations.

"The first Airmail glider from Manston to Reading, 1931"
In 1984 Barbara Cartland received the Bishop Wright Air Industry Award for her contribution to the development of aviation

Barbara Cartland in her ATS uniform

The women in the services in Bedfordshire were often depressed and miserable because they were allowed only twelve coupons a year for ordinary clothing, which was taken up mainly in stockings and handkerchiefs.

Then I discovered a hole in the rules regarding handicrafts and that I could buy any amount of pretty materials for about two pounds a yard from Peter Jones without coupons.

The girls measured it up on the floor of the Welfare Office and made themselves camiknickers. Every senior officer agreed that I had raised morale.

Next the women came to me in tears saying that they could not be married in their uniforms.

I therefore went to the War Office to ask if they could be allowed some extra coupons for their bridal gowns.

The answer was:

"Don't you know there's a war on?"

However, I said to the rather fierce-looking woman generals:

"I think perhaps I could get the gowns without coupons."

"You must have," one remarked sarcastically, "a touching faith in human nature."

To prove my point I advertised in the *Lady* and was delighted when I was able to buy two beautiful wedding gowns complete with veils and wreaths, one costing seven pounds, the other eight.

I sent them to the War Office with my compliments.

They replied that they would create a pool of wedding gowns for service brides—if I would provide them.

By the end of the war I had bought over a thousand white wedding gowns which could be borrowed for a pound for the day, not only for the War Office, but also for the WAAF and the WRENS.

I can still remember the delight on the women's faces when they knew they could be married in white and feel they were "real brides."

No. 4. In 1974 I was made a Dame of Grace of The Order of Saint John of Jerusalem.

I was very proud when I was one of the first ten women for a thousand years to become members of the Saint John Chapter General.

I joined the Saint John Ambulance Brigade when

*Barbara Cartland in the uniform of
The Order of Saint John of Jerusalem*

as chief lady Welfare Officer for Bedfordshire in 1943 I invited Lady Louis Mountbatten who was one of my oldest friends, to stay with me and talk to the ATS girls at Cardington who were making barrage balloons and were bored because they were seeing very little of the war.

Before she left I found myself with a Saint John uniform as County Cadet Officer for Bedfordshire, as well as my ATS uniform.

I was asked to raise the social standing of the brigade in the county.

First I recruited 2,500 cadets. Then I produced a Saint John Exhibition which was opened by the Queen at Saint James's Palace and then toured the country making thirty-five thousand pounds for local funds.

I tried to do the same when I came to Hertfordshire in 1950 and I am now Deputy President of the county and Chairman of the Saint John Council.

Over the years I have become more and more impressed that the Saint John Ambulance Brigade is the only large organisation in the world whose members give their services free.

Few people realise that you cannot hold a football match, a racehorse meeting, a gymkhana, or in fact anything where there are a large number of people, without the Saint John Ambulance Brigade

being represented.

They work at their normal jobs all day, then give their services free, and in many cases they themselves raise money in their own divisions to pay for bandages and other requirements.

It is an amazing organisation with 350,000 members, many of them in India, Sri Lanka, Hong Kong, and dozens of other countries all over the world.

No. 5. I won for the Conservatives the Socialist-held seat of Hatfield for the Hertfordshire County Council.

I became a County Councillor for nine years.

The first thing I discovered was that the Homes for the Old People were mostly in a very bad state and very little money was spent on them.

In fact, in some places a great many repairs to the kitchens, apart from anything else, needed doing.

I was very shocked at what I found and visited every Home in the county. My daughter, then Viscountess Lewisham, visited two hundred and fifty Homes over the whole of England.

When we sent our reports to the Home Secretary, then Mr. Duncan Sandys, he had an "Investigation" into the "Housing and Conditions of Old People," with the result that a great deal more money

With the Gypsies of Barbaraville, 1964

was spent, visitors were encouraged, and the picture changed over the whole of England.

No. 6. I am delighted that I managed to change the Law of England so that Gypsy children could go to school.

I discovered in 1961 that since the time of Henry VIII when the Gypsies first came to England, nothing had been done for them legally, except that it was a police rule that they should be moved on every twenty-four hours.

For me it was unjust and horrifying that every child in a democracy could have an education with the exception of the Gypsies!

In 1964, after a bitter three-year fight, Sir Keith Joseph, the Home Secretary, ruled that local authorities must "provide camps for their own Gypsies."

As an example I had my own Gypsy camp and I chose a family of Romany Gypsies who had been born in Hertfordshire, lived in Hertfordshire, and only wanted to stay in Hertfordshire all their lives.

They had been moved every twenty-four hours by the police and when I asked the Chief Constable of the county where they could go, he said:

"Nowhere!"

I replied:

"But this is ridiculous! They are human beings. How can they go nowhere?"

He said:

"That's the law."

After three years of bitter battling because nobody wanted Gypsies near them, I managed to get the law changed.

My Gypsies are in a small place not far from Hatfield and which they have christened *Barbaraville* after me.

We now have fourteen County Council camps in Hertfordshire and all the other counties are following suit so that thousands upon thousands of Gypsy children go to school.

I checked after a year with a number of schoolmasters and they all said that the children came to school looking "tidy, clean, and looked upon education as a *privilege."*

No. 7. In 1964 I thought of and founded The National Association for Health.

The Association was to be a front for all the health stores throughout the country and for anyone who produces a product of alternative medicine.

Today it has a 500-million-pound turnover, a fourth of which goes in export. At HELFEX in Birmingham in March 1988 thirty-eight countries were represented.

I first became interested in health in 1935 when my brother Ronald—who was the first Member of Parliament to be killed in the war—was the first Tory MP to visit the "Distressed Areas" and see people dying of starvation.

He was so horrified that I started to work with Lady Rhys Williams, whose son is the Member of Parliament for Kensington, giving vitamin B for habitual abortion and malnutrition in the shape of marmite.

I was so impressed that I took a course on herbal medicine at Culpeper with the famous Mrs. Leyel.

I was also in consultation with several doctors who were becoming interested in alternative medicine.

Dr. Dengler of Baden-Baden allowed me to study some of his cases. He was the first doctor ever to give unsaturated fat in the shape of olive oil for cirrhosis and afflictions of the intestines.

In 1955 I wrote my first health book: *Vitamins for Vitality.* The same year nonsynthetic vitamins first came to England from America.

In 1978, before his assassination in 1979, the Earl Mountbatten of Burma opened our Health Conference. He became a very enthusiastic advocate of vitamins after those I had given him helped him so much.

Now, we in the Association for Health are very grateful to HRH The Prince of Wales for his encouragement and championship of alternative medicine.

We try to make the public realise that while 2,000 million pounds a year are spent by the National Health Service on drugs, which are often dangerous, *our* products have no side effects.

I answer fifty thousand letters a year—twenty-five thousand are questions on health. I try everything new which comes onto the health market on myself, my family, and my household, and I write about them unpaid in three health publications and in any other magazines or newspapers that ask me to do.

The movement is growing year by year, and almost every month something new and exciting comes from one country or another.

If we have good health, we have happiness for ourselves and our children.

No. 8. In 1978 the Royal Philharmonic Orchestra approached me because they said it was the beginning of the Romantic era and would I choose Romantic songs of my period for them to sing.

I was so interested in doing it that I decided that I would sing twelve of the songs myself and EMI made a record with me singing with the Royal

Barbara Cartland with the Royal Philharmonic Orchestra

Philharmonic Orchestra, which sold both in England and America. I was then seventy-seven and the oldest woman ever to make her first *Album of Love Songs.*

No. 9. In 1981 I was chosen as "Achiever of the Year" by the National Home Furnishings Association of Colorado Springs.

This was because I had designed wallpapers and fabrics with the largest company of designers in America—Kirk-Brummel. I opened a display of my designs at Macy's and then my son Ian, who was with me, and I went to Colorado Springs to receive this award. All the women present wore pink.

No. 10. In 1983 in the U.S.A. Bill Blass voted me the Best-Dressed Woman in the world because he says I wear what suits and becomes me.

In 1927 I visited Egypt and found Howard Carter sitting on Tutankhamen's tomb which had recently been discovered.

I was so thrilled with the wonderful colours of the temples and tombs in the Valley of the Kings that I decided that their plain pink and scarab blue inspired me more than any other colour and have used them ever since in my house and my clothes.

I have had a great deal of ribbing one way or another because I wear so much pink but it has only just been realised in America that pink affects the character and personality of a person.

There is in Colorado now a whole prison being painted pink because it has such a good effect on the inmates.

No. 11. In January 1988 I went to the Mairie de Paris to receive La Médaille de la Ville de Paris (The Medal of the City of Paris).

I would like to be remembered for the honour bestowed on me by the City of Paris. This award, made by Monsieur Jacques Chirac, who was the Prime Minister as well as the Mayor of Paris, was for achievement.

Twenty-five million copies of my books, translated into French, had been sold in France, creating a great deal of employment.

It is something I will always cherish, and what touched me so deeply was that when I went to France to receive my medal my publishers bought for a million francs an hour of television. I had a charming interviewer and Charles Aznavour sang his romantic songs.

The studio was a mass of pink roses and rose petals floated down on me from the ceiling.

After the interview I was taken outside and sat in an open Rolls Royce in the park where, by permission of the Prime Minister, pink fireworks were exploded above my head. The initials "B.C." were entwined with a heart, and others were great bursts of pink roses!

I believe it was the first time such a tribute had been paid to an author.

No. 12. In March 1988 I was invited by the Prime Minister of India, Rajiv Gandhi, and his Government to open their health resort outside Delhi which is one of the largest in the world.

Because I have always loved India so much, it was not only a great honour, but also a delight to be able to accept the invitation to open *Body and Soul,* which is what this new resort is called.

This, I believe, is the real secret of the great success of alternative medicine.

The resort contains all the latest equipment for health and beauty, but there is also a section for meditation and yoga.

We in the health movement believe that this is another secret for health, because you must not only work at it with your body, but also with your mind and soul.

I am delighted to say that I was received with enormous enthusiasm by my Indian "fans," who fêted me with a reception in the city.

I also received a most attractive embossed plate from the Prime Minister and his Government.

I am very thrilled by what I have achieved in my life and, if nothing else, I would like to say a prayer of gratitude because I have helped a great number of people, both physically and spiritually.

To sum up my own philosophy I wrote this poem.

A Prayer

One thing I know, life can never die,
Translucent, splendid, flaming like the sun.
Only our bodies wither and deny
The life force when our strength is done.

Let me transmit this wonderful fire,
Even a little through my heart and mind,
Bringing the perfect love we all desire
To those who seek, yet blindly cannot find.

BIBLIOGRAPHY

Fiction:

Jigsaw. London: Duckworth, 1923.

Sawdust. London: Duckworth, 1926.

If the Tree Is Saved. London: Duckworth, 1929.

For What? London: Hutchinson, 1930.

Sweet Punishment. London: Hutchinson, 1931; New York: Pyramid Books, 1973.

A Virgin in Mayfair. London: Hutchinson, 1932; also published as *An Innocent in Mayfair.* New York: Pyramid Books, 1976.

Just off Piccadilly. London: Hutchinson, 1933; also published as *Dance on My Heart.* London: Arrow, 1977; New York: Pyramid Books, 1977.

Not Love Alone. London: Hutchinson, 1933.

A Beggar Wished . . . London: Hutchinson, 1934; also published as *Rainbow to Heaven.* London: Arrow, 1976; New York: Pyramid Books, 1976.

First Class, Lady? London: Hutchinson, 1935; also published as *Love and Linda.* London: Arrow, 1976; New York: Pyramid Books, 1976.

Passionate Attainment. London: Hutchinson, 1935.

Dangerous Experiment. London: Hutchinson, 1936; also published as *Search for Love.* New York: Greenberg, 1937.

Desperate Defiance, London: Hutchinson, 1936; New York: Pyramid Books, 1977.

The Forgotten City. London: Hutchinson, 1936.

Saga at Forty. London: Hutchinson, 1937; also published as *Love at Forty.* London: Arrow, 1977; New York: Pyramid Books, 1977.

Bitter Winds. London: Hutchinson, 1938; also published as *The Bitter Winds of Love.* London: Arrow, 1976; New York: Jove, 1978.

Broken Barriers. London: Hutchinson, 1938; New York: Pyramid Books, 1976.

But Never Free. London: Hutchinson, 1938; also published as *The Adventurer.* London: Arrow, 1977; New York: Pyramid Books, 1977.

The Black Panther. London: Rich & Cowan, 1939; also published as *Lost Love.* London: Arrow, 1969; New York; Pyramid Books, 1970.

The Gods Forget. London: Hutchinson, 1939; also published as *Love in Pity.* New York: Pyramid Books, 1976; London: Arrow, 1977.

Stolen Halo. London: Rich & Cowan, 1940; also published as *The Audacious Adventuress.* London: Hutchinson, 1971; New York: Pyramid Books, 1972.

Now Rough, Now Smooth. London: Hutchinson, 1941.

The Leaping Flame. London: R. Hale, 1942; New York: Pyramid Books, 1974.

Open Wings: A Twenty-third Novel. London: Hutchinson, 1942; New York: Pyramid Books, 1976.

After the Night. London: Hutchinson, 1944; also published as *Towards the Stars.* London: Arrow, 1971; New York: Pyramid Books, 1975.

The Dark Stream. London: Hutchinson, 1944; also published as *This Time It's Love.* London: Arrow, 1977; New York: Pyramid Books, 1977.

Armour against Love. London: Hutchinson, 1945.

Escape from Passion. London: R. Hale, 1945; New York: Pyramid Books, 1977.

Out of Reach. London: Hutchinson, 1945.

Yet She Follows. London: R. Hale, 1945; also published as *A Heart Is Broken.* London: R. Hale, 1972.

Against the Stream, London: Hutchinson, 1946; New York: Pyramid Books, 1977.

The Hidden Heart. London: Hutchinson, 1946; New York: Pyramid Books, 1970.

Again This Rapture. London: Hutchinson, 1947; New York; Pyramid Books, 1977.

The Dream Within. London: Hutchinson, 1947; New York: Pyramid Books, 1976.

If We Will. London: Hutchinson, 1947; also published as *Where Is Love?* London: Arrow, 1971; New York: Pyramid Books, 1971.

No Heart Is Free. London: Rich & Cowan, 1948; New York: Pyramid Books, 1975.

A Duel of Hearts. London: Rich & Cowan, 1949; New York: Pyramid Books, 1970.

The Enchanted Moment, London: Rich & Cowan, 1949; New York: Pyramid Books, 1976.

A Hazard of Hearts. London: Rich & Cowan, 1949; New York: Pyramid Books, 1969.

The Knave of Hearts. London: Rich & Cowan, 1950; New York: Pyramid Books, 1971.

The Little Pretender. London: Rich & Cowan, 1950; New York: Pyramid Books, 1971.

A Ghost in Monte Carlo. London: Rich & Cowan, 1951; New York: Pyramid Books, 1973.

Cupid Rides Pillion. London: Hutchinson, 1952; also published as *The Secret Heart.* New York: Pyramid Books, 1970.

Love Is the Enemy. London: Rich & Cowan, 1952; New York: Pyramid Books, 1970.

Elizabethan Lover. London: Hutchinson, 1953; New York: Pyramid Books, 1971.

Love Me for Ever. London: Hutchinson, 1953; also published as *Love Me Forever.* New York: Pyramid Books, 1970.

Desire of the Heart. London: Hutchinson, 1954; New York: Pyramid Books, 1969.

The Enchanted Waltz. London: Hutchinson, 1955; New York: Pyramid Books, 1971.

The Kiss of the Devil. London: Hutchinson, 1955; New York: Jove, 1981.

The Captive Heart, London: Hutchinson, 1956; New York: Pyramid Books, 1970; also published as *The Royal Pledge.* New York: Pyramid Books, 1970.

The Coin of Love. London: Hutchinson, 1956; New York: Pyramid Books, 1969.

Stars in My Heart. London: Hutchinson, 1957; New York: Pyramid Books, 1971.

Sweet Adventure. London: Hutchinson, 1957; New York: Pyramid Books, 1970.

The Golden Gondola. London: Hutchinson, 1958; New York: Pyramid Books, 1971.

Love in Hiding. London: Hutchinson, 1959; New York: Pyramid Books, 1969.

The Smuggled Heart. London: Hutchinson, 1959; also published as *Debt of Honor.* New York: Pyramid Books, 1970.

Love under Fire. London: Hutchinson, 1960.

Messenger of Love. London: Hutchinson, 1961; New York: Pyramid Books, 1971.

The Wings of Love. London: Hutchinson, 1962; New York: Pyramid Books, 1971.

The Hidden Evil. London: Hutchinson, 1963; New York: Pyramid Books, 1971.

The Fire of Love. London: Hutchinson, 1964; New York: Avon, 1970.

The Unpredictable Bride. London: Hutchinson, 1964; New York: Pyramid Books, 1969.

Love Holds the Cards. London: Hutchinson, 1965; New York: Pyramid Books, 1970.

A Virgin in Paris. London: Hutchinson, 1966; New York: Pyramid Books, 1971; also published as *An Innocent in Paris.* New York: Pyramid Books, 1975.

Love to the Rescue. London: Hutchinson, 1967; New York: Pyramid Books, 1970.

The Enchanting Evil. London: Hutchinson, 1968; New York: Pyramid Books, 1969.

Love Is Contraband. London: Hutchinson, 1968.

The Smuggled Bear. London: Hurst & Blackett, 1968.

The Unknown Heart. London: Hutchinson, 1969; New York: Pyramid Books, 1971.

The Innocent Heiress. New York: Pyramid Books, 1970.

The Reluctant Bride. London: Hutchinson, 1970; New York: Pyramid Books, 1972.

The Secret Fear. London: Hutchinson, 1970; New York: Pyramid Books, 1971.

The Pretty Horse-Breakers. London: Hutchinson, 1971; New York: Pyramid Books, 1975.

The Queen's Messenger. New York: Pyramid Books, 1971.

Stars in Her Eyes. New York: Pyramid Books, 1971.

The Complacent Wife. London: Hutchinson, 1972; New York: Jove, 1981.

A Halo for the Devil. London: Arrow, 1972; New York: Pyramid Books, 1977.

The Irresistible Buck. London: Hutchinson, 1972; New York: Pyramid Books, 1975.

Lost Enchantment. London: Hutchinson, 1972; New York: Pyramid Books, 1973.

The Daring Deception. London: Arrow, 1973; New York: Bantam, 1973.

The Little Adventure. London: Hutchinson, 1973; New York: Bantam, 1974.

The Odious Duke. London: Hutchinson, 1973; New York: Pyramid Books, 1975.

The Wicked Marquis. London: Hutchinson, 1973; New York: Bantam, 1974.

The Bored Bridegroom. London: Pan Books, 1974; New York: Bantam, 1974.

The Castle of Fear. London: Pan Books, 1974; New York: Bantam, 1974.

The Cruel Count. London: Pan Books, 1974; New York: Bantam, 1975.

The Dangerous Dandy. London: Pan Books, 1974; New York: Bantam, 1974.

The Glittering Lights. New York: Bantam, 1974; London: Corgi, 1975.

Journey to Paradise. London: Arrow, 1974; New York: Bantam, 1974.

The Karma of Love. London: Corgi, 1974; New York: Bantam, 1975.

Lessons in Love. London: Arrow, 1974; New York: Bantam, 1974.

The Magnificent Marriage. London: Corgi, 1974; New York: Bantam, 1975.

No Darkness for Love. London: Hutchinson, 1974; New York: Bantam, 1974.

The Penniless Peer. London: Pan Books, 1974; New York: Bantam, 1974.

The Ruthless Rake. London: Pan Books, 1974; New York: Bantam, 1974.

A Sword to the Heart. New York: Bantam, 1974; London: Corgi, 1975.

An Arrow of Love. London: Pan Books, 1975; New York: Bantam, 1976.

As Eagles Fly. London: Pan Books, 1975; New York: Bantam, 1975.

Bewitched. London: Corgi, 1975; New York: Bantam, 1975.

The Call of the Heart. London: Pan Books, 1975; New York: Bantam, 1975.

The Devil in Love. London: Corgi, 1975; New York: Bantam, 1975.

Fire on the Snow. London: Hutchinson, 1975; New York: Bantam, 1976.

The Flame Is Love. London: Pan Books, 1975; New York: Bantam, 1975.

A Frame of Dreams. London: Pan Books, 1975; New York: Bantam, 1976.

The Frightened Bride. London: Pan Books, 1975; New York: Bantam, 1975.

A Gamble with Hearts. London: Pan Books, 1975; New York: Bantam, 1975.

The Impetuous Duchess. London: Corgi, 1975; New York: Bantam, 1975.

A Kiss for the King. London: Pan Books, 1975; New York: Bantam, 1976.

Love Is Innocent. London: Hutchinson, 1975; New York: Bantam, 1975.

The Mask of Love. London: Corgi, 1975; New York: Bantam, 1975.

Say Yes, Samantha. London: Pan Books, 1975; New York: Bantam, 1975.

Shadow of Sin. London: Corgi, 1975; New York: Bantam, 1975.

The Tears of Love. London: Corgi, 1975; New York: Bantam, 1975.

A Very Naughty Angel. London: Pan Books, 1975; New York: Bantam, 1975.

An Angel in Hell. London: Pan Books, 1976; New York: Bantam, 1976.

The Blue-eyed Witch. London: Hutchinson, 1976; New York: Bantam, 1976.

Conquered by Love. New York: Bantam, 1976; London: Pan Books, 1977.

The Disgraceful Duke. London: Corgi, 1976; New York: Bantam, 1977.

A Dream from the Night. London: Corgi, 1976; New York: Bantam, 1976.

The Elusive Earl. London: Hutchinson, 1976; New York: Bantam, 1976.

The Fragrant Flower. London: Pan Books, 1976; New York: Bantam, 1976.

The Golden Illusion. London: Pan Books, 1976; New York: Bantam, 1976.

The Heart Triumphant. London: Corgi, 1976; New York: Bantam, 1976.

Hungry for Love. London: Corgi, 1976; New York: Bantam, 1976.

The Husband Hunters. London: Pan Books, 1976; New York: Bantam, 1976.

The Incredible Honeymoon. London: Pan Books, 1976; New York: Bantam, 1976.

Love in Hiding. New York: Pyramid Books, 1976.

Moon over Eden. London: Pan Books, 1976; New York:

Bantam, 1976.

Never Laugh at Love. London: Corgi, 1976; New York: Bantam, 1976.

No Time for Love. London: Pan Books, 1976; New York: Bantam, 1976.

Passions in the Sand. London: Pan Books, 1976; New York: Bantam, 1976.

The Proud Princess. London: Corgi, 1976; New York: Bantam, 1976.

The Secret of the Glen. London: Corgi, 1976; New York: Bantam, 1976.

The Slaves of Love. London: Pan Books, 1976; New York: Bantam, 1976.

The Wild Cry of Love. London: Pan Books, 1976; New York: Bantam, 1976.

The Castle Made for Love. Williamsport, Pa.: Duron Books, 1977; London: Pan Books, 1978.

The Curse of the Clan. London: Pan Books, 1977; Williamsport, Pa.: Duron Books, 1977.

The Dragon and the Pearl. London: Hutchinson, 1977; Williamsport, Pa.: Duron Books, 1977.

The Dream and the Glory. London: Pan Books, 1977; New York: Bantam, 1977.

A Duel with Destiny. London: Corgi, 1977; New York: Bantam, 1977.

The Hell-Cat and the King. Williamsport, Pa.: Duron Books, 1977; London: Pan Books, 1978.

Kiss the Moonlight. London: Pan Books, 1977.

Look, Listen, and Love. London: Pan Books, 1977; Williamsport, Pa.: Duron Books, 1977.

Love and the Loathsome Leopard. Williamsport, Pa.: Duron Books, 1977; London: Corgi, 1978.

Love Locked In. London: Pan Books, 1977; New York: Dutton, 1977.

The Love Pirate. Williamsport, Pa.: Duron Books, 1977; London: Corgi, 1978.

The Magic of Love. London: Pan Books, 1977; New York: Bantam, 1977.

The Marquis Who Hated Women. London: Pan Books, 1977; Williamsport, Pa.: Duron Books, 1977.

The Mysterious Maid-Servant. London: Hutchinson, 1977; New York: Bantam, 1977.

The Naked Battle. Williamsport, Pa.: Duron Books, 1977; London: Hutchinson, 1978.

No Escape from Love. Williamsport, Pa.: Duron Books, 1977.

The Outrageous Lady. London: Pan Books, 1977; Williamsport, Pa.: Duron Books, 1977.

Punishment of a Vixen. London: Corgi, 1977; Williamsport, Pa.: Duron Books, 1977.

A Rhapsody of Love. London: Pan Books, 1977.

The Saint and the Sinner. Williamsport, Pa.: Duron Books, 1977; London: Corgi, 1978.

The Sign of Love. Williamsport, Pa.: Duron Books, 1977; London: Pan Books, 1978.

The Taming of Lady Lorinda. London: Pan Books, 1977; New York: Bantam, 1977.

The Temptation of Torilla. Williamsport, Pa.: Duron Books, 1977; London: Corgi, 1978.

A Touch of Love. Williamsport, Pa.: Duron Books, 1977; London: Corgi, 1978.

Vote for Love. London: Corgi, 1977; New York: Bantam, 1977.

The Wild Unwilling Wife. London: Pan Books, 1977; New York: Dutton, 1977.

Alone in Paris. London: Hutchinson, 1978; Williamsport, Pa.: Duron Books, 1979.

The Chieftain without a Heart. London: Corgi, 1978; New York: Dutton, 1978.

Flowers for the God of Love. London: Pan Books, 1978; New York: Dutton, 1979.

A Fugitive from Love. London: Pan Books, 1978; Williamsport, Pa.: Duron Books, 1978.

The Ghost Who Fell in Love. London: Pan Books, 1978; New York: Dutton, 1978.

The Irresistible Force. London: Arrow, 1978; Williamsport, Pa.: Duron Books, 1978.

The Judgment of Love. Williamsport, Pa.: Duron Books, 1978; London: Hutchinson, 1979.

Lord Ravenscar's Revenge. London: Corgi, 1978; Williamsport, Pa.: Duron Books, 1978.

Love Leaves at Midnight. London: Hutchinson, 1978; Williamsport, Pa.: Duron Books, 1978.

Love, Lords, and Lady-Birds. London: Pan Books, 1978; New York: Dutton, 1978.

Lovers in Paradise. Williamsport, Pa.: Duron Books, 1978; London: Pan Books, 1979.

Magic or Mirage? London: Corgi, 1978; Williamsport, Pa.: Duron Books, 1978.

The Passion and the Flower. London: Pan Books, 1978; New York: Dutton, 1978.

A Princess in Distress. London: Pan Books, 1978; Williamsport, Pa.: Duron Books, 1978.

The Problems of Love. London: Corgi, 1978; Williamsport, Pa.: Duron Books, 1978.

The Race for Love. Williamsport, Pa.: Duron Books, 1978; London: Corgi, 1979.

A Runaway Star. London: Pan Books, 1978; Williamsport, Pa.: Duron Books, 1978.

The Twists and Turns of Love. London: Arrow, 1978; Williamsport, Pa.: Duron Books, 1978.

Bride to the King. London: Corgi, 1979; New York: Dutton, 1980.

The Dawn of Love. London: Corgi, 1979; New York: Dutton, 1980.

The Drums of Love. London: Pan Books, 1979; Williamsport, Pa.: Duron Books, 1979.

The Duchess Disappeared. London: Pan Books, 1979; Williamsport, Pa.: Duron Books, 1979.

The Duke and the Preacher's Daughter. London: Corgi, 1979; Williamsport, Pa.: Duron Books, 1979.

The Explosion of Love. New York: Bantam, 1979; London: Hutchinson, 1980.

A Gentleman in Love. London: Pan Books, 1979; New York: Bantam, 1980.

Imperial Splendor. London: Pan Books, 1979; New York: Dutton, 1979.

Light of the Moon. London: Pan Books, 1979; Williamsport, Pa.: Duron Books, 1979.

Love Climbs In. London: Corgi, 1979; Williamsport, Pa.: Duron Books, 1979.

Love Has His Way. London: Corgi, 1979; New York: Bantam, 1979.

Love in the Clouds. London: Corgi, 1979; New York: Dutton, 1979.

Love in the Dark. London: Hutchinson, 1979; Williamsport, Pa.: Duron Books, 1979.

A Nightingale Sang. London: Corgi, 1979; Williamsport, Pa.: Duron Books, 1979.

Only Love. London: Hutchinson, 1979; New York: Bantam, 1980.

The Prince and the Pekingese. London: Pan Books, 1979; Williamsport, Pa.: Duron Books, 1979.

The Prisoner of Love. London: Arrow, 1979; Williamsport, Pa.: Duron Books, 1979.

A Serpent of Satan. London: Pan Books, 1979; Williamsport, Pa.: Duron Books, 1979.

Terror in the Sun. London: Pan Books, 1979; New York: Bantam, 1979.

The Treasure Is Love. London: Arrow, 1979; Williamsport, Pa.: Duron Books, 1979.

Who Can Deny Love? London: Corgi, 1979; New York: Bantam, 1979.

Women Have Hearts. London: Pan Books, 1979; New York: Bantam, 1980.

Free from Fear. London: Pan Books, 1980; New York: Bantam, 1980.

The Goddess and the Gaiety Girl. London: Pan Books, 1980; New York: Bantam, 1980.

A Heart Is Stolen. London: Corgi, 1980.

The Horizons of Love. London: Pan Books, 1980.

Little White Doves of Love. London: Pan Books, 1980; New York: Bantam, 1980.

Lost Laughter. London: Pan Books, 1980; New York: Dutton; 1980.

Love at the Helm. London: Weidenfeld & Nicolson, 1980; New York: Everest House, 1983.

Love for Sale. London: Corgi, 1980; New York: Dutton, 1980.

Love in the Moon. London: New English Library, 1980; New York: Bantam, 1981.

Lucifer and the Angel. London: Hutchinson, 1980; New York: Bantam, 1980.

Money, Magic, and Marriage. London: Arrow, 1980.

Ola and the Sea Wolf. London: Arrow, 1980; New York: Bantam, 1980.

The Perfection of Love. London: Corgi,1980; New York: Bantam, 1980.

The Power of the Prince. London: Pan Books, 1980; New York: Bantam, 1980.

Pride and the Poor Princess. London: Corgi, 1980; New York: Bantam, 1981.

The Prude and the Prodigal. London: Pan Books, 1980; New York: Bantam, 1980.

Punished with Love. London: Pan Books, 1980; New York: Bantam, 1980.

Signpost to Love. London: Corgi, 1980; New York: Bantam, 1980.

A Song of Love. London: Pan Books, 1980; New York: Jove, 1980.

The Waltz of Hearts. London: Pan Books, 1980; New York: Bantam, 1981.

Afraid. London: Arrow, 1981; New York: Bantam, 1981.

Count the Stars. London: New English Library, 1981; New York: Jove, 1981.

Dollars for the Duke. London: Corgi, 1981; New York: Bantam, 1981.

Dreams Do Come True. London: Pan Books, 1981; New York: Bantam, 1981.

Enchanted. New York: Bantam, 1981.

For All Eternity. New York: Jove, 1981; London: Corgi, 1982.

From Hell to Heaven. London: Corgi, 1981; New York: Bantam, 1981.

Gift of the Gods. London: Pan Books, 1981; New York: Bantam, 1981.

The Heart of the Clan. London: Arrow, 1981; New York: Jove, 1981.

An Innocent in Russia. London: Pan Books, New York: Bantam, 1981.

In the Arms of Love. London: Hutchinson, 1981; New York: Jove, 1981.

The Kiss of Life. New York: Bantam, 1981; London: Arrow, 1983.

The Lioness and the Lily. London: Corgi, 1981; New York: Bantam, 1981.

Love Wins. London: Pan Books, 1981.

A Night of Gaiety. London: Pan Books, 1981; New York: Bantam, 1981.

A Portrait of Love. New York: Bantam, 1981; London: Corgi, 1982.

Pure and Untouched. London: Arrow, 1981; New York: Everest House, 1981.

The River of Love. London: Pan Books, 1981; New York: Bantam, 1981.

A Shaft of Sunlight. New York: Bantam, 1981; London: Corgi, 1982.

Touch a Star. New York: Jove, 1981; London: Corgi, 1982.

Winged Magic. London: Corgi, 1981; New York: Bantam, 1981.

The Wings of Ecstasy. London: Pan Books, 1981; New York: Jove, 1981.

The Call of the Highlands. London: Hutchinson, 1982.

Caught by Love. London: Arrow, 1982.

A King in Love. New York: Everest House, 1982.

Kneel for Mercy. London: New English Library, 1982.

Lies for Love. New York: Bantam, 1982; London: Corgi, 1983.

Looking for Love. New York: Bantam, 1982; London: Arrow, 1984.

Love and the Marquis. London: Pan Books, 1982.

Love Rules. London: New English Library, 1982; New York: Bantam, 1982.

Love Wins. New York: Bantam, 1982.

Moments of Love. London: Pan Books, 1982.

Riding to the Moon. New York: Everest House, 1982; London: Arrow, 1983.

Secret Harbour. London: Corgi, 1982; also published as *Secret Harbor.* New York: Bantam, 1982.

The Vibrations of Love. London: Corgi, 1982; New York: Bantam, 1982.

Diona and a Dalmation. London: Hutchinson, 1983.

A Duke in Danger. London: Pan Books, 1983.

Fire in the Blood. London: Pan Books, 1983.

From Hate to Love. London: New English Library, 1983.

Gypsy Magic. London: Pan Books, 1983.

Lights, Laughter, and a Lady. London: New English Library, 1983.

Love and Lucia. London: Pan Books, 1983.

Love on the Wind. London: Pan Books, 1983.

A Marriage Made in Heaven. London: Corgi, 1983.

A Miracle in Music. London: Corgi, 1983.

Mission to Monte Carlo. London: Corgi, 1983.

Tempted to Love. London: Pan Books, 1983.

Wish for Love. London: Corgi, 1983.

Barbara Cartland's Princess to the Rescue (for children; illustrated by Jane Longmore). London: Hamlyn, 1984, New York: F. Watts, 1984.

Bride to a Brigand. London: New English Library, 1984.

Help from the Heart. London: Arrow, 1984.

The Island of Love. London: Pan Books, 1984.

Journey to a Star. London: Corgi, 1984.

Light of the Gods. London: Corgi, 1984.

Love Comes West. London: Pan Books, 1984.

Miracle for a Madonna. London: Hutchinson, 1984.

Moonlight on the Sphinx. London: Hutchinson, 1984.

The Peril and the Prince. London: New English Library, 1984.

Revenge of the Heart. London: Pan Books, 1984.

Royal Punishment. London: Severn House, 1984.

The Scots Never Forget. London: Corgi, 1984.

Theresa and a Tiger. London: New English Library, 1984.

The Unbreakable Spell. London: Corgi, 1984.

The Unwanted Wedding. London: Corgi, 1984.

A Very Unusual Wife. London: Pan Books, 1984.

White Lilac. London: Pan Books, 1984.

Alone and Afraid. London: Pan Books, 1985.

The Devilish Deception. London: New English Library, 1985; New York: Jove, 1985.

Escape. London: Severn House, 1985; New York: Jove, 1986.

Look with Love. London: Pan Books, 1985.

Paradise Found. New York: Jove, 1985; London: Arrow, 1986.

A Rebel Princess. London: Corgi, 1985.

Safe at Last. London: Pan Books, 1985; New York: Jove, 1986.

Temptation for a Teacher. London: Pan Books, 1985.

A Witch's Spell. London: Corgi, 1985.

An Angel Runs Away. London: Pan Books, 1986; New York: Jove, 1987.

Crowned with Love. New York: Jove, 1986.

The Devil Defeated. New York: Jove, 1986.

A Dream in Spain. London: Pan Books, 1986; New York: Jove, 1986.

The Golden Cage. New York: Jove, 1986.

Haunted. London: Pan Books, 1986; New York: Jove, 1986.

Helga in Hiding. London: Arrow, 1986; New York: Jove, 1986.

Listen to Love. New York: Jove, 1986.

Love Casts Out Fear. London: Severn House, 1986; New York: Jove, 1987.

Love Joins the Clans. London: Pan Books, 1986; New York: Jove, 1987.

The Love Trap. London: Pan Books, 1986: Jove, 1986.

Secret of the Mosque. London: Pan Books, 1986.

Bewildered in Berlin. New York: Jove, 1987.

Dancing on a Rainbow. New York: Jove, 1987.

The Earl Escapes. New York: Jove, 1987.

Forced to Marry. New York: Jove, 1987.

Love and Kisses. New York: Jove, 1987.

The Love Puzzle. New York: Jove, 1987.

Starlight over Tunis. New York: Jove, 1987.

Wanted—A Wedding Ring. New York: Jove, 1987.

A World of Love. New York: Jove, 1987.

Sapphires in Siam. New York: Jove, 1988.

Under name Barbara McCorquodale:

Sleeping Swords. London: R. Hale, 1942.

Love is Mine. London: Rich & Cowan, 1952; also published under name Barbara Cartland. London: Arrow, 1970; New York: Pyramid Books, 1972.

The Passionate Pilgrim. London: Rich & Cowan, 1952; also published under name Barbara Cartland. London: Arrow, 1970; New York: Pyramid Books, 1976.

Blue Heather. London: Rich & Cowan, 1953; also published under name Barbara Cartland. London: Arrow, 1969; New York: Pyramid Books, 1975.

Wings on My Heart. London: Rich & Cowan, 1954; also published under name Barbara Cartland. London: Arrow, 1969; New York: Pyramid Books, 1975.

The Kiss of Paris. London: Rich & Cowan, 1956; also published under name Barbara Cartland. London: Arrow, 1971; New York: Pyramid Books, 1972.

Love Forbidden. London: Rich & Cowan, 1957; also published under name Barbara Cartland. London: Arrow, 1971; New York: Pyramid Books, 1973.

The Thief of Love. London: Jenkins, 1957; also published under name Barbara Cartland. New York: Pyramid Books, 1975; London: Sphere Books, 1980.

Lights of Love. London: Jenkins, 1958; also published under name Barbara Cartland. London: Arrow, 1969; New York: Pyramid Books, 1973.

Sweet Enchantress. London: Jenkins, 1958; also published under name Barbara Cartland. New York: Pyramid Books, 1976; London: Sphere Books, 1980.

A Kiss of Silk. London: Jenkins, 1959; also published under name Barbara Cartland. New York: Pyramid Books, 1974; London: Sphere Books, 1980.

The Price Is Love. London: Jenkins, 1960; also published

under name Barbara Cartland. New York: Pyramid Books, 1973; London: Sphere Books, 1980.

The Runaway Heart. London: Jenkins, 1961; also published under name Barbara Cartland. London: Sphere Books, 1967; New York: Pyramid Books, 1974.

A Light to the Heart. London: Ward, Lock, 1962; also published under name Barbara Cartland. London: Arrow, 1971; New York: Pyramid Books, 1973.

Love Is Dangerous. London: Ward, Lock, 1963; also published under name Barbara Cartland. London: Arrow, 1969; New York: Pyramid Books, 1976.

Danger by the Nile. London: Ward, Lock, 1964; also published under name Barbara Cartland. London: Arrow, 1971; New York: Avon, 1975.

Love on the Run. London: Ward, Lock, 1965; also published under name Barbara Cartland. London: Arrow, 1969; New York: Pyramid Books, 1973.

Theft of a Heart. London: Ward, Lock, 1966; also published under name Barbara Cartland. London: Arrow, 1969; New York: Pyramid Books, 1977.

"Camfield Romance" Series:

Lucky in Love. London: Pan Books, 1982; New York: Jove, 1982.

The Poor Governess. New York: Jove, 1982; London: Corgi, 1983.

Winged Victory. London: Pan Books, 1982; New York: Jove, 1982.

Nonfiction:

Touch the Stars: A Clue to Happiness. London: Rider & Co., 1935.

Ronald Cartland (biography). London: Collins, 1942; New York: Hutchinson, 1945; also published as *My Brother, Ronald.* London: Sheldon Press, 1980.

The Isthmus Years: Reminiscences of the Years 1919–1939. London and New York: Hutchinson, 1943.

The Years of Opportunity, 1939–1945 (autobiography). London and New York: Hutchinson, 1948.

The Fascinating Forties: A Book for the Over Forties. London: Jenkins, 1954.

Bewitching Women. London: Muller, 1955.

Marriage for Moderns. London: Jenkins, 1955.

The Outrageous Queen: A Biography of Christina of Sweden. London: Muller, 1956.

Polly, My Wonderful Mother. London: Jenkins, 1956.

Love, Life, and Sex. London: Jenkins, 1957.

The Scandalous Life of King Carol. London: Muller, 1957.

Look Lovely, Be Lovely. London: Jenkins, 1958.

The Private Life of Charles II: The Women He Loved. London: Muller, 1958.

The Private Life of Elizabeth, Empress of Austria. London: Muller, 1959; New York: Pyramid Books, 1974.

Vitamins for Vitality. London: W. & G. Foyle, 1959.

Husbands and Wives. London: Arthur Barker, 1961; revised edition published as *Love and Marriage.* London: Thorsons, 1971.

Josephine, Empress of France. London: Hutchinson, 1961; New York: Pyramid Books, 1974.

Diane de Poitiers (biography). London: Hutchinson, 1962.

Etiquette Handbook (illustrated by Francis Marshall). London: Hamlyn, 1962; revised edition published as *Barbara Cartland's Book of Etiquette.* London: Arrow, 1972.

The Many Facets of Love. London: W. H. Allen, 1963.

Metternich, the Passionate Diplomat. London: Hutchinson, 1964.

Sex and the Teenager. London: Muller, 1964.

Living Together. London: Muller, 1965.

The Pan Book of Charm. London: Pan Books, 1965.

Woman—The Enigma. London: Frewin, 1965.

I Search for Rainbows: 1946–1966 (autobiography). London: Hutchinson, 1967; New York: Bantam, 1977.

The Youth Secret. London: Corgi, 1968.

The Magic of Honey. London: Corgi, 1970.

We Danced All Night: 1919–1929 (autobiography). London: Hutchinson, 1970.

Barbara Cartland's Health Food Cookery Book (illustrated by F. Marshall). London: Hodder & Stoughton, 1971.

Barbara Cartland's Book of Beauty and Health (illustrated by F. Marshall). London: Hodder & Stoughton, 1972.

Lines on Life and Love (verse). London: Hutchinson, 1972.

Men Are Wonderful. London: Corgi, 1973.

Food for Love. London: Corgi, 1975.

The Magic of Honey Cookbook. London: Corgi, 1976.

Barbara Cartland's Book of Useless Information. London: Corgi, 1977.

Recipes for Lovers, with Nigel Gordon. London: Corgi, 1977.

Barbara Cartland's Book of Love and Lovers. London: M. Joseph, 1978; New York: Ballantine, 1978.

I Seek the Miraculous (autobiography) London: Sheldon Press, 1978; New York: Dutton, 1978.

Romantic Royal Marriages. London: Express Books, 1981; New York: Beaufort Books, 1981.

Keep Young and Beautiful, with Elinor Glyn. London: Duckworth, 1982.

Barbara Cartland's Etiquette for Love and Romance. New York: Pocket Books, 1984.

Getting Older, Growing Younger. London: Sidgwick & Jackson, 1984; New York: Dodd, 1984.

The Romance of Food. London: Hamlyn, 1984; New York: Doubleday, 1984.

Barbara Cartland's Book of Health. London: Javelin, 1985.

Editor of:

The Common Problem, by Ronald Cartland. London and New York: Hutchinson, 1943.

The Light of Love: A Thought for Every Day. London: Sheldon Press, 1979; also published as *The Light of Love: Lines to Live by Day by Day.* New York: Elsevier/Nelson Books, 1980.

Written with Love: Passionate Love-Letters. London: Hutchinson, 1981.

Turner Cassity

1929-

A LITTLE OF MYSELF

How does one become what one is? Not, surely, by way of childhood, in spite of what genetics, psychology, and economics may suggest. I find it difficult to believe that experienced adults can regard childhood as sufficiently interesting to describe as happy or unhappy. The temptation for me is to deal with it as Mrs. Wharton dealt with divorce (hers; not others')—to treat it as something hardly worthy of mention.

I did the things most small boys do, but I suspect I found them less satisfying than most small boys do. If you ask what was lacking all I can say is that Forest, Mississippi, population 2,500, had no architecture as I understood architecture from futuristic comics and the covers of *Popular Mechanics.* Nor was the landscape in any way satisfactory. To an eye conditioned by the other planets of the airbrush, the low hills and the forests of second-growth pine appeared featureless. I may add that they do still. Scenery begins at Shreveport.

Fortunately, there were gravel pits in the area, and these were settings of more appeal, having the glamour of deserts without their alarming distances, and the mystery of caverns without the darkness and the claustrophobia. My contemporaries and I would have thought it an absolute failure of the imagination to play in a park, let alone a playground. As a matter of principle I vote against bond issues for the construction of these instruments of regimentation. Let them have gravel.

Persons tended to be more satisfactory, the nature of the local gene pool being such that many looked acceptably like illustrations. Also, if the scenario of the day—*Tarzan,* for example—made vegetation inevitable, there were chinaberry trees, commonplace, but tropically exotic, and with low branches accessible to the least intrepid. To be avoided in blossom, of course, as the tiny lavender flowers, a definition of cheap perfume, attract insects in number and variety frightening even for Mississippi. By early summer, however, the berries themselves have clustered, hard and green, and lethal pellets for slingshots. Chinaberry wars raged over entire neighborhoods. I wonder all of us did not grow up blind. It was not air rifles which were the peril. At the end of the summer such of the berries as had not become

"A triptych of ears": Turner Cassity with his father, Hot Springs, Arkansas, 1930

missiles turned into a pulpy amber and fell to the ground, there to ferment and attract other insects, or to make the chickens drunk. A staggering rooster is less Disney-like than macabre. I had a book of Russian fairy tales centering on one Baba Yaga, who lived in the forest in a hut raised on four chicken legs. I always thought of her when I saw one of those intemperate birds, who seemed as sinister as the folkloric witch. The only Russian chicken folk art I care for is that of Fabergé, not for reasons of reaction but because his eggs look to me like models of nineteenth-century spaceships.

Pine trees were for lumber. My family on both sides were sawmill people for generations—longleaf yellow pine—and I can still hear the resinously oozing contempt with which they would pronounce "plywood." Pulpwood, like Teddy Wharton, was not even to be spoken of. It was an industry peopled by the cast of *Texas Chainsaw Massacre*. A real sawmill had six high smokestacks, elaborately guyed, and, smoking like Battleship Row in the Pearl Harbor newsreels, rose at the center of a great complex of planing mills, dry kilns, conveyors, scrap heaps, sawdust piles, millpond, and lumberyards, the smell of which is irresistible to me at this moment. At the whiff of a sawmill I will take the extreme measure of turning off the air-conditioning, rolling down the windows, and leaving the interstate.

My father's mother's family were cabinetmakers in Texarkana before the Civil War. During the war they evaded conscription and profiteered by turning their talents and their equipment to the manufacture of gun stocks. By the 1880s they controlled the means of production and were sawmilling in Louisiana, first in Webster and later in Bienville Parish. In 1915, in a reenactment of the Great Trek, or the remove of Father Abraham from Ur of the Chaldees, they relocated in Mississippi, carrying with them cattle, servants, pets, household goods, and the machinery of the mill itself. The company cut out in 1929, the year I was born, but there was some thought of yet another move, to Flagstaff, Arizona. Now there is a landscape one could have related to. Lowell Observatory is just outside town, and Meteor Crater, the ultimate gravel pit, is fifty miles away.

My great-grandfather Cassity, who did fight in the Civil War, was so unreconstructable that he afterwards joined Quantrill's Raiders. The story in the family is that he quarrelled with Quantrill over the killing of Yankees. Whether killing too many or killing too few is not certain. He then fled, depending on which story you accept, to Panama or to Nicaragua. I should like to think of him as filibustering with Walker or wallowing in the corruption of the Compagnie Universelle du Canal Interocéanique, but the chronology does not quite work out in either case. He spoke a little French, but it was Cajun, not De Lesseps's. He may well have been working for the Panama Railroad. Whatever he was doing I have no doubt that he was Hell on wheels, because the strain keeps surfacing in his descendants, one of whom was deputy-sheriff of Caddo Parish under Huey Long. There is also the achieving strain, represented by yours truly, and by Bert Jones, former quarterback of the Los Angeles Rams. But the adventurer lost his wife and young family to yellow fever and returned to the States to become a minister of the Gospel, beginning a second family, to which my grandfather belonged, and, presently, a third. Curiously, I am the last to bear the name, although, like all proper Southerners, I have many cousins.

My father's mother, who was badly crippled by arthritis, had notions about plant life as idiosyncratic as mine. She took great pleasure in gardening—well, in the gardening of her yard boys—but for her it was a morality play. Some flowers were more *worthy* than others, and their worth was more or less in direct proportion to the difficulty in raising them. A "volunteer," a plant that came up on its own, brought out the intonation reserved elsewhere for plywood. Tropical varieties were suspect, by reason both of their profusion and their vividness. Pallid English standards were best, although even hybrid tea roses had to answer for their lack of smell, a stricture with which I fully concur. Cannas counted as tropical, and, worse, brightened without effort the hovels of cooks and washwomen. Gardenias, before the days of embalming, were for funerals, not as ornaments but as necessities. When anyone dies, telephone the funeral home and be thankful that it is there.

Gardening was not my grandmother's only interest. The phrase was not available to her, but she could have drawn a flowchart of what happens to a log from the moment it leaves the forest, i.e., the stand of timber, until it is sold off the yard as lumber, and so could her sisters. Carriages and skidders and dummy engines were as familiar to them as embroidery hoops and crochet needles, and, I suspect, more interesting, as well they might be.

For the other side of the family, "lukewarm" elicited the tone of quiet reduction to powder that "volunteer" did in reference to the botanical moralities. I was ten years old before I realized the word referred to temperature. My great-aunts used it to describe families who had been less-than-passionate Confederates. In the kitchen or in the bath the term was tepid, and, in a climate like Mississippi, praise. One did not fail to notice that the lukewarm tended to have more money than the deeply committed, an observation that I have elevated into a principle. Where would I be if the cabinetmakers had not been lukewarm; and I am smug in the knowledge that at least one ingeniously tepid family hid its cotton bales in a gravel pit.

Neither side of the family escaped the Confederate curse of nicknaming and diminutives. God help genealogists who have to figure out that Abby was Albert and Moddy was Martha. I had a cousin Tincy who was very tall and have one a decade older than I am who is still Turner-Boy. Better him than me, but I blush to say that I myself as an infant was responsible for such horrors as Sue-Sue (Mary Sue) and Wo-Wo (Ora). Why did no one slap me. Nor were the Black folks guiltless. The washwoman of choice, anything but little, was Bo-Peep.

Elementary-school teachers in those days imparted facts and took no nonsense. To their great credit, they usually required even that we use the names we were christened with, creating identity crises in first grade. I doubt that all of those Bitsies and Tippies and PeeWees and Hoppies know who they are yet. Hoppy (Hopalong) perhaps does. He is I.

Excellent as my teachers were, my Sunday-school teachers were better. I intend it as praise when I say that they made the Old Testament seem a continuum with the adventure strips, nor was it lost on me that the Gustave Doré illustrations were in the same continuum. I was a very sharp-eyed little boy, for matters that held interest for me. I still cannot tell an oak tree from an elm. Hardwoods, you know. I knew at once, though, that without Doré the landscape of other planets was unthinkable.

Although the Sunday school was Presbyterian, original sin and total depravity were not stressed. The assumption was that if you had any sense and kept your eyes open you could hardly fail to arrive at Calvin's conclusions. I did not respond as readily to the New Testament as to the Old, and I hope I do not slander my teachers when I say it was obvious they did not. N.T. cities and plains are on a much smaller scale, and many of its characters do seem the most terrible busybodies. I intend no praise when I say they remind me of Jimmy Carter. The White South used to put a very high value on minding one's own business.

I did enjoy the book of Revelation, but only because so much of it is devoted to architecture (Philip Johnson obviously reads it), and to air-traffic control for the squadrons of angels. I have written three poems on the Tower of Babel and may write three more. If Mr. Johnson can keep building it I can keep writing about it. I suppose my favorite passage in the Bible is Elijah going at the Prophets of Baal: "Call him louder. Perchance he sleepeth, or is on a journey." That is a man who could have dealt with the Ayatollah.

Denominations existed, but were uniformly Protestant. A Catholic student in my elementary school would have been as outrageous as the Whore of Babylon on the courthouse square in a feather boa. In the fifth grade one did appear. Any new student was

an event, and this one was apocalyptic. We knew that Catholics fasted during Lent, and kept waiting for her to faint from hunger. She was in fact very thin. The interesting thing would be to know how we dated the onset of Lent, as not even the churches, let alone the schools, observed Good Friday, much less Ash Wednesday. That would have been rank papism.

The Presbyterian church, as a structure, would have been stark in Scotland, but the constraints were financial, not liturgical. Nothing constrained the psychological identification of Miss Mattie Christian (Mrs., actually) with the Prophet Isaiah, or the grandeur she brought to Joshua halting the sun on its course. The myth of Phäethon is a poor substitute.

It is traditional in literary autobiography to enumerate one's childhood reading. I am surprised that writers are so willing to tip their hands, but as I have already tipped mine I might as well come out and say that I chose books for their illustrations. I read the first two books of *Paradise Lost,* and *The Rime of the Ancient Mariner,* exactly as one would read any other science fiction. You will guess who the artist was. Even he could not get me through *The Divine Comedy,* though he managed to make London poverty more interesting than ever Dickens did. At this moment I would not read *David Copperfield* if you went macho and held a shotgun to my head. In a long career, Edgar Rice Burroughs outlived as many illustrators as he did ape-men, without ever getting what he really needed, which is Leni Riefenstahl. Burne Hogarth, who drew the newspaper panels, fatally suggests William Blake, and Johnny Weismuller suggested not sleeping in the crotches of trees so much as sleeping off hangovers in the crotches of trees. Where were you, Indiana Jones, when Edgar needed you?

My favorite reading was description of A Century of Progress, which closed two years before I was literate. At the age of fifty-nine, at the Cooper-Hewitt Museum in New York, I saw an exhibit that included Joseph Urban's original designs for the fair. The only comparable experience, except for the one I shall relate at the end of this essay, was discovering Rider Haggard when I was well past thirty. Like Kipling, he is the rare writer good enough not to benefit from illustration. I read Jules Verne, enjoying the Victoriana more than the wave of the future; I read Victor Hugo, even unto *Toilers of the Sea.* The great set piece about quicksand was highly relevant to those of us in swampy Mississippi. I would no more have read a children's book than I would have played in a playground. Tenniel attracted me to *Alice in Wonderland,* but after a few pages I found myself substituting Annie, Punjab, and the Asp for the Carroll figures, to the great improvement of the story. Well, Richard Strauss said once that he could conduct a Beethoven symphony only if he made up a program to go along with it (and wouldn't one like to know what those programs were). If I were filming either *Alice* or *Peter Pan,* or, for that matter, *David Copperfield,* I should place the setting in the Raj. England is a country whose relentless pastoralism deeply estranges me.

"He has too much imagination" was, except for lukewarm, the ultimate put-down, and I imagine it was said behind my back as often as to my face. The South had, and has, none, which is why I spend a great deal of time in California, and would love to spend more.

M y mother and her mother were musicians in silent-movie theatres. The more film courses universities offer the less people know about the silent screen. I should like to be able to give you, as a document, my mother's reminiscences, but as she dislikes the tape recorder as much as the audio equipment of original offense, this will not be possible. Students will know that the New York Roxy employed an orchestra (at one time Eugene Ormandy conducted it), and that in small towns the Saturday-afternoon serial had a piano accompaniment. The rest is silence, except, of course, it wasn't. Textbooks may mention that an extraordinary, i.e., road show, feature, like *Thief of Baghdad,* would have an original score composed for it. They will not mention that a studio sent out the parts in advance, along with the posters and lobby cards. Hollywood did not overestimate the ability of musicians to sight-read. The score was cued to the subtitles. The present controversy over surtitles in the opera house is a nonissue.

Remember that before TV seduced away their audience theatres had continuous showings. Before the orchestra came on for the two evening performances, and the live entertainment between, there were four earlier showings that had to be got through. The box office opened at noon.

In a theatre of some pretension, a small orchestra covered the matinees, alternating with an organ, the two overlapping and phasing in and out in such a manner that the audience, imperceptive at the best of times, never knew the difference. In regard to repertory the musicians were on their own, and, I have no doubt, faked a lot. Mood was the important thing. I have in my possession an anthology—it was once the property of Alfred Lehman Engel—indexed by such subjects as nocturne, orgy, and suspense. The distinction between copyright and public domain must have been hazier then than now. The estate of Isaac Albeniz, without whom the Latin lovers could hardly

have functioned, cannot have waived copyright. Either Spain or California was not signatory to the convention. The scores expressly composed called for "augmented orchestra," always advertised as such. The smallest house could get together a trio: piano, violin, flute.

Few works of art can hold up under the scrutiny of six showings a day, and this grandmother had many unkind things to say about the medium of her livelihood, especially about the sisters Gish. At the great console in the sky it must be a vexation to her that Lillian is simpering into her ninth decade. Mother's *bête noire* is Nita Naldi, who is dismissed as "greasy." When I finally saw Nita in *Blood and Sand,* at the Museum of Modern Art, I thought that she was rather sexy, but it may have been the Albeniz accompaniment.

Mother's career climaxed when, at a performance of the deMille *Ten Commandments,* the theatre burned down around her. As the villainess in the film is Miss Naldi, I can see how she acquired unfortunate associations. Sooty, perhaps, as well as greasy. When,

Father, Allen Davenport Cassity

thirty years later, deMille remade *The Ten Command-ments* as a sound film, I asked Mother if she was going to see it. "Not on your life," said she, feeling that, however colossal, it could only be an anticlimax. My own favorite among silent films is *Sunset Boulevard.* When it shows on late-night TV I turn off the sound.

I cannot abandon the thrall of silence without telling you that my father looked like Rudolph Valentino and my mother like Norma Talmadge. I look like Raymond Massey.

With the demise in rapid succession of the silent screen and of my father, Mother went to work for the Works Progress Administration. Scholars have dealt in detail with the Federal Theatre and the Federal Artists Projects, and in somewhat less detail with the Federal Writers Project. None, so far as I know, has taken on the Federal Music Project. Musicians being what they are, it would be the richest study of all, although of more interest, I daresay, to criminologists and psychiatrists than to sociologists.

The sociology was grim enough. The brothers

Mother, Dorothy Turner Cassity

Warner, over a period of hardly more than eighteen months, had put scores of thousands of instrumentalists on the streets. My grandmother maintained that sound would not last, a position she clung to until her death in 1934. Meanwhile, no Luddite, she took a job as sustaining pianist at a radio station. Keeping equally well ahead of the juggernaut of progress, my grandfather was building airfields. The radio station was WJDX in Jackson, the voice of the Lamar Life Insurance Company, founded by Eudora Welty's father, and for which Miss Welty wrote continuity. Technology was no more dependable then than now, and communication with the network frequently went dead. It was Grandmother and Franz Liszt to the rescue. (See "Rescue," page 101 of the anthology.) That is what a sustaining pianist is, and I suggest that Dan Rather hire one.

The Federal Music Project, in Mississippi, was under the direction of a Miss Jerome Sage, who had been head of the music department at Mississippi State College for Women, otherwise MSCW, aka Messy W. She assembled an orchestra of twenty-five or thirty, which would give concerts at orphanages and junior high schools, as well as broadcasting. I am uncertain as to how matters were worked out with the Musicians' Union, of which my grandmother was one of the first female members in the South. The local chapter may simply have folded. I know for a fact that its funds were embezzled. "Unprincipled," my mother's word, describes musicians best. The project paid for rehearsals as well as for performances, and although the players, conscientious veterans of the pit, worked hard, the project also employed, at full salary, a timekeeper who, in the best WPA tradition, did nothing whatever. The musicians hated him. He could take a watch from his pocket more ostentatiously than the White Rabbit.

The repertory was purest potted palm, as were the venues of performance. In the Visconti *Death in Venice* there is a scene in which the Mahler on the sound track finally shuts up (it doesn't finish; Visconti just stops it) and there is only the little string orchestra of the hotel, playing the Lehár *Viljalied.* It is a wonderfully authentic and unglamorized moment, and transports me instantly to rehearsals in the school auditoriums and rented lofts of fifty years ago.

I frequently attended rehearsals, not because, in those days, latchkey kids were suspect—and I certainly was one—but because the musicians were such a spectacle. Unprincipled or not, they were without exception beautifully kind to me, and, although I have outlived them, were lifelong friends. I preferred to hang out among the string players, because they were not always emptying spit out of crooks and valves, and because when they rosined their bows the smell reminded me of a sawmill. If my presence on these occasions seems to conflict with what I have so far told you about myself, you have missed the point. If the orchestra pit is not another planet, nothing is.

At the concerts I formed my opinion, never softened, that orphans are very unpleasant people. In college it was an irritation to me that my fraternity was determined to give them an annual party. I found that their attention span was no better than it had been for *In a Persian Market* and that they were still incapable of not spilling punch on me. I took my revenge as I had earlier, by seating them in chairs cracked so that they pinched. No one enjoys the sufferings of Annie more than I do.

The latchkey spared me becoming Andy Hardy, and the time I spent in boardinghouses and rooming houses was by far the most instructive of my childhood. Only Balzac could do full justice to my landladies. To their meals I owe my excellent appetite and my excellent health; to their rooms I owe my indifference to interiors and my indifference to much else. To live in a *house,* with a *yard,* in a *neighborhood,* seems to me sensory deprivation.

With the coming of World War II the ladies entered their high period. Mrs. Daniels, who may well have been the wealthiest woman in Jackson, having owned the land on which Sears Roebuck stood, slept, I swear to you, in a pantry behind a screen, so she could rent out one more room. Any true thing I tell you about her will make her seem an ogress of greed, but as a matter of fact she was a pink, pretty, white-haired, very plump old lady who was kindness itself to the hopelessly unremarkable young people whom she housed. She ran a photography business in the basement, and not for one moment would I put her beyond trafficking in kiddy-porn, if the profit margin were sufficient. She had a likely subject in her seven-year-old grandson, whose favorite activity was to run up and down stark naked on the sidewalk in front of adjacent Saint Peter's rectory, pursued by an enormously fat nun. I encountered him years later as, what else, a lifeguard. The main purpose of the rooming house, I am sure, was to launder money. Mrs. Daniels accepted payment only in cash. With widowhood she had given up a handsome house in a fashionable suburb to be, as we say, where the action is. She also owned, contiguous to the Sears property, a building she rented to a hat shop called La Mode. Its plumbing was undependable, and most of her day went into telephone conversations involving the commode at La Mode. I was reminded of the New York World's Fair of 1939, which boasted of "com-

modious busses to Flushing." It has all been downhill from A Century of Progress.

I took my meals next door, with a woman who was the sister of a Methodist bishop. This consanguinity in no way prevented her being the most accomplished black marketeer of 1942. We turned our ration books over to her and asked no questions. At breakfast—the last dry cereal I ever intend to eat—she was already on the phone to her purveyors, who were unknown even to others in the boarding business. I suspect they chained goats in upstairs rooms. At noon we would have a spread the Officers' Club at Jackson Air Force Base could not have matched. Never ask what "stew meat" is. I occasionally see people who used to eat there, indicating that the dangers of cholesterol have been much overstated. The husbands of boardinghouse keepers were a study in themselves. I never saw one lift a hand except to swat flies. They could have given Latin lovers lessons in being kept. Incidentally, it is not correct to say that Thomas Wolfe grew up in a rooming house. He grew up in the family enclave downstairs, a psychological environment wholly other. Look homeward, Swatter. The great poet of the rooming house is E. A. Robinson. *Amaranth* is full of characters I recognize, and the Arthurian poems would benefit by their presence. Those who dined at a Round Table will have known the boardinghouse reach. Schopenhauer boarded, but had no empathy with the milieu, nor with anything else. It will be the punishment in Hell of Rilke and of other social climbers to be moved from desirable front rooms to the third floor back.

In September of 1943 I entered Bailey Junior High School in Jackson, a building which had architecture with a vengeance. It is a monument of WPA *moderne,* and appears frequently in histories of the period. Entering the front foyer was like boarding the *Normandie.* I had the good fortune to go through junior high school and through high school in the great days of homogenous grouping. After the hearties in Forest and the losers at Mrs. Daniels's, I was in fully congenial company for the first time in my life, and it was imagination run riot. Every time we had to get up a program or perform a skit it got us into deep trouble with the establishment, whose notion of entertainment was an Armistice Day pageant.

All happy adolescences are alike. So are all unhappy adolescences, but writers seem unwilling to face this fact. Mine was the happiest of all, because on my sixteenth birthday my mother turned over the management of my inheritance to me, figuring that, with the example of Mrs. Daniels behind me, I would be more likely to move into a pantry than to squander my substance in riotous living. In a sense, move into a pantry is what I have done. I had the independence everyone else was rebelling for. As a rite of passage, money is not to be bettered. I had a job; presently I had a car; I had a girlfriend who was pretty enough that she could afford to let her intelligence show. In Jackson, that meant very pretty indeed. One of several wasteful peculiarities about the South was that it compelled smart women to act dumb. A joy of middle age is to encounter old acquaintances who have decided it is no longer necessary to be Betty Boop.

In the afternoons I solicited newspaper subscriptions door-to-door. The *Daily Clarion-Ledger* felt that wartime upheavals and residential mobility had reduced its circulation below optimal levels, and that the carriers needed help in building it back up. The basic problem, that the paper was lousy, escaped them. The experience taught me more about the streets of Jackson than I cared to know, but the door would frequently open to reveal former boarders become upwardly mobile, and thinner than they had been. The ideal was to make one's quota early and go to a movie. We solicited in pairs, and I was fortunate to work with a classmate who was a real expert, although watching him perform his tricks over and over became like Lillian Gish six times a day. He is now a munitions salesman. But sophisticated weapons systems. Nothing tacky and Rambo.

As a minimal concession to riotous living I would go once or twice a year to New Orleans or to the Gulf Coast. My mecca in Biloxi was the Edgewater Gulf Hotel, a 1920s Moorish wonder whose lobby had an immense bronze-hooded fireplace. Those who are familiar with the average temperatures in Biloxi can draw their conclusions as to the architect's competence. The hotel is the setting of the first act of *Sweet Bird of Youth*. I have this information from Tennessee Williams himself. I met him at a party in Atlanta and put the question directly. I saw the building for a last time a few weeks before Hurricane Camille entailed its dynamiting. The stucco, which had been buff-colored, had been painted boneyard white and the shutters a dark, dark green. The palm trees had grown very tall. It was Morocco.

Social consciousness was not exactly the Jackson thing, nor, as you will have gathered, is it mine. The great upheaval of my high-school years was a campaign to get rid of high-school fraternities and sororities, both of which, it was felt, promoted snobbery. The campaign was instigated by the Junior League. Think about it. After the passage of more than forty years, and several changes of name and numbering, the street of the former high-school frat houses, located in an otherwise respectable neighbor-

hood, suffers still from depressed real-estate values. A tribute, of sorts.

My other definitive Jackson story dates from later, when, as a college student, I was working at Jackson Public Library, in the Platonic Idea of a Carnegie Building. The head librarian, a capable and dedicated woman, told me that she calculated it took her, simply because she was a woman, exactly twice as long to negotiate with city hall as it would take a man. I add that the remark was made without bitterness, simply as a statement of fact. In fairness to Jackson I suppose I should say that the men in office at city hall were denser than most, although not as dense as they became later. A city commissioner, as I write this, is in prison for trying to fake his own death and collect the insurance. He was a fraternity brother of mine. I wonder if his wife is a Junior Leaguer.

I graduated from high school in June of 1947 and left immediately for Mexico City on a graduation trip with the aforesaid Baron Krupp. Mainly, it was a role reversal. He spoke Spanish and I did not, but I always ended by coping, as I *look* Mexican. I was the Albeniz accompaniment.

One afternoon at the bullring I saw a picador gored to death. He threw his arms wide, like the woman in *Day of Wrath*. The rhythm of the senoritas' fans never wavered. It came to me that any mob is a Roman mob, and that there is no reason it should not be. It is how we are. "There is only one beast out there, and it has a thousand heads." The best single subtitle ever projected on the silent screen. I will award my Vicente Blasco-Ibañez Prize, consisting of an eight-by-ten glossy of Nita Naldi, to the reader who identifies it. I sometimes attend the Indianapolis 500, where all I worry about is the structural failure of Styrofoam coolers. Once again, it is the orphans and their punch.

Of Millsaps College I have no criticism and no wish here to speak. It was high school with the road-show cast. I graduated on a Monday; on a Tuesday I bought a brand new convertible; and on Sunday I left for California. The most intelligent week, by a comfortable margin, I ever spent. The Golden State was not then in the grip of the dreaded Sierra Club, and the abominable Ralph Nader had not yet perverted automobile design. My decision postponed, by a calendar year, my being drafted.

On a Saturday six days later, in Yuma, Arizona, I stopped for lunch. I drank iced tea, and I realized that, for the first time in my life, the outside of the glass was not pouring condensation. If your environment has been such that you think of Yuma as an improvement . . .

I have written elsewhere of Stanford University

and of my experience with Yvor Winters. Over the more than thirty-five years since I was at Stanford I have been very frequently in "The City," but mainly in the straight, square, overfed San Francisco I saw the first time. The day after I arrived in Palo Alto I checked into a motel across the highway from the enormous hangar built for USS *Macon*—do not suppose my choice was an accident. You should know that there is only one writer whose home is really worth visiting, and that is William Randolph Hearst. The outdoor pool at San Simeon almost reconciles one to the outdoors.

After a year of enjoying California, I was drafted. That which had darkened my high-school days, had lifted, and had lowered again to darken my last years in college, was upon me. I was sworn in in Jackson and put on a plane for basic training at Fort Jackson, in Columbia, South Carolina. Like most scenarios of dread, this one proved illusory. The moment I was actually in the army I had a ball. I was so bored with going to school that an Antarctic expedition would have been diverting, and Fort Jackson was the world of the boardinghouse writ large, in uniform. I knew where I was, and could bring to my situation a lifetime of experience. Why had I not foreseen this?

The one setback was the first weekend I went on pass. Columbia, to my quivering disgust, was indistinguishable from Jackson. WHAT A DUMP. It was more fun to stay on the post, which is exactly what I did until I could get myself together and arrange a bugout. The decision was delicate. Atlanta, where everyone wanted to go, was just outside the three hundred mile pass limit; Augusta, where no one wanted to go, was just inside. That left Charlotte. There is one thing worse than a City of Homes, and that is a City of Churches. I swore I would never set foot in Charlotte again, and I have not. Thereafter I got on the bus and went every weekend to Charleston, which is rather like the Vieux Carré depopulated for a science fiction movie.

I would come back on Sunday night just before lights out. My training company was the diametric opposite of a representative unit in a World War II movie, with the wisecracking Jew from Brooklyn, the laconic Texas cowboy, and the preppie who always went chicken. Except for a Californian (another Californian, as I thought of him) and for me, everyone in the company hailed from within twenty miles of Burlington, North Carolina, and was farther from home than he had ever been. I was twenty-three, and thought of myself as travelled and sophisticated; they were eighteen and desperately homesick. As I walked down the aisle of the barracks toward my bunk, there was a tear in every same corner of every eye. The

sergeant would have loved the uniformity of it, had he not been too harried to notice. He was a conscientious man for whom I had, and have, infinite respect. God will get me for making fun of those boys, all too many of whom died in Korea, but I did have the charity to realize that what they needed was a landlady, which, up to a level, the army is. The knowledge of that is what makes *From Here to Eternity* a very good novel and a very great document.

At the company next to us a quiet horror was taking place. Through zealotry or through oversight, draft boards had consistently inducted borderline retardees. The army knew that if it released them it would have to pay pensions and hospitalization and who knows what else. Someone came up with the idea for a regimen that might turn the veggies into marginally effective soldiers. Put them into a unit with a leavening of men of normal intelligence and let them learn by imitation. The first to crack up were the drill instructors. The march past, if it resembled anything, resembled a *Totentanz*. Not one of the defectives ever learned to mitre sheets, which is just as well, because most of them were incontinent. You can imagine how pleasant that made life for the normals, who were confined to quarters whenever the morons screwed up, which was twenty-four hours a day. Panic spread next door when we realized we would have to run several training problems cheek by jowl with the veggies. I called several notes due so I could be positioned on the far right, with all of my own company, no giant intellects, but competent riflemen, between me and disaster. With the machine-gun fire chattering six inches above my head I thought of my grandmother's remark about the handicapped. Before she had arthritis, she said, she thought that cripples should be taken out and shot. But now that she had it, she knew they should.

Training ended, just before Christmas. One would surely go to Korea, a landscape of infinite boredom inhabited mostly by Protestant missionaries.

One did not go to Korea. On a dazzling January day—my birthday—my troopship stood off San Juan, above the thirty-thousand-foot-deep Puerto Rican Trench. I cannot swim, but it did not matter. On its white limestone bluff, above the blue Atlantic, the white dome of the Capitolio nosed in and out of the morning fog. The fog cleared; we sailed under the turrets of El Morro into the Bay of San Juan. At our left a small city rose from the flats of the bay to the low heights on the ocean side. The ocean was now out of sight. The waters of the bay had the ambiguous colors of a tortoise shell.

Disembarking at Fort Buchanan, we got on busses to go to Camp Tortuguero ("Place of the Turtle"), about twenty miles west of San Juan on the north coast. The drive took us through orange and red and yellow cannas springing out of green and bronze leaves, through poinsettias exploded out of pots into full-scale trees, through flamboyants in bloom—and they were like mimosas with their insipid colors intensified—through frangipani, and through tulip trees. I had an irrational desire to buy a bulldozer and plow under every stupid pink rosebush in the South. We arrived at Campamento Tortugue-ro, and I entered a life composed, in about equal parts, of the Foreign Legion, the Raj, and a Guianese penal battalion.

Having made it all the way through college and graduate school with a roommate for only one quarter of one year, I found that I would now be living in a 14-by-14-foot hut with seven other men, six of whom were tall. *All of those knees and elbows!* By observing a code of the mosquito net, we managed not to kill one another. If one withdrew into one's bunk and lowered the net it was as if one were not there. Nobody would make an inquiry or ask for a cigarette or expect one to make a fourth at bridge. The arrangement would not be possible now. Arguments would break out over smoking, and I personally plot at once the murder of anyone who brings a ghetto blaster within fifty feet of me.

Our huts at Tortuguero had many problems, but ventilation was not one of them. They had a concrete slab for a floor, board walls to a height of perhaps four feet, screen wire above that, and a tar-paper roof. The basic design is popular in *favelas* all over Latin America. The 196 square feet had to accommo-date—besides the eight bunks—eight footlockers and eight field packs, as well as eight rather elaborate civilian wardrobes. Korea was a long way off.

Outside it was sand and palm trees and a flamboyant that was a pillar of fire by day. Beyond the cleared area the Caribbean pines rose tall, their droopy needles making the trees look like watercolors of themselves. The only pine I ever saw that I do not reckon in board feet. The sea was not visible, but darkened the horizon a little from below. In January, when I arrived, the weather was cool and flawless. At other times it was hot and spaced about with rain-bows.

Our assignment was to teach English as a second language to Puerto Rican trainees. The all-insular Sixty-fifth Infantry Regiment, "Nuestro Regimiento," had mutinied in combat, and convenience dictated that the insurrection be ascribed to a failure of communication. More, not less, cultural imperialism

would solve the problem. Two civil service charlatans who had left the States during the Depression devised our method, which would be appropriate for the edification of mynah birds. In 118 hours of training a company received on the order of 40 hours of language instruction. A Spanish-speaking instructor would brief the company as a whole on the content of the lessons, then break them up into smaller groups for individualized instruction. We acted less as in-structors than as cheerleaders, pronouncing the phrases and sentences to be repeated individually and in unison by the "students." The brass of course loved it, for the appearance of activity and uniformity, and did not care whether it produced speakers who knew what they were saying. Like all people who grow up chewing sugarcane the trainees had no teeth. This spaciousness, in conjunction with the bewildering range of accents to which they were subjected, resulted in sounds as to whose usefulness I can only speculate. The speakers might have succeeded in propositioning Noam Chomsky—and would have, in a minute; their greed exceeded you know whose—but I cannot believe they ever broke the sound barrier sufficiently, say, to ask directions. Meanwhile, we picked up a Spanish whose usefulness was equally limited. If you like to hear obscenities in the Hispanic equivalent of Gabby Hayes, I am your man.

In the beginning all of the cadre, including the English instructors, wore pith helmets, as if we were searching out rebellious Moros. If my prejudices offend you, you can say we are what we wear. Apparently, we are also what we eat. We had a Puerto Rican mess, and although as, given my upbringing, you might guess, I loved it, the All-American boys found it totally threatening. Agitation for a "conti-nental" mess never ceased. When we got one, what the Puerto Rican cooks did with steak and potatoes started a stampede back to the indigenous, which I, of course, had never left in the first place. The red beans and rice, the candied plantain, fresh pineapple, and powdered-milk ice cream were the best publicly prepared food I had had since I had given up boarding. The *Piña fresca* was not 100 percent de-pendable. Although a pineapple plantation abutted the camp on one side, we frequently had Dole, from Hawaii. All of this, and permanent KPs, hired at a wage that would have made White Rhodesians blush.

I had a second assignment. I served on the firing squad that toured the island for military funerals. For reasons of tact, there had to be a continental on the squad, and I inherited the duty because I was the only one small enough to wear the pretailored uniforms. The gesture was statistic rather than outwardly sym-bolic, because by then I had such a convincing suntan

"Age ten: my last appearance outdoors"

that it got me Jim Crowed on a train out of Fort Knox when I was finally separated.

It took the army a full eighteen months to get dead bodies from Korea to Puerto Rico, and almost as long to return live ones, as many irate cadre could attest. A ship with coffins would dock at Fort Buchanan every six weeks or so; we would then go out for funerals once or twice a week, in a weapons carrier, into the remotest hills.

Our uniform could hardly be described as deep mourning: white spats, white gloves, a sky blue helmet-liner, and a sky blue scarf. Wildest of all, a white sling on the rifles. Just try to keep Cosmoline off of a white sling.

The rifles were M-1's, and I should willingly have exchanged mine for an Enfield, allowing even for the 1.5-pound difference in weight. The trouble with the M-1's was that they were cranky, and misfired frequently. We lived in dread that we would raise the rifles over the grave, that all six would misfire simultaneously, and we would look as foolish as our uniforms.

The eighteen-month time lag meant that the grief process, as the psychiatrists would say, was reopened just as it began to heal. Grief did not,

however, flood out courtesy. The poorest family served us coffee, and would make an effort to speak to me in English. I appreciated it then, and appreciate it now. As the casualties went on, I got to see more and more of the island. Hairpin curves such as one would expect in Switzerland, but overhung with the lushest vegetation this side of the Amazon. In the rear of the weapons carrier we used to grab for orchids. The highest villages were surprisingly nontropical. Protestant, one would say.

Nights during the week divided the catatonic, who took to their bunks, from those who tried to make a sort of life. One could go to the Service Club, but only if one were stone-deaf or deeply into mambo music. Just outside the gate was Miguel's, which was a clean, well-lighted place, but had nothing else to recommend it, although to walk down the long hill from the gate to the hutment area in bright moonlight, and in the Caribbean there is never any other kind, was an experience I think of more often than I care to admit to you. If one were sober one could walk backwards and see the Southern Cross rise over the unmistakable profile of the limestone outcropping that identified Tortuguero. It has been plagiarized at Ancon Hill in Panama and at the Peak in Hong Kong.

One left at noon on Saturday for San Juan. "Publicos," unmetered taxis, gathered at the gate, and as soon as they had a full complement, i.e., 104 persons, would roar off. The route took us past Caño Martín Peña and El Fanguito, by common consent the most appalling slums in the West Indies. To the extent I noticed, I thought them picturesque. I am prepared to defend my perception. The complicated catwalks over the mud flats of Fanguito were like a Mondrian deliberately shriveled, and Martín Peña was the Sausalito of the downwardly mobile. If a houseboat stranded it became a house; if a house floated away it became a houseboat.

You must understand that San Juan in 1953 was B.C.—Before Castro. The big tourist money went to Havana. Puerto Rico was a backwater, which is what one liked about it. What is now the Gold Coast had exactly two hotels: the Condado Beach, dating from the period of the Edgewater Gulf, and the pristine Caribe Hilton, completed in 1947. In uniform one went to the Condado; in civvies one went to the Hilton. The bar at the Condado was a quadrant of plate glass facing straight at the sea. Iridescent green inside the reef and agate blue without: fire nearer and veining farther.

In the evening, before air-conditioning, San Juan lived in its doorways and on its balconies. To walk the Calle Fortaleza was as much a social as an exercising experience. To walk the Calle Luna was an even more social experience, but that is not what I am talking about. I am puzzled as to what use households could have had for as many sewing machines as one saw: electric models, treadle models, hemstitching machines, portables, and versions that looked like—dare I say it?—chain saws. The number of flatirons was not in proportion; starched petticoats cannot have been the answer. Even then, guyaberas and ruffled shirts came from Taiwan. Was all of the city stitching for Pedro Albizu Campos, the local separatist? He kept himself wrapped in wet bed sheets under an impression the U.S. was bombarding him with death rays.

On weekends when I was too broke to do the hotels I would make the stroll from the Capitolio to El Morro. That route is on the high side of town, and the trade winds came whipping over. The breakers roared in on the Atlantic like the Red Sea closing over the Egyptians. One afternoon I saw a wave break all the way over the top of the lighthouse at El Morro. Until it broke it had seemed no higher than another.

To get back to camp one had to go to Bus Stop Number Fifteen and hail a publico. "Parada Quinze" was more than a bus stop. It was a way of life. Much of the city's night life blossomed here, the site of the iniquitous China Doll. The name on the canopy was in English, and was the one phrase you could count on the trainees to know. Returning the compliment, we chose to call it Muñeca China. It was an unremarkable dive with a sensational approach. The lighted canopy on the sidewalk led, not to a doorway and an interior, but to an external ramp that descended between two buildings to the waters of the bay itself. Fanguito was not all that distant, in several senses. At the bottom of the ramp one turned to the left, went through a battered door, and turned left again, into a dimly lit staircase that went upward forever. At the top it was right again, and one more step, on which everyone always tripped, into the dance bar. The dance floor was not large, and there was only one other room, the latter devoted wholly to gaming. The club was never especially crowded, since the coming and going—the raison d'être—took care of, and was, the overflow. The presence of merchant seamen suggested that the notoriety of the China Doll was international. U.S. sailors—the navy—seldom appeared, rarely being sober enough to negotiate the trapped approach. One saw a few at the gaming tables, but the shore patrol had its hands full merely dragging the gobs out of the gutters, and I am speaking literally. Marines, in from Vieques, and a cliquish lot, partied elsewhere in their own locales, nearer downtown. A good thing, because they were indefatigable brawlers. I suspect them of being or-

phans grown old.

The trip back to camp was invariably bloodcurdling, the publico drivers having spent the day pretty much as we did. However, I was always too pleased with myself to care.

I made two trips to Saint Thomas, in the Virgin Islands, where I made the invidious discovery that there were tours of duty cushier than ours. Then, at Christmas, training closed down at Tortuguero so the trainees could go home before being shipped out. The authorities told the cadre, in effect, to get lost and it would not come off leave time. On New Year's Day of 1954 I flew to Puerto Principe—Port-au-Prince; pardon me—and spent a week in Haiti.

When I got back I learned that I was being transferred to Henry Barracks, at Cayey, in the interior. I cursed myself for not remaining in Haiti and becoming a derelict, but the transfer turned out to be my high period in the military. Cayey was a loss, but the post was attractive and quiet. In the evenings it smelled of frangipani. One lived in a permanent barracks, not of the Von Sternberg grandeur at Fort Brooke, but on a par with Schofield, and one did a certain amount of serious soldiering. It was a glimpse at career men and at a peacetime army I should have hated to miss.

The barracks looked out on a favela known as El Polvorín. Occupying a conical hill, it was more vertical and better drained than Fanguito or Martin Peña, but more politicized. The word means "powder keg." The post commander would have loved to put up an off-limits sign, but his noncoms told him an appreciable percentage of his men had family there. You cannot put a man's own home off limits, unless you want to encourage desertion. El Coronel mounted instead a never-ending campaign about the VD rate, which was, I do not doubt, spectacular. But Polvorín too was picturesque. In the Virgin Islands it would have been a tourist attraction. To look at, I mean.

As my enlistment neared its end a curious little game began with Fortune, Empress of the World. Dienbienphu went under siege in March 1954, and there was a strong possibility that John Foster Dulles would take the U.S. into Indo-China, meaning that all enlistments would be indefinitely extended. I well remember sweating out the weeks after the French surrender in May, especially since, before the threat, I had considered reenlisting. If I could have been sure of staying in the Antilles, I would have. In the event my luck held—I guess; even now I have a little shadow of doubt—and I was separated in September of 1954. My first act on becoming a civilian (remember that it had to reassure me as to the wisdom of my decision) was to buy a Countess Mara tie.

I went back to work for the library in Jackson, moving us out of the *gemütlich* red brick Carnegie building into an off-putting Bauhaus module on North State Street. "If you can't circulate books across the street from Sears Roebuck," said the head librarian, "you had better give up."

Another two years in Mississippi and I was off to South Africa. From my desk at Jackson Municipal Library I was recruited on a three-year contract with the Transvaal Provincial Library, an arm of the Provincial Administration. The province would pay my way out and back.

It would have flown me, but I elected to go by ship, a Lykes freighter I had to chase around the gulf from New Orleans to Port Arthur, Texas. On British, Dutch, and even French ships you see instantly that in those countries the sea is an ancient and honored profession. On American ships you see people who cannot hold a job on land. I was the only passenger, and ate with the ship's officers. They were a talkative company, but talked mostly to themselves. Sparks, who must have been ten years beyond mandatory retirement, was undoubtedly the operator who failed to hear the *Titanic.* At boat drill I had, let us be blunt, a sinking feeling. Seniority in the maritime union has its place, but the burning deck is not it. Boy, namely me, would have to make his own arrangements if we went down.

There were men on the quarterdeck who had not been ashore in a decade. They joined the merchant marine to get away from all that. There is also the probability that waiting at the gangplank were subpoenas for nonpayment of child support. Never believe that sailors have a girl in every port. They cannot deal with one girl in one port. Surely that is what the myth of Lorelei is about. If you feel threatened every time a woman combs her hair . . .

Freighters proceed with a great sense of effort. This one could have labored in a calm sea with the current behind it. Our wake, to the extent we could generate one, looked a mess, always an indication of poor hull design. At seventeen days out we ran into really rough weather. One kept an eye out for the Flying Dutchman. We were in his latitudes. At twenty days out the storm dissipated, but we were battering into the notorious cape rollers, that build up from the Antarctic. I took to my bed. I have never been able to reread *Nostromo,* because it is associated in my mind with a certain sort of motion.

Table Mountain, which is ordinarily visible twenty miles out to sea, did not, because of a temperature inversion, reveal itself until we were practically upon

it. The navigation officer was sweating. Tafelberg, I must tell you, looks less tabular and more mountainous than it photographs. In four visits to the Cape I have not made it out to Blouberg Strand, which is where you have to go to get the full effect of the flat top. In the lifetime of General Smuts, people would go up on the mountain and have mystic experiences, but I believe there is less of that today.

Cape Town is quiet and self-effacing, content to let the scenery make its effect. The civil service sent a representative to ease my way through customs and immigration, which I expected to be inquisitorial. It was not. The officer asked if I was bringing in pornography, but his interest may have been personal rather than official. He twitched a lot. He asked if I were traveling with used beehive equipment. I resisted an urge to say, "I never go anywhere without it." He waved us through.

My chaperon checked me into a small hotel whose grounds backed up to the servants' quarters at the Mount Nelson. I went to bed, but without the motion of the ship I could not sleep. I got up, dressed, and went through the back door into the Empire. It was the first time in my life I ever actually saw moustache wax, and women at the Mount Nelson have the look of blue rinse without the use of it. I was glad I had had the ship's steward trim my hair, although I got my ear nicked in the process. No one spoke. Not to me, not to one another. That's the way the Empire is. The ranking waiters had a strange walk. After twenty-two days at sea, I had it myself. Union Castle Steamship owned the hotel, and I presume rotated personnel ship to shore as demand required.

The next morning I left for Pretoria on the Orange Free State local. Civil servants travel on a first-class concession. I had a compartment with varnished wood and green leather, and a rubber mounting for one's flawlessly accurate pocket watch. If I had known I could have taken my grandfather's out of the bank.

Once we left the Cape behind, the barrenness of the landscape was airbrush lunar and could not have pleased me more. The form of the koppies was familiar, as if Polvorín had fallen victim to slum clearance.

In the shuttered corridors of the train one expected to encounter Shanghai Lily at the very least, but I met instead a bright-eyed old Afrikaner who travelled because he liked steam locomotives. Destination was not important.

I have a rule of thumb that saves me a great deal of time. In reading any article about South Africa, at the first reference to the Afrikaners as dour, I throw the publication into the wastebasket. I have been a librarian for thirty-five years, and I do not hesitate to trash hardcover books. Afrikaners are about as dour as Neapolitans. They may be dour in dealing with the media, but so am I, and for the same reason: contempt. We should hail the heirs of those who wrote "Kiss me, My Fool" (the second-best subtitle ever projected on the silent screen) as oracles?

The trip occupied two days and two nights, although the expresses make it in twenty-seven hours.

By midafternoon of the second day we were nearing the Rand. Dusty yellow roads ran through yellow grass. Great numbers of Africans on foot and on bicycles hurried from no discernible point of origin toward no discernible destination. The women among them wore a sort of uniform: a turtleneck jersey, a straight skirt with a very wide leather belt, and a tam. Color was evidently a matter of choice. It was the exception to see anyone, male or female, in tribal dress. I shall not describe those commuters as smiling and happy and full of natural rhythm, but I shall say nothing could have been less like the changing of shifts in *Metropolis.*

The wind came up sharply; the air began to glitter; a fine granulation rang time after time on the pane. We drew abreast of a great golden butte: an Aztec pyramid of golden sand. A prodigious plume streamed off the summit, looking far more a natural phenomenon than the "tablecloth" in Cape Town. Eighty years of mining on the Witwatersrand had made of it a landscape unique in the world, and of every housewife an unwilling Danaë.

The train was now looping among a *massif* of the dumps. Some were terraced and hieratic, like Teotihuacán; others had heavily eroded sides, such as one might see in a rainy Babylon; a few were simply gigantic sand dunes. At Alberton, as at the end of a canyon, one saw for a moment the concrete skyline of Johannesburg itself. After a great deal of switching— "shunting," as I would learn to say—we pulled out of Germiston for Pretoria.

All civil service towns are alike. Pretoria, Ottawa, Canberra, Washington. Pretoria, having been a garrison town, and Herbert Baker's trial run for New Delhi, is far more interesting than the others. Past the Voortrekker Monument, as improbable on its hill as Wallace Stevens's jar in Tennessee, we coasted into Sir Herbert's Pretoria Station.

Life occurs in the first person, in the strictest chronological order. That is the sequence I have followed in this sketch. However, I want to jump ahead a few days, to the first visit I made to Johannesburg. From the first full day it was apparent

that Pretoria would have its attractions, but that there would also have to be a life of the weekends. So, on a brilliantly sunny Sunday, with the shadows already lengthening—it was increasingly colder, and the Rand is a thousand feet higher than Pretoria—I stepped out of Johannesburg Station into the city I still prefer to any other in the world. There is simply no real point in being anywhere else. By any conventional definition the central city is ugly: a concrete jungle comprising a bad copy of every bad building built in the twenties and thirties. But among them are the fractal cast iron and the raw tin roofs of the eighties and nineties, and above them a sky whose blue perhaps only diamond merchants can fully value.

The mining camp is wholly present: in the offset streets where the properties enjambed; in the tremors as the miles of tunnels collapse; in the dust in the air; in the hardhats on the streets; in the friendliness; in the ostentation; in the cruelty; in the persistence of hangover at three o'clock on a Sunday afternoon; in an avarice so complete as to be almost moral.

I walked from Park Station down Joubert Street to Commissioner Street, seeing, in what seemed to me the least likely setting, more Africans than I had so far seen in tribal dress. Groups of street musicians played as if shilling for Bourbon Street bars, of which there were none. At six o'clock the streets began to fill up with people who had come downtown for the "bioscope." If Jo'burg was Babylon, it was the Babylon of D. W. Griffith. I had been gawking at the most impressive building on Commissioner Street, His Majesty's Theatre. South Africa would be in the Commonwealth a few years more, and Elizabeth II was undoubted queen, but no one—except the magistrates and the Mount Nelson—bothered any longer to change pronouns. The building owed something, owed everything, to a building that still exists in Kreuzberg-Berlin, but the narrow streets of Johannesburg give its constructions a scale they do not earn. Neon crowns on the twin towers might have been at the height of the Chicago Board of Trade.

A discreet sign beckoned into "His Majesty's Cellar." One went down a short staircase past what I can describe only as a beaded curtain with enormous iron chain-links for beads. *Very* Weimar Republic. One hardly had the strength to part them, but the Boere and the Rooinekke are a hardy mix. A British pop group performed in vowels that offended even the Rooinekke, but the sustaining pianist played a medley from Lehár's *Land des Lächelns,* including "Dein ist mein ganzes Herz." I came within five minutes of missing the last train back to Pretoria, and the streets of Johannesburg after midnight can chill the blood of an old Parada Quinze hand.

"Most Intellectual" and "Highest Pompadour,"
Central High School, Jackson, Mississippi, 1947

Transvalse Provinsiale Biblioteek acted as a mother ship to public libraries all over the province. After a century of Boss Tweed and Boss Crump and T. J. Pendergast and Mayor Daley, Americans, with some justification, hold municipal government in disregard. In South Africa the burgermeester is a figure of consequence, with a chain of authority and a mystique that goes back to Rembrandt; and suburbs rush to incorporate with the frenzy U.S. counties reserve for resisting.

The Dutch Reformed congregations of Transvaal, as they grew prosperous, commissioned some of the farthest-out church buildings in the world (I told you South Africa was full of jolts), and as soon as the new kerke were financed, turned their attention to other amenities. We advised as to programs, architects, and interim arrangements. The province supplied a stock of fiction and other popular reading, exchanged at intervals, so that the local communities could spend their money on buildings, physical equipment, and reference materials. The most insensitive Raad had a cloudy conscience over the expendi-

ture of money on some groups and not others. The town council might be solidly Afrikaans-speaking, but the library boards would always have English-speaking members. The argument in regard to the Black population was that priority should go to primary reading materials—textbooks, etc.—and so far as it went, the argument may have been correct. If it had convenient side effects, so much the better for the party in power.

I have to say, however, that in the definition of short-term goals, the adjustment of ends to means, and the avoidance of inappropriate models, the Provincial Library System was by far the most sensible organization for which I ever worked. Academia in the sixties was an encounter between Chicken Little and the Swine of the Gadarene, and it is now the House of Baba Yaga, lurching on its chicken legs from intellectual chic to intellectual chic. You may argue, with Brecht, that it is not possible to do good in an evil society, but if that is true it is impossible to do good at all, as Calvin would remind us.

Only Union civil servants worked in the viceregal sprawl of the Union Buildings. Our headquarters were in a business building off Church Square, in Pretorius Street. At lunchtime we could walk through the Indian market, or eat in the square, an environment in which Leni Riefenstahl at either end of her career would have gone out of her mind.

Early in the week I and a supervisor or a driver-clerk would set out on an itinerary of small towns. Very soon I divided them by a classification of my own. The Rand towns, mining towns not on the Rand, and really rural towns. The last were like small towns in Texas, and, except for the language, known quantities to me. We stayed in hotels of blameless respectability that looked, however, like backdrops for dance hall girls and shoot-outs. The local librarian, or the board members, would entertain us, and one learned to deal with Barries and Peacocks whose mother tongue was Afrikaans, and with Krugers and Strydoms who appeared in the white flannels of the cricket pitch. The mayor of Vereeniging was named Chatterton. As one prepared to say, "And when did you leave England, Mr. Chatterton?" an archetypal Afrikaner came in. The remotest dorp has its English-speaking pharmacist, and in the heart of Johannesburg are *regte Boere*. American and European reporting vastly exaggerates the language division. White South Africa may not be a seamless scale, but it is certainly a continuum. Natal may have people who plant rosebushes and long for "home," but in the Transvaal the English-speaking know perfectly well where their roots are, and it is a slander to imply that they love the country less than the Afrikaners do.

They may love it more. They have more money there.

The Provincial Government had a good deal of the missionary spirit so far as *Ons Volk* were concerned, and tried to assure that no pocket of population, however isolated, was without access to information, as we should now say. We had library depots, consisting of a few shelves in a metal case we provided, at post offices, stores, and private homes. One morning I and my driver, who was white, stopped at a community that comprised two houses on a drainage ditch. One was like any other Afrikaner farmhouse, although there was no farm; its neighbor would have embarrassed El Fanguito. The lady of the house received us; her husband, whose employment one could only surmise, was also at home. The woman, of middle age, was vivid and attractive, a little broader in her gestures than I was used to seeing. The husband was blond and robust, but had a look of defeat. Mevrou served us coffee and set out a plate of *koeksisters,* twisted doughnuts dripping in a sugar syrup. I think of them whenever I find mention of Twisted Sister, the heavy-metal group. A call out the kitchen window brought over the neighbor, another bright-eyed old Boer. The eyes of Afrikaans men do not age. He himself brought over a banjo, and a bottle of *witblits,* otherwise white lightning. He played a few numbers, not *boeremusiek* but something I did not then recognize. The lyrics, though, were Afrikaans, and the woman joined in now and then. Two things struck me. The absolute isolation of the little group, although there was no real reason for it; Vereeniging was in full view down the veld. And the fact that my driver, who had not impressed me as a sensitive man, treated the woman with beautiful courtesy.

As we drove off he smiled at me. "You know that was a Coloured woman."

I lifted an eyebrow. "Do you know them?"

"No. But I can tell. The way she had the furniture placed: cater-cornered; you saw. The Cape Coloureds always do that. And the pictures on the wall."

I had a vision of the Vice Squad measuring the angle of furniture with a protractor and checking for Maxfield Parrishes, but I also remembered Ollewagen's courtesy.

"Well, you may be right. Obviously they never see anyone except the old man."

"No kids; they don't have to deal with schools. Probably the husband does the shopping. Or maybe not. Outside the Cape not many people would notice. And who cares. She's a nice woman."

"Do you think the old oomie knows?"

"Sure he knows. The place is his, incidentally.

He doesn't have to live like that. It's his names on the application forms, anyway." He tapped his clipboard. "He's just decided to go native. Can't be bothered. The church ladies would be much more likely to take her in than him. You can go much farther native than that, of course. The man who has the depot outside Louis Trichardt lives with a Venda woman, but he sends her out to the *pondokkie* on library day."

The Rand towns had a look all their own, as if each maze of tunnels underground had projected itself upward, to be adopted as a street plan. One felt, and was near the truth in so feeling, that the real townships *were* underground, and that the mine headgear were the gateways to them. The great dumps dwarfed without effort anything in their vicinity, and in Benoni, Brakpan, and Springs, buildings wisely rose no more than two or three stories. The eighties and nineties dealt with it better. A line of red corrugated-iron gables against a golden mine dump makes the very concept of "wilderness" seem the pretentious nonsense it is.

Hanging unspoken over the East Rand is the spectre of 1922: the full-scale Red revolt, i.e., White revolt, whose shadow conditions so much today. All of the antilabor legislation in South Africa did not originate with the Nationalist party. The spectre stalking the West Rand is that of the Jameson Raid. The insurrectionists were apprehended and detained in Krugersdorp. The raid took place on New Year's Day, when, then as now, the Last Trump could not rouse Johannesburg.

Mining has pursued geology westward down the reef in a great arc into the Free State. Isolated mines had depots in the Club, an institution that fascinated me, in that it combined in one hierarchy the analogue of the Noncommissioned Officers' Club and of the Officers' Club. The internal snobberies may have approached critical mass, but they did not apply to visitors. One never saw the mine officials; only their likeable, leathery wives. "Blondes don't last in this climate," one of them said to me, "but turning to leather is a small price to pay to get out of the English winter. Here I am, learning to *prat* the *taal,* but that's all right too. *Nie waar nie, meneer?*"

"Jolly well right," said my driver, perhaps in irony, perhaps not. His name was Steenkamp.

In Pretoria I had a flat off Arcadia Park and took my meals down the street at a private hotel. A private hotel is a boardinghouse. Frankly, there was not much to do in Pretoria except eat.

I read *The Magic Mountain* and I stayed out of bars. The game of darts is as frightening a follow-up to alcohol as floorboarding the car, and Pretorians play it like Puerto Ricans drive. I felt no need to become a Saint Sebastian of the civil service.

Much of downtown is as if that ethnic vending operation under the arcade of the Governor's Palace in Santa Fe had gone out of control and spread in all directions: a pallet party run amok. The Black population was inseparable from the blanket, on which took place business, meal preparation, child care, gossip, and siesta. One might say that the blanket provided everything except security. Pretoria made the interpenetrating invisible-to-one-another realities of the mathematicians seem the dimensions of everyday life. The Bantu filled every space not occupied by the White constructs, and believe me, for practical purposes they were simply not there. But that is true of servants everywhere. The convention of the Kabuki stage, whereby the stagehands are invisible, is universally applicable and universally applied. We have a common humanity, and nothing makes us happier than to fragment it.

For all of its small-town ambience Pretoria can put on a good show, and no city has a more secure sense of its own history. Government House makes Groote Schuur look like a remodeling job, which it is. The newer mansion postdates the Rhodes house by almost twenty years, and by then Herbert Baker really had his hand in. For nonroyals the office of governor-general has been thankless. The usual criticism was, too grand for the Afrikaners and not grand enough for the English. I do not know if the state presidents ever resolved the problem, and the executive president, I hope, has more important things on his mind. I do not think that Wallis Windsor would have found Pretoria much more congenial than she found Nassau; I mean, if she thought her sister-in-law was frumpy . . . But she would have understood Johannesburg utterly, and it her.

After ten months in Pretoria, I was reassigned to the Germiston Regional Library, to assist in planning and operating a bookmobile service in the northern suburbs of Johannesburg. You must understand that this is roughly comparable to running a bookmobile in Brentwood, Bel Air, and Beverly Hills, in terms of both the distances and the wealth. We mapped out likely routes and made trial runs, but had no real notion what to expect. The one certain thing was that the driver-clerks would have a high absentee rate, so as a contingency I took out a heavy-vehicle license.

Happily our service was a success from the first. The rich go after free services as eagerly as the poor, perhaps more eagerly, as they have the perception that the services are financed mostly from their taxes. Ladies left the tennis courts and swimming pools to storm our doors. I can report that both Muriel Spark and Iris Murdoch were popular, and that Ivy Compton Burnett was a positive cult. I belonged to the Compton Burnett cult myself, and still do. *The Mandelbaum Gate* suggests that Miss Spark could deal lethally with Johannesburg, but to do it full justice would require Dame Ivy. "I believe it would go ill with many of us, if we were faced by a strong temptation, and I suspect that with some of us it does go ill . . . Isolation and leisure put nothing into people. But they give what is there full play. They allow it to grow according to itself, and this may be strongly in certain directions."

The matrons of Illovo, Bryanston, and Buccleuch were as happy to be out of England as their sisters at the mines, and could afford more expensive skin care. Again, they were friendly as the English in England seldom are, outspoken in their antigovernment politics, and contemptuous of those who spoke of "home." They were as considerate of the feelings of my driver as my other driver had been of the Coloured woman outside Vereeniging.

One of our stops was at a township called Wynberg. Twenty years after its proclamation it consisted of three houses, of which one was occupied, by a veteran of El Alamein and his wife. Across the highway was Alexandra Township, an eyesore on the order of a flattened-out Polvorín, but desirable residential property for Africans, because they could own it freehold, until such time as the government could figure out a loophole in the proclamation, which went all the way back to the Widow Oosthuizen and the discovery of gold. No adults from Alexandra attempted to avail themselves of our service, but we turned away a few children, who may or may not have been literate.

I should insult the intelligence of my coworkers if I suggested that they were not aware of a disproportion in our efforts. They simply regarded library service for Africans as something in the future, and in the province of the Bureau of Native Affairs, as it then was. During the unrest after the Sharpville riots—the first Sharpville riots, those in 1960—we continued to make our stop. A few tanks and a few Saracens (armored troop carriers) sat at the ready on the borders of Alexandra, but I know for a fact that a friend of mine who had a trading license there—he was the Avon lady, as it were—continued to make his calls. The women of Alexandra would no more have given up skin care than those of Illovo. The veteran and his wife continued to read Angela Thirkell.

Germiston is twenty-five minutes from Johannesburg by train, and I lost no time in moving to Hillbrow, the most densely populated square mile in the British Commonwealth. I had a flat on Clarendon Circle, on the fourteenth floor, looking down Empire Road. The Rand commuter trains went through the heaviest concentration of mine dumps on the reef, and our headquarters in Germiston looked out on the most golden mound of all. It was not the newest, nor the biggest, only the goldest. I assume that it was the last created by some superseded process, since in the sixty miles from Springs to Krugersdorp it was nowhere duplicated. It reduced me to eyedrops, but what washed out was gold.

As I would rush for the 7:10 out of Johannesburg Station the Black labor force was pouring into town 300,000 strong. I can see that most people would find Johannesburg appalling, but I do not honestly see how they could find it depressing. There is too much vitality. The Blacks in Pretoria had seemed merely displaced and stunned. These were lively and purposeful: real urbanites. They too had to occupy an alternative reality, but were already making something of it. Influx control limited the number of live-in servants apartment houses or private homes could employ, and a good thing it did, or the residents would have had themselves carried from room to room in sedan chairs. As it was the limits were generous, and I did not have to make a bed nor wash a dish. The "locations in the sky," the servants' quarters on the roofs of the high rises, ripped and roared. In the life of Hillbrow, it was "Upstairs, Upstairs."

The domestics played their pennywhistles and played their radios, had a network of knucklebone games that could no more have been mapped than could have the tunnels underground, but whose attraction was so compulsive that the most intense lightning storms could not drive the players under cover, and had a trolley system of clotheslines by which bottles of liquor could be sped from roof to roof. Weight permitting, afternoon ladies of the evening could be trolleyed.

The humane objection to the Pass Laws was that they made it impossible for workers to have their families with them, but I have no doubt that for the younger men, abandoning family was an attraction of Johannesburg. Certainly the recruiters for the mining companies knew that it was not only economic necessity that drove workers into their hands, and were careful to stress the aspects of adventure and rakishness. I do not wish to downplay the force of poverty, but I do not for one moment believe that young men in Africa differ from those elsewhere, and what a blanketed "crocodile" of mine laborers being marched along the sidewalk toward Fordsburg most resembled was a line of recruits at Fort Jackson

waiting to go on pass.

On the other side of Louis Botha Avenue from the concrete escarpments of Hillbrow was Parktown, the onetime mandate of the Randlords. It had a sense, if not of ocean, of old trees, the more alluring that, in 1888, it was, like everything else on the site of Johannesburg, bare veld. There is very little that Sir Herbert and enough gardeners could not accomplish. When I reconnoitered Parktown it was block by block, with as clear a projection of its future as of its past. I had seen Saratoga Avenue, where the Randlords lived before they went onward and upward. Saratoga Avenue was Rooming House Row, which is where Parktown was clearly headed, in spite of the liveried servants, Bentleys, and guard dogs.

Baker's own house was there, as formidable a playpen as ever a kindergarten had, and far along the ridge to the east of it was a spreading, stretched-out copy, at the end of a dead-end climb where the site dropped off and you felt there was nothing between you and Rhodesia. It was the most extravagant view in Africa, and I allow for the Fairest Cape.

But the flagship house in Parktown is not Baker's. It is Dolobran, the work of Cope Christie. At the intersection of Oxford Road and Victoria Avenue, it waits the entrance of the gods into Valhalla. In 1922 the owner directed the military operations against the strikers. Artillery mounted on the lawn at Dolobran fired on Brixton Ridge. It is a neat reversal of the cliché: mansions firing on revolutionaries rather than vice versa. Most of Parktown is gone, but the red brick house on the crag is still there. Who would be foolhardy enough to eminent domain it? Another survivor, with onion domes on the turrets, was known to its owner as Turnip Towers. Parktown had a sense of humor. Houghton, the new money, has none.

Angst is no more interesting when it is justified than when it isn't, and I avoided Houghton liberals. Occasionally, nevertheless, would come an invitation I could not refuse. I wonder, now that events have passed them by, what has become of Johannesburg's drawing-room Africans, the trade guild that, by intent at least, enlivened our evenings as balloons and bellygrams enliven evenings of the well-to-do in Buckhead and Burlingame.

I can tell you that the Africans were professionals. Amateurs would have murdered the hosts. The ongoing crisis was the loo. If there were small children in the house the decision could be dealt with deftly. "Oh, Mr. Dimbaza. Nurse is bathing the children upstairs. Would you mind using the lavatory off the kitchen?" Mr. Dimbaza, who knew where his bread was buttered, never batted an eye. More often it was less subtle. "Oh, Mr. Dimbaza. We're putting in a sauna upstairs. [The sauna in the pool house is not adequate?] Would you mind using the lavatory off the kitchen?" The more experienced hostesses would designate a little boys' room and a little girls' room. After Mr. Dimbaza's first trip, none of the other men seemed able to remember which was which. The real pros of the guild would go early to both. Two can play a forgetting game, and "Mr. Dimbaza" would then have the pleasure of watching the Whites fidget, but would not be invited back.

The stories that were told disappointed. I could have told grimmer, but the guild knew exactly where to draw the line, not wishing to spoil dinner, especially their own. Mind you, I do not doubt that every slight, injustice, and brutality occurred. I do not think that every one occurred to every teller. No guest ever asked for corroborative detail intended to give artistic verisimilitude. They may have taken the narrations, like bellygrams, for what they were, a ritual gesture. One evening I heard the host say to "Mr. Dimbaza," in exactly these words, "You can use the servants' lavatory." I do not customarily leap to the defense of my hometown, but no husband of a Jackson Junior Leaguer would have done that. Buckhead would, if ever it invited Blacks in the first place. It is a pity that Houghton is in no way worthy of Helen Suzman, who for three decades has represented it in Parliament.

The interesting parties were not the Houghton guilt trips but the Hillbrow Saturday nights. Without particular effort one could find an evening in which the conversation drifted from English to Afrikaans to Flemish to Dutch (never try to persuade a speaker that those three are the same language) to German. If you really want to liven up things bring on the dour Afrikaners. One of the Dutch Reformed churches will drink but not dance; one will dance but not drink; and one will not do either. However, there is no need to try to keep the distinctions straight, as, after passing up the first round of drinks, the communicants will usually say, "Well, we all have the Devil in us," and drink everyone else under the table.

In Johannesburg bars there was a risk of fist fights, trampling, riot, methyl alcohol, police raids, and sexual assault, but one would at least not be impaled by darts. I was always meeting people who wanted me to join a fencing club (it must have been my crew cut; no one ever accused me of coordination) but here one had a choice. I could see myself with a duelling scar, but not with a sieve over my face. Besides, I was shown how to fake a scar with collodion.

If I were thirty again and going to South Africa for a first time, I would try to learn one of the Bantu

"The Old Hand when young," Tortuguero, 1953

languages. The Black TV channels in the Republic have many White viewers, who are able, if that is what they want, to pick up the language without having to consort with the speakers. It is a minor tragedy for the U.S., and time may prove it a major one, that the raising of Black consciousness in the sixties did not result in the widespread study of proper African languages, or their introduction into the curricula. Swahili is an Arabic creole, and surely there is no point in exchanging the language of one set of slavers for that of another.

As soon as I had a minimal competence, astute friends introduced me to the poems of Elisabeth Eybers. It was like reading Louise Bogan in Afrikaans, and I cannot give higher praise. I never met either of English-speaking Southern Africa's Great Ladies of Literature, and I am afraid that, however offensive and however little their fault, Nadine Gordimer and Doris Lessing must be described that way. They have become to the well-meaning what Pearl Buck used to be. I did, however, through the purest happenstance, meet the ex-husbands. The early short stories of both women are wonderful. The late novels of the one are about Patty Hearst, although the author seems not to have made the identification; the science fiction of the other is somewhere between Orson Welles's *War of the Worlds* and Louella Parsons.

In her diaries, Anne Morrow (Lindbergh), writing of her fiance, records the following: "He has become a kind of slop bowl for everyone's personal dreams and ideals." South Africa has become a slop jar for the pseudo-self-abasement of the White world and the very real envy of the Black. As the country produces contents of its own, I have tried not to add to the slops. It is as meaningless to criticize the Republic as to praise God and Mother, and about as efficacious.

As in Puerto Rico, a time came when I would have to go or stay. I returned to the U.S. on an American Enterprise passenger freighter. This time the trip was only seventeen days, and the passenger complement was filled. One of our number was the widow of a wealthy Pasadena florist, and Pasadena florists can of course be very wealthy indeed. "I have six boxes of colored slides," she told us at dinner the first night out. "All sunsets." We bribed the steward to tell her the projector was broken.

I arrived, inadequately prepared, in the U.S. of trampolines, ducktail haircuts, and *Rock Around the Clock.* I cursed myself for not becoming a derelict outside Vereeniging (I am willing to learn banjo), and within eighteen months had sailed for Europe on the motor ship *Kinderdijk,* out of New Orleans. Corrupted by my reading, I wanted to see Lübeck, a gambling resort and/or spa, Davos, and the Faubourg Saint-Germain. Corrupted by my listening, I wanted to see any ski resort associated with the composition of operas about women without shadows, and every opera house in Europe. I would have liked to see the *frühe moderne* architecture of Berlin, but assumed it had been flattened, and would have liked to see Yasnaya Polyana, but not badly enough to brave the Soviet Union in March.

I sailed up the Scheldt, like Lohengrin; I saw Lübeck, Wiesbaden (a kill of two birds with one stone), the Faubourg Saint-Germain, and a great many opera houses, whose summer closings had dictated my schedule. I did not make it into consumption country, but in Garmisch I had a lovely *lagniappe.* In the garden of his villa backed up against the Alp of the *Alpine Symphony,* I saw, as a portly gentleman of sixty, the very noisy baby of the *Domestic Symphony.*

My favorite sights in London do not and do make the guidebooks. The obscurity is W. S. Gilbert's magnificent house in Harrington Gardens, which looks more Flemish than anything in Flanders. The other is Cullinan I in the royal sceptre. It amused me to see by how many factors the bauble of the burgers exceeds that of the maharajahs, the Kohinoor, in the crown of the Queen Mother. The small crown of Queen Victoria was on display, evoking for me her cast-iron presence beside the House of Parliament in Cape Town. On leaving the Wakefield Tower I realized that I was in Tower Gardens, where the crew of Conrad's *Narcissus* broke up. Not without effort, I made it to Whitechapel, where Jack the Ripper ripped, and to Limehouse, which, after postwar reconstructions, is not so much *Broken Blossoms* as *The Shape of Things to Come.* What remains of the bad old days is, I am happy to tell you, wonderfully sinister. The route lies out West India Dock Road, which I could not have resisted in any event.

In pubs, open fireplaces and coal grates alarmed me as badly as dart boards, but needlessly. The British are too inhibited even to get up and poke the fire. Perhaps they have baked their brains. They go to the theatre mainly to applaud. It is one of rather few forms of self-expression which they have, perfidy being another.

I went to Ocean Dock in Southampton, to see where the *Titanic* sailed from, but except for this excursion did not leave London. Mayfair has impeccable potted-palm music. To hear *Roses of Picardy* in that setting is to forgive much. On the continent I had played a little game with myself. If, at dinner, I could identify every number the musicians played, I would treat myself to an after-dinner drink.

I fled Europe after a June snowstorm in Garmisch-Partenkirchen, where I occupied Sonja Henie's bedroom at the Alpenhof, as a photograph and a caption warned me. I admire Froken Henie, who contrived to die in midair on a transatlantic flight, panicking tax collectors on two continents.

I returned on SS *France,* the last of the superliners. The terminal at Le Havre built for the *Normandie* served for the newer ship. The portals did not line up, but may have not for *Normandie.* The French, as any librarian will tell you, can never do anything the same way twice. Their model—one would say archetype—is the German Big Bertha, the seventy-five-mile cannon whose barrel wore so fast that each shell had to be larger in diameter than its predecessor.

SS *France* is now SS *Norway,* and, on half of her engine capacity, fuel-efficiently cruises the Caribbean. Why the world's largest ship was thought suitable for the world's smallest harbors is something the owners of lighters and passenger launches will have to speak to.

At home push had come to shove. Public librarians in the American Library Association were already flagellating themselves over library service to illiterates, something I regard as on the same level with Death-of-God theology. Let them read cake. What are video parlors for? In September 1962, I went to work for Emory University in Atlanta, and will retire there year after next. It is a decision with which, after twenty-six years, I have no quarrel. Europe, whatever I say, had been productive. I completed the poems that "top up," as the filling-station attendants say, my first collection, *Watchboy, What of the Night?* published by Wesleyan University Press in 1966, and Emory has been what I intended it to be, productive. It has been what I have had instead of Caroline Balestier (Kipling) or Pauline DeAhna (Strauss), although I am no longer sure it approaches their intelligence.

Atlanta is a city which believes that only God can make a tree, but only Frederick Law Olmsted knew where to put one. Why have I spent my life in garden-club towns. Shrubbery and blind corners have surely caused more fatal traffic accidents than drunken driving and nonfastened seat belts in tandem. If I had not seen Pretoria in jacaranda season I might think more highly of dogwood time in Atlanta. Many people think it looks like Kyoto, but to me it looks like an explosion in the Handi-Wipe factory. In my childhood, I did not think highly of white wisteria, white crape myrtle, or white lilacs. Dirty Kleenex is dirty Kleenex. The jacaranda trees raise into the morning sky the sky of evening, and after rain confirm on the sidewalk Chicken Little.

As from Pretoria, one would have to get away. At the earliest opportunity I moved from the university neighborhood to the Hillbrow of the midtown. The first building I lived in, on Lombardy Way, put me in mind of a *Reader's Digest* piece I should write: "Call Girls Make Good Neighbors." They do. Their work is elsewhere, and the last thing they want is attention-attracting rowdiness. I had the heated pool to myself, and could swim—well, paddle—until late in October. The tone dropped sharply when, in the apartment next to me, the police raided a wig thief. Boxes and boxes from Wig Villa were hauled into the corridor. "It's NOT *Pink Mist*," the thief screamed in self-defense as the colors of the wigs were read out from a manifest. "It's *Pink Champagne*." The wig he was himself wearing I can describe easily: vegetable henna.

The building to which I removed had problems of its own. During construction the contractors found that the corings had been in error, and that additional fortunes would have to be spent on the foundations. The company went into receivership, and certain amenities, such as heat in the lower lobbies, never eventuated. On consecutive years, when in May the pool was filled for the first time, the bottom ruptured, flooding the storage rooms below. Residents lost furniture, clothing, pictures, and convertible tops. The litigation is still going on. The next year the water tank on the roof failed, flooding fourteen floors of apartments on the northeast corner of the building. Then a water main on West Peachtree burst. People came home to the parking decks to find their cars underwater to the level of the roofs. The fatal fires, of which there were three, took place only after I left. The building now has a pagoda roof and is converting to luxury condos. If I had any principles I would picket it.

Nor was the morality an improvement over Lombardy Way. Ten days after I moved in the vice squad closed a sex club on the eighteenth floor. This pie-in-the-sky was the fantasy of—beautifully—a couple named Breedlove, who had franchises going in Florida and in California. It is still not clear to me what was to franchise, sex being do-it-yourself if anything is. The Breedloves, however, dealt with a mimeographed list of sexual preferences, some of which were most specialized, and would try to match up complementary urges. They did their mimeographing in a basement room rented from the management, which, in a mimeographed notice, denied knowledge. It was somewhat before the period when people liked to think of themselves as swingers, and for weeks afterward, in the elevators, no one would press a button for any floor above ten.

My neighborhood bar was the Piccolo, franchised to the restaurant next door, Mama Mia. Mama herself would have been an ornament on Boarding-house Row. At the end of the business day she stashed her cash in the kitchen in the oven. One evening Mama forgot to turn off the gas and the take ignited. She was screaming and chasing bills about the room like a demented lepidopterist in pursuit of flaming butterflies, which her clientele presently became. Mama herself knew a learning experience when she saw one. She became Atlanta's arson queen, the *bête rouge* of insurance adjusters.

In 1981, thirty years after I was in the Caribbean the first time, as a student of twenty-two, I came to Cartagena, the Queen of the Indies. Having been the world's desire, the extraordinary old city lazes by the warm sea like a very old jewel-studded tortoise—one that knew Captain Cook socially—"in el casco." The walls could accommodate a chariot race. Mainly the city made me defensive about the provincial, easy, undesired San Juan of long ago. Barranquilla is Baton Rouge.

If my life as presented seems to you a discontinuity of airport security checks and chain motels you are wrong. It has had more continuity than most. Let us say it has been a chromatic scale. I still see occasionally friends with whom I went to elementary school, fifty-five years ago, and I see with some frequency friends with whom I went to junior high school, forty-five years ago. I am in contact with friends from every period and every locale I have survived. It is more than possible, though, that I am in the last generation of those who will know what it is to have lifelong friends. The mobility of the society is against it, and the drive to presentism. Presentism is if anything a worse affliction on writing than on historiography. Anyone who has taught composition knows that the students' idea of a short story is something about people who have known one another three days at a beach, nor is their youth an extenuation. Mann completed *Buddenbrooks* at the age of twenty-five.

You probably think that at this point I am going to launch an attack on the sixties. I am not. I rather enjoyed the sixties, although not as much as I have enjoyed the I-told-you-so. I decided early that the counterculture had more to do with the desire of manufacturers and advertisers to sell clothing than with ideology, and that, like the dance madness of the middle ages, it would pass, leaving lots of unemployable young people and a rich, widespread selection of new diseases. I did not foresee that the dears would come up with a 100 percent fatal venereal disease, but maybe that's the way Ages of Aquarius are.

I was living in Atlanta's midtown during the high period. I would say that at the absolute outside there were sixty full-time, live-in hippies, all of whom, jerking and twitching, eventually sought employment at Emory Library. The mobs on the strip on Saturdays were weekend hippies. I would see them park their cars (license plates from the suburban counties), take off their shirts and/or bras, put on their beads, muss their hair, and make the scene. If forced to choose, I would pick hippies over yuppies. They do not jog. Do I impute a dance madness to the wrong group?

No one lost less sleep over Vietnam than I did. If I could have managed to stay out of combat, and I suspect I could have, I would have enjoyed myself. At worst, I could have read Pierre Loti. The outrage of the draft resisters seemed to me rather selective, but outrage usually is, and the selectivity was certainly no news to a former South African civil servant.

I have a reputation for cranking out exotica, and I suppose anyone can see from my poems that I am a man who pursues his own interests. But, without really planning to, I have mounted a campaign that has taught me as much about heartland America as

the disciples of Walt Whitman and Dr. Williams can claim to know. For more than thirty-five years I have been making transcontinental automobile trips. Motel Row is darkest burgerdom, and no one knows it better than I do. You will learn more about America by sitting two hours in the cocktail lounge of any Holiday Inn than by reading all of De Toqueville, and you will have a more enjoyable learning experience. Do I deliberately set out to stalk material for poems? Yes, of course. Inner space exists to be supplied. Familiar as I am with human treachery, I certainly would not depend on the deeps of my psyche to fuel what I hope will be a sixty-year career. Its very delight would be to fail you when you most needed it. All the psyche can dependably do is act as a pilot light. Arranging fuel for the main blaze is a logistic problem like any other.

In my pursuit of the future as envisioned in 1932 I come nowhere closer than in Houston. To drive the expressway that parallels the sixty-story wall of skyscrapers that face on Louisiana Street is to live fifteen chapters of a Buster Crabbe serial between two exits. The Transco Tower on Post Oak Road rises as from the Plain of Shinar.

In the lounge of the Warwick Hotel I overheard the essential Houston conversation. It involved the proper method for the setting of an eight-carat diamond. "It was so heavy the *prawngs* wouldn't hold it," said the owner, "no matter how much they bent them in. They had to make this little platinum *jacket* faw it." The owner looked as Jean Harlow might have at sixty. I tell the story with a sneer, because Johannesburg does not regard any stone under twenty carats as a topic of conversation, and because Johannesburg knows that the place for platinum is in catalytic converters. No one has done more for the South African economy than the abominable Ralph Nader.

On the menu at the Warwick is smoked quail, and on the menu at the Cattle Guard is barbecued quail. The Cattle Guard, a restaurant on Milam Street whose parking lot is shaded by umbrella chinas (and no more efficient shade tree exists; sunlight that is feathered can only whisper, like the serpent . . .). The Cattle Guard, I say, should be a compulsory stop for every Houston visitor, especially Rust Belt academics. Like scores of places in Tulsa and Rapid City and Cheyenne and Flagstaff it is the locus of people who are exactly where and what they want to be. Was any academic, Plato least of all, *ever* where and what he wanted to be? Not bloody likely. It will be the punishment in Hell of ambitious academics to have the response of Paul Kruger to the envoy, a belted earl, who preceded his credentials with a long list of titles. "Really," said Oom Paul. "I was a shepherd."

At the end is California, where I impose on the hospitality of old friends and mend my literary fences. In 1980 I had a grant from the National Endowment for the Arts. Jimmy Carter was in the White House; there had been criticism of the previous year's awards for being geographically skewed. I do not think that my Georgia address did me harm. Any fool could see that the criticized awards had been demographically dead on the mark, but none of us in the boonies is about to tell. I took the money and streaked for Palo Alto.

In Mountain View I had an apartment in an "executive relocation facility" where Silicon Valley types could take furnished efficiencies on short-term lease. My balcony faced down Moffett Boulevard toward Hangar Number One at Moffett Field, and do not think my choice was accidental. As soon as the miraculous California reversal of the midday heat sent me for the late-afternoon sweater, I would pour a drink, prop up my feet on the balcony rail, and wait for the *Macon* to come in. Since, like those who believe in the existence of Tinker Bell, I had faith, it not infrequently came. With the hangar to give the scale, there was no problem. The great silver shape, "than a storm more vast," hovered just at the edge of vision. If the herald came nearer I knew exactly what to say. "Du Bote aller Boten . . . Gibt es kein Hinüber? Sind wir schon da?" There is nothing Freudian in any of this. It was the *Akron* my father lifted me out of bed to see. I was three years old.

Popular Mechanics could never decisively make up its mind about the automobile of the future, but leaned toward a teardrop design. I was having none of that, and the magazine should have let well enough alone, as it was publishing at the zenith of classic design. The sight of sixteen Dusenbergs side by side at Harrah's display in Reno came as near to wrecking my mind as the sight of a BOAC Comet I taking off from Jan Smuts Airport. The streets of *my* future are no Way of Tears, unless they be those of the abominable Ralph Nader.

In the first fuel crisis, in 1973, I found I was miles from work without particularly good bus connections. My next-door neighbor in my high rise was an alcoholic who was a chain-smoker. It seemed a good time to move. I bought a condominium in Decatur and, within a few years, had to serve as president of the condominium association.

It was like inheriting a banana republic: God's punishment on me for playing the Lord of Creation in the colonies all those years. People are only very minimally gifted at living in society. There ought to

be an equivalent of the Tarzan myth for those of us who dislike nature. There is: Howard Hughes. But who of us has the income to act it out. As if searching for one good man in Sodom, we tried repeatedly to find a solution to the problem of parking, pets, and children. After tears at bedtime, seasickness in the bunks above me, knees and elbows, call girls, wig thieves, Mr. and Mrs. Breedlove, and Noah's Flood these irritations did not seem to me great, but others have not had my experience. Children grow up; for pets we purchased a "Pooper-Scooper," the details of which you do not wish to know; and parking? You have it with you always. Each of our units has covered parking for two cars (I am myself a two-car family of one; anything to spite the Abominable); it was visitor parking that reduced us to savagery. By and by the difficulty partially solved itself. We became so unpleasant that nobody came to see us.

I learned in Africa, however, that there is a great difference between the least society and no society. Those trekking Afrikaners who felt crowded if they could see their neighbors' smoke assembled quarterly for a communion service, and religion was not its only function. It made exogamy possible. In the most contentious condo there is a nostalgia, perhaps unrecognized, for the life of a small town, although for those of us who grew up in small towns, the idea of a global village is frightening. Most of the world's present problems are due to that well-known small-town vice, meddling. When we say good-bye, that is, God be with you, we indicate that we do not regard God as company in the fullest sense, and any parent will tell you that small children are not company in the fullest sense.

Art is, or it can be, hence the high proportion of artists who are unmarried. I phase out when aspiring poets say to me, "I want to write about relationships." In forty years I have seen no evidence that they have the willingness or the ability to create characters to have the relationships. It is not altogether their fault. They have no models. The English lyric is too relentlessly first person and too relentlessly centered on the internal. As in *Patience,* one might almost mistake it for indigestion. The possibility that poetry might deal with settings and characters as well as drama or fiction is alien. For those who wish to put the emotion or the act or the image directly on the page—an impossibility; ink is all one can put on the page—the very word medium must be offensive, as it denotes something that intervenes. I find a demanding medium liberating rather than otherwise. The more secure the technique the wider range of subjects I am prepared to deal with. Few poems I read, however, have a subject. Flaubert wanted to write

"The Old Hand grown old," Decatur, Georgia, 1986

about nothing. Poets do. But *Un coeur simple* is not about nothing. It is about the passage of time. When I returned to Camp Tortuguero after twenty years I realized that if I had waited five years more it would have taken a professional archaeologist to identify anything. When I returned to South Africa after twenty years I found it rich and uncontrite, but unsegregated to a degree I would not have believed possible in 1967. There is a sense in which, like Félicité's parrot, one's past, if it can be preserved at

all, is a triumph of taxidermy, but meter is one thing which can put life into it. It is a heartbeat.

It seemed to me when I came to Emory University that it was a rather good second-line university which taught English and history and math and premed. I am sure that, mummied in the tatters of interdisciplinary studies, interdisciplinary centers, centers for the study of war, centers for the study of peace, and centers for the study of centrism, there is still a rather good second-line university which teaches English and history and math and premed. We could not get from one day to the next if that were not true. But unfortunately the university received a great deal of money, and sinks ever deeper into the abysm of relevance and good works. As I near retirement it appalls me to think how much effort has gone into charades which have nothing whatever to do with education as I understand it. Let me say first that I do not consider "learning experiences" education. If you make up an alphabet, that can be a learning experience, and, possibly, can transfer. If you learn an alphabet already in use, that is education. Education is the sum of other people's learning experiences. Voter-registration drives, the last gasp of elitism, can teach you things. Not, probably, those you wish to learn. It was the nineteenth century that understood how to get people to the polls: buy them liquor.

In the seventies, when rapid transit was going to deliver us from the social evils of the automobile and bring about the millennium, Atlanta neighborhood coalitions blocked construction of an expressway. The university, as the university, took no part in the maneuvering, nor should it have taken part, as none of the land is contiguous to the campus. Having been eminent domained, the land was cleared, and after long disuse, became a kudzu-cum-hobo jungle.

In the eighties, some of the land was designated as the site of the Carter Center, whose relationship to Emory University would make some of the arrangements in the Austro-Hungarian monarchy seem simplistic. The Department of Transportation, under a mostly imaginary pressure to get mostly imaginary visitors to the center, revived the expressway plan, expanding it to include a widening of Ponce de Leon Avenue through the Olmsted parks. Doers of good on the faculty picked up the Sword of Righteousness. Various city planners had suggested earlier that the land might be turned into a park, and the "Great Park" concept became to the anti-expressway contingent what the League of Nations was to Woodrow Wilson. From very early they began to speak of it, to think of it, as if it already existed. I have never seen reality more rapidly abandoned. The amenities, the benefits of the Great Park became as real as the Fourteen Points.

Nothing is sillier than the notion that architecture and landscape are somehow capable of improving people. The briefest visit to a public-housing project, or, for that matter, to a country club, will demonstrate that they are not. Nothing is sillier, except a notion that architecture and landscape which do not even exist can accomplish the same thing.

Pursuing one of the Fourteen Points of the

eighties, that everything must somehow be or become political (Are my poems political? Only when they deal with politicians), the well-meaning forced the university into the issue, although it was no more contiguous to the Great Park, nor to the Olmsted parks, than it had been before. Druid Hills Country Club, which is contiguous, took no position, and felt no need to. It was a nonissue. For a solid year the university was paralyzed for the sake of a few ditches and a few trees, and by the same people who would think nothing of running an unsightly escalator up the grand staircase of the Paris Opera to allow access to the halt and the lame. Before I would see that happen I would form an International Richard Widmark Society to push the handicapped over precipices. I suggested that the entire area in controversy be flooded and stocked with snail darters, but no one was amused. We are in the grip of Sentimental-Pastoral, the worst outbreak of it since the romantic poets. The original environmental-impact statement was, "What God had joined together let no man put asunder," and it was wrong. After seventy-five years Gatun Lake and the Panama Canal look much more natural than the River Nile, and are. What is natural about a river that runs two thousand miles through the middle of a desert? The Nile exists, but so does pregnancy, and as a friend of mine said to her sentimental obstetrician, "Doctor, what is natural about walking around with another person inside of you?"

The rending of garments and the lacerating of the flesh is *still* going on, but the Carter Center was built, and much resembles the Palais des Nations in Geneva. The only persons to emerge with credit were the judge who ruled that land eminent domained for one purpose cannot be used for another without offering it back to the original owners at the original price, and Jimmy Carter himself, who, in a case where it was clearly called for, took the position of Pontius Pilate. Everything is political? Not while there are silver salvers around it it isn't.

No one who travels as much as I do deeply, sincerely believes that the bluebird of happiness is in his own backyard. You would not either if you had to live in a place where the emotional climax of the year is a dogwood festival. But just as it appeared that, on retirement, I should have to go for the sake of my aesthetic well-being to the proletarian glories of Stockton and Bakersfield, wicked capitalism came across and Atlanta built the IBM Tower, a skyscraper that in terms of "Come, let us make a name" is exceeded only by the Chrysler Building itself. In spite of its beauty it is to me as the Gorgon, because I cannot keep my eyes off of it, it is visible from all over town, and it is going to cause me to wreck my car. As the owners light it up like a world's fair, it is reassuring to know that it is permanent, although at my age permanence is relative. A Century of Progress ran for two years, which is longer than presidencies and pontificates I could name.

For many years I was a periodicals librarian, a position which gave me a unique insight into the grandeur and the triviality of American civilization. There is no profession, no cult, no hobby, no religion, no business, no political persuasion, no sickness, no perversion, no domestic animal, no sport, no school of poetry which does not have its newsletter or house organ. I learned early to respect those which, however loony, keep their billing, subscription lists, and voluming in order. I have to tell you that academic publications are the worst offenders. Naturally. Their authors and editors are busy defending ditches, in whatever meaning you wish to understand the term. Of only slightly less concern to those persons than the benefits of landscape is that burning question, "What did the Hartford Accident and Indemnity Company mean to Wallace Stevens?" I can answer. Wallace Stevens's job meant to him exactly what mine has meant to me: everything, since it is what made everything else possible.

If your message to the world is "Thou Fool" you are not going to be the most popular poet around, especially if you say it in meter. Thou Fool is in fact a perfect iamb. No, it is not a spondee. If a lifetime of writing in meter has taught me anything it is that spondees do not exist. One always comes down on one side or the other, as rarely in life. I may be unfashionable, but no more unfashionable than I was forty years ago.

Psychiatrists, whose profession is to point out the obvious, observe that Hitler's paintings contain no people, only buildings. They could make the same charge against this sketch. Well, Hitler was a perfectly competent watercolorist, and what my life has taught me is, Hitler was not uniquely evil. He was routinely evil. Unless we face that, nothing can be done. People are no damned good. One can react to Calvin's *aperçu* by crawling into the corner of a box and assuming a fetal position, like the figure in the Steig cartoon, or, in the words of the seldom-photographed Elizabeth Daryush, "go out to elemental wrong." If you elect to go, go all the way.

Like an ever-lengthening orbit, the passage of years bears one farther from his focus, or nearer to it. One cannot speak of *the* focus of an ellipse. It has two. The outer sweep of the fifties—mine, not the century's—jetted me south across the River Maritza (*Servus,*

Gräfin), out over the Black Sea, and straight down the Bosporus. At the last moment, as we turned for the airport, Byzantium disappeared in its own smoke.

In the early evening, showered and Turkish-towelled, I went out on the top-floor terrace of the Istanbul Sheraton, looked across the Golden Horn, and there it was: the Planet Mongo—every pinnacle, every parapet, every flattened dome. Every desirable thing in our unconscious actually exists, and needs only to be sought out. Something put it there, did it not?

I watched for a long time; it grew dark; and as the first rocket ship landed beside the galleys in from the Sweet Waters of Asia, I went to bed. In two days I would have to leave for those other planets—dual planets?—Budapest and Vienna.

Another year, another transit. A few days before Christmas, and I am in Honolulu. Keeping a promise I made to myself decades earlier, when I saw the *Lurline* sail under the Golden Gate Bridge for the Farallones, I am staying at the Royal Hawaiian, in the neon heart of unspoiled Waikiki. A display in a corridor off the lobby commemorates the opening of the hotel in 1927. It has menus, a setting of the original china, and a selection of photographs. Among the beachboys is Buster Crabbe. It seemed wholly fitting that Flash Gordon grew up in a Territory—a colony—beside the warm sea, out of which all life emerges. Another photo is Norma Talmadge, on one of her honeymoons. My mother never remarried. The banyan tree in the court brings depressing images of sages and saints, but the palm trees on Kalakaua Avenue curve out to sea like a row of very large but very discreet asterisks. The profile of Diamond Head is familiar from elsewhere. I know it is hollow, the outcrop, but I can pretend.

I was the adored only child of young, intelligent, middle-class parents and of grandparents whose means I inherited at an early age and have managed well for almost fifty years. Poetically, I was very talented, and my training was the best. There is no secret to success in poetry or in life. All that is necessary is to be dealt the high trumps.

Emory University
5 August 1988

BIBLIOGRAPHY

Poetry:

Watchboy, What of the Night? Middletown, Conn.: Wesleyan University Press, 1966.

Steeplejacks in Babel. Boston: David Godine, 1973.

Silver out of Shanghai: A Scenario for Josef von Sternberg, Featuring Wicked Nobles, a Depraved Religious, Wayfoong, Princess Ida, the China Clipper, and Resurrection Lily, with a Supporting Cast of Old Hands, Merchant Seamen, Sikhs, Imperial Marines, and Persons in Blue (illustrated by Steve Fritz). Atlanta: Planet Mongo Press, 1973.

Yellow for Peril, Black for Beautiful: Poems and a Play. New York: Braziller, 1975.

Two Are Four (poem card). Binghamton, N.Y.: Bellevue Press, 1977.

The Defense of the Sugar Islands: A Recruiting Poster. Los Angeles: Symposium Press, 1979.

Phaëthon (broadside). Binghamton, N.Y.: Iris Press, 1979.

Keys to Mayerling. Florence, Ky.: Robert L. Barth, 1983.

The Airship Boys in Africa: A Dramatic Narrative in Twelve Parts. Atlanta: Hendricks Publishing, 1984.

The Book of Alna: A Narrative of the Mormon Wars. Florence, Ky.: Robert L. Barth, 1985.

Hurricane Lamp. Chicago and London: University of Chicago Press, 1986.

Lessons, with R. L. Barth. Florence, Ky.: Para Press, 1987.

Raymond Federman

1928-

A VERSION OF MY LIFE—THE EARLY YEARS

*Buffalo, today—Raymond Federman
practicing his saxophone*

To Whom It May Concern

I often wonder if being a writer, becoming a writer is a gift one receives at birth, or if it happens accidentally in the course of one's life. I am always envious, and suspicious too, of those who say to me, "I wrote my first poem when I was eight years old, and published my first story when I was fifteen." It makes me feel that perhaps I wasted the first twenty-five years of my life.

Even today, after the millions of words I have scribbled (in English and in French) over the past thirty years, with six novels in print, one more in progress, one abandoned, two volumes of poems, several books of essays and criticism, hundreds of loose pieces of prose and poetry in magazines, and much more still unpublished, I often doubt that I am a writer. Thirty years of trying to convince myself of this fact. Thirty-one years, to be exact, since my first published poem in a college magazine in 1957, a five line poem entitled "More or Less." It went like this:

> From Cambrian brain-
> Less algae sprung the ten-ton
> Flesh and bone reptile
> Then man from ape till bodi-
> Less brain shall inherit the earth

A ponderous little poem which certainly does not indicate that I was then or would ever become a writer. Even now I believe I am still working at becoming one, and perhaps I shall die never knowing whether or not I was a real writer. It seems to me that everything I write (and few days pass that I do not sit at my desk to work) is a preparation for the great book that someday will make of me the real writer. Meanwhile my books are published, reviewed, discussed, analyzed, translated, praised and attacked, a couple received literary prizes, and still I am not sure.

The other day my best fan, my lovely twenty-five-year-old daughter, Simone, on the phone from New York City (collect of course) says to me, oh without malice, lovingly in fact, "Hey Pop, I think I know what your epitaph will be, I mean, you know, what should be written on your tombstone: OUT OF PRINT." What gentle brutality! She's got it right though, there is brutality in what writers do. Writing is such an inhuman thing to be doing, so brutally asocial, unnatural. So much against nature. No wonder writers suffer fits of doubt and despair.

No, I do not think I was born a writer (even though I too can doubt and despair like a true writer), but the accidents of my life may have helped make of me a writer. If I was given a gift at all which forced me to write, it was what happened to me, often in spite of myself, during the first twenty-five years of my life. Much of the fiction I have written found its source in those early years.

"With daughter Simone at the wedding of stepson Jim," Los Angeles, 1986

In a recent article about my work, the critic Marcel Cornis-Pop states, rightly so I suppose, that "unlike some of his metafictional contemporaries, [Federman] has been blessed (or cursed) with enough biography for several epic cycles, condemned to stringing out the story of his life endlessly in various fictions." In retrospect, the first twenty-five years of my life certainly contained enough drama, enough adventures, misadventures, and misfortunes to inspire several novels. I lived those years oblivious to myself and to the sordid affairs of the world around me, unaware that the experiences I was living, or I should say enduring, would someday make a writer of me. My life began in incoherence and discontinuity, and my work has undoubtedly been marked by this. Perhaps that is why it has been called experimental.

And I Followed My Shadow

I was born in Paris, France, in 1928, May 15, a Taurus, which means one who lives in the world with his feet firmly on the ground and his head in the clouds. But if this is my official date of birth, it was not until July 16, 1942, that my life really began. On that day, known in France as *le jour de La Grande Rafle*, more than twelve thousand people (who had been declared stateless by the Vichy government and

forced to wear a yellow star bearing the inscription *JUIF*) were arrested and sent to the Nazi death camps. That day, my father, mother, and two sisters were also arrested and eventually deported to Auschwitz where they died in the gas chambers. There are records of this. I escaped and survived by being hidden in a closet. I consider that traumatic day of July 16, 1942, to be my real birthdate, for that day I was given an excess of life.

A poem I wrote years ago entitled "Escape" opens with these lines: "My life began in a closet / among empty skins and dusty hats / while sucking pieces of stolen sugar." On July 16, 1942, at 5:30 in the morning, while the French militia and the German gestapo were coming up the stairs to our third-floor apartment in Paris to arrest us, my mother pushed me into a little closet on the landing of the staircase. As I sat there in the dark, still half-asleep, wearing only my underwear, I listened to my mother, my father, and my two sisters go down the stairs on their way to extermination.

X-X-X-X, these are the symbols I have used throughout my work to mark that moment. For me these signs represent the necessity and the impossibility of expressing the erasure of my family. I believe I have spent the last thirty years of my life (and will probably

Paternal grandparents in Poland with some of their children, about 1920.
The author's father is seated at far right.

spend the remaining years) writing in order to understand my mother's gesture when she hid me in that closet, and in order to decipher the darkness into which I was plunged that day.

Almost everything that precedes "the closet moment," as I have referred to it over the years, seems to have been erased from my memory. The first fourteen years of my life are like a blur. I have only vague, disjointed recollections of what I did with my parents, with my sisters and my cousins, with my school friends, before that fatal day. And I often suspect that some of these recollections are pure inventions. I know certain facts about my parents, their origin and background, and about the place where I was raised. Facts I learned after the war from surviving relatives, and from old family papers and photographs I found in a cardboard box in our apartment. Over the years, I have returned to France many times, and on several occasions went back to the neighborhood of my childhood on the outskirts of Paris to see the apartment building where we lived. I even reentered the closet where I was left to survive, and visited the school where I first learned to read and write, and wandered in the streets where I used to play, but I never found anything there of any significance. No vivid traces of joyful or even unhappy events that took place before the closet moment.

Nothing singular that demands to be told. Only facades and facts are what I found there.

I have no remembrance at all of playing with my sisters, of arguing and fighting with them, as brothers and sisters do. I found only one photograph of my sisters in that cardboard box. It shows the three of us at the ages of six, seven, and nine—I was the middle child. My sisters look pretty in that picture. It must have been taken around 1935. Sarah was sixteen when she was deported in 1942, and Jacqueline thirteen. I know nothing of their thoughts, their dreams, their desires, their ambitions. I cannot remember a single sentence that passed between us. I think Sarah wanted to become a teacher or a scientist, and Jacqueline a ballerina, but I may have invented this about them.

Much of what I know about my parents, and the rest of my family—grandparents, uncles, aunts, and cousins—I gathered after most of them had disappeared. It is in conversations with the few relatives who survived the Holocaust that I learned something of my parents, of my sisters, and of myself too, before the closet moment. I do not mean to suggest that I suffer of amnesia, or that I have a bad memory. On the contrary, I have a terrific memory. Undoubtedly many events of the early years of my life have been

*Raymond with his sisters, Jacqueline and Sarah,
in Paris, about 1935*

blocked, but also lost in the turmoil of World War II, for there is an obvious reason for the ignorance I have of my own childhood.

It was not until I got married, in 1960, and found myself suddenly raising a family (Erica had three young children when I married her, Steve was ten, Jim seven, Robin three, and then our own daughter, Simone, was born in 1962) that I began to understand that we do not really remember our early years, but that these are remembered for us by our parents as they tell us over and over again who we were and what we did when we were little, tell us again and again how happy or unhappy we were, how *smart*, how *cute* we were, especially when they show us photographs of ourselves when we were children. Eventually, as we get older, we take over our own memories, and even take from our parents the photographs they preserved. But by then these have become second-hand memories. I suppose the reason I know so little of who I was and what I did when I was a child is because my parents disappeared too soon for them to be able to tell me, and continue to tell me, the stories of their lives before I was born and the stories of my early years, and show me the pictures of their childhood and mine. These stories and pictures have vanished with them.

What I know now from vague memories, and from what I managed to gather afterward, is that my parents were poor, very poor. And worse, until their deportation, they were considered foreigners in France—*des étrangers*. Jews who had come from the ghettos of Eastern Europe, and who had never been able to become assimilated in the French culture.

My father, Simon, was born in Siedlce, a small town in Poland near the Russian border. He was the second-youngest of nine children. (Only one of my uncles and four cousins on my father's side survived the Holocaust.) My father was eighteen when he came to France in 1922, but he was never able to obtain French citizenship because of political reasons. He was a fanatic Trotskyite. An anarchist, I was told. My mother was born in Paris, but of parents who, in a strange reversed journey, immigrated to Europe in the late nineteenth century from what was known then as Palestine. They went first to Poland for a few years, and after that to France. Their first two children were born in Palestine, then three more in Poland. My mother was the first of eight children to be born in Paris, but she lost the French citizenship she had acquired at birth when she married my father, and like him became stateless. The French have very subtle and complicated laws to protect *la patrie* from being taken over by foreigners. My sisters and I had to be naturalized French citizens even though we were born in France.

Politics was at the center of my father's life. He spent most of his time participating in demonstrations or sitting in cafés arguing with foreigners. I know this because when I was a little boy he sometimes took me (to the despair of my mother) to these demonstrations, to teach me, as he used to say, about the great revolution, or took me to the cafés in Montparnasse where I would sit quietly next to him drinking *une limonade* while he argued with the people there. I could not understand a word of what was being said in these foreign languages, but the arguments were loud and passionate. My father spoke seven languages. But as I learned later, there were other passions and obsessions in his life.

Tall and handsome, with pale grey eyes, he was a great womanizer. This I was told by aunts on my mother's side who did not care much for my father and who described him to me as a "lazy, irresponsible, and irrational man." He was an artist. A surrealist painter who never attained fame and recognition, who "never became anything." Nonetheless, he was an artist, though all his paintings and drawings are lost. Stolen or destroyed during the war. I have searched in many places for traces of my father's work but have failed to find anything. It was suggested to me that perhaps he painted under a different name than Federman. I suppose my father was what used to be called romantically a "starving artist." His work barely brought enough money for his wife and children to survive. During the hard years of the 1930s when my sisters and I were growing up, often

"Wedding picture of Mother and Father,"
Paris, about 1925

my mother shamefully took us to stand in line at the *soupe populaire.* Faithful to the romantic image of the starving artist, my father was also afflicted with tuberculosis, and constantly spat blood. One of his lungs had been collapsed. It was known as a pneumo-thorax, and every other week he had to have oxygen pumped into his lungs. I think my father suffered a great deal in his short life, physically and intellectual-ly. He was thirty-eight years old when he died at Auschwitz. He was described to me, by the uncle who brought me to America (a brother-in-law of my father who knew him when he was a young man in Poland), as a wild, reckless, but sensitive man. A dreamer. He was also an inveterate gambler. He played the horses, cards, dice, roulette, baccarat.

I have one vivid memory of my father and his gambling. One day he came home to our one-room apartment and emptied his pockets on the table. Stacks of large bills. We had never seen so much money. My mother started crying, but we the children were screaming with joy. My father announced that we were all going on a vacation to the seashore. Deauville, in Normandie. We left by train that very day, and stayed in a hotel which appeared to my

sisters and me as a fabulous, unreal palace. We had a two-room suite for the whole family with beautiful furniture and a balcony overlooking the sea. But we didn't stay there very long. The next day we were back on the train to Paris. While my mother sat on the beach watching us children play in the sand, my father was losing the money at the Deauville casino. It was the first time I saw the ocean. I must have been six or seven years old. The next time I saw the sea was when I boarded the boat to America, in 1947.

If I have managed to preserve or reconstruct an image of my father, of my mother I hardly remember anything, except that she was short, wore thick glasses, was plain-looking, always spoke in a soft voice, and that she worked hard all the time doing laundry for other people so she could feed her children. After the war, her brothers and sisters, all of whom managed to survive the Holocaust (they were well-off and found places to hide somewhere in southern France), often referred to my mother as a saint, but of course that's just an expression. *"Pauvre Marguerite,"* they would say, *"elle a tellement souffert."* I think it was a way for them to appease their guilt for not having helped my parents escape as they them-selves did. All my aunts and uncles on my mother's side died of old age in their large, comfortable beds.

My mother's father, I was told, died very young, in 1910, of pneumonia, leaving my grandmother with eight children, the youngest only a few months old. Four of the children were placed in an orphanage. My mother was one of them. She stayed in that orphan-age for twelve years, until the age of eighteen, when she came out into the world to work. That's all I know of her, except that she had big dark eyes and cried a lot.

The Voice in the Closet

July 16, 1942, is the last time I saw my parents and my sisters. I can almost relate, day by day, everything that happened to me from that moment on. I stayed in the closet all that day and until late into the night. I was afraid to come out because I knew that the people who lived downstairs did not like Jews and they might see me and denounce me. As I look back on the long hours I spent in that closet sitting on a pile of old newspapers, I do not think that I was really scared, but that I was in a state of total incomprehension. I felt that what was happening was temporary, that my parents would soon return and everything would be just as before. I lived with this feeling, this deluding hope, for the next three years until the end of the war, when it slowly became clear that my parents and sisters were never coming back. Eventually I was given documents that confirmed their extinction.

Groping in the dark, I found old clothes piled in a corner of the closet, and behind these a box full of sugar cubes. Sugar probably bought on the black market and hidden there by my mother. I sucked on the sugar when I became hungry during that long day. Later, in the afternoon, I had to defecate, but felt ashamed not to be able to do it in the proper place. Unable to hold back, I unfolded a newspaper, crouched over it holding my penis away from my legs so as not to wet myself, and did it right there. Then I rolled the paper into a parcel and placed it near the door, and when finally it was night outside, and all was quiet in the building, I opened the door of the closet and listened while holding my package of excrement in one hand. The landing was on the top floor of the building, but there was a short ladder that led to a skylight in the roof. I climbed that ladder holding the newspaper away from my face, but feeling its warmth and wetness on my hand, and when I reached the skylight I lifted the glass pane and placed the parcel on the roof. Three years later, when I returned to Paris, this is the first place I went. I wanted to know if my package was still there. Of course, there was nothing on the roof. I have often wondered what happened to this symbolic package in which I had wrapped my fear.

It would take pages and pages to describe in detail what happened from the moment I stepped out of the closet to the day when I returned to see if the parcel I had left on the roof was still there. Briefly then so that I can get on with the story, the story of my life, I must rush through the next three years—the years of wandering and surviving during the war.

It was the middle of night when I tiptoed down the stairs holding in my hands a pair of man's shoes too big for me which I found on the floor of the closet, and wearing one of my father's jackets which had been hanging from a nail in the wall. Underneath the jacket I only had my boy's shorts. I was going down as quietly as I could when I tripped on one of the steps and almost fell. As I slipped I let go of the shoes and they tumbled down the stairs with a frightening noise. A door opened above me and someone shouted, "Who is there!" In panic I ran the rest of the way down and out into the street. At that time there was a curfew every night, and only people with special permits were allowed in the streets. As I was running I heard footsteps around a street corner. I quickly pushed open the door of a building and hid inside a

corridor under the staircase. I waited there until morning. Somehow I had the presence of mind to remove from the jacket the yellow star sewn on it. I left it under the staircase with the shoes, which were useless to me. I knew I had to go to the Marais, the old Jewish neighborhood in the center of Paris, where most of my aunts and uncles lived, and warn them about what had happened. Our apartment was in Montrouge, just outside the city limits. It was a long walk, and of course I had no money to take the metro. Still I had to go and tell my aunts and uncles to get away, and take me with them.

Even though I was walking without shoes, and wearing a jacket so large that it looked like a winter overcoat, no one paid attention to me. It was a nice warm day. The sky clear and indifferent. It took me a long time to reach the Marais, but as I approached I became aware of the frantic activity of the ongoing roundup. Army trucks were parked everywhere, and people wearing yellow stars and carrying suitcases or bags were being led to these trucks by uniformed guards.

I went to my aunt Basha's apartment, at the corner of rue Beaubourg and rue Rambuteau. (I mention the exact location because on the very spot where my aunt's building once stood now stands the Centre Pompidou and the National Museum of Modern Art. Fabulous substitution. The insolence of history replaced by the playfulness of art.) Aunt Basha was my father's youngest sister whom we often visited to play with her children, two boys and one girl about the same age as my sisters and I. I found my aunt, my uncle, and the two boys sitting in the apartment waiting, their suitcases packed. They told me that our other relatives in this neighborhood, all the aunts and uncles and cousins, had already been arrested. The boys had seen them being taken away when they went out to investigate what was going on.

My cousin Sarah, the youngest of the three children, was not at home. She was in the country, my aunt told me, and I learned later that's how she too survived. She stayed at a farmhouse with an old widow who made her work as her servant and took her to church every day. My cousin Sarah and I found each other at the end of the war and for a while lived together until I left for America. She could not come to the United States because she was denied a visa for reasons of health. At the required medical examination at the U.S. Consulate in Paris, the doctor discovered a tuberculous spot on her left lung. Soon after I left France, my cousin Sarah went to Israel. She was seventeen then. She fought in the war of independence of 1948, and afterward joined a kibbutz. She's been living and working on that kibbutz for the past forty years. We were reunited, in 1982, after thirty-five years of separation, when I went to Israel on a Fulbright Fellowship to teach at the Hebrew University of Jerusalem. I found a fifty-year-old woman of great strength and unusual character.

Not long after I arrived at my aunt's apartment the police came to arrest them. I had told my aunt and uncle what had happened and how my mother hid me in a closet, and I had pleaded with them that we should all try to get away, but they had explained that they didn't know where to go, and even if there was a place in the free zone, they didn't have the money to go there. Not enough to buy train tickets for all of us, and pay someone to get us through the line of demarcation between the occupied zone and the free zone. Many Jews were deported during the war not because they could not escape (there were many ways one could buy survival, even from the Germans), but because they were poor. The police asked who I was, but since I didn't have a yellow star on my shirt, and my aunt explained that I was just a friend of the boys, not Jewish, they left me alone. Besides, my name was not on their list. I was now wearing one of my cousins' short pants and shirt, and a pair of his espadrilles which my aunt gave me when she saw what I had on as I came in. I walked with my aunt, uncle, and cousins to Place des Vosges, that sumptuous historical square with its beautiful arcades, whose entire perimeter was lined with army trucks. I waited with them until it was their turn to go. I kissed my uncle, my aunt, and my cousins good-bye, and then watched them being pushed up into one of the trucks. I have often wondered if that day, when I was left standing there, I had not been chosen so that someday I could tell that story.

Among the Beasts

After the trucks left I walked all the way back to Montrouge. I was still thinking that perhaps my parents and sisters had been sent home. I wanted to make sure. I was standing at a distance from the building where we lived because I didn't want to be seen by the neighbors, when a woman approached me. She was someone with whom my mother washed people's clothes at the nearby *lavoir*. Of course, she knew what had happened, and was surprised to see me standing there. I told her about the closet. She grabbed me by the arm and quickly led me to her apartment, just a block away. She gave me some food. I remember, a bowl of warm milk and a piece of bread. She kept saying that we had to find a way to

hide me. But then after a while she explained that perhaps the best thing to do was for me to go to the police and tell them that I had been left behind. This way, she went on, they would put me with my parents and everything would be fine. She told me she would take me to the militia headquarters herself. I suppose she had realized that she could be in serious trouble if she kept me.

Feeling lost and confused, and tired, too, as I had not slept for almost two days, I agreed with her that it was the best thing to do. We were walking towards the Montrouge police station, on Avenue de la République, the woman was holding me by the hand, when suddenly I pulled away from her and started running in the opposite direction from the station. I knew that I could not let this woman take me there. I heard her call behind me, "Where are you going? Come back, they'll catch you." But I kept running until she was out of sight.

The next few days, until I managed to reach the non-occupied zone, unfolded like a wild adventure movie, and I lived every moment totally unconscious of what I was going through. There was the frantic wandering in various neighborhoods of Paris trying to find someone in my family who might still be there and who would take care of me. There were the two days and two nights I spent at the bustling train station hoping to be able to sneak up on a train leaving for

Raymond during World War II

the free zone. There was the night when all the men in the station were rounded up and questioned by the Germans and some of them arrested, and I was one of those they questioned but let go. And there was the night when I found myself on a freight train going in the wrong direction, away from the free zone, but when that train stopped in the middle of the night to let another train go by in the other direction, I jumped across the track and managed to force my way inside one of the cars. It was full of huge bags of potatoes. I was so hungry I climbed on top of the bags, tore one open, and for a long time sat there eating raw potatoes until I became sick to my stomach and vomited. Later, when the train slowed down around a curve I jumped off and wandered in the countryside until morning when I was picked up by an old farmer in a horse carriage on his way to the city. I had jumped from the train full of potatoes just a few kilometers from Paris. Again I went to the train station, still hoping to find a way to get to the free zone, and that night, during an air raid, with two young men from Belgium I met in the station, I hid inside a freight car while all the people were rushing to the shelters. The train must have already been inspected by the Germans because as soon as the blaring sirens announced the end of the air raid it left the station. The next morning I got off near Toulouse in the southwest of France. The two Belgian young men stayed on the train. They were trying to reach Spain and from there North Africa to join the Free French Forces. They thought I should come with them, but I told them that I wanted to stay in France because my parents might come back soon and they would be worried about me.

I have no idea why I got off the train where I did. It had stopped in a small station, and it was so peaceful there, and since no one paid attention to me, I decided to try and find a place to stay until things were back to normal. Later that day, after wandering for a while in the fields, eating fruit from the trees along the way, I found a farm which needed help. It was a time when farms were run by old men and women because most able-bodied men had been taken away to work in German factories. Therefore, when someone came along, even a clumsy, inexperienced, fourteen-year-old city boy like me, who was willing to work just for food and a place to sleep, no questions were asked. I looked strong and healthy enough to do a good day's work. There were many people wandering about in those days. It was not until the Germans invaded the free zone, late in 1942, that the situation got difficult for those who were hiding in the country or who had joined the French underground.

I stayed on that farm for three years, until France was liberated. I worked hard in the fields and in the barn, from early morning till late evening, except for a few hours on Sundays when the old man who owned the farm, with his daughter and her two small children, would put on their best clothes to go to the village church. They would take me along. Since I was never asked what my religion was, I thought it would be better to not say anything and go with them. And so every Sunday in that church, I mouthed the Latin words of their prayers.

During those three years I became a good farmer, but I was lonely all the time, sad and homesick, and my body hurt constantly from the brutal work. Especially my hands. They were always full of sores, cuts, and blisters. The crude and vulgar mode of existence of the people and animals had gradually taken over my whole being. I was confused, and could not understand the indifferent violence of reproduction and of death which surrounded me. Every day animals were born, died, or being killed. And as I participated in this incessant process of birth and death, I became accustomed to its violence and simplicity. I felt dirty all the time. Prisoner of that dirtiness. Day after day I toiled in the fields or in the barn absent from myself. I did not suffer of hunger for there was plenty to eat on the farm, but some intolerable discontent was at work in my body and it seemed to center on the most immediate organ of contact with nature: my hands. Their physical appearance upset me. On the farm, my hands were always dirty, rough, sore, and red, and I could never get my fingernails clean.

I finally returned to Paris in May 1945, riding all the way on top of an American tank. It was a joyful journey. The German occupation was over, the country was free, people in the little towns and villages were singing "La Marseillaise" and dancing in the streets, and I was convinced that my parents and sisters were already home waiting for me. Of course, no one was there when I arrived.

All this sounds so much like the script of a bad movie. But I suppose, in retrospect, one's life always becomes a series of clichés. Even the most horrendous moments appear banal. After all, many boys and girls were left hidden in closets or abandoned in train stations during the war, and many farmers, kindhearted prostitutes, and nuns took cognizance of these children and saved them, so that ultimately all these stories become trivial.

A few weeks after my return to Paris I was working in a factory, the night shift, making tubes for toothpaste. All my aunts and uncles on my mother's side had also returned from wherever they were hiding, and were quite surprised to find me alive. They held a family council to decide what to do with me, but since they all found reasons for not being able to take care of me, I left in the middle of their gathering. What I wanted most was to go back to school, but that was not possible. I had to earn a living. I was seventeen now and had a huge gap in my education. I took a room in Montparnasse, the neighborhood where my father used to spend most of his time before the war. Since I worked at night, I slept part of the day, and the rest of the time I sat in cafés with the friends I had made in the factory and planned ways to make extra money on the black market.

When I got back to Paris, I spent a lot of time trying to find out what had happened to my parents and sisters. I went from one office building to another, waiting in line with other people who were there to obtain information about their families. Eventually I was given documents which ascertained my parents' and sisters' death at Auschwitz. Still, once in a while I would go to my old neighborhood to see if perhaps my mother or father or one of my sisters had come back. Many whose parents, brothers, or sisters were deported during the war lived with this false hope that one of them had survived and would someday return. It took me years to get rid of this delusion.

Amer Eldorado

One day, the concierge of our old apartment building in Montrouge gave me a letter addressed to my father. It had come from America, but was written in Yiddish. Since I do not know Yiddish, I had someone translate it for me. It was from an uncle I didn't even know existed. His name was David Naimark. I learned later, when I finally met him in America, that he had married one of my father's sisters back in Siedlce, and was still living there when the war started.

This uncle explained in his letter that he, but not his wife and children, had managed to escape deportation in Poland, and that now safe in America he was anxious to know if my father and his family were well. He had written to the old address. David Naimark was a journalist, and in his letter he told how, in 1939, when the Germans invaded Poland, he was doing a reportage in Russia and got literally locked out of his country. That's how he survived. For the next few years he wandered in Russia, then in China, lived in Shanghai for a while, and finally made it to the United States in 1945. When he wrote to my father,

David Naimark was working as a political writer for the *Jewish Daily Forward,* the leading Yiddish newspaper in America.

I immediately wrote to this uncle in America, telling him what had happened, and that I was the only one left from our family. I wrote in French, and he replied in Yiddish. Then he started sending packages with clothes, canned food, cartons of cigarettes, chocolate, most of which I would sell on the black market. Eventually he asked if I and my cousin Sarah wanted to come to America. When we said yes, he made the necessary arrangements for us to obtain immigrant visas. We waited nearly two years before being called to the U.S. Consulate. This is when my cousin Sarah learned that she could not go because of her health. For weeks the two of us agonized whether or not I should go alone. She insisted that I should. I left on the SS *Marine Jumper,* an old liberty ship, on August 19, 1947. A few months later, my cousin Sarah went to Israel with a group of young French Zionists. I have often wondered if I made the right decision. Would I have become a writer if I had gone to Israel with my cousin Sarah?

On the boat that was taking me to America, I met a young man my age with whom I had gone to school when I was a boy. He too had managed to survive alone and had discovered an uncle in America. His name was Lucien Jacobson. He became a painter in America, an abstract expressionist of some renown. He appears in my novel *Double or Nothing* under the name of Loulou.

My uncle David Naimark died in 1960. At his funeral in New York, attended by a large number of people, many of them eminent Yiddish writers, I learned that he was one of the most respected political analysts of his generation. All his writing was, of course, in Yiddish. From the moment we met until his death, I was never able to communicate with my uncle. He had arrived in America at a rather advanced age, and since he lived and worked mostly in a Yiddish environment, he barely learned to speak English. I came without any knowledge of the English language, but when I became fluent enough, I discovered that I could not talk with my uncle. I never learned Yiddish, and he did not know French. I have often regretted not to have known who he was.

My uncle met me at the boat. We had sent each other photographs, and were able to recognize one another. We embraced. He was a short, round man. He wore gold-rimmed glasses, and had a big nose. All the years I knew him, he always wore the same wrinkled brown suit with the same striped tie. Most of the money he earned he sent to Europe or Israel to members of his family who had survived. He spoke to me in Yiddish, and I spoke to him in French. I think we understood what we had to say. From the pier where the boat landed my uncle took me to the Bronx by subway to spend a few days with friends of his, Polish Jews who had survived the Holocaust and had recently come to America. When we got into the subway and I found myself surrounded mostly by black people, for a moment I wondered if I had come to the wrong country. I had no idea what America was all about. I only knew what I had seen in the American movies shown in Paris after the war—movies about gangsters, cowboys and Indians. At the time when I arrived, my uncle was the editor of the Detroit branch of the *Jewish Daily Forward*—that branch folded in the 1950s. After a few days in New York, sight-seeing (my uncle took me to see the Empire State Building, the Statue of Liberty, and we even went one afternoon to Coney Island), we left for Detroit by train. Since my uncle lived alone in a one-room furnished apartment, he had reserved a room for me (with kitchen privileges) in the house of a Hungarian family. Two weeks after I arrived in Detroit, I was working on the assembly line at one of the Chrysler factories. I often wondered then why I had come to this great land of opportunity, and what I was doing there, in Detroit. In 1947, Detroit was a rather depressed and depressing city.

Again I worked the night shift, which means that I slept most of the day. Once a week, on Fridays, I would meet my uncle and he would take me for dinner to a kosher restaurant near his office in the Jewish neighborhood. We managed to exchange a few words. He would ask how I was doing, if I had made friends, if I was saving money. It was a sad, lonely period of my life. Working all night, and sleeping late into the afternoon, I would spend the rest of my time wandering alone in the city, or else reading, mostly adventure novels, in French, since I could not yet manage a whole book in English. It took several months before I dared check out from the public library a novel in English. I chose it at random on the shelves. I remember, it was Thackeray's *Vanity Fair.* I really don't know why I chose this particular book that day. Perhaps its subtitle intrigued me: "A Novel without a Hero." Or else because of the opening sentence of the preface, which I read standing in front of the bookshelves and must have found relevant at the time to my own state of mind: "As the manager of the Performance sits before the curtain on the boards, and looks into the Fair, a feeling of profound melancholy comes over him in his survey of the bustling place." I suppose the expression "pro-

found melancholy" is what attracted me.

I had no idea then that someday I would become a writer, but reading was important to me, and I spent a lot of time at the public library. I had arrived in America with two French books in my suitcase. I still have them: Jean-Paul Sartre's *La Nausée*, and a pornographic novel entitled *J'irai cracher sur vos tombes* (*I Shall Spit on Your Graves*). The copy I have is by Vernon Sullivan. Some years later, when I was studying French literature at Columbia University, I discovered that it was the pseudonym of Boris Vian, the eccentric existentialist friend of Jean-Paul Sartre. At the time I bought these two books, everyone in France was fascinated by existentialism.

One day, a few weeks after I arrived in Detroit, while wandering in the streets, I noticed the word "HIGH SCHOOL" inscribed on a building. I went in. By then I had enough English to manage to make myself understood (with a rather thick French accent which, I must confess, I have carefully cultivated over the years, "for social and sentimental reasons," as the protagonist of one of my novels says of his own accent). I spoke to the principal, who said that even though at nineteen I was older than most students, he would accept me in his high school. He suggested a program of courses—English, American history, government—and took me around the school to meet some of the teachers. However, because I worked at night I could only come to class in the afternoon. The principal was very understanding, and made it all possible. The next day I was a student at Northern High School on Woodward Avenue. Most of the students were black, which I discovered on my first day in class.

Double or Nothing

During the two years I spent at Northern High School (I received my diploma in 1949), I was known only as Frenchy. There I not only learned to read and write English, learned about American history and government, but I also learned to play the clarinet and the saxophone. At Northern High School jazz entered into my life.

After class on the first day of school as I was walking out of the building, I heard loud music coming from the auditorium. I opened the door and saw students gathered in small groups in corners of the auditorium, improvising on their instruments. They were playing jazz. I had heard jazz before, in Paris, but I had never heard it played like this. I sat quietly in one of the seats and listened. A man, a white man (all the

High school graduation picture, Detroit, 1949

teachers at Northern High School were white), was sitting at a desk on the stage of the auditorium. He was large and chubby, with curly hair, and a very red nose. His name was Mr. Lawrence, the music teacher. After a while he banged loudly on his desk several times with a stick, and all the students gathered around him in a half circle and began to play. Not jazz, but what sounded to me like military music. I remained in my seat and listened. What I didn't know then was that among these students were young men who would someday become leading figures in the world of jazz. Tommy Flanagan was there playing the piano, and Kenny Burrell was playing the guitar, and Frank Foster the tenor saxophone, and the Heath brothers were there too, and Roland Hanna. Eventually I came to know all of them, and when I learned to play my saxophone well enough I joined a small combo they had formed and played in jam sessions with them all over the city. One night, in 1949, Charlie Parker, who was in town for a concert, came into the Blue Bird, a jazz club on Dexter Boulevard where we were jamming, and as he stood next to me asked if he could "blow my horn." That night, Yardbird played my tenor saxophone for forty minutes. I did not wipe my mouthpiece for weeks afterward. I have recalled and fictionalized that unforgettable moment in my novel *Take It or Leave It* in a chapter entitled "Remembering Charlie Parker or How To Get It Out of Your System."

But back in the auditorium on my first day of school.

When the band stopped playing I approached Mr. Lawrence and asked if I could learn to play an instrument. He pointed to a room offstage and told me to go in there and choose something I would like to learn. The room was full of musical instruments, most of them broken. I came out with a clarinet. Mr. Lawrence showed me how to put the mouthpiece in my mouth and how to place my fingers on the keys, then he wrote some scales on a piece of paper and told me to practice, and to come back when I had learned these. Every day after school I worked with Mr. Lawrence, and a few weeks later I was playing clarinet with the Northern High School marching band.

My best friend at Northern High School was Ernest Blake. He played the alto saxophone but never became a professional jazz musician. During the Korean War he was drafted into the army and made a career of it as a captain. He was standing next to Mr. Lawrence when I asked if I could learn to play an instrument, and after I got the clarinet, Mr. Lawrence told Ernest to teach me the scales. Later that afternoon we went to Ernest's home to practice. Ernie, as he was known to everyone, noticed my thick French accent (how could he not) and asked all kinds of questions about France, and about me, and how I had come to Detroit. Ernie was the first person I met in America who showed interest in who I was and where I came from and how I felt. When we finished practicing my scales, Ernie asked if I liked jazz. I told him I did but didn't know much about it. We sat on the floor next to his record player and for hours listened to the music of Charlie Parker and Wardell Gray and Dizzy Gillespie and Thelonious Monk and Miles Davis. Ernie explained that this was the new jazz and that it was called "bebop." That day I knew I wanted to become a jazz musician and play bebop.

I never made it as a jazzman. Even though I studied and practiced for long hours, I never became as good as my high-school friends in Detroit. Eventually the tenor saxophone I bought with the money I had saved working as a waiter in the Catskills during the summer of 1948 went into a pawnshop on Sixth Avenue in New York just before I was drafted into the army in 1951. But jazz has given me a great deal of pleasure in my life, and is certainly responsible for the somewhat delirious improvisational quality critics have attributed to my writing.

After I graduated from Northern High School in 1949, I spent one semester studying music at Wayne University, which was at the time just a city college mostly for black students. By then I had stopped working in the factory. I had a job in a grocery store on the east side, in the black neighborhood, where I rented a small room near Ernie's house. But even though I had friends now, and spent most of my time practicing my saxophone, I was unhappy in Detroit. The factories with their promise of a good salary were always there to tempt you, and eventually one always went back to work in one of these, even for a few months, until one was laid off again. The winters were particularly hard and depressing. Finally, in January 1950, with fifty dollars I had saved, I left for New York. There I was reunited with Lucien Jacobson, the childhood friend I had found on the boat to America. Loulou had stayed in New York when I went to Detroit. Together we rented a furnished room in the Bronx, near the Grand Concourse.

Loulou was living a bohemian life, carefree and irresponsible. He was trying to become an artist, and refused to take a job. He lived off other people, or the little money his uncle gave him whenever he went to visit him in Queens. While Loulou stayed in our room in the Bronx to draw or paint, I would go out in search of a job, any job, to pay the rent and buy food for the two of us. During the winter of 1950, there was a recession in America, and it was almost impossible to find work, and for months we lived only on noodles. Every morning I would check the *New York Times* want ads and then go stand in long lines with other young men until we were told there were no more jobs for that day. Meanwhile, in order to keep going, Loulou and I became regular customers of the New York City pawnshops. Gradually most of my things—my winter overcoat, my first American suit, the new suitcase I had bought in Detroit to move to New York, my wristwatch, and eventually my brand-new saxophone—ended up in a pawnshop. This went on for several months until finally I got a job as a dishwasher in a cafeteria—the Automat on Sixth Avenue. But that job didn't last long. I was fired a few weeks later when I got caught taking food to bring home to Loulou. Eventually Loulou and I were thrown out of our furnished room for not paying the rent. I moved to Brooklyn when I got a job in a lampshade factory (I suppose that's postmodern irony). Meanwhile Loulou left for Florida. He was fed up with New York and starvation. I bumped into him, in 1954, after I got out of the army, on Forty-second Street and Times Square. By then I was studying at Columbia University on the GI Bill. Loulou had just returned to New York. He was with a girlfriend, a woman much older than he, who, he explained to me, was supporting him until he became famous. This was the last time I saw Loulou, but some years later I read in a magazine about a successful show he had in a New York gallery.

Take It or Leave It

While living in the Bronx with Loulou I was taking evening courses at City College of New York, but now that I had moved to Brooklyn I wanted to continue. So after work I would ride the subway from Brooklyn to the Bronx and back. I did a lot of good reading on that subway (novels, political writing, some philosophy), but without any sense of direction. At CCNY I got involved with an anti-McCarthy group and participated in some demonstrations. I was beginning to like living in New York. I had a job, a place of my own, friends, even a girlfriend in Brooklyn, and I was involved in something, but all this ended when, in March 1951, I was drafted into the army. Since I had applied for U.S. citizenship I was now eligible for military service. The day I was inducted I volunteered for the paratroops, almost in spite of myself, just to get away from the sergeant in charge of the recruits who kept mocking my French accent and referring to me as a "frog." After basic training I was sent to jump school at Fort Benning in Georgia, and then assigned to the 82d

"As a paratrooper before first jump,"
Fort Benning, Georgia, 1951

Airborne Division in Fort Bragg, North Carolina. It was my first encounter with the South. Even though I had lived for almost two years in the black ghetto of Detroit, I was unprepared for the kind of prejudice and racial discrimination I discovered in the South, especially among my tough fellow paratroopers, most of whom were barely literate farm boys or hillbillies from the deep South. I have recounted, in my novel *Take It or Leave It,* in a burlesque and ironic fashion, the adventures and misadventures of Frenchy in the 82d Airborne Division. Frenchy made forty-seven jumps as a paratrooper.

In February 1952, I was shipped to Korea and spent a few months on the front line, near Inchon, until I was ordered to Tokyo, where I was assigned to the 510th Military Intelligence Group as an interpreter for the U.N. French-speaking forces. The army had discovered that I had one useful qualification: I could speak French. It was as though I had been given a new lease on life. In the muddy foxholes of Korea I was convinced that I would be killed one night. But now as a member of the victorious occupying forces in Japan with lots of money to spend which I made on the black market, I had a good life (and a beautiful Japanese girlfriend). So good in fact that I decided to reenlist for one additional year just to stay in Tokyo. I was discharged from the Army in 1954.

I became an American citizen in Tokyo, in 1953. That year a new law was passed by Congress permitting foreigners who were serving abroad in the U.S. Army to become citizens on foreign land. I was among the

ninety foreigners gathered in the Hardy Barracks Theater in Tokyo who received citizenship papers from Brigadier General Homer Case as he told us what a historical moment this was. Moinous, the antihero of my novel *Smiles on Washington Square,* recounts how he too became an American citizen in Tokyo while serving in the U.S. Army, and how that day he was given a little American flag on which was written "Made in Japan."

It was in Tokyo that I began to write. Short pieces that look like poems, though at the time I had no idea what poetry was or how it should be written. These poems were about the prostitutes, the pimps, the transvestites, the hustlers, the black marketeers in the streets of Tokyo. I suddenly felt a need to express and record for myself what I was seeing there. I wrote my first short story on the ship which was bringing me back to the States to be discharged. I was unhappy to go back to America. There was nothing awaiting me. I had tried to find a way to remain in Tokyo, but was told that only if I reenlisted in the army for life could I stay overseas. The story was naively entitled "You Can't Go Home Again." During the three years I spent in the army I had read everything Thomas Wolfe had written, but also novels by Hemingway, Faulkner, Fitzgerald, and many others, especially war novels—the classics such as *The Young Lions, From Here to Eternity, The Naked and the Dead,* anything I could find in the Fort Bragg library, or in the Ernie Pyle Recreation Center library in Tokyo.

After I was discharged in March 1954, I went back to New York. I was broke. I had lost all the money I had made in Tokyo on the black market playing poker on the ship back to the States. A few days after I was a civilian again, I was working as a waiter in a French restaurant on Lexington Avenue. Totally disenchanted with America, I was then seriously considering returning to France and abandoning the Great American Dream. But one day, near Times Square, where I spent a lot of time going to movies after work, I stumbled into an army friend from Tokyo. His name was George Tashima, an American nisei. In Tokyo George often told me that he wanted to become a writer, and that he had started a novel about an American Japanese who, during World War II, when he was still a boy, spent time with his family in an internment camp in Arizona. It was George who told me in Tokyo that I should try to write down my experiences there, that perhaps I too could become a writer.

George was discharged from the army a few months before me, and when I bumped into him he was studying creative writing at Columbia University

"*Receiving U.S. citizenship papers from Brigadier General Homer Case,*" Tokyo, 1953

U.S. Army Photograph

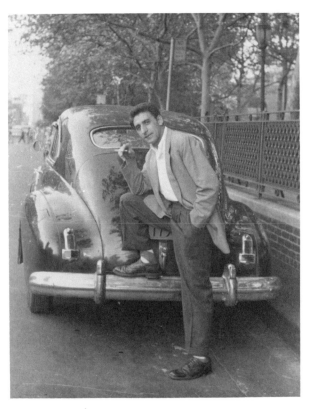

"With the Buick Special immortalized in
Take It or Leave It," *New York, 1954*

under the GI Bill. He explained that I too could study there since I was also eligible for the GI Bill. The next day, George Tashima literally led me to the registrar at Columbia University. I had to take an entrance exam because even though I had a high-school diploma I had been away from school too long. I barely passed that exam (especially the parts dealing with science), but in the fall of 1954, I became a freshman in college. I was twenty-six years old. That year I read Shakespeare for the first time, and for the next three years I read Homer and Dante, the Romantic poets, and all the great Russian novelists, and Flaubert, Proust, Thomas Mann, Joyce, and Kafka, and many others. I majored in comparative literature since after all I was fluent in a foreign language. But more importantly, at Columbia University I studied creative writing and spent much time writing poetry, short stories, and even a novel which was never finished.

As I was going through the course catalog to prepare my first semester's schedule, I came across the description of a poetry workshop offered by Leonie Adams which stated that students needed the instructor's permission to register. When I went to Leonie Adams's office to ask if I could take her course, I had

with me some of the things I had written in Japan. Leonie Adams was a tiny woman who always wore purple clothes and whose long grey hair fell over her eyes. I sat next to her desk while she read my poems, shaking her head in apparent approval. Finally she told me that I could come to her workshop. She said that my poetry was quite unusual, especially the subject matter, that it was very realistic and had a curious loose form. Then she added: "You write a bit like Walt Whitman." "Who?" I asked. She repeated the name. I asked her to spell it as I wrote it on a piece of paper. After I left her office, I rushed to the library and took out the complete works of Walt Whitman. I spent most of that night reading *Leaves of Grass* aloud to myself, and though I was fascinated by the beauty and the daring of this poetry, I found little affinity with my own writing.

I learned a great deal about writing poetry from Leonie Adams, who emphasized symbolism and ambiguity, but also from Babette Deutsch, whose poetry workshop I took during my second year at Columbia. From Babette Deutsch I learned about form and discipline. She would often invite me and other students to her apartment to have tea and talk poetry, and I would always leave with a book under my arm which she insisted I should read. Also she started me on translations, saying that it was the best way to learn how to write. As one of the projects for her workshop, I put together a collection of poems I translated from various French poets.

My first instructor in fiction writing was Dick Humphreys (who still teaches at Columbia and has published numerous novels). In 1976, when the Fiction Collective published my novel *Take It or Leave It*, Dick Humphreys attended the publication party. He reminded me of a note he had written on one of the stories I submitted to his class. It said: "There is something totally illogical about the way you write fiction." I had written a story in which the first-person narrator commits suicide in the middle of the story by jumping off a boat and yet continues to tell the story after his death. Dick Humphreys explained that it was not possible, even in a work of fiction, to have a character die and remain the narrator. This had never occurred to me. I had discovered that writing fiction was a way to gain freedom, and therefore thought that anything was possible. It may explain why a critic once referred to me as "a writer who is capable of making a mess out of chaos."

I graduated from Columbia University (cum laude, Phi Beta Kappa) in June 1957, with my head full of books, and boxes full of manuscripts (hundreds of

Federman in a café with Samuel Beckett, Paris, 1978

poems, short stories, and one unfinished novel entitled *And I Followed My Shadow*). During my senior year, a story I submitted to a contest at a writers' conference held at Columbia won a one thousand dollar prize. The story, called "Young Man without a Horn," was about a jazz musician who cannot find the money to retrieve his saxophone from a pawnshop just when he is offered a splendid job. With the prize money I bought a 1951 Pontiac which I drove to California.

I had been offered fellowships to do graduate work at Columbia, Harvard, and the University of California at Los Angeles. I went up to Cambridge for an interview with the people in comparative literature at Harvard. They told me that they would be very pleased to have me in their program and hoped that I would be able to devote all my time to my studies. I replied that I would certainly study hard, but that I had to find some sort of job to support myself because the fellowship I was being offered only covered my tuition and textbooks. I was told, "At Harvard one does not take on spare-time jobs." At Columbia, even though my tuition was covered by the GI Bill, I needed three different jobs in order to survive. I turned down the Harvard fellowship, and instead went to California as a teaching assistant at UCLA, where I received my M.A. in 1958, and my Ph.D. in 1963. I wrote the first doctoral dissertation in English on the fiction of Samuel Beckett, and it was

published as a book in 1965, under the title *Journey to Chaos*.

The Twofold Vibration

I first encountered the work of Samuel Beckett in 1956, when I saw the Broadway production of *Waiting for Godot* with Bert Lahr, E. G. Marshall, Kurt Kasznar, and Alvin Epstein. I was overwhelmed. I knew I had seen something important even though I did not fully understand what it was. I have not stopped reading and studying the work of Beckett since that day. In 1979, I was elected "Honorary Trustee" of the Samuel Beckett Society. If the Holocaust and the closet experience greatly marked my emotional and psychological life, the work of Samuel Beckett and my personal relationship with the man have deeply marked my intellectual and creative life. From reading Beckett's work and talking with him (we first met in Paris in 1963, and have remained in contact since) I learned that being a writer means never to compromise one's work, and that no linguistic utterance, however convincingly representational it may seem, can ever successfully accommodate the chaos of life.

At UCLA, busy taking graduate courses while teaching French to freshmen, I had to set aside the novel I had started at Columbia. After I got my M.A. in 1958,

Family portrait, Santa Barbara, California, 1963: Raymond, Jim, Erica, Simone, Robin, and Steve

I decided to return to France and see if, perhaps, I might be able to live and write there. I sold my old Pontiac, some of my clothes, most of my books, even some of my jazz records to buy a plane ticket from Los Angeles to Paris, and left in May 1958. This was my first return to France after eleven years in exile. The three months I spent in Paris that summer were a total disaster. I only found disenchantment and sordid memories there. I was unable to write. I returned to UCLA just on time to register for the fall semester and continue working on my Ph.D., and again abandoned for the time the writing of fiction.

Soon after my return from France, I met Erica at UCLA where she was studying French. She had just gotten a divorce, and had gone back to college while taking care of her three young children. Marrying her is certainly the most successful thing I have ever done. While still working on my dissertation, I found myself suddenly raising children and learning to care for a family. But Erica and the children made me discover that there was laughter in me, and even tenderness. I had lived all the years since I emerged from the closet thinking that life was only unhappiness and loneliness. But now I was surrounded with affection and joy. No one has been more supportive of my work, especially when the writing doesn't go well, than Erica, who is also my best and most severe

critic. She reads everything I write, and not a word goes by that she has not carefully scrutinized and questioned. She always cuts where I have the tendency for excess or sentimentality, though sometimes, behind her back, I cannot resist reinserting certain words she has deleted. Together we have enjoyed golf and tennis, of which we are both fanatics, and good food, and good friends, and we have gambled in casinos all over the world. Erica and I have traveled to most European countries (Erica was born in Vienna), but also to Japan, Egypt, India, Israel.

Our daughter Simone was born on December 7, 1962—Pearl Harbor Day. I finished the final draft of my doctoral dissertation on Beckett two days before her birth. The dissertation is dedicated to Oscar, the name Simone was referred to before she arrived in this world.

From 1959 to 1964, I taught in the French department of the University of California at Santa Barbara. During those five years I not only finished my dissertation, but wrote a lot of poetry, both in English and in French, some of which was published in a bilingual volume in Paris, in 1967, under the title *Among the Beasts*. In Santa Barbara, I founded and edited *Mica*, a literary magazine that has since become a collector's item. Through *Mica* I became

Bruce Jackson

With Michel Foucault and Olga Bernal, Buffalo, 1970

acquainted with a number of writers with whom I have remained in contact. At that time I was also doing a lot of translations from the French. Some of these, including prose pieces by Jean Genet and poems by André Breton, Max Jacob, Boris Vian, and others, appeared in issues of *Big Table* and the *Evergreen Review.* In 1965, I published *Temporary Landscapes,* a book of poems by Yvonne Caroutch I had translated from the French. I was suddenly becoming part of the contemporary literary scene, and it was a new experience for me. But now that I had my Ph.D. and was teaching full time in a university, I also had to write and publish criticism.

Though I kept writing poetry, I was anxious to return to fiction, and the novel I had already abandoned several times. I felt torn between the necessity of having to write criticism, and the more profound and personal need to write fiction. Meanwhile in 1965, my Beckett book, *Journey to Chaos,* was published, and received favorable reviews, including one in the *New York Times.* Suddenly I found myself being recognized as a Beckett scholar.

In 1964, I accepted a position in the French department at the State University of New York at Buffalo. (After my first novel was published, I moved to the English department.) In the sixties, SUNY-Buffalo was an exciting center of literary activities—and it is still. Important writers from all parts of the U.S. and from abroad came to Buffalo, and some settled there. Charles Olson was still teaching in the English

department when I arrived, and a number of poets and novelists joined that department in the following years—Robert Creeley, John Logan, Irving Feldman, Carl Dennis, John Barth, and many others. Leslie Fiedler came the same year I did, and we have been friends ever since, even though we have not always agreed about what literature is or should be, and have argued much and passionately during the years we have been together. Buffalo has been good to us. Recently Leslie mentioned that he had written eleven books while in Buffalo. I told him I had written exactly the same number.

In 1966, one year after my Beckett book was published, I was awarded a Guggenheim Fellowship to spend a year in France to finish a second book on Beckett and write on contemporary French poetry. We left on the *United States,* in June 1966, and on the boat I began writing notes toward a new novel. Besides finishing the book on Beckett and writing articles, I spent part of the year in Paris working on that novel, which eventually became *Double or Nothing.*

With its pulverized syntax, its wild, exuberant typography, and its outrageous self-reflexiveness, *Double or Nothing,* which was finished in 1970, had difficulties finding a publisher. Richard Kostelanetz, who had read the manuscript, went from one publisher to another for over a year trying to get the book accepted, and though most of them found it original and interesting, they thought it would be too expensive to produce. I was beginning to think that *Double*

"A discussion with Leslie Fiedler," Buffalo, 1980

or Nothing would never be published when Michael Anania, who was then literary editor at Swallow Press, accepted it. The book appeared in 1971, and won two prizes—the Frances Steloff Fiction Prize, and the Panache Experimental Fiction Prize. I was forty-three years old. At the publication party in Chicago, Jerome Klinkowitz, who had already read the novel, suggested that I send a copy to Ronald Sukenick, whose work, he said, I would find interesting and not unlike my own. And indeed, not only did I find Ron's fiction fascinating, but we immediately became friends. Meanwhile Jerome Klinkowitz and Larry McCaffery, whom I met soon after the publication of *Double or Nothing,* have remained my most devoted readers and supporters.

When Ronald Sukenick received the copy of *Double or Nothing* I had sent him, he wrote back saying that he had already gotten the book from the publisher, and in fact had reviewed it for the *New York Times.* In his review Ron wrote of *Double or Nothing*: "It is a considerable achievement, a deliberate and complicated doodle, a perversely trivial book that forces you to take it seriously. And that also opens interesting possibilities for contemporary fiction." Because of this novel which, according to the reviews, "defied all the conventions of fiction with effrontery and laughter," I found myself associated with a group of experimental writers known then as metafictionists, and subsequently as surfictionists (a term I coined in

an essay-manifesto published in *Partisan Review,* in 1973, under the title "Surfiction: A Position"). Though greatly discussed and analyzed, and even taught in literature courses, *Double or Nothing* has been regarded, and still is today, as a curiosity. The German translation, entitled *Alles Oder Nichts,* which appeared in 1986, also won two prizes, and made the list of best books published in Germany that year.

Since 1971, I have not stopped writing fiction in order to achieve the vocation of my name—Federman/*Homme de Plume*! But that's another story. Perhaps, next time, I shall tell that version of the story.

And all will be *Smiles on Washington Square*!

BIBLIOGRAPHY

Fiction:

Double or Nothing ("A Real Fictitious Discourse"). Chicago: Swallow Press, 1971; also published in German translation as *Alles Oder Nichts.* Nördlingen, Germany: Greno Verlag, 1986.

Amer Eldorado ("Récit exagéré à lire à haute voix assis ou debout"). Paris: Editions Stock, 1974.

Take It or Leave It ("An Exaggerated Second-Hand Tale to Be Read Aloud Either Standing or Sitting"). New York: Fiction Collective, 1976.

The Voice in the Closet/La Voix dans le Cabinet de Débarras

"At home in Buffalo with Erica, Simone, Sam, and George," 1987

(bilingual novel; bound with *Echos à Federman,* by Maurice Roche). Madison: Coda Press, 1976.

The Twofold Vibration ("An Extemporaneous Novel"). Bloomington: Indiana University Press, 1982; Brighton, England: Harvester Press, 1982; also published in German translation as *Die Nacht Zum 21. Jahrhundert Oder Aus dem Leben eines alten Mannes.* Nördlingen, Germany: Greno Verlag, 1988.

Smiles on Washington Square ("A Love Story of Sorts"). New York: Thunder's Mouth Press, 1985; also published in German translation as *Eine Liebesgeschichte Oder Sowas.* Nördlingen, Germany: Greno Verlag, 1987.

Poetry:

Among the Beasts/Parmi les Monstres (bilingual poems). Paris: Millas-Martin Editions, 1967.

Me Too (concrete poems). Reno: West Coast Poetry Review Press, 1975.

Nonfiction:

Journey to Chaos: Samuel Beckett's Early Fiction. Berkeley and Los Angeles: University of California Press, 1965.

Samuel Beckett: His Works and His Critics: An Essay in Bibliography, with John Fletcher. Berkeley and Los Angeles: University of California Press, 1970.

Translator of:

Postal Cards (poems), by F. J. Temple. Santa Barbara, Calif.: Noel Young Edition, 1964.

Paysages provisoires/Temporary Landscapes (poems), by Yvonne Caroutch. Venice, Italy: Mica Editions, 1965.

Detachment (essays), by Michel Serres; translated with Genevieve James. Athens: Ohio University Press, 1989.

Editor of:

Cinq Nouvelles Nouvelles (fiction). New York: Appleton-Century-Crofts, 1970.

Surfiction: Fiction Now and Tomorrow (essays). Chicago: Swallow Press, 1975; revised and expanded edition. Chicago: Swallow Press/Ohio University Press, 1981.

Cahier de L'Herne: Samuel Beckett, with Tom Bishop. Paris: Editions de L'Herne, 1976.

Samuel Beckett: The Critical Heritage, with Lawrence Graver. London and Boston: Routledge & Kegan Paul, 1979.

Mica magazine. Santa Barbara, Calif: 1959–64.

Dick Higgins

1938-

The boy that became me wrote his first poem and set it to music:

Andante

Star, star, come to me, In the dark of night I see.
Moon, moon, come to me, In the dark of night I see.
Etc., ad lib.

He was, I'm told, about four years old when he wrote that. His mother wrote poetry and stories at the time, and gave him rewards for memorizing such poems as Edgar Allan Poe's "Annabel Lee." His father was a businessman, but he composed some naïvely modernist vocal pieces. The really musical one in the family was the grandmother, Clara. She hailed from St. Louis, had written her high-school class graduation song, and, if she had not been from a traditional southern family, might well have become a serious musician. As it was, "Grammy" Higgins had a seat on Friday afternoons at the Boston Symphony, and was not averse to taking the child along with her from time to time to hear Serge Koussevitzky conduct there. So it was that the child was exposed to fine music (including the moderns) from a very early age, while the mother encouraged his literary side. And, though he only wrote that song down much much later—at seven or eight, perhaps—it is not surprising that the first composition should be both text and sound.

The grandfather was important too. In the Higgins family, Saturday afternoons were a time to work at home. But his father tried to get him to box (he had been a college athlete), to work in the rock garden, or to fix things around the house. Little Dick *hated* that kind of thing and, though he eventually learned to garden a little, he still can't drive a nail straight into a wall. But while the grandfather, John, also encouraged handiness, he was a collector of things medieval, especially armor, and his John Woodman Higgins Armory still exists in Worcester, Massachusetts. Dick's preference was to spend Satur-

days with "Grandaddy" Higgins whenever possible, learning about characters of legend, such as King Arthur, or of history, such as the Emperor Maximilian, who is said to have taken a year to get to his wedding with Mary of Burgundy because of his wish to participate in so many jousts and tournaments along the way, and whose name is associated with a fluted style of armor that is particularly beautiful. Grandaddy Higgins taught Dick how to polish suits of armor and handle them safely. And one memorable day, when Dick came into Grandaddy's "loggia" and found him sorting some old books (some of which had pictures of armor in them), he asked: "Grandaddy, how are those books put together?"

Grandaddy thought a minute, selected a handsome but not too valuable book from the seventeenth century, took his very sharp penknife (of which he seemed to have an inexhaustible supply), and slit the binding open. This he presented to Dick to inspect, saying, "See, *this* is how these books were made." That was Dick's real introduction to the world of binding, and was perhaps the start of his interest in the processes of design and publishing which led to Something Else Press. Actually, fine books were nothing rare in the Higgins family; his great-grandfather's name was Aldus Manutius Chapin, named, obviously, for the great Venetian printer and scholar. The Higginses had been blacksmiths for generations near Standish, Maine, and their New England roots went back to the *Mayflower*, which was broken up for scrap and burned in 1630 after Richard Higgins, for whom Dick was named, came over. Dick's father was the first Higgins in a century or so who had never shoed a horse, and Grandaddy Higgins loved to tell stories about watching *his* grandfather, Lewis, at work. His own father, Milton, had been the one to "leave the farm," in this case the smithy, and become a professor at Worcester Polytechnic Institute. And Lewis and Milton had instilled in Grandaddy a profound love of fine crafts and workmanship which Dick, in his own way, found congenial.

Dick's mother, Katherine, was also involved in the visual-art life of Worcester, which centered around Umberto Romano, then teaching at the Worcester Art Museum. Summers were spent first on the New Hampshire coast with Grammy and Grandaddy, and, later, at Gloucester on Cape Ann, where the Romanos and other artists also stayed. Dick sometimes posed for Romano's class there, and spent his earnings on comic books and art supplies for his own first endeavors.

So it is that the boy was involved in musical, visual, and literary art from his earliest childhood. In fact it was all "art," as he saw it, each art was only a form, and the whole picture needed all the arts to complete itself. He was shocked when, later on, he found that most artists tried to specialize in one or another art or form. That kind of thing never occurred to him. Now baseball, *that* would be getting far afield. Horses seemed sensible enough, skiing or swimming okay, forestry, sure, but at baseball and team sports Dick took a kind of satisfaction in being the last person chosen for the team. And because he didn't want to be like the other kids, they tended to pick on him. Fortunately he inherited his father's size, and could take care of himself in a scrap. But this situation did not further Dick's social graces. In fact he was pretty miserable most of the time in Worcester, so his mother took him to a boarding school in Putney, Vermont, Hickory Ridge School, which he adored. It was something of a Summerhill; the kids learned to farm, to research subjects for themselves, to discover the differences and similarities among boys and girls, and to prepare to fulfill themselves. Here Dick acted in school plays, wrote a few of them, made a puppet theater which presented the ongoing saga of *Hootchafoo* in the Land of Winowilla, learned to play the violin and piano, started to compose seriously, and, in his final year, raided the school's junkyard with his cronies. Everything metal that was small enough to be dragged by a few of the kids was taken to a big maple tree near the school's main building, where Dick and his friends had built a tree house. When enough was accumulated, the objects were dragged up into the trees and hung there with ropes so that when the wind blew, the objects banged

into each other. The school had a rest hour before dinner, and the other kids who had not been in on the project were regaled with a very strange concert; somehow, I think it is with that piece that I first became myself.

Dick Higgins and his father, Carter, at Hickory Ridge, about 1949

Also important to me then was the presence in school of Aube Breton, daughter of André Breton of surrealism fame. I liked "Aubie," who was a little older than myself, she was a great square dancer and also was French and therefore a little mysterious. I became curious about what her father wrote, so somehow I acquired a copy of his *Young Cherry Trees Secured against Hares,* and with my reading of that book I began my commitment to modern poetry—I loved it!

Now (1948) my parents were divorced. It had been a long time coming, and my mother had been away or ill a lot (Worcester was not her kind of town). In Gloucester I had become friendly with a German woman, Mary. She was Jewish and had nearly died in a concentration camp. A woman of considerable culture, she had been active on the Berlin scene before Hitler came to power. Her stories became part of my own cultural experience, and the grimmer ones awoke me to the less attractive parts of political reality, from which I had, up to then, been sheltered. When my mother departed from the Worcester scene, Mary came to take care of my younger brother, Mark, and, when she was there, my sister, Lisa, who usually lived with my mother, first in St. Augustine, Florida, and, after 1951, in my mother's native New York. Mary married my father in due course, and, concerned that Hickory Ridge was uncivilizing me, sent me to Saint Paul's School, in Concord, New Hampshire, an Episcopalian prep school of the older sort, boys only, noted first and foremost for its hockey team. The year after I left Hickory Ridge it burned down, and Phil Chase, the founder and head of the school, reluctantly closed it down. As for Saint Paul's, I *hated* it, and, after a little over a year, I ran away with a friend to Putney, and slept the night in a barn belonging to Phil Chase. There my father came and picked me up, and then followed six of the happiest months of my life, attending North High School in Worcester.

North High was public education at its best, egalitarian and yet with enough good academic courses available to satisfy even a mental glutton like myself. I decided also that this would be a good time to deepen my musical involvement, so I studied harmony and orchestration with the conductor of the local orchestra, Harry Levenson. Wanting more lessons, I searched about to find some way of paying for them (my father would have discouraged *too* serious an involvement), and I got a job with a printer rubbing up presensitized offset plates. That, too, was right up my alley—I loved the presses, the typesetting. Unfortunately Mary and my father decided I must return to Saint Paul's if I was to get into one of the "right" colleges. So I did, and spent my last three years there involved in the Dramatic Club, the literary magazine *Horae Scholasticae,* and hiding in the school's excellent library, doing no more of the requirements than was absolutely necessary to get by. Vignette: my Latin teacher was a former Roman Catholic priest, a very prim gentleman. Having decided that Latin poetry was A-Okay, I snuck into the library room where dangerous books were kept, and devoured Ovid's *Ars amatoria.* But what was this? There were words there that were not in my trusty *Cassell's.* Well, I made a list of them and gave them to my teacher to translate for me. Of course the poor man turned red as a beet with embarrassment. But he *did,* at the next class, discretely present me with a neat little list of the words. Also at Saint Paul's there was a very gifted German teacher, Herr Schade; between him and my stepmother I acquired a fascination with that language and literature that is with me still; it is a rare week when I don't write something in German, even if it is only a letter, and most of my radio plays are in German, not to mention that one of my books is a

translation of the German Romantic poet Novalis's *Hymns to the Night.*

*Dick Higgins' graduation picture from
Saint Paul's School, 1955*

From Saint Paul's I went to Yale College, then in its worst RA RA BOOLAH BULLDOG FOOTBALL-SMASHING SATURDAY DRUNK phase. That too I hated. The music school was staffed with Hindemith followers to whom even twelve-tone music (then already over forty years old) was wild and far out. I switched to being an English major, got various part-time jobs in the library, including some work transcribing medieval manuscripts, which Grandaddy had shown me how to do, had my own radio program playing modern music, and worked in the Dramatic Association as costumer, composer, playwright, and radio adaptor of Shakespeare and of Nicholas Rowe. I was also utterly miserable at Yale. I missed the lively new art scene which I had been coming to know on visits to New York. There I would come to visit my mother and her very cultured lawyer husband, Nicholas Doman (I assumed *all* Hungarians spoke a dozen or so languages as he did), and then I would contact Mary's sister Ilse Getz, who was very much a part of the avant-garde scene in the mid and late 1950s. Ilse sent me to concerts at the Nonagon Gallery downtown, to see the now-legendary "White Show" by the then almost unknown Robert Rauschenberg. New Haven was a bad dream from which I could not seem to awake. There must be other people like me somewhere, I felt, but even the other gays (I came out at Hickory Ridge at eleven or so) seemed to have no interest in what concerned me. The result? I cracked up, and it was among the best things that ever happened to me.

It led in due course to my coming to New York, which was in an especially lively time (1958). Abstract Expressionism was winding down, and in its wake there was an enthusiasm for "the next thing," whatever that might be, coupled with a high degree of connoisseurship in all the arts which is hard to imagine now. First I got a job in a public-relations firm, Ruder and Finn, where I learned to write news releases (a useful skill for an artist and publisher) and also to research in the New York Public Library. Then I enrolled at Columbia University's School of General Studies (the adult-education division). Ilse told me John Cage was to give an important concert at Town Hall, so I went to that. This changed my life, in that previously I had assumed I wanted to write musical comedies of some sort, perhaps modelled on the Kurt Weill–Bert Brecht collaborations. But with Cage's work, with its fusions of the arts and its chance operations, I realized that there were other ways to combine my multiple interests.

I admired very much the music of the composer Henry Cowell, who had taught Cage a quarter century earlier and who was now teaching at Columbia; so I enrolled in Cowell's course there. But Ruder and Finn offered to pay for any course which its employees chose to take at the New School for Social Research, and Cage was teaching there—"Experimental Composition" and "Mushroom Identification." I took both courses. It was fascinating to study with both Cage and his teacher, since I could thus see through some of Cage's ideas to their probable source. In Cage's class I came to know George Brecht, Al Hansen, former Cage students Jackson Mac Low, Richard Maxfield, and Allan Kaprow, and I found myself composing "music" without notes, often with words or actions. Two of my pieces from this time, fairly typical of such things though composed at the end of this period, read:

Concretion No. 6
"Telephone Music"

An old telephone, a new telephone, a hot plate or stove, a large saucepan, a die, and a single performer are required for this piece.

The performer listens for the phone to ring. As soon as it does, he throws the die. If the number thrown is a two, he disconnects the phone. If the number is a four, he answers the phone and makes concrete suggestions over it, speaking as rhythmically as possible. If it is a six, he answers the phone and listens, not saying a word, until the other party hangs up.

If it is a one, three, or five, he does not answer the phone but fills the saucepan with water, puts it on the hot plate, and heats it to boiling. Now he puts either phone, the new one or the old one, into the water and leaves it there to melt, listening all the while.

New York City
December 28, 1960

Constellation No. 7
"New Constellation"

Any number of performers agree on a sound, preferably vocal, which they will produce. When they are ready to begin to perform, they all produce the sound simultaneously, rapidly, and efficiently, so that the composition lasts as short a time as possible.

Boulder, Colorado
October, 1960

Al Hansen was especially active at that time (still 1958), and so was the Coffee House scene in New York's Greenwich Village. One could sooner or later hear most of the Beat and Black Mountain poets reading in these shops, one weekend or another. But they were older than myself by far, and their needs and perspectives seemed closer to Abstract Expressionism. They weren't over, but they weren't me or Hansen. Hansen was and is primarily a visual artist; and he was close with some other artists, notably Lawrence Poons, who had the E-pit'-o-me Coffee Shop on Bleecker Street, which had a reading series and which was also identified with post-Beat, post–Black Mountain ideas. So it came about that during most of 1959 whatever pieces we made in Cage's class during the week were performed at the E-pit'-o-me for a more general audience on weekends. Hansen and I called ourselves (plus whoever joined us for the occasion) "The Audio-Visual Group" or, if we wanted to play with a long name, "The New York Audio-Visual Ensemble." We had stationery printed up, sent out press releases, and once even rented a room at the old Hotel Albert (named for Albert Ryder, the painter), where we did a piece using around a dozen motion-picture projectors. Virtually no documentation remains of this activity, however.

In the meantime, Kaprow had progressed from doing extended visual-art constructions and collages through environmental ones to the point where they began to include performers; lacking a term to describe this kind of thing, he called them "happenings." His first New York presentation of the new form, *18 Happenings in 6 Parts,* took place at a cooperative gallery, the Reuben Gallery; I was among the performers. However, I did not feel entirely comfortable with the Reuben Gallery director, since she seemed somehow to think that the happenings should serve ultimately as a publicity gimmick for serious, salable art; besides, I was based as much in music and literature as in visual art. So I stayed somewhat aloof from the later happenings.

Time passed. In 1959 I met Alison Knowles, who was then painting; we were married the following year, when I graduated from Columbia. I wanted to go to graduate school, but my father, who kept hoping to make a businessman of me, supported my alternate plan, to go to the Manhattan School of Printing, which I did. In 1960 my brother, Mark, was killed while working for President Lumumba in the troubles that accompanied the independence of the Republic of the Congo (a soldier mistook him for a Belgian paratrooper). This shook me up, and explains the radicalized political content of my writings of the next ten years or so. And in the meantime, the hard-to-define performances kept on taking place, being done by new arrivals on our scene, by La Monte Young, Ayo, Yoko Ono, Philip Corner, and others. Similar work was, by now, happening elsewhere, in Japan and in Europe, where Benjamin Patterson, Wolf Vostell, Nam June Paik, and others were active.

I won't go into great detail about this time, since it is covered in detail in my book *Postface* and elsewhere too, both by myself and others. Suffice it to say that, as an outgrowth of this activity, Young and Mac Low put together an anthology of such pieces, called simply *an anthology,* which was designed by George Maciunas, who had earlier produced performances of many of the pieces in the book as a sort of ongoing festival at his art gallery in New York, the A. G. Gallery. When the gallery went bankrupt, as such galleries are apt to do, he decided to edit a magazine, to be called *Fluxus,* which would be devoted to this kind of work and also to visual poetry,

which also fused two arts, poetry and visual art, supporting his publishing habit through his skill as a commercial designer. Maciunas went to Europe, where in due course (1962) he wound up presenting a festival, the first "Festum Fluxorum," at the art museum at Wiesbaden in West Germany, intended originally as a promotion for the magazine and his other Fluxus publications. I quit my job printing and designing bank checks, and Alison and I went to Wiesbaden to take part in the goings-on there, bringing with us new pieces by others of the Americans as well as by ourselves. But the concerts caused a tremendous sensation, and the world press began to call us "the Fluxus people." What else could they call us? Well, it didn't bother us that this was not a name we had chosen for ourselves. What we were doing finally had a name.

But because Maciunas had come along at a time when most of us had been doing Fluxus work for several years already, he never had the authority within the group that, for example, André Breton had in surrealism. His was just one of many voices, and even he usually referred to Fluxus as a collective. A manifesto was written, but somehow it seemed too late for all that, so only a few of the group signed it. Too closely defined a program would have seemed confining, both for Maciunas's editorial concerns and to some of the members of our group, which was a fairly disparate one. So we simply moved around, giving Fluxus performances in Amsterdam, London, Copenhagen, Paris, and (without Maciunas) Stockholm. Alison and I returned to the U.S.A. in March 1963, and Maciunas came to the U.S.A. the next year, after other Fluxus festivals in Amsterdam, Nice, and elsewhere.

I had a little loft on Canal Street in New York, which I used as a studio. Upstairs from a plastics store, it was an excellent work environment for me. Directly downstairs was another loft, which Maciunas now occupied, and this is where many of the Fluxus concerts took place over the next two years. They were called "concerts," reflecting their past in music and distinguishing them from the more visual art-based happenings. Also, like concerts, almost all of the performances presented works by many Fluxus artists, not just one or two, so that they really did resemble concerts.

Maciunas began to produce the Fluxus publications at this point—the irregular newspaper *CC V Tre,* the *Fluxus* yearboxes and *Fluxkits* (which replaced the *Fluxus* magazine that never did appear), and a few publications in traditional book form, one by La Monte Young and one by François Dufrêne and Daniel Spoerri. A book by myself was also supposed

Higgins in his Canal Street studio, around the time when Something Else Press was started, 1963

to appear, *Postface,* to be bound together with a year's worth of works, *Jefferson's Birthday,* everything I had written between April 13, 1962, and April 13, 1963. I delivered the manuscript to George in the summer of 1963. But Maciunas kept putting off getting to work on the publication, and I became desperate. "When can you get to the book, George?" I asked.

"A year from next spring," he answered.

"That's no good," I said.

"Too bad," said George.

So I wandered downstairs to a neighborhood bar, had a few drinks, then went back up to George's loft, removed my manuscript, and brought it upstairs to my own loft and worktable. Then I went home,

down the street, to Alison's loft, where we both lived, and I announced we were founding our own press.

"Oh really? What's it called?"

"Shirtsleeves Press."

"Oh that's no good—you should call it something else." I did. Something Else Press always tried to publish something else—other than whatever the going thing of the moment was. Deliberately iconoclastic, it focussed on Fluxus artists and works, happenings, concrete poetry, chance poetry, and various new forms of novel or prose constructions. The first book was indeed my own. *Jefferson's Birthday/Postface* (1964). It came out after a long, hot summer when my father died suddenly and when

Alison's and my twin daughters, Hannah and Jessica, were born (and, a month later, exhibited on pedestals as living works of art, but that is another story). I paid the printer's bill and made the down payment on a house with the money I got from an insurance policy which I held on my dad's life. I inherited a piano and a painting, but little else. Most of his estate went to my stepmother, Mary. She, in turn, could not ever get over my father's death, and committed suicide in 1966, leaving everything to her brothers and sisters. This would not normally be important in a short biography, except that there is a legend of my being some kind of millionaire, based on an article Grace Glueck wrote about me and the Something Else Press in the *New York Times* in 1966, in which I am described as a steel heir; my father did indeed run a small steel-fabricating plant associated with my grandfather's museum, but it was a money loser, and such proceeds as there were went to my daughters and paid for their education, which I could never have covered myself. Ah, if only . . .

Anyway, my book was followed by a collection of mail-art pieces by Ray Johnson, *The Paper Snake* (1965), and we proceeded, over the next years, to publish ninety-seven books with virtually no public-funding support, books by Daniel Spoerri, John Cage, Henry Cowell, Claes Oldenburg, our very inexpensive "Great Bear Pamphlets" by Vostell, Hansen, Oldenburg, Knowles, Sweden's Bengt af Klintberg, by Robert Filliou, and others. The original editor, working with me, was the now critic, Barbara Moore. When she left to have a child in 1966, her replacement was our fellow Fluxus artist Emmett Williams, who had also been among the original group of concrete poets. The press commissioned his *Anthology of Concrete Poetry* (1968), which sold eighteen thousand copies, not bad for a literary or art press that was never too large to fit all its staff into one taxicab, which would be my definition of a small press. We had a project of reissuing avant-garde classics of the past, to make clear our own lineage. With this in mind we reissued facsimiles of Richard Huelsenbeck's *Dada Almanach* of 1920, and five books by Gertrude Stein, including *The Making of Americans* in the complete, 1907–9 version. For those who want to know more about the Something Else Press, there is a fine book on the subject by Peter Frank, *Something Else Press* ("DocumenText." New Paltz, N.Y.: McPherson and Company, 1983).

We also did the *Something Else Newsletter,* which gave my theoretical opinions concerning the books we were publishing, but also concerning Fluxus and other problems of new art which concerned me. The first issue of the newsletter was my "Inter-media" essay, which revived that term from S. T. Coleridge (who, however, only used it once, in 1813). "Intermedia" arts are arts which represent a conceptual fusion of previously existent ones, not easily separable into their constituent parts as are "mixed media" arts such as opera or expanded cinema. What happenings, graphic musical notations (such as Cage's, Corner's, or some of mine), Fluxus, and concrete poetry (and more recent forms of visual poetry too, for that matter) have in common is their intermedial nature.

By the end of the 1960s, however, it seemed to me that Something Else Press had made its point. I was being run ragged fund-raising, and I did not have enough time left to do my own work; without that I tended to become depressed. Also, New York was too expensive for me and too busy, its tendency to be trendy and to stress fashion too much was annoying to me, and I missed my native New England. So I bought a tumbledown house in Vermont. I wanted to move there. Alison wanted to stay in New York. Instead of either, we both moved to California to teach at the then-new California Institute of the Arts. The marriage did not survive the move, and I wound up living with Hannah and Jessica in a very suburban canyon north of Los Angeles, feeling terribly sorry for myself. While Something Else Press did produce a few books at this time, the hopes that the Press would be associated with "Cal Arts" as a university press were not fulfilled. But I did organize gourmet tours of the desert as part of one of my courses, and I performed with a troupe of Cal Arts students, working over in Tujunga and doing Satie's ballet *Parade* at the San Bernardino Valley State College. The students loved it, and the reason we were circulating around in the first place was that in the pecking order at Cal Arts I was the low man, and the other faculty members would not give us space on campus. But once we were getting all the attention, jealousies developed. Then, too, I could not get used to the forest fire in my canyon that had me on the roof overnight hosing my wood shingles down, or to the snowstorm that hurt my live oak trees, or to the big Los Angeles earthquake of 1971, whose epicenter was a few miles from my house and whose aftershocks had me nearly hysterical for months. I now wanted to do something about my drinking, which had become serious. I wanted out. And I got it, after only a year in Southern California.

The twins, myself, and my friend, the amigo of the *amigo* poems, all moved to my little house in Vermont. There I reorganized (once more) the Something Else Press. But my heart wasn't in it. I

Dick Higgins on his arrival in Vermont, 1971

Eugene Williams

didn't want to be known mostly as a publisher, but mostly as an artist who published and did other things as well. Something Else Press had become too much for me to handle. So I worked up a good list of people whose cigars were worth lighting, and I turned over the Press to a new editor, Jan Herman, who had moved to Vermont to work with me. Alas, he didn't get on with John Kimm, who had also moved there, to be the business manager, and who certainly was loyalty personified. One sad day both of them came to me, an hour or so apart, and each told me that if I didn't fire the other, he would leave. I made a mistake: I let John Kimm go, on the assumption that Jan could run the business in a pinch but John could never edit. What I should have done was call the bluff of both, and, if they called *my* bluff, let Jan go. John would have used free-lance editors until a permanent one was developed, and perhaps Something Else Press would still exist today. Instead Jan stayed home, planted a garden, never went out to light important cigars, did the small jobs, ignored the big executive decisions, and, in spite of his own good will, let the Press go to pieces. I left it in late 1973, and spent most of 1974 recovering from my drinking and from a subsequent depression. One day at a time I have managed not to drink since then. But one sad day late in 1974 I had to come out of the hospital (which was in Connecticut) and sign the Press into bankruptcy. Since then my material situation has forever been unstable, since, whatever the problems with the Press may have been, it usually made it possible for me to do what I had to do in the way of getting readings, lectures, and so on.

In these years Alison and I were reforming our relationship. She came to Vermont in 1972, but that didn't work. Eugene ("amigo") was still too much a part of the scene to forget. And she missed New York; so she bought a loft in the Soho section of New York City, and she moved there. I missed her. Then, starting in 1975, we began to keep company again, as they say. By then I had rebuilt and overbuilt my little house in Vermont; I could no longer afford it. So I moved to another, smaller place nearby and sold the old place.

Already in 1972, at the suggestion of my very capable secretary, Nelleke Rosenthal, I had founded a second small press, Unpublished Editions, to bring out small editions of my works that nobody else wanted; these I could and did sell through the same outlets that Something Else Press had used. It worked for me; why not for Alison? She joined me in the project, and it worked for her too. So we invited others aboard, and we changed the name to Printed Editions (1978). As a cooperative it worked very well, and the members were, besides myself and Alison, John Cage, Philip Corner, Geoffrey Hendricks, Jackson Mac Low, Pauline Oliveros, and Jerome Rothenberg. We sold our out-of-print books through the group and did American editions of our European ones in this way, as well as producing original titles. Every year we did a catalog, listing the fifty-something books we did in all, along with various posters and special editions. This second press was dissolved at the start of 1987, not because it didn't work, but because it did—so well that we no longer had any books to put into the catalog, since other presses wanted just about everything we did. I may yet revive Unpublished Editions for another kind of publishing, but that remains undecided. And for Printed Editions I did do two more numbers of *Something Else Newsletter* for the kind of theoretical work I wanted to do for which there was no other outlet.

Theory. That was much on my mind in 1975 as I recovered from my depression. There was no theory of the new arts which satisfied me, but I did not feel that I could generate one without improving my methodology. So I used the money I had gotten for my old place in Vermont, and I enrolled in the graduate program in English at New York University, working towards a Ph.D. In 1977 I got my M.A., which I celebrated by teaching at the University of Wisconsin at Milwaukee for a semester. I loved it and I think my students got a lot out of it; but I also learned that teaching English would be a hard row for me to hoe, since I would have to compete with people whose deepest ambition was to teach English, while I was more anxious to share what I had found out about English and the arts, and I would probably have a hard time fitting into a department. I continued to study at NYU, getting mostly A's in my course work, but in 1979 I took the Comprehensive Examination for practice, and failed all six sections. "Why?" I wondered.

So I asked to see my paper; and it was marked throughout with "NR" beside many of my answers. "NR" meant "Not Relevant." And the comment was made wherever I had mentioned *anything* that was not English-language literature! How can one study Coleridge, for instance, without mentioning German romanticism? One can't. The program was silly, silly and stodgy, it seemed to me. I had stopped auditing the department head's course when he asked us to read three hundred pages of Emily Dickinson in one week—that is *not* how to read Emily Dickinson. While there were indeed a handful of distinguished people in the department, the Victorian scholar William Buckler for instance, most of the department was terribly pedantic. Many of the best people had left a few years before in some kind of departmental blowup: J. Max Patrick went to Milwaukee, Leon Edel retired, and there were others. I kept wishing I were in comparative literature, but it was too late for that. So I dropped out.

First I returned, alone, to Vermont, to the smaller house we owned, which in some ways was the finest home I've ever had. I had new friends there, Paul and Roger Berard, both in their teens, with whom I performed and worked on such projects as *Ten Ways of Looking at a Bird* (1981), a violin-and-harpsichord work using photographs of Roger as a notation, the large visual novel *of celebration of morning* (1980), *geographies* (1984). But my daughters were growing up, and I realized that after a while Vermont would be too far away, they would not want to be there in the summers where work was scarce and where they no longer had much in common with most of the friends they had gone to school with. Alison could only be there summers. And, while I had friends with whom I could weep, I did not have to weep very often, and I missed professional friends. There were only a very few of these in my area. So I decided to leave Vermont and move to the Hudson Valley, to the hamlet of Barrytown, where a small-press friend, George Quasha, told me a church and parsonage could be had for a fairly reasonable price. Alison had been depressed about my not wanting to live in New York, as I was by her not wanting to live in Vermont. So when I told her about the Barrytown property, she virtually levitated off the bed where she was resting. That was in mid-April 1980. Since June that year I have been living in Barrytown. Alison has

her studio and our darkroom in the former garage. We remarried in 1984. We live in the church, which is also my studio for my paintings. The parsonage is rented out for income. It is not quite enough to live on, but it certainly helps, and I can occasionally find teaching work, especially now that Fluxus has become an "in" subject. For instance I was asked to give two courses on Fluxus at Williams College in 1987, which I very much enjoyed doing. The situation works, we are only two hours from New York City, we're a few miles from Kingston and not far from Poughkeepsie, both of which have lively and developing arts communities. New York is, obviously, far more expensive than it was twenty years ago, so many young artists cannot afford to live there as they once could. Solution? Many are settling in this area, going into New York City only to present their works. My church is not as beautiful as the Vermont place, but it is large, it is surprisingly practical in the winter, my books are all in one place for the first time in my life, and it is beautiful enough for me. And my daughters like it here as well.

So much for the living situation, what of the work? Well, the theoretical work started with intermedia, and the first book on this, *A Dialectic of Centuries: Notes Towards a Theory of the New Arts* (New York: Printed Editions, 1978), stressed that. It was an expanded collection of essays, based on those which had come out in the *Something Else Newsletter* over the years. It was revised in 1978 as a second edition, and, as such, it is my key collection of essays. But it lacked a teleology, and did not answer the question: *why* intermedia? What are the intermedial arts for? Granted that they work sometimes, how do they work for an outsider? To address this problem, I published a second book of theoretical essays, *Horizons: The Poetics and Theory of the Intermedia* (Carbondale: Southern Illinois University Press, 1983). That book also collects my articles on Fluxus, and finally begins the other thrust of my work in intermedia, which is scholarly and historical: I wanted to provide a model history of an intermedial form, partly to counteract the impression that intermedia forms were a phenomenon of the 1960s, or at least of twentieth-century "modernism," whatever that is, thus allowing for a "post-modernism," which I see as an illusion. Since visual poetry is so frequently assumed to be primarily a twentieth-century phenomenon, I collected all the pattern poetry (definition: visual poetry from *before* the twentieth century) I could find, and documented it, first in brief in my M.A. essay from New York University, published as *George Herbert's Pattern Poems: In Their Tradition* (West Glover, Vt.: Unpublished

Editions, 1977), and finally in *Pattern Poetry: Guide to an Unknown Literature* (Albany: State University of New York Press, 1987). This collects documentation on some two thousand pattern poems, far more than most people realize exist, illustrates a hundred fifty of them from European, American, and Oriental literatures, and opens the Pandora's box of these things to comparatists and theoreticians. While my interest in this area is ongoing, those are the two works to start the area. I would also, someday, like to do a historical work on sound poetry, poetry in which the sense *is* the sound more than the semantic content. But that may not happen.

Also, I applied the hermeneutic approach I had used in my *Horizons* to Fluxus in an unpublished essay, "Fluxus: Theory and Reception," in which I also, among other things, give a list of criteria of what constitutes Fluxus pieces; not all Fluxus pieces match all the criteria, but the more that each does, the more Fluxus the piece probably is. And, since 1977, the poet Charles Doria, who also has a doctorate in Latin, and myself have been working on an English-language edition of the last work by Giordano Bruno (1548–1600) that was published in his lifetime, *On the Composition of Images, Signs, and Ideas* (1591). Besides having intrinsic interest as a work on mythology, and also having a fascinating semiotic which prefigures Saussure's in the nineteenth and early twentieth centuries, the work has a section which is the earliest statement I know of intermedia, and, as a mixture of poetry and prose, literature and philosophy, it is in its own right an intermedial work.

But where does this leave my art? I hope that is what the rest of my life is about. My founding of Something Else Press offended Maciunas for a time, though by the late 1960s we were working together again. However, during the middle of that decade, because of the estrangement, I felt particularly free to make work which was by no stretch of the imagination Fluxus work, such as the radio plays *Die fabelhafte Geträume von Taifun-Willi*, which is deliberately a period piece and which describes a nonexistent happening, and *City with All the Angles*, a satire on Los Angeles and pop culture, or the visual-poetry cycle "moments in the lives of great women," published by Something Else in 1969 in my *foew&ombwhnw*, which is Emmett Williams's selection from my work of the 1950s and 60s. But I was not very prolific in the years when I ran Something Else Press, which was, of course, part of my problem at the time. From that time there is almost no visual art and rather little music, let alone fusions of these.

But between the time when I left Something Else Press in 1973 and my medical problems of 1974, I became quite insanely productive. I did many of the chance and systematic poems collected in *Modular Poems* (Barton, Vt.: Unpublished Editions, 1974), and also many of the very intermedial pieces in *everyone has sher favorite (his and hers)* (West Glover, Vt.: Unpublished Editions, 1977), which brings together many of the more experimental or conceptual pieces I wrote in my Vermont years. But primarily I worked in silk screen and did a cycle of one-of-a-kind prints using a set of common screens and images; the cycle, called *7.7.73*, five sub-cycles in it—the four usual seasons plus "mud season," a fifth season in Vermont in the early spring, when maple syrup is made. Then, during my years at New York University, 1975–79, since my studio was in Vermont, I did rather little visual work, but I wrote music, the theory essays (they went along with my studies, after all), and many many poems, especially the very symmetrical visual poems which I called "snowflakes." These began in the macaronic cycle *classic plays* (West Glover, Vt.: Unpublished Editions, 1976), and most of them were collected in *some recent snowflakes (and other things)* (New York and West Glover, Vt.: Printed Editions, 1979). This is a fairly typical "snowflake":

But then, after doing the celebration book, I decided to concentrate on my music. After the move to Barrytown, where I had a very sophisticated darkroom, it made sense for me to complete many musical pieces which had previously lived only in notebook form, or which needed a lot of darkroom work for their realization as scores. At that time I was attempting to make my living by travelling around performing, often with Roger Berard, who was an excellent percussionist, or Paul Berard, who could read very well. So I published *Ten Ways of Looking at a Bird* (which suggests my fondness for Wallace Stevens and which has been widely performed), *Piano Album* (which collects short pieces), *Variations on a Natural Theme* for orchestra, *Sonata No. 2 for Piano*, and three others, all between 1980 and 1982.

In 1975 I had received a fellowship from the Deutscher Akademischer Austauschdienst to spend a year in Berlin, a favorite city; I was too ill at that time to spend more than a few weeks there, though I did stay long enough to write a cycle of chance poems, "The Colors" (unpublished). But in 1982 I went there with my daughter Hannah for the remaining eleven months of my fellowship, she attended a local Gymnasium to perfect her German, and I spent the time performing, working on the intermedia projects, writing short pieces, and working on the *Graphis* series, a series of graphic performance notations which I had begun in the summer of 1959 when I was in John Cage's class, and on which I have worked

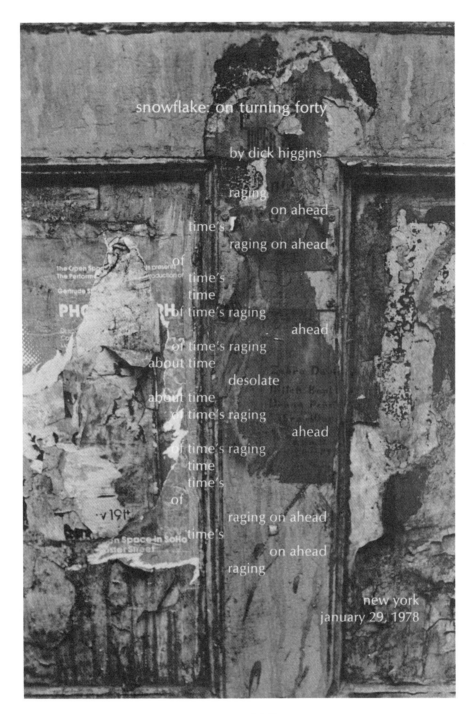

snowflake: on turning forty

by dick higgins

raging

on ahead

time's

raging on ahead

of

time's

time

of time's raging

ahead

of time's raging

about time

desolate

about time

of time's raging

ahead

of time's raging

time

time's

of

raging on ahead

time's

on ahead

raging

new york
january 29, 1978

A "snowflake"

intermittently ever since. The series is described up to 1969 in *foew&ombwhnw.* But now the *Graphis* series took off in another direction, usually using arrows to indicate vectors. As time went on, the pieces became more and more autonomous works of visual art, and their performance aspect became increasingly unimportant. I began to make them not in ink on paper, but in acrylic paint or sometimes even in oil on canvas. Some were shown in an exhibition I did in Berlin in 1982. Others were in a large show I had in

Graphis #181 "Pennsylvania Dutch"

New York at Emily Harvey Artworks in 1987. A typical one is this, *Graphis 181 "Pennsylvania Dutch":*

Most recently I have been writing a new set of chance poems based on word sets generated by the game Scrabble; they are also visual poems, using the typesetting capabilities of my Macintosh computer. At the same time I have also devoted this year (1988) to making acrylic paintings, some of which are an outgrowth of the *Graphis* series using arrows, but most of them use maps and other cultural artifacts that, in one way or another, suggest the ways in which we today constantly re-invent a past for ourselves which we call history. They will be shown at Emily Harvey's in April 1989. I also plan a series of sound poems and radio works, what we now call, following the Germans, hörspiels.

No doubt there will be other projects as well.

But I long ago gave up waiting for myself to settle down and be just a painter, just a poet, or just a composer. Of course I do not confuse those matters, and Gotthold Ephraim Lessing's points, raised two centuries ago in his *Laocoön* essay, pointing out the differences between our literary and our visual-art experiences, are still well taken and as valid today as they were then. But there do exist other possibilities, and for me it would not be natural to work in only one of these areas, simply in order to be professional.

Not all my work is intermedial. Some of my poems are as purely literary as works by favorite poets such as William Carlos Williams and Wallace Stevens, neither of whom wrote visual poems. But others of my works are just that, and as long as this is the case, my sensibility remains a wandering one. To be true to it I must follow it wherever it leads me, and so I must do all three of these things.

Barrytown, New York
15 August 1988

BIBLIOGRAPHY

I find I never feel quite complete unless I'm doing all the arts—visual, musical, and literary. I guess that's why I developed the term "intermedia," to cover my works that fall conceptually between these.

—Dick Higgins

Books:

What Are Legends. New York and Calais, Me.: Bern Porter, 1960.

Jefferson's Birthday [and] *Postface.* New York: Something Else Press, 1964.

Dick Higgins, 1988

foew&ombwhnw. New York: Something Else Press, 1969.

Pop Architektur, edited by Higgins and Wolf Vostell. Düsseldorf: Droste Verlag, 1969; also published in English translation as *Fantastic Architecture.* Millerton, N.Y., and New York: Something Else Press, 1971.

Die fabelhafte Geträume von Taifun-Willi. Stuttgart: Reflection Press, 1969; Somerville, Mass.: Abyss Publications, 1970.

Computers for the Arts. Somerville, Mass.: Abyss Publications, 1970.

amigo. Barton, Vt.: Unpublished Editions, 1972.

A Book about Love & War & Death. Barton, Vt.: Something Else Press, 1972.

The Ladder to the Moon. Barton, Vt.: Unpublished Editions, 1973.

For Eugene in Germany. Barton, Vt.: Unpublished Editions, 1973.

Le Petit Cirque au fin du monde, un opéra arabasque. Liège, Belgium: Aarevue/Aafondation, 1973.

Spring Game. Barton, Vt.: Unpublished Editions, 1973.

City with All the Angles. Barton, Vt.: Unpublished Editions, 1974.

Modular Poems. Barton, Vt.: Unpublished Editions, 1974.

classic plays. West Glover, Vt.: Unpublished Editions, 1976.

Legends and Fishnets. West Glover, Vt.: Unpublished Editions, 1976.

Cat Alley. Willits, Calif.: Tuumba Press, 1976.

The Epitaphs/Gli epitaphi. Naples: Edizioni Morra, 1977.

everyone has sher favorite (his or hers). West Glover, Vt.: Unpublished Editions, 1977.

George Herbert's Pattern Poems: In Their Tradition. West Glover, Vt.: Unpublished Editions, 1977.

The Epickall Quest of the Brothers Dichtung and Other Outrages. West Glover, Vt.: Unpublished Editions, 1977.

A Dialectic of Centuries: Notes Towards a Theory of the New Arts. New York: Printed Editions, 1978.

Hymns to the Night (translation by Higgins of *Hymnen an die Nacht,* by Novalis). New Paltz, N.Y.: Treacle Press, 1978.

some recent snowflakes (and other things). New York and West Glover, Vt.: Printed Editions, 1979.

Piano Album: Short Pieces, 1962–1984. New York: Printed Editions, 1980; Verona: Edizioni Factotum-Art, 1980.

of celebration of morning. New York: Printed Editions, 1980.

Ten Ways of Looking at a Bird. Barrytown, N.Y.: Printed Editions, 1981.

26 Mountains for Viewing the Sunset From. Barrytown, N.Y.: Printed Editions, 1981.

Sonata for Prepared Piano. Barrytown, N.Y.: Printed Editions, 1981.

Variation on a Natural Theme, for Orchestra. Barrytown, N.Y.: Printed Editions, 1981.

Selected Early Works. Berlin: Galerie Ars Viva, 1982.

1959/60. Verona: Editioni Francesco Conz, 1982.

Sonata No. 2 for Piano. Barrytown, N.Y.: Printed Editions, 1983.

Song for Any Voice(s) and Instrument(s). Barrytown, N.Y.: Printed Editions, 1983.

Horizons: The Poetics and Theory of the Intermedia. Carbondale: Southern Illinois University Press, 1983.

Intermedia. Warsaw: Akademia Ruchu, 1985.

Poems, Plain & Fancy. Barrytown, N.Y.: Station Hill Press, 1986.

Czternascie tlumaczen telefonicznych dla Steve'a McCaffery/ Fourteen Telephone Translations for Steve McCaffery, edited and translated into Polish by Piotr Rypson. Klodzko, Poland: Witry Artystów, 1987.

Pattern Poetry: Guide to an Unknown Literature. Albany, N.Y.: State University of New York Press, 1987.

Fluxus: Theory and Reception. Berkeley: Inkblot Editions, 1988.

Five Hear-Plays. Berkeley: Inkblot Editions, 1988.

On the Composition of Images, Signs, and Ideas (translation by Charles Doria of *De imaginum, signorum, et idearum compositione,* by Giordano Bruno), edited and annotated by Higgins. N.p., n.d.

Art graphics and other multiple publications:

Homage to Erik Satie. Milan: Ed 912, 1966.

January Fish. Stuttgart: Edition Hansjörg Mayer, 1967.

Der Dom im Himmel (postcard format). Heidelberg: Edition Tangente, 1968.

Dieses ist kein Kunstwerk von mir/This Is Not an Art Work by Me. Remscheid, West Germany: Vice Versand, 1969.

Dear Osman. Aachen: Galerie Kuhn, 1970.

glasslass. Vancouver: Ace Space Company, 1971.

Frauenkirche (postcard format). Heidelberg: Edition Klaus Staeck, 1971.

structure. Providence: Diana's Bimonthly, 1972.

Self-Portrait. Barton, Vt.: Unpublished Editions, 1973.

definition. Barton, Vt.: Unpublished Editions, 1974.

#426, 427, 428, 429, [and] 430. 7.7.73 series. Barton, Vt.: Unpublished Editions, 1974.

Five Traditions of Art History: An Essay. Barton, Vt.: Unpublished Editions, 1976.

Wanting to Become Art. West Glover, Vt.: Unpublished Editions, 1976.

one two one two. West Glover, Vt.: Unpublished Editions, 1976; Genoa: Mohammad, 1978.

Some Poetry Intermedia. Barton, Vt.: Unpublished Editions, 1976.

E-Stampe. West Glover, Vt.: Unpublished Editions, 1977.

[Postcard.] 7.7.73 series. Vancouver: Image Bank, 1977.

the nature of fish. New York: Printed Editions, 1978.

snowflake: on turning forty (postcard format). New York: Artists' Postcards, 1978.

The Book of Life, Part Two. New York: Printed Editions, 1978.

#607 (postcard format). 7.7.73 series. New York: Printed Editions, 1979.

Graphis 172 "Copenhagen Graphis." Copenhagen: Svend Hansen, 1982.

Blue Graphic. Cavriago, Italy: Pari & Dispari, 1982.

Florence. Verona: Editioni Francesco Conz, 1987.

Labyrinthus I. Verona: Editioni Francesco Conz, 1987.

Sound recordings:

Eine zweite heutliche deutliche Sprache (reel-to-reel tape). Düsseldorf: PRO, 1972.

Plug: An Acid Novel, with Emmett Williams (cassette tape). Calgary: Parachute Art Center, 1977.

Poems and Metapoems. New York: New Wilderness Foundation, 1983.

Bodies Electric: Arches [and] *Requiem for Wagner the Criminal Mayor* (cassette tape). Florence: Recorthings, 1985.

Music by Dick Higgins (reel-to-reel tape). Verona: Factotum-Art Records, 1988.

Piano Music of Dick Higgins and Erik Satie (reel-to-reel tape). Berlin: René Block, forthcoming.

Sound Publications:

Graphis 144 "Wipeout for Orchestra" [and] *Graphis 143 "Softly for Orchestra."* New York: Something Else Press, 1967.

Suggested by Small Swallows. San Diego: Dorn Editions, 1973.

Emmett Williams' Ear/L'orecchio di Emmett Williams. Cavriago: Pari & Dispari, 1978.

Hörspiels—first broadcasts:

Die fabelhafte Geträume von Taifun-Willi. Südwest Rundfunk, 1970.

City with All the Angles (produced in German translation as *Los Angeles mit allen Engeln*). Süddeutscher Rundfunk, 1973.

Scenes Forgotten and Otherwise Remembered. Westdeutscher Rundfunk, 1985.

Girlande für John. Westdeutscher Rundfunk, 1987.

Three Double Helixes That Aren't for Sale. Westdeutscher Rundfunk, 1989.

Films:

A Tiny Movie. 1959.

The Flight of the Florence Bird. 1960.

The Flaming City. 1961–62.

Invocation of Canyons and Boulders for Stan Brakhage. 1962.

Plunk. 1964.

For the Dead. 1965.

Scenario. 1968.

Hank and Mary without Apologies. 1969.

Mysteries. 1969.

Men & Women and Bells. 1970.

Martin. Forthcoming.

Mugs. Forthcoming.

Videotapes:

Gentle Talk. 1977.

The Something Else Press and Since (lecture). 1981.

The Flaming City. 1981.

Ursula Holden

1921-

The five Holden children: sisters Irene, Ursula, Unity, and Sheila, with baby brother, Hyla

Percy S. Smith, West Dorset Studio, Bridport

In the past I have said that I would never write about my life. What did happen is only interesting in that it provides ideas for the work. Nothing that has happened to me is as colourful as what I can make happen on the page, though I have known extreme contrasts. Like many writers I tend to be secretive; I prefer to hide like a burrowing insect away from fact. W. H. Auden said that art springs from humiliation; for me that is largely true. I was flattered to be asked to write something about my writing life and will be as truthful as I can.

I was born, one of five, in 1921. I was the fourth girl before the long-awaited boy arrived. Until he came I was called "Baby." Apparently my father said, "Another girl I'm afraid," when he told my sisters that I had been born. Perhaps that was the start of the damaged ego which drove me on to be a writer.

My brother and I were kept in the nursery, we were the "little ones," my older sisters were "the children"; they stayed in the schoolroom. Our upbringing was much coloured by middle-class Victori-

an codes. My father was in the Egyptian Civil Service and he was away for most of the time. We saw him in the summer, when he came on leave to our home in the south of England. My mother spent part of each year with him in Egypt. I don't remember a time when there weren't taxis arriving and departing with luggage labelled P & O, and these taxis gave me a sense of dread. A repeated childhood nightmare was of being chased upstairs and everywhere by a taxi from which there was no escape. We were left in the charge of governesses and nurses. The servants and gardener pointed to an affluent life-style but my mother instilled in us the importance of economy. I believed we were poor, my clothes were rarely new but passed down from my sisters. I remember suffering because of my black stockings at a party where the other children wore silk stockings or socks, and my brother had no Eton suit like the other small boys. All the families we knew lived as we did. Only when the war came did I mix with the less-affluent or very poor people.

Corin Haslemere

Ursula (left) and Hyla, with Nanny

I hated the nanny that my brother and I had. She was strict and she liked my brother best, the heir could do no wrong, but she punished me harshly. If I bit my nails she would slap my buttocks on each side for either hand, and an extra slap if I cried. The slaps hurt worst on wet skin, these inspections took place in the bath. Another punishment was to be sent to bed in the afternoon until the morning for wetting my knickers, or eating loganberries in the garden. If I was slow to change my dress or button my white kid shoes she stopped me from going down to play in the drawing room with my mother for the hour before bedtime. I would watch her carry my brother down (I was then three or four) to be cooed over and adored. I don't think my mother can have realised this harsh regime and I never dreamed of telling her. I was in awe of her, she was dignified and perfect and she expected perfect behaviour from her children. She loved us, she was remote.

In the drawing room there was a Noah's ark which belonged to me and was kept for the teatime hour. Made by the blind, the wooden animals were unpainted but perfect in my eyes. They were roughly shaped, the two doves were just blobs of wood, but I loved and cherished them all. Nanny gave me an

expensive doll called Bambina, which I was in awe of because she had brought it. Another drawing-room game was walking along lines of playing cards laid on the carpet. My mother used to tell me about her own childhood ("Tell me about the olden days") as well as Bible stories. I had to learn my catechism at an early age and to love God as well as my father in Egypt, whom we rarely saw. Loving these two became a guilty feeling, an emotion you pretended to feel because you were told. I remember running to him when he got out of the taxi and being unable to hug his knees because of my sisters' skirts getting in the way.

My mother was dominant, it was important to please her, to remember the prayers that she taught, to smile and not sulk, to have good manners. To say thank you when you were asked out to tea was as important as loving God. I loved my mother but didn't feel at ease with her. My jealousy of my brother, Hyla, must be concealed. I played imaginary games alone, as children do, stuffing cherries up the nostrils and bottom of my wooden horse, knowing that Nanny would smack me for it, growing a small garden of sharp pieces of china and glass instead of flowers. My imaginary friends were two gnomelike men behind some lavender bushes who smiled but never spoke, and the child that looked back at me from the mirror (called Varelie, I couldn't say Valerie). Obedience, silence, cleanliness were rewarded with, "Good child." But it was a privileged existence with plenty of toys. Drawing books, crayons, Plasticine, and a substance called Glitterwax, which must be warmed before moulding, were all plentiful. I loved the Glitterwax flowers that I made, lumpy and smelling of candle grease. You had to keep your things neat inside your toy cupboard.

When I was about five Miss Caryer was governess to my brother, Hyla, and me. I don't remember Nanny leaving. My sisters started school. My brother and I learned reading and simple arithmetic from Miss Caryer, a kindly woman who didn't punish us. She was in charge of the household when both parents were absent, but I was never afraid of her. She was a constant presence that brought day and night calm. No taxis came to take her over the sea, no P & O trunks were in her room. She loved me and my brother. Each afternoon we went for walks to collect and identify nature specimens. We pressed and labelled flowers in our books, we collected broken shells of eggs, but not the whole egg; that would be theft. We recognised bird song. I still prefer wildflowers to any other. Each Christmas my mother organised parties for adults and children. Games were

The Holden family home

played, ending with hide-and-seek in the dark all over the house. But for Miss Caryer I would have been terrified. I can still feel her woollen dress and her hand securely round mine as she took me to hide in a simple place, behind a door perhaps, nowhere extreme like attics or cellars, and no seeker was allowed to pounce on me.

Religion was not as onerous when my mother was away, though we always went to church. Miss Caryer didn't lecture us. If you tried anything sneaky like eating cake before the bread and butter, she just smiled and handed the plate. When I asked why Nora, the housemaid, had left, I was told, "Nora told lies."

Sex and procreation didn't exist for Miss Caryer. Birds laid eggs, flowers were pollinated, anything else was taboo. A blood orange was a "rhubarb" orange. When passing a refuse collectors' cart we had to hold our breath. We drew from still life, no freedom of expression, accuracy mattered. I wrote a poem, "When I'm nine I'll have a pet, When I'm nine, but I'm not nine yet." But we did have pets in a sort of zoo at the end of the garden, where rabbits and various rodents were caged, as well as cats and dogs. I had no idea for years how they got their young. My sister Irene had charge of the zoo, she wouldn't tell me.

I used to agonize each time my mother left for

Egypt, but less so for my father. These partings patterned my life until the Second World War.

I was about twelve when Miss Caryer's taxi came; she left without P & O labels on her trunks, she was in tears. I felt sick and guilty for hiding in the zoo to avoid saying good-bye. I owe her much. The day school where my sisters already were was a shock to me. The girls in form three were malicious and bossy. I had never come across cheating at lessons before. Hockey was hell. I saw little point in competition and no point in team spirit at all. We were put into "Houses." Abbot House meant you wore a yellow sweater and were expected to be loyal, collecting A pluses towards the interhouse competition. I rarely got A plus, except in English. My poems were sometimes read aloud to the class but this gained little kudos. My sisters were popular, they were voted for form leader, they captained games teams, they were made prefects and head of the house. When I left this school the headmistress said, "Well, there is not much to be said for you is there?"

The boarding school was on the south coast and was noted for a preoccupation with the arts. If you wanted you could learn cookery and art instead of sitting public examinations. It was High Church, with chapel twice a day and a sung mass on Sundays and holy days. I was chosen for the choir to my joy. The

"At the Pyramids": on camels from left, Sheila, Irene, Hyla, and Ursula, 1939

drama and musical productions were outstanding, but my mother never came to them, nor any of my family. I was there nearly three years, but only worked hard at my poems and violin lessons. I would think about the poetry lines day and night, trying to get it right, the start of a habit that is part of my nature now. Music means a great deal to me.

My mother didn't know what to do with me (she never saw the poems). My sister Unity married early, the others went on to further education, and my brother was at Charterhouse. I had no confidence or particular interest. My parents stayed in Egypt and I was sent to the Constance Spry School of Floral Art, where I learned to arrange flowers, making wreathes and exotic sprays, living in digs in South Kensington. There was an Australian painter, Vincent, who had a great influence on me. He was the first man to take an interest in me, he talked to me about truths in art in a way that no one had, showing a glimpse of another world.

The war came and I left London to rejoin my mother at home. My father was in Egypt throughout the war. I never saw Vincent again but I tried to remember what he had said. I didn't think I'd ever get a proper boyfriend like everyone else. Marriage was the expected goal in those days. I joined the WRNS, which was an eye-opener. At last I met people from other walks of life, in a way it was a

coming to life for me. The friends I made knew nothing of the narrow background from which I had escaped, they seemed more real, not so inhibited, not so accent or behaviour conscious as I was. I was stationed near Portsmouth and latterly in Largs in Scotland. Naval standards of efficiency are rigorous, total accuracy was demanded, anything less was reprimanded. You were never praised. Accustomed so early to Nanny's rule I didn't object. We were told that if a single digit in a code group was inaccurate a ship could sink (this was in a signal department). This discipline was useful when later I started to write, the importance of getting it right. A girl called Stella had been a dance teacher and she taught me to dance round our bunk beds. The best part of the war was climbing into the backs of lorries and going to dance with Canadians and Americans. Jiving was popular, I adored it. I fell in love a few times but no one seriously asked me to marry him. By the end of the war my sisters had married and were starting families, my brother was a medical student (and had also become my great friend). My parents wanted me to join them in Egypt but I couldn't bear the thought of being sucked back into their tight insular world, I wanted a new identity, I was immature and totally unsure.

I went to Ireland, where my grandmother lived. I had been there for holidays since I was three and loved it more than anywhere else (Ireland figures

Holden at the beginning of World War II

largely in my fiction). I became a model at a Dublin art school and it was rather a happy time. My family were horrified but it was part of my breaking away. I loved listening and talking to the students in the sculpture life class, this was the world that Vincent had spoken of, where truth in art counted most.

I met and married a Dublin man, he was gentle but he suffered from the twin addictions of gambling and drink. Quite soon I knew about real anxiety and poverty. The drinking bouts were worst, but of the two sicknesses gambling is the most vile, being covert. It is said that the artist must suffer in life and this was a testing time for me, going on for many years. I still have nightmares about those days and probably will all my life. I didn't tell my family (who had not approved of the marriage) and kept hoping he would change. Two daughters were born in Dublin and we moved to London. The poverty came too. I took in lodgers and did various odd jobs. Like many others I kept vowing that I would write a book about my troubles, but for years it remained a wishful thought. The binges and debts got worse. I got help from a group formed to help relatives and friends of alcoholics. By now my mother knew the situation. ("He is weak so you must be doubly strong.") Marriage was for life, our family didn't divorce. When she became ill with cancer we became friends and I

lost my fear of her. She said, "You could write. I can tell." I showed her a little sketch about a neighbour, she said, "Yes, but it should go with more of a hop and a jump." My father lived for ten years after her death and I got to know him better too.

I started going to a "craft of writing" class when I was forty-three, it was another turning point. I knew then what I wanted to do, no matter how long I must wait for success. The tutor, Paul Sheridan, picked me out, praising my efforts (short sketches), ignoring my lack of confidence, urging me to write in spite of any obstacle. Talent was useless without continued application. I listened raptly to what he said about writers and writing. "It is important to aim beyond your seeming capacity, to reach forth, read widely beyond what you feel you can understand. Listen, sense, notice so that you learn about character." He harangued me to dig deeper, not to fear self-exposure, to show rather than state, so that the words hop from the page. My mother had been right in that early criticism, the piece I showed her lacked life. He was unconcerned about rejection slips. Work must come first, even in a terrible way before loved ones. He is dead now, he was a rare person and his teaching came at the right time. Through him I got a ticket to the British Library, where I still work sometimes.

I started writing a novel to give me a rest from those rejections. They fluttered through the letterbox from newspapers and magazines for years and years. Then I got an agent, John Johnson. His wife had died and he was working nonstop, taking on unknown

Sheila, Hyla, Unity, and Ursula Holden, in the armed forces, about 1944

Thomas A. Wilkie

"At the golden wedding anniversary of my parents, Andrew and Una Holden," 1962. The author is seated to her mother's left, with daughter Maureen directly in front of her; husband, Sydney, is standing at far right; daughter Deirdre is standing at far left; daughter Kathy is in the front row at left.

writers. When the letter came saying, "I think you have written a good novel and I hope to get it published," I was overcome. I had become secretive about my writing; no one wanted to publish it. I put the letter in the pocket of my jeans and said nothing. I rushed up to the room where my daughter kept a large cage full of gerbils to look at the letter. In my excitement I left the cage door open and our ginger cat, James, leapt in and caught our best gerbil, the father of the family. The blood, the noise James made, and my daughters' screams were awful. I couldn't get James out of the cage, I was scratched and cut. The gerbil died of course. I wondered if fate was saying, "That's what you get if you want to write. Just you wait."

And it was a long wait, that first book, "Down a Steep Place," didn't find a publisher though it went out to about twenty. Some of these wrote saying that they would like to see my next book, this kept me going as I worked on the second. I was divorced in 1970, which was a dreadful year. I had my youngest daughter on my hands still. I let out half the house to tenants and took jobs in department stores. Life gradually became more ordered, though money was

still short, but I always wrote each day. The first time I was put on a till I was nervous. It shot like a dragon at the lightest touch and I used to give out fifty pence pieces instead of tens. The till never balanced at the end of the day and my buyer said, "For god's sake don't let that woman near it again." I worked in various departments, filling in where needed. I ended up on the fancy-linen section, where the buyer asked me to stay, and never mind the till. I loved displaying the towels, tea cloths and table napkins as beautifully as possible, even getting to work early for it. Sometimes I used to hate the customers touching my displays and spoiling them. I would stop them, but it was against my interests, as I was on commission. Perhaps this is another example of the power of art to make order from chaos which Vincent had spoken about. When I left the store they gave me a present of some tea towels. In some ways I was sad to leave shop work. I had made friends but it is the lowest kind of labour for anyone middle-aged, unskilled, and down on their luck. It was a good stopgap for me at a terrible time in my life. I got a job in the music section of my local library, which is in the next street from where I live, and this was an improvement. I stayed there for four years, asking for late shifts so that I could keep my resolution of writing daily. Henry Miller said, "Let the employer have the writer when he is tired from his own work"; this applied to me. I wasn't very good at the job, nor did I like it, but the music was marvellous and I learned to know a lot of new composers, listening as much as possible.

My agent, Andrew Hewson, of the John Johnson Literary Agency, at last found a publisher for the second book. After offering it to a great many, a small poetry press said that they would like it as their first work of fiction. I was still secretive about writing, I called myself Maris Flag and received a thirty-pound advance and all went ahead to the stage of being entered in the publishing catalogue. But fate made me wait again and the venture fell through. Publication had been scheduled for October 1974 and the day that I heard the news I kept coming across that advance date on borrowers' library tickets. It looked so mocking, I couldn't believe the awfulness of it. But it strengthened my resolution, I worked like fury on the third novel, *String Horses*. At the beginning the inscription reads, "Cast a cold eye / On life, on death. / Horseman, pass by!" from W. B. Yeats. I like that.

Eventually Alan Ross of the *London Magazine* took on the second book, *Endless Race*. He insisted that I drop the pseudonym Maris Flag. I took my maiden name, which I am glad about. The next two books followed via Alan and I had made the break-

The author with James the cat, about 1968

through. The first time I met him I was so uneasy that, incredibly, I managed to set the tablecloth on fire. A poet himself, we got on well and he was a good and helpful editor. The three books claimed the attention of top reviewers. The *Times* wrote that *Endless Race* was a contribution to English literature that would not be forgotten. For a person of my low self-esteem this was heady stuff. When I saw the book on a shelf in Foyles I burst into tears, I had to rush out and buy some fudge. I wanted to write full-time, the first three books had only earned me seven hundred pounds in all, but the Arts Council gave me a bursary. This was the spur and I left the library. I am glad that no one warned me how poorly my kind of fiction sells, in spite of continued rave reviews. I survived, you always do, but it was tough.

After Andrew Hewson arranged a contract with Methuen in New York for my first five books I went to the States on three occasions, staying at the Millay Colony first, then MacDowell. I went to Yaddo one February and I didn't know such cold existed. Meeting other artists so far off made me realise how different we are as a breed; work is our life regardless of remuneration. The single-minded expression in the eyes of the artist talking about work is the same anywhere. I made some American friends.

Then Methuen discontinued their fiction list, and I haven't been back there again. Unexpected spin-offs occur from time to time. *Penny Links* was translated into Russian. Recently De Boekerij in Holland arranged to have three books translated into Dutch, starting with *Tin Toys*, which is the first of a trilogy about three sisters. About twice a year I go to the Tyrone Guthrie Centre in Ireland, which is run along similar lines to the artists' colonies in America. I absolutely love it there, I like having work with me wherever I go, so that these resorts are ideal and I regard them as one of the perks of my writing life. You never know what a telephone call or a letter will bring, but it is a hard life, and lonely. Gertrude Stein said that one writes for oneself and strangers, I find this quite true, my many relatives seem to find my work disconcerting and don't mention it. My brother is supportive and I am lucky in my three daughters, Deirdre, Kathy, and Maureen.

I have just finished my eleventh book, *A Bubble Garden*, and when this piece is finished I shall return with some relief to some more fiction.

Living alone as I do now, I can arrange life round the work. I like to sleep near the typewriter and a little tape recorder that I keep especially for dreams and nightmares, which can sometimes be useful. (Fortunately I have at last outgrown the sleepwalk-

Ursula Holden, 1988

ing.) I dislike modern machines, the typewriter that I'm using now is over sixty years old and I have four others, all with faults but I'm fond of them. I have never owned a car.

I depend increasingly on the unplanned attack on my fiction. Random ideas are often the truest and once I have got my characters going I must trust them to chart their own course, even when the plot appears to take an absurd turn. I have to learn to trust my subconscious and believe that it cannot lie. I prefer to avoid what did happen or what was experienced though of course this colours the work. The characters are conglomerates of many parts, a remark here, an eyebrow there, or a movement of the feet, and once they start to take over, to dictate to me, I know they are coming alive. Sometimes I start a novel with a terrible situation, for instance, the cat James inside the cage. The work is like an addiction. For me, fiction is like a fix, I hate starting off each day but after an hour or so, with luck, the machinery will be

oiled. I work straight onto the typewriter, doing thirty or more drafts before I am satisfied. This striving for perfection is best kept for work alone and anything else must lump behind. I adore movies, I do a lot of yoga, and there is music, which never lets me down.

Some people quiz me about the compulsion that I feel to work, they don't understand the sense of order that creative work brings; whether working at a childish poem or arranging tablecloths in a shop, you search for a pulse of truth. This kind of truth is elusive, you never capture it but you might come near it and you go on. (I am reminded of John Bunyan's *Pilgrim's Progress,* which my mother read to us when we were quite young.)

Writers crave praise like worms craving food, it is beguiling but praise doesn't last. Adverse criticism can rankle but if it comes from an informed source it should be valued.

The sense of identity I now have compensates for my early inadequacy, but a damaged ego can act like a lever, that part of the psyche that motivates. It is important for me to be unpretentious in approaching the craft, to beware of arrogance. Searching to get it right is what matters, perfection is a dream. I remember Paul Sheridan in the early days. "It is a matter of time. But watch that ego, we are just termites among other termites."

BIBLIOGRAPHY

Fiction:

Endless Race. London: London Magazine Editions, 1975.

String Horses. London: London Magazine Editions, 1976.

Turnstiles. London: London Magazine Editions, 1977.

The Cloud Catchers. London: Eyre Methuen, 1979; New York: Methuen, 1979.

Fallen Angels (includes *Endless Race, String Horses,* and *Turnstiles*). New York: Methuen, 1979.

Penny Links. London: Eyre Methuen, 1981; New York: Methuen, 1981.

Sing about It. London: Eyre Methuen, 1982.

Wider Pools. London: Methuen, 1983.

Eric's Choice. London: Methuen, 1984.

Tin Toys. London: Methuen, 1986.

Unicorn Sisters. London: Methuen, 1987.

A Bubble Garden. London: Methuen, 1989.

Edwin Honig

1919-

Edwin Honig in Brooklyn, New York, about 1926

Say that writers are used to inventing the mythologies of their losses. Because they understand the worst, since knowing what actually works in making things believable, they are constantly operating on, dealing—even bargaining—with what doesn't work. They also know that sometimes the things that at first seem clear as glass and then turn out to be shifty or misty, may still be rendered as plain facts or even as bone-hard truths.

But what about those other things that are now barely discernible, though once deeply felt but no longer vibrant, like quickly glimpsed insects that streak out of the light to find hiding places they can't be dislodged from: the intangibly poignant lost events of another time? Such occasions that lurk somewhere in the memory cannot be grasped or pried loose without immense concentrative effort, even great physical stamina. Of these things a writer

will say that they are signally provocative and deserve a name—Nemesis, maybe—and so, like a ghost hunter prowling for real blood, the writer will set out to embody them through the haze.

Acquiring a name quickly identifies a thing, makes it familiar. A unique history is created out of named, often insignificant things, like a gun the writer had that was lost or stolen, or traded for a typewriter during the war. So the loss is absorbed, or better, transformed in a myth that may last a lifetime. Often the writer's life itself becomes a myth.

Where to begin? With a pencil. But first it must be sharpened. I look for a sharpener.

If, when looking at an old pencil sharpener, rusty, stationary, screwed down on the desk, you think of the time you live in, the "age," as the self-conscious historian calls it, and sense how limited the feeling-thinking-being is and must be, how in fifty, twenty-five, even ten years from now all this present sensing of yours will have so little substance it will almost be nonsense—then you know how small, closeted, and unamplified your voice is, even the voices of all the more and most eloquent alive must be. Then a certain rush of feeling springs from you, from your tensed thighs, from the back of your throat, behind the mucous in your face, and you are sorry for all the people nearest you, pretending as they do that everything is so urgent and necessary, and you are touched by the drooling pathos of all human life striving to assert itself, simply to be, be anything, against oblivion.

But where to begin, with what, when? The beginnings.

I was born in Brooklyn, New York, at—as my mother used to say—*exactly* 5:30 in the morning, on September 3, 1919, the day the Versailles Peace Treaty ended World War I and germinated World War II.

The first half of the 1920s was a *pot pourri* of shrill quarrel-torn days and nights for my young parents Abe and Jane; frenetic moves from one rented apartment to another; the traumatic death under the wheels of a Mack truck of my brother, Stanley, for which I was blamed when I was five; then,

Edwin in the back seat of the car; with his mother, Jane, tending to his infant brother, Stanley; and his maternal grandfather, Paul Freundlich; Brooklyn, New York, about 1922

I had begun writing in high school when I was twelve or thirteen. Miss Newman, an alert young teacher, was intent on introducing some of us to modern poetry. Meeting with her once a week after school, we discussed our reading and showed off our writing. The idea of expressing myself in long swelling lines often kept me writing through the night while the BMT "L" trains racketed past the big plate-glass windows of my grandparents' flat on Broadway, Brooklyn. I'd done some less self-conscious writing earlier, when I was eight, scribbling my own versions of two detective serials heard on the radio—the sinister "Eno Effervescent Crime Club" and "The Shadow Knows." Another model was the short-short story featured on a single page in the New York *Daily News*. My first try at publication was a reversal-of-fortune piece called "Just a Tramp." It didn't make the *News* but got into the Boody Junior High School *Beacon*. For years I told myself they'd printed it because Jane had transcribed my illegible manuscript in her beautiful round hand.

Another piece, a courtroom farce called "Who

at eight, a long, dark hospital bout with nephritis and subsequent recuperation on a diet of steaks and Dugan's double-layer cakes; and the birth of my sister, Lila, a year or so before our big sweaty move "to the ocean" in upwardly mobile Brighton Beach, Brooklyn.

The later twenties continued grim. Bitter recriminations followed Abe's restive hunting for salesmen's jobs and Jane's efforts to keep a household going on ten dollars a week. Then the grimness softened a bit (by my learning to live with it in another guise?) during the last months in junior high, with their heated and violent separation.

Stranded by their divorce in 1932, I went to live with my paternal grandparents in Williamsburg, Brooklyn, making my way through high school on my grandmother's rice and beans at home and the Automat's rolls and catsup downtown. Experience enforced certain necessities. One was to write instead of choking; another, to make some sense of the world around me, but sense that would not be deprived of my imagination. It seemed necessary to grow up fast.

"With my sister, Lila, off the Coney Island boardwalk, the day of my graduation from junior high," 1932

Killed Hogan?'', was put on during the last home-room period of the year. It barely escaped rowdy adolescent highjinks by the studied miming of my chubby classmate Seymour Brooks, who improvised the stellar role of accused-murderer-turned-missing-victim.

When I graduated from junior high, we were living in Brighton Beach, Brooklyn, a station-stop away from Stillwell Avenue, Coney Island. Endless nighttime street games and widely echoing gang fights sustained our dreams of prowess in the neighborhood. I could be wild, or else gentle and considerate. I could abstain from being either, stay home, especially on snowy days, and read novels near the whistling steam radiator in the kitchen—all the Sherlock Holmes and Poe mysteries together with the Frank and Dick Merriwell growing-up stories. My mother practiced the piano, self-taught. She played sternly, often passionately, giving lessons when she could find students in the neighborhood. I started with her four times, and four times made mistakes grievous enough to have my wrists slapped, and quit. Disengaged, I ran out to join my gang playing wild ringaleevio in the nighttime streets. Some of the gang ended up as lifers in Sing Sing; others, like me, who became professors, never left college.

Not long ago at a reception for visiting faculty I met a man from Princeton, small, leathery, keen-eyed, gray and smiling. He came at me: "I know all about your work—poetry, scholarship, translations. What I'd really like you to tell me is this: Are you any kin to the Honig I remember as a boy playing baseball in the sandlots? Was he the pitcher on the other team who always struck me out?

"So tell me," he added, shaking hands, "if you are indeed that chap, why did you always beat me up after every game we played? Was it—may I say this?—because you were so tall and I was, and still am, such a shrimp?"

I was reading Hart Crane by 1932—also Vachel Lindsay, T. S. Eliot, Gerard Manley Hopkins. It was the year Crane killed himself. Crane's suicide touched me, and I discussed it with friends, including Brom Weber, a classmate at Abraham Lincoln High, who later became Crane's biographer. The following year I ran headlong into Rimbaud and Lorca. Based on the French and Spanish I had taken in school, I kept reading the foreign poets, and was trying to learn German on my own by reading and translating Rilke. I reviewed books and plays for the *Lincoln Log,* the school weekly, and wrote stories and poems for the magazine *Cargoes,* which I edited in my senior year. Surely there was some connection between this literary awakening and my living with Moriz and Ester

Honig in Williamsburg, Brooklyn.

Moriz, whom we called Zaide, was born in Russia and migrated to Palestine. There, in Jerusalem, around 1885, he married Ester Mohliver, whom we called Nona. (Nona's family had come from Morocco sixty-five years earlier, to settle in the Holy City.) Nona's eleven children brought thirty-two grandchildren into the world. A carpenter all his life, Zaide built the façade of the small Jerusalem synagogue with the sundial, visible until recently across from the Machne Yehuda, the city's main open-air market. As a child, my father tells me, he accompanied Zaide to Bethlehem in a goat cart. There Zaide completed the job of reinforcing the wooden barrier around the ancient tomb of Rachel.

Living with them in Williamsburg, I heard Ladino, Arabic, and Yiddish spoken, but English only minimally. Nona spent most of her life in America indoors. Immigrant mothers with large families seldom went outdoors except to attend family weddings and funerals. She had all the washing, cooking, and cleaning she could do in the cold-water flat. Zaide did the shopping regularly with his cracked Leatherette bag.

The Leatherette bag remains an early symbol of a time when speed counted. During the Depression, around 1934, I accompanied my grandfather early Friday mornings so as to be among the first to dive for the free grapefruits and cabbages in the handout bins of the Relief Store. Slowly unbolting the doors for the pressing and jostling takers to pour in, the fat guard wisecracked, "Here it is, folks, go take what you want but don't kill yourselves trying to take it all!"

Digging into the bin was more frenzy than fun with twenty other hands, big and hairy, lumpy and grimy, groping for the same grapefruits even as I occasionally managed to rip one away and dump it into the black bag Zaide held open. There was some outrageous fun in being accidentally scratched and scratching back: since part of the game of hauling off the swag was to immobilize the next guy's grabby hand in the boiling bin. If I played it right, I'd stuff not only Zaide's Leatherette bag but also the two or three extra paper sacks I'd brought along, just in case. So there we'd be, scurrying down the street, my scraggly, white-bearded, hunched-over grandpa in a black derby, and I in a worn, purple-and-gray turtleneck my sporty dentist uncle once tossed me, serious and wildly balancing the near-bursting bags, slowing my stride, pretending I was trying to keep up with Zaide. Then, after bringing the bags home, exalted and groaning them up onto the kitchen table, there was Nona to kiss my diligent hands in her quick Near Eastern sort of way.

"Zaide"—Moriz Honig, 1932

"Nona"—Ester Honig, 1932

Every Saturday, clomping up the stairs to their third-story, cold-water walkup, came drifting all day, duos and trios of aunts, uncles, cousins, in-laws, to take their places around the white tablecloth decked with pea-studded mounds of saffron rice and steaming red beans.

"Eat more, my child! What? You can't? Tell me, where does it hurt, child? Come, show me now—let me see where!"

All day through the endlessly replenished meal, the squabbling, squeals, self-confirming hilarity, I was there, like a surfside bather with waves breaking over him, exhilarated but doubting anything I saw was really happening. Maybe because most of the sound was unintelligible jabber out of an old world I'd never seen. While taking it all in, I would think of Nona the night before, blessing the twin Sabbath-eve, chaste, white candles, a linen kerchief draped loosely over her neatly tied, henna-dyed thinning gray hair done up in a bun, the twilight flickering through the third-story windows. And, as she sighed her prayer, both hands scooped up the candlelight and splashed it around the cold-water flat, as if to make everything Sabbath-clean.

Women who later attracted me often bore some

resemblance to Nona: Sara, the light red hair; Moira, the wide mouth and two rows of tiny teeth; Helen, her quick warm brown eyes; Beulah, the sensuous shoulder swerves, dancing. A decade later I wrote "For an Immigrant Grandmother," the elegy that ended,

For her heart was a mediterranean cradling the earth
With wishes that tumbled like fish and ancient sea fairs
Where pirates were drowned and angels were spared by
*   her prayers*
Till she slipped unaware on the edge of a sigh to her
*   death.*

Was it out of some bedraggled need for her that I concentrated on a single love who never matched her all-engulfing spirit, her singular gift of affirmation? Perhaps even more, it was all that sloshing around her of the languages spoken in their house that made life seem so magical, luminous, and fruitful.

Hearing languages spoken brought Europe alive. Something in me quickened to the idea that they withheld a mysterious but potent resource latent in my pre-American past. The promise of what lay overseas touched my imagination and drew me to study foreign languages. The same potency drew me to poetry; the odd density of its verbal challenge absorbed me, but differently, requiring another kind of study and mastery.

In college I took Attic Greek, German, Russian, then more Spanish and French. In my freshman year at the University of Wisconsin I won the school's literary essay contest with a paper on "modern experimental poetry." By the time I graduated I'd written several hefty term papers later shaped into a book on García Lorca. The Lorca translations started in class also were revised for publication in a New Directions Annual.

Tales of the flamboyant linguist and poet William Ellery Leonard and of the noted philosophical idealist Alexander Meiklejohn's experimental college had brought me to Madison lugging a black cardboard suitcase one monumentally icy winter day in 1936. I somehow never got to Leonard, though I observed him at a distance being casually followed by his beauteous blonde wife Grace Golden. And soon I also discovered that the experimental college, having run out of funds, had expired in 1932. After grubbing and thawing my way through the spring, only partly enrolled, I returned to Brooklyn and Nona's beans and rice.

But I was back in Madison in the fall. Having determined to advance my age so I could qualify for the job, I managed to join the WPA Federal Writers Project as an eighty-four-dollar-a-month junior writer. An older writer, the poet Lorine Niedecker, became a close friend. She was of slight build then, with motions quick and birdlike. Bifocals made the pupils of her milky blue eyes appear much larger than they were. Her hair was naturally blonde and wispy, her lips noticeably large. She laughed readily, often explosively, but quickly suppressed her laughter, one hand clapped over her mouth, her head averted. She had a good wit, a high-pitched voice, and a sense for the incongruous, which made her a good storyteller. Anecdotes she told invariably concerned country people and their expressions. Although ideologically a Marxist, her strong loyalties as a person and as a poet were always turned toward human beings rather than abstractions.

She sometimes took me on a visit to her parents' home in Fort Atkinson, Wisconsin. They owned a few rural cottages and sheds by a stream, with great wooded areas, outside of town. Lorine's mother was awesomely tall, gaunt, and silent; her father, an easygoing farmer, not regularly employed, was a good storyteller. I don't recall if Lorine had any sisters or brothers. But I do remember a supper of greens, rutabaga, potatoes, and mud-hen.

Lorine, who must have been in her mid thirties then, sometimes spoke of writing children's books, though I don't recall seeing any by her, either published or in manuscript. She had been a librarian for a while, perhaps only temporarily, in Milwaukee, but she clearly preferred living at home in Fort Atkinson. Because she was identified with the rural scene where she had grown up, and was also a published poet (Decker Press did a small book of hers called *Goose*), people on the Writers Project kidded her about being another Emily Dickinson. But Lorine wasn't at all reclusive or shy. She was friendly, quick to express her concerns, both personal and political. She believed in her work and felt connected with the poetry being written in and around New York City. Louis Zukofsky was Lorine's guide and mentor, then and always. She exchanged letters with him joyously all her adult life; I was often impressed with how much she counted on Zukofsky's words as a source of living sustenance. From her and indirectly from Zukofsky, I learned about "open forms," the work of the Objectivists, Pound, and Williams, and, indirectly again, the poetry of social consciousness.

In late August, a fellow worker who drove his own car took Lorine and me and Charlotte, the woman I would marry in 1940, on a visit to New York City. On the way we learned that war had been declared in Europe. The day was also my twentieth birthday.

We wrote sporadically over the years, and once in the late sixties I received a short letter from Lorine about the archive of her work being established in the Harris Collection at Brown University. Later I was deeply annoyed with myself for not having answered her; Lorine died soon after I received word of her final illness.

In 1938 I met Charlotte Marion Gilchrist, a young woman from Milwaukee who was studying library science at the University of Wisconsin, and we were married in the spring two years later. Meanwhile, two friends from Brooklyn had come to Madison, partly at my urging, to try their luck in an uneasy quest for work and the hope of enrolling somehow at the university. One was the writer Joseph Frank, now a distinguished biographer of Dostoevsky, and the other my high-school friend Milton Miller, recently retired from the University of California, Riverside. Estranged from the scene like me, Joe and Milton reinforced my somewhat studied outsider's view of our adopted midwestern home.

After joining Charlotte in Washington, where she had been called to a civil service appointment as a special librarian with the Adjutant General's Office, I landed a minor librarian's post in the Documents

Division at the Library of Congress. Daily work in the stacks brought on a heavy case of rhinitis from library dust and mold; this soon degenerated into asthma and a lifelong distrust of libraries.

If there was any literary life in Washington, I was unaware of it. I was befriended by several local literati, among them Frederick A. Blossom, an august, tall, elderly man with a mane of wavy white hair, who happened to be a translator of Proust and an ideological follower of Scott Nearing and of Bill Haywood, the industrial anarchist of the teens and twenties. There was also the jovial Joseph Auslander, the Library's poetry consultant, with Audrey Wurdemann, his wife and a Pulitzer prize–winning poet. Archibald MacLeish, the new head of the Library, could be seen daily entering through the back door of the main building and tipping his homburg as I slipped by pushing a trolley of books. I was glad to remind him of his genteel greeting when, a decade later, we were colleagues in the Harvard English Department. Then his nongenteel reply, taking in his experience at the Library, was, "Yes, by George, but wasn't *that* a hell-hole?!"

In the late spring of 1942 I gave up my grubby post to enroll in a government-sponsored summer session at the University of Michigan. The government was looking for rapidly trainable personnel to send to Latin America and teach English as a foreign language. Herbert J. Muller, the literary critic–historian and fellow student that summer, helped me get a job at Purdue, his university in West Lafayette, Indiana. I managed to limp through a semester of English teaching, and during the year wrote my book on Federico García Lorca, the Spanish poet murdered by Franco's fascists in Granada. J. Laughlin accepted the book for New Directions just as I was going off to France with an infantry battalion in 1944.

Drafted into the army at Indianapolis in November 1943, I was conveyed to Camp Crowder, Missouri, for Signal Corps training, and from there assigned to a cryptographic school in suburban Virginia. Charlotte rented a small apartment and taught high school in Warrenton for a term. We saw each other some weekends, even overnight occasionally, if I could get leave. Meanwhile, from back in West Lafayette, Indiana, Charlotte was getting irate letters from her neglected eighty-four-year-old grandmother, Mary Schmidt, demanding she return to care for her in the apartment where we had all been living before I was drafted.

As a girl, Mary had seen the local Wisconsin troops of the Union Army returning from the war and marching, many of them crippled and amputees, through the streets of Milwaukee. Mary had a long, sharp memory. She told us, in her short, white locks, palsied hands, and distracted head shaking, of the grinding poverty of the people she lived with during the Reconstruction period. She spoke of an Indian who came out of the forest one day, made his way without hesitation into the general store, lifted a hundred-pound sack of flour and, silently descending the steps, disappeared unhindered into the forest.

Charlotte, before I had met her, already had a degree in secondary education from Milwaukee State Teachers College. The year following her time in Madison, she lived in Wauwatosa, outside of Milwaukee, and worked in the town library. I would hitchhike from Madison on occasional visits to be with her. Charlotte's grandmother, with whom she had always lived, regarded me for years as an intruder, and then barely tolerated my staying overnight, even after we were married on April 1, 1940.

At twenty-four, Charlotte was still heavily tied to Mary Schmidt, through intricate bonds of indebtedness and filial obligation, and to these were added those of her mother, Charlotte, Sr., an entertainer and "exotic dancer" in Chicago. Mary's husband, a German immigrant, had come to Wisconsin in 1848 to escape the European famine. Later they adopted Charlotte's mother, a dark-skinned girl of five who had been working with a large farming family of boys unrelated to her. Being childless, the Schmidts took the child, a strong-minded character who invariably explained herself as "a born gypsy." Mary Schmidt amended the view, willingly granting that Charlotte, Sr., may have been *kidnapped* by gypsies, who left her on the steps of an orphan asylum. There she was subsequently adopted by the farming family, who then returned her to the asylum for some reason, and there the Schmidts found and adopted her.

Charlotte Honig, with her lifelong fascination for gypsies, somehow wanted to be associated with her mother's putative origins. Her father, Lawrence Case Gilchrist, the son of a well-to-do family, a dropout from Princeton, sometime playwright and magazine writer, had eloped with her mother, a girl of fifteen. "He stole her right out of my house!" Mary Schmidt put it; and shortly afterward, when Charlotte, Jr., was born, he left the two with Mrs. Schmidt, by then a widow, living on her husband's small pension.

Charlotte's marrying me had the effect of easing the inevitable departure from her grandmother. The circumstances of the war added a constant unpredictability to the events which led to the break-up of the household, leaving her grandmother alone in our apartment in Indiana. With Mary Schmidt's illness and eventual death soon after, in 1943, Charlotte was to spend the rest of the war years on her own, first as

Charlotte Honig in Vinalhaven, Maine, 1952

a high-school teacher in Virginia, while I was stationed nearby, then as a psychologist in Rockland State Hospital, New York, during the time I spent overseas.

Like most draftees, I used to think of my thirty-two months in the army as an utter waste, an open wound, a sorrowful vacuum in my life. Later hindsight showed me it was something else, a good deal more and different. I'd survived the worst war in history without going crazy or becoming maimed or dying, as countless millions had. My "service"—a barely suppressed resistance—was a fiasco of tedium, a near calamity, but also a constant learning of survival tactics that lasted years into my resumed "civilian" life. I could fend for myself, I could "stranger out" both when necessary and without warning, and I could assume authority and act decisively in most crises. My army unit had survived an incredibly bitter winter in tents in open country below Le Havre, without basic heat and without adequate food. I was compelled to go into the French

countryside to negotiate elaborate exchanges with cigarettes for bread, cider, cheese, eggs, all accomplished with my rather formal literary French. In March we moved to the Siegfried Line, relieving a battle-worn division near Saarlautern. Bombarded daily by the entrenched Germans, we had to learn ways of overcoming routine attacks by making ourselves scarce without running amok.

In a crisis I could pretend to believe in an action I was forced to undertake and convince others to join me. I could also resist orders if I disbelieved in them, or modify them at times so as to lessen personal risk. I was once made to deliver from the regimental message center a message to the captain of an infantry company pinned down across the river from us. I was ordered to drive the signals unit jeep alone, but the difficulty was that I couldn't drive at all, and overcoming the hysterical accusations of the sergeant that I was lying, persuaded him to supply me with a driver. Under enemy fire we crossed the bridge at midnight, delivered the slightly incredible message, which read, "We attack at dawn," turned around and recrossed the Rhine in the jeep, under fire again, and made it back to the message center without further incident. Of course either or both of us might have been killed or wounded, but I had saved myself from being court-martialed, as the sergeant had threatened, for failing to follow the order to drive the vehicle that I had never learned how to drive.

For a while afterward I seemed to believe that I was living a charmed life and thought I might be invulnerable. Once under bombardment, as shells were being lobbed into our streets, houses, and laps, I heard the sound of an organ playing Bach. To discover how to cope with divine or angelic intervention, I made my way during a lull in the firing to the house across the courtyard: an elegant building I rightly assumed served churchly purposes. As I drew near and the organ music grew louder, I did not hesitate to open the heavy door and duck inside. From the vestibule I recognized the Protestant chaplain, seated in his captain's uniform and playing Bach.

"Forgive me, soldier," he said with a tremor, seeing me approach. "I'm alone in here and the music comforts me."

"Please, sir," I replied, "play on. I need comfort too!"

I could hear the shells explode again outside while he went on playing. The chaplain did not ask me to go but I left in good time, comforted by the music if not by my disbelief.

At war's end I found myself writing up the Sixty-fifth Infantry Division's posthumous battlefield awards in Austria and Bavaria. During that period, to occupy restless GIs in Europe, the army arranged for brief "education" leaves. While studying variously at Edinburgh, Stratford, and Bristol, I bought bags of books of the English classics for later reading in conquered Hitlerland. Such reading sparked a passion for Ben Jonson, Edmund Spenser, and Jonathan Swift. Without knowing it, I was getting ready to teach again and to follow ideas of allegory and satire that would lead to my book *Dark Conceit: The Making of Allegory*.

Returned to wife and country in June 1946, I worked sporadically teaching at NYU, IIT, the University of Wisconsin, and kept struggling to make sense of routine courses in composition I'd scarcely studied, though continuing to write stories, poems, essays. I was mainly hoping to keep heart, soul, and Charlotte together long enough to get us to Spain one day, just to see if it still existed. In the Hispanic environment of Albuquerque and Sandoval, New Mexico, I came closest to feeling at home in America before turning thirty. Ramón Sender, the exiled

Spanish novelist, taught at the University of New Mexico. He kept turning out oblique existentialist novels, plays, stories, and books of poems. A strong-minded Aragonese, a "Roman Spaniard" (as he called himself), Sender was a bruised intellectual hero of the Spanish Civil War, distrustful of Marxists and academics. Most days when not writing, he could be found painting murals at home in a highly fanciful mix of the late styles of Picasso and Miró. We were friends and fellow-founders of the spontaneously created brotherhood Ramón called *Las Tortugas* ("The Turtles"), sworn to uphold the motto *nec spec nec metu* ("without hope without fear"). At monthly meetings we drank wine while responding to his implacable injunction that each of us tell the worst truth about himself that we could—the more painful the better. It was like living somewhere in the country of Tom Sawyer and a pack of Dostoevskean anarchists. I translated a fable of Ramón's for the *Partisan Review* called "In the Hot Land." Blessed the following year (1948) with a Guggenheim fellowship, I wrote stories about the war and edited poetry for the *New Mexico Quarterly Review*.

Honig (right) with novelist Ramón Sender, outside of Albuquerque, New Mexico, 1948

Somewhere in the night back then—possibly later too, there came to me, and still occasionally comes, something unspoken but seen, heard, or simply felt: a sense of the fascination of new beginnings, the beginnings that invite us to be free. They tell that simply by living we are visited by the possibility of freedom each day without knowing how to take it. The moment tells us that we are not merely locksteppers in a constant duty drill but free agents able to erase time for an hour, a day, a year, erase time with full consciousness of who we are. And however locked in we are, or determined to be so, a quick flash of recognition continues to invite us to seize the freedom we abjure.

The recognition may come unannounced in an ordinary glimpse—say, while driving by in a car—of a girl in her early twenties walking, bent, or squatting on the street. And the girl is suddenly transformed into another me, starting out again, desperately wanting things with the ravenous need that will last a lifetime. She becomes some opposite young me in whom I embrace again the lost vision of the burden that comes with freedom—wishing for it and wanting to avoid it, both.

It may be the vision present in Hopkins's recognition of the child's sense of loss in "Spring and Fall": "Márgarét áre you gríeving / Over Golden-grove unleaving?"—writing his lovely statement on the unchangeable periodicity of life and nature. It fully concerns that sense of what at a certain age one must go through with the same puzzlements that both my wives endured (Charlotte, already forty when Margot was turning twenty) and, at different times, observing the way it was with them and unable to affect the outcome beginning to change them: for Margot the divorce that was about to bind instead of free her life; for Charlotte, the cancer that was about to end hers.

The freedom that may have existed for the girl glimpsed from the car, and again for Charlotte and Margot, differently, could only be seized by me in the creative consciousness, the agitation to make life exist in poems, out of the doubts and normal plights of others. "Our doubts," wrote Henry James, "is our passion and our passion is our task. The rest is the madness of art."

We thought we had found our paradise in rural New Mexico but an unexpected invitation uprooted us: the chance to teach at Harvard, and to buy, as it turned out, a small fire-station-red house on Prentiss Street, Cambridge. It was also to become the occasion of my turning into a New Englander, since I have continued living in Massachusetts and Rhode Island to this day. The deciduous (twice renewable) instructorship begun in 1949 became a Briggs-Copeland Assistant Professorship three years later. With the new dignity of the five-year appointment came the chance to teach my own courses in poetry and creative writing, and seminars on allegory and Ben Jonson, all somehow abetted by my random army readings.

Cambridge at the time was full of poets and other writers: Dick Wilbur, Dick Ellmann, Cal Lowell, Dick Eberhart, John Ciardi, Albert Guerard, John Hawkes, May Sarton, Radcliffe Squires, Byron Vazakas, Monroe Engel, and others who would remain unknown to me. Frank O'Hara and John Ashbery were among the undergraduates who, with Violet Lang and Roger Shattuck, started The Poets Theatre, where my one-act play *The Widow,* was given a staged reading in the mid-fifties. With these and other talented youths were some who enlivened my courses: Nora Sayre, Edward Hoagland, Christopher Lasch, Arthur Kopit, Arthur Freeman, Jean Valentine, John Updike.

So it soon appeared that Boston and Cambridge, unlike wartime Washington and postwar New Mexico, were leaping with literati—many escaped from New York, Paris, and London, and others beginning to burgeon more or less on the spot. T. S. Eliot appeared for a while biannually in the mid-fifties, and Auden, Spender, MacNeice, and Dylan Thomas came by more than once. J. Laughlin advised me that in an area of fifteen miles of Boston lived some of the most talented and original minds in the country. I half believed him, though the idea daunted me, being neither a professional scholar nor as yet a semi-known poet. Uneasy about my lack of learning and lack of social savvy, and underscoring in literary gamesmanship, I tended to keep to the side-lines with a few other marginal characters at the time. But there were many memorable meetings with visiting poets, as the one with Wallace Stevens whose unexpected appearance one day in April brought on a lengthy conversation between us that may have been the most illuminating for me during the eight years I spent in Cambridge.

The chance meeting with Stevens occurred during the spring term, 1955. I was teaching the modern poetry course and the class was overcrowded. I had to resort to lecturing, a practice I almost successfully avoided until then. But I had already started on the poetry of Stevens, most of it unread and rarely discussed at the time. While working up my lectures, I had students respond to poems of their own choosing by submitting brief, weekly evaluations on a double set of three-by-five cards. The responses had to be written in terse, telegraphic prose in order to fit the cards. They may have learned a new kind of shorthand doing it, but the pattern of response was in many ways predictable: they were gloatingly familiar with Frost and Cummings, excessively knowledgeable

"With Oscar Williams, in front of my house in Cambridge, Massachusetts," 1954

about Eliot, offended by Pound, baffled by Stevens. One graduate student had warmed up to the long poem "Owl's Clover," almost as though it had been written especially for her. We were conferring over a paper she was planning to do about it.

It was around that time when the annual dinner given by the Board of Visitors to the English Department took place at the Harvard Club in Boston. The Visitors were a mixed group of old grads, mostly former composition students of Copey or Briggs in the twenties—the ghosts most frequently invoked to the detriment of newcomers like me, holding a temporary appointment as the Briggs-Copeland Assistant Professor. Established novelists, publishers, magazine and newspaper editors, they were a liaison group between the Department and the Overseers. During their week at the university each year they visited classes, then presumably told the Overseers about what they saw and heard. They might make a case of the Department's undersupply of graduate fellowships (always painfully scarce)—and this was generally the burden and drift of the professors' afterdinner speeches. The Visitors had the jocular air of successful men of the world, which of course they were, who are temperamentally down on academics, and though joshing them, still regarding the more eminent with obvious respect.

On this occasion, April 11, 1955, cocktails and dinner were confined to a small dining room of the club because of some banquet going on simultaneously in the main dining room. So there was more crowding and jostling than usual and a rather quicker downing of drinks and upsurging of camaraderie. On entering the room I was immediately introduced to Wallace Stevens, present there as a new member of the Board.

A large, heavy, powerful looking man, he struck me as being monolithic, a real lion, an Olympian. I was not prepared for his striking physical appearance. The poet Byron Vazakas, who'd grown up in Reading, Pennsylvania, had spoken of the Stevens brothers in that town, of Wallace Stevens's magisterial manners, of his cheerful but stolid Pennsylvania Dutch taciturnity. John Sweeney, the Poetry Curator, had told me of numerous attempts to bring Stevens to Harvard to read. He had only recently succeeded, as was evident in the Harvard Vocarium record, used later by Caedmon, of a Stevens reading which Richard Wilbur had introduced. It must have been around this time that Archibald MacLeish was trying to get Stevens interested in the Charles Eliot Norton Professorship for the following year. And I, fresh from a long talk with my student about "Owl's Clover," was speaking to the poet who had written it.

Most of the hour or so before dinner we stood shifting a bit near the east wall of the narrow dining room. Though somewhat over six feet tall myself, I had the impression Stevens was a good half-head taller. I recall that at one point in our conversation he interrupted himself to ask, "Who is that man leaning against me?" Someone as tall as Stevens was not so much leaning as now and then rocking back and forth and accidentally brushing shoulders with him. "That's Professor Kenneth Murdock," I said. Murdock, hearing his name spoken, looked towards us surprised. It was then I noticed that Stevens's long impassive cheeks occasionally twitched and trembled uncontrollably.

Earlier, when I'd been introduced, Stevens recognized my name; but it turned out to be Abe Honig, my father, who had been an insurance agent in the early thirties (and who, when later asked, told me he'd never met Stevens, though "the name rang a bell"). Talking about critics, Stevens said, "I used to read my critics at first, but then I stopped because they never seemed to hit it right." Before I could ask him about some of the better ones he went on, "I never read Yvor Winters's piece about me. Isn't he a snob . . . ?" Then, as if to correct himself before the little stain of the word could spread, he added, "Well, no, I respect him—both as a poet and a critic."

I mentioned the new poems William Carlos Williams was then writing, and this brought forth the slowly measured observation, "The young are wild about Williams's new line. What is it, after all, but the old line broken into two or three parts?" I described my students' typical responses to the poets we'd been reading, particularly Eliot and himself, and he replied, "Hugh Kenner wrote in the *Quarterly Review* lately, last month—no, not *Quarterly*, it was *Poetry* magazine (he's about the worst-writing critic there is)—he wrote that Eliot and Pound concentrate on the line. Now I never worried about the line. I've always been interested in the whole thing, the whole poem. Eliot and Pound are very learned, very cultured men, and they put all their culture into the poetry. I never had any to worry about."

That made me think of his "Esthétique du Mal," the poem I'd just assigned the class as a counterbalance to Eliot's "Four Quartets" and an alternative meditation on the Second World War. Some student had questioned the near-uniformity of lines in the long stanzas and sections of the poem. And so I asked Stevens about it. His stanzas were normally quite symmetrical, as in "Notes Toward a Supreme Fiction," for example. But in "Esthétique" the first three sections run to twenty-one lines each, while the remaining twelve sections dilate occasionally to twenty-five and contract to twenty. Was this deliberate?

"The reason for that," he said in his deep, unchanging voice, "is that I was writing on a pad of paper, and the contents of each sheet became a separate stanza. Some had more lines than others—I didn't bother to count them up." I couldn't tell from his voice or facial expression if he was pulling my leg or not. Now my question struck me as being silly. Why had I asked it? Though I thought myself informed, I was certainly no more knowledgeable than my student. It then occurred to me that where a difficult poem is concerned there's no such thing as "the informed reader." The poem reduces us all to being guileless and gullible. Another student-instigated question, about "Owl's Clover," brought the response—rather unreassuring to the student—"I took it out of the *Collected Poems* because it was too rhetorical. Something I wanted very much to write— and I rewrote it, but never really brought it off."

Discussing other places and countries, I mentioned New Mexico and my having lived there for two years just prior to my coming to Cambridge in 1949. He remembered having driven through the state once—the shrubbery, the mountains, the red soil. "Yes, I was out out west once—around 1924—but not on vacation. I've never had a vacation in my life." He stressed that. No vacation. Then what about "venereal Florida?" What about being down in Key West with Hemingway and Frost? But there are questions one does not ask—after a point.

The time came to sit down to dinner. The dapper, white-haired columnist who would be the toastmaster surfaced and was tapping a signal on his water glass just as I had asked something about "The Comedian as the Letter C." "Nobody," Stevens said, "has understood 'The Comedian' very well. I meant the letter *c* to stand for hard and soft sounds both." I mentioned that *crispus*, from which the name Crispin is derived, means "with curls" in Latin. He said he didn't know that. "I just picked the name Crispin because I liked it."

In the vague pressing toward the T-shaped table and chairs Stevens was indicating a place beside him for me when someone abruptly led him away to the other side. Later I heard from Douglas Bush, who had been his dinner companion, that when they'd been introduced Stevens impassively tucking in his napkin intoned, "And I suppose you're an entomologist?"

In 1957 the bell tolled for me at Harvard. It was the final year of my appointment, and I was hired to start a writing program at Brown University. The same year Charlotte's doctor found she had breast cancer. She had done psychological counselling in Boston, and when we moved to Providence, she began work as a psychologist at the Butler Hospital. In 1962, the year before her death, I was lucky to get a second Guggenheim Fellowship. It seemed we could leave Providence and live in the country nearby. Early that spring, on his visit to Brown, I met Saul Bellow who suggested that John Berryman wanted to spend some time in the east, and so it was arranged for him to get leave from the University of Minnesota to come to Brown and take over my courses for the academic year. Bellow had come to discuss the possibility of teaching a mini-course at Brown for a token salary in exchange for a university grant to subsidize the publication of his magazine the *Noble Savage*. But Brown's literature professors chose instead to start *Novel*, a periodical devoted to historical and esthetic studies of the same.

Berryman arrived in Providence in late August 1962, and with Kate, his pregnant young wife, took over our rented house on Congdon Street while Charlotte and I moved into a furnished house in West Woodstock, Connecticut, where we lived until she died there the following April.

From the beginning Charlotte had taken to my writing—more to it, maybe, than to me. Believing I had a gift needing nourishment and support, she often plotted with me in trying for grants with time off for writing. Always my best editor, she spotted the faulty, the clogged, the overly decorative, and the sentimental twist wherever they occurred. We fought over each instance in my work but invariably ended by rooting out the offensive element. She had a stubborn belief in the validity of language to express what was expressible, totally, and without subterfuge. Her vehemence often surprised me, but it was the same vehemence she voiced against the phoniness in people we both knew. She was convinced I could get things written, no matter how complex or how long it took to get right, if I worked hard enough. It took ten years and almost two dozen drafts to round out *Dark Conceit*, the allegory book—not only because the subject was abstruse and manifold, but also because I was more the callow adventurer—like Spenser's Red Cross Knight, "a tall clownish young man . . . falling before the queen of fairies"—than the real professional at the scholarly game. Although I gave up every year, ego-bruised and in despair, having quarreled with her over every sentence, the book was published—unbelievably!—in 1959.

Her lifelong difficulties with a demanding grandmother and a wandering, psychotic mother, along with her preoccupations over a lost father, often kept Charlotte from demonstrating and developing her own gifts. She was a warm-spirited, serious woman with a wildly theoretical but quite logical mind that constantly questioned people and demanded explanations regardless of age, status, or authority. She had few close friends, being socially shy, defensive, and mostly withdrawn at parties. She worked long hours at home on her diagnostic reports, having little confidence in their efficacy, disturbed by the terminology she was expected to use, and trying to circumvent jargon in favor of something plainspoken of her own.

As her cancer spread, leaving her maimed and exhausted with pain, she often wrote in snatches. She also had me read to her—novels, plays, and frequently poems I'd been trying to write. She died one morning while I went out to get her a glass of water after having read her a poem she said she liked. She was forty-seven, and we had been married twenty-three years. The doctor couldn't say if it was the cancer or the medication that killed her.

In June I went off to Portugal and Spain, retracing the route I had taken with Charlotte in 1958. I went to Lisbon, then down along the coast to Sagres and stayed at the Penguin Inn in Praia da Rocha (where, incidentally, I then heard of the poet Fernando Pessoa from a drunken fisherman who recited Pessoa's verses at the bar). From there I went through most of the Algarve, turned north through the Alentejo and drove back again to Lisbon. I proceeded to Madrid and Barcelona, and took the overnight ferry to Palma de Mallorca. I rounded the island and stayed briefly in Puerto Alcudia, where we'd lived the fall and winter of '58–'59, and returned to spend the early summer in Palma. Now my notion was to buy an orange orchard in Israel and divide my time between Rhode Island and the orange business each year. But before the year was up I'd returned to Brown and, after having met Margot Dennes at a party at the Robert Lowells' in New York, I married her two months later. That December, Hi Sobiloff, the merchant poet friend of Oscar Williams, threw us a sumptuous party in his town house in the Upper Sixties; the Berrymans came, also the Ellisons, the Eric Bentleys, the Doctorows, and a hundred other well-wishers.

Margot and I spent the following summer in a primitive house off Lake Atitlán, Guatemala. We walked shoeless to town, fording streams under the towering aguacate trees where tiny Indian children watched us carrying our big shoes. " *¡Mira los gigantes!*" ("Look at the giants!"). I know that much of the mail to and from the States never arrived because the stamps were ripped off at the local post office, their value often exceeding a postal employee's daily salary there in Panajachel, Guatemala. For this reason I had not learned of Oscar Williams's terminal illness until we had returned to the States in September.

I was to teach a year at the University of California in Davis where Brom Weber, my high-school classmate, was chairman of English. I lived with Margot in a small rented house near the tracks where the locomotive thundered into our kitchen daily like a heavy hobo, shunting freight cars at the doorstep. I walked to class under blossoming fruit and nut trees lining the streets along the tracks. Margot's parents lived in Berkeley, where she had grown up and where her father, Will Dennes, the philosopher, was dean of the Graduate School. While visiting them and later traveling long the coast, we discovered Bodega, a small ranching community five miles inland from the Bay. Both were sites for Alfred Hitchcock's popular thriller *The Birds.* There we rented Louis Albini's old ranch house, with three hundred working acres of livestock pasturage and surrounding sheds.

I'd begun work again on literary projects; the most pressing was the long poem *Four Springs,* eventually published as a book in 1972. The immediate provocation for doing a poem of that length grew out of a realization that much of my significant (at least, dramatic) experience over the years had not found its way into poetry. Some of the material had crept into a few short stories and one aborted novel. Attempts to use historical events had dredged up matters that needed attention in my other writings. In the sixties and early seventies, with the renewed holocaust war in Vietnam and the assassinations of the Kennedys, an urgent sense of political reality forced itself on me, as it had done once before, in the thirties. I saw that the Depression, the Second World War, and my troubles with government bureaucracy ("Have you ever been taken for somebody else and felt / the oddness of being, / even briefly, not yourself?"—from *Four Springs*) had cleared an area for something unprecedented in my poetry. Instead of angling in the old Eliotic backwaters of loss and dismemberment, seeking for retrievals out of the past ("These fragments I have shored against my ruins"), I discovered in current history new imaginative potencies of terror and beauty.

I envisaged the possibilities of a poetic form offering almost infinite extensibility. The note that heads *Four Springs* alludes to these matters:

In 1966 or so I began writing a poem that very soon went beyond my conception of where or when it would end. To cope with its extensibility and rein it in as it galloped

The author with Brom Weber, Davis, California, 1979

along, I made up a flexible long-and-short line combination, a five- alternating with a two-stress line. I did not think of it deliberately at the time, but I may have been remembering something of those loose long forms which Louis MacNeice adapted to everyday subjects in *Autumn Journal*, a poem I loved immediately when I read it at nineteen.

The scheme accommodates a variety of inset poems, like the dream enactment of my brother Stanley's death ("Spring Two," 9); another relates the death of Charlotte ("Spring Two," 14). I invent poems in which a personal past achieves new focus through the historical present. The prospect offers an unusual means of creating poetic belief. As a poem framed in terms of public events, *Four Springs* deals with the crucial happenings of personal history interlinked with world events covering half a century.

The first part ("Spring One") appeared in a book in 1968 with other poems under the title *Spring Journal: Poems.* Three other parts were added in 1972 to form *Four Springs.* By then my imaginative projections, along with great shifts in world events, were being dispersed over new areas of concern—the end of the Vietnam War, the election of Nixon, the breakup of my marriage. The poem drew the encouragement of fellow poets; some saw in the openness of the long poem something analogous to what Lorca had once called, in his later work, "my opening-of-the-veins poetry." Others, including former students and some colleagues who'd found my work till then

"obscure," were pleased to praise the "lucidity" of the long poem in which they found substance they could identify with. Good, I thought, maybe I've really broken through to the legendary "average reader." But the work was clearly not going to be infinitely extensible along the lines in which it had been conceived. Other work was pressing.

For one, I had to return to Calderón de la Barca, both to the translations and to the book about the plays. *Life Is a Dream*, the last of my translations of Calderón's five plays, done in Spain and Portugal, was actually completed to accompany my insomnia brought on by a spell of asthma while living in Pragal, across the Tagus River from Lisbon. As a sequel, I wrote a book about honor *(Calderón and the Seizures of Honor)*, the principal theme of the plays. In addition, *Calisto and Melibea*, a libretto I had adapted from Fernando Rojas's sixteenth-century Spanish novel *La Celestina*, was being set to music by the composer Jerome Rosen in Davis, California, and was later performed there. I also saw through the press at that time the first of my translations of Portugal's best modern poet, Fernando Pessoa. In the next seventeen years I went on to publish three other books of Pessoa translations.

B ut to return to Brown in the mid-sixties:

When in the summer of 1965 it became clear we'd go back to Providence and I'd resume teaching at Brown, I was ready to join others seeking to improve the environment in literary studies. I'd been hesitant about starting anything new, half-hoping to find a job in attractive northern California, but while there I'd made few attempts to inquire, enjoying a new marriage and the convincing Mediterranean ethos.

Brown, a fairly conservative school, was slow to move in a new direction, having had a tradition of paternalistic presidents and deans. But the presidency of Barnaby Keeney had begun to favor the humanities. Keeney was later to go to Washington as the first Director of the National Endowment for the Arts and the Humanities. In any case, Brown was at least not averse to considering new ideas in the humanities since it had been so headstrong in the sciences, especially applied mathematics and engineering. The administration had supported my choice of John Hawkes as a second writing teacher in 1958 and had agreed in principle to the practice of giving more frequent leaves to creative writers. It was also following through on a plan, initiated by Juan López Morillas and me, to enlarge the comparative literature offerings and create a full-fledged department. I drew into the department the noted Hispanist Alan Trueblood, and together we began to give courses in literary translation. Subsequently the brilliant Renaissance scholar Rosalie Colie joined the department and became a dynamic chairperson. Her ill-timed death drew a good deal of the life and possibility out of whatever accomplishments we had rallied to make by 1972.

While Jack Hawkes was changing colors and turning into a tenured professor, I began to look for other writers to join us in what was becoming known then as "a writing program." Earlier in California I'd met James Schevill, poet and playwright, who was a codirector of graduate writing at San Francisco State College. Now he was persuaded to come to Brown with his wife, the opera singer Margot Blum. In 1967, I volunteered to head the English Department, although for one year only. I was accepted and given the opportunity, as the last of Brown's traditional autocratic chairmen, to hire a breed of young professors that would make a difference. Among them were: a flaming painter with a Ph.D. in English (Brent Harold); a former lawyer and new Ph.D. (Roger Henkle); a poet publisher from Wesleyan University (Keith Waldrop and Burning Deck), and a well-known fiction writer and Iowa workshop teacher (R. V. Cassill). When Michael Harper, the poet, George Bass, the playwright-theatre director, and Barry Beckham, the young novelist, were added the following year, Brown had a full stable of writers and—as one old prof was overheard to remark sorrowfully—"would never be the same again."

Once, some years before, when we were casting about for a bright particular star to add to the comparative literature staff, and I had suggested the Chilean poet Nicanor Parra, my colleague Leicester Bradner, the Elizabethan and neo-Latin specialist, burst out impatiently, "Oh, Edwin, you're always thinking of hiring poets!" I felt a momentary rush of sympathy for Bradner. What if I were the world's authority on the poems of Queen Elizabeth I, and some of her worthies in the cool tombs, how would I take this crazy Honig and his insuppressible passion for alive-and-kicking anarchic poets? I'd no doubt think like him: too many writers, too few scholars, though of course there were others who were both, like Albert Cook and Willis Barnstone. But this wasn't the precise answer. The answer was—especially then, in the sixties it was—to provide the school with "a radiant and productive atmosphere." It was why Brown's president, Barnaby Keeney, had approved my appointment in 1957; Keeney liked my plans to build a program that would include teachers of literature who were also practitioners of literature. In

any case, by the time Mark Spilka, my successor as head of English, had served his five-year term, solidifying and amplifying such developments, the department had become a different and most particularly luminous part of the establishment.

My administrative functions, as department head (very brief glory) and as codirector of the writing program with Jim Schevill, were ended by 1971–72. I returned more fully to my own writing.

The suicide of John Berryman coincided with a collection of orphic poems I had been writing. These I collected with an earlier verse play *Orpheus Below*—once published in a New Directions Annual—in a book called *Shake a Spear with Me, John Berryman* (probably a weak pun on a sympathy shared, since Berryman had been writing a book on Shakespeare). My book was retitled subsequently, *The Affinities of Orpheus.* I had gone back to using a short gnomic line and writing more lyric, nontopical, quietistic poems. I also brought out a *Selected Poems* and a collection of short, loosely connected fictions I called *The Foibles and Fables of an Abstract Man.* The orphic poems and the fictional pieces were no doubt colored by the long sad unraveling of my marriage with Margot and separation from our two young sons, Daniel (born 1966) and Jeremy (born 1967).

Other projects included a number of translations. In addition to the *Selected Poems of Fernando Pessoa,* there was a reworking of an earlier set of Lorca

The Honig family in Cranston, Rhode Island, 1968: Edwin, Daniel, Margot, and Jeremy

pieces: his last collection of twenty Arabigo-Andalusian poems called *The Divan at the Tamarit*. To these I added several short dramatic pieces, a story, and a puppet play. The book was called *Divan and Other Writings*. I began a long difficult translation, with Alan Trueblood, of Lope de Vega's autobiographical novel *La Dorotea*. We worked sporadically on it for several years, then more closely, though still mostly in patches, time taken from academic vacations and weekends, and some intensive periods here and there, as at the Virginia Center, the artist colony at Mount San Angelo, and a month or so in Cálig, a small Mediterranean town not far from Valencia, Spain. It wasn't till 1985 that the work, in all its baroque splendor (and never before translated fully into English or any other language) began to take final shape. Of all of Lope's prodigious literary works—four hundred and more plays, epic and lyric poetry, pastoral novels—*La Dorotea* is his most revealing personal invention, a novel in dialogue inset with thirty-two poems of various lengths and several hundred proverbs, both traditional and made-to-order by Lope himself. As a fiction based on an incident in Lope's early professional life when he was an up-and-coming young dramatist in Madrid, it also contains stream-of-consciousness devices used by few other writers until the modern period. When Harvard University Press published our translation in 1985, its reception as a literary event was as noticeable as a pearl earring dropped in the corner of a plush carpet at the Metropolitan Opera in New York.

Other collaborations during this period of the

Edwin Honig and Alan S. Trueblood, cotranslators of
La Dorotea, *by Lope de Vega, 1984*

seventies were more open, more public: the founding of a small publishing venture, Copper Beech Press, in 1973, and the inauguration of an informal play production group, Wastepaper Theatre.

"Spirit spirit / lord of this place / flame in the center / father of our world / with your eight winds / eight corners of our world / draw near now / help us." These are the first words published by Copper Beech, part of a poem from a book of Northwest Coast Indian shaman songs, freely adapted by the young poet David Cloutier in his collection *Spirit Spirit*. I remember that the first glimpse of his manuscript brought these words to me like an arrow. Cloutier conveys the magic of the shaman's song out of a tame anthropological text into an equivalent verbal context and charm-set no doubt intended by the original singer, the "root of the cry." With the aid of an older graduate student, Harry Reese, interested in printing (and now, incidentally, publisher of his own Turkey Press, an elegant hand-printing establishment in Isla Vista, California), Copper Beech was started. Since most commercial publishers let into their small stable of poets very few new ones every five or ten years, and as the population grows and new poets multiply, where will they be published? And with poets living longer, where will the old ones publish? Launched with a private contribution of $1,200, Copper Beech published over forty titles in its first decade. Publishing new volumes of poetry was the first concern, but also on the list were two books of short fiction, two novels, and several books of translation. It has become a commonplace since to observe that through translation the possibilities of writing in our own language are expanded; by the actual re-creation of a work in English, the roots of our own tongue are enriched.

James Schevill, David Cloutier, and I were the working editors, with the production aspects of management in the hands of Cloutier. Schevill's view that cultural emphasis in theatre and poetry was shifting from cosmopolitan to regional centers—a view held by many subsequently—was confirmed at Copper Beech. We published the new poetry of Jane Miller and Paul Petrie, and the Chinese translations of David Lattimore, writers who with Schevill himself have commanded national attention. We were on the way to publishing the new poet Robert Pinsky's first book when news came that he'd won the first Princeton Poetry Series prize, and we yielded our priority on the manuscript to the more prestigious press, as Pinsky wished.

Generally in each instance of accepting a manuscript there was the pleasure of evolving the physical book from the beginning. This was a process I had not experienced before: books being made in the correspondence that ensued between the author and the editors. To this collaborative editing the concluding act was the discovery of a new organic entity when the contents of the work fell into place. It was not all a bed of roses, but many of the roses were real. When I retired from Brown in 1983, I gave the press over to Mutlu Blasing, of the English Department, once a student of mine, and to the poet teacher Randy Blasing, her husband. Like the tree outside my window after which the press was named, it is still very much alive today.

The other public literary development of the seventies was the co- (or *con*) founding in Providence of the Wastepaper Theatre, a pseudoGoethean, environmental product of James Schevill, Keith and Rosmarie Waldrop, and myself. We had in common an uncommon desire: to enjoy the company of each other's inventions in a setting free from cant, commerce, and coercion of any kind. A free theatre, in which to present fresh, original—often just-completed—plays to be performed in any drawing room, sculpture garden, film-studio loft or, if nothing better offered itself, an auditorium: such were our immodest aims.

"Mock heroic, spastic Quixotes," I wrote, "in love with the language of comic deployment," the plays I hatched and had the gall to publish later, as *Ends of the World and Other Plays* (against the proscription inherent in the Theatre's name), were in principle like those by my fellow playwrights, "pieces that take off from contemporary events, with the grandiose lurking in the commonplace, to light up the very places where vital concerns are often discarded." And so much for wastepaper! If stages and prefaces to books of plays are often the places for sounding off, I was then satisfying a craving without too much concern for the literary consequences.

The Waldrops, Schevill, and Honig kept at it each year and each season, as we and the Theatre together advanced (in age, albeit), while an inveterate audience of housewives, children, pets and other professionals appeared out of the Providence fog, just before Christmas or right after Easter—and continues to do so to date.

Perhaps a shorter act of public collaboration, though extending up to a decade as well, was the gathering of my conversations with eleven notable literary figures, mainly poets, on their practice as translators. The initial contacts had been made in the late 1970s, but the process of tape editing, the reorganizing of the pieces, and the writing of introduction and conclusion had lagged because of the

discouraging response to the project from the handful of publishers most likely to favor it. Who would buy such a book, they asked? And, "we cannot consider manuscripts that have evolved from conversations among participants, no matter how eminent." I was sorry to hear this, I wrote back, because in that case the publisher would have had to turn down Plato's *Dialogues*. Finally a young (and, as one used to say, "courageous") publisher, Bruce Wilcox, of the University of Massachusetts Press, brought the book into being in 1986: *The Poet's Other Voice: Conversations on Literary Translation.*

In 1978 I had a thirteen-weeks' stay at the Mishkenot Sha'ananim, the international artist—and intellectual—colony in Jerusalem, under the nominal supervision of the Mayor, Teddy Kollek. Since Jerusalem is my father's birthplace, he still counts heavily on visiting his Israeli cousins while there. I learned for the first time, on his eightieth birthday, what his particular sense of "roots" must be. He lived in a modified state of euphoria among an extended family, in which the nation of Israel itself was always on the verge of being included. But when asked if he would like to take up residence there again, he thought the idea slightly preposterous, since he regards himself "first and foremost a loyal American." Although only a boy of thirteen when he left for America in 1910, he could still make himself understood in Arabic and Hebrew, and so felt at home wherever he went. He showed me the buildings where his family had lived, where his brother Hyman had kept a pigeon cote, and where his eldest sibling, Fanny, had learned how to sew from a seamstress in the Old City. He prayed at the holy places; he showed his affectionate and generous nature by leaving gifts of all sorts among relatives and their friends wherever he visited. They in turn met him with unrestrained fondness and amusement, indulging his penchant for family storytelling, and countering it with an endless line of their own. As a child I found his demonstrative nature hard to take; now I observed that it was by no means a singular trait but characteristic of the Mediterranean disposition everywhere, particularly there in the Levant.

As a child I habitually withdrew from most emotional displays of any sort since I felt implicated, or about to be victimized, by them. Now again, alone in Israel, I kept mostly to myself while at Mishkenot, preferring to work days and nights on *Aging Embryo,* a novel I have yet to finish satisfactorily, and abjured visits, social engagements, and the little pleasures of foreign travel. The one public appearance I made was to speak to an audience of writers, diplomats, and academics about the problematic coincidence of fame

"My father, Abraham Honig, as a cantor in Florida, eighty-three years old," 1980

and suicide among well-known contemporary poets: Hart Crane, John Berryman, Sylvia Plath, Randall Jarrell, Anne Sexton, and others. The main question implicit in my rambling presentation was this: Why in the world's richest nation in the twentieth century do such poets have (and fulfill) the overwhelming yearning to do themselves in? Something in our culture incites the talented Sextons and Berrymans to wallow in the pathos of their fame in order to gain a large public following, like all the dead young rock stars and actors of recent years. I did not think that drugs, alcohol, "the curse of sundered parentage," or any bad genetic inheritance, alone or in combination, was the answer. There was something else at fault, some indefinable element in America itself that is lethal to talent and its development or pursuit. Few in the audience, which included the philosopher Walter Kaufmann and the Israeli poet Dan Pagis (now both dead), seemed inclined to entertain my questions directly. Then after a prolonged silence, I invited one and all to a party in my quarters. The party was a total success.

I know that I have strayed in a good part of this narrative from my initial resolve to embody the

facts out of lost events and, in effect, failed "to tell the truth." We all know how the manysidedness of experience repels the mere recounting of stories in pursuit of plain facts or the flat truth. Not long ago I discussed such matters with a young writer (call her Kora), known for her published memoirs and the autobiographical nature of her poetry. When I met Kora we seemed to understand in the same way the sorts of things that go into the making of a genuine literary work—and this feeling warranted our keeping up a correspondence thereafter.

In one letter I spoke of the writer's need "to be true, down to the bone, in the life and in the writing," assuming the one cannot help but affect the other. But even as I repeat the caution now I feel that I am overstepping whatever authority is needed to be convincing. Perhaps it's less the achievement of intense truth-telling than the ability to sustain the possibility that matters.

I want to be true. I try to make it so. I score against myself if I falter or noticeably dismount from my honorable (think of Pegasus) true-white steed. "So it's all right," I tell myself, "you're not being dishonest now or very far from the mark: you're taking a side-road to it." If it were a matter of willing it so, I'd exercise the necessary power, I know. But the other relevant aspect of this endeavor is the technique, the ability to trim and sharpen the writing, tone it up or down, according to one's experience over the years. Here I must say I don't quite know enough to determine what enforces such ability. So let me try using Kora's experience to make the point. (Of course, it's easier to find the fault in someone else's writing than in one's own, particularly through the living character of the person and the work known to you for a long time.)

Kora asks if what her friend Alma says is true about Kora's going off the deep end every time her writing becomes precious. I'm impelled to agree as it concerns the writing and the person both. Kora's gift of exuberance, overflow, abundance, identifies her in the quick outgoing process of word-dancing. One word leads to another. There is a trickle, then a stream, then a joyous but calculated flow. Spectacular! It looks and feels like the real thing, truly.

Perhaps it's a matter of temperament, and the same kind of exuberance is to be found in Dickens, in Thomas Wolfe, in Whitman, in Ginsberg even. But in Kora it's not the exuberance itself that may offend, but the style of its usage. And Kora herself may be admitting as much when she says that what her father dislikes in her writing is that she is always putting herself "on top of the situation," lording it over the thing she's describing. She calls this, playing the ingenue—and I suppose it's true, if they are talking about the same thing.

I don't care for the way she inserts herself deliberately into the first part of her long review of a recent suicide poet's *Journals*. When I tell her this, I also warn her that I was schooled in the New Criticism, whose primary law is that the poet's life and what he or she creates as art are two distinct things and must never be allowed to meet in the process of evaluating the art. But again, this is perhaps a matter of temperament. Red won't act Blue; Blue won't be caught dead being Red—though any real chameleon wouldn't have much of a problem on that score.

Something else is at issue: call it the manner or spirit of the times. Because of all the swift changes, the mass dying and brutality, the holocausts of so many peoples in contemporary history, any writing that shows insensitivity to such matters must be declared suspect, if not intolerable.

To get back to the bone-truth: when, where, and how is it to be created? Magic will help; nothing great is done without some magic. But that's not all; all is many things. And perhaps even Kafka was fudging when he was being clearest and truthfulest, down-to-the-bone. The "truth" is that we cannot even know it, trying to be truer than we are. Being such impersonators, we have stuffed so much fiddle-faddle of what we call "natural" about ourselves into creating the usable style and thrust and trick of the persona that we rarely recognize that, or how, we have phonied and failed.

The twenty-fifth chapter of Ernst Pawel's life of Kafka, *The Nightmare of Reason,* describes the impact truth-telling made on him, particularly in his relationship with Milena. What emerges from the grand letters and exchanges between them, from their intuitive and educated understanding both, is something that suddenly explodes their intense relationship. It is the understanding itself that *misunderstands,* cutting them off and bringing them up sharply and back to where they started, as strangers to one another. The real has emerged, with the illusion-of-the-real groveling before it.

At the end of his life, Kafka was reading Jonathan Swift. He delighted to point out to his sister Ottla that Swift agreed with him about child-rearing. But Swift agreed even more than Kafka knew, being like himself a despairing soul, constantly deriding himself for being unable to accept his own truth, even when he had discovered a totally loving companion.

Concerning such painful discoveries, I often ask how—out of what immense patience of heart, strength of body, trick of the genes—did Jane, my mother, who died immediately in 1984 of a massive stroke, manage to live her eighty-four years without caving in earlier, undergoing the misery that kept humming to and through her, like a sweetheart, all her life, telling her the lies about herself which she willed herself to believe, keeping her subservient to her intensely cloddish, disagreeable, counter-life parents, brothers, husbands—how did she manage to survive, what truth was she seeking, what peace did she ever find in being herself? What was she seeking? Love? Some response from children, any children, as she got older? Well, no—that's not convincing enough. She kept pulling herself away from involvements too. But she did take herself in hand: first, after her second marriage came apart; then, again, after her terrible, slave-driving, browbeating brother died. She made a father-authority out of the "good Lord," and came to Providence to live and be near me—though never too near, or near enough, fearing to be hurt again. Housebound in her small apartment, she prayed and kept away from people as long as she could, at least from empty, bossy neighbors. Even so, the wrong ones came to her, when she was in need, and made things worse. So she played the piano or, as she said, she "practiced" it. And when I

"My mother, Jane," 1938

brought an occasional friend around, she gave us a recital—some Beethoven, some Mozart, a hymn. We applauded. "You liked it?" She swept her falling braid back. "Listen to this—it's Brahms—I've been practicing for weeks, and still don't have it right. Be patient with me." Maybe practicing the piano was her way of looking for "the truth," something better than looking for love, because in practicing one just gives what one has to give, never mind what one gets in return.

Maybe the same goes for Kora: the genie for her, the trick of being, is what she enacts or personifies as *it* knows how, or "how best," to do. What's called "the quest for truth" or "the brush with the unspeakable" may only be highsounding phrases used to show how much we sweat while covering up reality as it naturally is, things as they are, things that we yearn more intuitively and more directly to express. And the so-called techniques are only what we often frantically learn to use in order to deal with what we have no choice but to express. Maybe this great mind-questing labor spent on unfolding the selfness of consciousness is, after a point, no longer a skating on ice but a using up of the skates' sharpness, clean-edgedness, the sad bounty of overly expressed effort to make figures on ice.

In a recent letter Kora described her "day": one part spent shopping for a dress fuses with another part spent listening to a benefit poetry reading lasting two-and-a-half hours. And she records, out of vexed impatience with herself, all the possible reactions she might have had to what she allowed herself to do with her time. The drama of consciousness, as it unrolls untended, and then tended for the use of oneself alone, becomes the great solitary amusement of the self and its few precious friends, whoever they may be. I admire the consciousness being tended and masterfully expressed in its details and contents. I enjoy and encourage, when I can, its genuine uses. But I also ask, toward what end? A great wounded solipsism? A spidery tautology? To express is its own end, like using the lungs simply and automatically to breathe.

At some point in the seventies, perhaps a bit earlier, it seemed that something of the quality one took for granted in students entering an ivy league school was atrophying. Fewer came with literary interests grounded in premodern literature or in the major authors in English, never mind any other literature. Few showed any feeling for language, and those who did seldom thought it necessary to improve their acquaintance with other literatures and languages. Students at Brown were bright as ever but there was less joy in teaching them because what they did not know and had to make up before going further did not seem to challenge them. Nothing inside or outside required them to know more; the fun and savor had gone out of the idea "Gladly would I learn and gladly teach."

I'd begun teaching at Purdue in the fall of 1942, and the year was now, suddenly, 1982. Some writers I knew, many in the academy, had died on the brink of their retirement. I saw that if I were going to follow through on plans to catch up with my writing I should be freer to use my time. Another long poem was emerging, *Gifts of Light*, which began to draw on my energies. I was sixty-two: the bell rang to close the door on teaching. So I departed from Brown and Providence in that same year and moved to a small house on Newport's First Beach. The place was full of bathers and summer people in summer, almost deserted in winter. One Christmas day the ocean steamed like freshly cooking gelatine under constantly sweeping, thin veils of mist. Gulls let themselves be blown around in great updrafts and downpourings of air, like pieces of gray paper, never landing. Later I learned that the effect is called Arctic mist, and the temperature was seven below zero. When spring came, the beach was strewn with long carpets of microscopic copper-colored algae, locally referred to as "the red tide." I could no longer walk in solitary splendor since the effluence of the tide choked my lungs and sent me breathless indoors for days.

I sold the Newport house and moved to a rented apartment in Providence near the university. After my mother died in April 1984, I went off to China with a fairly congenial company of elderly widows, middle-aged professional couples, a few academics and their wives, a brace of college students, and one retired merchant mariner named Ed.

I thought of Kafka when I visited the Great Wall. Like a newly rediscovered bazaar teeming with international tourists, the Wall spoke to me in his words: "Human nature, essentially changeable, unstable as the dust, can endure no restraint; if it binds itself, it soon begins to tear madly at the bonds, and its very self." (tr. E. and W. Muir) Man, who makes such a wall *for* himself, also makes a wall *of* himself. He becomes the wall he makes, which continues to stand, unless he destroys it, ages past his lifetime on earth. The wall becomes his monument, his final residue. Now, perhaps, the news is widely known that the Great Wall of China is the only man-made object visible from the moon (at last sighting, that is).

In 1984 the Chinese reminded me of the first Spaniards I encountered in Spain in 1957. Both peoples have a similarly long, sentimental heritage of solicitous care for superficial details, which invests their fervid politeness with a strong abiding sense of duty, generosity, pride, and distrust of foreigners.

On July 4, we had come up from Souzhou to climb the Yellow Mountain, five miles up and down. In Souzhou we had visited a wrought-iron-picture workshop. I noted down my impressions of the art work: something to the effect that it is an art that overcomes supreme difficulties one prefers it would not have dealt with. The thought immediately occurs that someone must surely have said this about the novels of Henry James!

From Souzhou we traveled eight hours by train to make the winding trek up the mountain in rain and mist all the way. The rain often poured down mercilessly. On the way, through my fever and vertigo, I repeated tirelessly the old line from Heraclitus, "The way up and the way down are the same way." But I was wrong. The way down, I discovered, was worse, infinitely worse.

On top of Yellow Mountain there was a melting-pot hotel bristling with local and international climbers, coughing, spitting, farting. In the big communal bathroom, there was no running water. As soon as we arrived I plopped into bed, unable to rise for the evening meal. My room-mate Richard, the twenty-five-year-old adolescent clown, kindly brought me a plate of supper. Still half-asleep I rose, changed clothes, went into the washroom. Meeting my tour companions there, I made civil sounds to reassure them, undressed, went back to bed, and fell asleep to the sound of small firecrackers and drunken song appropriate to American Independence Day in the courtyard. I slept heavily, like a keg of rusty nails, but still not long or fully enough, because when I woke I was still semi-conscious and totally unprepared for the descent.

Going down the same mountain differently, I learned I had a fierce nay-sayer inside me, cursing, resistant, rebellious. *He* wanted to give up and not budge again: become stone. *His* bones locked, his muscles flowing into his liquified shoes. The steps down were more numerous and steeper than any of the steps upward. *He* carried a plain bamboo stick he'd bought somewhere for ten cents. Perversely it failed to support him, so heavy was his downgoing body. The stick was a surly weapon, erratic pseudo-friend, intent on misleading his steps, a drunk buffoon staggering into smiling Japanese tourists coming up. Passing a small waterfall, I threw it away. It had begun to knock things down, turning into an eye-poking assailant of innocent children. The action freed me immediately; I stopped to notice that on the way down, as on the climb up, there shone through shafts of intermittent sunlight, the beauty of the mist, the rocks, the trees, the waterfalls—with their mythic names and shapes often more sensed than seen, as if perceived through the skin or the tips of one's hair,

In Little Compton, Rhode Island, 1981

even as the dulled, recalcitrant body rebelled. *Truth to tell*, had it not been for the college student and fellow tourist John Vergola, who patiently accompanied me and would not leave me, I would never have gotten down in one piece.

Now it turns out that I've been left standing long enough to write this piece, which is itself a way of downing the nay-sayer inside me. And besides, whatever art still remains to be practiced alongside the pencil sharpener, I shall meanwhile do what I once threatened to do (at the end of "Spring One" of *Four Springs*):

                                        jump into my pants,
run out and dance
in the foggy streets of Providence, play God—
maybe bring out the sun!

BIBLIOGRAPHY

Poetry:

The Moral Circus. Baltimore: Contemporary Poetry, 1955.

The Gazabos: Forty-one Poems. New York: Clarke & Way, 1959; also published as *The Gazabos: Forty-one Poems* [and] *The Widow: A Verse Play in One Act.* New York: Clarke & Way, 1961.

Poems for Charlotte. Privately printed, 1963.

Survivals. New York: October House, 1964.

Spring Journal. Providence: Hellcoal Press, 1968.

Spring Journal: Poems. Middletown, Conn.: Wesleyan University Press, 1968.

Four Springs. Chicago: Swallow Press, 1972.

At Sixes. Providence: Burning Deck, 1974.

Shake a Spear with Me, John Berryman. Providence: Copper Beech Press, 1974; also published as *The Affinities of Orpheus.* Providence: Copper Beech Press, 1976.

Selected Poems 1955–1976. Dallas: Texas Center for Writers Press, 1979.

Gifts of Light. Isla Vista, Calif.: Turkey Press, 1983.

Interrupted Praise: New and Selected Poems. Metuchen, N.J.: Scarecrow Press, 1983.

Fiction:

The Foibles and Fables of an Abstract Man. Providence: Copper Beech Press, 1979.

Plays:

Calisto and Melibea: A Play in Verse. Providence: Hellcoal Press, 1972.

Ends of the World and Other Plays. Providence: Copper Beech Press, 1983.

Art Book:

Cow Lines, with Jean Zaleski. Providence: Copper Beech Press, 1982.

Nonfiction:

García Lorca. Norfolk, Conn.: New Directions, 1944; London: Nicholson & Watson, 1945; revised edition. Norfolk, Conn.: New Directions, 1963; London: J. Cape, 1968; New York: Octagon Books, 1981.

Dark Conceit: The Making of Allegory. Evanston, Ill.: Northwestern University Press, 1959; London: Faber, 1960; Dartmouth: University Press of New England, 1981.

Calderón and the Seizures of Honor. Cambridge: Harvard University Press, 1972.

The Poet's Other Voice: Conversations on Literary Translation. Amherst: University of Massachusetts Press, 1986.

Translator of:

The Cave of Salamanca, by Miguel de Cervantes Saavedra. Boston: Chrysalis, 1960.

Calderón: Four Plays (*Secret Vengeance for Secret Insult, Devotion to the Cross, The Mayor of Zalamea, The Phantom Lady*), by Pedro Calderón de la Barca. New York: Hill & Wang, 1961.

Cervantes: Eight Interludes, by Miguel de Cervantes Saavedra. New York: New American Library, 1964.

Life Is a Dream, by Pedro Calderón de la Barca. New York: Hill & Wang, 1970.

Selected Poems of Fernando Pessoa. Chicago: Swallow Press, 1971.

Divan and Other Writings, by Federico García Lorca. Providence: Bonewhistle Press, 1974; Providence: Copper Beech Press, 1976.

La Dorotea, by Lope de Vega, translated with Alan S. Trueblood. Cambridge: Harvard University Press, 1985.

The Keeper of Sheep, by Fernando Pessoa, translated with S. M. Brown. New York: Sheep Meadow Press, 1986.

Poems of Fernando Pessoa, translated with S. M. Brown. New York: Ecco Press, 1986.

Always Astonished: Selected Prose, by Fernando Pessoa. San Francisco: City Lights, 1988.

Editor of:

The Mentor Book of Major American Poets, with Oscar Williams. New York: New American Library, 1962.

Edmund Spenser. New York: Dell, 1968.

The Major Metaphysical Poets of the Seventeenth Century, with Oscar Williams. New York: Washington Square Press, 1968.

Judson Jerome

1927-

Judson Jerome with Marty, Yellow Springs, Ohio, 1986

Discharged from the United States Air Force in 1946, I thought first that I would go back to college. I had had two years at the University of Oklahoma before being drafted. The campus had few students in 1943–1945, mostly women, and seemed a friendly place. But when I went back to Norman to visit it and found it teeming with Real Men—veterans puffing jaunty pipes, leather cases for slide rules slapping on their massive thighs—I decided it was time to go East and become a writer. I was just a little guy. I had started college at sixteen, looking eleven, five feet tall, weighing a hundred pounds, and a year in the occupation force on Okinawa hadn't done much to change my physical appearance or level of maturity. But I was ready, anyway, to leave behind the Southwest where I had grown up.

The East was to me the land of the pale and the literate, the sophisticated and sinful, the mandarins who, thin and yellow, were familiar with evil and ruled the nation with elegant cynicism and culture. They probably all knew "Prufrock" by heart. (My major literary achievement to date had been to learn that poem.) I still could not be served in bars. In the East, I figured, everyone was served in bars. They were above Tchaikovsky and Aldous Huxley and Thomas Wolfe, and I was trying very hard to get above such cultural figures. I was trying to get above Gershwin and Kenneth Roberts. I was trying to advance from Will Rogers to Thurber. I didn't know whether they would let me in the East, but I wanted to go there to endure the damnation real writers endure, to answer the Call of the Tame shouting in my heart, "Go East, young man!"

So I went to the Oklahoma City depot and asked the price of a one-way ticket to New York. Sixty dollars. How about Chicago? I asked. That was twenty. Well, Chicago was, from my perspective, East enough for me. I arrived in the wee hours of a bitter February night, 1947, just before my twentieth birthday, with about twenty dollars left from my mustering-out pay in my pocket, to start a new life. What did one do? One took a cab to the YMCA. I don't know that I had ever ridden in a cab (other than a rickshaw—while on rest and recreation in Shanghai), and I was afraid of being cheated, but I got in one. "Where to?" "The Y," I said. "Which one?"

Which *one?* I couldn't imagine a city having more than one Y. "The closest one," I said—and that turned out to be the Lawson Y.

Pause, while I sketch in lightly the years before that scene. Since many of my poems recall my youth, as do the autobiographical essays that intersperse the verse dramas in *Plays for an Imaginary Theater*, it seems appropriate to use the space available to me here to write about aspects of my life not covered elsewhere.

My mother was, during my childhood, a very

pretty dark-haired woman, a day shy of twenty when I was born. She had finished high school at sixteen, started work as a secretary, and in 1926 married my father, who was two years older, but who had left high school without graduating to join *his* father as an oil royalty broker. Both Mother's family, the Stewarts, and the Jeromes had come to Oklahoma from Missouri in the era of the "runs" (1893–1901), when land expropriated from the Indians (who were given compensating land grants) was offered free to settlers from the States who raced to stake out claims. The Jeromes settled near Yale, Oklahoma. John Stewart, my mother's father (my Stewart grandparents both died in 1925), worked on a farm near Haskell.

Bampaw, as I called Frank Jerome, my other grandfather, had done well as an oil producer—with no more than five years of schooling. He was reputedly a millionaire when poor health forced him to return with his family to Missouri and to leave his business in the hands of a brother, who so mismanaged it that when Frank brought his family back to Tulsa in 1924, for money to live on they had to sell off a library of fine books, paintings, a piano, and other belongings acquired as investments. By the time I was born there were only a few leather-bound books around the house to evoke the family's more prosperous past. My memories are of relative poverty, but not hardship, through the Dust Bowl and Depression years.

Among those books was a soft-leather-covered pamphlet, *Grains of Sand*, poems Bampaw wrote to various family members. My father wrote humorous dialect poems (reminiscent of James Whitcomb Riley) that were published in the Tulsa and Oklahoma City newspapers. My father's three sisters, teenagers when I was small, read me poems, helped me memorize poems, before I could read. My favorites were the scary ones like "The Raven" or "Little Orphant Annie" or "Little Boy Blue." Poetry meant being cuddled on the couch while your aunts scared you. Poetry meant writing you could learn by heart—and get up in front of people and recite.

In trying to understand my own roots I come back most often to my father, the fisherman in this poem:

On Mountain Fork

discipline:

       the whispering S of line
above the canoe, the weightless fly thrown
                  through

"With Dad and Stew (right) shortly after Dad's marriage to Evelyn Dietz," 1942

a gap in the branches, spitting to rest
on the still pool where the bass lay,

                                        wrist true
in the toss and flick of the skipping lure.

love:

        silence and singing reel, the whip
of rod, chill smell of fish in the morning air,
green river easing heavily under, drip
of dew in brown light.

                        At the stern I learned
to steer us—wavering paddle like a fin.

art:

    tyrannous glances, passionate strategy,
the hush of nature, humanity slipping in,
arc of the line, ineffectual gift
of a hand-tied bug, then snag in the gill, the
    snap
and steady pull.

                        His life was squalid, his

temper mean, his affection like a trap.
I paddled on aching knees and took the hook.
My father shaped the heart beneath my skin
with love's precision:

                        the gift of grief, the art
of casting clean, the zeal, the discipline.

Mountain Fork is a broad river in the Kiamichi
Mountains in western Oklahoma where we often went
for Dad to dry out from alcohol.

The two people I have learned most from, both
of whom I loved dearly, have been the two that
caused me the most pain—my father and our brain-
damaged daughter, Jenny, now, also, deceased. They
are the only figures who recur in my dreams. Jenny is
always comic in those dreams, full of mischief as she
was in life, and I always wake feeling better about life
for having dreamed her back. My father appears in an
overcoat with upturned collar and felt hat, its brim
down over his eyes. He stands at a distance, his hands
in his coat pockets, and says nothing, but I know he is
saying, "I'm sorry," and though I say nothing I am
hoping he can hear my thoughts: "I know. I know."
From those dreams I wake with a sense of profound
loss of a relationship I would not relive for the world.
Sober, he was the sweetest man alive, a loving father
who shared with me ideas (he was an avid reader),
feelings, experiences. During one of his benders,
which grew more frequent until one of them killed
him in 1947, he was a monster of sarcastic cruelty and
obscene crudity.

The first nine years of my life were spent moving
back and forth from Tulsa (where I was born) to

"On a date in a Chicago restaurant," 1947

Oklahoma City. Mother finally got a divorce in 1936
and took my three-year-old brother, Stew (John
Stewart Jerome, now a successful writer), and me to
Houston, where I lived until I returned to Oklahoma
to start college. I went to some fifteen different
elementary schools and called as many places home
until Mother remarried (to Otto Luer, a square-
headed German refinery worker whom I never liked)
in 1939 and life settled down somewhat.

But let's return to that fellow lugging his huge
suitcase into the Lawson Y in Chicago at 2:00
A.M. Within a few days I had found a job as a typist in
a legal publishing house (in a huge pool equipped
with electric typewriters—the first I knew that such
existed). And I located, from the Y bulletin board, a
room in a rooming house run by a woman with half a
face. The other half was being destroyed by cancer,
which had already eaten through the roof of her
mouth. She smelled dreadful—and turned out to *be*
dreadful—but it was through her, Louise Rogers, that
I met Marty, whom I was to marry the following year.

Louise was Marty's stepaunt. A sixteen-year-old
junior at Francis Parker High, Marty came by the
house often to help Louise with chores, and Louise
told her about her new roomer, a young veteran,
who, she thought, had money. We were introduced,
and I began taking Marty on dates. Theater. Concerts. Dinner with gypsy violins and photographers
who snapped you at the table and sold you prints on
the spot. This pretty little girl with the long light
brown curls taught me about all such things.

And she introduced me to her parents—her
mother, Marion (that's how she spelled it), and

stepfather, Mischa. I was awed by the sophistication of this family. Marty was not only above Grieg and Chopin and Maugham and Cummings, but was rather blasé about Beethoven, Eliot, and Joyce. And her parents had gone on to Thomas Aquinas, Prokofiev, Scarlatti, and Henry Miller. Even beyond Henry Miller. They had copies of the *Communist Manifesto* and Mark Twain's *Sixteen Hundred and One*. The University of Chicago seemed like an elaborate kindergarten where I might prepare to be them, so I applied for admission to its three-year M.A. program in English (which one could enter, as I did, without a B.A.).

The University of Chicago had no sororities (as a condition of a large bequest), so the fraternities were little more than boardinghouses—to my surprise, cheaper than other boardinghouses in the area. I joined Delta Upsilon, and it was largely in the D.U. house near campus that our courtship was conducted. We became engaged on New Year's Eve, 1947, as I say in "Love, the First Decade (1948–1958)":

> . . . We stole
> upstairs in the frat house, there said those droll
> and ceremonial words of tender troth,
> then called your parents, who were shocked. Oh youth,
>
> they cried: We had not had a period
> of trial. We said we'd tried. In this we lied
> and spent the midnight wondering whether it
> were more sophisticated to resist,
> comply, or lie. We lay all night, quite dressed,
> before a mock-wood fire and made commit-
> ments, listened to Sibelius, were distressed
> by Henry James. Our hearts were full of wit.

That is literally true. Marty's parents did not want her to get engaged without having had premarital intercourse, and we made up a story about our having gone to a hotel to check each other out. Both of us would have been scared silly to go to a hotel.

But we did manage, before our marriage in June, to consummate the relationship. Marty's left arm was in a cast from the shoulder down (she had just had bone surgery), and we were on a narrow couch in her parents' apartment while they were away. I remember, after coming almost instantly, asking for a couple of raw eggs to swill down to restore my virility.

Marty and I were married June 20, 1948, in Rockefeller Chapel on the University of Chicago campus. On the GI Bill, living in apartments with our own 78 RPM record player and growing record collection, books, and few other possessions, we spent the next two years struggling to survive while I finished the master's program. Both of us worked,

"Before we were married, I took Marty (then Pierce) down to meet my far-flung family in Texas and Oklahoma. Mother, tall Stew, and Bill Luer are with us on the Luer Farm," New Braunfels, Texas, 1947.

Marty at various office jobs she hated, me at the Food Research Institute at the University, mostly as animal man, tending rhesus monkeys, rabbits, cats, and frogs used for experiments concerning staphylococcus and salmonella food poisoning.

But my poetry was at a standstill. I had been pouring out free verse since leaving the University of Oklahoma—on Okinawa and in Chicago. I sent a batch of this back to my favorite professor, Bob Daniels, at the University of Oklahoma. His dissertation at Harvard had been a long poem I much admired. He said two things that disturbed me deeply. "I can tell you have been reading a lot of Eliot," he wrote. (I didn't know it was *that* obvious.) And he asked, "How do you decide where to break the lines?"

I could weed out the influence of Eliot, but I knew no answer to his question about line breaks. It was fundamental. The major formal difference between poetry and prose is, I realized, that poetry uses line units. I just cut lines where I felt like it. I thought that was what all modern poets did. Already, when I started college in 1943, almost the only poetry taught was free verse. No one had ever taught me about meter, though I had assimilated it from poems I memorized as a child. I had no idea how line length was determined. Baffled, I had put poetry aside for the time being, though I think I knew that it was my true calling.

Now, at Chicago, I enrolled in an introduction to poetry class taught by a disciple of Yvor Winters's, J. V. Cunningham. On the first day of the course he said, "If this were a course on elephants, we would have to know what an elephant is. What is poetry?" Then he sat there, leaning his long, lean frame (with pants too short and socks rolled on his ankles), smoking cigaret after cigaret and flipping each skillfully across the room to arc over the glass windbreak on the window and sail outside, listening to us exchange moonlight-in-frog's-belly opinions for most of the hour. At last he said, "So far as I'm concerned, poetry is metrical writing. If it's anything else, I don't know what it is."

I was outraged. That definition sounded reactionary. It sounded like something my parents might say. But I was also challenged. The following day I gave this poem to Cunningham:

My Doubt Ranged Free

My doubt upon the land ranged free. It fed
where others trusted and believed: a child
for lunch, a test tube, home, and church were
    piled
upon its dinner plate alive and dead,
for all was sham except my love and me.

The land was bare. My doubt was fat with pride,
and, ardent beast, it purred at my delight;
but, fond of praise, and whetted, vain of might,
it looked again. It was not satisfied
until it turned, consumed my love and me.

To my astonishment, when I next went into class, that poem was on the blackboard (without my name). Professor Cunningham lectured about it for an hour, pointing out niceties of meter and form I did not understand. For example, the first two lines he called "parasitic." He did not mean the term pejoratively, but was indicating how a pentameter line is overlaid on a tetrameter structure. He drew our attention to a similar technique in Eliot: "April is the cruelest month, breeding / Lilacs out of the dead land, mixing / Memory and desire, stirring / Dull roots with spring rain." He used the term *refrain* for the fifth line in each stanza. All this was news to me. But, most

importantly, I learned about the tension between line measure and meaning. I now understood where and why to break lines.

I don't remember his saying much about content (except to point out that the whole poem was built on an extended metaphor), but the theme of that poem was to recur in many of my poems to come: the problem of faith, or belief. I had long been struck by the yearning of Don Marquis's archy, who, writing about a moth who seemed to want nothing so bad as death as it circled a flame or lightbulb, says, "i wish / there was something i wanted / as badly as he wanted to fry himself." In response to a revival meeting I had joined the Methodist church as a teenager, but soon experience and knowledge undermined any faith I might have felt.

Faith meant believing in something you could not know for sure. It seemed to me that it was almost by definition a form of delusion, but it could be heroic. One of my poems, "Ishmael to Ahab" (written for a course at Chicago and later published in *College English*), expresses Ishmael's envy of Ahab, who had sufficient belief in his mission to go down lashed to the whale. I thought that one might rest in something one believed that strongly. The beast of doubt might then be placated, even if it required one's death.

I was reacting to the systematic demolition of innocence going on around Marty's parents' living room and dinner table. I thought they were going to throw me out one evening for saying that I liked Plato

Marty (center) with her parents,
Marion and Mischa Rubin, and Hrothgar,
in front of Antioch's Glen Helen House, 1954

better than Aristotle. The arena for faith for Marion, Mischa, and their friends seemed to be social rather than spiritual. Oh, how I wanted to believe in the Progressive party's candidate, Henry Wallace, in 1948! I favored him loudly and eloquently throughout his campaign, then, when it came to casting my first vote, in the privacy of the booth, I hedged my bet and voted for Truman.

We were very political in those days. Several of the friends of Marty's parents had been Communists in the thirties, which made them seem quite racy to me. Communism itself never interested me, though I loved the Communist-tinged folk songs of the labor movement and of the Lincoln Brigade. But I had been an anarchist since an ROTC major at the University of Oklahoma said to me, as he dressed me down, "You can't do whatever you want. That would be anarchism." As soon as I looked up the word in the dictionary I knew I had discovered my brand of politics.

The point was not so much to be political as to be radical, to challenge authority, to be unconventional, to be artistic, to be sophisticated. Often I felt like a boy from the sticks lost in the metropolis (and the teasing of Marion and Mischa reinforced that feeling). I cultivated a tragic view of life. I remember working up a good case of despair when I received my master's degree. So what do I do now? What does this degree fit me for? Ah, life's futility! Did I dare to eat a peach? Should I wear white flannel trousers, and walk along the beach . . . ?

The degree fitted me for more study, of course, and I already had an appointment as a student assistant in a Ph.D. program at Ohio State starting in the fall of 1950. Teaching a heavy load for little pay (fifteen hundred dollars a year for two five-credit courses each of three quarters), taking more and more demanding courses, boning up for my prelims—all this occupied most of my time during the three years we were in Columbus, Ohio. Marty took some courses as a music major (we acquired a spinet), but soon dropped out to help support us. We shared apartments with various other graduate students, and, eventually, with a couple I'll call Stash and Billie, conceived of ourselves as a group marriage.

The four of us planned to save up and buy a sailing ship and take off from South America to Africa (where Stash had been stationed during the war). Such dreams lasted through the miserable spring and summer of 1952. Both Marty and I had serious sexual problems with our new mates, and they came to seem like leeches to us—rather sloppy leeches at that. Tensions between us continued to mount, and Stash and Billie moved out that fall. By that time the two

couples hated each other. Stash and Billie moved in with another couple, and *that* group marriage went off to Borneo together.

In 1953, an ABD (as we referred to one who had completed all requirements for a doctorate except for a dissertation), I took a job (for what seemed a munificent forty-five hundred dollars) at nearby Antioch College in Yellow Springs, Ohio, and found my spiritual home. Antioch was completely different from anything I had experienced in academia—informal, free in structure, yet terribly intense (and radical). I was, for a change, working with people in academia whom I genuinely liked and respected. One, Paul Treichler, who taught drama, offered a course in playwrighting, and I sat in with his little group of five students and started writing the verse play that became, eventually, *Candle in the Straw*.

Marty was pregnant when we moved to Yellow Springs. Our first year we shared a mansion owned by the college out in the country, on the edge of the college's huge Glen Helen, with Jessie and Paul Treichler. The river near our house froze deeply that winter; the Treichlers and Jeromes held a party on the ice—bonfires, skating, food and drink—for nearly a hundred faculty, students, and other friends. Marty skated on the day before Michelle was born, January 26, 1954.

But that birth was a wicked introduction to young parenthood. The infant was allergic to life, including mother's milk. From her first weeks she was covered with eczema and could not digest either any form of milk or the soy substitutes we tried. Finally we settled on Nutramigen, a chemical to be mixed with water, which she could at least tolerate, but her first year was miserable. I remember her lying screaming on my chest as I sat back in a recliner; I read Dylan Thomas to her in a booming voice, and that seemed to soothe her. I can still summon up the strange odor of Nutramigen, for years her life's blood.

One of the conditions of my hiring was an agreement to use S. I. Hayakawa's *Language in Thought and Action* as a text in my section of Current Reading and Writing, or freshman comp. Our department chairman, Basil Pillard, had collaborated with Hayakawa on the revision of the old *Language in Action* and was a great believer in general semantics. It proved to be a sprightly text for a composition course. I also taught a course called "Donne to Pope," which came out on the registrar's class list and on many student transcripts as "Done to the Pope."

I arrived at Antioch as the kind of professor that would later come to be called a "Young Turk." Those were the days chronicled by David Riesman as *The Academic Revolution* in a book by that title published in 1968. By the time it came out the "revolution" he meant was over. That was the year of the Columbia and Sorbonne riots, and what Riesman called a revolution blew apart as it confronted a new one. But Riesman wrote approvingly about the postwar phenomenon of academic domination of the world of research, hence the increasingly close ties of academia with business, science, and the military. One of my professors at Ohio State, Richard Altick, had written a book called *Scholars in Business Suits,* whose title neatly summarizes the academic temper of the Eisenhower years.

I was certainly not in a business suit, nor was anyone else at Antioch, but I had picked up from graduate school the notion that the function of undergraduate education was to prepare students to become Ph.D.'s. Everyone was to read and write and think like an English professor. I was a tough grader, writing long, detailed comments on papers, forever demanding that students push their ideas harder, deeper, that they read all that had been written about a topic, duly note that in bibliography and footnotes, and then push on to say something fresh and new.

Of course you can only do what students will let you get away with. I overprepared for my first session of Donne to Pope. I had been teaching composition for the past three years at OSU, so was used to that, but this was my first effort to teach *literature,* and I was running scared, so I had pages of notes on seventeenth-century background to go through as a kind of introduction. After about fifteen minutes of this one of the students interrupted me. "When are we going to get to the poetry?" he asked.

Hastily I put aside my notes and said sheepishly, "Why, right now," and honed in on "The Canonization," having been taught to read that poem—and most other poetry—by Cleanth Brooks's book *The Well Wrought Urn* and by *Understanding Poetry,* the text Brooks wrote with Robert Penn Warren. Writers coming into academia in those days were the students of the New Critics, of the poets anthologized by John Ciardi in *Mid-Century American Poetry* (such as Wilbur, Lowell, Rukeyser, Roethke, Shapiro, Nims, Jarrell, Eberhart, Bishop, and Ciardi himself), and of the scholars in business suits. And we were setting out to create others in our images. But we were profoundly wrong-headed—about education if not about poetry—as I came later to see (and to write about in *Culture out of Anarchy*). I had been hired to replace novelist Nolan Miller, Antioch's creative writing teacher, while he was on sabbatical—though I did not teach creative writing, that year or ever. It was a one-

year contract with no possibility of renewal, but because of student demand I was kept on.

Meanwhile, mornings I was up at five finishing my dissertation ("Rochester and the Generation of Wit," completed in 1955) in the dank basement of our house on faculty row. Then one evening in that basement I sat down and wrote four "Kiamichi Sonnets." I sent them to *Poetry*—my very first submission of poetry anywhere since, at seventeen, I had had a puerile poem published in *Red Earth,* a regional literary magazine in Oklahoma. *Poetry*'s editor Henry Rago took one of the four. After "Deer Hunt" appeared, editors began writing me to ask for submissions to *their* magazines. The poem was picked up by several anthologies and textbooks, chiefly because it concerns a boy's ambiguous feelings about manhood: "and then gripped once again the monstrous gun, / since I, to be a man, had taken one." It was years before I learned that the success of this poem was not a good indication of how things go in the literary world.

When Nolan returned from sabbatical, he drew me in on a project he had proposed to Bantam Books: *New Campus Writing,* a series of anthologies of work by college students across the country. I was to be primarily the poetry editor (though we both read and reached agreement on all submissions), and so began having my first experiences judging the poetry of other young poets. Many well-known writers today had their start in that series of collections (appearing in paperback from Bantam and Grove Presses and hardback from Putnam's between 1957 and 1966).

The books required several trips to New York City with Nolan, so I was introduced to such publishing amenities as three-martini lunches. A little of such amenities and book-talk with Nolan's many literary friends (and his agent at the time, Diarmuid Russell) went a long way with me. I still feel like putting my thumb in my mouth when I go to New York—everyone seems so sophisticated and successful and prosperous. How lucky I was that I couldn't afford a ticket to that city when I set out East. But I am deeply indebted to Nolan for bringing me into the literary world. He initiated writers' workshops at Antioch and brought to campus as staff such notables as W. D. Snodgrass (who met Anne Sexton on our campus—the beginning of an important and long-standing literary friendship).

Our daughter Beth came into our lives in 1956. I associate her babyhood with studying Shakespeare. We spent the summer of 1958 on Bustin's Island, Maine, where our friends Bob and Charlotte Maurer (Bob taught with me in what we had come to call the Department of Literature) had a "cottage" (a huge two-story house with its own tennis court). The cottage we rented was a little one right on the shore. Each morning I would rise with the first light and sit on the front porch of that cottage studying Shakespeare because I was to start teaching the Shakespeare course in the fall. I scanned miles and miles of pentameter that summer, marking the accents, circling related vowel and consonant sounds, noting the interplay of images, and making copious marginal notes about thematic development—all before Beth woke up and needed attention, the day began, and study time was over.

Shakespeare courses came to be my favorites, maybe because I loved reading the speeches aloud. I preferred to use class time in discussion, and, anyway, would never have had time to read all the speeches and make all the comments I wanted during class hours, so I recorded readings from and comments on some twenty plays, going over them line by line, and made the tapes available to students in the library. I did the same thing with a number of novels I assigned in other courses—and I recorded the whole of Chaucer's *Troilus and Criseyde* in somewhat uncertain Middle English pronunciation so that students could listen as they followed the written text in modern English.

My teaching of Shakespeare culminated in 1969 in a "Shakespeare Weekend" at the elegant home of a local woman who was taking the course. The class gathered there with bedrolls; we were to read every word of *Othello* aloud between Friday and Sunday afternoon, spread around in a gigantic conversation pit, stopping to discuss as interest led us, or taking a break for a swim in the pool. Saturday evening a sixteenth-century feast was prepared and consumed. The course went straight downhill after that: no one wanted to be in a classroom ever again.

Polly was born in June 1959, and I took off almost immediately thereafter for a fellowship at the Huntington Hartford Foundation in Pacific Palisades, California. This old estate (that once belonged to Will Rogers) was, like Yaddo and MacDowell and other extant artists' colonies, intended to provide private and isolated working quarters for artists in various fields. Lunch was brought to each cabin in a basket so we could continue working undisturbed, though there was considerable socializing among the residents in the evenings. Accustomed to working with children underfoot, the phone ringing, the household humming with activity, I nearly went out of my mind in all that peace.

My main project was to rewrite *Candle in the Straw*, a verse tragedy based on the life of James

Naylor, the seventeenth-century Quaker preacher. I had finished that to my satisfaction within a week or so, invited the other artists in for a reading, and received a standing ovation. Next I decided to rewrite in verse my musical comedy, *Winter in Eden* (Adam, Eve, Archangel Michael, and Satan are the characters, along with a chorus of angels and another of devils). It had already been produced at Antioch in prose form, but I was dissatisfied with it and rewrote extensively. Another reading. Another round of applause. Then I started on a sequence of lyrics, "Instructions for Acting," and was turning out two or three poems a day. Each time I finished one I panicked. Because I was supposed to be writing, I couldn't concentrate on reading—or anything else— and feared that I wouldn't come up with new ideas. After a couple of weeks of this I was much relieved when Marty called to say that Michelle was sick and I'd better come home—after being there only six weeks of a three-month fellowship. The directors of the foundation didn't like it much when recipients of their fellowships didn't stay their allotted time, but I had, as it were, a doctor's excuse, and happily returned to normal domestic confusion. (The illness turned out not to be serious.)

We lived in faculty housing until Christmas Eve 1959, when we moved to our first real home—a house we were to own for a decade, though we lived abroad for three of those years. And, as the fifties ended, I began writing for *Writer's Digest*. Dick Rosenthal, publisher and editor of the magazine and as much of a shavetail as I was, came up from Cincinnati to meet me and request an article on poetry. I wrote and sent him "Are You a Poet?"—later a chapter of *The Poet and the Poem*, published in the December 1959 issue. I had nothing but scorn for *Writer's Digest*, having seen only a few issues years before. It was commercial, not literary. Its whole emphasis was on selling and success. Poetry is too good for this magazine, I thought, too good for its readers, and I'll take this opportunity to tell them that poetry is almost impossible to write well, requires a great deal of technical mastery, is very hard to get published, and usually pays nothing at all.

They loved it at *Writer's Digest*. It conveyed the opposite message from everything else in the magazine, and that was apparently exactly what Dick wanted. Kirk Polking, who had taken over as editor, invited me to write a regular column on poetry (for twenty-five dollars a month), and I began doing so enthusiastically, beginning with the January issue for 1960, mailing in columns from England and Spain, where we were living from June 1960 to August 1961 on a sabbatical supplemented by the Amy Lowell

Poetry Travelling Scholarship.

My first columns systematically covered the technical elements of poetry and illustrated them with the best poems I could find from the past and from contemporary poets. These columns were to become the core of *The Poet and the Poem*, the first edition of which appeared in 1963. There was undeniably a haughty tone in those early columns. I was still being a Young Turk in my column as in my classroom.

I was writing mostly fiction during our year abroad, "Theodore and the Mermaid," a novel that was never published. My first collection of poetry came out after we returned. The editor of Golden Quill Press requested a book manuscript for their Poetry Book of the Month Club, leading to the publication of *Light in the West* in 1962. The acknowledgement page provides a cross-sectional view of my career to that point:

> Most of these [44] poems have appeared in *Antioch Review, Atlantic, Colorado Quarterly, Epoch, Harper's, Humanist, Mademoiselle, Nation, New Mexico Quarterly, New Orleans Poetry Journal, Poetry, Poetry Dial, San Francisco Review, Saturday Review, Shenandoah,* and *Virginia Quarterly Review,* and are reprinted with their permission.

In 1963 we moved to the Virgin Islands. Michelle's doctor had recommended that we try another climate, as her asthma and eczema were getting steadily worse. Our friends and neighbors in Yellow Springs, Phil and Frankie Ruopp and their four children, were going down to help start the new College of the Virgin Islands. Our families were so close we hardly knew their kids from ours, so it was a pleasure to be their neighbors again in former army officers' quarters on the hill above the airport and golf course on Saint Thomas. My position was chairman of the humanities division and professor of English. Phil was dean of students, and Larry Wanlass was president; we three were initially the total staff. As the first faculty member hired I had the pleasure of ordering the library. I sat in the spring sun in our backyard in Yellow Springs leafing through *Books in Print* and checking the titles in every field that I thought a well-rounded college library should own.

The climate change had an almost immediate beneficial effect on Michelle. Her growth stunted by years of cortisone, she was quite tiny for her age (eleven). We made friends with Beverly and Henry Nieves, who owned a bookstore on the island and sailed most weekends with charter passengers on their thirty-foot cutter. Michelle and I began joining

"On our porch overlooking the golf course on Saint Thomas," 1965: Jud holding Beth; Michelle; Marty holding Jenny; Polly

them for those sails to surrounding islands, where we would anchor and snorkel in crystal bays. Already a good swimmer, Michelle became quite a little athlete. Her skin cleared and her asthma attacks were less frequent. I crewed for Captain Hank and led tourists on guided tours of ruins of a sugar plantation on Saint John, making up history I didn't know.

Teaching the islanders was a challenge. Most came from English Caribbean islands as well as the U.S. Virgins, and over ninety percent were black. Their Calypso-like dialect was at times almost unintelligible to me, and many had no concept of an English sentence. One of the first works I assigned was *Pygmalion,* as it seemed so pertinent to their condition, but its relevance was lost on most. Again I was into the ordeal of making long, detailed comments on the margins of papers, handing out low grades, and making impossible demands.

One way to get students to familiarize themselves with a variety of English quite foreign to them was to have them memorize it, to wrap their tongues around the sentences and vocabulary of Shakespeare, for instance. I had acted in plays—at the University of Oklahoma and at Antioch—but I had never directed one. Now, at the College of the Virgin Islands, I directed a series of scenes I had selected from Shakespeare. The theater we put together for this purpose, in the loft of a former army barracks then used as a classroom, had many remarkable productions in the years I was there, including one of my one-act verse play, *The Glass Mountain* (with a black princess).

The day before the assassination of Kennedy, Marty gave birth to premature twins with a blood incompatibility (something like the Rh factor). We didn't realize at first how serious the problems were, and I remember writing my colleague Milton Goldberg, back at Antioch, how delighted we were to find ourselves suddenly with *five* redheaded daughters. But one of the twins died within a week, and it had become evident after we returned to the mainland that the surviving girl, Jenny, was seriously brain-damaged, aphasic, in addition to being epileptic and having slight cerebral palsy.

I had taken a two-year leave from Antioch, and at the end of that period Michelle was beginning to have allergic responses to the island environment, so it seemed wise to return home. Her doctor had explained that no particular environment was bad or good for her allergies, but that a change now and then would probably be beneficial. My island students threw a surprise party to bid me farewell. I have never felt so loved, appreciated, and honored by my students as I was by these whose language I had struggled to force into the Procrustean bed of the narrow dialect I call "editorial English."

But we experienced culture shock when we returned to Yellow Springs and Antioch. The counterculture had taken over. Long-haired boys and hippie attire. Pot. Acid. And heavy doses of militancy on the one hand and spaced-out love talk on the other. One of the most heartrending images I have of those days is of daughter Beth, then eleven, trying to explain to me why she found "Eleanor Rigby" such a moving song.

I was, indeed, the Mr. Jones of Bob Dylan's song, who didn't know what was happening, with my head looking to the longhairs like a cigar. I figured I had better get serious about education or get out of it, so I joined the radical group of faculty who were involved in trying to bring more innovation and freedom to campus—the antitheses of Young Turks. Something else was needed, I thought, besides freedom and innovation: community. Rapes and thefts were occurring in the dorms. Drugs were rife. The campus population had doubled from the five hundred students it had had in 1953. Most people on campus were strangers to one another. Blacks took over dorms and refused entrance to whites. Peaceful, friendly Yellow Springs was a mass of tensions.

My response was to form a college within the college, an effort to rebuild, at least on a small scale, a sense of belonging, of caring about one another. Antioch made available to us two of its smaller dorms

(large old houses that could accommodate twenty students in all). Four other faculty members from contrasting disciplines joined with me in this venture. The Inner College, largely my design, was the first coed housing at Antioch, the first program to offer nongraded credits, the first in which requirements were largely self-defined by students. They were free to study anything they wanted to and then to apply for credit *ex post facto* with evidence of what they had done.

That fall, 1968, an essay I had written about the problems in higher education, "The System Really Isn't Working," was published in *Life.* Accompanying it were photos of Inner College students and faculty, suggesting a model to be followed elsewhere. I found myself suddenly catapulted into as much fame as I have ever enjoyed (if that's the term for what I experienced). I began getting invitations to speak at colleges and before organizations all over the country—even in Hawaii, where I addressed the National Association of Drug Manufacturers Representatives on the need of change in higher education. With other faculty from several colleges I helped disrupt an educational conference at the New College of the University of South Florida, Sarasota, with a bit of street theater I invented. Wearing long hair now, travelling and speaking and giving readings around the country, I embarked on a course of philandering that at the time seemed in keeping with the counterculture and the Age of Aquarius.

The Inner College did not last, partly because it offered more freedom than students could handle and partly because I was moving on to yet another educational experiment. Antioch had set up an extension campus (at first called a Kleenex college because it was disposable) on Kauai and sought to begin such ventures elsewhere. One of these satellite campuses was to be in Columbia, Maryland, a "new town" the Rouse Corporation was developing—a somewhat utopian vision of a city of "the next America" that I found quite attractive. Antioch moved in at the invitation of Jim Rouse himself. I joined with vice-president Morris Keeton to initiate this venture, and we moved our families to Columbia.

I am skimming a complex tale that is more fully rendered in my writing that grew out of it—first a series of activist poems, "Rumors of Change," in *Change,* a new quarterly devoted to innovation in higher education; then an article, "The Fifth Estate," that took up half of one issue of that magazine (and sent me, on a handsome expense account, to campuses of every variety all over the country—including the Antioch facility on Kauai); then the book in which, at the suggestion of its publishers, Herder and

Herder, I gathered all this material together and expanded it: *Culture out of Anarchy: The Reconstruction of American Higher Learning.*

That was the sixth of my books to be published. The others were a novel, *The Fell of Dark;* and a textbook, *Poetry: Premeditated Art,* published by Houghton Mifflin; *Plays from an Imaginary Theater; Light in the West;* and *The Poet and the Poem* from Writer's Digest Books. I was one of the most widely published of American poets with hundreds of poems in dozens of magazines, most notably and frequently *Saturday Review.* (I owe much of what success I have had to my intermittent friendship with John Ciardi, who was poetry editor of that magazine when it took poetry. It was John who had recommended me for the Amy Lowell and had me on the staff at Bread Loaf in 1967 and 1968.)

And I was sick at heart. My profession seemed to be taking me further and further from the literature that attracted me to it in the first place; and while all this running around being famous was exciting, it was hardly fulfilling. Meanwhile our family was having its own problems. Jenny was in a public-school program for handicapped students, and it wasn't working. Her teachers asked us to find some other alternative. She had serious behavior problems, and she was making no progress toward learning language. Meanwhile a son, Topher (we took the "Christ" out of Christopher), had found his way through the foam spermicide, was now three years old (and quite healthy). Jenny was bigger than he was, but he could talk. She could beat up on Topher, but he could outsmart her. If Jenny got out of the house alone she was inclined to run away, and there was no telling what the neighbor children—or any strangers—might do to her. The time had come for us to find a residential facility for her—a shattering realization, for, difficult as were her communication and physical problems, Jenny was a warm, loving child, full of sparkle and humor, and the whole family (and our friends) adored her.

We took her to Beaver Run, near Philadelphia. This is one of the Camphill Special Schools run on the anthroposophical principles of Rudolf Steiner. As soon as we visited there we knew—and she knew—this was to be her home: a rural village of cottages for staff families and the handicapped, scattered on a woody hillside. At just under seven, she was the youngest placement they had ever taken, and she was happy there from the moment she arrived. Though she was at home for Christmas and Easter each year, and during the summers when the school was closed, she was always delighted to return, and the staff

obviously loved her and found her just as amusing (and troublesome and troubling) as we did.

But Beaver Run had an even more profound effect on our family than to provide a haven for Jenny. It is a commune. The staff members, who live with their normal children in cottages with the "villagers" (as they refer to the handicapped children) are not paid. Their living expenses are provided by the organization. Each household, like the community as a whole, is self-governing in the context of the larger Camphill movement. In the course of visiting campuses I had often stayed in student communes. And the film I had written about Arthur Morgan (produced and directed by my good friend Richard Kaplan) was titled *I See a Village* . . . because of its focus on Morgan's work in development of small communities.

All this seemed to be of a piece. I think we all felt in our family that Jenny had found her place, and it was up to us to find ours—some way of life more wholesome and communal than Columbia, Maryland, was proving to be. Michelle, with our blessing, on her sixteenth birthday had dropped out of school, gotten her driver's license, and found a tiny apartment and a job in nearby Washington, D.C.—all on the same busy day. Beth, in high school, was finding herself increasingly in a jungle of drugs, sexual and racial tensions—and was quite miserable. Polly, the most scholastically inclined of our children, was becoming a lovable brat. And Topher, five, in kindergarten, was turning into a different child from the one we recognized: suddenly possessive, competitive, smart-aleck, giggly about sex . . . a normal kid. We wanted to get him out of school before it was too late.

I decided that I wanted to write a book on communes and use the occasion to visit many with a view to joining one, and Marty encouraged this plan. I applied for a grant from the Twentieth Century Fund—sixty thousand dollars for eighteen months' support—and got it, thanks to recommendations from David Riesman (who was on the board of the foundation), Lewis Mumford (who had written me about my "Rumors of Change" poems), and others. We bought a VW camper and set out to study communes and, on our return trips to Columbia, began meeting with other people—dozens, to our surprise—who were becoming disillusioned by Columbia and thinking of some communal alternative. Libby and Jim Rouse were among those who came to our meetings.

Much of that experience is summarized in *Families of Eden: Communes and the New Anarchism,* the resulting book, published by Seabury Press in this country and Thames and Hudson in England (and

"Examining hollow-log planters at Downhill Farm," 1976:
(from left) David Kingslake, Marty, Judson, Topher

disowned by the Twentieth Century Fund when its director found out I had gone native). Our many visits to communes revealed there were few children in most, and these few generally went to public schools. One of our chief motives in seeking rural communal life was to enable Polly, Beth, and Topher to stay out of school if they preferred to do that. So we decided to start our own commune.

We began looking for farmland, preferably with buildings on it so people could move in immediately. We wanted an isolated location that would permit casual nudity. And we wanted the most acreage we could get—preferably mostly woodland—for the least money. One other constraint was that the land had to be within half-a-day's drive from Beaver Run, for we would have to make several round-trips a year to pick up Jenny and take her back. After considerable search we found a hundred acres that met all these requirements. It was at our distance limit, about two hundred miles—a four-hour drive—west of Beaver Run. After we named it Downhill Farm (on the assumption that life would be all downhill from that time on) I remembered with amusement that Archy MacLeish, with whom I frequently corresponded, lived at Uphill Farm in Conway, Massachusetts. Somehow it seemed

appropriate to write from Downhill to Uphill, considering the stature in my mind of that great gentleman and poet.

The steep land was mostly covered with scrub pine. It had three large and several smaller buildings on it so people could move in immediately, and many were eager to do just that, people whom we had met on our travels in the counterculture and those attracted by speeches I had given as far away as southern California. Someday I'll write a book about our experiences there—fun, painful, trying, rewarding, enlightening as they were—but for now I will stick to the effect of Downhill Farm on my career.

I had resigned from Antioch (after twenty years), and so (after the funds from the foundation were exhausted) took a 90 percent cut in income. I suppose that many professors did that in the late sixties and early seventies, but I personally know of none who did—resigned a tenured position after twenty years of teaching at a college.

For a time after we moved to the farm I had occasional consulting jobs and speaking invitations from colleges, but, out of touch with my colleagues, I soon was mostly forgotten by the academic world. I had written what I still regard as one of my best poems, "The Village," based on our experiences in taking Jenny to Beaver Run, and none of the better-known magazines would take that poem. It finally appeared in a little commune magazine that folded after one issue. But I was trying to put bitterness about or even concern with such matters behind me. I realized that a major item on my agenda at Downhill Farm was to get out of my system what I had come to call "the fame game." "Put your ego away; you won't need it today," was a slogan I burned onto a wooden plaque, and I hung it on one of the Downhill buildings. Another was, "Either do what you like, or like what you do."

I stopped sending poetry or other writings to magazines or publishers that hadn't asked for me to contribute, and those that did were mostly small countercultural publications. The very words *submission, rejection,* and *acceptance* came to sound degrading. I took up self-publishing under the name of Trunk Press. ("Get ahead the way Emily Dickinson did," I had written in a column: "Try your trunk.")

And I rejected all forms of elitism, even in poetry. My column, my long letter to the world, mellowed noticeably, and the comments I had from readers expressed appreciation of the change. I began writing poetry again with an appetite and excitement such as I had never known. Once I stopped worrying about publishing it—knowing that I could always self-publish it in pamphlets and give them away—I felt liberated and renewed. I again began working in longer narrative and dramatic forms—and continue to do so in the hope that someday those vast areas poetry has lost to prose can be recaptured.

I had time to think and read and write at Downhill such as I had not had in years, yet our lives there were very full of hard work, too. Our first year we had more than twenty members and no industry: we survived by contributing savings until we could get a business under way. Between 1973 and 1975 we averaged a dozen adults with attendant children. In the final period of the commune proper, 1976–78, there were six to eight adults and six children. We supported ourselves from the fall of 1972 until 1975 by making planters out of sections of logs, and I was the principal band sawyer (taking out the cores). Later we made wind chimes as a studio for a Washington metal sculptor, Bill Cook, who provided the original designs and training. These were shipped for wholesale sales to over three hundred stores around the country, and my wife continues making and shipping those chimes today. We assessed ourselves one hundred fifty dollars per person per month from the income of these industries and paid

ourselves five dollars an hour for time put in beyond the required thirty hours. All other work was voluntary—and there was a lot of it: gardening, animal care, fencing, firewood gathering (for, at one time, seventeen wood-burning stoves), vehicle repair, building maintenance, and many other jobs. The voluntary system functioned only moderately well. A few high-energy people did most of the work, and a number of others, who tended to move on their way fairly soon of their own free will, contributed very little to community work. Many were drifters, refugees from the cities, and many never set foot in our large organic garden. In that time of social turmoil they were looking for intimacy, family, something to replace marriages, professions, trades, or studies that had gone stale.

In 1977 Topher, then ten, was the only child on the farm and was quite lonely. For a few months we lived at Deep Run Farm, a commune near York, Pennsylvania, that ran an alternative school where he could be with other children. There we met Bonny. Marty and I very much liked Bonny and her girls (aged five, ten, and twelve). One evening while Bonny and I were collating one of my self-published pamphlets, *Public Domain,* I began talking about my own views of communalism and family, views very dimly realized at Downhill Farm. The more we talked the more Bonny felt that she had been waiting all her life to find others who shared these views with her.

Since the beginning of our marriage Marty and I have believed that monogamy is not necessarily the best arrangement for human happiness—and that sexual jealousy and possessiveness are symptoms of insecurity that one should address, not surrender to. Our incorporation of Bonny and her daughters into our family (that is, our family at Downhill—Topher, Marty, and me) actually had little to do with sex. Though Bonny and I were attracted to one another, and I much enjoyed sleeping with her every other night, our primary reason for melding our families was the welfare of our children. For various reasons all of Bonny's girls were miserable in school. And, as I have said, Topher wanted the company of other children. If Bonny and her family moved to Downhill there were ways of dealing with the problem of all the children concerned.

Moreover, as one of my poems points out, three people are somewhat like a three-legged stool or three logs on a fire; they provide a kind of stability impossible for only two. This is especially true when two are women, or it was for us, because, well-trained and willing house husband though I am, there is much cooking, housework, and child-rearing that the

At Downhill Farm, about 1978: (top row) Bonny, one of her daughters, and Marty; (middle) Judson and Topher; (bottom) Jenny, another of Bonny's daughters, and Michelle

women could do better than I, and Marty and Bonny found much of such work fulfilling. When one of the adults was sick or away, there were always two left. We were good company for one another during long country evenings (we played a lot of three-handed bridge, and the women played a lot of Scrabble). We were all involved in the wind-chime business. The women enjoyed gardening together and raised herbs (some for sale fresh to Washington restaurants) and flowers in addition to vegetables.

We bought a house trailer to accommodate our new family members and eventually connected it to our log cabin with added rooms. Our little unit of three adults and four children overpowered the remainder of the commune. First a couple moved out, then some months later the other four adults and two children left to set up a wind-chime studio, still for Bill Cook, in California, where they lived a few years communally and then split up. We made no effort to

recruit more members, so the commune consisted only of our extended family from 1978 until 1984. During that time we put in a large above-the-ground pool, and nude swimming became quite popular—especially with a group of gay men, friends from Washington, D.C., who often came for weekends.

When Jenny, at nineteen, was supposed to "graduate" from Beaver Run, she went around to all the cottages and said good-bye, then went to bed and peacefully died of a seizure in her sleep. Our by then widespread family gathered at Beaver Run for a beautifully simple memorial service and burial; rather than grief, both family and staff felt a kind of misty elation that Jenny had, as if by choice, moved on.

In December 1981, we took off as a family (seven of us) to the Dominican Republic, where we bought a house on the north coast almost immediately. Our plan was to winter there, but the second year we were there, 1982–83, our stay ended in disaster. Polly and the man she lived with had come down for a visit. We were returning to our house from a distant beach, Topher driving our little pickup truck, when a government limousine—a Ford LTD—slammed into our rear. Polly was nearly killed. She was thrown out of the bed of the truck, slid some seventy feet on her back, and her neck was broken in two places. Polly's friend nearly lost a toe, my collarbone was broken, and the three others in the truck were injured in lesser ways. A week later—as soon as Polly was able to travel—we fled. There was no recourse against the Dominican government. Our insurance proved to be worthless. We were wiped out physically and financially and were unable to return to the island until I went down to sign sale papers on the house in November 1986.

Our triad was overall a very practical arrangement, and it ended when there was no further need for it, after eight-and-a-half years. Bonny's youngest was by that time the only child still at the farm. Now *she* was lonely—and very much wanted a social life, hence a school. That meant a rather redneck public school near the farm or a Christian school in a nearby city. We tried both, and neither worked out. So we moved back to Yellow Springs, where Marty and I knew the school and the environment had been good for our daughters.

But the world had changed. Drugs, sex, alcohol, running away, or sleeping out with friends . . . all these problems had not existed for our daughters, but they certainly hit Bonny's daughter hard. Bonny felt it was better to live alone with her to give her more attention, and our triad came to a natural end. We are all glad to have broken up, but we have no regrets or bitterness, and we remain friends.

The years since we moved to Downhill have been the most productive of my life, increasingly so since we returned to Yellow Springs. At Downhill I prepared the third edition (each of the three editions is very different from the others) of *The Poet and the Poem* (a book now out of print; it sold about twenty thousand copies in its twenty years of life); wrote *The Poet's Handbook;* started work on the first *Poet's Market* (an annual); wrote *On Being a Poet;* and, at the request of David Yates, got out a collected poems: *Thirty Years of Poetry, 1949–1979.*

David was then editor of *Cedar Rock,* a quarterly literary tabloid for which I wrote a poetry column for many years. Cedar Rock Press had published a number of books, and David urged me to let him bring out a collected poems. I would do so only if he would let me share the investment in printing, as I knew he was a journalism professor at a small college in Texas, and it might be years before such a book would recoup the initial investment it required. Also, in my antiestablishment mood of the time, I wanted to prepare the copy on my IBM Selectric to avoid typesetting costs. The latter condition was a serious mistake. The photoreduced pages are too light, and the whole thing looks amateurish. While I loved the opportunity to bring all the poetry I chose to save into one volume, and loved the chance to type and arrange it all myself, I even made typos and got pages numbered wrong (which reduced my swellhead-edness considerably). The book was reviewed *nowhere.* We sold enough copies by mail order to earn back expenses and make a small profit, but that book remains one of the best kept secrets in the literary world.

The most fulfilling publishing experience I have had, however, has been with my most recent book, *The Village: New and Selected Poems,* published by Dolphin-Moon Press in Baltimore in 1987. In looking at samples from publishers for *Poet's Market* I was impressed by the work of Dolphin-Moon and so asked its owner-editor, James Taylor, whether he would be interested in doing a book of mine. He was enthusiastic about the proposal, and in collaboration with James and other editors in Baltimore I chose a hefty sample of new and old poetry and was quite pleased by both the hardback and paperback editions. Moreover, James brought me to Baltimore to publicize the book, arranging interviews, readings, a workshop—all kinds of hoopla that my various other publishers never bothered with. He made me feel like an *author.*

I have tried to refrain in these pages from including much of the writing I am most tempted to put in, my poems. But I have a very good reason to close with one that means as much to me as the title poem of *The Village.* I knew I wanted to give myself a poem as a present for my sixtieth birthday, February 8, 1987, and I had worked out much of what this poem says before I started—literally at nine on the morning of my birthday. But it was when I performed the act mentioned at the beginning, for the reason given, that I knew I had a first line and could get under way. It is a very realistic snapshot of our lives these days, and it expresses themes very important to me in coping with the dangerous passions at loose in the world.

This poem opened a continuing season of harvest. I have written more—both poetry and prose—since then than in any comparable period of my life. I have been to more writers' workshops (which I love) than ever before, and have travelled more in general, both for the Kettering Foundation (I am associate editor of their *Kettering Review* and do part-time free-lance writing and editing for that organization) and for private and family reasons, such as visiting our far-scattered children and grandchildren. Marty and I spent twenty days in October 1987 in China on a tour organized by the Writers Guild.

In short, turning sixty brought me to the happiest and busiest period of my life, and this *carpe diem* begins, then, a whole new autobiography:

Darkling Plain Revisited

Now let me punch the mute on CNN,
the screen still flashing images of terror,
and let's make love as nearly four decades
have taught us how—serenely, without error,

with passion deep, relentless as Gulf Stream
warming the wintry wastes of northern shores,
precise as chefs manipulating enzymes
like syllables of juggling troubadours.

Now while grey February dawns breaks over
a village numbed by Sunday, you and I,
for whom all days are sabbath equally,
our morning sacrament demystify.

(My rod and staff still stands to comfort us.)
We knead the molehills of our flesh to mountains
and delve recesses that flame blackly pink
until the youth within our old bones fountains,

and damply we unpeel, then sighing sink
back to diurnal hazards we defuse
methodically: I brush my teeth and shave;
you shower while, again, I watch the news.

There is no safety. That is headline fact.

The screen that bubbles color like a flower
bears only tidings of our helpless dodging
colliding ricochets of random power.

On what, then, may grey budgerigars rely?
To Whom or What on Sunday sing their praise?
We build upon the Rock of moderate habits
a frail cathedral of our Ginnie Maes,

and in this high-tech jungle must we prey,
avoiding all exposure to the Game,
consuming little that corrupts or fattens,
protecting loins from Milton's spur of Fame.

casting our ballots, gossamer in the flood,
for levies offering a ghost of choice,
opening hymnals to humanity
although we know that we are not in voice.

Yes, Plato, I know that I am nowhere when
it comes to rivalry with madmen. I
subsist outside the temple changing coins.
Inside are all the anthropophagi

trading futures, Kuwait's for Des Moines',
inflamed by credence, credence is what sells
and licenses a CIA jihad.
I hear the street cries wrung by temple bells.

And so to work, you to your craft, I mine.
By nine my cursor pecks across the screen.
Dear Matthew Arnold, I write, the armies are
no longer ignorant; their strikes are clean;

the world which lies about us does not seem
other than what it is—both drab and dread.
The fight for peace will kill us, and we fear
the certitude each carries in his head.

But you were right about the need of truth
between those bonded pairs who would survive.
Ah love, I turn to you, may we preserve
our sweet cell insulated from the hive

and dream of hard earth cracking into spring,
sap surging in the dry old trunks anew.
May I, with reason, cry on winter air
Familiar words to you: *I do, I do!*

BIBLIOGRAPHY

Poetry:

Light in the West. Francestown, N.H.: Golden Quill Press, 1962.

The Ocean's Warning to the Skin Diver and Other Love Poems. Point Richmond, Calif.: Crown Point Press, 1964.

Serenade. Point Richmond, Calif.: Crown Point Press, 1968.

I Never Saw . . . (for children; illustrated by Helga Aichinger). Chicago: Albert Whitman, 1974.

Myrtle Whimple's Sampler. Hancock, Md.: Trunk Press, 1976.

The Village and Other Poems. Hancock, Md.: Trunk Press, 1976.

Public Domain. Hancock, Md.: Trunk Press, 1977.

Thirty Years of Poetry: Collected Poems, 1949–1979. New Braunfels, Tex.: Cedar Rock, 1979.

Partita in Nothing Flat. Daleville, Ind.: Barnwood, 1983.

The Village: New and Selected Poems. Baltimore, Md.: Dolphin-Moon Press, 1987.

Plays:

Plays for an Imaginary Theater. Urbana and London: University of Illinois Press, 1970.

Fiction:

The Fell of Dark. Boston: Houghton, 1966.

Nonfiction:

The Poet and the Poem. Cincinnati: Writer's Digest Books, 1963; revised edition. Cincinnati: Writer's Digest Books, 1974; revised edition. Cincinnati: Writer's Digest Books, 1979.

Poetry: Premeditated Art (textbook). Boston: Houghton, 1968.

Culture out of Anarchy: The Reconstruction of American Higher Learning. New York: Herder & Herder, 1970.

Families of Eden: Communes and the New Anarchism. New York: Seabury, 1974; London: Thames & Hudson, 1975.

Publishing Poetry. New Braunfels, Tex.: Cedar Rock, 1977.

The Poet's Handbook. Cincinnati: Writer's Digest Books, 1980.

On Being a Poet. Cincinnati: Writer's Digest Books, 1984.

Screenplays:

I See a Village . . . (film biography of Arthur Morgan). New York: Richard Kaplan Productions, 1969.

Confrontation (documentary). New York: Richard Kaplan Productions, 1969.

Editor of:

New Campus Writing, with Nolan Miller. Vol. I. New York: Bantam, 1956; Vol. II. New York: Bantam, 1958; Vol. III. New York: Grove, 1959; Vol. IV. New York: Grove, 1962.

Poet's Market: Where and How to Publish Your Poetry (annual directory). Cincinnati: Writer's Digest Books, 1985–.

For the Ages

You snap me writing verses at my desk,
my cursor dancing on a chip of quartz,
though I am not exactly picturesque—
decked out in naught but glasses and my shorts.
Or I snap you out hoeing lima beans,
catching you sweaty, soiled, with tousled hair,
bent to your work in floppy, paint-stained jeans
while I immortalize your derriere.
We bought the camera for we thought we should
have one to take to China, and, besides,
at our age we believe it would be good
to let grandchildren see how youth abides
when love makes all the biosphere Edenic,
and we, like them, are cute—and photogenic.

Gabriel Josipovici
1940-

"My Russian grandfather,
Alexei Rabinovitch," Paris, 1914

"My grandmother, with my mother and aunt,"
Alexandria, 1916

There is a passage in one of the poems of Samuel Hanagid, a Jewish poet who lived in Spain at the turn of the eleventh century, which runs:

> She said: "Rejoice, for God has brought you
> to your fiftieth year in the world!" But she
> had no inkling that, for my part, there is no
> difference at all between my own days which
> have gone by and the distant days of Noah
> about which I have heard. I have nothing in
> the world but the hour in which I am: it
> pauses for a moment, and then, like a cloud,
> moves on.

I used this as an epigraph for my novel *Conversations in Another Room,* and could use it even more appropriately for this essay, since it is probably true that Marcel's walks by the Vivonne, Dante's climbing up the steps of another man's house in his bitter exile, and David's inability to come to terms with the thought that his beloved son Absalom is dead and swinging by the hair from the branches of a tree, are more real to me than my own past.

Nor would I particularly want it any other way.

I have never been able to understand people who write their memoirs or autobiographies. Writing, for me, has to be an exploration. It has to involve making, not telling. It must look forward, not back. Simply to recount a story you already know seems to me a funny way to spend your time. There is obviously something to it, since so many people seem to indulge in it, but it is not something I can understand.

* * *

Is it possible to separate one's earliest memories from the stories one is later told about one's own childhood? I don't think so. Besides, these memories, if they really are such, come in the form of images, moments of clarity emerging from a sea of darkness. We make a story of our lives by fitting the images together. But what if meaning is bought at the expense of truth? Are there not many stories which might link the images to each other? Why select one and ignore the others? And why do we need such stories in the first place? Why not be content with the images alone?

*

One of the earliest images I think I recall is of myself and my mother walking along a road. The bank rises steeply and is perhaps covered with grass, or perhaps made of steps. It is difficult to say because there are massed rows of men sitting there. As we pass they hold out fruit to me, oranges or perhaps apples or pears. My mother tells me I can accept what they are offering me. The men smile and laugh. There is a feeling of well-being.

Later I am told that these were Italian soldiers. I was two or three at the time. The place is Cannes, in the south of France. The year is 1942 or 1943.

I also learn later that we Jews were safe in the south so long as it was under Italian control. When Italy fell, though, the Germans swooped down on the area, where Jews from all over France had gathered, under the impression that they would be safe, and picked them up in their thousands.

*

Another image: I am walking along a grassy track with my mother and father. We come to some large wrought-iron gates. My father takes hold of these and shakes them. They do not move. He says to me: "We'll have to climb over." Laboriously, I do so. When I am safely down on the other side he pushes open the gates and steps through, laughing. In my rage I bend down and pull up a clump of grass. One of the blades of grass cuts my fingers.

This was in La Bourboule, in the Massif Central. When the Germans made their first raid on Nice my mother left the hotel where we were staying—she and my father were already separated—and took me for a walk along the promenade. When she returned the Germans had gone, taking as many Jews as they could cram into their trucks. But no one doubted that they would soon be back for more.

My mother ran into an old friend, Ida Adamoff, the wife of Claude Bourdet, the Resistance fighter and later editor of *Combat.* Ida told her she must get out, and put her in touch with friends of hers who were escaping to La Bourboule.

"My parents with Tossi," Aix-en-Provence, 1936

*

Today the train journey from Nice to La Bourboule, via Lyon and Clermont-Ferrand, takes a few hours. In 1943 it took two days and a night. At any moment our train might have been stopped and the passengers searched. My mother sat a little way away, leaving me in charge of the others. She knew she would not be able to deny her Jewishness if asked.

I remember waking up in the night. We are still in the railway carriage, but the train is stopped. There are bright lights outside, and a lot of noise. I ask where we are and am told: Lyon. The thought of lions frightens me.

Even today I find journeys difficult. The fear of those people in the railway carriage must have seeped through to me, for I cannot have known in any conscious way that we were in danger of our lives.

It must be to those early years in France that I owe my very strong sense of how thin is the veneer provided by civilization and how quickly it can disappear.

*

My first novel is called *The Inventory.* There I

The beach, Cannes, 1942

tried to explore the curious fact that men gather possessions round them all their lives but that in the end these avail them nothing. They die as naked as when they came into the world. The things we pick up in the course of our lives remain to provide our descendants with the traces of what we had once been. They are perhaps no more than triggers for memory and imagination.

Ten years after that, in 1977, I wrote my fourth novel, *Migrations*. Though the immediate experiences behind that novel were as personal and diverse as the death of a beloved dog and the overwhelming impression made upon me by Harrison Birtwistle's *Triumph of Time*, as I wrote the book I discovered that my real theme was in fact that most common of twentieth-century experiences, the experience of being on the move and not knowing where you will end up, or indeed if you will ever reach a point of rest.

As I try to sort out these memories and images I see suddenly that between *The Inventory* and *Migrations* there is a link, and that perhaps all my work has been concerned with the attempt to explore and so lay to rest the feelings of a three-year-old child in war-torn France.

*

As an epigraph to *Migrations* I used a passage from the prophet Micah: "Arise and go now, for this is not your rest."

Shortly before writing the novel, I had begun to get interested in the Bible. My mother had told me the Bible stories when I was a child, but I had had no religious instruction, had never taken my *bar mitzvah* or even been inside a synagogue. But at the University of Sussex a colleague and I had started a course on "The Bible and English Literature," and another colleague, an Anglican priest who was also a Semiticist, was encouraging a group of us to learn Hebrew. For me the language was less alien than for some of the others, since I had spent ten years learning Arabic at school, and one Semitic language is much like another.

But the main reason why the Hebrew Bible seemed to speak to me was that it seemed to be almost entirely about the kinds of experiences I had myself undergone. Abraham, after all, is told by God to *lekh lekha*, to get up and go, leaving the country of his birth, his home, and his extended family. That is the start of the Hebrew nation. Of course Odysseus too travels to far-off lands, but that is only in order to come home again to his waiting wife and son. Aeneas is a little closer to Abraham. He too has to leave home and wife behind, knowing he will never return. But though Virgil has an uncanny awareness of the pathos of displacement and exile, it is the founding of the new home that is the main theme of his epic. Only the Bible, though of course it also celebrates the founding of a city, accepts that it is the fate of all cities to be destroyed, and suggests that the shadow of the wandering in the desert must always lie across man's fervent visions of rootedness and permanence.

In the Bible *going* and *resting* form part of the same whole. Arise and *go*, for this is not your *rest*, Micah tells the Hebrew nation. The dove sent out from the ark "found no rest for the sole of her foot," and Naomi tells her daughters-in-law, who wish to leave their native Moab and return with her to Israel: "The Lord grant you that ye may find rest, each of you in the house of her husband." It is because rest, a house, a family, are so important, that the notion of wandering, of going, is so poignant. It is extraordinary though that exile and migration and the longing for an end to such a condition, which seems to be a quintessentially modern experience, should have been most fully explored in a book written over twenty-five hundred years ago. That is the wonder of literature.

In my own case I feel that my most successful

pieces have been those in which I have been able to incorporate the maximum of movement, or unrest, in a form which eventually generates, in the reader, a sense of poise and rest. And one writes, of course, for the reader in oneself who is dissatisfied with what already exists.

*

There is a golden statue of the Virgin high up above the harbour of Marseilles. For a week I stared at it from our hotel window, and on one of the last days of our stay my mother took me there. As is usually the way with these things, it is the expectation rather than the fulfilment which I remember.

The war was over. The popping of champagne corks, I recall, frightened me more than anything I had previously known. That was in La Bourboule. Men climbed up greasy poles for prizes, but in my memory at least they always slither down before they can reach the top.

My mother later told me that the greatest horror of the war for her was the reprisals against suspected collaborators, which were a feature of those days. Much the same was said by many of those interviewed in the moving film *The Sorrow and the Pity*, which we watched with particular interest because it focussed on the town of Clermont-Ferrand, not far from La Bourboule. The mayor of La Bourboule, who was aware that we were Jewish yet never denounced us, in fact went out of his way to help, was one of those murdered.

As the war ended, my mother's sister, in Egypt, was able to get word to us that she had booked us a passage on an English troopship leaving Marseilles. We were to make our way there and wait.

I had been born on the day when the last ship sailed for Egypt which my parents might have caught before the war engulfed them. Now, almost five years later, my mother and I were at last to leave Europe and its horrors.

I remember eating a whole fish. I remember the perfect skeleton on the plate before me when I had finished. But it may only have been something I saw in a restaurant window.

*　　*　　*

The ship was called the *Arundel Castle*. Every morning we assembled on deck for safety drill. There was no certainty that we would not hit a mine.

When, eighteen years later, I got a job as lecturer in English at the newly formed University of Sussex, one of the first things my mother and I did was to

"With my mother," Alexandria, 1946

drive out to see Arundel Castle, not twenty miles from Brighton. It is the seat of the dukes of Norfolk, the senior Catholic family in England. On that September day in 1945 when we boarded the ship, there seemed to be no earthly reason why I should ever come to live in England, far less earn my living as a teacher of English literature. I was, after all, a French-speaking Jewish child on his way to Egypt, where both my parents had been born. What had England or the English language to do with me?

I had never tasted chocolate. The rumour spread through the ship that my fifth birthday would fall on the day we docked at Suez. The English soldiers strung up bars of chocolate round the deck and I and the few other children on board jumped and climbed up to get at them. The soldiers were kinder than the planners of the victory celebrations at La Bourboule and we no doubt ate more than was good for us.

It was three years since the Italian soldiers, probably thinking of their own children left at home, had stretched out their arms to give me some of their fruit. Several million soldiers and civilians had died in that time. We were among the lucky ones.

*

I remember a strange lady at Cairo station. She and my mother fell into each other's arms, leaving me to look on.

Until then my mother had been my only family. We had walked together in sunshine and snow, she had taught me to read and write, she had told me stories and carved dolls for me out of pieces of wood. Now I discovered I had an aunt, an uncle, and two girl cousins, seven and nine years older than myself. I discovered what this all meant: communal laughter, furious rows, the disappearance of the sense of threat.

Though the war had of course come almost to the edge of Cairo, most people in Egypt had little conception of what those in Europe had gone through. My mother was thirty-five when she returned, but her hair was almost as white as it is now at seventy-seven, and both mentally and physically she was far from well. And I don't think one ever "recovers" from profound experiences such as this had been. One merely learns to live with them, for better or worse.

Consciously, I was unaffected. I had not been old enough to know what fear and danger meant. But at Groppi's, the tea shop which stood for so long as an emblem of the old, cosmopolitan Cairo (its place now, symptomatically, taken by the Cairo Hilton), I still scooped up the sugar as we left the table and slipped it into my pocket, amazed that no one tried to stop me.

*

Maadi, where I was to live for the next ten years, was built by the English at the turn of the century. You cannot get lost in Maadi. It lies six miles south of Cairo and it is built on a simple grid plan, interspersed by a network of irrigation canals. The roads are lined with trees and many of the houses have sloping roofs and English gardens. In 1945 some of them were still inhabited by English families.

Maadi lies between the Nile and the desert, and all its main arteries run north to south. Furthest west is the Nile. Then comes the railway line, which links Cairo to Helwan, another eight miles further south. This is where my mother's father, a Russian-Jewish doctor from Odessa, had come to settle in 1907. He had been wounded in the Russo-Japanese War, and had then decided to travel. He had found Helwan, with its sulphur springs, the healthiest place in the

world. Now it is a mass of crumbling, high-rise blocks, often built in the gardens of the old villas without even any attempt to demolish these. It is here that the new Egyptian work force live, here that the bread riots start.

After setting up his practice my grandfather married a local girl. Her paternal grandfather had come from Ferrara, and my family, like so many Italian-Jewish families, tends to regard *The Garden of the Finzi-Continis* as *its* book. On her mother's side my grandmother's family was said to have been in Egypt since the time of Moses.

Here in Helwan, in the villa called La Gabalaya, "the grotto" (there was indeed a grotto in the garden), my mother and aunt were born. Strangely, English was the first language they spoke, for they had an English nanny. My grandparents were so besotted by things English that they bought all their wedding furniture at Maples.

My mother still possesses an English Bible with an inscription "from her Godmother, Sister Margaret Clare, Feb. 1921." The reason for this is that when her father died, when she was five, her mother was befriended by a missionary and had her two little girls baptised. An inquisitive aunt reminded the family of this when my mother came to get married (her mother had died, after remarrying when she was ten), with the result that she had to go to the rabbinate in Cairo and undergo a ritual immersion in a filthy pool, while someone chanted outside the window, before the proper Jewish wedding could take place. My aunt had in the meantime met a Catholic boy and, before marrying him, converted to the Roman faith. One of her daughters in turn married a Moslem and converted to Islam, the other married a Greek Orthodox journalist, but has remained a Catholic.

*

The trains from Cairo to Helwan ran every quarter of an hour. I know, because our first independent flat (we had begun by living with my aunt) was right next to the railway line. In the mornings we had breakfast on the terrace. Beyond the railway line were fields of maize. Beyond that, the stately movement of the tall masts of the hidden *felucca*s attested to the presence of the Nile.

When people came to visit they stopped talking when the trains thundered by and took time to get started again afterwards. We couldn't understand why they stopped. The trains, after a few weeks, did not even trouble my sleep.

My mother went to work in a milk shop at five in the morning. Though my grandparents had been well

The terrace, Road 9, Maadi, 1947

off, the Russian Revolution, the devaluation of the Deutschmark, and the fecklessness of my mother's relatives meant that we now found it very difficult to make ends meet. We must have been the only European family in Egypt not to have a servant, though that was less because we couldn't afford one than because my mother had a horror, which I have inherited, of being in a position to give orders to anyone just because you are paying them.

Once, when I couldn't get my trousers buttoned in the morning, I went out into the street and got a passerby to help me. He complied, politely, but I was given a good talking to and did not try again. However, as far as I can recall, nobody ever got raped, or mugged, or murdered. We rode about on our bicycles all day when we weren't at school. Maadi was a friendly place to grow up in.

But violence could erupt at any time. Every now and again we learned that the Moslem Brothers had assassinated a leading politician. At Ramadan the Arabs would find their nerves wearing thin, and fights would break out in the streets. The Egyptians are a gentle people, but when they get angry they will do things they later regret. Fathers would turn on their children and beat them about the face and head; a donkey that was too laden or tired to advance would be thrashed till it fell on its knees. There was nothing vindictive about this, but there was not much self-

control either.

We moved to another flat, this time just the other side of the railway line. It was a basement flat in a house owned by a patriarch who lived on the top floor with his thirteen children, their spouses, and their innumerable offspring. When a member of the family fell ill, the witch doctor would be called in. He would slaughter a turkey in the garden and chant over it. Usually the person recovered.

We had a dog (we always had dogs in Egypt; my mother was known as the "mother of the dogs," my aunt, who at one time had forty cats—people would come from far and wide to watch the feeding of this army—as "the mother of the cats") who was driven wild by the sight of a *galabiyeh*. He would growl and sometimes, it must be said, try to bite the ankles of its wearer. I remember one scene, more obviously frightening than anything in the war. One of the landlord's adult sons is standing at the top of the garden stairs leading down to our basement flat, kicking at my mother's head and screaming that he is going to kill our dog. My mother tries to calm him while pushing the dog into the house behind her.

This must have been after 1948 and the first Arab-Israeli war. I cannot remember ever feeling any hostility to Jews in Egypt, though. After 1952 there was of course hostility to Westerners, and school would often be cancelled (to our great joy) because there were riots and burnings in Cairo and the buses couldn't get through. But I had many Egyptian friends and I never felt that they were hostile to me as a Jew.

*

The next north-south artery after the railway was the central canal, with its border of giant eucalyptus trees. The irrigation system must have been excellent because I remember Maadi as constantly in flower. On one day of every week the gardens of a different section of the town were flooded. Within twenty-four hours the water had disappeared, but the earth clearly needed no more. The garden of one flat we lived in had a guava tree. In the beautiful bungalow we owned and lived in for the last two years and which gave onto the central canal just at the point where a little wooden bridge crossed it, there was both a mango and an apricot or *mish-mish* tree. This last gave onto the road, and the children on their way to one of the Arab schools would throw stones up into it to get the fruit down long before it was ripe. My mother would remonstrate with them, urge them at least to wait until they could eat the fruit, but they never seemed to take the point. Once too my mother got up in the middle of the night because she thought she heard someone in the tree. She went out onto the verandah and saw a white shape among the branches. "Who's there?" she called out. "Me," answered a sheepish voice, and the night watchman slowly clambered down.

In this house too the police came once in the night and took away the young and charming couple we had taken in as paying guests at a friend's request. They had been tipped off about the woman but it turned out that the real catch was her companion, one of the most wanted Communist agents in the country.

*

The fourth and final main artery of the town was the great dyke, beyond which lay the desert. The dyke had been built before our arrival, after a flash flood had hit the town. Overnight the water had built up in the nearby *waddi*s and rushed down out of the desert. For days afterwards, apparently, toilet rolls from the stores of one of the nearby army camps festooned themselves round trees and blocked up drains. The resourceful headmistress of my cousins' school got the girls to collect these and dry them in the sun. For ages afterwards this slightly wrinkled, brown-edged paper acted as a daily reminder of what had happened.

In 1950 some of the land on the other side of the dyke was irrigated and in no time at all there were green fields, and then strange modernist buildings started to spring up. This was to be the new Victoria College, Cairo, an outgrowth of the famous Alexandria school of that name, founded in 1901, on the good Queen's death. During the war it had been evacuated to Cairo and lodged in the premises of an Italian school. Now the Italians wanted their school back and the authorities decided to build in the more spacious area of Maadi. Thus when I was ready for my secondary education, the school, with its English teachers and its attempt at a public-school ethos (houses, prefects, etc.), though without a single English pupil, was on my doorstep.

When we had landed in Egypt I spoke only French and it was natural that I should be sent to a French school. My mother was horrified, however, when she discovered that they were giving me at least an hour's homework a day. What she felt I needed, after the anxiety and solitude of the war years, was to play with other children. So she took me out and sent me to the little English primary school in Maadi.

On such decisions hinge the directions taken by a whole life. My father had been educated at one of

The canal, Maadi, 1947

the *grands lycées* in Paris, and then at the University of Aix-Marseilles. His father, Albert Josipovici, had written, when still a very young man, a novel called *Le Livre de Goha le simple,* in collaboration with his brother-in-law. Octave Mirbeau had contributed an enthusiastic preface, and the book enjoyed a great success in France when it came out, even being short-listed for the Prix Goncourt in 1919, the year when Proust won it with *A l'ombre des jeunes filles en fleurs.* It was an archetypal case of one member of the team having the style, the other the ideas, for when, in later life, each tried to write a novel on his own, one was stylish but dead, the other brimming with life but appallingly written. Both were failures. Now, by sending me to an English school at the age of five, my mother ensured that if I in turn were ever to try my hand at writing it would be in English and not in French, and that the natural place for me to end up in would be an English-speaking country. That, however, was not something she had in mind at the time.

*

One of the things that most surprised me about

England, when I came here in 1956, was that all the schools were English. In Cairo there were at least three English and three French schools (the Lycée, the "Pères," and the "Frères," as they were affectionately called), a German school, an Italian school, an Armenian school, a Greek school, and no doubt many more. Everyone spoke at least three languages, all badly, since it was always easier to say a word in a language other than the one one was using at the time if one couldn't think of the right word in that language. I'm afraid that is still how I speak to my cousin on the phone.

The fact is that Alexandria, Cairo, and Beirut were the last great cosmopolitan centres in the world, the last of the Hellenistic cities, as Cavafy instinctively sensed. Now all have vanished and in their place, for better or worse, are three Arab cities.

Victoria College is now Victory College. Maadi has become a suburb of Cairo. On the desert side, where we used to cycle out for picnics or to look for prehistoric arrowheads (the area was rich with archeological remains), there is now only barbed wire topped by signs which warn one to keep away from the military zone. The central canal has been filled in with rubble. It is apparently no longer necessary and was a breeding ground for mosquitoes. But the mosquitoes are still a pest and the dust merely rises up into the neglected eucalyptus trees. The drains don't work and water gushes out of holes in the roads and pavements.

*   *   *

I saw all this when I returned to Egypt in 1976. I had won a travelling scholarship for my first volume of stories, *Mobius the Stripper,* and decided to use it for more than a trip to Paris.

It was twenty years since we had left.

Almost as soon as I had landed in England, Egypt had become unreal. In the following years my time in Egypt became the subject of anecdote but, because it was unrelated to anything else, it was as if it had never existed.

It was not even as if I had been born there. And I had left at fifteen, just at the moment when one begins to do more than take one's environment for granted. I had won a lot of medals swimming for my club. I had played tennis and football and even represented the school at athletics. I had spent a lot of time riding round on bicycles and whistling at the girls. But the "I" who had done these things seemed to have no connection with the person I now was, the student and then the teacher of English literature, the writer who looked for his models in the art and

literature of Western Europe.

If I felt different from the English people I met, it was because I was as interested in continental literature as I was in English. I felt "foreign," but that seemed to have nothing to do with Egypt, only with a kind of rootlessness or, if one wanted to be positive about it, a cosmopolitanism which, I gradually realised, was not something I could take for granted even in those I found myself closest to intellectually and emotionally.

But as the years went by I found that, far from gradually becoming assimilated to England and the English, they were growing more and more strange and incomprehensible to me. I also began to sense, obscurely, that I had perhaps not quite understood the basis of my own difference.

I suppose it was during the Six-Day War that I, like so many others, had it driven home to me that I was Jewish. I began to read the Bible and writers like Franz Rosenzweig, the greatest modern exponent of Judaism. I began to learn Hebrew and to read Israeli writers like Yehuda Amichai and Aharon Appelfeld, who wrote in Hebrew but whose roots, like my own, lay in a peculiarly Jewish and not Israeli experience.

In that way my sojourn in Egypt, and the Eastern Mediterranean roots of my family, began to make a sort of sense. They helped explain to me certain aspects of myself, my instinctive response to writers as diverse as Cavafy, Pessoa, and Montale, and my aversion to the Puritan strain in English culture, Milton in particular. And they helped explain too why I also felt so alien to the dominant Anglo-American Jewish culture, which is, of course, East European, and harks back nostalgically to the warmth of the *shtetl.* My own family culture, as I learned about it from anecdotes and photos, was radically different: urban, cosmopolitan, cultured, wealthy. I found it mirrored, perhaps surprisingly, above all in Proust: that tolerance, wit, and irony, a quality of mind which takes for granted the benefits of civilisation yet is all too aware of the abysses covered over by culture, which emanates from Proust's work, made me feel at once, when I first read him, that he was *my* writer, that neither the English nor even the French could quite understand him.

And Proust was very much on my mind during the month I spent in Egypt in 1976. I had gone back partly to see my aunt and her family, partly to bring those ten lost years back into the mainstream of my life, and partly to try and understand my own distance from the European culture of which, whether I liked it or not, I was now a member. I accomplished all these things, but, naturally, not quite in the ways I had expected.

One of the most wonderful moments in *A la recherche du temps perdu* comes at the start of *Le Temps retrouvé*. The ageing Marcel goes to stay with Gilberte, now married to his old friend Robert de Saint-Loup, at their country estate of Tansonville, close to Combray. On his evening strolls with Gilberte, his first love, Swann's daughter, she shows him how, in a few minutes, one can walk from what in his childhood he had known as Swann's Way to the Guermantes Way. This is shattering to Marcel. For him the two Ways were as distinct from each other as two separate universes. And yet, he now learns, they had all along been as accessible to each other as two adjoining Parisian streets. It takes the rest of the novel for Marcel to come to terms with this fact, the gulf between our childish perceptions of the world and the way it "really is," and to understand why it is necessary to be mistrustful of that word "really." For at some deep, instinctive level the newfound reality quite fails to annul the childhood perception.

I thought of this episode when I went back to Egypt. In my memory Maadi was divided into six or seven different "ways." Here was where we lived when we first arrived: here I fought with my enemy of the day; here I used to wait for a girl in pigtails as she cycled home from school, my heart beating, wondering whether I would dare speak to her. Here I had lived when I was twelve: on this corner I had drunk Coca-Cola with my friends; down that stretch of road we organised our slow bicycle races (the winner is the last home but falling over disqualifies you). Here was the little wooden bridge over the central canal and the bungalow we had lived in for the last two years; the sporting club was just five minutes away, and on summer nights, when an open-air film was showing, you could hear the music clearly and, if you strained your ears in bed, over the distant barking of the dogs, even some of the dialogue.

But now I found I could walk from one "way" to another in a few minutes. A house I had played in as a child of seven was actually in the very same street as another house, belonging to quite a different epoch, where I had found myself alone with a girl I was in love with and not dared to take advantage of the situation. The swimming pool, where I had spent a good part of every year training and playing, turned out to be no different from other open-air swimming pools, filled with quite ordinary water and bounded by a quite ordinary wall and fence. I walked and walked and found it impossible to reconcile memory and reality, past and present.

And that is the absurdity of memoirs. Words convey the common, not the unique. I could have written a journalistic piece on Egypt in 1976, as a

number of well-meaning friends urged me, but though that might conceivably have been of interest to others, it would have left out precisely what meant most to me about the return journey, the mysterious sense of disparity between what I was encountering and what I still felt in my bones about the place.

That is why Proust had to write a novel, not an autobiography, and why it took him half his life to find the form he needed. Simply to write down what he "remembered" would not have done; he had to construct a fiction in order to make sense to himself of the nature of memory and thus of his own life. But that of course is why we will go on reading Proust long after the memoirs of Canetti, Spender, and Patrick Leigh Fermor have been forgotten.

*

My mother and I left Egypt in September 1956, eleven years after we had arrived, halfway between Nasser's seizure of the Suez Canal and the Suez crisis.

By the early fifties it had become clear that there was no future in Egypt for non-Moslems. Besides, all my education had been in English, and there was the unspoken assumption that I would finish my studies at Oxford. This was not snobbery, it was just that Oxford and Cambridge were the only English universities known in Egypt, and the myth still persisted that Oxford was for the arts and Cambridge for the sciences.

A few enquiries sufficed to make it clear that the only way to get a grant was for me to take my A levels in England (and a university education without a grant was out of the question). So the headmaster of Victoria College promised that he would try to find me a place in a sixth form at an English school. Eventually he reported that Cheltenham College, where he had previously been headmaster, would take me on as a day-boy from September 1956.

My mother had never felt well, physically or spiritually, in Egypt (unlike my aunt, who loves the place in spite of everything). England, since her childhood, had been a dream. She decided to uproot herself once more and try to settle in England, if that could be achieved. Now that I am older than she was when she took that decision I see what courage it required. What energy too. In nine months she succeeded in selling the property we had, which was our entire capital, and getting it out clandestinely (losing a good third, naturally), and acquired a passport for herself (hers had been confiscated when we landed in 1945) and for me (it turned out that my father had taken French nationality, so I was myself French). For weeks the authorities stalled about

The pool, Maadi, 1955

giving us exit visas, and we wondered if we would ever get away. And even as we boarded the boat in Alexandria we expected to be stopped at any moment and thrown into jail (taking capital out of Egypt was of course a crime). I felt sick too at leaving my dogs and friends, my whole life, behind. But that, it seemed, was what periodically happened, and one simply had to accept it as a law of existence.

*

I think I was in a state of shock when I got to England. At school everyone was very kind, though, and I survived by smiling a lot and playing a great deal of sport. One of my reports said, in a wonderfully British way, "Should do well if he does not work too hard." But I could not afford not to work. I had to get a place at Oxford and a State Scholarship to enable me to take up that place. If I failed to do either there was no knowing what my mother and I would do or where we would end up.

Fear, I discovered, is a great spur. I got the place at Oxford and the grant, and, after a lot of effort, my mother's request for a year's residence, renewable, was granted by the Home Office. After that it was relatively easy to do well at Oxford and move on from there to a job at the first and most interesting of the New Universities. I have been at Sussex ever since, and my life as a writer has so swallowed up my life as a person that there is, in a sense, nothing more to be said. Except perhaps to sketch in briefly the origins and growth of that new life.

*

I was too young to go up to Oxford in 1957, so we moved to London and I had a year between school and university. It was a wonderful period.

The only culture in Egypt was the cinema. As a child I saw no plays, went to no concerts, saw no paintings, but did get to see most of the Hollywood films of the forties and early fifties. This was not altogether a bad thing. Though it meant I knew nothing, it also meant that I had no built-in prejudices (about Renaissance painting being an "advance" on medieval art, for example, or modern music being "cacophonous"). In that year in London I got to know all the great galleries, started going to concerts, and read my way through the masterpieces of world literature.

I read Tolstoy and Dostoevsky, Shakespeare and Donne, Eliot and Pound. And then I read Proust.

The impact which Proust made on me then—and still does—has, as I have suggested, partly to do with the fact that he seems to describe a familiar world. But much more important is the fact that here, for the first time, I came upon a writer who was not afraid to admit to failure.

Other novelists, of course, have dealt with human, personal failure. But they have done so in works which never seem to doubt their own ability to convey whatever it was that needed conveying. In Proust's great novel I found the story of someone who recognises the central place of creativity in our lives and yet who also recognises the perpetual frustration of that creativity, despite the best will in the world.

Marcel realises early on that he wants to write more than anything else in the world. Yet as soon as he tries to write he finds either that he is not saying what he wants to say or that a sense of terrible tedium comes over him. But since he has at moments felt that writing was the one thing that could enhance life, could bring real and lasting joy, something seems to be wrong. The feelings of intense happiness which seize him every now and again seem to cry out to be made permanent, to be brought into the realm of words. Yet as soon as he tries to do this the joy departs, leaving only boredom and frustration. What is he to do?

In the end his great book grows out of exploring precisely this contradiction. It demonstrates that the cardinal sin is indeed despair, and that this is closely followed by laziness, the acceptance of what the world thinks rather than what you have felt. Swann, falling out of love with Odette, can dismiss the whole experience of his passion for her with the words: "She was not my type." But for Marcel the experience of passion is as important as the realisation that it has little to do with the object of passion. Why did I feel what I felt if she was not my type? is the question he keeps asking.

Proust gave me the confidence to fail, the confidence to be confused, the confidence to know that if one trusted one's instinct and refused to be satisfied with immediate solutions, one would probably get somewhere in the end.

But even a lesson of this magnitude cannot be automatically translated into action. Though Oxford was important to me—it was there that I began to learn to think as well as to feel, there I met people who were driven by some of the same concerns as myself, such as the composer Gordon Crosse—it was not till 1966 that I was able to internalise that lesson.

I had taken the job at Sussex imagining, like so many hopeful writers, that the academic life would give me time to get on with my writing. And, like many hopeful writers, I soon discovered that the reality was rather different.

First of all there was the heady stimulus of working with lively colleagues and teaching a huge variety of great works, from Dante to Eliot. The trouble with that was that my own efforts then seemed pointless and trivial, lacking the very qualities I admired in other writers. Even more insidious, though, was the sense that while a day or even a week spent on a critical essay or preparing for a lecture would never be wholly wasted, even if I made very little progress, weeks or months might be totally wasted on fiction that didn't turn out as I had hoped.

The garden, Lewes, with Pilly, 1969

The temptation to win the respect of colleagues, students, and friends, and even of myself, by writing a good critical essay, giving a good lecture, instead of producing bad fiction, was immense.

And yet somewhere deep inside me there was a need to write fiction, a need almost as strong as the need for air and food. After three years at the university I began to feel that I would have to get out for the sake of my sanity.

The crunch came when I was granted my first term of paid leave, to get on with a critical book I had been toying with on and off ever since I had started a B.Litt. at Oxford. I was terrified. I sensed that this was my last chance. I had been promising for too long. I was twenty-five. I had to write my novel or get out.

The problem was that when I tried to write instinctively, as I wrote my short stories, the novel would peter out after a few pages. Yet when I worked out a plot beforehand I lost all interest in the thing. How then to keep the excitement of writing which the short stories gave me, with the comfort of working at something bigger than a short story?

Fear, as I had already found when working for my A levels, is a great stimulus. It pushes one past the barriers of what one thinks one can do to the discovery of what it is one can really do. But it has to be genuine fear. And this was it all right. I would wake up in the mornings in a cold sweat, wondering how I would be able to cope with the day to come. Every hour became a test.

I read—quite by chance—I still don't know what

made me take the book off the library shelves—the autobiography of an American thriller writer—I don't even remember his name. He had been at Harvard Business School but had decided that he liked the outdoor life and wanted to be his own man, so determined to become a successful thriller writer. A friend then gave him the best piece of advice I have ever come across: You had better write the first seven books fast, he said, because only the eighth is going to be any good.

I decided then and there that I wouldn't worry about *how* my book came out. I would simply be concerned with getting it written. And I worked out that if I wrote ten pages a day for fifteen days I would have the draft of a novel in a fortnight. In this way I hoped to beat the size bogey.

A word had come into my head: inventory. Just to repeat it to myself filled me with excitement. The reason for this, I realised, was that it pointed in two opposite directions at once. An inventory is a list of objects, the most impersonal and external thing imaginable. But hidden in the word is the ghost of the word "invent," the most subjective and internal thing imaginable. The word spawned a rudimentary plot: a man dies and his relatives gather round and make an inventory of his belongings. In the course of this one of them tries to understand her relations with the dead man, and to do this she recalls (or perhaps invents) one scene after another.

Thus the woman's search would become mine, or mine hers, and I wouldn't lose the excitement of exploration. Yet now I encountered another block, which I had not reckoned with (there is nothing like tackling a big piece of work for forcing problems—and therefore solutions—on you). I realised as soon as I began to write the first sentence that something in me revolted at the thought of telling a story, describing houses and people. It quite literally made me feel sick to write down the equivalent of "She laid her lovely white hand on his sleeve, her rings sparkling in the lamplight." I didn't mind reading this in Tolstoy—it occurs in a crucial scene between Anna and Vronsky—but I could not be party to it myself.

Critics sometimes accuse me of writing difficult books, even books specifically designed to annoy the reader. But would anyone spend a large part of his life shut up by himself in a room simply to annoy people he doesn't know? Writers may be daft, but they aren't that daft. Clearly one writes because one has to. One writes to bring a little order and clarity into what is otherwise murky and confused, and to make something clean, bright, and true. But if that is so, how could I put down a sentence like Tolstoy's? I have never seen that hand or those rings sparkling in

the lamplight. What childish nonsense to pretend I have merely to persuade an imaginary reader. Surely writing ought to be concerned with more important and interesting things?

So I learned for myself the implications of the Proustian dilemma, which I had responded to with excitement ten years earlier but which had to be learned the hard way: I needed to write for my own survival, but it had to be a different kind of writing from Tolstoy's.

Give me specific problems, not general ones, Stravinsky once observed. In *The Inventory* I solved the specific problem of narration and description by eschewing description and dealing only with what interested me, the interplay between characters and the generation of plot expressed only by means of dialogue and inventory lists. When I grasped what it was I wanted to do, the book changed from being a painful and boring task to being a wildly exciting (though frightening) one. The book became possible, it became something I wanted (wanted desperately) to do, because it was now no longer a question of telling, as if it were true, a story I had made up in my head, but of bringing into the world something which did not and could not have existed before, of making something which, if I succeeded, would have a life of its own and be irreducible to paraphrase. It turned out that if one trusted one's instinct—and, perhaps, was scared enough—then it might be the first and not just the eighth book which would be good enough to publish.

*

Though I had found teaching inhibiting at first, once I began to have confidence in my own writing I realised how lucky I was to be at Sussex. For here, in the sixties and seventies, I found an atmosphere in which genuine and valuable work could be born. It seemed to be the natural continuation of what my friends and I had come to believe in at Oxford, but which neither Oxford itself as an institution nor English literary culture at large seemed prepared to understand.

I had gone up to Oxford raw and confused, but with the sense of tremendous possibilities in myself and in the world at large. There was so much to discover: Greek drama, medieval art, Hölderlin, Kleist, Valéry, the music of the Renaissance and of the Far East—it was endless. In Gordon Crosse and the other musician in my year at Saint Edmund Hall, David Phillips, and in John Mepham, a biochemist from Magdalen (now a philosopher and literary critic), I found people who were equally curious,

"The garden in Lewes, with (clockwise from right) Timothy Hyman, Gillian Barlow, Stephen Finer, my mother, my cousin Anna, and (in the foreground) Nimrod," 1979

equally willing to explore and discover. Gordon persuaded me to join the Contemporary Music Club, where I heard the music of Varèse and Stockhausen for the first time, and where most of the leading British composers came and talked. We went over to see Peter Maxwell Davies at Cirencester, where he was teaching, and I remember introducing him to my former tutor, Del Kolve, knowing they both had a passion for the art of the Middle Ages—a passion I had come to share. Webern and Messiaen were the rage then, but Webern forced one to go back to late medieval polyphony and Messiaen to the music of Southeast Asia. It was clear to us that you could only understand the new if you understood the old and distant, and *vice versa.* People who said they loved Beethoven but loathed Stockhausen, loved Dickens but sneered at Robbe-Grillet, in effect only demonstrated their prejudice and laziness. It was not a question of old and new, traditional and experimental, but of the ability or otherwise to read, listen, and see.

At Sussex I found a new university fired by the same principles. The student would read Homer and Proust, Dante and Eliot. Not in some general Great

Books course, but in courses designed to make him grasp the specific cultural and historical matrix of each author, how Homer *differed* from Proust and Dante from Eliot, as well as what they had in common.

Sussex gave me the confidence to write my first critical book, *The World and the Book,* which I had been turning over in my head since my undergraduate days, and which I dedicated to Peter Maxwell Davies because it seemed to me that he embodied in his own work and person much that the book was trying to say: how an understanding of pre-Renaissance modes of thought and artistic purpose could help one in one's own art today, and how a response to modern art could open the doors to an appreciation of pre-Renaissance and non-Western art in general.

What Sussex (and in particular the School of European Studies under its first dean, Martin Wight) was setting out to do in the sixties was paralleled by developments in English musical life. William Glock had become Controller of Music at the BBC and instigated the wonderful Thursday Invitation Concerts. The secret of these weekly events lay precisely in their juxtaposition of works. The first concert consisted of two Mozart quintets and Boulez's *Le Marteau sans maître;* later, I seem to remember, we had Ockeghem and Stravinsky, Beethoven and Schoenberg, Messiaen and Javanese music. Boulez became principal conductor of the BBC Symphony Orchestra, and concerts became more frequent and more adventurous. The London Sinfonietta was formed and Peter Maxwell Davies and Harrison Birtwistle formed the Pierrot Players, giving memorable performances of medieval and Renaissance music and the music of the Second Viennese School, as well as that of the two founders themselves. Stockhausen, Boulez, Berio, Ligeti, and Lutosławski were regular visitors and often gave preconcert talks. The halls were packed and the sense of excitement at each concert immense.

Alas, that excitement did not spread to the literary scene. It has become clear to me over the years that with the coming of the war English literary culture turned decisively away from Europe. The great Modernists are intensively studied at university, but as classics, not living presences. As far as the literary establishment is concerned it is as if Pound, Eliot, Joyce, and Woolf had never existed. England is once more the country it was when Pound and Eliot first arrived: smug, self-satisfied, distrustful of foreigners and their ways. True, a number of foreign writers, such as Grass, Marquez, and Kundera, are almost idolised in certain circles, and used as sticks with which to beat the timidities of the English, but there is little sense of any understanding of the literary context from which they have sprung, and many better, though quieter, writers are totally ignored. All this is reinforced by a peculiar brand of English Marxism, profoundly moralistic and puritanical in its inclinations typified by Raymond Williams and Terry Eagleton, which imagines it is fighting the establishment but is in fact (at least to my outsider's eye) the victim of precisely the same insular prejudices.

This, sadly, is beginning to affect every aspect of English life, and even the University of Sussex is starting to look very much like any other English University, while the musical life of the country, since Glock's retirement and Boulez's departure, has markedly deteriorated.

*

One thing Maxwell Davies taught me by example was not to be afraid of trying anything new, for it is often only by trying one's hand at a new form or even medium that one discovers one's potential. So I have, when the opportunity has arisen, written stage and radio plays, as well as stories, novels, and essays.

Most of the time, of course, one has to live with frustration and the sense of failure: one has not done what one had hoped to do; somehow, at some point, one has betrayed the work. Yet every now and again the opposite happens: it all works out infinitely better than one could ever have imagined.

This occurred with the play I wrote for the Actors' Company in 1973, *Flow,* where a very precise commission led to a work which embodied material so profoundly buried I did not know it was there; and it happened again with my last novel, *Contre-Jour.*

I had been gradually turning from music to painting as a stimulus for my work. This was partly under the impact of meeting a wide range of figurative painters, from the septuagenarian Polish-Jewish painter Josef Herman to R. B. Kitaj and younger artists such as Timothy Hyman, Andrzej Jackowski, Christopher Couch, and Stephen Finer. I found again, as I had at Oxford with Gordon Crosse, that artists who were not writers seemed to have a much wider sense of the possibilities of art, and to be much more in tune with my own aims and ambitions, than most English writers.

One day, on the radio, I heard someone talking about a Bonnard exhibition at the Pompidou Centre in Paris. In passing he mentioned that one of the main reasons why Bonnard painted so many nudes in bathrooms was that his wife had been a compulsive washer.

Within two or three hours of that talk an entire novel had taken shape, where before there had been absolutely nothing. I dropped everything else I was working on. I knew I simply had to keep my days clear and give myself entirely up to it, and the novel would write itself. It was almost as if I were reading from a very faded page on which, nevertheless, everything could be made out if I only concentrated hard enough.

The novel is not "about" Bonnard at all. For one thing, half of it consists of a monologue by the painter's daughter, and Bonnard and Marthe had no children. Yet the more I learned about Bonnard's work and about the man, the more I liked and admired them: his reticence, his modesty, his un-Romantic sense of dedication, and the way he combined the classical and monumental with the impressionistic and the fugitive. You start to look at a painting, focussing, as usual, on the centre, and quickly find your eye drawn outward, to the periphery, where a head peers in, or a tiny figure can be made out in the shrubbery, or a dog is about to disappear. So many of Bonnard's paintings are in effect impossible objects, yet with none of the slickness of Escher or the high polish of Magritte; so

The Sussex Ox, with Henrietta Foster, 1981

many of them express deep suffering, but transmuted into a kind of acceptance, and even happiness.

I did not want to write a fictional biography. I did not want to pretend that I could "be" or even "understand" this painter. We cannot ever understand the people or the artists we are fondest of. Perhaps the best we can do is recognise the nature of their distance from us.

And that, in the end, is what the book is about, and (I think) explains its form. I knew from the start that the daughter was absolutely essential, but I didn't know why. I think now that she is perhaps my lead into the centre of the book. For she feels excluded from the close relationship of her parents, just as I felt excluded from the relationship of Bonnard and Marthe. But then her feeling is strangely reduplicated in her mother, who in turn feels shut off from the life of her husband. And yet she knows, as he knows, even though a part of her refuses to acknowledge this, that there is a deep bond between them, and even that it is this which makes his work possible.

When it was done the book felt like a Paradise to the Hell of *Migrations* and the Purgatory of *The Air We Breathe*. A sombre paradise, but at any rate the nearest I would ever be able to get to it.

*

What I find interesting about the way the novel came to me is that once the right objective correlative had been found (or given), it allowed material which had obviously always been there, but which I had not known about, to find the light. The book came in a single clear jet because I found myself able to talk about many things that were close to my heart. But the corollary is frightening. Had it not been for that chance overhearing of a talk on Bonnard, had the speaker not mentioned a strange fact about Bonnard's married life, would it have remained buried for ever?

That is an amazing thought. It suggests that most of us, for most of the time, are completely out of touch with what is most central to ourselves. The Romantic and Realist error is to imagine that one has something to express, and that then it is simply a question of finding the best way to express it. But the truth appears to be very different. It seems that even when one imagines that one is quite open to oneself, one is still likely to pass over nine-tenths of what is really important to one. And, most probably, to die without ever becoming aware of this.

It seems that only the act of making can lead to discovery. The act of memory cannot. That is why autobiography is so misleading. It can tell us what a person thinks he is like, perhaps what he would like to be like. It can provide a form of gossip, telling one who knew whom, and when, and even who went to bed with whom, and when. But that is all.

Autobiography and memoirs can never make manifest their own limitations. They always give the illusion (to their authors as well as to their readers) that they are adequate to the task in hand. Only fiction can point to its own limits, can remind us that not everything has been said or can be said. Autobiography fosters the illusion that our lives are stories and as such can be told. It thus does nothing to appease the deep sense we all have that this is not so. Only fiction, in the right hands, can awaken in us the sense of how little we know of ourselves and the world, and how intense is our desire to change that condition. By so doing it brings us back in touch with both ourselves and the world.

That is why I have felt the need—it grew on me as I was writing—to organise even this brief memoir into a tight and somewhat arbitrary form (derived from Schoenberg's *Pierrot lunaire*).

Even so, I am relieved to bring it to an end (for I cannot help but be suspicious of its implicit as well as its explicit claims), and to return to the rigours and pleasures of fiction.

BIBLIOGRAPHY

Fiction:

The Inventory. London: M. Joseph, 1968.

Words. London: Gollancz, 1971.

Timothy Hyman, Gabriel Josipovici, and Andrzej Jackowski on the Downs above Lewes

Mobius the Stripper: Stories and Short Plays (includes the plays *One, Dreams of Mrs. Fraser,* and *Flow*). London: Gollancz, 1974.

The Present. London: Gollancz, 1975.

Four Stories. London: Menard Press, 1977.

Migrations. Brighton, England: Harvester Press, 1977.

The Echo Chamber. Brighton, England: Harvester Press, 1980.

The Air We Breathe. Brighton, England: Harvester Press, 1981.

Conversations in Another Room. London: Methuen, 1984.

Contre-Jour: A Triptych after Pierre Bonnard. Manchester, England, and New York: Carcanet Press, 1986.

In the Fertile Land: Stories. Manchester, England, and New York: Carcanet Press, 1987.

Nonfiction:

The World and the Book: A Study of Modern Fiction. London: Macmillan, 1971; Stanford, Calif.: Stanford University Press, 1971.

The Lessons of Modernism and Other Essays. London: Macmillan, 1977; Totowa, N.J.: Rowman & Littlefield, 1977.

Writing and the Body. Brighton, England: Harvester Press, 1982; Princeton, N.J.: Princeton University Press, 1982.

The Mirror of Criticism: Selected Reviews, 1977–1982. Brighton, England: Harvester Press, 1983; New York: Barnes & Noble, 1983.

The Book of God: A Response to the Bible. New Haven, Conn., and London: Yale University Press, 1988.

Editor of:

The Modern English Novel: The Reader, the Writer, and the Work. London: Open Books, 1976; New York: Barnes & Noble, 1976.

The Sirens' Song: Selected Essays of Maurice Blanchot, translated from the French by Sacha Rabinovitch. Brighton, England: Harvester Press, 1982; Bloomington, Ind.: Indiana University Press, 1982.

Plays—Selected Productions:

Evidence of Intimacy, first produced at the Gardner Centre, University of Sussex, in Brighton, England, 1969.

Dreams of Mrs. Fraser, first produced at the Royal Court Theatre Upstairs in London, 1972.

Flow, first produced at the Lyceum Theatre in Edinburgh, 1973.

Echo, first produced in London, 1975.

Marathon, first produced at the Marlborough Theatre in Brighton, England, 1976.

A Moment, first produced at the National Theatre Platform in London, 1979.

Radio plays:

Playback, first broadcast on BBC Radio 3, 1973.

A Life, first broadcast on BBC Radio 3, 1974.

AG, first broadcast on BBC Radio 3, 1977.

Vergil Dying, first broadcast on BBC Radio 3, 1979. Published by SPAN, the Windsor Arts Centre Press, 1981.

Majorana: Disappearance of a Physicist, translated and adapted by Gabriel Josipovici and Sacha Rabino-vitch from *La scomparsa di Majorana,* by Leonardo Sciascia, first broadcast on BBC Radio 3, 1981.

Kin, first broadcast in BBC Radio 3, 1983.

The Seven, with Jonathan Harvey, first broadcast on BBC Radio 3, 1984.

Metamorphosis, adapted from the story by Franz Kafka, first broadcast on BBC Radio 3, 1985.

Ode to Saint Cecilia, first broadcast on BBC Radio 4, 1986.

Mr. Vee, first broadcast on BBC Radio 3, 1989.

H. R. F. Keating

1926-

H. R. F. Keating, 1987

In a way I have been ready and waiting these many years to give the world my autobiography. Or at least I have had a title stored away in my mind, *Ancestors and Influences.* And that title already, I have a notion, says a good deal about myself. First, that I am one who for long harboured the secret hope I was of autobiographical stuff, that I counted or would one day count. For that I can plead in excuse only that I believed firmly I would never be called on to set finger to typewriter. (But now . . .) And, second, my putative title also says that I am, indelibly, a viewer from a distance.

So I find I can commit this self-description only by looking at myself from afar, by pondering what influences made me the writer that I am, by asking myself what contributions came from ever more distant ancestors. My life in terms of the events that have occurred has been no different from thousands, from millions, of others. It is worth no particular record. But the books that it has come to me to write

are, perhaps, perhaps, worth considering. An account of how they came to come to be must constitute my life story.

I see that in writing fiction, as well as in my manner of looking at life as it trundles by, the distant view is my way. Thus it was only when I chanced to start writing crime novels set in a far-off India I had never even so much as visited that my career in this branch of literature really came into its own. Equally, this is the reason why I have enjoyed setting some books—an occasional crime novel, three test dives into more popular waters under the name of Evelyn Hervey, two of my mainstream novels—in the Victorian age.

The pseudonym that I used is, again, I suppose, another distancing device, making the author of those books a figure who might be of the other sex from my own. Perhaps that is the real reason, too, why I chose to write the books in which I believed most under my surname and initials rather than under the name I am called, though when asked about that I have always answered till now that at the time I began to write it was not quite "the done thing" to use an informal name, my "Harry" in place of the "Henry" which at my birth in 1926 I was christened, together with "Reymond" and "Fitzwalter."

And here I can begin with the ancestors. I come of a family on the paternal side that puts much store in ancestors. So the "Henry" was in honour of half a dozen Henry Keatings over the generations, and the "Fitzwalter" reflected in particular my Anglo-Irish forebears, who came as conquerors to the isles of Britain from Normandy at the time of 1066 and all that. They left me with an ineradicable belief in that mysterious concept of the "gentleman," one with duties in life which, if acted on, deserve respect. No wonder I responded from childhood on to Sherlock Holmes, brainchild of that Irish-ancestored Scot, Conan Doyle, with his totally scathing condemnation, once uttered, "How an English gentleman could behave in such a manner is beyond my comprehension."

There remains "Reymond." No spelling error, but a variant my father, John Hervey Keating, simple schoolmaster, found, it is said, in some family history. He gave me the name, which it was intended I should use (the "Henry" was more in hope of attracting at some future day a substantial bequest—only the wealthy bachelor took it into his head to marry) in order, so my father is reputed to have announced at the christening ceremony, "to look good on the spines of his books." Because my father, alas, was a writer manqué. I can remember, vividly, vividly, him showing me once a bound volume of, I think, the *Boy's Own Paper,* with an article, a short article, in it headed "How To Keep Rabbits" by John Keating aged ten. It fired him. But, sadly, the necessary trick did not enter his being. When he died, at an early fifty-six, going through his desk I found three or four yellowing typescripts, rejected all round. And they were abominably arch.

But the seed was sown. Though little was openly said, the impression was deep-stamped in me that there was no one more mighty, more deserving of praise and acclaim, than the writer. I have made no great effort to scrub that away. Let who will be president or prime minister . . . Seeing from my hotel window once when I was invited to speak at the Edinburgh Festival the huge statue of Sir Walter Scott, I thought, "It is fitting."

So as a boy I learnt to count up and revere ancestors. There was on my paternal grandmother's side no less than Robert the Bruce. Have I got

A portrait sketch by Sir William Rothenstein of Keating's great-aunt Lady Hilton Young, formerly Kathleen Scott, nee Bruce, sculptor

the patience that hunted monarch acquired watching the spider? I think not. Yet, to have needed to learn that lesson, the Scottish king must have lacked long-haul patience in the first place, and that is a trait I am willing to accuse myself of.

Then, youngest of the fourteen children of whom my grandmother was the eldest, there was Kathleen Bruce, sculptor, pupil of Rodin (and more than pupil, scandal hints), and in the end wife of Scott, the heroic Antarctic explorer. (Her statue of him is to be seen in London's Waterloo Place, just south of Pall Mall.) Some artistic impetus from the Bruce side then. And was it because of Scott that Sir Vivian Fuchs, explorer of two generations later, became one of my heroes, an exemplar of the power of the will? An unlikely idol for one of limited physical prowess.

Yet it was on the other side of the family, my mother's, remembering little of ancestry and forebears, that the one talent for fiction appeared, since I cannot feel my paternal grandfather, Canon John Fitz-Stephen Keating, Chancellor of Saint Mary's Cathedral, Edinburgh, author of *The Agapé and the Eucharist in the Early Church,* stern theological tome, really contributed. But my mother's father, a businessman, W. H. Clews, was author of two historical

Horsburgh, Edinburgh, Scotland

Paternal grandfather, Canon John Fitz-Stephen Keating, about 1906

romances no more, bound together as a single volume and, as I recall, a good read. So where did the inexpugnable writing urge, which blazed fitfully and ineffectually in my father, and has burnt steadily in myself, come from? Who knows? Who can tell?

Certainly it burnt in me from my earliest days. If it was at age ten that my father saw himself in print with solid advice on rabbit keeping, it was at age six that I typed out, tremendously laboriously, *Jims Adventure* (no apostrophe). I still have the half-sheet of thin paper. Jim's adventure began with him securing a berth as a cabin boy on a ship bound, possibly, for the Spanish Main and becoming "fast friends" with another lad. Then inspiration failed.

The fire spurted up at intervals, however, from then on. At boarding school at the age of nine or ten at about the time I was revelling in a book, author now unknown, called *The Purple Fleet,* a pirate tale in which the knife-in-mouth villain turns out to be a goody (was it from this I gained my love of reversals, especially those where the good unexpectedly triumph?) I produced a story that earned me, I remember, sudden approbation from above. It ended something like this: "And he was beside himself with rage, and when he saw himself he killed himself." (I pinched the idea from a bigger, more literary boy, but even then, I see, I was attracted by oddities of

phrasing.) At Merchant Taylors' School during World War II I saw print in the school magazine with a dramatic piece about the garotting of an enemy sentry, even then working out as harmless words on paper the violence I fear and detest.

From where comes that hatred of violence and the timidity that goes with it? From, I suspect, my mother, infused through and through with a desire for things to go well and be well to the point of being able to blot out the contradictory even when it was directly in front of her. It is from her, no doubt, I get, too, my inability to believe that anybody can be totally bad, which produced eventually a short story called "Inspector Ghote and the All-bad Man." The trait, perhaps, is at its worst a desperate naivety. Its good side, I believe, is a generous allotment of author's empathy, the ability to see very quickly in the day-to-day world the other side of any case and, writing fiction, the gift of putting oneself on occasion into utterly alien shoes.

It was from my father, also a person of remarkable niceness, however, that I got my occasional outbursts of violent temper, eventually the driving force behind my crime novel *Under A Monsoon Cloud.* I was famous at school in my earlier days, I recall, for these rages, at one time getting private instruction when one master refused—I believe this must be right—to have me any longer in his classes.

There is, too, another vivid memory: the conversation in the scorers' box. This was during a cricket match against the school along the road in the Sussex resort of Bexhill-on-Sea, a place pullulating with boarding schools. I, as a hopeless player, had been relegated to keeping the score, a fairly formidable task considering the seriousness with which cricket was taken (still is, for all I know) at even the most junior level. So we sat in the special compartment in the pavilion set aside for the two rival scorers, this stranger eleven-year-old and myself, and at one moment of lull—I probably missed the solemn recording of a ball bowled to no effect—my companion pointed out to me a boy from his school as being "the one who's got a terrible temper," and who, he asked, in your school do you have? I can remember at this moment the way I relished the irony of being able to reply that that was me.

And irony I savour, deeply, to this day. It forms a major strain in my books, notably in the very central situation of my hero, Inspector Ghote, being a person prone to mistakes, and yet more prone to becoming the underdog, who nevertheless always and invariably gets his man, achieving a final triumph. But where does this strain in me come from?

Of course, it could be a windblown seed. Something must be allowed to chance. Something, too, to nurture rather than nature. But I cannot see any of the circumstances of my life particularly nurturing a delight in the ironic. So I put it down to my Anglo-Irish ancestry in general.

A great list of names here, springing from that happy combination of Anglo-Norman hauteur and Ireland's obfuscating climate, from Dean Swift to Oscar Wilde. With them I claim no parity (even that modest denial is impudent, though I savour their writing to the last morsel). But I believe that particular strain of humour is to be found in my pages. Most perhaps not in astringent wit (though here and there . . .) but in that special form of Irish humour, not ever to be confused with humour about the Irish simpleton, that consists in a sort of wild whimsy. (Oh yes, as a boy I worshipped Dorothy L. Sayers's Lord Peter Wimsey.) The Irish fairy is no twee creature like your English little wingy thing but a sharp and stout small leprechaun. Irony, in the sense of topsy-turvy-dom, of the unexpected reversal, was, I suspect, much reinforced in me by an early much-loved author, Lewis Carroll (still read with high pleasure), and years and years later I came to delight in the paintings of Joan Miró, a reproduction of one of whose upside-down men hangs in my study.

The Irish influence was much strengthened in me, I believe, by the chance of my receiving my higher education at Trinity College, Dublin. I got there by luck. My father, who had a generous streak of the naive in his makeup, had removed me from Merchant Taylors', where it was customary to stay till the age of seventeen or eighteen, when I was barely sixteen. He had a theory about the tremendous usefulness of "the University of Life" and he felt, too, acutely the burden of school fees. So he found me a job as a wartime youth-in-training in the engineering department of the BBC, something for which I was fitted only by having rapidly mugged up Ohm's law. But I was at least capable of operating the studio controls, and in the quiet moments in the middle of the night (I worked in the overseas service) I wrote a novel, unfinished, a comic epic. Two of the characters were called McVitie and Price, well-known biscuit manufacturers of the day. There were many interpolated authorial comments. Well, I was sixteen, almost seventeen.

It seemed then that the more usual universities, which in those days still required fees from parents, were not to be for me. However, my father, slightly backing two horses, had also enrolled me for a correspondence course for external students at London University, for which I had answered a few question papers before I was conscripted into the army (on, as it happened, the day the war with Japan ended). This slender attachment to the educative process entitled me at the end of my military service to a government grant at any university that would take me.

That military service, which lasted some two and a half years, was totally undistinguished. For a month or two I rose to the rank of acting lance-corporal (unpaid) in anticipation of passing the tests for officer training. I failed. Otherwise I peeled a good many potatoes, made a mess of mending some radio sets, kept out of trouble. My ancestor, Sir Henry Sheehy Keating, would have been ashamed that none of his fighting spirit had trickled down. He was knighted for his services in war and made a lieutenant-general, having, as family history records, been "present at the affair of La Trinité, the attack on Mont Rouge and Mont Calabasse (wounded) and the defence of Berville Camp (severely wounded and taken prisoner)." In 1811 he was granted four hundred guineas, for the purchase of a piece of plate, by the East India Company. (Perhaps in view of my later contribution to the story of India I might, after all, have been forgiven my lack of wounds, my plethora of peeled potatoes.)

My years in the army left me only with a habit of

*H. R. F. Keating, "Even as a baby
all too willing to please"*

being "five minutes early on parade." But that is a trait I possessed in any case, an aspect of a particularly well-developed desire to please (aka Conscience), one thing more inherited from my mother. Inherited from her, but reinforced and influenced certainly by my favourite book at the age of five, Heinrich Hoffman's *Struwwelpeter* (I still can read it with pleasure), with its fiercely moral verses about such children as "Augustus, Who Would Not Have Any Soup." Yet Edward Lear's amoral nonsense was an equal favourite then, and now.

Cambridge University, where my father had been, would not, with the minimal qualifications I had, accept me at the end of my time in the army. Dublin, where my father's father had been, would, after I had painfully tussled with Virgil and passed, with 40 percent, an examination. So at Trinity College I spent four fulfilling years, grasping at last what literature and even life were about, eventually to the point of gaining a First Class Honours degree.

Trinity at that time was a good place for one of my innate modesty. No high-flying intellectual whizz kids were there greatly to overshadow me. There was time enough, too. Time to send a poem or two to the college magazine and see them printed. Time to debate. Time to act. Time to write short stories. Time at least to begin another novel, called *The Deep Despair of Oliver Mudd* (so that its hero could say, "My name is Mudd"), very symbolic, very Kafka. Time to found a college literary magazine. Time to gain a scholarship and be entitled to wear an extra-voluminous gown. Time, above all, to talk. Talk is the great Irish virtue, and vice. I blossomed swinging from talk's benign branches.

I wrote, I edited, and I was beyond doubt one of Trinity's literary set, as well as gulping up such of the great masters of literature as I had not yet devoured. Proust and Joyce's *Ulysses* had already capitulated in front of my relentless intellectual snobbery. Dickens I had delighted in from boyhood. I recall, indeed, myself sitting quietly reading *The Pickwick Papers,* aged eleven or even less, with my father absorbed in the newspaper opposite, and in my intense pleasure voicing just aloud the exclamation "Pickwick!" My father thought I had uttered the then rudest word. Happily he accepted my explanation. But the Dickensian vividness had set me a tremendous target, little though I knew it then.

At the end of those four dizzy Dublin years (interrupted by splendid depressions) I had decided, however, that I was not to be a writer. I had, I judged, nothing to say. I would settle for life as "a gentle failure." But, since I had to earn my living and since

the only skill I thought I possessed was with words, I took it into my head to be a journalist.

Modesty, as I have said, is one of my major virtues, or my besetting sin. I am not sure even yet which. But it was modesty that led me at that period—I was twenty-five—to choose the quiet, silent life. It was modesty as well as snobbery that had made me read any author set before me as "great," though it was from the influence of Conrad that I eventually gained a not-at-all-modest notion of what a writer of fiction should strive for. "You must," he wrote once, "squeeze out of yourself every sensation, every thought, every image—mercilessly, without remorse."

But it is modesty, still, that leads me to accept as gospel, ninety-nine times out of a hundred, anything I read or am told with any show of authority. It is modesty that marks out Inspector Ghote as the detective least likely to succeed (but he does) and which, I think, has earned him also the reviewers' frequently used "endearing."

But Ghote has a saving streak of shrewdness, as I have that hundredth time after ninety-nine naiveties. Ghote needs it on purely novelistic grounds in order plausibly to solve his cases. It comes from within, however. To both of us. Unexpectedly, every now and again I see through someone's pretensions, I wriggle ahead in the game. Where does this come from? Perhaps from that strain in my paternal family that brought Sir Henry Singer Keating to the judicial bench and the office of solicitor-general in Lord Palmerston's administration.

For some eight years after leaving college, then, I was a journalist. For most of the time not a reporter, which that ineradicable self-doubt unfitted me to be, but a sub-editor, a composer of headlines, a chopper-down of other people's copy, rising eventually to become a "copytaster," the selector of minor items in such great newspapers as the *Daily Telegraph,* the *Times,* the *Sunday Telegraph.* And, as such, not writing a word.

But did those years as a provincial journalist or in Fleet Street influence me? Not much, I think. For some time after I began writing fiction I found it hard to use such emotive words as "very," sternly banned from the pages of the *Telegraph.* And I pride myself, still, on submitting neat copy and to time. But, beyond that one negative influence and that sideline positive one, the great newspaper industry passed over my head in a roar of printing presses ducked underneath and ignored.

But this is to anticipate a little. Leaving college, I had made up my mind never to write anything in the shape of a novel. But that great influence in the

*H. R. F. Keating with his wife, Sheila, and their firstborn
son, Simon, Broad Town, Wiltshire, 1955*

affairs of men, Eros, had yet to take a decisive hand in
my life. As a diversion from the sub-editors' table in
Swindon, Wiltshire, where I began my journalistic
period, I was sent to review the plays put on each
week at the local repertory theatre, and one of the
actresses there caught my eye. Or, to be accurate to
my memories of those days, a whole succession of the
actresses there caught my eye in a matter of weeks,
but one in particular responded to my tentative
advances.

In something of a whirlwind courtship, I met
Sheila Mitchell in May of 1953, having reviewed her
performance in a play called *Breach of Marriage.* I see
from the cuttings book which I kept for a few months
at this the start of my journalistic career that it was on
the twentieth of that month I wrote: "Michael Barber
and Sheila Mitchell handle powerful emotions without once dropping the tension—no mean feat in a
repertory theatre." Sheila and I became formally
engaged that June. On October 3 we were married.

I had linked myself, I soon found, to more than a

fine actress. I had married a powerful influence. She
it was who very quickly disabused me of my comfortable and modest notion of living out my days as "a
gentle failure." And soon afterwards she had extract-
ed from me the secret ambition planted in me by my
father, author of "How To Keep Rabbits"—to be a
writer. But, I bleated, I have nothing to say. "Well,
you like those detective stories, don't you? Write one
of those. They don't say anything." (To my wife's
credit, let it be said, she had read little of the genre.)

So I wrote a detective story. It was set in a
repertory theatre, and I rather think—the typescript
seems to have gone missing—that the murder was
committed by taking away the weights that balanced a
descending platform, such as had been used in one of
the weekly plays my wife had been involved in. It was
a murder method I reused when I came to write a
mystery set in the world of opera, *Death of a Fat God,* a
title for both book and imaginary opera invented so
that a *deus* could descend from a *machina,* his car
eventually crashing down onto the book's victim. As
will have become evident, no publisher was interested
in that first venture.

But by then two forces were driving me on. My
once-suppressed but now raging desire to be a writer,
and my wife. So another book was written. I have just
unearthed it from my study cupboard—a distasteful
task—and I find it was a mystery set in the hunting
community in some unspecified part of rural England. Not a bad idea. But the execution—I have read
a few pages—is, to be polite to myself, uneven. An
agent took it on, was hopeful, was less hopeful,
returned it.

By then, however, I was remorselessly on to Book
No. 3. I had decided, still unaware of how much
could be done with the detective-story form, to use as
a "background" a trip I had taken in 1953, the year of
Queen Elizabeth's coronation, by coach-and-four
conveying loyal greetings from Bath to London. It
was an expedition I reported for the *Wiltshire Herald*
only as far as halfway, since the paper's funds did not
rise to overnight stays. But I thought I had acquired a
few facts about coaching from it, and I determined to
make use of them to adorn a simple murder mystery.

Setting to work, I remember, I began jotting
down in note form some things that would go into the
opening description of a coach and its four champing
horses waiting to receive a party of visiting Americans
at Southampton Docks. But, seeing those jotted,
verbless phrases, it struck me that they themselves
constituted a vivid piece of writing, and I decided to
use this style for all the narration and description in
the book.

The author on the coach-and-four trip that was the basis of his first book,
Death and the Visiting Firemen, *1953*

It got written. A title had come to me as I lay in the bath, *Death and the Visiting Firemen* (so I made my Americans fire-prevention experts). I sent it to the agent who had had such high hopes of my previous effort. He rejected it. For a month it lay on the table in our flat in the London suburb of Willesden. Then I thought I would at least try a publisher or two myself. I sent it to the firm of Gollancz, publishers in the past of Dorothy L. Sayers, of Julian Symons, and of Michael Innes, much admired. And, on the day of the Feast of the Epiphany, January 6, 1959, as I was hurrying off to Mass (I was still then a practising Catholic), I stopped to tear open a letter that had dropped onto the doormat. It was from Victor Gollancz himself. He wanted to publish my book, if I would make a few changes.

It was a high point of my life. The tiny flame which my father had lit at my christening with the forename Reymond, never actually used, had lit its fire. The prayers I had poured upwards night after night walking back from where the late-night bus from Fleet Street set me down had been answered. I was—how willingly I made Mr. Gollancz's suggested improvements—a writer.

It was, however, some six or eight months later when I held in my hands an actual copy of the book

that it came to me that I could do more as a writer than merely produce detective stories in the mode of those I had read as a boy, lapping up from my mother's example the happy simplicities of Gladys Mitchell, Agatha Christie, E. R. Punshon, Dorothy Sayers (as I then believed, only later realising how much more she did), E. C. R. Lorac, Margery Allingham, names forgotten and names that have survived. Years later I had the pleasure of interviewing Margery Allingham when I was still near the start of my writing career. She told me then, and it went deep, what an almost forgotten writer of, among other things, Sexton Blake juvenile detective adventures, G. R. M. Hearne, had once said to her: "They never mind you putting all you've got into this sort of stuff. They never pay you any more for it, but they don't stop you."

I realised then, as I looked at this book of mine in print, in real print, that perhaps I did have "something to say." So it was at this time that Graham Greene, whom I had read and simply liked before, began to take on the shape of my beau ideal as a novelist. This was not for the religious content of his books, but for his relentlessness in going for the truth, in writing, as he says in *Ways of Escape,* "truthfully enough for the truth to be plain." I admire, too, this side idolatry, Greene's literary savvy. Long ago I painfully copied into my writing notebook from *A Burnt-out Case,* much reread, "A writer doesn't write for his readers, does he? Yet he has to take elementary precautions all the same to keep them comfortable."

Simenon, too, at this time became for me an exemplar of what it is possible to do in crime fiction. I have never succeeded in achieving his splendid simplicity of style, and, indeed, I think with my innate tendency to have reservations about almost any plain statement (call it tolerance or inhibiting conscience, as you will) a sentence structure not without parentheses is my way. But Simenon's search for the truth of people, that, yes, he makes me aspire to.

I realised with my first book in my hands that I could use the next one to better purpose. And I knew almost at once what it was that I wanted to say through it. My mind went back to an incident that had lain in my subconscious ever since I was, I think, eight years of age.

I had been brought up, as all good children were in those golden days in England shortly before World War II, to believe it was "a sin to tell a lie." But, one summer day—summer lasted then, with one short interval for Christmas, from one year's end to another—I was out with my father and an uncle in the car, and my father, chatting away, shot a red light right under a passing policeman's eye. When we arrived home it was teatime, a marked point in every single day in that halcyon era, and we sat under the big cherry tree to have it. My father recounted to my mother what had happened. And, to my amazement, it was not what I had seen happen and what my father, talking with my uncle on the way home, had spoken of as having happened. Now, mysteriously, that minor infringement of the traffic laws was not at all my father's fault. A lie had been told. Uttered by God. Or at least by my god.

My book sprang directly from that sun-soaked teatime. Its theme of lies and lying, an obsession ever since that day, arrived at, I cast about for a subject, a background to the murder puzzle that would constitute my story and let me put forward attitudes to the telling of lies, as many as I could find. Soon I hit on that subject. At that time Zen Buddhism was all the intellectual rage, and I saw I could seize on it to give me a nice topical touch. I read a few "First Steps" books, and saw that Zen with its paradoxes, such as getting a bird out of a bottle by saying, "There, it's out," led me beautifully into lies and lying, truth and deception. I sat and wrote. I wanted to call the book *Zen and the Art of Murder,* paralleling a then much talked of work, *Zen in the Art of Archery.* Mr. Gollancz wanted it to be called *Zen There Was Murder.* It was called that.

At yearly intervals other detective novels followed. On the strength of my first advance of one

"With my father, John Hervey Keating, and my younger brother, Noel, under the cherry tree that played such a part in my life"

hundred pounds, a small but not pitiful sum in those days, I resigned my sub-editor's post at the *Times*. For some years I held various part-time journalistic jobs, but in spirit from then on I was no longer a journalist. I was a writer, a novelist.

So one by one the books came out, each saying a little more about the insights on life that had blossomed in me. There was *A Rush on the Ultimate* in 1961, about violence, in a croquet setting; *The Dog It Was That Died* in 1962, about not seeing things in black and white; *Death of a Fat God* in 1963, about pride. Each provided a murder puzzle in the classical manner. And none of them found, at that time, a publisher in America, where they were thought to be too British.

So, seeking fresh fields to conquer (and income enough to abandon all journalism), I hit on the notion of adding to the various interesting backgrounds I had used up to then, the coach-and-four, Zen, croquet, brainwashing, opera, one more—India. I knew almost nothing of the country (a cousin on my mother's side, my age, had been born there and taught me to count to five in Hindustani), but I saw it as a fine symbol of the imperfect. And one of the things I had it in mind to write about was perfectionism, that conscience of mine continually having to be squashed when I failed to do anything to perfection.

The idea of India was only a vague notion in the back of my head, seen partly as a way of writing a book that would not be "too British." But, offered a lift to a party by a couple who were then total strangers, I learnt that the husband had just returned from working in an advertising firm in Bombay and I mentioned the thought I had had. He was all enthusiasm. It was his nature. He offered me help towards getting details of Indian life right. I succumbed.

So, in the expectation of increased income from a possible American sale, I took time to mug up India. I suppose already I had realised there was only one possible title for a book with the theme I had in mind, *The Perfect Murder*. But then, a tremendous piece of luck, I found that one of the surnames in the Parsi community in India was "Perfect." So my murder need not be a perfect one in order to be called the Perfect Murder: it could be an imperfect affair. The victim could actually be not quite killed, an idea that greatly pleased my Irish sense of tough whimsy, of the ironic, and which also reflected my theme.

I read book after book about unknown India, whatever I could lay hands on. Ruth Prawer Jhabvala, that German-born Briton married to an Indian, taught me much. The wonderful writer, R. K. Narayan, gave me insights into Indianness with his marvel-

The author's mother, Muriel Marguerita Clews Keating, holding his second son, Piers

lously lucid tales of the little town of Malgudi. Read and reread since, his books have not perhaps influenced me (I am, I suppose, too old to take in new influences) but this notion of each person having an ordained place in the world (mine, I know, to be a writer) and his almost holy simplicity, the simplicity of truth, not the simplicity of simplemindedness, have both chimed in singingly with what was already in my nature.

A few geographies passed through my hands, too, in that period of preparation, and I began to wonder where in the huge Indian subcontinent I should set my story. A city, I thought, since all cities, East and West, have some things in common. Calcutta, too horrible. Delhi, too diplomatically dull. Madras, too densely Indian. Bombay? India's most cosmopolitan city? Yes, why not Bombay? I seized the atlas to make sure just where Bombay was.

And then, as I was reading yet another geography book (I have come to believe), sitting in my red armchair by the window of my study (I know that), into my head there stepped my hero. He would be diffident. He would have bony shoulders. He would be pretty naive. This not, I thought then, because I was naive, but because in this way he could ask the questions readers knowing little of India would want to ask. It was only later that I realised that in bringing this man to life I had, in many ways, put myself on the pages. My hero should be called, I decided, Inspector

Ghosh. I saw him as saying, often, "Oh, gosh," in simple surprise, though I suspected I would have to keep that rather crude character-affirming device to myself eventually.

It was only when I sent an outline of the book to my newfound friend, the enthusiastic ex-India hand, that I learnt that Ghosh is a Bengali name. To give it to a Bombay police officer would be the equivalent of giving a Parisian cop the name Ivan Ivanovitch. My friend suggested "Ghote." It seemed right.

In some ways it has proved right indeed. To begin with, it is a genuine Maharashtrian name, and most Bombay policemen are from Maharashtra, the state that surrounds the city. But Ghote is not an enormously common name, and in particular it is not one of the names of the families that tend to enter, son after father, the police service. So no libel problems. On the other hand, no one outside India knows whether to pronounce that final *e* or not (you do). At paranoid times I see huge lines of would-be buyers outside bookshops, unable out of shyness to ask for one of Ghote's adventures by name. But perhaps I attribute more shyness to the average book buyer than they possess, subject as I am to such complications in my own life.

So *The Perfect Murder*, intended as a single excursion to exotic India as a background, came into being. It did even better than I had hoped, however. I had aimed to secure publication in America, and I did. But it had never entered my head that the book would win the Gold Dagger of the Crime Writers Association in Britain or that it would gain a Special Edgar award from the Mystery Writers of America. Or that Ghote would be hailed by reviewers as a new star in the crime firmament.

Yet, looking back now, I see that, with the simple luck which the novelist V. S. Naipaul once said was what a writer needed most, I had found myself a hero through whom and in whom I could express my every thought, or most of them, and who is someone also, perhaps by virtue of springing from my innermost self, who is a recognisable, three-dimensional, multi-faceted human being.

So from that day in 1964 when *The Perfect Murder* appeared my life has been entwined with Inspector Ghote's. Other things have intervened. There have been books in which he has made no appearance, though I have some difficulty now in keeping India out of anything I write. To begin with, I was embarked on my next detective novel before I realised what the creation of Inspector Ghote had done for me. So in the next year there appeared *Is Skin-deep, Is Fatal*, set in the world of London beauty

contests and with a plot blatantly pinched from Agatha Christie. And, later, when I knew I was to visit Bombay at last and did not want to write another India book until I had, there was a historical crime story, *A Remarkable Case of Burglary.*

Later still, in an effort, perhaps misguided, to write books that would reach the American paperback reader, there were three stories about Miss Harriet Unwin, Victorian governess, into whose shoes I enjoyed stepping, though I found the plain, ongoing stories I believed necessary for the mass market I half-wanted unsatisfying to write. I have never really sought to acquire huge sums of money, though I have wanted, badly, to have enough to live on with my family of four children without too many worries. I feel, I think, that it is reward enough for me to be a writer. The money is, fundamentally, only a sign that I am achieving the ultimate aim of writing: being read.

But otherwise there was the yearly Ghote novel, each one, I think, showing the reader, and myself, some new aspect of the man. There was *Inspector Ghote's Good Crusade* in 1966, an exploration of the impulse to be kind, its benefits and drawbacks. There was *Inspector Ghote Caught in Meshes* in 1967, my nearest approach to the espionage novel, concerned with the net of differing loyalties we are all in this life entangled in. There was *Inspector Ghote Hunts the Peacock* in 1968, in which I, perhaps unwisely, listened to all those, my publisher among them, who said, "Why don't you bring Ghote to London?" and in which I tackled again the problem of pride, how much of it you should have, something that modesty of mine frequently forced to my attention. In 1969 there was *Inspector Ghote Plays a Joker,* a reaction from someone who finds, for all his fondness for jokes, that it is hard not to be serious about what I saw as the too absorbed frivolity of the times. *Inspector Ghote Breaks an Egg* came in 1970, another worry at the problem of violence after *A Rush on the Ultimate.* I had thought such dilemmas could be "written out of the system," but either I had failed before to write with enough intensity or that theory is a concoction.

It must have been about this time that, in response to a suggestion from a neighbour who was a director of the publishers William Heinemann, I began writing a mainstream novel. Partly I felt it a challenge, to step as it were onto a wider stage. Partly I had found that crime novels, unless they came from an Agatha Christie or a Ngaio Marsh, did not reach an enormously wide audience. And then, too, I believed the theme I wanted to get my teeth into, the true nature of strength of personality, did not suit the Ghote format, though looking back I cannot see why it should not have done. However, the combination of circumstances led me to produce a long novel with an adventure-story thread, *The Strong Man*.

I do not know to this day quite how good it is. In that Heinemann asked me to cut it before publication and that it failed to find an American publisher, it must be considered a partial failure at least. It got some good reviews in Britain, and some less good ("Readable, forgettable": that hurt), though how much either sort was deserved I cannot say, though I have reread the book more than once. I think probably I was unable to give it the power it ought to have had. But was this out of an inherent inability? Or was it, simply, a failure of technique? A series of misjudgments? I cannot say. But when every now and again I come across someone who remembers the book my heart leaps up. That is, after all, what one aims to do: to plant in another mind something memorable. And in that in a few minds here and there I appear to have done this, I am happy to regard the book as a success, a small success.

But then it was back, not unwillingly, to Inspector Ghote, whom I had now discovered to be called Ganesh, though I seldom use the name. To do so would, I think, diminish the distance at which I like to find myself from whatever and whomever I write about. Yet am I right? Were I able to write about Ghote more immediately, more warmly (though from my distance I do not think I fail to see him in a warm light), would he have achieved the sort of wide popularity that once belonged to Lord Peter Wimsey or Nero Wolfe? A question I cannot answer, especially not, being what I am, by writing at less of a distance from my subjects.

So there came in 1971, the year *The Strong Man* appeared, *Inspector Ghote Goes by Train*, a hymn to the huge and fascinating Indian railway system and an examination of the merits of "going by train" steadily, as Ghote and I do, as against "flying," as my villain in the book metaphorically does and as the world's high flyers do.

It was followed in 1972 by *Inspector Ghote Trusts the Heart*, a book that until I wrote *Under A Monsoon Cloud* in 1986 said as much as I had ever managed to do about Ghote and, I suppose, about how I think life ought to be conducted. Its theme, of course, is how much should the heart be trusted over the head. Its story was that of a kidnapping, of the child of a poor tailor in Bombay in place of a rich man's son. And, because I did not need for this story the intricate detection plot I had felt up to this time I owed my readers, I was able here, I believe, to write more directly from the subconscious than I had been able to do before. Consequently the book expresses more

"Researching for a Victorian novel"

© *Universal Pictorial Press & Agency, Ltd., London, England*

of my own feelings. It was, I am happy to say, well received.

At about this time I was also working on a second "straight" novel, *The Underside*. I wrote it, as I remember, in intervals between the drafts of the current Ghote book. (Would that I were able to follow the poet Horace and leave first drafts for nine years.) *The Underside* was set at a favourite period of the past, the years round about 1870, when Victorian England was perhaps at its apogee. I read widely for it, especially as its hero was to be a painter (=writer) called Godfrey Mann (=Everyman). Its theme was the value that should or should not be given to the underside of our nature. Its story took Godfrey Mann to the heights and the lowest depths of Victorian London. It was my first attempt to come to terms in fiction with the sexual instinct. I remember to this day the moment when my typewriter, it seemed, spelt out to me the famous four-letter word. I looked at it. I felt it was right in the context. It remained. The book came out in 1974. It failed to find an American publisher, despite some good reviews in London.

Bats Fly Up for Inspector Ghote appeared in that

same year, an examination of suspiciousness, the seed of which had been planted a good many years earlier when I met a Pakistani customs officer who told me how he had resigned when he found he was suspecting members of his own family of serious smuggling offences. It was after writing this that, one morning, I received a letter from an official of Air India saying he had heard of this writer about India who had never visited the country and asking if I would be interested in a flight to Bombay.

My immediate reaction, of course, was delight. I had made an attempt to finance a trip—proceeds from the books hardly justified the expense when I had a family of four to consider—by taking a job in Delhi teaching journalism, but when that fell through I had seen myself as writing "at a distance" for the foreseeable future. Immediate second thoughts made me ask myself whether seeing the actual poverty of the Bombay streets and smelling their smells might not debar me from writing about the place ever again. But I thought this a little cowardly even for myself and accepted the offer.

Still, it was not without inward trembling that on October 12, 1974, I stepped out of the Air India plane onto the soil of Bombay Airport. I had intended, parodying those first words spoken on the moon, to say, perhaps even aloud, "One small step for Harry Keating, a giant leap for Inspector Ghote." Instead, overwhelmed by the thick, damp heat, I thought simply, "Cripes," and immediately afterwards was summoned back on board by the Air India photographer who had missed me stepping out so as to reenact the moment. If I had seen India once as a symbol of the imperfect, my notion seemed now to be realised.

I found, however, my fears about visiting this unseen scene of my imaginative labours were unfounded. Thanks to having envisaged in my inner mind's eye the beggars and some of the squalor, I was able to cope with them in reality. On my first morning in the city I decided, timid fellow that I am, to take a walk just round the block and then retreat again to the air-conditioned safety of the Taj Mahal Hotel. I was waylaid, though, by an agreeable Indian who began to talk to me about the buildings round about. Naive Harry Keating failed, of course, to realise he was in the hands of a professional guide. But, under a stream of implacable discourse, I was led far that morning, saw lepers up against the railings round Saint Thomas's Cathedral and did not blench.

I saw much else during that visit—and on four subsequent visits, the most recent two to make the Merchant-Ivory film of *The Perfect Murder*—that might

have disgusted me and did not. I saw, as well, things that happily confirmed what I had written, and I saw some things, not many, that I had got wrong. I filled, of course, notebook after notebook with those little, different touches that make vivid a strange environment to readers of fiction, the women selling bundles of grass beside the holy cows wandering at will the metropolitan streets, the roadside cobblers, thread held taut round a big toe, ever ready to mend the strap of a frail sandal, the rust red splashes of betel juice from chewed *paans* on the pavements everywhere, the padlocks on the letter boxes.

So now I have a large store of facts about Bombay and other parts and aspects of India to draw on as I write. Where before I had to use such single facts as I had discovered, from Indian newspapers I subscribed to, from Indian films, from television programmes of all sorts (once a documentary in Welsh for a schools audience), now I have often some three or four apposite illustrations to choose from.

Yet on my return from my second trip—it came within months of the first, to make a TV documentary about this writer who had described Bombay for some ten years without ever going there—I found I had got myself into a quite unexpected difficulty. I had decided to test the new Ghote on a short story. It began, as many of his adventures do, with a summons to see the head of the CID. Only, with the BBC camera crew I had spent hours myself in his very office. So I wrote a description of it, right down to the names of the police dogs on the crime board behind the desk. It took pages, and Ghote still had not been sent on the mission that was to constitute the story "The Noted British Author." (Such I myself had been called in a Bombay newspaper piece.) I saw the error of my new way, and I hope afterwards did not allow myself to be dragged down by sticky facts from the real world instead of being buoyed up by airy ones passed through the transfiguration factory of the imagination.

I trust this was true of the first post-India book, *Filmi, Filmi, Inspector Ghote.* I had reserved the extraordinary world of the Bombay film industry, out-Hollywooding Hollywood at its most absurd, until I had seen something of it for myself. In many ways it exceeded my most riotous imaginings with its marvellously self-absorbed stars, its shift system by which they make as many as forty films at a time moving from one to another from morning to evening, its playback singers voicing for the dancing stars the obligatory songs that interrupt even a story like the *Maqbet* I invented as a typical rip-off from Shakespeare's tragedy.

Filmi, Filmi (the word is a Hindi hybrid) was a

POINT OF VIEW: **M.V. Kamath** on *The Times That Are Sadly Out of Joint*

Bombay
The City Magazine

H.R.F. KEATING   ZAFAR HAI

What's the big idea? ②

The 2nd of 5 unique contests on Bombay

THE PERFECT MURDER

Inspector Ghote Comes to Town

NASEERUDDIN SHAH

WOMEN ENTREPRENEURS:
They Mean Business

CHEQUE FORGERIES:
You Can't Bank on Banks

BOMBAY URBAN DEVELOPMENT PROJECT:
Low Cost Solution

Bombay, The City Magazine, Bombay, India

On the cover of Bombay *magazine during the filming of* The Perfect Murder, *1987*

comic Ghote. So next I turned to a more serious story, *Inspector Ghote Draws a Line*, and a setting outside Bombay, an isolated house deep in the arid countryside, where a retired judge views with contempt a threat to his life. He was an attempt to portray a figure that, with increasing age, had begun to fascinate me, the former idealist turned realist, the liberal who had moved quarter-inch by quarter-inch to conservatism.

Still fired with ambition to succeed as a pure novelist, I next wrote *A Long Walk to Wimbledon*, a

book springing from an idea that had flashed upon me out walking one day and had gradually come to occupy a large place in my mind. I had stopped at the kerb about to cross the road near my home in London's Notting Hill and had seen in my mind's eye a truck, waveringly driven, mount the pavement and almost knock me down. I imagined its driver under the influence of a marijuanalike drug and saw that this might happen in a future London wrecked by the excesses of its own civilisation.

The book sends its hero, one not unlike myself of course, on a long walk across the ruined city from

Highgate to Wimbledon (the latter chosen in an attempt to interest American publishers: it failed). Again, I think the book was a success, if not the overwhelming one in both literary and sales terms I was hoping for. And, again, I ask: have I got the right stuff for that in me? Unanswerable question, except in terms of a book that does it.

Before I wrote about Ghote again I produced a crime story with an Indian background but set in the past, *The Murder of the Maharajah.* I had been asked by my British publisher, Collins Crime Club, celebrating in 1980 its fiftieth anniversary, for something to mark the occasion, and, remembering an outline I had written for James Ivory, who had wanted at some earlier time to make "a big picture," I chose the year 1930 and wrote a classical puzzle tale set in the palace of the ruler of an Indian state. The book is, perhaps, less tightly tied to a theme than its predecessors, though it does touch throughout on the playing of games as a mode of living. It won for me a second Gold Dagger and an aborted film option with a production company other than Merchant-Ivory.

I returned to Inspector Ghote with a book which I am in some doubt that I ought to have written. People had said to me over the years, "You should send Ghote to America," and I had thought it was not a bad idea, especially when I saw I could use a visit to California to comment on the mystical versus materialism, but making the West the centre of mysticism (all those Californian ashrams) and the East the materialist centre (Bombay is as business oriented as could be). I think that aspect of *Go West, Inspector Ghote* came off, though some critics jibbed horribly at an incident of translocation of the body. But, away from his true setting, Ghote perhaps lost something.

One of the things I have come to realise the Ghote books do is to show us our common humanity through emphasising the differences in the relatively less important areas of life between the Indian way (say, arranged marriages) and the Western (love matches). The books show, I hope, that the real fundamentals, the actual love of one human being for another, the anger that comes to us all wherever we live, the yearning for perfection that can bloom in an Indian as easily as in a Briton or an American, are what we all share. And in showing that, I trust, they earn their keep in the world.

There followed yet one more attempt at the novel pure, *The Lucky Alphonse.* This was mildly experimental. I had long wondered whether a novel could be written in the manner of a symphony with, say, three movements in place of a continuous story. The theme I chose to illustrate and underline in this manner was one dear to my heart, the position of

being in the middle. The title is the punch line of a well-known dirty joke, so-called, which culminates in a hotel room-waiter named Alphonse being found lying between the chef and the headwaiter, and the manager merely exclaiming, "Ah, the lucky Alphonse, in the middle again."

The book tells three stories, each with a hero whose name is a variant of Alphonse, all in different ways "in the middle." There is an Indian diplomat blackmailed by wife and mistress equally, who ends in suicide or something near it. There is, a humorous version, a little Irish informer caught between crooks and police and neatly coming out safe. There is a German history professor summoned by a former pupil to a small state in southern Africa poised between Communist and anti-Communist big powers and at last just triumphing by retaining independence. Again, a reception not unequivocally enthusiastic, though I received one very heartening letter of praise from a correspondent in Namibia.

I returned to Inspector Ghote, managing for the first time to put sex into his situation in a story set in Bombay's red-light area, the Cages. *The Sheriff of Bombay* has as its theme the subjectivity of our way of looking at things, particularly suitable for a detective novel, seeing, for instance, a sheriff either as a Wild West law-keeper or as an honorary officer of the Bombay High Court, seeing certain sexual activities either as rollickingly sportive or as utterly beastly. Seeing the other side.

There followed a book that might be looked on as my testament, and Inspector Ghote's, *Under A Monsoon Cloud.* I had now abandoned, perhaps for ever, the idea of writing a mainstream novel that would establish for me a reputation (fame is, as they say, the spur) and a wide readership (other minds filled with one's thoughts are the lure), but I hoped I could write a crime novel that did as much as the mainstream novel.

I like to think I succeeded, if only in part. Certainly, a long review in the *Los Angeles Times* said it "is not really a mystery as such but a kind of moral suspense story, virtually a straight novel that happens to center on a familiar figure from another range of fiction." In it I put Ghote on trial, if not for his life, for his whole career, and I let him make out his case for the honest police officer in a difficult and sometimes dirty world. I hoped, too, to have put into readers' heads some thoughts about anger, its dangers and its uses, that occasional force in myself inherited from a sometimes suddenly irascible father.

Of the two last Ghote novels I have written to date I will say little. They are too close to me still. Each of them is a good deal lighter in tone than *Under*

A Monsoon Cloud in response to commercial pressure (perhaps illusory) from America. There, it seems, there has been a fashion for the classic British mystery, and I endeavoured to respond with *The Body in the Billiard Room*, an Agatha Christie–style puzzle which simultaneously reflects back on her particular genre, and with *Dead on Time*, again a classical whodunit, though also a consideration of punctuality, being a slave to the clock or being too much freed from its trammels.

I suppose I ought to say something about a parallel strain in my writing life that sprang from the success my novels have gained. In 1967 I was invited (at my own asking) to review crime fiction in *The Times*, a task and a pleasure I carried out for some fifteen years. In the wake of that I have written a good many introductions to new editions of various crime books—what a chance to be asked, in effect, to write a long review of, for instance, Wilkie Collins's *Moonstone*—as well as a strictly nonfictional life of the greatest of the fictional detectives, *Sherlock Holmes: The Man and His World*, a book I immensely enjoyed writing and pondering, and, what is in some ways my literary testament, a small volume, *Writing Crime Fiction*. Spin-off from what I see as my reason for being in the world, but contributions nonetheless.

And that brings me to the time of writing this essay in self-analysis, and to two thoughts. One is that autobiography is, of its nature, unsatisfactory in that the account cannot come to a proper end, unless I should happen to drop dead tomorrow. In the next ten, twenty, or even thirty years much may change in my writing life, and I may come to see what I have done and the influences and ancestors that brought me to it in quite a different light. The other thought is this: how dangerous it is to allow a writer of imaginative fiction to tell his own story. How many of us doing it will be able to abandon the practice of a lifetime, that urge to take bits of the world and bang them into some sort of shape? What if the shape I have made here is wrong? What if, even, in the higgledy-piggledy of daily existence there is no shape?

BIBLIOGRAPHY

Fiction:

Death and the Visiting Firemen. London: Gollancz, 1959; New York: Doubleday, 1973.

Zen There Was Murder. London: Gollancz, 1960.

A Rush on the Ultimate. London: Gollancz, 1961; New York: Doubleday, 1982.

The Dog It Was That Died. London: Gollancz, 1962.

Death of a Fat God. London: Collins, 1963; New York: Dutton, 1966.

Is Skin-deep, Is Fatal. London: Collins, 1965; New York: Dutton, 1965.

The Strong Man. London: Heinemann, 1971.

The Underside. London: Macmillan, 1974.

A Remarkable Case of Burglary. London: Collins, 1975; New York: Doubleday, 1976.

A Long Walk to Wimbledon. London: Macmillan, 1978.

The Murder of the Maharajah. London: Collins, 1980; New York: Doubleday, 1980.

The Lucky Alphonse. London: Enigma Books, 1982.

The Governess, under pseudonym Evelyn Hervey. New York: Doubleday, 1983; London: Weidenfeld & Nicolson, 1984.

The Man of Gold, under pseudonym Evelyn Hervey. New York: Doubleday, 1985.

Mrs. Craggs: Crimes Cleaned Up. London: Buchan & Enright, 1985; New York: St. Martin's, 1985.

Into the Valley of Death, under pseudonym Evelyn Hervey. New York: Doubleday, 1986.

"Inspector Ghote" Series:

The Perfect Murder. London: Collins, 1964; New York: Dutton, 1965.

Inspector Ghote's Good Crusade. London: Collins, 1966; New York: Dutton, 1966.

Inspector Ghote Caught in Meshes. London: Collins, 1967; New York: Dutton, 1968.

Inspector Ghote Hunts the Peacock. London: Collins, 1968; New York: Dutton, 1968.

Inspector Ghote Plays a Joker. London: Collins, 1969; New York: Dutton, 1969.

Inspector Ghote Breaks an Egg. London: Collins, 1970; New York: Doubleday, 1971.

Inspector Ghote Goes by Train. London: Collins, 1971; New York: Doubleday, 1972.

Inspector Ghote Trusts the Heart. London: Collins, 1972; New York: Doubleday, 1973.

Bats Fly Up for Inspector Ghote. London: Collins, 1974; New York: Doubleday, 1974.

Filmi, Filmi, Inspector Ghote. London: Collins, 1976; New York: Doubleday, 1977.

Inspector Ghote Draws a Line. London: Collins, 1979; New York: Doubleday, 1979.

Go West, Inspector Ghote. London: Collins, 1981; New York: Doubleday, 1981.

The Sheriff of Bombay. London: Collins, 1984; New York: Doubleday, 1984.

Under A Monsoon Cloud. London: Hutchinson, 1986; New

York: Viking, 1986.

The Body in the Billiard Room. London: Hutchinson, 1987; New York: Viking, 1987.

Dead on Time. London: Hutchinson, 1988.

Nonfiction:

Murder Must Appetize. London: Lemon Tree Press, 1975; New York: Mysterious Press, 1981.

Sherlock Holmes: The Man and His World. London: Thames & Hudson, 1979; New York: Scribner, 1979.

Great Crimes. London: St. Michael, 1982; New York: Harmony/Crown, 1982.

Writing Crime Fiction. London: A. & C. Black, 1986; New York: St. Martin's, 1987.

Crime and Mystery: The One Hundred Best Books. London: Xanadu, 1987; New York: Carroll & Graf, 1987.

Radio plays:

The Dog It Was That Died (adapted from the novel of the same title). British Broadcasting Corp., 1971.

The Affair at No. 35. British Broadcasting Corp., 1972.

Inspector Ghote and the All-bad Man. British Broadcasting Corp., 1972.

Inspector Ghote Makes a Journey. British Broadcasting Corp., 1973.

Inspector Ghote and the River Man. British Broadcasting Corp., 1974.

Editor of:

Blood on My Mind: A Collection of New Pieces by Members of the Crime Writers Association about Real Crimes, Some Notable and Some Obscure. London: Macmillan, 1972.

Agatha Christie: First Lady of Crime. London: Weidenfeld & Nicolson, 1977; New York: Holt, 1977.

Crime Writers: Reflections on Crime Fiction. London: BBC Publications, 1978.

Whodunit?: A Guide to Crime, Suspense, and Spy Fiction. London: Windward, 1982; New York: Van Nostrand, 1982.

The Best of Father Brown, by G. K. Chesterton. London: Dent, 1987.

Richard Kostelanetz

1940-

PERSON OF LETTERS IN THE CONTEMPORARY WORLD: A MEMOIR IN TEN PARTS

Richard Kostelanetz with Mary Emma Harris: "The classic from the mid-seventies of me in the hammock, titled 'The Poet and His Muse—The Photographer and Her A-muse-ments.' What I like here is the suggestion that since I do the work of three men, I must be triplets."

I

The people who make the discoveries, those of whom one says on reviewing their lives, that they were not born for nothing, are prudent, sedentary men, men who can stay awake patiently and remain in one place for a long time.

—Paul Nizan, *Aden-Arabie* (1931)

Not unlike other writers who have produced work and pursued a career that are both customarily regarded as unusual (a.k.a. avant-garde), I have previously written about my art and my professional life, not only in short essays but in the catalogue to a traveling exhibition of my art, *Wordsand* (1978), and then, differently, in the book *Autobiographies* (1981). In writing about my work I have tried to be frank and clear, treating it as though it were done by someone else, explaining what I could while acknowledging the possibility of myster-ies beyond my understanding; for I have always admired artists such as John Cage and Ad Reinhardt who spoke about their own art with more critical acumen than did their initial reviewers. Most of these earlier personal essays have observed two conven-tions—they are chronological, and my works are discussed by genre, with the poetry in one section, the fiction in another, and so forth. Now, with another invitation to look back on my activity, it seemed opportune to do something else, not just to say what has not been said elsewhere, perhaps with more frankness than is customary, but also to beat scholars to my carcass by defining some unities amid the variety. All my professional life I have tried to do what no one else has done, to do what I did so differently my work would always stand apart from everyone else's, with me accepting the risks of that position along with the rewards.

First it would be appropriate to rehearse the basic facts. I was born in New York, 14 May 1940, the

179

son of Ethel and Boris Kostelanetz, she a sometime modern dancer and he a lawyer. We lived first in the Bronx, near Yankee Stadium, and then in Inwood at the top of Manhattan, and finally on Riverside Drive and Ninety-first Street, escalating socially through northern New York City during the post–World War II boom. In 1951, we moved to suburban Scarsdale, which was a misfortune that set me back in more ways than I care to count. Aside from playing football, there was little to engage me there; and once my mother refused to sign the parental release allowing me to be on the high-school team, I was bored silly. One subsidiary benefit was that it gave me reason to be highly critical of the world around me—a skepticism that did not exist before but has been highly evident ever since. From my earliest years my taste for numbers exceeded that for words; in my senior year of high school and then again in my senior year at college my score on the mathematical aptitude test was one hundred points higher than the verbal. My principal recollection of childhood is that mostly I stayed in my room, playing with my toys. That, come to think of it, is how I spend most of my time today.

In 1958 I went to Brown University and learned first of all to like to read, which I then proceeded to do with gusto, customarily staying up into the night, night after night; and all this reading revived a latent desire to be a writer. So I began by publishing mostly book reviews in the undergraduate newspaper and became an editor of both the undergraduate literary magazine and then a rebel "off-campus" magazine. To undergraduates seriously interested in literature, it seemed that the English department at Brown, and especially its creative writing program, was best avoided. The brainy Pembroker who became my wife (and is now an English professor in California) majored in philosophy; I went into American civilization, graduating with only a B average but with honors, thanks to a thesis on Henry Miller. My principal teachers were in four different fields—Juan Lopez-Morillas in comparative literature, William G. McLoughlin in American history, Dennis H. Wrong in sociology, and especially S. Foster Damon, a poet and William Blake scholar whom I knew mostly from weekly dinners that I cooked to his recipes at his house.

Unwilling to become cannon fodder, I had to go to graduate school and decided in favor of American history, as I had more college credits in it than anything else. I chose Columbia, not only because I wanted to be back in New York City, but because, as I had become accustomed to reading into the night and thus sleeping through the morning, it was more practical to go to a university whose graduate classes were held after noon. Since so many graduate students were on the rolls at Columbia—nearly a thousand in my own department—it became convenient for the professors to ignore us, which bothered me none, as I didn't want to be there at all. (At Yale or Harvard, say, with only a few graduate students, there would have been a closer surveillance of my waywardness and thus a quicker discovery of my disinterest.) Had I needed to pay Columbia's tuition, this ruse might not have been worth anyone's money, but fortunately I won a Woodrow Wilson Fellowship for the first year, an International Fellowship for the second year, and New York State Regents Fellowships throughout.

Most of my days at this time were spent at home, in an apartment on the tenth floor of a low-income Harlem public-housing project down the hill from Columbia, writing by day, reading by night, every night, to six or so in the morning. At home listening to classical music, I read books through the 1964 Harlem riots only a few blocks away. (Later it was said I could have read my way through the Revolution.) Out of this period came not only a few articles and numerous book reviews but the anthologies *On Contemporary Literature* (1964) and *The New American Arts* (1965), in addition to an M.A. thesis, "Politics in the Negro Novel in America." (Most of its chapters eventually appeared in scholarly magazines.) My wife initiated our applying for Fulbrights to London in 1964, she going to the Courtauld Institute of Art, me to King's College; but since King's had little to interest me (and not even two stipends were sufficient for basic survival), I spent most of my time at home, again reading and writing not only for magazines but for the BBC. My professional development became a problem for my wife, who was unusually successful at being competitive; and as our Fulbrights ended, our marriage did as well. (I've since been a free-lance serial heterosexual monogamist.)

In 1966, now alone, I moved downtown, to the top floor of a brownstone on East Fifth Street, six blocks south of the private elementary school to which I had commuted fifteen years before, a mile or so east of where my parents had moved by then; and I organized my life around the desire to be a writer, nothing else. Regarding myself as inherently nervous, in need of quiet and relaxation to write at my best, I isolated myself from interruptions, refusing to go out or to answer the telephone until late afternoon; and whenever I came across anyone who seemed destructive, whether male or female, I unhesitantly moved away. Living a good life in New York became an ideal important to me. As I passed twenty-six unscathed, the military issued me a classification that made my

J. Nebraska Gifford

" 'The Thirteen Studios of Richard Kostelanetz,' by
J. Nebraska Gifford, showing my home along with me, all
composed to my prescription around 1982"

being drafted unlikely. By the 1970s that East Village apartment became so crowded that no more than three people could fit into it comfortably. In 1974 I found in north SoHo, only a mile away (and a few blocks closer to my parents), a space three times the size. Able to afford the co-op down payment of eleven thousand dollars (a sum that now seems incredibly cheap), I moved into the eighteen hundred square feet where I have lived and worked ever since, from time to time serving as an officer of our Good Deal Realty Corporation (no joke).

Most people think that this apartment contains my life. There are thousands of books, hundreds of records, dozens of compact discs, shelves of audiocassettes and videocassettes; all of them worth keeping, I swear, I swear. There are five rooms and several worktables—one for writing, a second for rewriting, a third for proofreading, a fourth for art projects, a fifth now for computers, etc. In the back of the putative "living room," behind John Furnival's classic screens of visual poetry, *Tours de Babel Changées en Points* (1964), is yet another table for viewing and cutting 16-mm film; across from it is a deck for editing ¼ inch audiotape. On other shelves is equipment for all these toys. On the walls is visual art,

mostly mine.

I spend nearly all my time in this loft kingdom, working on one thing or another; for most of the days of the year, there is nothing else I would rather do. Typically, I get up around ten or eleven, write at the typewriter or word processor until late afternoon, then return telephone calls collected by my answering machine and answer letters that can take an immediate reply (both as matters of etiquette). Most of each day is spent simply doing what must be done, whether fulfilling a commitment, completing a project, or helping a colleague. Going out only in the evening, I customarily rewrite manuscripts or read late into the night. Classical music plays most of the time. I don't smoke or do drugs, scarcely drink, and have no vices other than watching sports, in a somewhat selective way. Nothing has regularized my life recently as much as having a VCR, which allows me to record an afternoon game that, given my schedule, would best be watched in the evening. (My next toy will be a two-piece projection television with a screen at least six feet wide.) I go south at least once every winter and to Europe for a few weeks of work, generally in May. In the summertime I sometimes break regimen to swim or read in the sunshine. Otherwise, I'm usually home working. In good health, I plan to live to be one hundred, working all the way (as my father still is, now at seventy-seven). The instructions are that I be buried in the same Shearith Israel cemetery that contains my father's parents and some of my mother's relatives.

II

We changed our expectations of men's abilities. The man who had done only one thing in Europe had to do a hundred in the New World. In pioneer times, he did all of them at once; today, he does a number of them in turn, shifting from occupation to occupation, but either way a new flexibility enters in.
—Margaret Mead, *And Keep Your Powder Dry:
An Anthropologist Looks at America* (1942)

When I first imagined becoming a writer, I was thinking in terms of criticism and ancillary journalism, such as book reviewing and cultural features. My first specialty as a critic was current American fiction; but thanks in part to a 1965 Pulitzer Fellowship in critical writing, I became interested in writing about the other arts as well. As a magazine writer, I began to do extended profiles of major American artists and intellectuals, extending my training in intellectual history. These two experiences informed my academic work, as I made a specialty of the arts, all the arts, in America. I would have gladly done a Ph.D. thesis on the American imagination as reflected in the works and careers of Walt Whitman, Herman Melville, Charles Ives, and Albert Pinkham Ryder—a sort of *Banquet Years* about American figures—had I not in 1968 flunked a preorals that was, alas, devoted mostly to American political history! (Though I have written about the arts individually, I am still more interested in writing about all of them together or about rare individuals I call "polyartists," who have done distinguished work in more than one nonadjacent art.)

Free of academia, living downtown, I was by 1969 entirely on my own. I should add that I have never thought of myself as "free-lance," as my services are not for hire. Even in writing for magazines, I rarely do topics suggested by editors, in part because it takes too much time and research to write well about something I have not thought about for a long, long time. Another practical rule is never do anything that anyone else can do better, in any medium, not only because the people hiring you will come to regret not choosing the better guy, but also because, unless you are starving, it is always a pleasure to give jobs away.

In 1967 I began creative writing, initially in poetry, but later in fiction, experimental prose, and book-art. In 1975, I began to work in audio and video, not as a collaborating scriptwriter but as the principal author or maker of tapes; before long, film and holography became part of my repertoire. Instead of being just a writer, I had reason to call myself a "writer/artist." Nonetheless, I continued to do expository prose of all kinds. Adding new activities without fully abandoning old ones, I have evolved for myself a pluralistic working situation, where I can go from one thing to another, from one art to another (or, in my house, from one worktable to another), without any strain or anxiety. There are only projects demanding attention, and my daily job is, simply, laboring toward their completion. Though other authors may be more prolific, none known to me is quite so various, "all over the place" being an academic euphemism that is at once deprecatory and appropriately distinctive.

I would be remiss if I did not talk about surviving as an independent noncommercial writer in America. It is commonly said that it is impossible, and I suppose it is, even though I've done it for over twenty years now. How? Not from book royalties, which amount to less than one thousand dollars a year. (By comparison, I earn more annually from selling copies of books of mine that were dropped by their original publishers—RK Editions, as I call them.) Not from articles and reviews, which never earn more than ten thousand dollars a year. Not from lectures, which likewise never amount to more than ten grand. Not from grants either, even though I've gotten more than two dozen of those over the past two decades, the sum of them falling below a hundred thousand dollars, which is to say less than five thousand dollars a year to me, or less than a full professor's salary for a few years. (Now the problem is that, in spite of the recent proliferation of cultural foundations, all of them staffed by well-heeled executives, independent noncommercial writing is respected more in piety than in fact; in this neglect, reflecting our ambivalence toward the ideal of independent integrity, America resembles Russia more than Western Europe.) If nothing is sufficient, how do I survive? Simply from the respect that colleagues have for what I do and, on the other side, from having always survived on income that would be utterly intolerable for anyone else my age, apart from my professional achievement. To put it another way, I've lived like a struggling graduate student long after the fact. Thankfully, I have no dependents, I rarely get ill, and I have never needed to own a car.

Why not teach? At first I thought it would take too much time; I also feared such hidden costs as working for people who might have too much control over my future or economic livelihood. Temperamentally no more suited to being an underling than a boss, I feared as well a softness that follows rewards that come from having a title after your name, rather than from the quality of your work. In 1972, when I felt my independent career had reached a low point, I nonetheless accepted a "teaching associate" job at City University's John Jay College of Criminal Justice, lecturing mostly to policemen about the arts one night a week, in exchange for a few thousand dollars; but as my situation improved in 1973, I was relieved when that obligation ended. For 1977, after a financial crisis in Good Deal Realty had tripled my monthly maintenance, the American studies program at the University of Texas at Austin made me an offer that could not be refused—a "visiting" full professorship at a salary of several hundred dollars a week; but during that semester in Austin, an otherwise charming place, so little got done that I gladly returned to New York. At the time I was a candidate for a university chair whose price included living at a college three hours from New York. Fearing yet more inactivity, I withdrew my name. I have since fantasized about jobs appropriate to my experience—running a writing program in an arts college or supervising major independent projects (in, say, a

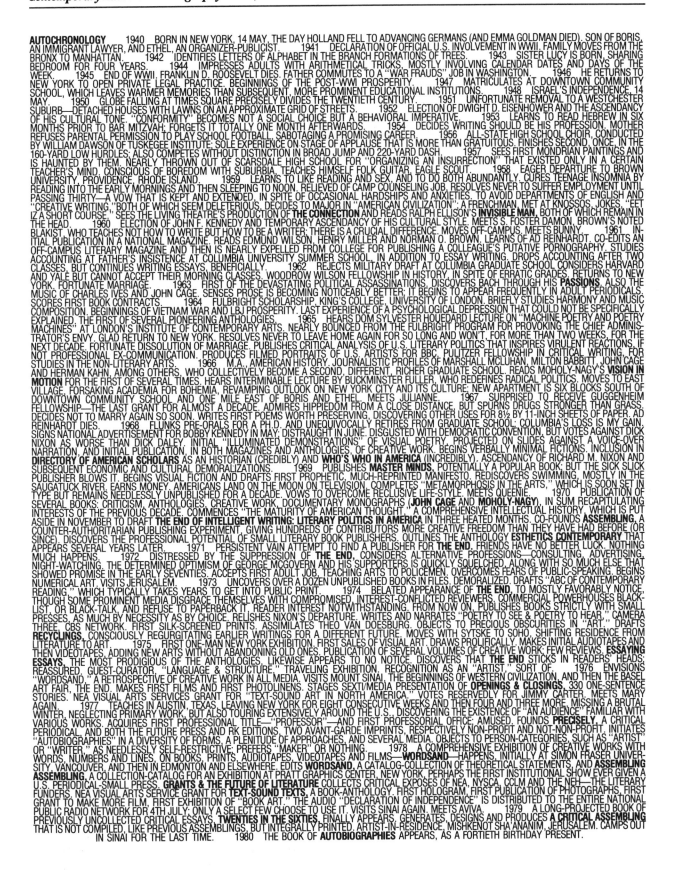

AUTOCHRONOLOGY 1940 BORN IN NEW YORK, 14 MAY, THE DAY HOLLAND FELL TO ADVANCING GERMANS (AND EMMA GOLDMAN DIED). SON OF BORIS, AN IMMIGRANT LAWYER, AND ETHEL, AN ORGANIZER-PUBLICIST. 1941 DECLARATION OF OFFICIAL U.S. INVOLVEMENT IN WWII. FAMILY MOVES FROM THE BRONX TO MANHATTAN. 1942 IDENTIFIES LETTERS OF ALPHABET IN THE BRANCH FORMATIONS OF TREES. 1943 SISTER LUCY IS BORN, SHARING BEDROOM FOR FOUR YEARS. 1944 IMPRESSES ADULTS WITH ARITHMETICAL TRICKS, MOSTLY INVOLVING CALENDAR DATES AND DAYS OF THE WEEK. 1945 END OF WWII. FRANKLIN D. ROOSEVELT DIES. FATHER COMMUTES TO A "WAR FRAUDS" JOB IN WASHINGTON. 1946 HE RETURNS TO NEW YORK TO OPEN PRIVATE LEGAL PRACTICE. BEGINNINGS OF THE POST-WWI PROSPERITY. 1947 MATRICULATES AT DOWNTOWN COMMUNITY SCHOOL, WHICH LEAVES WARMER MEMORIES THAN SUBSEQUENT, MORE PROMINENT EDUCATIONAL INSTITUTIONS. 1948 ISRAEL'S INDEPENDENCE, 14 MAY. 1950 GLOBE FALLING AT TIMES SQUARE PRECISELY DIVIDES THE TWENTIETH CENTURY. 1951 UNFORTUNATE REMOVAL TO A WESTCHESTER SUBURB—DETACHED HOUSES WITH LAWNS ON AN APPROXIMATE GRID OF STREETS. 1952 ELECTION OF DWIGHT D. EISENHOWER AND THE ASCENDANCY OF HIS CULTURAL TONE. "CONFORMITY" BECOMES NOT A SOCIAL CHOICE BUT A BEHAVIORAL IMPERATIVE. 1953 LEARNS TO READ HEBREW IN SIX MONTHS PRIOR TO BAR MITZVAH; FORGETS IT TOTALLY ONE MONTH AFTERWARDS. 1954 DECIDES WRITING SHOULD BE HIS PROFESSION. MOTHER REFUSES PARENTAL PERMISSION TO PLAY SCHOOL FOOTBALL, SABOTAGING A PROMISING CAREER. 1956 ALL-STATE HIGH SCHOOL CHOIR, CONDUCTED BY WILLIAM DAWSON OF TUSKEGEE INSTITUTE; SOLE EXPERIENCE ON STAGE OF APPLAUSE THAT IS MORE THAN GRATUITOUS. FINISHES SECOND, ONCE, IN THE 160-YARD LOW HURDLES; ALSO COMPETES WITHOUT DISTINCTION IN BROAD JUMP AND 220-YARD DASH. 1957 SEES FIRST MONDRIAN PAINTINGS AND IS HAUNTED BY THEM. NEARLY THROWN OUT OF SCARSDALE HIGH SCHOOL FOR "ORGANIZING AN INSURRECTION" THAT EXISTED ONLY IN A CERTAIN TEACHER'S MIND. CONSCIOUS OF BOREDOM WITH SUBURBIA, TEACHES HIMSELF FOLK GUITAR, EAGLE SCOUT. 1958 EAGER DEPARTURE TO BROWN UNIVERSITY, PROVIDENCE, RHODE ISLAND. 1959 LEARNS TO LIKE READING AND SEX, AND TO DO BOTH ABUNDANTLY. CURES TEENAGE INSOMNIA BY READING INTO THE EARLY MORNINGS AND THEN SLEEPING TO NOON. RELIEVED OF CAMP COUNSELING JOB, RESOLVES NEVER TO SUFFER EMPLOYMENT UNTIL PASSING THIRTY—A VOW THAT IS KEPT AND EXTENDED, IN SPITE OF OCCASIONAL HARDSHIPS AND ANXIETIES. TO AVOID DEPARTMENTS OF ENGLISH AND "CREATIVE WRITING," BOTH OF WHICH SEEM DELETERIOUS, DECIDES TO MAJOR IN "AMERICAN CIVILIZATION"; A FRENCHMAN, MET AT KNOSSOS, JOKES, "EET IZ A SHORT COURSE." SEES THE LIVING THEATRE'S PRODUCTION OF **THE CONNECTION** AND READS RALPH ELLISON'S **INVISIBLE MAN**, BOTH OF WHICH REMAIN IN THE HEAD. 1960 ELECTION OF JOHN F. KENNEDY AND TEMPORARY ASCENDANCY OF HIS CULTURAL STYLE. MEETS S. FOSTER DAMON, BROWN'S NOTED BLAKIST, WHO TEACHES NOT HOW TO WRITE BUT HOW TO BE A WRITER; THERE IS A CRUCIAL DIFFERENCE. MOVES OFF-CAMPUS. MEETS BUNNY. 1961 INITIAL PUBLICATION IN A NATIONAL MAGAZINE. READS EDMUND WILSON, HENRY MILLER AND NORMAN O. BROWN. LEARNS OF AD REINHARDT. CO-EDITS AN OFF-CAMPUS LITERARY MAGAZINE AND THEN IS NEARLY EXPELLED FROM COLLEGE FOR PUBLISHING A COLLEAGUE'S PUTATIVE PORNOGRAPHY. STUDIES ACCOUNTING AT FATHER'S INSISTENCE AT COLUMBIA UNIVERSITY SUMMER SCHOOL, IN ADDITION TO ESSAY WRITING. DROPS ACCOUNTING AFTER TWO CLASSES, BUT CONTINUES WRITING ESSAYS, BENEFICIALLY. 1962 REJECTS MILITARY DRAFT AT COLUMBIA GRADUATE SCHOOL CONSIDERS HARVARD AND YALE BUT CANNOT ACCEPT THEIR MORNING CLASSES. WOODROW WILSON FELLOWSHIP IN HISTORY, IN SPITE OF ERRATIC GRADES. RETURNS TO NEW YORK. FORTUNATE MARRIAGE. 1963 FIRST OF THE DEVASTATING POLITICAL ASSASSINATIONS. DISCOVERS BACH THROUGH HIS **PASSIONS**. ALSO THE MUSIC OF CHARLES IVES AND JOHN CAGE. SENSES PROSE IS BECOMING NOTICEABLY BETTER; IT BEGINS TO APPEAR FREQUENTLY IN ADULT PERIODICALS. SCORES FIRST BOOK CONTRACTS. 1964 FULBRIGHT SCHOLARSHIP, KING'S COLLEGE, UNIVERSITY OF LONDON. BRIEFLY STUDIES HARMONY AND MUSIC COMPOSITION. BEGINNINGS OF VIETNAM WAR AND LBJ PROSPERITY. LAST EXPERIENCE OF A PSYCHOLOGICAL DEPRESSION THAT COULD NOT BE SPECIFICALLY EXPLAINED. THE FIRST OF SEVERAL PIONEERING ANTHOLOGIES. 1965 HEARS DOM SYLVESTER HOUEDARD LECTURE ON "MACHINE POETRY AND POETRY MACHINES" AT LONDON'S INSTITUTE OF CONTEMPORARY ARTS. NEARLY BOUNCED FROM THE FULBRIGHT PROGRAM FOR PROVOKING THE CHIEF ADMINISTRATOR'S ENVY. GLAD RETURN TO NEW YORK. RESOLVES NEVER TO LEAVE HOME AGAIN FOR SO LONG AND WON'T, FOR MORE THAN TWO WEEKS, FOR THE NEXT DECADE. FORTUNATE DISSOLUTION OF MARRIAGE. PUBLISHES CRITICAL ANALYSIS OF U.S. LITERARY POLITICS THAT INSPIRES VIRULENT REACTIONS, IF NOT PROFESSIONAL EX-COMMUNICATION. PRODUCES FILMED PORTRAITS OF U.S. ARTISTS FOR BBC. PULITZER FELLOWSHIP IN CRITICAL WRITING, FOR STUDIES IN THE NON-LITERARY ARTS. 1966 M.A., AMERICAN HISTORY. JOURNALISTIC PROFILES OF MARSHALL MCLUHAN, MILTON BABBITT, JOHN CAGE AND HERMAN KAHN, AMONG OTHERS, WHO COLLECTIVELY BECOME A SECOND, DIFFERENT, RICHER GRADUATE SCHOOL. READS MOHOLY-NAGY'S **VISION IN MOTION** FOR THE FIRST OF SEVERAL TIMES. HEARS INTERMINABLE LECTURE BY BUCKMINSTER FULLER, WHO REDEFINES RADICAL POLITICS. MOVES TO EAST VILLAGE, FORSAKING ACADEMIA FOR BOHEMIA, REVAMPING OUTLOOK ON NEW YORK CITY AND ITS CULTURE; NEW APARTMENT IS SIX BLOCKS SOUTH OF DOWNTOWN COMMUNITY SCHOOL AND ONE MILE EAST OF BORIS AND ETHEL. MEETS JULIANNE. 1967 SURPRISED TO RECEIVE GUGGENHEIM FELLOWSHIP—THE LAST GRANT FOR ALMOST A DECADE. ADMIRES HIPPIEDOM FROM A CLOSE DISTANCE, BUT SPURNS DRUGS STRONGER THAN GRASS. DECIDES NOT TO MARRY AGAIN SO SOON. WRITES FIRST POEMS WORTH PRESERVING, DISCOVERING OTHER USES FOR 8½ BY 11-INCH SHEETS OF PAPER. AD REINHARDT DIES. 1968 FLUNKS PRE-ORALS FOR A PH.D. AND UNEQUIVOCALLY RETIRES FROM GRADUATE SCHOOL; COLUMBIA'S LOSS IS MY GAIN. SIGNS NATIONAL ADVERTISEMENT FOR BOBBY KENNEDY IN MAY; DISTRAUGHT IN JUNE. DISGUSTED WITH DEMOCRATIC CONVENTION, BUT VOTES AGAINST DICK NIXON AS WORSE THAN DICK DALEY. INITIAL "ILLUMINATED DEMONSTRATIONS" OF VISUAL POETRY, PROJECTED ON SLIDES AGAINST A VOICE-OVER NARRATION, AND INITIAL PUBLICATION, IN BOTH MAGAZINES AND ANTHOLOGIES, OF CREATIVE WORK. BEGINS VERBALLY MINIMAL FICTIONS. INCLUSION IN **DIRECTORY OF AMERICAN SCHOLARS** AS AN HISTORIAN (CREDIBLY) AND **WHO'S WHO IN AMERICA** (INCREDIBLY). ASCENDANCY OF RICHARD M. NIXON AND SUBSEQUENT ECONOMIC AND CULTURAL DEMORALIZATIONS. 1969 PUBLISHES **MASTER MINDS**, POTENTIALLY A POPULAR BOOK; BUT THE SICK SLICK PUBLISHER BLOWS IT. BEGINS VISUAL FICTION AND DRAFTS FIRST PROPHETIC, MUCH-REPRINTED MANIFESTO. REDISCOVERS SWIMMING, MOSTLY IN THE SAUGATUCK RIVER. EARNS MONEY. AMERICANS LAND ON THE MOON ON TELEVISION. COMPLETES "METAMORPHOSIS IN THE ARTS," WHICH IS SOON SET IN TYPE BUT REMAINS NEEDLESSLY UNPUBLISHED FOR A DECADE. VOWS TO OVERCOME RECLUSIVE LIFE-STYLE. MEETS QUEENIE. 1970 PUBLICATION OF SEVERAL BOOKS: CRITICISM, ANTHOLOGIES, CREATIVE WORK, DOCUMENTARY MONOGRAPHS (**JOHN CAGE** AND **MOHOLY-NAGY**), IN SUM RECAPITULATING INTERESTS OF THE PREVIOUS DECADE. COMMENCES "THE MATURITY OF AMERICAN THOUGHT," A COMPREHENSIVE INTELLECTUAL HISTORY, WHICH IS PUT ASIDE IN NOVEMBER TO DRAFT **THE END OF INTELLIGENT WRITING: LITERARY POLITICS IN AMERICA** IN THREE HEATED MONTHS. CO-FOUNDS **ASSEMBLING**, A COUNTER-AUTHORITARIAN PUBLISHING EXPERIMENT, GIVING HUNDREDS OF CONTRIBUTORS MORE CREATIVE FREEDOM THAN THEY HAVE HAD BEFORE (OR SINCE). DISCOVERS THE PROFESSIONAL POTENTIAL OF SMALL LITERARY BOOK PUBLISHERS. OUTLINES THE ANTHOLOGY **ESTHETICS CONTEMPORARY** THAT APPEARS SEVERAL YEARS LATER. 1971 PERSISTENT VAIN ATTEMPT TO FIND A PUBLISHER FOR **THE END.** FRIENDS HAVE NO BETTER LUCK. NOTHING MUCH HAPPENS. 1972 DISTRESSED BY THE SUPPRESSION OF **THE END**, CONSIDERS ALTERNATIVE PROFESSIONS—CONSULTING, ADVERTISING, NIGHT-WATCHING. THE DETERMINED OPTIMISM OF GEORGE MCGOVERN AND HIS SUPPORTERS IS QUICKLY SQUELCHED, ALONG WITH SO MUCH ELSE THAT SHOWED PROMISE IN THE EARLY SEVENTIES. ACCEPTS FIRST ADULT JOB, TEACHING ARTS TO POLICEMEN. OVERCOMES FEARS OF PUBLIC-SPEAKING. BEGINS NUMERICAL ART. VISITS JERUSALEM. 1973 UNCOVERS OVER A DOZEN UNPUBLISHED BOOKS IN FILES. DEMORALIZED. DRAFTS "ABC OF CONTEMPORARY READING," WHICH TYPICALLY TAKES YEARS TO GET INTO PUBLIC PRINT. 1974 BELATED APPEARANCE OF **THE END**, TO MOSTLY FAVORABLY NOTICE, THOUGH SOME PROMINENT MEDIA DISGRACE THEMSELVES WITH COMPROMISED, INTEREST-CONFLICTED REVIEWERS. COMMERCIAL POWERHOUSES BLACKLIST, OR BLACK-TALK, AND REFUSE TO PAPERBACK IT, READER INTEREST NOTWITHSTANDING. FROM NOW ON, PUBLISHES BOOKS STRICTLY WITH SMALL PRESSES, AS MUCH BY NECESSITY AS BY CHOICE. RELISHES NIXON'S DEPARTURE. WRITES AND NARRATES "POETRY TO SEE & POETRY TO HEAR," CAMERA THREE, CBS NETWORK. FIRST SILK-SCREENED PRINTS. ASSIMILATES THEO VAN DOESBURG. OBJECTS TO PRECIOUS OBSCURITIES IN "ART." DRAFTS **RECYCLINGS**, CONSCIOUSLY REGURGITATING EARLIER WRITINGS FOR A DIFFERENT FUTURE. MOVES WITH SYTSKE TO SOHO, SHIFTING RESIDENCE FROM LITERATURE TO ART. 1975 FIRST ONE-MAN NEW YORK EXHIBITION. FIRST SALES OF VISUAL ART. DRAWS PROLIFICALLY. MAKES INITIAL AUDIOTAPES AND THEN VIDEOTAPES, ADDING NEW ARTS WITHOUT ABANDONING OLD ONES. PUBLICATION OF SEVERAL VOLUMES OF CREATIVE WORK; FEW REVIEWS. **ESSAYING ESSAYS**, THE MOST PRODIGIOUS OF THE ANTHOLOGIES, LIKEWISE APPEARS TO NO NOTICE. DISCOVERS THAT **THE END** STICKS IN READERS' HEADS; REASSURED. GUEST-CURATOR, "LANGUAGE & STRUCTURE," TRAVELING EXHIBITION. RECOGNITION AS AN "ARTIST," SORT OF. 1976 ENVISIONS "WORDSAND," A RETROSPECTIVE OF CREATIVE WORK IN ALL MEDIA. VISITS MOUNT SINAI, THE BEGINNINGS OF WESTERN CIVILIZATION, AND THEN THE BASEL ART FAIR, THE END. MAKES FIRST FILMS AND FIRST PHOTOLINENS. STAGES SEXTI/MEDIA PRESENTATION OF **OPENINGS & CLOSINGS**, 330 ONE-SENTENCE STORIES. NEA VISUAL ARTS SERVICES GRANT FOR "TEXT-SOUND ART IN NORTH AMERICA." VOTES RESERVEDLY FOR JIMMY CARTER. MEETS MARY AGAIN. 1977 TEACHES IN AUSTIN, TEXAS, LEAVING NEW YORK FOR EIGHT CONSECUTIVE WEEKS AND THEN FOUR AND THREE MORE, MISSING A BRUTAL WINTER, NEGLECTING PRIMARY WORK, BUT ALSO TOURING EXTENSIVELY AROUND THE U.S., DISCOVERING THE EXISTENCE OF "AN AUDIENCE" FAMILIAR WITH VARIOUS WORKS. ACQUIRES FIRST PROFESSIONAL TITLE—"PROFESSOR"—AND FIRST PROFESSORIAL OFFICE; AMUSED. FOUNDS **PRECISELY**, A CRITICAL PERIODICAL, AND BOTH THE FUTURE PRESS AND RK EDITIONS, TWO AVANT-GARDE IMPRINTS, RESPECTIVELY NON-PROFIT AND NOT-NON-PROFIT. INITIATES "AUTOBIOGRAPHIES" IN A DIVERSITY OF FORMS, A PLENITUDE OF APPROACHES, AND SEVERAL MEDIA. OBJECTS TO PERSON-CATEGORIES, SUCH AS "ARTIST" OR "WRITER," AS NEEDLESSLY SELF-RESTRICTIVE; PREFERS "MAKER" OR NOTHING. 1978 A COMPREHENSIVE EXHIBITION OF CREATIVE WORKS WITH WORDS, NUMBERS AND LINES, ON BOOKS, PRINTS, AUDIOTAPES, VIDEOTAPES AND FILMS—**WORDSAND**—HAPPENS, INITIALLY AT SIMON FRASER UNIVERSITY, VANCOUVER, AND THEN IN EDMONTON AND ELSEWHERE. EDITS **WORDSAND**, A CATALOG-COLLECTION OF THEORETICAL STATEMENTS, AND **ASSEMBLING ASSEMBLING**, A COLLECTION-CATALOG FOR AN EXHIBITION AT PRATT GRAPHICS CENTER, NEW YORK, PERHAPS THE FIRST INSTITUTIONAL SHOW EVER GIVEN A U.S. PERIODICAL-SMALL PRESS. **GRANTS & THE FUTURE OF LITERATURE** COLLECTS CRITICAL EXPOSES OF NEA, NYSCA, CCLM AND THE NEH—THE LITERARY FUNDERS. NEA VISUAL ARTS SERVICE GRANT FOR **TEXT-SOUND TEXTS**, A BOOK-ANTHOLOGY. FIRST HOLOGRAM, FIRST PUBLICATION OF PHOTOGRAPHS, FIRST GRANT TO MAKE MORE FILM, FIRST EXHIBITION OF "BOOK ART." THE AUDIO "DECLARATION OF INDEPENDENCE" IS DISTRIBUTED TO THE ENTIRE NATIONAL PUBLIC RADIO NETWORK FOR 4TH JULY; ONLY A SELECT FEW CHOOSE TO USE IT. VISITS SINAI AGAIN. MEETS AVIVA. 1979 A LONG-PROJECTED BOOK OF PREVIOUSLY UNCOLLECTED CRITICAL ESSAYS, **TWENTIES IN THE SIXTIES**, FINALLY APPEARS. GENERATES, DESIGNS AND PRODUCES **A CRITICAL ASSEMBLING** THAT IS NOT COMPILED, LIKE PREVIOUS ASSEMBLINGS, BUT INTEGRALLY PRINTED. ARTIST-IN-RESIDENCE, MISHKENOT SHA'ANANIM, JERUSALEM. CAMPS OUT IN SINAI FOR THE LAST TIME. 1980 THE BOOK OF **AUTOBIOGRAPHIES** APPEARS, AS A FORTIETH BIRTHDAY PRESENT.

"The graphic that became the cover for Autobiographies *and was also widely exhibited, mostly mail art." Typeset by Sasha Newborn*

small liberal arts college); but nothing has yet materialized. I expect that someday soon, as it becomes harder to live like a graduate student (or I assume expensive responsibilities), my independence will fall to an offer-with-tenure; but what cannot be estimated, what frankly makes me anxious, is the deleterious effects this might have upon my professional activity.

III

He wrote on all subjects, in all forms, and for all purposes. For him there was no separation of art and action; they were identical.
—Roger Shattuck, *Selected Writings of Guillaume Apollinaire* (1950)

As I look back over my work, I see subtle reflections of my academic training. It is commonly said that one goes to university to learn to think in a certain way; and even though I was only a fair student who mostly read books outside his field, there is no doubt that I still think like a historian who majored in American civilization. From the beginning there has been a recurring critical interest in what is unique about American culture—initially in American fiction and theater, then in American art and American literary politics, and more recently, for a series of features initially for German radio stations, in the art of radio in North America. This historical training also accounts for why I tend to cast explanations in chronological sequence; it accounts as well for my taste for empirical analyses of art and the relationship between art and politics. Perhaps it accounts for my preference for Anglo-American styles of thinking; nothing turns me off quicker than "frogthink," especially when written by native English-speakers.

Out of this training also comes an interest in alternative historiography, shown initially in *Autobiographies* (1981), which is a book-length portrayal of my life in the counterlinear form of a mosaic that includes chapters written at various times, often for purposes other than this book, and thematic dredgings of my own experience, in addition to chapters written by others. The general suggestion is that autobiographers exploring structures other than chronological narrative might make discoveries about understanding of their lives. (The German *Autobiographien New York Berlin* [1986] has different material.) This notion of alternative historiography also informs a 1972 proposal to write a history of the U.S. backwards, from the present to the past (an obvious experiment that someone else ought to try sometime). The idea of alternative history stands behind my audio portrait of the 1960s, *A Special Time* (1985),

which is a montage of participants' voices talking about the uniqueness of that era. (I remember William G. McLoughlin, bless him, recently telling me that "oral history" did not have much status within the profession.) I think this interest in alternative historiography inspired my film about pre–World War II Berlin as evoked by the great Jewish cemetery there, portraying as it does a graveyard as exemplifying visual history. There is no question in my mind that, more than two decades out of school, I think more like a historian than anything else.

From the start of my critical career, I made the avant-garde a principal subject. *The New American Arts* had my own essays on the latest developments in fiction and drama; *The Theatre of Mixed Means* (1968) was about a yet newer theater. *Metamorphosis in the Arts* (1980, but written in 1969) I wrote entirely by myself, with critical surveys of innovative directions in painting, sculpture, music, dance, and film, in addition to the new intermedial arts of word imagery, environments, mixed-means events, machine art, artistic machines, and inferential art. The second half of *The End of Intelligent Writing* (1974) is about innovative developments in literature. The difference between what is truly avant-garde and what is not informs as well two recent collections of my critical essays, *The Old Poetries and the New* (1981) and *The Old Fictions and the New* (1987), in addition to my selections for *The Yale Gertrude Stein* (1980). The companion 1970 documentary monographs about John Cage and Moholy-Nagy honor men who will always be avant-garde heroes; a sequel to the former is *Conversing with Cage* (1988).

The term avant-garde defines what is decisively new, not only with respect to previous work but with relevance to the changing times. With that definition in mind, we can see how most of my anthologies are about an avant-garde, favoring that which is furthest-out within the subject customarily announced in their titles: *Future's Fictions* (1971), *Breakthrough Fictioneers* (1973), *Essaying Essays* (1975), *Scenarios* (1980), *Text-Sound Texts* (1980). Years later, all of them still stand as way-out landmarks. My sense of the importance of understanding the avant-garde informs as well such anthologies of criticism as *Younger Critics in North America* (1976), *Esthetics Contemporary* (1978, 1988), *Visual Literature Criticism* (1979), *Aural Literature Criticism* (1981), and *The Avant-Garde Tradition in Literature* (1982), in addition to my coediting of the periodical *Precisely: A Critical Journal* (since 1977). The principle of an avant-garde also inspired the collections of futuristic social thought: *Beyond Left & Right* (1968), *Social Speculations* (1971), *Human Alternatives* (1971), and *The Edge of Adaptation* (1973). Since the tradition of innovation has no end, I suspect that my work on this theme is not yet done.

IV

The sociological imagination enables its possessor to understand the larger historical scene in terms of its meaning for the inner life and the external career of a variety of individuals.
—C. Wright Mills, *The Sociological Imagination* (1959)

Perhaps because I've been a full-time literary worker surviving on the margins, fully immersed in a world where many only dip their toes, the problems and politics of the profession have been a continuing concern. Remembering C. Wright Mills's dictum about recognizing the public issues implicit in private problems, I have written, often at length, about closure in the literary world. This has perhaps been the most risky element of my activity, challenging as I do the powers adjacent to me, rather than those far away (in Moscow, or Nicaragua, or even Washington, D.C.). Many of these essays fed into the first half of *The End of Intelligent Writing*, which was released in paperback under its subtitle "Literary Politics in America" (1977); and these issues were discussed again in *"The End" Appendix/"The End" Essentials* (1979).

In 1978 I began a critical analysis of publicly funded literary granting in America, a subject that concerns everyone I know, which no one seems to have examined as closely (not for the least reason being that I've received many personal grants); but making this criticism public has turned out to be even more problematic. The publishing house commissioning it in 1980, even featuring it in its catalogue, was foolishly advised not to publish it (and for similar wisdom later went out of business), while magazines accepting chapters have dallied them to death (and others take pride in not discussing realities immediate to them). Jerome Klinkowitz, editing a series for a university press, found his bosses rejecting him, and so forth. The commercial houses judged there was insufficient public interest in the subject, while one middle-sized publisher wanted a book exposing Ronald Reagan's evil effects, which was contrary to my point that the problems of these agencies had little to do with politicians (and contrary as well to my disinclinations to make up opportunistic lies or kiss ass). Meanwhile, the folks running such funding agencies feel that, immune from criticism, they can act with impunity, their particular problems getting not better but worse. Given a growing concern about

the subject, as well as a continued demand for the text, I issued a limited edition, produced on my computer, in 1987; but I suspect there will be another version before long.

V

But it is the business of the man of letters to call attention to whatever he is able to see: it is his function to create what has not been hitherto known and, as a critic, to discern its modes.
—Allen Tate, *The Man of Letters in the Modern World: Selected Essays, 1928-1955* (1955)

Another continuing preoccupation has been the culture of cities. Back at Brown, I did an independent study, a fifty-page paper, on the image of the city in modern American literature; and my honors thesis dealt with Henry Miller, an urban writer if ever there was one. An early piece of literary journalism analyzed the portrayal of different neighborhoods in recent fiction, and in the early eighties I edited for the literary magazine *Shantih* a special issue on the literature connected to the neighborhood in which I live, SoHo. (The preface sketched a sociology of literary production in New York City in the 1970s, the Upper East Side being different from the Upper West Side, and both being different from the Village.) The Berlin graveyard films are another brick in this house.

The culmination of this interest, however, has been *New York City*, an audiotape composition of and about the sounds unique to my hometown. Originally commissioned by Westdeutscher Rundfunk, as part of its Metropolis series, my *New York City* now exists in several lengths—a 60-minute international version that was broadcast over WDR in 1984 (and subsequently exhibited at Documenta in 1987), an 87-minute tape made in 1983 as a first draft that has still the most satisfactory overall structure, a 30-minute tape of excerpts that was used to accompany an exhibition about Forty-second street at the Whitney Museum of American Art at Philip Morris in 1982, and a 140-minute American version that I mean to differ from the others not only in its length and accompanying richness but its inclusion of a greater amount of indigenous speech. In a 1984 concert for Pro Musica Nuova, Radio Bremen's biannual festival, the tape was accompanied by hundreds of slides of distinctly New York images. Someday I would like to reverse the conventional filmmaking procedure by adding to my *New York City* a visual track of kinetic images equally unique to this city; I've already begun synthesizing more abstract video accompaniments to other audiotapes. In progress is yet another tape about the sound of New York City speech, in which perhaps a hundred native New Yorkers state when they were born, in what neighborhood they grew up, where their parents came from, etc., my acoustic/sociological point being that there is not one New York accent but many, each reflective of different times and neighborhoods and ethnic backgrounds. (Someday too I would also like to do a long critical essay about the painter Ad Reinhardt, whose sensibility, with a taste for geometric purity accompanying an avoidance of Nature, has always represented for me the epitome of the urban imagination in visual art.)

VI

The artist is not a propagandist but more than any other person a seismograph of his time and its direction, who consciously or unconsciously expresses its substance. Apart from this limitation of predetermined social and ethical existence, the creative artist is free as to its formulation. This freedom is the genesis of the unpredictability of genius.

—László Moholy-Nagy, *Vision in Motion*
(1947)

The process of writing extended profiles of major American artists and intellectuals, the pieces collected in *Master Minds* (1969), gave me a richer, more various, and ultimately more useful education than graduate school. Mostly because I profiled only people whom I admired (e.g., Milton Babbitt, John Cage, Allen Ginsberg, Marshall McLuhan, Reinhold Niebuhr, Glenn Gould, Richard Hofstadter, among others), with whom I would spend time talking one-on-one, I was prepared to learn from them as well.

In the course of telling me about his own ideas, Marshall McLuhan advised me to read Moholy-Nagy, and I remember enjoying his posthumously published *Vision in Motion* while sitting on my Fifth Street roof in 1966. That masterful book not only revealed to me the foundation of intermedia, or new arts between old arts, but it also introduced me to constructivism as the most fertile and valid of the modernist movements. Out of the discoveries associated with these two traditions came first my creative work in visual poetry and then in comparable fiction. From these traditions also comes my belief that excellence in art comes largely from distinctive, if not innovative, use of the materials indigenous to an art; content is something else. Simply, what you hear in music, for instance, is not the composer's heart but the beating of the drums. This bias accounts for why the poetics of T. S. Eliot, say, remain more sympa-

thetic than rationalizations of expressionism.

A first reflection of constructivism in my own creative work is the use of severely limited constraints, such as fictions with only two words to a paragraph ("One Night Stood" [1969], whose text was later reprinted in a book), and then one word to each paragraph ("Excelsior" from 1970, reprinted in *More Short Fictions* [1980]), and, later, several kinds of fiction composed of only single-sentence stories: "Openings and Closings" (1975), which appeared as a book in 1976; "More Openings and Closings," which may be a book in 1989; *Foreshortenings and Other Stories* (1977), in which the same sentences are systematically rearranged to make other stories in essentially modular fictions; "Epiphanies," which have been appearing in literary magazines all through the 1980s, some German translations of which were collected in a book (1983); and more recently "minimal fictions." Constructivism mixes with Dada in the first three chapbooks of my visual poems: *Visual Language* (1970), *I Articulations* (1974), and *Illuminations* (1977). The influence of constructivism also confirmed my earlier commitment to the principle of "working things up"—to work and rework something until it became greater than what could be done spontaneously. Innate genius will take you only so far in art and writing, where so much excellence depends upon the ability to make something better—smarter, more resonant, more percipient—than you are.

More explicit symptoms of constructivism include the poems and stories composed of numbers alone and the fictions composed of line drawings that evolve in systemic sequence. I've called this last kind of work "constructivist fictions" in direct acknowledgment of their source, thinking that they represent the kind of thing Moholy-Nagy might have produced had he decided to do visual fiction. *Constructs* (1975) and *Constructs Two* (1978) are both collections of stories, while *And So Forth* (1979) uses a similarly geometric visual vocabulary for pages whose ordering can be shuffled. (*Tabula Rasa* [1978] and *Inexistences* [1978] are both conceptual fictions, filled with gloriously white blank pages framed within a constructivist polemic.) Constructivism also informs the geometric poems with single words in the four corners of the page (or eight words, with the four additional words configured like points of a compass in the middle of the page, or sixteen-word poems with four rectangles within a single page). *Turfs/Arenas/Fields/Pitches* (1980) was an initial collection of only quartets; *Arenas/Fields/Pitches/Turfs* (1982) contains selections from all three strains.

The numerical literature epitomizes the theme of alternative materials for traditional genres. As my

An image from the book Exhaustive Parallel Intervals

early poems are composed of words visualized, which is to say that the enhancement associated with "poetry" comes not from syntactical or rhythmic manipulations but from something else, so my precedent for the constructivist fictions was visual fictions whose full-page sequences tell a story. For "Obliterate" (in *Short Fictions* [1974]), for instance, incremental patterns of vertical, horizontal, and then diagonal lines cross out the printed instructions for birth-control pills, the essentially visual story thus depending not only upon a verbal title but the verbal background. Similarly, the initial idea behind *Numbers: Poems and Stories* (1976) and *Exhaustive Parallel Intervals* (1979) was simply to see whether I could write semblances of poetry, fiction, and book-length novels by using numbers alone.

From this emphasis upon generating art, rather than "expressing" it, come my experiments with nonsyntactic prose, initially for *Recyclings* (1974, 1984), which consists of single-page reworkings of my own writings, but also for the adaptations of biblical texts, most of them collected in *Aftertexts/Prose Pieces*

(1987). Another concern here has been alternative bookish forms: beginning with ladder books such as *Modulations* (1975) and *Extrapolate* (1975); and including *Come Here* (1975), a visual fiction whose narrative unit is not sentences but words arrayed in two-page spreads; and *One Night Stood* (1977), in which the same verbal text appears in two radically different formats—one a three-by-five-inch perfect-bound book with only one two-word sentence to each page, the other tabloid-sized, loose-leaf newsprint with several sentences to each page.

VII

I believe that life is indestructible, and the force that makes it indestructible is human constructive consciousness. . . . Art is an effort of our consciousness directed toward a specific goal—to know and to make known, to give shape to the shapeless, structure to the discomposed, and to lend form to the amorphous origin of chaos.
—Naum Gabo, *Of Divers Arts* (1962)

From the example of Moholy-Nagy, more than anyone else, also follows my explorations of the literary uses of media other than printed pages. It began with audiotape in 1975, as I produced, at WXXI-FM in Rochester, the single-word paragraphs of the sexual interchange of "Excelsior" by putting one voice on the left side of a stereotape and the other voice on the right side. Since I spoke both voices, creating the charming ambiguity of self-seduction, one charm offered by audiotape was that this "auto-duet" could not possibly be done live. Six years later, with the sixteen interwoven narratives of "Seductions" (a text also reprinted in *More Short Fictions*) I made sixteen different amplifications of my own voice, declaiming the interrupted seduction stories one sentence at a time in a multivoiced acoustic narrative that would likewise be impossible in live performance.

Once I was invited to be a guest artist at the Electronic Music Studio of Stockholm, I became a true composer, putting language on audiotape in ways that could not be represented in any text. For *Invocations* (1981, 1984), I recorded over sixty ministers speaking prayers in over two dozen languages, and from these recordings mixed a sixty-minute piece structured roughly along the lines of J. S. Bach's *Saint Matthew Passion*. There are solos, duets, trios, quintets, and whole choruses, all of them composed of only prayer-speaking, the acoustic theme being that there is a sound unique to such speech, regardless of differences in language. (The literary influence is, of course, James Joyce's *Finnegans Wake.*) In his *Electronic and Experimental Music* (1987), Thomas B. Holmes places me between King Crimson and Kraftwerk (!) and then praises *Invocations* as "an excellent example of text-sound composition using the tape medium to control the structure of a work." Thanks, stranger. Later audiotapes include: *The Gospels* (1982) and *Die Evangelien* (1982), in which the opening books of the New Testament are heard simultaneously, respectively in English and German, the musical model being Beethoven's *Grosse Fugue; The Eight Nights of Hanukah* (1983), an incremental passacaglia that portrays the Jewish Diaspora through a variety of accents for Hebrew; and *Americas' Game* (1988), which regards sounds unique to baseball as reflective of American life.

I also began making videotapes in 1975, initially as a guest artist at the Synapse studios at Syracuse University. As with audio, the opening pieces were for texts I'd written before entering the studio. For "Excelsior," the seduction story with single-word paragraphs spoken alternately by a man and a woman, I designed electronically one geometric shape for the male and another for the female, and then, in an example of constructivist eroticism, had their kinetic appearances alternate in correspondence with the changing voices. For "Plateaux," with its single-word paragraphs spoken by an omniscient narrator, I used video feedback to introduce a moiré pattern that visually metamorphosed in repetitious ways that corresponded to the circularity of the text's plot.

The most ambitious 1975 video realization was *Recyclings,* the nonsyntactic prose text whose words necessarily had equal relation to each other. As in the audio realization of the same text, a first page is read by one voice and a second page by two voices, one beginning just behind the other. As we were working with tape, both voices could be mine. For the third text, there were three voices in the canon, for the fourth, four voices—up to six voices. On the screen appeared only pairs of lips visibly moving in unison with the texts—one pair for the first, two for the second, etc.; thanks to the possibility of video over-dubbing, all of these lips could be mine. While I was still using a text written initially for pages, I was also exploiting capabilities indigenous to video.

The practical difference between writing manuscripts and producing video is that you need a studio for the latter; and if you don't have the machinery at home, you need an invitation to a place that is appropriately equipped. Not until 1979 did I have another opportunity to do video, during a visit to Eastern New Mexico University, ostensibly for a literary interview recorded at the school's television

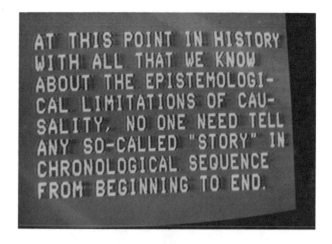

From the video Epiphanies

station, KENM. When my hosts, Stanley Berne and Arlene Zekowsky, asked to incorporate an excerpt of me reading my works, I replied that I don't read my poems and stories live, in part because visual poems and visual fictions can only be seen (not heard), but mostly because the work exists apart from me. Since the experience of it should have nothing to do with me, seeing me in connection with any text of mine can only compromise the transmission. On "reading tours," I prefer to display my pieces—on slides, videotapes, audiotape, and film—while I am standing apart from them (ideally in the darkness behind the machines). For the same reason, if photographs are to accompany an article such as this, I would prefer that they be not of me but of my work. What is at issue here is not modesty but an ethic particular to the esthetics of constructivism.

Instead of doing a reading at KENM, I proposed making a piece of literary video art, in this case using my text "The Declaration of Independence" (1978, reprinted in *Prose Pieces/Aftertexts*), which is essentially the historic document backwards, word by word; but this time I read the text three times in approximate unison. The image on-screen has only bearded lips (that happen to be mine), or actually three pairs of lips, each different in size from the others. As nothing framed this unusual tape, I figured that it needed some explanation, and the best solution to that problem would be using the character generator, or electronic letter-making machine, to run an explanatory text along the bottom of the screen. This last decision introduced me to the video technology that would inspire my future work.

In 1980 I used a primitive character generator to write a video *Epiphanies*, in which the single-sentence stories appear on the screen in various arrays, for

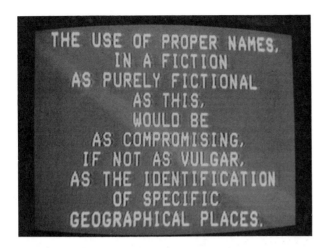

THE USE OF PROPER NAMES,
IN A FICTION
AS PURELY FICTIONAL
AS THIS,
WOULD BE
AS COMPROMISING,
IF NOT AS VULGAR,
AS THE IDENTIFICATION
OF SPECIFIC
GEOGRAPHICAL PLACES,

Again, from the video Epiphanies

various durations of time, my point being to make a tape that consisted only of reading matter. This bias informed as well *Partitions* (1986), a tape about words within other words in increasingly complicated configurations. Since 1985 I've been working at the Experimental TV Center in Owego, New York, using not only the character generator to make video poems and stories, but also various image synthesizers to make abstract, mostly constructivist images as visual accompaniments to my audiotapes. (The last are best played on one of those giant video screens that I want for myself.) I find these videotapes wonderful when I'm making them; but once I get home, surrounded by deadlines, damnit, I postpone the job of editing these syntheses into definitive compilations suitable for duplication and thus distribution.

VIII

The older the craft, the more restraining is its influence upon the imagination of the designer. It is easier to design a new product which is based upon the new sciences and technologies than, for example, to redesign the production-ways and shapes of pottery, one of the oldest handicrafts.
—László Moholy-Nagy, *Vision in Motion* (1947)

Already introduced to audiotape and videotape, I looked into film. Registering for a film-school animation class, I worked first with words on film using the printed texts of my *Openings and Closings,* with the openings, as black letters on white, appearing in alternation with the closings, which are white letters against a black background. As letters on-

screen recalled silent movies, the gag was that this film was "all titles, no action." Films with words and only words remain a good idea that I've scarcely explored; for while electronically generated letters are typographically limited to what is available within the machine, in film the image can be whatever words can be drawn. For the other early film, I enlisted a fellow student, Peter Longauer, to collaborate with me in animating the constructivist fictions in patterns unique to film. Shown now and then, *Constructivist Fictions* (1977) won an honorable mention in the Classe Indépendante at the Twenty-fifth Festival Mondial du Cinéma de Courts Métrages in Huy, Belgium. Thanks, strangers.

When I went to Berlin as a guest of the Deutscher Akademischer Austauschdienst Künstler-programm, living away from my typewriter and my mail, my involvement with media became greater; for in Europe, there is more respect for the principle of a known writer working not as a secondary collaborator (mostly on commercial projects, as here) but as a fully responsible media artist. It wasn't my intention to become a *Hörspielmacher* and *Film-macher;* only American neglect forced that identity upon me. (The U.S. differs from other culturally third world countries only in being shameless about our insufficiencies.)

First I worked on making a film of *Epiphanies,* my collection of single-sentence stories; but rather than shooting footage for each verbal vignette already recorded on audiotape, I wanted to make a film equivalent, which I figured would consist of footage that likewise suggested climax moments in otherwise nonexistent stories—the film track thus having no correspondence to the sound track other than similarity in structural kind. However, I resisted making such footage myself, since anything shot by a single filmmaker would have more consistency than I wanted (and also because I find the process of shooting film to be intolerably boring). It became more appropriate (as well as feasible) to gather "outtakes" from various sources, beginning with other filmmakers, and from that footage to extract individual epiphanies, whether intentional or not; in sum manipulating my material from a distance that is more constructivist than, say, surrealist.

My initial assistant for *Epiphanies,* the West Berlin filmmaker Martin Koerber, became my partner for the next film, which likewise capitalized upon the fact that in filmmaking, unlike live theater, picture and sound can be produced separately. Called *Ein Verlorenes Berlin* (1983), this unusual documentary regards the great Jewish cemetery there as the principal surviving relic of pre–World War II Berlin. On the visual track is the cemetery as it appears now, the inscriptions and designs on its gravestones speaking not only of individual lives but of historical changes within the culture. For the film's sound track I recorded sometime Berliners speaking in German about the cemetery and the world represented there. When we were asked to redo the film in English, we ruled against using subtitles, as the film already had too much to read, and against using overdubbing, which sounds affected. Since the informants never appear on-screen, it became convenient to interview another set of Berliners in English, and from their testimonies to produce a wholly fresh sound track that complimented the autonomous visual track and yet was different from the German. Given the success of that film, *A Berlin Lost* (1985), we were commissioned to continue the compositional principle in Swedish (1984), French (1986), Spanish (1987), and Hebrew (1988). In using only authentic testimony and in regarding a graveyard as representing a world, these films are eminently constructivist. Incidentally, when I first recognized the significance of the cemetery, I thought of doing a book mostly of

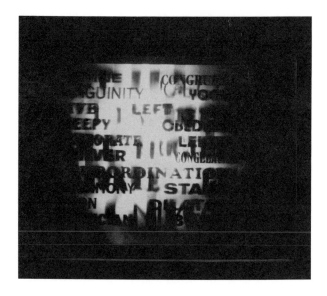

"One side of Antitheses, *in exhibition, with frame edges visible"*

photographs; but Koerber convinced me that the image really belonged in a film which, since it contains so much to read, should perhaps be regarded as a cinematic book.

I could not work in holography until I received an invitation in 1978 from Hart Perry's Cabin Creek Center for Work and Environmental Studies. This time I began not with a text already in manuscript but with an appreciation of a capability unique to multiplex holography—making a 360-degree image that would revolve suspended within a drum. For that space I wrote five syntactically circular sentences, one of which reads:

> . . . the hologram creates a world of incorporeal activity that exists only within . . .

So, as the drum turns, the viewer is reading five visually parallel, semantically complementary statements. Given my esthetic biases, it was inevitable that I would make a hologram whose visual material would be entirely language, and whose language would be about the uniqueness of holography.

Dependent as I am, I was not able to make another hologram until I won a 1985 competition for a residency at the Museum of Holography. This time, working with Fred Unterseher (as great a technician as I have ever known), I wanted to capitalize upon two capabilities unique to this technology—throwing an image in front of the plate, and using both sides of what appears to be a single piece of suspended glass.

Robert Haller

"Me and my first hologram, On Holography," *1979*

On one side I cast a field of words suggesting chilliness, having them fall into four levels—one directly on the glass itself, a second with fuzzier edges two inches in front of the glass, a third yet more vaporous perhaps six inches in front, and a fourth barely visible two feet in front (in a state-of-the-art feat). On the other side is a comparable field of words suggesting warmth. As the words were typeset in typographic pairs (with one on each side of the glass), it is possible, as you move from one side to the other, to "read" a considerable amount of verbal wit.

One way that *Antitheses,* as this work is called, differs from most holograms is that its image is more literary than photographic—it not only must be *read* over time but the perception of it requires a good deal of physical movement, both up and down to read words hidden behind other words and from one side of the glass to the other. This perhaps accounts for why, in the single long review of its first appearance in a group exhibition, the critic Arthur David Fornari said he found *Antitheses* more involving than the other works. Thanks, stranger. (It would be appropriate, I know, to testify at this point in the memoir that I've used my computer to do writing that could not be done "live," to so speak; but I haven't, though I should, damnit. Wait 'til next year, as we say.)

In all my media art, there is usually a base in language or in literary ideas (e.g., visual *fiction*); and since I've introduced into critical discourse the concept of the *polyartist,* or the person who excels at more than one nonadjacent art, the question is whether that term is applicable to me. I think not, because unlike such pure polyartists as László Moholy-Nagy and John Cage, I approach my work in various media not with encompassing esthetic ideas (in their cases, respectively, constructivism and diffusion) but with language, which is just material. To put it differently, I would say that I am a writer, a person of letters, whose work reflects the possibilities revealed not only by the example of polyartistry but by the new media available to us in the late twentieth century.

IX

In my experience, a professional becomes radical when he tries to pursue his profession with integrity and courage; this is what he knows and cares about, and he soon finds that many things must be changed.
—Paul Goodman, "The Black Flag of Anarchism" (1968)

Another theme of my work has been politics—not only in writing about them in literature, as in the M.A. thesis mentioned before, but in evolving a personal praxis for action. Once I read Paul Goodman, midway through college, I knew myself an anarchist; which is to say someone who believes in less government rather than more, in less social control rather than more, in egalitarian structures as preferable to hierarchies, in the diffusion of power rather than its concentration, in behavioral independence over conformity, etc. This anarchism informs not only the four anthologies of future-centered social thought noted before; it also informs an essay, first written in 1966 (and reprinted in *Twenties in the Sixties* [1979]), called "Technoanarchism," which tried to show how certain anarchist ideals could be realized through technological advance, rather than, as most anarchists thought, in opposition to it.

Since the early 1970s, I've been voting the Libertarian line, especially in local elections, simply because it is the only party on my ballot to represent anarchist values. What initially attracted me to that new indigenous party, which mixes "right" with "left" in a relevant way, was its stand on drug usage. Having lived in New York all my life, I suspect that the only true "solution" to the crime that threatens our lives is the abolition of laws prohibiting drugs. If marijuana, cocaine, and, yes, even heroin could be made freely available, addicts would have no need for exorbitant sums required to purchase drugs on a black market—no need at all. (Remembering that the black market is a free market, I also suspect that every time the police confiscate a large amount of drugs off the street the only result is cutting down the supply, driving up the price and thus causing an increase in crime. Conversely, it would be cheaper for New York City to give these drugs away than pay for the law enforcement! Why have the lessons taught by the failure of alcohol prohibition been so completely forgotten?) On the other hand, I also agree with my party over the virtues of owning property and of running a small business (as I've done for over two decades now, the business being me), the sense that America is a land of opportunity (as someone like me could happen only here), the beneficence of American democratic capitalism, the need to halt America's role as the Western world's policeman, and to eliminate as well all laws proscribing victimless crimes, and much, much else.

During the seventies the most immediate vehicle for my politics was the annual *Assembling* that I cofounded with Henry Korn in 1970. Initially a reaction to the artificial authoritarianism of most literary magazines, it invited artists and writers whom we knew to be doing "otherwise unpublishable work" to contribute a thousand copies of whatever they wanted to include. In return, we promised to bind

From Word Prints

their submissions into a thousand books, returning two to each contributor. My feeling was that if anyone felt strongly enough about their work to make a thousand copies of it, they deserved membership in *Assembling*'s community. What I had not fully realized at the beginning was the more profound libertarian implications. Since the contributions were printed in alphabetical order, there was no way of featuring one over the others. Indeed, what every contributor risked in this egalitarian structure was being compared with all the others. Secondly, as we never

refused anyone, there was no cachet in appearing in *Assembling*—no stamp of approval. A contributor earned only what other readers chose to recognize; and needless to say, given a diversity greater than that in any other magazine, most readers found certain contributions much stronger than others.

The libertarian politics implicit in *Assembling* were so attractive that we wanted to extend them to other vehicles. Thanks to a grant, we sponsored a *Critical Assembling*, where we invited artist-critics to submit no more than two pages of whatever camera-ready

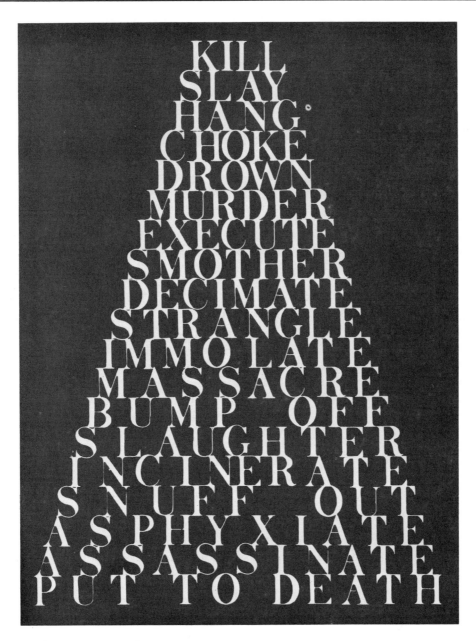

From Word Prints

criticism they wanted to see published, 8½ by 11 inches, which we then reproduced. (We knew that we didn't want any writer unable to produce camera-ready copy and so by that requirement let them disqualify themselves.) We sponsored a *Pilot Proposals* (1981), again requiring camera-ready copy, in response to the question: If you could apply for a grant of $500,000, what precisely would you propose to do? The answers were reproduced alphabetically in a perfect-bound book. We also applied to the National Endowment for the Arts to do "American Writing in 1980," which would invite a thousand American writers of note to represent themselves with one camera-ready page of their own choice, published or unpublished, that would be bound alphabetically into a hardbound book that would become a kind of current inventory in which every contributor had equal space (thus remaining true to the politics); but this was not funded. By 1981 Korn had retired to a career in arts administration and, as I was spending more and more time working in Europe, I gave the Assembling Press away to people who continue to run it.

There has also been a politics implicit in the way I handle *Epiphanies*. Manuscripts of these single-sentence stories have been customarily offered to editors with the advice that they can choose whichever ones they like and then set their selections in whatever order they wish. I am willing to abdicate the authority of ordering not because I'm lazy but because I think that editors, if they are true to their trade, might discover an arrangement beyond my own designs. Some of them have, my favorite being the *Portland Review*, while others have not; and someday I would like to exhibit the two dozen or so places in which the stories have appeared, along with correspondence, illustrating what happens when an opportunity comparable to that of *Assembling*—do your own thing within the guidelines—is extended to American literary editors.

Now when the libertarian revolution succeeds, all the publishing houses will be dismantled, their salesmen and publicists put out to pasture; and everyone in the competition for literary respect will have to start from scratch. Close readers of my work can find signs of my libertarian anarchism not only in proposals like that but all through, say, *The End of Intelligent Writing*, which after all advocates an opening of the field, and especially in my interpretations of John Cage.

There are probably other themes that run through my work, some of them no doubt less apparent to me, as I hope that this extended self-analysis will not close off critical discussion; but in this survey, in accounting for nearly everything, I have tried to suggest that my activities are more interconnected, or less diffuse, than they superficially seem.

X

There is something about the literary life which, although it offers the writer freedom and honor enjoyed by very few, at the same time brings him a cup of bitterness with every meal. There is too much betrayal, there is a general atmosphere of intellectual disgrace, writers have to make too many concessions in order to support themselves and their families, the successful acquire an air of being elevated into public figures and therefore having lost their own personalities. The unsuccessful are too spiteful and vindictive and cliquey, and even the greatest, when they are attacked, reveal themselves often as touchy and vain. . . . If success is corrupting, failure is narrowing. What a writer really needs is a success of which he purges himself.

—Stephen Spender, *World within World: The Autobiography of Stephen Spender* (1951)

Though I spend much of my time working alone, I feel surrounded by colleagues whom I can call upon for advice, whose opinion is important to me, whose presence in my work and mind persists. Among them, in no particular order, with apologies to those who might feel themselves omitted, are the composers Francis Schwartz, Skip Brunner, Joseph V. DiMeo, Charles Dodge; the media artists Reynold Weidenaar, Sorrel Hays, Frances Alenikoff, and Klaus Schöning; the visual artists Manfred Mohr and Esta-rose Wolfson, Rimma and Valery Gerloven, Paul Zelevansky, Michael Metz; the filmmakers Peter Longauer and Martin Koerber; and writers A. D. Coleman, Dick Higgins, Charles Doria, Mary Emma Harris, Samuel R. Delany, Donald Porter, Jerome Klinkowitz, Rochelle Ratner; the holographers Rebecca Deem, Fred Unterseher, and Scott Lloyd. (Note that few of these people are professors and that fewer are cultural bureaucrats or salesmen.) Would I not fear lamentable omissions, I would add here a longer list of those who helped crucially with contracts, commissions, and grants—none of them too remunerative, but all contributing to my continued functioning. As the work does not "sell" (and there is no position that includes the power to bestow remunerative rewards), you necessarily survive on the respect that many people have for you and what you have done. May my biographer(s) honor each of them with the credit he or she deserves. Thanks, friends.

I said at the beginning that this essay represented a reinterpretation of my own experience. Other, more chronological essays about my art appear in the catalog to *Wordsand* (1978), *The Old Poetries and the New, The Old Fictions and the New, Autobiographies,* and *Autobiographien New York Berlin,* (1986). Interviews from the mid-seventies appear in *Twenties in the Sixties* and *"The End" Appendix/"The End" Essentials.* Uncollected essays include the latest version of "Art Autobiography" in *Unsound,* vol. 3, no. 1 (1986) and "Expanded 'Writing' in Nontraditional Media," *Leonardo,* vol. 14, no. 4 (1986). Regarding creative radio alone, examine "Excerpts from Texts and Proposals for Radio," *Perspectives of New Music,* vol. 23, no. 1 (1984); "Audio Art in America: A Personal Memoir," *Dictionary of Literary Biography Yearbook* (1985); the booklet *Radio Writings* (1989); and the audiotape *Audio Writing* (1984). Regarding video, see "Literary Video, 1984," *Lotta Poetica,* Third Series, vol. 1, no. 1 (January 1987), "Literary Video [updated]," *The Kindred Spirit,* vol. 7, no. 2, (Summer, 1988); and the videotape *Video Writing* (1987). Regarding my first two holograms, see "Literary Holography," *Holoblad* (Antwerp, Belgium: December 1985). Regarding films, see "My Nonsync Films" scheduled for a future *Confrontation.* Regarding compilations, see "On Anthologies: A Memoir," *Centennial Review,* vol. 31, no. 4 and vol. 32, no. 1 (1987–88). *Assembling Assembling* (1978) contains a detailed history of that magazine. An elaborate professional resumé appears in the first edition (only) of *Who's Who in U.S. Writers, Editors, and Poets* (December 1987), begun under my name and then extended under the letter *X;* a cassette tape of me reading this resumé (no joke) has been published by Illuminati (a small press in Los Angeles). Some previously uncollected memoirs will probably appear in "Autobiographies at Fifty," which will hopefully be published in 1990.

Even though a lot of cultural produce has flowed out of my house, I've always felt underutilized; so much remains unfinished. My tendency has been to start a project, gathering enough materials to see an end, and then to try to find appropriate backing. Usually support comes through from somewhere, but sometimes too late to be useful and other times not at all; and one reason my house is so cluttered is the number of projects awaiting sufficient support to be completed. In criticism, I can find "An ABC of Contemporary Reading," a much-revised theoretical essay about the uniqueness of contemporary avant-garde literature; "The New Poetries and the Old," which collects fugitive poetry criticism of the past decade; "The New Literature," about avant-garde American writing in all genres since 1959; "The Emergence of a New Theater," which would publish contemporaneous notes about avant-garde performances of the past two decades; "Booknotes" on three decades of reading; "On Music(ian)s," which gathers critical essays about music and musicians; "The Art of Radio in North America," which would bring together the essays based upon those extended features written for German radio. I would like to do a new edition of *Master Minds* (1969). Meant to be my most popular book—the one that my father, say, can read with greatest ease—this should now include the profiles I've written since its first publication: Edwin Land, Noam Chomsky, Northrop Frye, Kenneth Burke, Gershom Scholem, among others. I should soon put together the chapters from the intellectual history of post–World War II America, most of which appeared in cultural magazines a decade ago, even if "The Maturity of American Thought" would necessarily be subtitled "an unfinished history."

On my shelves I also find manuscripts of "Epiphanies," thousands of single-sentence stories; a collection of "Minimal Fictions" of various kinds; a book version of "More or Less," a cycle of single-sentence erotic fictions that is scheduled to appear in *Iowa Review;* in addition to two more collections of constructivist stories and two novels in this visual mode. There are uncollected examples of the geometric poems, a book of two-word, three-word, and circular poems called "Duets, Trios, and Choruses," in addition to "Wordworks: New and Selected Poems," and a book or two of previously uncollected numerical works. I also find an "R. K. Reader" of writings in several areas, entitled "All Along the Edge," that was put together for a German publisher that did something else instead.

Support for work in sound is no better. "A Special Time: The 1960s," a one-hour pilot, never found a backer willing to complete the project, whether in thirteen-hour series or a six-hour single production. I have field recordings toward a "Kaddish," based upon the Hebrew prayer for the dead spoken in various accents; and other tapes toward "The Sound of German Poetry in America/American Poetry in Germany," which is based upon imperfections in speaking classic texts in another language. The book *Radio Writings* has pages of audio proposals that have been circulating for years.

In film I have been trying for nearly a decade to get sufficient support to complete *Epiphanies,* which should be four hours long. Financing it wholly on my own, I've gotten two hours done, but there are limits to my pockets, while grant applications have struck out. I have a proposal toward another film about Berlin, this about its nadir in April 1945, based upon the extraordinary footage taken from American airplanes of a bombed-out city. There are many hours of raw video synthesis that need sufficient support to be edited. In Hamburg, as I write, are holographic negatives that must be transferred to make works that can be exhibited. After I die, I hope that my executors will publish a book of my proposals, to reveal what could (and perhaps should) have been done.

Have I been a "success" or a "failure"? Obviously, with so much incomplete, with so few worldly rewards, the last epithet comes to mind. On the other hand, the work has been (and still is) original and noncommercial and underpublicized, which is to say all those things that inhibit advance in America. Since little of what I've done has been commercially promoted (and no one, aside from me, discusses it all together), people tend to know only bits and pieces of it. Indeed, which works they say they know often tells me where in life they are—those knowing *The End of Intelligent Writing* being literary people, those knowing *John Cage* being musicians, while visual artists know some of the book-art books, and little-magazine

An installation of Wordsand, *a traveling exhibition of
Richard Kostelanetz's art, at the
University of North Dakota*

editors know *Assembling,* etc.; in sum indicating that I have not one reputation but several. Living with professional inequities that others might find intolerable, I would like to think that as a person of letters born in the mid-twentieth century I have tested the possibilities of how far you can go in this country while remaining independent, and proceeding with integrity, and doing a lot of unconventional, challenging work that is respected less by many than a few, the sum of my activity reflecting certain profoundly American assumptions about freedom and self-realization; but final judgments about these questions are not for me to make.

For the forseeable future, I envision more of the same, which is to say a lifetime of days being a man of letters in the late twentieth century, handling words in special ways, playing with my toys, finishing off those projects on which I've been working for years and years and years. Amen.

Copyright © Richard Kostelanetz, 1989

BIBLIOGRAPHY

Poetry:

Visual Language. Brooklyn, N.Y.: Assembling Press, 1970.

I Articulations / Short Fictions. New York: Kulchur, 1974.

Portraits from Memory. Ann Arbor, Mich.: Ardis, 1975.

Numbers: Poems and Stories. Brooklyn, N.Y.: Assembling Press, 1976.

Rain Rains Rain. Brooklyn, N.Y.: Assembling Press, 1976.

Illuminations. Woodinville, Wash.: Laughing Bear, 1977; New York: Future Press, 1977.

Numbers Two. Columbus, Ohio: Luna Bisonte, 1977.

Richard Kostelanetz. New York: RK Editions, 1980.

Turfs/Arenas/Fields/Pitches. Battleground, Ind.: High/Coo Press, 1980.

Arenas/Fields/Pitches/Turfs. Kansas City: BkMk Press/University of Missouri at Kansas City, 1982.

Fiction:

In the Beginning. Somerville, Mass.: Abyss Publications, 1971.

Accounting. Sacramento: Poetry Newsletter, 1973.

Ad Infinitum: A Fiction. Friedrichsfehn, West Germany: International Artists' Cooperation, 1973.

Metamorphosis. Milwaukee: Membrane Press, 1974.

Obliterate. Sacramento: Ironwhorsebook, 1974.

Come Here. Des Moines: Cookie, 1975; Brooklyn, N.Y.: Assembling Press, 1975.

Constructs. Reno, Nev.: West Coast Poetry Review, 1975.

Extrapolate. Des Moines: Cookie, 1975; Brooklyn, N.Y.: Assembling Press, 1975.

Modulations. Brooklyn, N.Y.: Assembling Press, 1975.

Openings and Closings. New York: D'Arc, 1975.

One Night Stood. New York: Future Press, 1977.

Constructs Two. Milwaukee: Membrane Press, 1978.

Foreshortenings and Other Stories. Willits, Calif.: Tuumba Press, 1978.

Inexistences: Constructivist Fictions. New York: RK Editions, 1978.

Milestones in a Life. Lethbridge, Alta.: Lethbridge Herald, 1978; Pittsburgh: Carnegie-Mellon University Press, 1979.

Tabula Rasa: A Constructivist Novel. New York: RK Editions, 1978.

And So Forth. New York: Future Press, 1979.

Exhaustive Parallel Intervals. New York: Future Press, 1979.

More Short Fictions. Brooklyn, N.Y.: Assembling Press, 1980.

Epiphanies. West Berlin: Literarisches Colloquium Berlin, 1983; New York: RK Editions, 1983.

Nonfiction:

The Theatre of Mixed Means: An Introduction to Happenings, Kinetic Environments, and Other Mixed-Means Performances. New York: Dial Press, 1968; London: Pitman, 1970.

Master Minds: Portraits of Contemporary American Artists and Intellectuals. New York: Macmillan, 1969.

Recyclings: A Literary Autobiography. Vol. 1: Brooklyn, N.Y.: Assembling Press, 1974. Vol. 2: New York: Future Press, 1984; augmented edition published as *Recyclings, 1959–61.* New York: Future Press, 1984.

The End of Intelligent Writing: Literary Politics in America. New York: Sheed & Ward, 1974; also published as *Literary Politics in America: The End of Intelligent Writing.* Shawnee Mission, Kan.: Andrews & McMeel, 1977.

Prunings / Accruings. Geneva: Ecart Publications, 1977; New York: RK Editions, 1977.

Grants and the Future of Literature. New York: RK Editions, 1978.

Wordsand: 1967–1978: Art with Words, Numbers, and Lines, in Several Media: An Unillustrated Catalog with Related Documents. Burnaby, B.C.: Simon Fraser Gallery/Simon Fraser University, 1978; New York: RK Editions, 1978.

"The End" Appendix: "Intelligent Writing" Reconsidered / "The End" Essentials: "Intelligent Writing" Epitomized (extracts from *The End of Intelligent Writing*). Metuchen, N.J., and London: Scarecrow, 1979; Brooklyn, N.Y.: Assembling Press, 1979.

Twenties in the Sixties: Previously Uncollected Critical Essays. Westport, Conn., and London: Greenwood Press, 1979; Brooklyn, N.Y.: Assembling Press, 1979.

Metamorphosis in the Arts. Brooklyn, N.Y.: Assembling Press, 1980.

Arts History. New York: RK Editions, 1981.

Autobiographies. Santa Barbara, Calif.: Mudborn, 1981; New York: Future Press, 1981.

The Old Poetries and the New. Ann Arbor: University of Michigan Press, 1981.

Reincarnations. New York: Future Press, 1981.

American Imaginations. West Berlin: Merve Verlag, 1983; New York: RK Editions, 1983.

Autobiographien New York Berlin. West Berlin: Merve Verlag, 1986.

The Grants-Fix: Publicly Funded Literary Granting in America. New York: RK Editions, 1987.

The Old Fictions and the New. Jefferson, N.C., and London: McFarland & Co., 1987.

Prose Pieces / Aftertexts. Calexico, Calif.: Atticus Press, 1987.

Conversing with Cage. New York: Limelight Editions, 1988.

Radio Writings. New York: University Arts Resources, 1989.

Editor of:

On Contemporary Literature: An Anthology of Critical Essays on the Major Movements and Writers of Contemporary Literature. New York: Avon, 1964; revised edition. New York: Avon, 1969.

The New American Arts. New York: Horizon Press, 1965; London: Collier Macmillan, 1968.

Twelve from the Sixties. New York: Dell, 1967.

The Young American Writers: Fiction, Poetry, Drama, and Criticism. New York: Funk, 1967.

Beyond Left & Right: Radical Thought for Our Times. New York: Morrow, 1968.

Assembling: A Collection of Otherwise Unpublishable Manuscripts, with Henry Korn. New York: Gnilbmessa, 1970.

Imaged Words & Worded Images. New York: Outerbridge & Dienstfrey, 1970.

John Cage. New York: Praeger, 1970; London: Allen Lane/Penguin, 1971.

Moholy-Nagy. New York: Praeger, 1970; London: Allen Lane/Penguin, 1970.

Possibilities of Poetry: An Anthology of American Contemporaries. New York: Delta/Dell, 1970.

Future's Fictions. Princeton, N.J.: Panache, 1971.

Human Alternatives: Visions for Us Now. New York: Morrow, 1971.

Second Assembling: A Collection of Otherwise Unpublishable Manuscripts, with H. Korn and Mike Metz. Brooklyn, N.Y.: Assembling Press, 1971.

Social Speculations: Visions for Our Time. New York: Morrow, 1971.

In Youth. New York: Ballantine, 1972.

Seeing through Shuck. New York: Ballantine, 1972.

Third Assembling: A Collection of Otherwise Unpublishable Manuscripts, with H. Korn and M. Metz. Brooklyn, N.Y.: Assembling Press, 1972.

Breakthrough Fictioneers: An Anthology. West Glover, Vt.: Something Else Press, 1973.

The Edge of Adaptation: Man and the Emerging Society. Englewood Cliffs, N.J., and Hemel Hempstead, England: Spectrum/Prentice-Hall, 1973.

Fourth Assembling: A Collection of Otherwise Unpublishable Manuscripts, with H. Korn and M. Metz. Brooklyn, N.Y.: Assembling Press, 1973.

Fifth Assembling: A Collection of Otherwise Unpublishable Manuscripts, with H. Korn and M. Metz. Brooklyn, N.Y.: Assembling Press, 1974.

Essaying Essays: Alternative Forms of Exposition. New York: Out of London Press, 1975.

Language and Structure in North America: The First Large Definitive Survey of North American Language Art, November 4–30, 1975. Toronto: Kensington Arts Association, 1975.

Sixth Assembling: A Collection of Otherwise Unpublishable Manuscripts, with H. Korn and M. Metz. Brooklyn, N.Y.: Assembling Press, 1975.

Younger Critics in North America: Essays on Literature and the Arts. Fairwater, Wis.: Margins, 1976.

Seventh Assembling: A Collection of Otherwise Unpublished

Manuscripts, with H. Korn. Brooklyn, N.Y.: Assembling Press, 1977.

Assembling Assembling. Brooklyn, N.Y.: Assembling Press, 1978.

Eighth A–J Assembling. Brooklyn, N.Y.: Assembling Press, 1978.

Eighth K–Z Assembling. Brooklyn, N.Y.: Assembling Press, 1978.

Esthetics Contemporary. Buffalo, N.Y.: Prometheus Books, 1978; revised edition. Buffalo, N.Y.: Prometheus Books, 1988.

Complete Assembling, with others. Brooklyn, N.Y.: Assembling Press, 1979.

A Critical (Ninth) Assembling. Brooklyn, N.Y.: Assembling Press, 1979.

Visual Literature Criticism: A New Collection. Carbondale: Southern Illinois University Press, 1979; London: Feffer & Simons, 1979.

Scenarios. Brooklyn, N.Y.: Assembling Press, 1980.

Tenth Assembling. Brooklyn, N.Y.: Assembling Press, 1980.

Text-Sound Texts. New York: Quill/Morrow, 1980.

The Yale Gertrude Stein. New Haven, Conn., and London: Yale University Press, 1980.

American Writing Today. 2 vols. Washington, D.C.: Voice of America Forum Series, 1981.

Aural Literature Criticism. New York: Precisely/RK Editions, 1981.

Eleventh Assembling: Pilot Proposals. Brooklyn, N.Y.: Assembling Press, 1981.

The Avant-Garde Tradition in Literature. Buffalo, N.Y.: Prometheus Books, 1982.

The Literature of SoHo. New York: Shantih, 1983.

The Poetics of the New Poetries, with Benjamin Hrushovski. New York: RK Editions, 1983.

Precisely Complete, with Stephen Scobie. 6 vols. New York: RK Editions, 1985.

Films produced and directed:

Openings and Closings, with Bart Weiss, first screened at Anthology Film Archives in New York, 1976.

Constructivist Fictions, with Peter Longauer, first screened at Global Village in New York, 1979.

Ein Verlorenes Berlin, with Martin Koerber, first screened at the Berlin Film Festival, 1984.

Epiphanies, first screened at Sender Freies Berlin, 1983.

Ett Förlorat Berlin, with M. Koerber, first screened at the Goethehaus in Stockholm, 1986.

A Berlin Lost, with M. Koerber, first screened at the Edinburgh Film Festival, 1985.

Berlin Perdu, with M. Koerber, first screened at the

Maison Goethe in Paris, 1987.

Berlin Sche-Einena Jother, with M. Koerber, first screened at the Jewish Museum in New York, 1988.

El Berlin Perdido, with M. Koerber, first screened in 1988.

Plays:

Epiphanies, first produced in Grand Forks, N.D., 1980.

Sound recordings:

Experimental Prose. Brooklyn, N.Y.: Assembling Press, 1976.

Foreshortenings and Other Stories. New York: RK Editions, 1976.

Openings and Closings. New York: RK Editions, 1976.

Audio Art. New York: RK Editions, 1977.

Asdescent [and] *Anacatabasis,* engineered by Ceil Muller. New York: RK Editions, 1978.

Monotapes. New York: RK Editions, 1978.

Praying to the Lord. New York: RK Editions, 1981.

Seductions, engineered by Bill Brunson. New York: RK Editions, 1981.

The Gospels [and] *Die Evangelien.* Westdeutscher Rundfunk, 1982.

Conversations [and] *Dialogues.* New York: RK Editions, 1983.

The Eight Nights of Hanukah. Canadian Broadcasting Corporation, 1983.

Invocations, engineered by B. Brunson and Ragnar Grippe, composed in 1981, revised definitive composition in 1984. New York: Folkways Records, 1983.

Relationships, engineered by Frank Cunningham. New York: RK Editions, 1983.

Seductions [and] *Relationships.* New York: RK Editions, 1983.

Two German Hörspiele. New York: RK Editions, 1983.

Audio Writing. New York: RK Editions, 1984.

New York City. Westdeutscher Rundfunk, 1984.

Complete Audio Writing (includes nine audiocassettes). New York: RK Editions, 1985.

A Special Time. American Public Radio, 1985.

Le Bateau Ivre / The Drunken Boat, edited by Maya Reed. New York: RK Editions, 1986.

The Gospels Abridged, edited with Skip Brunner. New York: RK Editions, 1986.

Americas' Game, engineered by Thomas Hammar and Magnus Fredriksson. New York: RK Editions, 1988.

Resume. Los Angeles: Illuminati, 1988.

Turfs/Arenas/Fields/Pitches. New York: RK Editions, 1988.

More Complete Audio Writing (audio-only VHS cassettes). New York: RK Editions, 1989.

Epiphanies, edited by Maya Reed and Kathleen Monroe. Forthcoming.

Kaddish. Westdeutscher Rundfunk, forthcoming.

More or Less. Forthcoming.

Radio features:

Audio Art. Australian Broadcasting, 1978; also broadcast as *Hörliteratur.* Sender Freies Berlin, 1983.

Text-Sound in North America. Australian Broadcasting, 1981; also broadcast as *Amerikanische Klangtexte.* Sender Freies Berlin, 1983.

Glenn Gould as a Radio Artist. Westdeutscher Rundfunk, 1983; Ostreichischer Rundfunk, 1984.

Hörspiel USA: Radio Comedy. Westdeutscher Rundfunk, 1983; Sveriges Radio, 1984.

Audio Writing. Australian Broadcasting, 1984; Sender Freies Berlin, 1984.

Nach Weissensee, with M. Koerber and Michael Maassen. Rundfunk im Amerikanischen Sektor Berlins, 1984.

Radio Comedy Made in America Today. Westdeutscher Rundfunk, 1986.

Hörspielmaschiner Tony Schwartz. Westdeutscher Rundfunk, 1987.

New York City Radio. Sender Freies Berlin, 1988.

Orson Welles as a Radio Artist. Westdeutscher Rundfunk, 1988.

Orson Welles as an Acoustic Filmmaker. Westdeutscher Rundfunk, 1989.

Videotapes:

Poetry to See and Poetry to Hear, scripted and narrated by Richard Kostelanetz, directed by Merrill Brockway. WCBS-Camera Three/New York State Department of Education, 1974.

Openings and Closings. New York: RK Editions, 1975.

Three Prose Pieces. New York: RK Editions, 1975.

Declaration of Independence. Portales, N.M.: KENW, 1979.

Epiphanies. New York: RK Editions, 1980.

Partitions. New York: RK Editions, 1986.

Home Movies Reconsidered: My First Twenty-Seven Years. New York: RK Editions, 1987.

Seductions [and] *Relationships.* New York: RK Editions, 1987.

Video Writing, scripted and narrated by R. Kostelanetz, directed by Robert Boynton Wyer. New York: RK Editions, 1987.

Video Fictions. New York: RK Editions, 1988.

Video Poems. New York: RK Editions, 1988.

Portfolios of prints:

Numbers One. San Francisco: Cory Gallery, 1974.

Word Prints. New York: RK Editions, 1975.

Holograms:

On Holography, first exhibited at the Museum of Holography in New York, 1978. New York: RK Editions, 1979.

Antitheses, first exhibited at the Museum of Holography in New York, 1986. New York: RK Editions, 1985.

Abracadabra. New York: RK Editions, 1987.

Ambiguity. New York: RK Editions, 1987.

Hell/Elle, with Eduardo Kac. New York: RK Editions, 1987.

Ho/Log/Rap/Her. New York: RK Editions, 1987.

Ho/Log/Rap/Hy. New York: RK Editions, 1987.

Madam. New York: RK Editions, 1987.

Maxine Kumin

1925-

Maxine Kumin with her husband, Victor, 1976

I once read something Wilfrid Sheed wrote about "the self-importance problem" that is "endemic to all autobiographies." On guard against it, a good Jewish Calvinist, I have until now resisted telling my own story.

What changed my mind was an invitation in the fall of 1987 to read my poems at Radford University, formerly a small women's college, now a thriving part of the Virginia university system. My mother was born in Radford in 1895, number six in a family of twelve children. Her father, Abraham Simon, was a merchant—indeed, the main merchant—in town. His name, as she had once pridefully informed me, was carved in stone over the door. Just this year, a kind soul in Radford sent me photographic evidence dated 1911.

My uncle Saul Simon, the only one of the clan who neither married nor left his native heath, served with the cavalry in World War I. He was a spectacular joiner of organizations, an excellent horseman, a super patriot, and quite possibly the most caring man in that corner of rural Virginia. His reputation in Radford as unofficial ombudsman for veterans of his and all subsequent wars, as silent philanthropist to the needy, as friend to the lonely or the housebound, persists in the community. Because of him I was very warmly received in Radford. So were my poems, particularly the ones that dealt with what I like to call tribal material. It is out of that tribal feeling, and to tell the little tale of my origins, that I now undertake this account.

Everyone deserves a flamboyant ancestor and it seems to me, even upon superficial inquiry, that everyone has one. I hereby lay claim to Elias Rosenberg, my maternal great-grandfather. Possibly half of what I know about him is fiction, embroidered by his daughter, my grandmother, Pauline Rosenberg Simon, as told to my mother, Belle (Doll) Simon Winokur. Certainly I have added to the fiction in my own retellings.

201

On Being Asked to Write a
Poem for the Centenary
of the Civil War

Good friend, from my province what is there to
   say?
My great-grandfather left me here
rooted in grateful guilt,
who came, an escaped conscript
blasted out of Europe in 1848;
came, mourned by all his kin
who put on praying hats
and sat a week on footstools there;
plowed forty days by schooner
and sailed in at Baltimore
a Jew, and poor;
strapped needles up and notions
and walked packaback across
the dwindling Alleghenies,
his red beard and nutmeg freckles
dusting as he sang.

There are no abolitionists in my past to point to.
The truth is that this man,
my only link with that event,
prospered in Virginia, begat
eight young and sewed eight years
on shirts to get them bread.
When those warm states stood up to fight,
the war made him a factory
in a pasture lot where he sat,
my part-time pacifist,
stitching uniforms for the Confederates.
The gray cloth made him rich;
they say he lived to lose it all.
I have only a buckle and a candlestick
left over, like old rhetoric,
from his days
to show how little I belong.
This is the way I remember it was told,
but in a hundred years
all stories go wrong.

The facts in the poem are unvarnished, except
for the buckle, which I added in the interest of
thickening authenticity. The candlestick is actually a
brass menorah my ancestor is reputed to have carried
in his pack as he traveled, shank's mare, from
Baltimore to Virginia. Much mended, it does appear
to be of an honorable antiquity, "but in a hundred
years / all stories go wrong."

Great-Grandfather reappears in "For My Great-
Grandfather: A Message Long Overdue." The actual
letter that gave rise to the poem hangs framed on my

study wall. I marvel at the lavish language it contains,
and at the anguished effort this man is making in his
non-native tongue to heal a family rift. The rupture
was apparently occasioned by his remarriage to a
woman said to have been the same age as his oldest
daughter.

"It was a cold relentless hand of Death robbing
us of wife and Mother that broke up the home Circle
and scattered us abroad," he writes from Newport
News in September of 1895. The reconciliation
centered on my mother's birth the preceding June.
My grandmother has apparently sent a picture of
some sort, certainly not a snapshot—". . . it is
impossible for me to gaze on the picture before me as
portrayed by the Artist and not be impressed with the
realization that they are *My* People and to pray that
God in his Infinite Mercy may bless them even as he
blessed Jacob." In return, Elias Rosenberg, Rosenberg the Tailor, a Full Line of All the Latest in Suiting
and Pants, as his bill of sale attests, sends his new
wedding picture.

I remember his second wife, my step-great-
grandmother, who lived her last years in the Sinai
Home for the Aged in Baltimore and came by train
once or twice a year to Philadelphia to stay with us.
Most vividly I remember her recounting her own
fondest childhood recollection, that of sitting on her
father's shoulders to catch a glimpse of Abraham
Lincoln passing by on parade. The setting was
Baltimore. Is this historically possible?

My grandmother, I know, went by horsecar every
Friday afternoon in her girlhood to buy the Sabbath
bread. She was born on Fayette Street in Baltimore,
home of many of the Jewish families that came by ship
from Hamburg. But Great-Grandma's story thrilled
me. How American it was! How deep my roots! It
never occurred to me to fault my opportunistic
ancestor for sewing Confederate uniforms. A tailor-
forebear—no wonder, years later, I loved Ciardi's
description of his own father, who was "born with a
spade in his hand and traded it / for a needle's eye to
sit cross-legged on tables / till he could sit no
more. . . ." How easy it was to write, at the close of
the poem for my great-grandfather, "Welcome, ancestor, Rosenberg the tailor. / I choose to be a
lifetime in your debt."

It is hard to reconcile the grande dame my
mother became in my view of her with the simple
small-town childhood she had had. When she could
be induced to talk about it, her story was an idyll of
chickens and rabbits, a family pony, and her father's
matched pair of Saddlebreds. My earliest visions of
my mother place her in an evening dress, about to
depart in a cloud of French perfume for an important

Mother, Belle (Doll) Simon Winokur, about 1920

social event—a gala evening at the symphony under Stokowski's baton, the opening performance of a stage play featuring Katharine Cornell or the Lunts, or someone's anniversary party. She wore an evening cape of black velvet, its full length sprinkled with what looked like multicolored nonpareils. As she swept out the door in it, I was suffused with longing to look in on whatever it was the grown-ups did on these occasions. I knew they drank foamy concoctions called Brandy Alexanders or Grasshoppers, for I had tasted these and found them unbelievably bitter. But did they play Going to Jerusalem? Twenty Questions? Monopoly? What kept them out so late? I remember how hard it was to fall asleep until the parents, those Olympians, were once again safely under the same roof as we. And after the Lindbergh kidnapping, when my father had iron bars installed on my bedroom window overlooking the porch roof, sleep was even more elusive.

I never knew either of my grandfathers. My mother's father died long before I was born. My grandmother Simon came to live in Germantown, a suburb of Philadelphia, in an apartment not far from our house. I remember her pet Pekingese which she carried about everywhere, like a mandarin lady, lacking only the full sleeves and the pillow. I remember that she was quite hard of hearing, though I seem to have invented the ear trumpet (see "The Chain"). Nothing else about her comes back to me, except her somewhat imperial manner. I suspect children often misread this trait into adults who are not intimate with them. She was grandmother to seventeen progeny, and she had been notorious, according to my mother, for her inability to call her own dozen children by their correct names the first time, so it is not surprising that it fatigued her to sort us all out.

I was named for my father's father, Max Winokur, who died shortly before I was born. His naturalization papers, dated the fifteenth of September, 1888, stating he was formerly a citizen of Russia, hang on my study wall under the great-grandfather letter. In the text, he renounces forever "all allegiance and fidelity to any foreign prince, state or sovereignty whatsoever, and particularly to the CZAR OF RUSSIA. . . ." (caps in the text).

My mother, who was not given to hyperbolic praise, apparently adored him, for she eulogized him to me often as a scholar and a gentleman. His widow, my paternal grandmother, Emma Bachrach Winokur, spoke an accented English that rang wryly on my ear.

Max Winokur ran a shirt factory in Philadelphia at Eighth and Dauphin streets; Emma was his forelady. When the employees went out on strike, he shut down the enterprise and went into the pawnbroking business. My oldest brother, Fred, reports that he wore shirts custom-made by our grandmother for his growing frame until he was a teenager.

Grandma Winokur died in 1937 when I was twelve. Visits to her apartment in Atlantic City still rank among the high points of my life. As I remember it, my brother Peter, three years my senior, and I were packed off with our fräulein to spend the entire summer in the salubrious ocean air. From Grandma's living-room window a child could peer up and down the Boardwalk for miles. On a clear day the Steel Pier was visible jutting out into the Atlantic. A vista of sand and waves was reinforced by the ceaseless throbbing.

We children—often, our two cousins, Jimmy and Billy, were also in residence—lived only to go to the beach each day. Although lifeguards were stationed up and down the strand and huge ropes ran out into the surf to guard unwary bathers against being caught in the undertow, we were never allowed to roam free. The hardest task I had at age four, five, six was to

*Maxine on the Boardwalk in
Atlantic City, New Jersey, about 1929*

contain myself until the dilatory adults were ready, seldom before 11:00 A.M., to mount the daily safari to Paradise.

For the sand offered infinite, inventive pleasures. Drip castles, packed castles, tunnels, holes, turrets and moats, traps, multilayered dungeons added to the exquisite joys of lurking under the Boardwalk in the suspiciously pungent, slatted shade, overhearing snatches of conversation as the boulevardiers passed by overhead.

The adults lounged in elaborate folding chairs under umbrellas. They came encumbered with reticules from the depths of which emerged towels, handkerchiefs, rubber bathing slippers, bathing caps, ointments and creams, and sometimes, swathed in white linen towels, lunch. Each encampment loomed, a veritable oasis, on the sand. Bent double under his great, square pack, an ice-cream man could be seen approaching in the early afternoon, picking his way from group to group. Popsicles were three cents, an ice-cream sandwich, a nickel.

On weekends, when hundreds of fathers appeared, pale, stern, important figures conveyed by train from the city, we children were often forced into roller chairs with a parent or grandmother or stray great-aunt, to be pushed along the Boardwalk by a cheerful, sweating black man. Even then, this seemed at least odd to me, in some way degrading to both of us. I detested having to sit still so long and I loathed even more the white dress, white socks, and freshly whitened shoes I had to wear in observance of these occasions.

A few times, I remember being taken further down the Boardwalk to the man with the ponies, and I suspect this is where it all began. Young as I was, I knew these were sad, tattered creatures who stood about all winter in a dark stable, barely tended to, and that they were hauled here by open truck to spend the warm months wearily plodding round and round with screeching, stupid children on their backs. My fantasy then was to kidnap them all and carry them off to the Wild West to run free on the prairie. Somehow the vision of horses running free had already taken root in me. Almost half a century later, those dreams came true. Much as I delight daily in turning out our mares and youngsters on spacious, well-tended pasture, I treasure even more the abuse cases we have rehabilitated.

My grandmother loved the perpetual auctions that took place each afternoon along the Boardwalk. I remember several dreary rainy sessions spent in storefronts watching the grown-ups bid on Oriental rugs, objets d'art, and various painted renditions of the ceaseless surf. Left to ourselves, we children played overheated rounds of a new game called Monopoly, in which all the place names were geographically correct Atlantic City sites. Tiring of the cheating and wrangling that invariably overtook the board game, in which The Banker became as ruthless as the "CZAR OF RUSSIA," we would turn to working on our shell collection.

Scallops, clams, and angel wings were painstakingly sized so that they nested by species in my father's cast-off wooden cigar boxes. The entire collection was housed in the hall closet, neatly labelled by my second oldest brother, Herbert, who was quite good at lettering. The full cigar boxes were kept in a humidor, an imposing piece of furniture done in dark walnut. Every evening after supper my father would select a cigar to take into the living room to his reading chair, where he drowsed over the *Philadelphia Evening Bulletin.* We children waited, surreptitiously counting the number of cigars left in the box, for the day when it was at last empty and we could take possession. The names on the lids, Ramon

Allones, or Havana Roma, were another romance, to be rolled over the tongue, conjuring up foreign places. Best of all, a little metal clasp shaped like a comma held the lid tight. One could keep any secret in such a box.

My father was a funny mixture of sybarite and Calvinist. He left school at the age of thirteen in order to help in his father's pawnbroking establishment, Federal Loan, while his older brother, Joseph, to whom he remained devoted the rest of their lives, became the family scholar. Joseph went on to college and law school at the University of Pennsylvania, but he was never financially successful. Behind the scenes, my father continually made up the difference, which surely contributed to the tension between the wives.

"Early to bed and early to rise," my father used to say with a wink, "and you never see any of the regular guys." Nevertheless, he was up at dawn every day except Sunday. He worked long hours without a lunch break, pausing only for a milk shake at noon, never returning home before 6:30 Monday through Friday. On Saturdays the store stayed open until 10:00. Sometimes my mother and I would drive to South Philadelphia to meet my father as the store was closing and the heavy metal guard gates were being locked. We then drove to a section of the city known as Strawberry Mansion, where, in my father's favorite delicatessen, we enjoyed a late supper of whitefish, exotic sturgeon, Swiss cheese, half-sour pickles, and cream soda. The wooden booths were worn and chipped. There was sawdust on the floor. Outside, on warm spring evenings, a bearded old man sat on an upturned keg and played his violin quite mournfully. I was told he played to usher out the Sabbath. How blessed I felt in this safe harbor!

But my mother was racked with ambivalent feelings. First of all, she, of proud German-Jewish origins, had married a latecomer, a descendant of Russian Jews, and this virtually constituted a mixed marriage. Her mother-in-law still kept a kosher house except when the grandchildren came to visit and milk magically appeared on the table next to the boiled flanken. This old lady still spoke Yiddish, a forbidden tongue in our upwardly mobile household, although my father insouciantly peppered his speech with Yiddishisms. My mother was clearly uncomfortable with my father's profession because of its Shylockian stereotype and she hid it in conversations with strangers, referring to him as a "broker" or "merchant."

According to my oldest brother, who remembers him vividly, our grandfather Simon was a deeply religious Orthodox Jew who laid tefillin every morning of his life. Doubtless this accounts for the twelve children. Theirs was the only Jewish family in Radford; every fall they journeyed forty miles to Roanoke to attend synagogue for the High Holidays. But my grandfather countenanced my mother's playing the organ for all Methodist church events on grounds that some form of worship was better than no worship.

My father was the least self-conscious man I have ever known. Everything about him conveyed the sense that he was very much at home with himself and with his appetites. He believed in salvation through hard work, and while he drove himself and others mercilessly, salvation consisted not only of living well but also of extending a benevolent hand to selected unfortunates. He was a generous giver to public charity and a quiet philanthropist on the side. Years after his death I continued to be confronted by strangers in Philadelphia who, upon hearing that I was Pete's daughter, had still another tale to tell of a crushing mortgage being lifted, a medical bill paid, a college tuition contributed to, and so on.

My father had great scorn for parsimony. He delighted in pointing out to me a bank president or corporate executive who had pledged only a hundred dollars to the Community Chest. When I looked at these florid, important men, it was like seeing a secret stain. For a long time I thought "a blot on the escutcheon" was a kind of birthmark the stingy wore under their white shirts.

My father was generous with himself as well. He ate well, he loved to host big parties at which the best liquor flowed in unlimited quantities; he and my mother stayed, on their infrequent trips, in the best hostelries. He was generous with his own mother, providing her with a live-in companion, a spacious apartment, and an allowance that covered her little forays to the afternoon auctions. When the Depression struck and my mother's two youngest brothers moved in with us, my father, I suspect, hustled jobs for them in addition to providing room and board. The chalk marks on the sidewalk that led to the back door of our house on Carpenter Lane indicated that ours was a good handout. One of my earliest memories is of two or three men down on their luck sitting on the steps of the back porch, eating enormous sandwiches.

My parents met at a Saturday-night party on Tulpehocken Street in Philadelphia in 1914. According to her account, my mother, then a student at the Combs Conservatory of Music in Philadelphia, was playing the piano when my father burst in jovially and had to be shushed so that the concert could continue.

The Winokur children in Germantown, Pennsylvania, about 1930:
(from left) Peter, Herbert, Maxine, and Frederick

"Who is this haughty dame?" my father is said to have inquired, while my mother glared daggers in his direction. It didn't seem a propitious beginning, but they were married soon thereafter and remained a very loving couple until my father's death in 1962.

Four of us children arrived, at quite explicit three-year intervals, beginning with Frederick William in 1916, followed by Herbert Simon, succeeded by Edward Elias, who so resembled my father that he was dubbed Little Peter (despite a Jewish injunction against naming a child for a living person, his name was legally changed to Peter Winokur, Jr., when he was six). I was the last of the line, alternately cosseted and resented by my older brothers, and the only child who was actually born in the house on Carpenter Lane that featured so large in my early life.

Built in the last decade of the nineteenth century for a wealthy invalid—this accounted for the circuitous, sloping brick walk that would allow a wheelchair to be pushed from the street curb to the back door—152 Carpenter Lane was essentially a Georgian Colonial set atop an imposing brick terrace above two sets of stairs. A round portico supported by Ionic pillars sheltered the front entrance. A huge

side porch looked into the second-story windows of the house on the down slope. On the other, uphill side a privet hedge with numerous useful gaps in it divided our land from the Convent of the Sisters of Saint Joseph.

The house had six chimneys, all elaborately manteled and tiled, an ornate divided staircase with curving balustrades we were forbidden to slide down but frequently did, a dark, panelled back hall and back staircase where I was certain bears lurked, a cavernous stone cellar with coal bins and terrifying storage compartments full of the skeletons of bad children who had preceded me. On the third floor my oldest brother and, for a time, my two youngest uncles lived, next to a huge attic room equipped with a Ping-Pong table. There were three bedrooms and three baths on the second floor. Everything about the house, it seems to me now, was on the grand scale. The ceilings were high, all the doors were imposingly heavy and the hardware was equal to the task. The dining room held a massive dark-walnut table and at least eight chairs. On family occasions this configuration could be extended, stretching out into the front hall to accommodate up to thirty diners.

The kitchen, apparently rebuilt in the twenties,

was restaurant-size. The stove stood on its own raised brick hearth and contained warming ovens, baking ovens, a griddle, and six gas burners. The range and depth of the glassed-in cupboards matched the prodigious stove, as did the refrigerator, a converted four-door icebox powered by a compressor in the cellar. Wedged between the kitchen and the dining room, a breakfast room served as the true heart of the house. It was sunny, cozy, and abutted the walk-in pantry from which each of us children regularly filched supplies. My brother Peter was an inveterate tippler of vinegar, which seemed a simple gluttony to me then. One of my two oldest brothers was a raisin devourer, the other, nuts. I stole sugar lumps, though not for myself—I fed them to every horse that passed up or down the steep lane, delivering bakery goods, milk, or hauling the garbage wagons.

Just outside the back door grew what I believed was the only ginkgo tree in Germantown. Every fall it dropped squashy, odoriferous fruits that had to be raked up and disposed of. I admired this tree greatly for its antiquity and Oriental origin. On the other side of the house a spreading copper beech provided a leafy bower of privacy for my cousin Barbara, who lived just two backyards away, and me. It was a favorite climbing tree until one of my boy cousins, who also lived nearby, fell out of it and broke his arm. Climbing the tree joined the seemingly long list of things forbidden us.

In the lower garden my mother maintained stiff beds of peonies, delphinia, roses, and other perennials, and a wide cutting bed of zinnias, cosmos, asters, and petunias. A gardener named Clinton came each week to look after the lawn and garden beds, but my mother was there frequently, decreeing which flowers to cut, and carrying in great basketfuls of blooms for her "arrangements." She had some rigid opinions about what constituted a proper bouquet and would not tolerate mixed species. Every night at bedtime the great glass vases of flowers were removed from the living, dining, and music rooms and were stored in the front vestibule to preserve their freshness.

Behind the formal garden there was enough space left for badminton, croquet, and, all fall and winter, football. Because there were never enough boys to make up two teams, I was frequently pressed into service as center for both squads. After I had spun the ball between my legs to the waiting receiver, I had to run to the sidelines until the play was completed. It was just barely better than not being allowed to take part at all.

At the very back of the yard, brambles, lilacs, and unnamed greenery made a good cover for violets, Johnny-jump-ups, and lilies of the valley, which I picked carefully in separate bunches for my mother. In the deepest corner of this tangled growth, my brothers had built a tree house which Barbara and I burgled regularly. We stole peanut butter and comic books and forbidden jackknives and buried our treasure under the lilacs, where some shards may still remain.

Germantown then was a smug and sleepy sort of suburb, upper-middle-class Protestant in tone, although several Jewish families, even some not related to us, had invaded the precinct. Saturdays and any day when school was out, I could take a sandwich and an apple and go hiking in Carpenter's Woods, which abutted Fairmount Park. There were miles of trails in the woods and parkland, a good, deep creek bed, little frog ponds, shallow caves in the rock outcroppings, providing a rich playground for resourceful kids on their own.

Grown-ups went horseback riding in the park from several livery stables that ringed it, and the Park Guards, an elite group in splendid uniforms, patrolled the area on horseback. Every man was responsible for his own horse and they were beautifully turned out. Sometimes, although it was against regulations, a favorite guard would let a child sit on his horse as it stood dozing in the sun. These halcyon moments fed my lifelong obsession.

Out-of-doors, away from the constraints of a Germanic household, my childhood was untrammeled. Dogs followed me home (with a little persuading) but I was never allowed to keep a stray. A succession of dogs scarred my home life. One, a German shepherd, was poisoned. Another, a wire-haired fox terrier, developed an incurable mange and had to be destroyed. A favorite Irish setter wandered off and was never found.

Cats were forbidden. My mother didn't trust them, for they jumped into perambulators and sucked the infants' breath. My grandmother had a canary, which sang ceaselessly, nourished on what were very likely marijuana seeds. And my great-aunt Manya, my grandmother Winokur's step-sister, had a pet monkey, which seemed to me the ne plus ultra of house pets. I vowed I would fill up my adult life with animals; this has proved extremely easy to do.

Inside, however, life was quite regimented. In addition to the live-in cook and butler and the once-a-week laundress, my mother hired a "governess" to look after my brother Peter and me, although she was not called by that title. A young German girl who had immigrated to the States in 1920, she came to live with us a few years before I was born. My mother addressed her as Agnes, other adults, Fräulein, but we four children called her Froy. She shared my room, sleeping in the other twin bed until I was seven years old, when she left to marry a German restaurateur, and she was a constant, favored visitor in our house as long as I can remember. We stayed in touch faithfully. After I was married, I continued to visit her. Victor and I took the children—the youngest was still in arms—to see her in Haddon Heights, New Jersey. I was quite taken aback by her permissiveness, for I had remembered her as kind, but strict.

Nothing in my childhood surpassed my love for Froy. She was truly my mother. Her departure left a deep wound which was almost unbearable for many years; somehow I had become convinced that she had gone away because of a flaw in my character. My mother, who had little patience with children and a busy social life of her own, reinforced this notion by exclaiming at least once a day that I had "changed" since Froy departed.

I lost my ability to speak German almost instantly, although it had been my mother tongue. I lost completely the considerable vocabulary I had had, and over a lifetime I have never regained it. Froy's brother had been a U-boat captain in the First World War. Her parents still lived in Bremen. With the news coming from The Fatherland in the early thirties, it was hard not to think dark thoughts of her rejection. And what about her husband? Someone with the same last name was a member of the German-American Bund. These and other false rumors swirled around my head. Years later, I learned how painful this period had been for Froy and her family.

At the age of five, over my father's mild objections, my mother sent me next door to the nuns to attend their kindergarten. It was immensely convenient; I ducked through a gap in the privet and managed to arrive at my place in line (we were sized by height before marching into our classroom) before the bell had stilled. Moreover, I felt very much at home in the convent, as I was a frequent guest on Sundays after Mass, when the sisters enjoyed a lovely brunch. The mother superior of the order, Mother Rosarine, spoiled me outrageously—I heard this repeated at home, almost daily—and I usually sat on her lap at the table. My schooling continued at the convent through second grade, at which time the crucifixion of Jesus became as much an issue for me as animal cruelty. No matter that I was told, on one side of the hedge, that the Romans had done that to Him. On the other side, quite matter-of-factly and without casting blame on my innocent state, it was the Jews who had fastened Him to the Cross. A larger-than-life-size replica of the crucifixion hung in the

main corridor of the schoolroom; daily there was no escaping this piteous sight.

The Jesuits are reputed to say, "Give us a child until he is eight and he will be ours always." I was deeply touched by my early experience at convent school, but the final effect of my bifurcated religious education was quite simply to feed my skepticism. Jesus became for me a symbol of goodness and humility that I never quite relinquished, a very human figure in an otherwise quite mysterious faith full of saints available for special intercessions.

The appeal of the nuns was their seemingly neutral gender; they, most surely, were not troubled by the itch of sexual feelings. Indeed, in their black habits and starched white fronts, their stiff wimples beneath which not even one hair showed, they appeared to me to be seamless, all of one skin, like a fish. The nuns were good neighbors. In 1934, when my brother Herbert lay gravely ill with pneumonia, they came in pairs to sit day and night at his bedside. The doctor put him on a new, still experimental medication called sulfanilamide and he recovered, claimed equally by science and religion.

It was hard not quite to belong in that calm, faith-centered world next door. Voices were not raised there, nor doors slammed. There were no late parties which grew boisterous as the alcohol circulated. No father furious over department-store bills, no constantly bickering brothers tormenting each other to the point where my exasperated father made them put on boxing gloves and pummel each other mercilessly. Then, hating each other more than ever, they were forced to shake hands and declare an end to combat.

To be a Jewish child in Germantown in the thirties was sometimes painful. More than once I was pursued with cries of "Christ-killer." Even harder to sort out was the omnipresent but invisible line that divided Jews from non-Jew-hating Christians. Both of my parents spoke with pride of their "good Christian friends." But it was clear that this level of friendship differed from friendships within the brotherhood. There were things they didn't say in front of "the Gentiles." There were in-group jokes, sprinkled with Yiddishisms, which could only be told in the right company, and there were tacit admissions of abhorrent traits.

My mother, for example, was driven wild by any of us gesticulating in the course of a conversation. "Don't talk with your hands!" she hissed. "You look like an immigrant." Until I was in my teens I believed that only Jews used gestures or stood close enough to breathe on each other as they conversed.

All of us attended Sunday school at Temple

Rodeph Shalom during the reign of Rabbi Louis Wolsey. Here, too, we received a double message. We were exhorted to be proud of our Jewish heritage but enjoined savagely from Zionism. We were not in favor of planting trees in (then) Palestine. As late as 1940, we were required to write an essay titled "America, Not Palestine, My National Homeland."

Reform Jews in that congregation did not learn Hebrew beyond the alphabet and a few simple prayers. These were taught by rote; there was no effort to treat Hebrew as another language with its own grammar. Pronunciation was still old-style Ashkenazi. There were no chuppahs, no yarmulkes, certainly no stamping on glasses at weddings, which we were told was a leftover paganism. The services at Rodeph Shalom were almost indistinguishable from Unitarian services—we even sang some of the same hymns—but in our house we did light candles every Friday night and say the Sabbath blessing. We celebrated Hanukkah, we ate homemade Hamentashen at Purim, and we held enormous Seders—one night only, of course—attended by all of the Simon family within reach, as well as by my father's brother, with his wife and two sons, two sets of courtesy aunts and uncles, and an occasional stray, someone stranded in Philadelphia over the holiday. It was a family practice always to include one or two "good Christian friends" to celebrate Passover with us. Somehow I felt we were actors performing a famous play for their edification.

My mother spent days getting ready for this dinner party of all dinner parties. The best damask linen, the best Bohemian cut-glass goblets, the family silver, huge and heavy. My father bought the wine—Chablis and cabernets, for he could not abide the sweet taste of Concord grape wine—and there was grape juice for the children who were young enough to prefer it. He was in his glory at the head of the table, a benevolent patriarch given to jokes and raillery throughout the service.

The gefilte fish was made according to my maternal grandmother's recipe, German style, which involved stuffing the ground fish back into its skin before poaching it, a terrible penance for the cook. The matzoh balls, klaes, they were called, were also prepared à l'allemande, and they were magically light. Dessert was always a kistorte, an enormous confection made of meringue in the shape of a castle, the fallen center larded with fresh strawberries suspended in whipped cream. And during Passover week, my mother, who cooked nothing else, made fahnkuchen, skillet-size pancakes of matzoh meal, sugar, and egg whites, which puffed up during the baking and melted on the tongue.

Not that we were deprived of Christmas. For many years we had a tree, somewhat hidden from view, on the upstairs landing, complete with winking lights, tinsel, and ornaments. We children got presents, as did the cook and her husband. But our Christmas was a private, almost shamefaced celebration informed by the sneaking sense that we had no right to it. We lived in a Christian world; we were in it, if not of it. Unfortunately, we were not exactly "of" the world in which we did belong.

These dichotomies pursued me into adolescence, and I think my experience was not atypical for American Jews of my generation. Parents made great efforts to assimilate into the suburban culture, but only up to a point. They went to their own country clubs, they organized their own dancing classes for their offspring (and these, in my circle, were further stratified into most desirable, less, and least, a hierarchy based on elusive criteria of social standing). They did not approve of mixed dating, which led to mixed marriages, but they desperately wanted their sons and daughters to go to Ivy League or Seven Sister colleges, where they were most easily enticed away from their parochial views.

Hardest of all, there were gradations of Jews. We were expected to observe these as rigorously as we observed certain behavior when in the company of Christians. These injunctions were laid down by my mother, who was extremely conscious of origins and income. In the case of, for example, the Mendeses, who were descended from Sephardic Jews (this term in its earlier version referred to Spanish Jews who came to the New World before the American Revolution) and were, in my mother's euphemism, "not well-off," origins cancelled out income. The Mendes family was not only acceptable, but sought-after company. In the case of (here I will invent a name) the Glitskis, who owned a department-store chain and lived garishly in a mansion, income overrode origins and they too were written into the canon. But the vast land between these two extremes was pocked with pitfalls: nouveaux riches who were too nouveaux for polite society, Sunday-school classmates whose Russian and Polish surnames indicated their families were recent arrivals, and so on. Philadelphia Jewish society, it seems to me at this safe remove, was as intricately structured and as frail as the towers my brother Peter built with his Erector Set.

Third grade commenced for me at the public school a mile away. Peter was assigned to walk with me for the purpose of seeing me safely across half-a-dozen intersections. Since I was not allowed to accompany him the length of the blocks for fear of subjecting him to the ridicule of his peers, we were a strange pair leapfrogging along, he waiting for me to catch up at the cross streets, I admonished to stay back while he strode ahead unencumbered by a little sister.

In private, Peter and I were best friends and confidantes. Within a fairly boisterous and aggressive family we were each other's bulwark, a sympathetic contract that continued through our mutually dreadful adolescences and into early adulthood.

While many of the children in our neighborhood were sent off to Germantown Academy, Friends Central, or Penn Charter, all four of us attended public schools. My father did not approve of private-school education; it did not prepare you to meet the real world. In many ways he was fiercely plebeian, proud of his humble beginnings, his decision to leave school early (he finished high school by attending night classes) while his older brother stayed on. I suspect it was not need but restlessness that impelled my father to drop out of school. An autodidact, he was something of a mathematical wizard. He used to astonish us children by doing enormous sums in his head. He could multiply and divide, carry decimals into six places, split percentages into splinters without benefit of pencil and paper. Alas, I did not inherit any of his mathematical genes.

Our grammar school was notable for its principal, a little, white-haired spinster who conducted bird walks in spring and fall and managed, she boasted, by judicious use of transfers, to keep black children out of her classrooms. I was a model of scholarship and deportment. In fifth and sixth grades, however, I met my nemesis in the form of the sewing teacher. I could not master coordination of the treadle sewing machine; my thread invariably broke, requiring me to start over rethreading. I can still see that menacing chart on the wall with incomprehensible instructions of steps one through eight. I have managed to live my life relatively free of needle and thread. The men in my family sew on their own buttons.

Germantown had a good public library, the Lovett Memorial, within bicycling distance for me. A child could borrow six books at a time, which fitted nicely into the basket strapped to my handlebars. The library smelled wonderful. The aroma was a mixture of varnish and white paste, newsprint and ageless dust. The librarian was kind and let me take out Paul de Kruif's *Microbe Hunters,* even though it was not in my age category.

I don't remember learning how to read, but I know I could do so before I went next door to kindergarten, because this fact was much remarked by the nuns. After A. A. Milne and Kenneth Grahame

and the Bobbsey Twins, I finished all my brothers' *Tom Swift*s. British books were better than American ones, I decided, basing this on my two most favorite texts, *The Bastable Children,* by E. Nesbit, and a long-lost horse book called *Silver Snaffles,* by Primrose Cumming. I didn't care for the Walter Farley books; they were too violent. *Black Beauty* was too sad. But I was writing a horse book of my own, and managed three chapters in a lined copybook before I ran out of steam.

Writing poetry was much more to my taste. I was a facile rhymer, and effusive nature poems came forth almost unbidden. My brother Herbert illustrated a sheaf of these when I was eight, which gained me even more notoriety. Within the family I was alternately respected and mocked as a budding intellectual.

My aunt Bea—my father's sister-in-law and my mother's archrival—began to take an interest in me as I emerged into adolescence. She gave me her own set of Louisa May Alcott novels. Until then, I had read only *Little Men, Little Women,* and *Jo's Boys.* Little by little she fed my romantic nature with Edna St. Vincent Millay and Elinor Wylie, Willa Cather and Ellen Glasgow. The mother of two sons, she was lonely for a daughter. My mother, who was, I thought, fiercely critical of me for not conforming to her standards of femininity or social grace, was nevertheless reluctant to share me.

But I was not the prime battleground between these two strong-minded women. Aunt Bea fancied herself a linguist. She had spent several years in Paris during a period when her mother had made a disastrous second marriage, and she was of course fluent in German, for her mother had been born in Berlin. Moreover, Aunt Bea had a college degree and many of her friends were educated women. My mother had left the conservatory at nineteen in order to marry my father. She had grown up in a small town in Virginia among chickens and cows, not cathedrals and museums. Although she had won an elocution prize for reciting "The Curfew Shall Not Ring Tonight," although she had played the organ for the Methodist Church every Sunday, she had not sojourned in Paris nor set foot in the Louvre. And while she maintained a lavish table and raised abundant, bright flowers, her bookcases did not wrap around the living room, crammed with alphabetized authors, many of whom had signed their volumes. This undeclared vendetta sustained these women well into their old age.

I remained in the vortex of the little tempest they generated. Each time I returned to Germantown from college, I re-entered Aunt Bea's cloister like a celebri-

As a member of the Radcliffe crew, Cambridge, Massachusetts, 1942.
The author is the rower closest to the coxswain.

ty. She mixed and served, in place of tea, a Dubonnet-and-gin concoction that was sweet enough to drink and powerful enough to induce giddiness. My mother so fulminated against these visits that, twenty-five years later, when each of them was widowed and lived a few blocks apart in central Philadelphia, I had to resort to considerable subterfuge to continue to see my aunt. It was a terribly sad ending; little by little she grew senile and toward the end recognized no one. I think even my mother, who longed for revenge against her lifelong adversary, was shocked by this ignominy.

Looking back over my long tenure in the German-town public schools (elementary school then included seventh and eighth grades), it seems to me that I fared quite well. Sewing class was the major trauma of those years. Cooking classes in the final two years were delightful excursions into white sauce and bread pudding, skills I have never since used.

Once a week, after school, I ran uphill to Ross-Del Riding Academy, where I was allotted my one, one-dollar-an-hour lesson. I earned others by staying late to feed and muck out, groom horses and clean the muddy, worn tack, but I lied about these activi-

ties. My mother, who had doubtless seen a good deal of menial stable duty in her girlhood, did not approve. Sometimes I stayed overnight with my best friend, Nancy Farquhar, who lived in a tidy row house on Germantown Avenue across from the fire station. Our favorite activity was spying on the lives of the firemen, whose second-floor dining and rec rooms were clearly visible from an upstairs window. Less often, Nancy stayed at my house. In retrospect it seems odd to me that my mother did not disapprove of this friendship, for it met none of her social criteria. Often, though, she surprised me with little acts of largesse and affection which tapped into the immense reservoir of love I felt I had always to hold back.

The summer I turned eleven I was sent off to Camp Watitoh in Becket, Massachusetts, directed by the de Sola Mendes family of New York City. Unlike my brothers, who had had for the most part to settle for two weeks at a time at Boy Scout or Y camps, I enjoyed a full eight-week season in the Berkshires. This setting was to become the safe house of my stormy adolescence. (Indeed, my husband likes to say that he married me to rescue me from summer camp.) Long before Earth Science and Environmental Studies became worthy categories, camps like Watitoh were focusing on what was known as Nature. Here too I became a proficient swimmer, earning, as the years advanced, all the American Red Cross certificates, including that of Water Safety Instructor. And here, for the first time since my relationship with Nancy Farquhar, I formed some abiding friendships with bunkmates.

Camp Watitoh was a coeducational camp for Jewish boys and girls. Friday-night services were held in an outdoor amphitheater; candlelight combined with the strong aroma of citronella to create the appropriate ambiance. Campers were encouraged to write their own services. At Watitoh I fell out of the bosom of the Almighty into the strong arms of Pantheism. I wrote reams of purple prose in praise of the Oversoul, although I did not know that far more systematic thinkers had preceded me.

The Mendes family were Sephardic Jews (old-style Sephardic) and ardent Zionists. I felt as though I were in the enemy camp, where coins were collected to plant the very trees in Palestine that our Philadelphia rabbi had vigorously denounced. As my skepticism grew, Jesus looked more and more temperate to me by contrast.

It wasn't just the Zionist issue. I didn't know much about the Spanish Civil War, but I knew we sided with the Loyalists. The rise of Nazism in the thirties colored all our lives. My father had always been a news hound. Now he followed the Fascist acquisitions of the Sudetenland and Czechoslovakia with worried interest. The America Firsters outraged him. Neville Chamberlain was a traitor. As the dreadful truths began creeping out of Nazi Germany, my father received a spate of letters from relatives, or relatives of relatives, in Poland, begging for his assistance. One of my most vivid memories from this period is of coming upon my powerful parent, uncharacteristically seated at the dining-room table long after the dishes had been cleared away, with crumpled pages of a letter spread before him. His head was in his hands and when he looked up at me I saw that he was in tears. It was a wordless moment, but I understood. Finally he spoke.

"They will all die," he said. "This is the pogrom to end all pogroms."

For long before it was public information, news of the concentration camps had sifted into the Jewish community. No one else seemed to care. Even my father's beloved Roosevelt failed him. I began having horrendous nightmares of being pursued and captured by the Nazis, just as after the Lindbergh kidnapping I had had nightmares of pursuit and capture by the mailman, who stuffed me into his mail

sack and carted me away. A deep sense of guilt over having been born a safe American Jew haunted me. By an accident of fate I was to survive while millions went to labor camps—we did not quite know about the ovens yet. Out of sympathy with my father I began to share his news broadcasts. I was educated in the root causes and outbreak of World War II by such radio commentators as Raymond Gram Swing, H. V. Kaltenborn, Elmer Davis, Max Lerner and Fulton Lewis, Jr., who boomed into our living room telling the same tale over and over but from divergent viewpoints.

At the close of eighth grade, my future became the subject of parental debate. My mother, to her credit, argued that I not be sent to Germantown High School, where my brother Peter, lacking the athletic prowess of his two older brothers, was having a miserable time. My father, adamantly opposed to private schools, at length compromised. I was sent out of the township to Elkins Park Junior High, where I repeated the eighth grade and thus grew a year closer to my proper age-group. (I had skipped twice in elementary school and was two years younger than most of my classmates.) The tuition in Elkins Park for commuting students was two hundred dollars a year. I continued from junior high to Cheltenham High School, a participant in the final group of the experimental Columbia Eight Year Study Plan. In this program students proceeded at their own rate, retaining the same teachers, through the various curricula. Dutifully I plodded through plane geometry, but in Latin and English classes my soul leapt up.

I have written elsewhere about Juanita Mae Downes and Dorothy Lambert, two heroic figures who made a profound difference in my life. With Miss Downes I studied Latin year by year, moving from Caesar's *Gallic War* through Cicero to Virgil (including the forbidden chapter set in Dido's cave; Miss Downes was a purist and omitted nothing). My senior year in high school was largely devoted to translating Ovid's *Metamorphoses* into matching hexameters. In Mrs. Lambert's English class I read all of Dostoevsky and, for ballast perhaps, Hopkins, Arnold, Housman, and Hardy. This wonderful teacher believed as devoutly in the rules of prosody as any of my nuns had believed in the Second Coming. Once again, I was an enthusiastic convert.

Scholastically, the switch to another township was a sound move. Psychologically, however, it nearly destroyed me. Because I commuted both ways by trolley and train—an hour each way—I had little or no social life involving my peers. The passage through adolescence was a lonely, involuted time for me. None except other outcasts—a paraplegic boy crippled by polio, who reported sports events for the school paper, an epileptic black girl who played in the orchestra—held out a hand in friendship to me. Although I was on the staff of the school newspaper and the literary magazine, I had no one to eat lunch with, and took my sandwich to the locker room, where I pretended to be busy writing an article.

Forced to attend dancing class on alternate Saturday nights, where all of the popular girls were indifferent students in my French or history section, I hid in the ladies' room until the ordeal ended. I think I was enabled to survive this dreadful period of isolation, if not ostracism, by the underpinning of my happy Other Life in summer. In July and August I became someone else. The other ten months of the year, shut out by the snobbism and cliquishness of my classmates, I took refuge in scholarship.

Although I had applied to Wellesley College, which not only had a fine swimming pool but also an underwater observation room for analyzing swim strokes, I was not accepted. For while they did not openly practice the quota system, virtually all the top colleges and universities at that time sharply limited the number of Jews and other minorities they accept-

Maxine with her father, Peter Winokur, on her wedding day, Philadelphia, Pennsylvania, 1946

ed. Instead, I attended Radcliffe, where the basement pool wasn't even regulation size. Nevertheless, I swam for the team all four years and captained it in my senior year. I also stood lifeguard duty—the pay was a dollar an hour—and taught swimming to those few students who had somehow never mastered the rudiments. One could not then receive a diploma without passing a simple swimming test in deep water.

At Radcliffe epithets with which I had been branded—bookworm, greasy grind, brain trust—now became a badge of honor. Dorm life brought me into contact with girls from vastly different backgrounds and geographies. Hemmed in by rigid parietals, we quite easily fell into the pattern of late-night bull sessions in the smoking room. Politics, the war, our public and personal aspirations all came under scrutiny. And boys; although they called us girls, we called them men. Cambridge was full of uniforms. The navy was turning out ensigns at the business school; they were known as ninety-day wonders. The army had language training programs in Russian and Chinese at Harvard. Because of the war, Cliffies no longer had to attend separate classes, but were finally integrated into the regular lectures in Harvard Yard.

With Victor Kumin in Harvard Yard, 1945

At Radcliffe my parochial Jewishness fell away. Unself-consciously, I found friends of varying beliefs and hues, some in the camaraderie of the swimming team and the freshman crew, my new sports enthusiasm, others through proximity in the dorm, and still others in the course of developing a social conscience.

In 1942, the Fore River shipyard workers went out on strike in an effort to vote in a union of their own. With a few other Cliffies, most of them juniors and seniors, I rose at dawn, caught the 6:00 A.M. subway to Ashmont, where an antique station wagon belonging to the CIO met us, and reached the factory gates in time to hand out leaflets as the shift changed. Later, after breakfast in a diner (my first diner!), we helped with the writing and layout of the union newspaper, a weekly. My high-school experience with layout served me well; I became the chief headline composer.

I did not report this new activity in my weekly letters home; some uncharacteristic caution caused me to withhold my enthusiasm, even though my father was a Democrat and believed firmly in the New Deal. To my astonishment I received a furious phone call from him. My father had never before initiated such contact. He demanded that I stay away from Fore River and give up all union activities. The FBI had taken out a dossier on me. An agent had paid my father a personal call alerting him. The union effort, he said, was being marshalled by Commies and fellow travelers.

Even now, I don't really understand from what reservoir I drew the strength to argue back.

"I'll yank you out of that fancy college so fast your head will spin!" shouted my irate parent at extra-decibel level. Just talking long-distance always caused him to raise his voice across the miles, but this time he was bellowing. "You hear me?"

"You do that," I said. "My grades are all A's. I'll just apply for a scholarship and a work-study job and stay right here."

He never broached the subject again.

The following summer—1943—I applied for a job on the assembly line making weather balloons for the army at ninety cents an hour, nonunion. I planned to share an apartment in Cambridge with three classmates who had signed on for similar jobs, but at the end of May I came down with a mysterious fever. Initially diagnosed as polio, only after an anxious week of chills and delirium did it resolve itself as a severe case of measles. I don't remember how I passed the three weeks I had to spend in a darkened room, forbidden to read, but my relief at having been spared the paralysis everyone dreaded is still fresh in

At home in Newton, Massachusetts, about 1965: Judith, Jane, Victor, Maxine, and Daniel Kumin

my mind.

Once I had recovered I went back to Camp Watitoh. Shorthanded because of the war, the directors were glad to take me back.

The balance of physical and intellectual activity seemed to be something I not only craved but required. That pattern has persisted. I still find that three hours at my desk leaves me keyed up and restless and that to go to the garden or to the barn restores my sanity.

My undergraduate years were brightened by such notable professors as Albert Guerard, Jr., Michael Karpovich, F. O. (Matty) Matthiessen, and Harry Levin. I wrote my senior honors thesis under Professor Levin's benevolent eye. He and my oldest cousin, Joseph Hyman, had been Rhodes scholars together, which gave me an extra edge.

In April of 1945, on a blind date, I met an army sergeant, Harvard '43, Victor Kumin. Our mutual infatuation was instant and headlong. In June I rushed out to Amarillo, Texas (two days by train, via Chicago), ostensibly to visit my cousin Barbara, who was working as a clerk at the air-force base where her father was a colonel. Victor, one of George Kistiakowsky's and Oppenheimer's soldier-scientists, who had been whisked out of their other geographies in a highly secret deployment, was stationed at Los Alamos. He was able to wangle a three-day pass and hitchhiked across the desert to see me. At the end of this all too brief liaison, my uncle Sam managed to reserve a hotel room for us in Albuquerque, which was as close as civilians were permitted to come to the facility at Los Alamos. If Victor signed back in at camp, he could get another forty-eight-hour release, so we set off by bus. This conveyance broke down midway. Everyone disembarked and we spread blankets and pillows on hummocks of sand and admired the cactus roses by moonlight.

Although I had been offered a fellowship for the fall of 1946 to study at the University of Grenoble, passion prevailed. We were married in June of 1946, just after I graduated and Victor was mustered out of the army; we set out for Woods Hole, where he was employed by the Oceanographic Institution. In the late fall we came back to Boston, and, after a dreary period of working as a general factotum for an organization called United Service to China—Chiang Kai-shek's China, that is—I returned to graduate school.

By the summer of 1948 I had completed all the requirements for an M.A. in comparative literature,

except for the ancient-language proficiency exam, which I flunked to my chagrin. Harry Levin interceded for me. I was by then visibly pregnant. On grounds that I was not planning to press on for my Ph.D. at that time, he had the requirement waived and the degree was conferred. Lucky for me, as some ten years later the M.A. enabled me to get a job at Tufts University teaching freshman composition to the dental technicians, engineers, and phys-ed majors. I was not considered qualified to teach liberal-arts students there.

In the ensuing five years we had three children, moved several times, and finally bought a modest house in a suburb of Boston so that we could take advantage of the highly touted Newton public schools. During this period I free-lanced as a medical writer for a variety of ambitious, busy physicians, doing research at the Boston Medical Library whenever the baby-sitter came, and settling down at night to ghosting articles for my employers.

In the fall of 1952, pregnant for the third time, I began to suffer from a terrible anomie, a sense of rootlessness and futility. I wasn't what could be called clinically depressed, but I felt woefully unfulfilled.

The staff of the 1970 Bread Loaf Writers' Conference, Middlebury College, Middlebury, Vermont: (back row, from left) John Nims, Galway Kinnell, Judith Ciardi, Perry Knowlton, Miller Williams, Dan Wakefield, Sandy Martin, Harry Crews; (middle row) Maxine Kumin, William Sloane, John Ciardi, Joanna Foster; (front row) John Williams, Shane Stevens

The life I was leading was the post–World War II life I had been programmed to lead: suburban housewife, mother, active in PTA and community organizations, supposedly keeping the intellectual flame alive by way of Great Books discussions (I was a workshop leader) and my own underground poems. These I shared with no one. For hadn't The Famous Writer who taught my English A-1 class told me in my freshman year that I had no talent in this arena? Nor was I writing the book reviews and intelligent articles on trends in modern literature that I had vaguely fantasized would make my debut as a writer. I had not found the courage to strike out on my own, like Conrad's *Secret Sharer,* in search of a new destiny.

On impulse I sent away for a little text by Richard Armour called *Writing Light Verse.* I made a pact with myself that if I had sold nothing by the time this baby was born I would turn my back on the Muse and find a new vocation.

From articles in the *Writer,* I deduced that magazines and newspapers had their own advance timetable for poems. What I needed to do, in the early winter, was to think about spring. On March 17, 1953, the *Christian Science Monitor* bought the following quatrain:

Factually Speaking

There never blows so red the rose,
So sound the round tomato
As March's catalogues disclose
And yearly I fall prey to.

Soon I was appearing in the *Monitor* on a regular basis. My filler verses ran in the *Saturday Evening Post, Good Housekeeping,* the *Wall Street Journal,* the *New York Herald Tribune,* and a dozen smaller periodicals. By the end of the year I had set up a card file of markets and established a cottage industry that netted me twelve hundred dollars, all without *neglecting*—the buzzword of the fifties—husband and children.

But my discontent and my guilt over these feelings continued to nag me. I wanted to write real poems. I haunted the Grolier Book Shop in Cambridge on my one day off each week from motherhood. I read all the post–World War II poets, only subliminally aware that there were virtually no women among them. I skulked around the fringes of poetry readings at various universities. I went on writing poems in the dark, keenly aware that I lacked focus, lacked direction; I did not then understand that I needed a mentor.

The winter of 1956 I heard about a poetry workshop at the Boston Center for Adult Education,

*The author with two of her many pets,
Warner, New Hampshire, 1981*

to be conducted by John Holmes, a poet and professor from Tufts. I believe the workshop first came together in January 1957. Anne Sexton and I met in that group and there began the intense personal and professional friendship that sustained us both as we came of age as poets. Women poets, it seems important to add. I have written elsewhere about our relationship and my hard grief over her suicide in 1974, and about our very different associations with John Holmes, who won me my first teaching post at Tufts.

The rest of my life is an open book. Now, in my sixties, trying to balance the life of the mind against the physically taxing demands of our farm, it occurs to me that my discontent over my chronic inability to make the pieces fit neatly together is not unlike the angst I endured in the early years of my marriage. The women's movement did not yet exist. The notion of role models was not yet being explored. I probably could not have articulated my unease and resentment even if a sympathetic hearing had been provided.

The three adults who are still our children have

informed and changed my life in more ways than they will admit to, but establishing a balance point is not one of them. It seems to me that I am forever pursuing the fulcrum. Since I suspect that this is the source of my creative energy, I pray it will continue to elude me for a long time to come.

Copyright © Maxine Kumin, 1989

BIBLIOGRAPHY

Poetry:

Halfway. New York: Holt, 1961.

The Privilege. New York: Harper, 1965.

The Nightmare Factory. New York: Harper, 1970.

Up Country: Poems of New England (illustrated by Barbara Swan). New York: Harper, 1972.

House, Bridge, Fountain, Gate. New York: Viking, 1975.

The Retrieval System. New York: Viking, 1978; Harmondsworth, England: Penguin, 1979.

Our Ground Time Here Will Be Brief. New York: Viking, 1982; Harmondsworth, England: Penguin, 1982.

Closing the Ring (illustrated by Barnard Taylor). Lewisburg, Pa.: The Press of Appletree Alley/Bucknell University, 1984.

The Long Approach. New York: Viking, 1985.

Nurture. New York: Viking, 1989.

Fiction:

Through Dooms of Love. New York: Harper, 1965; also published as *A Daughter and Her Loves.* London: Gollancz/Hamish Hamilton, 1965.

The Passions of Uxport. New York: Harper, 1968.

The Abduction. New York: Harper, 1971.

The Designated Heir. New York: Viking, 1974; London: Deutsch, 1975.

Why Can't We Live Together Like Civilized Human Beings? (short stories). New York: Viking, 1982.

Fiction for children:

Sebastian and the Dragon (illustrated by William D. Hayes). New York: Putnam, 1960.

Follow the Fall (illustrated by Artur Marokvia). New York: Putnam, 1961.

Spring Things (illustrated by A. Marokvia). New York: Putnam, 1961.

A Summer Story (illustrated by A. Marokvia). New York: Putnam, 1961.

A Winter Friend (illustrated by A. Marokvia). New York: Putnam, 1961.

Mittens in May (illustrated by Elliott Gilbert). New York: Putnam, 1962.

No One Writes a Letter to the Snail (illustrated by Bean Allen). New York: Putnam, 1962.

Archibald the Traveling Poodle (adapted from a story by James Krüss; illustrated by Erich Holle). New York: Putnam, 1963.

Eggs of Things, with Anne Sexton (illustrated by Leonard Shortall). New York: Putnam, 1963.

The Beach before Breakfast (illustrated by Leonard Weisgard). New York: Putnam, 1964.

More Eggs of Things, with A. Sexton (illustrated by L. Shortall). New York: Putnam, 1964.

Speedy Digs Downside Up (illustrated by Ezra Jack Keats). New York: Putnam, 1964.

Paul Bunyan (illustrated by Dirk Gringhuis). New York: Putnam, 1966.

Faraway Farm (illustrated by Kurt Werth). New York: Norton, 1967.

The Wonderful Babies of 1809 and Other Years (illustrated by Carl Rose). New York: Putnam, 1968.

When Grandmother Was Young (illustrated by Don Almquist). New York: Putnam, 1969.

When Mother Was Young (illustrated by D. Almquist). New York: Putnam, 1970.

Joey and the Birthday Present, with A. Sexton (illustrated by Evaline Ness). New York: McGraw, 1971.

When Great-Grandmother Was Young (illustrated by D. Almquist). New York: Putnam, 1971.

The Wizard's Tears, with A. Sexton. New York: McGraw, 1975.

What Color Is Caesar? (illustrated by E. Ness). New York: McGraw, 1978.

The Microscope (first appeared in *The Wonderful Babies of 1809 and Other Years;* illustrated by Arnold Lobel). New York: Harper, 1984.

Nonfiction:

To Make a Prairie: Essays on Poets, Poetry, and Country Living. Ann Arbor: University of Michigan Press, 1979.

In Deep: Country Essays. New York: Viking, 1987.

Dorothy Livesay

1909-

Dorothy Livesay in Victoria, British Columbia, 1988

How She Grew Up

Dorothy Livesay was the first-born child of literary parents who had gone west to Winnipeg in the early 1900s. Her mother, Florence Randal Livesay, came from a United Empire Loyalist family who had left Vermont for the British enclave of Quebec. Florence, the second of six children, was educated at Compton Ladies College, Quebec, a Victorian-style girls' school which emphasized languages and the arts. Already in her teens she was writing poems and stories, eventually published in *Massey's Magazine*, Toronto. From 1900 to 1902 she became a society editor for the *Ottawa Journal*; and in 1903, after a year teaching English in a refugee camp near Johannesburg, she set forth to go west to Winnipeg. On the staff of the *Winnipeg Telegram* she met a "fascinating Englishman," J. F. B. Livesay.

Fred, or "Live" as he was nicknamed, had emigrated from the Isle of Wight to Ontario in 1898; went harvesting on the prairie and ended up as a full-fledged reporter with the *Winnipeg Telegram.* After a lengthy courtship and often-delayed marriage date, these two disparate characters were wed on September 1, 1908. Dorothy Kathleen May Livesay was born on October 12, 1909.

Her literary life began early as she was often encouraged to tell her own stories which her mother published on a women's page of the *Free Press.*

The family moved to Toronto in 1920–21 when J. F. B. Livesay was appointed general manager of the Canadian Press. Her mother meanwhile became known as a translator of Ukrainian folk songs, published first in *Poetry Chicago*, then in a volume called *Songs of Ukraina*, published by Dent. So it was in Toronto, at the girls' school Glen Mawr, that Dorothy met her "bosom friend," Eugenia Watts (Gina), and began reading contemporary literature, both English and French; and writing poems, which she looked upon as playful games.

As Dorothy—or Dee, the way she is familiarly known—has looked back upon her life in order to write her memoirs, she has found herself haunted by remembrances. That close student friendship with Gina lasting through the formative years of 1929–39 seemed to have been the strongest influence upon her development into poet and activist. It was as if that friendship had remained hidden, a closed fan; until the moment came, years later, when the fan opened. The question now was: how to write it down? The only sure way was to set it forth as a letter to Gina; imagining her friend still alive, and listening.

Other events did intervene. From the University of Toronto Dorothy twice sojourned in France. Her Sorbonne thesis, "Symbolism and the Metaphysical Tradition in Modern English Poetry," was completed in 1932, just when the Great Depression had hit Canada. So, instead of seeking university teaching, she registered with the newly established School of Social Work at the University of Toronto. After a year's apprenticeship in Montreal, she went to New Jersey in 1934 and was employed as a caseworker at Memorial House, a community centre in Englewood. It was after that experience that she returned to Ontario to write her first "depression documentary," "Day and Night." This was published in 1936 in the first issue of the *Canadian Poetry* magazine, edited by the veteran poet, E. J. Pratt. Of this work he wrote that it was good to find Canadian poetry being written about city life rather than about maple leaves. From then on Dorothy left the "maple-leaf school" far behind. Gina would have approved.

Gina

1925–1940

Ah, Gina, is it only after seventy years of living that I begin to understand you? We met when we were about twelve, in the spring of 1921. The place was Clarkson, then a small village on the highway between Toronto and Hamilton. Both your parents and mine were using the Blue Dragon Inn as a place to stay pending house-hunting in Toronto. Our family—myself and my young sister—boarded there for the spring months. Father commuted by train to his office in Toronto where he was to become General Manager of the Canadian Press.

I was a timid, lonely child. Somewhat at a loss because of the uprooting from Winnipeg where I had

Sisters Dorothy and Sophie, 1916
(Photograph courtesy of the Archives and Special Collections Department, University of Manitoba)

had one close friend or chum. In this Ontario village I knew no one, did not know how to make friends; and at the one-room country school the older children scared me. I buried my nose in my scribbler and tried to comprehend the arithmetic: *reduction* it was called: gallons to quarts to pints. Useless exercises, I thought.

And then, for two or three weekends, there you were! Tall, thin, boyishly built, with silver blonde short hair; a gamin, your fair and rosy skin contrasting with your brown eyes, soft as velvet and deep as a woodland stream. But what a tomboy you were! I have never met a girl so rough, forcing me to wrestle with you as you seized hold of my arms. Only two years later, when we ended up in the same girls' school, I discovered the other side of your nature: you, sylphlike, darting through woodland, leaping over streams, delighting to find rare wild flowers and birds. And reading poetry all the time, as I was.

When we had settled in the Annex, I spent my first year at Saint Mildred's School, run by Anglican sisters. Then my mother heard about Glen Mawr, a small boarding school on Spadina Avenue near Hoskin, where the principal, Miss Gertrude Stuart, emphasised the arts—music, painting, drama, and the history of art. For the first term I was put into the Fourth Form, very timid with my classmates but determined to please my teachers and to shine. As a result, after Christmas I was promoted to the Lower Fifth, where I immediately recognised you, my Gina, the talkative tomboy who was always in hot water, always questioning. The teachers called you Eugenia, for you had been christened Myrtle Eugenia. How you hated that name! We suspected that the existence of the Empress Eugenie, in your mother's day, had something to do with that handle. To make up for it, your classmates called you variously Gene, Jeanie, Jim, or Gina. And you came to be, for us, the voice of resistance against authority.

Was it your wit, sometimes mingled with malice, that fascinated us? I remember how, perhaps on a streetcar or sitting in the Owl Drugstore over a chocolate soda, you would make caustic remarks about people, not too softly. Or you would recount how "Every Monday morning I lean out from my window over the ravine and say Hello to the garbage-men. They have the greatest way of talking back and joking. They make words exciting. Honestly, Dee!"

One day, at school, we were looking out of the upstairs classroom window before teacher came in.

Then we noticed a man in the lane below, waving at us. Suddenly he unbuttoned his trousers and pulled out his *thing.* "Don't look!" you warned, loudly pulling down the sash and drawing the blind. I think only the girls with brothers knew what was going on. The rest of us sat in stunned silence until the teacher entered the room. She must have wondered at the unusual quiet. "Eugenia, pull up the blind," was all she said.

Lesson hours at our private school were from nine o'clock to one; after which the day girls walked home to lunch. More often you had to stay on, lunching at school, to take music lessons or play basketball. I was never good enough at these pursuits to be burdened by them. Actually, we both preferred to walk and talk. We must have been an incongruous pair, you so tall and slim and I broader and shorter with disproportionately long legs and arms. By the time we were in the Upper Fifth we were very conscious of our bodies and uncomfortable with them. No matter how much the hearty and healthy gym teacher told us that menstruation was normal, "It proves you have entered into womanhood, not a time for misery," we knew differently. Some girls suffered more than others and I was one of those. You were, as always, stoical.

During this period of late adolescence I was probably only aware of delight in your companion-

J. F. B. Livesay, General Manager of the Canadian Press

ship. But you have recorded what you experienced through participating in the Livesay household games. Your own homelife was strictly Victorian, with hours laid down for housework, study, shopping, piano practice; whereas my life must have seemed wildly bohemian. I love the way you have described these years, with exaggerated gusto:

> You see, the father and the mother were so completely different. There was a constant pull for the two girls between them. And the father was, well, he was quite a neurotic character, with a rather marked speech impediment. But a very brilliant man. And the mother, while she wrote, it is true, I would think she was a very minor writer. The main thing about her was that she was extremely traditionally religious; she was a very staunch Anglican. Of course, Livesay's aim at home was to horrify her at every step. So every meal was a kind of bravado anti-religious thing on the part of Livesay with Mrs L kind of sighing and tearing her hair. Oh, and he used to do things like pasting up rather insulting but quite funny poetry on the walls about one or other of the family. Of course, she couldn't reply; this wasn't her means of defense. In fact, she had no means of defense. As well as that, she was the most appalling housekeeper; the house was mad. They used to have new Canadian maids, a series of them. None of them ever stayed long. As soon as they learned English—and a lot of them seemed to be writers, poets and things in their own languages—they weren't really cut out to be maids. And they would do things like move the bathtub to wash under it, thereby pulling out all the plumbing. But the house had some lovely old English things, stuff Dee still has, old chests. Still, it was a mad place, but full of books.

> Well, I grew up there because it was so much pleasanter than my house. Livesay was terribly interested in the girls. His whole life centred on those two girls and their friends. And he used to treat us all like grown-ups and invite us to lunch at the Royal York and have green turtle soup and strawberries in December, and that sort of thing. When you're fourteen and you've been out to lunch with a real grown-up man, it is a tremendous thing. And they never really treated them as children really. They

were part of the adult world.

As for boy-girl relationships, we didn't know any boys, did we? Except your elder brother. In any case, we wouldn't have known what to say to them, but we envied them their freedom (as we saw it) from the pains of growth.

What I remember is extreme nervousness in the presence of boys. However, we admired their firm, straight bodies and in order to look the same we strapped our budding breasts under tight cotton brassieres. I recollect my shock when you went so far as to wear only boys' striped cotton shorts instead of rayon panties. But then, I followed your lead. Of course we had to wear skirts, well below the knee. (We would have revelled in the blue-jean era!) Nevertheless, whatever clothes you wore, Gina, you always looked striking.

Perhaps you don't remember how, by the time we were in the Sixth Form and reading Michael Arlen's *Green Hat* (read aloud to us, of all things, by our English teacher, Mary Jennison), you took on the role of *femme fatale,* wearing flared skirts, orange sweaters, and, of course, a dashing green felt hat with a feather in it! At one point you even persuaded your parents to give you a white Russian wolfhound with which, on leash, you sauntered along Bloor Street between Markham and Spadina. O dizzying delights!

Throughout these changing phases of yours I remained the sober, plodding one. I was aware, of course, that I was dressed dowdily. (My mother still bought my clothes.) Once when I had some pocket money I went downtown myself and bought a garment that fit, and suited my mood. It was one of grey broadcloth, straight lined, long sleeved, high necked, quite a uniform. At this time we were reading and acting out *The Merchant of Venice* in our English class, so you immediately dubbed my new costume "Dee's Jewish gaberdine."

Soon afterwards you led a movement to have the school adopt uniforms, as did other private schools such as Havergal or Bishop Strachan's. Essentially this involved wearing a white tailored blouse, a short navy blue serge tunic, and long black stockings. My mother objected to the expense but my father, the Englishman, emerged from his usual detachment in such matters to state that I should conform to the school pattern. This solution left me free from worry about my clothes. My hair, however, was still long, drawn back in a barrette; whereas the other girls went along with the trend and were *bobbed.* But my hair was the only part of my physical being that afforded me any satisfaction. It was fine and wavy, nut brown in colour, with golden lights when I dried it in the sun.

Florence Randal Livesay, 1916
(Photograph courtesy of the Archives and Special Collections
Department, University of Manitoba)

My eyes did not please me, being neither dark blue nor grey but something in-between. In the summertime my face and arms were heavily freckled. Fine gold hairs had begun to show above my upper lip. So on a frosty winter day as we walked up Spadina, you cried out in glee, "Dee, you should see yourself. You've got a white moustache!" You were often disposed to putting me down in this way, and loudly. But I developed a defence: laughter. Rippling laughter surrounded us wherever we went.

We both loved the woods and the Ontario countryside. That was the great bond between us. Other schoolmates would spend their Saturday afternoons skating or going to "the show," which in those days was the stock company theatre; you and I would take the streetcar to the top of Yonge Street and go walking in Hog's Hollow, or saunter in the spring rain, over the Rosedale Bridge. The trees waving below in the ravine seemed themselves to be weeping green rain. Then, after my father built Woodlot, the first half of a house-to-be in the Clarkson woods, you

would manage to get permission from your very strict parents to spend some weekends with me, especially in the spring and fall. In your recollections of this period you speak of us two "sleeping in the woodshed." It was not properly such. My father had built, from rough-hewn logs, a woodshed beside the creek, away from the main house. To this he added a room alongside, big enough for two cots. We called this room *Cherokee.* Through the windows at night we could see the white birches gleaming in the moonlight, hear the purling stream, and the whippoorwill, sending his loops of song into the silence. It was a fine place in which young girls could whisper their secrets.

Our first secrets concerned school, largely; our classmates, our teachers, and our poems, in which we vied with each other to astonish, amuse, delight. We even tried publishing a class newspaper, but after the second issue the principal announced at morning prayers that it was being confiscated and must never appear again. It had dared to make mild fun of some of the teachers' idiosyncrasies! You and I, however, after our first bursts of fury, were not really downhearted. We had discovered that our ruling passion was to write. My diary records that complication in these words:

> Again, I am under the influence of Gina's brilliance. Her passionate need is to write, but she says that she *cannot.* Compared with her I should be uncertain and depressed. But I am not. Most people have a reason for living, that is to say, a philosophy, a creed. Mine is beauty. Gina, so coldly scientific, hasn't even that. There is nothing to balance her, to hold her. She should have been gifted in some definite way. It is terrible that she isn't.

Nonetheless, you participated with me in most of my literary explorations: the short stories, novels, plays of Shaw, Chekhov, and Ibsen. But it was the shared poetry that meant the most to us emotionally. We memorized some of Shakespeare's songs and sonnets; Herrick, Marvell; and the poetry of the Georgians: de la Mare, Humbert Wolfe, Edward Thomas (my favourite). Then we discovered the women: Elinor Wylie, Katherine Mansfield, Emily Dickinson. This is how you recollected those experiences:

> I am sure we were reading Emily Dickinson
> in school. I can't really say why we liked,
> why I still like, Emily Dickinson, and find

her absolutely fascinating to read. It's just the small, the compact, the beautiful little structures. And yes, of course, Emily D influenced Dee. Everything you read influences you. But it is quite obvious, isn't it, that in spots Dee is pure Emily Dickinson. Then, she doesn't stay within this little mould. I'm pretty sure we were reading Emily Dickinson long before going to university, because when we got to university we were reading what were then contemporary writers, just eating up everything. Huxley and Virginia Woolf were at that point bringing out books. You got first editions. We'd passed through the historical period— all the ones who were dead, we'd read them all. Once I discovered Dee's family, I spent all my time there and read everything that they had, from Trollope on up because Livesay was very interested in anybody who read books and was interested in books and he just couldn't wait to press books upon you constantly. It was wonderful. It was like having your own private public library. And of course he discussed books with you, quite seriously. He would want to know your opinions. It is really rare when you are young that anyone wants to know your opinion, except to write it in an essay. It was a tremendous thing knowing that family.

Remembering all this, so vividly now after your words, I ask: Is it any wonder we were called bluestockings? It is clear that though there were only two of us who were mavericks in that Sixth Form class of a dozen girls, we formed a solid and indestructible minority, an underground, if you like, in a small girls' school that had always been stamped with gentility. Not for university were these girls of *old* Toronto families destined, but for "coming out" and going abroad and getting married. When Edward, Prince of Wales, visited Toronto, our senior graduating class was invited to the ball at Government House. Next day, great was the excitement when one of our Lower Sixth classmates reported that her sister, Helen, had danced with the Prince! You and I were not impressed (though doubtless we were envious).

Ironically our principal, Miss Stuart, whom we both respected and feared, was not herself a society-oriented type at all, but a graduate in classics from Gerton College, Cambridge. She taught us scripture, with a choice of Greek or Latin. I chose Latin and appreciated her teaching; yet I was easily subverted by you into seeing the principal as Enemy Number

One. One morning we were expecting her to arrive at any moment to visit the alcove, a small seminar attic corner where we would be carrying on with Caesar's *Gallic Wars.* We got to making puns, especially about the Roman manoeuvre of attack on the rear. You searched the floor and produced a tack. "Let's put it on her chair," you murmured, conspiringly. The half dozen girls were amused, then stunned, as you cunningly placed the tack pointed end up, on the principal's chair. "A tack on the rear!" With suppressed laughter but mounting apprehension we watched the time go by. The principal was often late for a lesson because of administrative crises in her office. We waited and waited. Finally her portly body appeared in the doorway and she marched to the small table around which we were sitting.

"Now. What chapter were we at?"

"Attack on the rear," someone murmured.

"Well, let me see . . ." Standing over the book, Miss Stuart ruffled through the pages. "Oh, yes. Will you start translating, please. On page five."

Our notebooks flew open, our eyes bent low. Would she or would she not sit down? Then, piercingly, the bell rang. End of lesson.

"Very well, then. That is your homework." And she sailed out of the alcove.

"Whew!" I was trembling with fear and relief. But you screamed with laughter.

It was other escapades such as that one, though, that frequently did get you into trouble. Most serious was the punishment you received one noonday:

"If you think you are so important, Miss," the principal told you in front of us all, "I will ask you to be my guest today at lunch." And when all the boarders were seated in the dining room, the principal marched in, side by side with you, clothed in hat and gloves. You were ushered to the staff table and forced to eat with the teachers. Do you remember how you did not go home after lunch, as you were supposed to? Instead, you flew up the street to our house on Walmer Road. I was waiting for you, fearfully anxious. We sobbed and sobbed in each other's arms.

The next step for us acolytes was, of course, not to be writing to each other, but to be writing to the beloved. It was an accepted part of life in a girls' school—even in Toronto—that one developed *crushes* on older girls or young teachers. You and I were perhaps more overtly and ardently turned in that direction because we stimulated each other's emotions and fixations. I still remember a sense of the utter shattering of one's privacy, yet the exaltation derived therefrom when we admitted to each other that we were in love with a fellow student. There had been others in the two previous school years and there were the two teachers who were wonderfully helpful in widening our knowledge of the world. But it was Leslie, a new girl who came to Glen Mawr in our last, sixth year, who really aroused our awakening sexuality.

This was the year in which I had to study for Honour Matriculation, doing senior courses in English, French, Latin, German, and modern history—as well as the horrors of algebra and geometry, for which both you and I had had to take remedial coaching. So the tension of looming examinations was ever with us. Perhaps even more powerfully with you, for you had decided—against your parents' advice of course—to take a pre-med course at the University of Toronto. And for this we well knew our polite ladies' finishing school had in no way prepared you. Science was not taught and we received generally poor mathematics instruction until the teachers Ford and Messervy came along during our two Sixth Form years.

The way out of this tension was to indulge in an infatuation or crush. It was quite natural that the nearest object was a girl, perhaps a year older than we were, and very sophisticated. Leslie belonged to one of Toronto's "old families" living in Rosedale. She told us that her parents had broken up, that she had had a mysterious illness, and that she had been sent to this boarding school for her finishing off before she would become a Deb and enter the exclusive rounds of Toronto society. All this of course added to Leslie's fascination; for never would *we* be admitted to such circles. Leslie was patently headed for that sort of life. She was in no way a student intellectually inclined. She was swarthy, square jawed, sombre: brown hair cut short like a boy's and with the most extraordinary dark eyes, "smouldering," in your phrase, the genuine *femme fatale*.

For once you agreed with me that we should keep our passion to ourselves and not flaunt it before any of our classmates. This might have reached Leslie's ears and destroyed the sense of mystery she emanated. We wrote poems to Leslie, but showed them only to each other. Things came to a climax, however, when the school year ended with its annual exercises, heavy with lilacs and the scent of make-up as the school play was performed. I was Lydia in Goldsmith's *She Stoops to Conquer*. Or was it Sheridan's *Rivals*? Parents came to the prize-giving and the reading of marks. We were quite excited when my short story "Siki" was awarded the prize presented by Katherine Hale, Mrs. John Garvin. But none of this mattered to us much, for we were scouring Bloor Street for flower shops. We had decided that Leslie

required one parting gift, one dozen yellow roses. We finally found this rarity, despatching the offering with bated breath. On the card we printed a cryptic verse, but signed no names. Since we weren't boarders, we were unable to witness the opening of the gift! Then, suddenly, school was over.

We would have seen nothing more of Leslie were it not for the fact that my parents were moving to our summer place in Clarkson and it was decided that I should stay in Toronto to prepare for the senior matriculation examinations. The principal agreed to taking me in as a boarder along with any other Sixth Form girls who would be writing exams. Among them was Leslie.

Was I right in thinking you were really envious of my opportunity to be so near the beloved? As time would reveal, the decision was most unfortunate for me, as I was the only serious crammer in the school and the other girls, including Leslie, sought to conspire together to keep me from studying. We had orgies of midnight feasts. I remember that after an unusually filling Sunday dinner in the school dining room, the girls went upstairs and immediately opened cans of tomato soup which they heated on their secret alcohol stove. The result was that the next day I failed to get a first class in my modern history examination. Only, I believe, did I succeed in English, French, and Latin. Miss Stuart had drilled us so thoroughly in memorizing Horace, Virgil, and Caesar that very likely we all sailed through that examination.

Once free of this ordeal, you eventually managed to meet me to receive all the details that I had gleaned of our beloved's life. But the intimacies of boarding school regime had somehow disillusioned me. Your pride must have smarted when I recounted, with insufferable superiority, the attitudes the girls had expressed during one jam session on marriage and babies. "Oh," Leslie said, "Have you ever seen a new-born baby?" None of us had. "Well, it's just a red blob. Not white, like us. Not *human*. The ugliest thing you can imagine." At that time I never consciously connected that description as being a confession. But *you* did! "So that was Leslie's baby!" The mystery of the girl's illness was solved. But by now you had had experience as a counsellor at a children's welfare camp. You knew what was *really* happening in the world. I was to learn somewhat later.

That summer, I think, marked the beginning of the end of our intense friendship. When I went to Trinity College my courses, classmates, and professors were so differently orientated from scientific ones at the pre-med level that we would only see each other perhaps on a Saturday afternoon—going for a walk in the ravine or sitting in your rooming-house digs listening to Beethoven's Fifth on your portable gramophone. Once a week also at Convocation Hall there was an organ recital where we went together to listen to Bach, Haydn, and Mozart. "You are like that music, Dee," you said once—your first praising, rather than mocking, words. I flushed; my heartbeat quickened.

By our second university year something else was happening to your emotional life that distressed me deeply. You were in love with a camp counsellor and had been on the verge of a lesbian relationship that summer. I hated to think of it. And here, now, on campus, you were going around with a known lesbian crowd. True, they were not regarded with the sense of taboo associated with "fairies"—our name for homosexuals. It was a peculiarity of women's state that there were no laws prohibiting them from cohabiting. Perhaps this was because women did not pervert children, as it was believed men did? In any case, *The Well of Loneliness* was *the* book, yet it did not help me to accept your new role. This caused a rift. Then, the September of my third year, I went through my own rites of passage by leaving home for the first time and studying at Aix-Marseille from October to May. The possibility of travel was what had led me into taking modern languages in the first place.

You, however, stayed home, struggling with medical courses. I received few letters from you. Then I heard from my sister at Christmas that you had had a breakdown, you had quit university and were sent to recuperate living with relatives in California.

Not having your address, I wrote to my mother in Toronto, asking her to get it from your mother. Here is her reply:

Dorothy, dear: Both your letter and parcel came an hour ago. They shall be sent on at once. By the way, her address is 147 Ricardo Ave., Piedmont, Cal. She did not (as you see) go south, but out to the coast, where she is visiting Herbert's brother and his wife. She will, no doubt, tell you of her changes of plans. We all felt a complete mental change was indicated, for her. Yes, dear, I do agree with you. The medical work is far too heavy to be undertaken, unless one had a body of (practically) cast iron. I never did feel it was the work for her, but the knowledge she already has will never come amiss.

Seemingly, on receipt of this letter I wrote you at once, probably in apprehension but seeking to assure you of my affection. Your reply must have thrown me considerably; but it is a moving example of your insight and resilience: ever seeking a way out.

Feb. 28, 1930

I forbid you to delude yourself like this about me, just because you haven't seen me for a while. You must never, never call me 'darling' nor think that I am necessary at all.

You know that, for me, living with you is the only real living, and always will be, but it isn't so with you. How you tempt me with Europe. You and Europe together would cause me to die of surfeit of ecstasy.

Really, though, I don't get any money when I am 21 so that, unless the family would consider it, it would be hopeless. As a matter of fact, they thought of you when they were about to send me away, but I refused to land on your doorstep and announce my presence calmly.

And then, funny things have been happening to me, so that you wouldn't like to be with me, and it might be dangerous. Since I left, I have no one, and am living quite secretly, and find myself constantly tormented like an adolescent boy, or a man about to enter a brothel. So that I am forced into religion, out of very preservation. Catholic churches are conveniently numerous here, so that in extremis I can rush into one. I keep seeing people, *my* sort of people, suddenly, anywhere, and wanting to begin to talk to them and have an affair. And it seems always that these people somehow know, and a very secret signal passes between us. Is there an underlying, hardly recognised sisterhood of these people?

You see, I am already a bit mad. Every time I go out I wonder, almost subconsciously whether I shall somehow meet—anyone.

So you see, I *am* in a bad way, and, having confessed all to you, want not your revilement, but . . . well, whatever else you have to give. How did you know that I'd left Meds, before I told you? Write me more, Dee.

Here is part of a letter, perhaps an earlier letter, written on campus at the U of T.

Woodlot during a winter in the 1940s

Although such things are only ugly to you, the affair I had this summer will always remain very perfect and very beautiful. Unlike the business with V., it did not turn to ashes and disgust when I had a proper perspective upon it—on the contrary; it gained its true significance then. We were very perfect lovers, and always I shall keep last summer in my mind as one of the best and richest times I have ever had. Will 20 years hence find me like the former Jenny, turning to Catholicism for relief? It was funny of you to think that I should marry. You know anyhow that V. is a burnt-out cinder for me, though we have very good times together, he being now a very prominent man-about-Varsity. I am reading "Hedylus" (by H.D.) slowly sipping it as you advised. It's very lovely, isn't it—but a decadent sort of sophisticated beauty.

Another letter lovingly describes the women writers we shared.

March 11, 1930

Thank you for an unknown birthday present, which the family won't send on account of it being somewhat enfeebled as to wrapping after such a journey.

Here is a picture of Gertrude Stein. Did you know she was thus? I wish you could dash up to Paris sometime and have a look at these people and find out just what G.S. is trying to do, and be the only one in captivity that knows and then tell me in words of one syllable and indelible ink.

Have you seen a picture of Elinor Wylie? She strangely like Katherine [Mansfield]—dark and quiet. Here is the last poem in her posthumous book, *Angels and Earthly Creatures*—do you not think it charming?

Little Elegy

Withouten you
no rose can grow
no leaf be green
if never seen
your sweetest face
no bird have grace
or power to sing
or anything

be kind or fair
and you nowhere.

Recently I have dived into Amy Lowell. Such lovely free verse things alternating with awful rhymed hexameters (I think). There is one which begins "Hey my daffodil crowned, slim and without sandals"!

My next epistle to you must have been written to tell you about the experience I was having in the south of France, living *en pension* with a delightful family of the *petite noblesse* out in the country next to *Le Château Noir* where Cézanne had lived. That *Route de Tholonet* is now called *Route de Cézanne,* for it leads to the foot of the *Mont St. Victoire,* which he painted so often. Madame's daughter Agnès was seventeen, two years younger than me, passionately fond of the countryside and of the arts, but destined to go, in a few months, to a girls' Agricultural College in the north of France. In the meantime she was at home, between convent life and technical college. She did not know a word of English, but I soon understood her enough to be able to follow her story of boarding-school life in a French convent; and of a love affair far more intense than any we had known at school. I loved Agnès dearly, but not in the way she began to love me. I was very careful: "*Très sage, cette Dorothée,*" Madame was heard to remark. It was this story which called forth your letter of March 12.

Another letter from you, so now I have an excuse to continue. Tell me more about Agnès, won't you? for I don't know her origins at all, only that you gave her your rabbit. Thank you for telling me about this. Of course you realize that all my crushes were quite unphysical, up to perhaps Leslie. And with C. there was and is no being in love, only that passion. Apparently such things are common in convents and girls' schools, and wise nuns recognize it and do what they can.

It was very nice of you to be strong and suppress it, Dee. But then you were always like that. How I love you. Will you read *The Well of Loneliness* which presents the problem in an altogether different light? I'm not sure that scientists agree, but it's very well done—emotional energy quite extraordinary.

Of course, the fact that you haven't a man this year accounts for this—but still can't

you feel that all this is somehow useful—or does that sound like Henny "stardust"? Will you be a "lad with a star-duster" and remove same, vigorously?

As for my adventures as you persist in believing I am having—they consist of dining about with professors, and deans, since I'm related to large numbers of them. I am dying to get back, really, but am sticking it out to the first of April.

Len says I have a victory bond, which I may be able to get from dad—only worth about 100.—Still it would help. I'm glad you still want me. But tell me—do you feel the least emotional about me, because I should hate us to spoil things after so many years. What a curse self-consciousness is! Until last year I never in the least analysed my affairs—not even with C.

Now, O lord, I am a huge writhing mass of desire, and life's very strained. I go to your church now, and when I am home to Catholic church with Anne. It helps somewhat.

It's become very necessary for me to see you and to get away from the family etc., for I've got to get organized into the universe. You might write to my family or something.

Wouldn't it be funny if I'd never met you. I would have been lost in the mire long since, I fear. You manage to illuminate things, you know.

Do you understand that with A. there is that tremendous physical factor, but also friendship. I took damn good care that there was something more than in my affair with C.— which is a perfect example of pure passion. That is why no one was even able to understand my interest in her—it was only explainable through that unexplainable physical attraction; but I didn't want that horrible experience again, so that, when Anne and I do come to an end of passion, we will still be friends.

By the time you got back to Toronto in April you had regained your self-confidence and optimism— linking up with the old college crowd and having "a rather jolly time." That was to be our direction in the future, for our fourth and final year as undergraduates.

April 7

My friend, your letters have arrived. I am home.

I am in a state of lostness.

You know, of course, that I want to join you as much as you want to have me, but Dee, I have no particular desire to learn Italian, whereas I have to have fluent French or German next year for Psychology. I can't wander about, can I—I want to see France. And the family, though perfectly willing that I should go, absolutely won't contribute anything. So that I shall more or less be sacrificing my financial independence for a year or two and would probably have to live at home, next year, which would be bloody awful!

Thanks for the suggestion about Meg, but you don't seem to realize that I'm not going to be one of those artistic dabblers, on the contrary, I am all set for a continuance of scientific pursuits.

You were quite right, it was not difficult to discover that I was slightly neurotic as a result of seven weeks of repression. Your fears are groundless, however, so disperse them from your frigid couch. I am no longer suffering from a sense of sin or a sense of my own importance (same thing, according to Cabell) but have learned after divers buffeting to be, as you say, more unobtrusive. I also discovered in the course of my psychological reading, that I am not homosexual, but bi-sexual, a condition very common, apparently, among the Greeks—Plato and Socrates, etc. It was not then considered, and probably is not essentially abnormal at all, but has come to be considered so for reasons which would be interesting to find.

But be of good cheer, for I am, even to your discerning eye, in no way abnormal, and having a rather jolly time in the first rush of being home.

P.S. Did you know a cynic is a place where you wash the dishes? (not quite up to Paul). I am learning the wisdom of madness but the catch is, it's difficult to be mad while alone—Paul does. You know, it's awfully hard for me living alone. I'm not really asocial—quite the opposite, once my inferiority complex is overcome. So I continue to be scarcely ever alone.

I have the same fear of your Italian school as you have of London society (your mother read me your letter), so do you not understand my reticence? I quite agree with your father about getting your degree—it's good discipline for you to return here for another year, before becoming a pure *litterateur,* or companion of Meg in Jewish and Negro little theatres.

Farewell for the present.

By my fourth year we were friends again, but on a different level. You had left home and were living in rooms at the Old Elm on Harbord Street. This was a "tea-room" frequented by the students of Trinity College—the red-brick men's residence across the street. In this curious way you and I, Gina, moved for the first time with the same crowd. Literary and political discussions, chianti parties, sleigh-riding on moonlit snowy nights when we sang to the jingling of the horses' bells—these were some of the delights. By now you had broken with your lesbian circle and were ready to take on the men. Alas for Dee! For as soon as there seemed to be a young man interested in me, the time came to introduce him to you. And there was no way I could be your rival. You were like a rocket among candles: lithe, sinuous, graceful you had become now. Your pale silver-gold hair worn longer than a bob, your brown eyes the colour of a river in sunlight, your rose-petal skin: how do I find the words to describe the young woman you had become? You were avid for love and sex and you thought of me as a sister in whom you could always confide. I think that you were simply not aware of how you were hurting me. I think that just to look at you, and then to hear you talk, the young intellectuals frequented the Old Elm. There were two young Englishmen constantly in that orbit: Frinkie (Frank Grimble) and his pal J. K. Thomas. There was Victor Lange, headed for an academic career, and Gilbert Murrell-Wright for whom I had had a secret passion in my second year and who was now publishing the *Privateer,* the first literary magazine on the campus. Most significant was the introduction I had, through my French professor, Felix Walter, to his friend Otto van der Sprenkel. As I remember it, he had come from Holland to teach in the Department of Economics. A bearded, heavily spectacled man of the world, he held seminars on life in the Soviet Union, to which I was invited. After the sessions he would invite some of us to his apartment to listen to music, talk politics, play poker. Eventually, I brought you along to meet him, and while I browsed amongst his books (discovering T. S. Eliot for the first time) Otto entered into a sophisticated repartee with you. I knew what would happen: soon you were staying the night.

Although these "steals" pained me, they did not create a rift between us because by now we were having a lively social and intellectual life, of which we had been starved in our early university years. Otto, by introducing us to wide areas of knowledge about Marxism, socialism, and communism, increased our thirst for travel. He was very convivial and open with students—unlike any professor we had met at the University of Toronto (except, perhaps, E. K. Brown and Barker Fairley). Otto was a teddy-bearish and loveable sort of guy. But he was quicksilver. He did not really care, I think, who his woman was. And when you and he did go to Europe that summer he ended it by leaving you in Paris, alone. Do you remember how devastated you were? You cabled and telephoned from France, frantically. "Dee, you have to come to Paris and help me!" I had been having a continual battle with my parents that summer because, with my sister, Sophie, I was running a coffee-shop near campus "in order to make money to get to the Sorbonne for a post-graduate year." Instead of waiting until October, I now wanted to go in August, to be with you. My father had already agreed to give me the Paris year if I would study for the *Diplôme d'études supérieures;* but he had been enraged by the coffee-shop project. It was my mother who persuaded him that I might have a nervous breakdown if I didn't go to my friend's support. She offered me the ship's fare, Cunard Line, from her own savings as a free-lance writer, and so I went.

Thus began another chapter of our loves and rivalries.

It is difficult for me to write about our reunion in Normandy. A journalist friend of my father's, Mrs. Josephine Hambleton, had recommended an auberge at *Arromanches-les-Bains.* We were to spend a week or more walking around the countryside, visiting museums, exploring the French way of life until such time as I would get myself enrolled at the Sorbonne in the Department of Comparative Literature (where Professor Louis Cazamian held sway). But now you and I found it really hard to relate to each other. That summer, while you had been travelling through Germany and Spain as the mistress of a brilliant, youngish professor, I had stayed in Toronto to run Charlotte's coffee shop with the help of my sister, Sophie. True, I had by then met up with a new group of friends—young newspaper people. With one, I had

my first affair. Though I was not in love with him, I felt a strong sense of friendship with him. He was twenty-seven and ready to settle down. I certainly was not ready.

Otto's abandonment of you was cruel indeed. In your panic when you had phoned me long distance, you had asked me for Tony's Paris address. You had already met this student friend of mine while staying with Otto in Barcelona. Alone in Paris you contacted him again and began exploring museums and art galleries through his very perceptive eyes. Indeed, his exuberance and wit had been sufficient to rescue you from your depression, so that by the time I arrived in September you had put thoughts of Otto aside. You were still, however, in a very uncertain frame of mind, with fluctuating moods from despair to hilarity. I remember long walks through Normandy fields, fleeing from bulls; never really bridging the gap between our differing views on life-styles. Actually, we became just plain bored with rural touristing and decided to get back to Paris soon. There we found the hotel where Tony was staying and spent a week or more living the café and boulevard life: three most innocent, though not virgin, Canadian students.

You and Tony seemed to be good friends—your wit made sparks fly at every meal. But between Tony and me a growing attraction (which had begun back in Canada) now fanned our maturing sexuality. One evening I felt ill and at my lowest ebb of hope for the future. I left the two of you and went to my room to break loose and have a sobbing fit. I knew I was in love.

You were concerned. You came to sit at my bedside. "What's the matter? What's the matter, Dee?" And I finally blurted it out: "It's just so crazy. Such a weird cycle. Grant is in love with me and I am in love with Tony and he is in love with you and you are in love with Otto!" You denied this vehemently, "It's not true. It's perfectly obvious that Tony is in love with you."

I didn't think you really believed it, but of course I wanted to believe it. Did you at that point decide on action on my behalf? Much later that night there was a rap on my door. It was Tony, in pyjamas and dressing-gown. We caressed, passionately; but were still too shy to do other than lie down side by side and whisper our love.

Next morning, I went to your room to share *le petit déjeuner* and found you in bed, raving feverishly. You had swallowed half a bottle of aspirin.

O Terror! To be in a strange country, knowing nothing, no one, let alone how to find a doctor. I rushed up to Tony's room and somehow he, who spoke excellent French, found out by telephone how

*Dorothy, on her return to Toronto
from the Sorbonne, 1932*

and what to give as an emetic. Trembling, we prepared a mustard drink and made you swallow it.

Oh Gina! From what depths of despair and loneliness did you do such a thing? Tony and I were now closer than ever before, working to save you. And yet—perhaps it was only a token, a dramatic gesture on your part? Perhaps you had not swallowed all those aspirins? We were too distracted really to find out. In a day or so you had recovered and we took you to the *Gare St. Lazare* to catch your train to *Le Havre* and the voyage home.

Tony felt he could not bear to return to his third university year. He could do as I had done two years before, getting leave from the University of Toronto to take his third year modern languages in Paris. That was how we came to set up housekeeping together on *Boulevard St. Germain*, in the sixth-floor two-roomed flat. In between love-making and eating in cheap restaurants on the *Boul Mich* (remember the automats?) we started in seriously to work at our diplômes. A wonderfully happy and stimulating time, isolated though it was from friends and colleagues.

We looked forward to that Christmas, 1931,

because you and Jinnie, another student journalist friend of mine, decided to come to France for the holidays. That meant one week in Paris and twenty days at sea! How we were overjoyed to greet you on the station platform. "We're married!" I whispered to you. "Not *really?*" "No," I laughed, "Not really." You have described my changed self with your usual acumen:

> Then later her sex life took a fine upswing
> and she had a wonderful year in Paris. This
> was really very satisfying and she blos-
> somed, she just blossomed.

It is true that I had blossomed, but it was also true that my sexual needs were stronger than those of my partner. So the tensions grew if we were together too long—as on weekends. But we did begin to take a great interest in the French political scene. Tony was constantly reading Marx and Engels and applying their theories to the current collapse of the capitalist system; unemployment, strikes, and the build-up towards war—Hitler's goose-stepping youth. We read *L'Humanité* daily and began to go to rallies of the Left, and to witness police brutality against the organized workers. On the five-mile parade commemorating the Paris Commune I heard for the first time the voices of young *blouses bleues*, chanting their Brechtian slogans, songs, and skits. Although I was writing love poems at the time, my social conscience was roused. I felt that a poem must speak more about the times. My first longer effort was entitled *Père-Lachaise*, the great Paris cemetery where the 1871 martyrs are buried. But in between these emotional highs we were both working doggedly at our Sorbonne theses.

Before the winter was over we decided to live separately again. Tony, I had discovered, did not want an adoring, mothering love-mate. He thought I should learn to "stand on my own pins." I know he was right, but at the time I could not accept an independent feminist role. I was still in the romantic throes of the clinging-vine myth. Fortunately, perhaps, the demands of our research kept us parting and meeting that spring. I had to do a stint of research on the Sitwells at the British Museum, staying in London with a Livesay aunt. Tony's daily letters came boating across the Channel. Then, he had to take off for Italy. By the time he returned to Paris I had moved into a modern flat at the *Porte D'Orléans.* It was rented by two sisters from Montreal, Andrée and Yvette Levy. The third sister, Simone, was in student housing, for she was studying art. Tony returned from the south, not a little jealous of my new milieu, my growing independence, and my socializing with the Levys' friends—mostly Canadian artists and graduate students like Leon Edel. For our last month in Paris, May–June, Tony persuaded me to return to him. This time we found a suite far from the student world, on the east side, the working-class area of Ménilmontant. At home, writing our theses, we saw no one but ourselves. For that short time it was blissful rather than claustrophobic. I had a scare about being pregnant, but happily the French birth-control system we had adopted, a small white cone inserted beforehand, had fulfilled its function. We were still deeply devoted when we set sail for Canada, bearing high marks from the Sorbonne. (Cazamian even wanted me to stay on and do a Doctorat d'Etat.)

But at home in Canada, as you, Gina, were finding out, the Depression had struck and there were no more funds available from parents for student travel. We had made it, just by the skin of our teeth!

That was a stormy summer, back living with my parents at Woodlot, or staying alone part of the week in their Toronto house, 20 Rosemount, near St. Clair.

Tony invited me to stay at his parents' summer cottage in Muskoka, but the visit was not a success. I did not know how to handle his relationship to his mother. She clearly disapproved of his moodiness and urged me to cater to his wishes and to "coax him

Gina (standing at left) with the Workers' Theatre troop, 1933 (Photograph courtesy of the Archives and Special Collections Department, University of Manitoba)

around." Impossible role! Although I was seeing beautiful northern lake country in fine summer weather, I wasn't good at swimming or canoeing; and my menstrual period prevented any love-making (we believed). The rift widened.

Where were you that summer, Gina? I had not found you in Toronto. You must have been working at the children's welfare camp in Bolton? But by late August we all got together again, this time in an entirely new environment with a new set of goals. We became members of the Progressive Arts Club, meeting in an upstairs room near the Toronto Art Gallery, Grange Park. You, with Toby and Oscar Ryan, were in the theatre section; I was in the writers' group chaired by Ed Cecil-Smith, later of the Mackenzie Papineau Battalion fame. There I learned how to write *agit-prop* for the magazine *Masses.* We were by now firmly attached to the party line and adamantly rebellious against our parents and their conservative views. You and I decided to share a flat over a store at Charlotte and College Streets, close to the university. You would be finishing a year in psychology and I was enrolled in Toronto's new School of Social Work. But before Christmas I had to face the fact that Tony had definitely broken off our relationship. You didn't put obstacles in my way, Gina, when in my misery I gave up living in our flat, and went back to my parents' house on Rosemount. I scarcely saw you any more and only my studies in social work and my new friendship with Maysie Roger saved me from doing more than consider suicide. For I was still desperately trying to see and talk with Tony—only to discover that he was having an affair with you. I did not get over what seemed a terrible betrayal on both your parts—until in the autumn of 1933 I left Toronto and went with Maysie to Montreal, to work in a Protestant family welfare bureau as an apprentice case worker.

There we were thrust into the depths of the Depression under its most repressive regime in Canada: Montreal's unemployed in daily confrontation with Tachereau and the laws of R. B. Bennett's Section 98. This experience was the most traumatic of my life up until then, but one I could no longer share with you. As far as I was concerned I was by then an active militant out on the picket line, writing and delivering leaflets, writing and reciting chants. That was the year when I was promoted from the Young Communist League to membership in the Communist Party. One of many like-minded young people who wanted to build the movement against war and fascism. The policy in 1934–35 was still that of the United Front of workers and progressives from the middle-class, and being one of the latter I was chosen to contact organizations such as the YMCA, YMHA,

George Freeland

From the Toronto Star, *February 28, 1936: "The Theatre of Action presentation,* Waiting for Lefty, *was well received in Margaret Eaton Hall last evening. The play which is directed by Miss Jean Watts (above) will continue this evening and Saturday night."*
(Photograph courtesy of the Archives and Special Collections Department, University of Manitoba)

church groups, welfare groups, with a view to setting up a youth peace movement in Canada. When I returned to Toronto in June 1934, I met you again and we talked politics, without rancour.

By now you had married Lon, a man your own age with the same political beliefs. Together you were on your way to live for the winter in New York. Meanwhile I spent the summer months engaged in the same activist directions as before, but with the added sort of experience as organizer-secretary for an office and shoe salesman's union. The Worker's Unity League slogan was "Organize the Unorganized." However unsuited I likely was for such work, I undertook it for the summer, having planned also to go to New York and look for a job in social work. My plan worked. With my union card safely in my pocket, I landed in the great city by bus and made haste to your place. The apartment was in Chelsea, a few

doors away from the offices of the *New Republic,* at that time a favourite journal of left-wing intellectuals. From the windows it was possible to see its much admired literary editor, Malcolm Cowley, striding past on his way to work. While in New York, you were studying acting and directing with Elia Kazan, Clifford Odets, John Garfield, and other luminaries of the Group Theatre. This experience you used in helping to found the Theatre of Action on your return to Toronto and to direct its first production: Odets's *Waiting for Lefty.*

This was the last time, I think, that you and I and now Lon were in complete agreement about the role we had to play in combating fascism and the outbreak of war in Spain. In those days intellectuals were made to feel needed; we felt ourselves to be a part of a world-wide struggle. For me this had its focus in the small town of Englewood, New Jersey, where I found employment for the next year as a case worker in a community neighbourhood house. Most of our clients were *coloureds,* from the south, as were two of the social workers themselves. My eyes were opened to the agonies of racism—a story of its own which I felt compelled to record the next year in the poem "Day and Night." I wrote it on my return to Woodlot in Clarkson the winter of 1935.

In the meantime, much had been going on in left circles in Toronto. You were now something of an heiress, having reached the age when your grandfather's money could be released for your living expenses and for literary projects. With great zeal and enthusiasm for the United Front, you and Lon started a monthly magazine which was intended to rally middle-class intellectuals in Canada, as did the Left Book Club in England and *New Masses* in the United States. The result was a co-operative effort, *New Frontier,* a monthly journal to the left of the *Canadian Forum* and aimed at teachers, social workers, writers, and artists. Even reading it today, we would have to admire its lively content of informed opinion. And you, Gina, were already a correspondent from Spain. You had left Canada at this time to go with Dr. Bethune to Spain, where you drove an ambulance, at first for his Blood Transfusion Unit and later for the Mackenzie-Papineau Battalion.

But in 1935–36, with Spain being murdered by Franco, working for that magazine gave me my first real opportunity to see myself in print, speaking out on the ills of the Depression. I travelled west, through Manitoba, Saskatchewan, and Alberta to British Columbia, writing documentary reports about strikes, lock-outs, demonstrations by the unemployed. All during those years I was in the main writing prose: fiction and journalism.

Well, as you know, I never returned east to live. As a government-employed social worker in Vancouver I married an unemployed Scot: Duncan Macnair, who had been helping me sell subscriptions to *New Frontier.* He was thirteen years older than me and a longtime friend of A. M. Stephen, the Vancouver "people's poet" of the day. Both were ardent workers in the League Against War and Fascism. (Later it was named The League for Peace and Democracy!) When we learned that Duncan would have a much better chance of getting an accountant's job if he was a married man, we decided to marry, on August 14, 1937. Sure enough, in three months time he had a job and as soon as the Department of Health and Welfare heard about it, they fired me! In the thirties, a married woman in the professions could never be hired if her husband was employed. This was true of teachers, nurses and social workers. It was a blow to my self-respect, my feeling that a woman was a human being having equal rights with a man to be a person. You had an independent income and when the war came along you threw yourself with great enthusiasm into the Women's Army.

Nineteen thirty-eight must have been the watershed of our youth. What we had worked for and dreamed it could lead into was a decade without war, without dictatorship, when man's urge for power and destruction might be curbed for good. Instead, the scene was dominated by Mussolini, Franco, Hitler,

The Macnairs—Duncan and Dorothy
(Photograph courtesy of the Archives and Special Collections
Department, University of Manitoba)

and Stalin. You will remember, Gina, the tension of that year when all across Canada the forces of left and right were lining up, not for unity, but for power. Magazines like *New Frontier* folded, the United Front collapsed and in my seaport town, Vancouver, the Progressive Arts Club and the West End Community Centre, which we had built up in the old bathhouse at English Bay, were in disarray. This is not the place to re-argue the validity of the Party Line, Chamberlain's appeasement of Hitler, whether we should vote "Peace" or take a stand, a war if necessary, to stop fascism. I remember well that in August and September of 1939, you came out west on a speaking tour and stayed with Duncan and me on Pendrell Street, near Stanley Park. There were violent disagreements between us, but, now, in my seventies, I cannot remember which sides we took! For when the phoney war ended, when Stalin and Churchill formed their united front, when in Canada our friends and comrades were released from jail, we were all in favour of stopping Hitler.

Lon, who had become quite ill in the Don Jail, was released to join the army and you joined the CWACs. I stayed at home, with a son born in 1940 and a daughter in 1942. So our lines of communication were broken for many years. Until, in the sixties, after Lon had emerged from university as a psychiatric social worker, you moved with your adopted children to Victoria, British Columbia.

Our lives criss-crossed, but never with the old intimacy. I admired the way with which you devoted your life to the Ban-the-Bomb antiwar campaign of the sixties and in supporting the Voice of Women movement. Yet it was ironic that your fighting spirit and aggressiveness hardened—all in the cause of peace! You were hard to live with, Gina, and hard on your own heart. You died too soon.

Today, in my seventies, it seems only fair that you, who knew me so intimately, who gave such impetus to my early poetry-making, should have the final word. Here it is, as told to Charlie Boylan:

> You couldn't possibly compare Canada in the 30s with Canada in the 60s. This continent is untouched by any real kind of political conflict, just like it's untouched by any kind of war. We're innocents. Brecht was doing a political act. He was really involved in the Folk Theatre. If you are just writing poetry, you're not involved in this way. So I don't think Dee was terribly interested in political theory. I don't think she's got that kind of mind, that kind of interest. She was interested in people. And

Gina and Lon Lawson at Woodlot, about 1935

this is the thing about Africa: she wasn't terribly interested in the politics of Zambia or what kind of liberation movement was going on. It was how it affected the individuals that she knew. I think her interest is always a personal one. It has to be. You can't write poetry and have any other kind of interest. She is successful in her poetry mainly I guess because of the imagery. In most of her poetry she is not dealing with ideas, impersonal ideas, because she is not that kind of a poet. I don't remember it because there are ideas in it; I remember it because of the images.

And something of your old, stringent self, Gina, came out in these words:

I don't care if a person writes erotic poetry at a hundred. You don't read poetry thinking, "How old is the writer," do you? This is not the important thing. After all, if you had

to look at Dylan Thomas' face while you were reading his poetry, it would take away a good deal because he is horribly homely. But this is not important.

And in this question and answer session:

Do you think she represents the woman's point of view?

For me that's a rather meaningless generalization. I don't know what *the* woman's point of view is.

Well, then, a woman's point of view.

Well, obviously she represents *a* woman's point of view!

Take the love poetry at the end of her last book, do you identify with it, understand it?

Yes, certainly. But can't men identify with it, too? I mean, is love poetry so divided between the sexes? Such things are only significant to women? I don't think so, but then of course I'm not a man.

Not a man, my Gina. But with a toughness and intransigence that is still, in our age, attributed to the masculine. An uncompromising mind in a very sensitive and sensual frame. You, Gina, in the thirties and forties were the New Woman. Disagree as we did, your vibrant pace swung me along the same road.

BIBLIOGRAPHY

Poetry:

Green Pitcher. Toronto: Macmillan, 1928.

Signpost. Toronto: Macmillan, 1932.

Day and Night. Toronto: Ryerson, 1944; Boston: Bruce Humphries, 1944.

Poems for People. Toronto: Ryerson, 1947.

Call My People Home. Toronto: Ryerson, 1950.

New Poems. Toronto: Emblem, 1955.

Selected Poems, 1926–1956. Toronto: Ryerson, 1957.

The Colour of God's Face. Vancouver: Unitarian Service Committee, 1964.

The Unquiet Bed (illustrated by Roy Kiyooka). Toronto: Ryerson, 1967.

The Documentaries: Selected Longer Poems. Toronto: Ryerson, 1968.

Plainsongs. Fredericton, N.B.: Fiddlehead Poetry Books, 1969.

Disasters of the Sun. Burnaby, B.C.: Blackfish, 1971.

Collected Poems: The Two Seasons. Toronto and New York: McGraw-Hill Ryerson, 1972.

Nine Poems of Farewell, 1972–1973. Windsor, Ont.: Black Moss, 1973.

Ice Age. Erin, Ont.: Press Porcépic, 1975.

The Woman I Am. Erin, Ont.: Press Porcépic, 1977.

The Raw Edges: Voices from Our Time. Winnipeg: Turnstone, 1981.

The Phases of Love. Toronto: Coach House, 1983.

Feeling the Worlds: New Poems. Fredericton, N.B.: Goose Lane Editions, 1984.

The Self-Completing Tree: Selected Poems. Victoria, B.C.: Press Porcépic, 1986.

Fiction:

A Winnipeg Childhood (short stories). Winnipeg: Peguis, 1973; also published as *Beginnings: A Winnipeg Childhood*. Toronto: New Press, 1975.

Nonfiction:

Right Hand Left Hand: A True Life of the Thirties (miscella-ny), edited by David Arnason and Kim Todd. Erin, Ont.: Press Porcépic, 1977.

Editor of:

Collected Poems of Raymond Knister. Toronto: Ryerson, 1949.

Forty Women Poets of Canada, with Seymour Mayne. Montreal: Ingluvin, 1971.

Woman's Eye: Twelve B.C. Poets. Vancouver: Air, 1974.

Down Singing Centuries: Folk Literature of the Ukraine, translated by Florence Randal Livesay, edited with Louisa Loeb. Vancouver: Hyperion, 1981.

Plays:

Call My People Home (radio play), broadcast in 1949. Toronto: Ryerson, 1950.

Joe Derry. In *Eight Men Speak and Other Plays from the Canadian Workers' Theatre*, edited by Richard Wright and Robin Endres. Toronto: Hogtown, 1976.

Sound recordings:

A Winnipeg Childhood. 1975.

Films:

The Woman I Am. Montreal: National Film Board, 1982.

Robert Peters

1924-

AN AUTOBIOGRAPHY

Robert Peters in East Lansing, Michigan, 1987

Robert Turney

O n October 20, 1924, my birthdate, Eagle River was an impoverished Wisconsin town of some fourteen hundred people, situated in a spectacular area of fir trees, white birch and sugar maple forests, with thousands of freshwater lakes, many of them unnamed. Even then Eagle River was renowned for its sportsfishing, deer hunting, bars and taverns, and scenery. While most locals struggled for a living, the rich enjoyed summer homes on the most desirable lakes, inhabiting them only during the three short summer months before returning to Milwaukee, Chicago, and points south. A few summer

resorts flourished, appealing to a rich clientele served by the local citizenry. Since the town lacked any industry, the degree of winter want endured by the locals was in inverse proportion to the presence of tourists—the always unpredictable weather (semi-Arctic blasts might arrive as late as June) and the uncertain state of the fishing (muskellunge were the primary game fish, attracting visitors from all over the country) determined whether paying tourists would appear and stay for any length of time. The more tourists there were and the longer they stayed, the more money they spent and the easier winter would be. Most of the resorts were anti-Semitic, as was the town. Rich Jews, it was declared, dressed far too scantily, were noisy, wore too much makeup, seduced the local girls, and would shove you off your own sidewalk if they had a chance. Not until after World War II did "Restricted Clientele" signs disappear, declared illegal by federal and state laws.

My father, Sam Peters, aged twenty-one, brought my mother, Dorothy Keck Peters, aged seventeen, to Wisconsin in 1923. Dad was an itinerant farm laborer who worked for my mother's dad threshing wheat on their North Dakota farm. Dorothy, one of a family of four brothers and four sisters, on reaching sixteen was informed by her parents that she would either have to work or get married—the family was too poor to support her. Before that summer ended, Dad proposed, and shortly thereafter set out with his bride, in a Model T, for northern Wisconsin, where his brother Geshom had already settled and where his father had built a house from hand-hewn, stripped pine logs chinked with moss and plaster. Here I spent much of my childhood.

Dad's mother had died when he was two, leaving him to be raised by an older sister in a sod house built into the side of a North Dakota prairie hill. His dad, seldom home, off pursuing women and odd jobs, was eventually reduced to scavenging the residue of closed mines for scraps of coal to sell. Sam, at age seven, was left alone for days with nothing to eat but sourdough pancakes. He had less than two years of schooling, and because of his own scanty education, insisted from my earliest years that I must be educated, and avoid the serf-labor he endured. My mother's education concluded after a freshman year at a rural high school, the year she married.

Shortly after my birth (my mother had just turned eighteen), my maternal grandmother arrived to help. I had been named after Robert Louis Stevenson, and his *Child's Garden of Verses* was one of the three books we owned—the others were *Tom Swift and His Sky Train* and *Robinson Crusoe,* all gifts of my mother's youngest sister, Nell, who eventually stayed with us, completing high school in Eagle River, and assisting Mother with her two babies. My sister Marjorie arrived in September 1925. *Swift* and *Crusoe* bored me; I was never able to read either of them beyond the first few pages. My *Crunching Gravel* (Mercury House, 1988) is filled with details from these boyhood years.

My education began when I was three and learned the ABCs. I filled an entire fat pencil tablet with nothing but the alphabet for Santa Claus, thinking he would be pleased. I learned words from those ABC cards that came between layers of Shredded Wheat biscuits. I would copy the words onto scraps of paper bags, butcher paper, and old wallpaper sheets. During that year my mother arranged with the teacher of the local one-room country school to borrow all the first-grade primers. Before I turned four, in October 1928, I had so mastered the books that the teacher admitted me to first grade. For the remainder of my public-school years I was out of synch with students my own age.

Our incredible poverty was alleviated when Dad bought a cow and a pair of pigs; at least we were assured a regular supply of milk, and a certain amount of meat as the animals produced offspring. We supplemented the larder with venison (shot sometimes out of hunting season) and fresh fish from nearby lakes and streams. Yes, the diurnal rounds were cruel. Animals suffered and died to support our lives, and there were perpetual worries about where money would come from for clothes and food. I was always shy of guns, hated hunting, and showed none of the mechanical aptitudes my dad excelled in. To his enormous credit, despite his lack of education, he never teased or mocked me for being less the "boy" he might have hoped for. If I preferred to lie in a hammock reading my mother's *True Story* magazine, that was OK with him. And since I was late in learning to drive a car, he patiently drove me to town band rehearsals and to rehearsals of class plays, waiting for me, never with a complaint. On the whole, I was my mother's boy rather than my dad's. Thanks to President Roosevelt's programs, my dad had a job helping build roads for forty dollars per month, we received staple foods and clothing from Welfare, and the Home Owners' Loan Corporation made it possible

Robert's first years were spent in this log house built by his grandfather Richard Peters (center). Also pictured are the author's father, Sam Peters (left), and a friend, Les Brooks. Eagle River, Wisconsin, 1923

for us to buy forty acres of land near Minnow Lake, where Dad built us a new log home.

High school brought horizons. A very special teacher, Esther Austin, took an interest in me, coached me through orations, and arranged silently for my fighting a horrid self-consciousness. She was a quasi-mother, and only after I graduated did I realize that she had kept an ongoing journal, complete with charts and graphs to show my development. She submitted the journal to the University of Wisconsin and earned a master's degree.

During these years I had vague hopes of being a writer, and actually started a novel based on the Nazi destruction of the Czech town Lidice. Aesthete that I was, I believed that the execution of such a work must in itself be beautiful, so I procured an out-of-date wallpaper-sample book from a store in town and proceeded to write the first pages of *Lidice* via quill pen, avoiding the wallpaper designs whenever they were obtrusive. I managed no more than a score of pages before stopping, defeated by my ignorance of characterization. In my final scene a Nazi speared a baby on a bayonet.

During my senior year, I heard of Gertrude Stein and actually sent off to her publisher for *Ida* and later bought an old 78 recording of Virgil Thomson's opera *Four Saints in Three Acts.* I played the opera endlessly on our old windup Victrola and memorized chunks of *Ida,* which I spouted to any fellow students who would listen.

During this period my gifted dad interested me

Mother, Dorothy Keck Peters (age thirty-two), with her children: from left, Everett Louis (age nine), Nellie Emma (six), Marjorie June (twelve), and Robert Louis (thirteen), La Crosse, Wisconsin, 1938

Mays Photo Shop, La Crosse, Wisconsin

in playing guitar. He was a self-taught musician, adept at violin, accordion, mandolin, and banjo, and with a cousin, Charles Mattek, played at tavern dances. His plan was that I manage to strum a few obvious chords on a banjo guitar (no amplification then) and join them, earning a bit of extra money for school clothes. I also played bass horn in the high-school marching band, an instrument chosen for me by the instructor strictly on account of my size—I was 6 feet 2½ inches tall, and husky.

I graduated in 1942, and spent the year in Wausau, a city some sixty miles south of Eagle River, working for the Employers Mutual Insurance Company. My plan was to become a claims adjustor. I knew so little of college and university, attending seemed impossible—and there was always the problem of money. I performed tedious typing and filing chores at the company, until I was drafted into the army in the spring of 1943.

During basic training in South Carolina, I soon realized that I was inept at calisthenics, firing weapons, and the presentation of arms. Assigned to an infantry unit, the 422d Regiment, later destroyed at Bastogne in the Battle of the Bulge, my ineptitude at shooting a target, and climbing ropes hand over hand, earned me the worst position of all, carrying the baseplate in a mortar platoon. Curiously, though I was desperate to succeed as a soldier, I never ceased to flinch as I pulled the trigger of the M1 rifle, and with designs of becoming a Lutheran minister, had

real inner hassles over the issue of killing, which I was never able to resolve. I spent my months learning to play bass drum for reveille, training to be the company barber (men were "sentenced" to have my haircuts), and working on the regimental newspaper, the *Fighter,* a paper cooked up by a PR officer anxious to be promoted to corps headquarters.

Hours before we left for England in 1944, the company clerk surprisingly changed my MOS from rifleman to clerk-typist, an act which undoubtedly saved my life. In Europe, I found myself in a replacement-depot company processing men for the front. A second memoir, *The Turquoise Lake: A Memoir of World War II,* recently completed, reviews my three years in the military.

I still harbored notions of being a writer, though remained abysmally ignorant of how to go about it. While books were available through a marvellous series of paperbacks produced for servicemen, I was rarely able to complete reading a single novel, preferring biography and history. My lack of real curiosity was most manifest in my failure to cross Paris to one of the famous soirées Gertrude Stein held for GIs. I did though manage to sit in the front row at one of Marlene Dietrich's performances in Paris. I kept no journals, although I wrote triweekly letters home, all of which were thrown out by my family on one of their postwar moves.

Thanks to the GI Bill I enrolled at the University of Wisconsin–Madison, in the fall of 1946, and came within a single semester of achieving the Ph.D., government-paid. During those years Madison was in

Staff Sergeant Peters in Mussbach, Germany, with Replacement Battalion Headquarters, spring 1946

the full afterglow of the controversial president Glenn Frank, who had appeared from the East bringing hordes of New York intellectuals with him, changing the face of the university forever. Before Frank, Madison was a typical, stodgy Big Ten school; during and after Frank it was the most exciting, liberal, and innovative of all midwestern campuses. Appearing there as a culture-clod (my two years in Europe had done little to sophisticate me), and majoring in English (I chose literature over history, thinking that there would be fewer term papers to write), I was soon intimidated by bright students with an East Coast cultural veneer, both hating them and admiring them.

My circle of friends (most of whom were interested in writing) eventually included Easterners. I assumed postures as a "writer"; loved seeing Wisconsin author August Derleth appear in a local bookstore looking incredibly successful and huge-necked (and devoted to Wisconsin); liked knowing that now-forgotten, eccentric, agoraphobic sonneteer William Ellery Leonard breathed the same air; that Frederic Prokosch and the Lunts were Wisconsinites; and that Frank Lloyd Wright with acolytes dwelt nearby, some of his pupils writers. Yet, despite the writing workshops I took, I never completed any story on my own terms—I had not learned at all how to "feel" my own experience. And the poems I wrote were lousy imitations of Longfellow and Tennyson. Among the attitudes I shared with other students pretending to be writers was an inordinate fondness for Virginia Woolf and Truman Capote. To shock bourgeois students, who we assumed were everywhere, we'd appear in our tiny group in the student rathskeller, prominently displaying our copies of *To the Lighthouse* and *Other Voices, Other Rooms,* holding them to our chests like small shields, self-advertisements and warnings to the uninitiated to keep their distance.

My one serious writer friend of those years was Leonard Casper, now a professor at Boston College and a specialist in the work of Robert Penn Warren. Len was a Wisconsinite who was already publishing occasional poems and stories. Through his warm encouragement and example I first saw what real professionalism was. We were part of a serious writing group, meeting in apartments. I dropped my Capote and Woolf, and made my first really serious attempts at writing. Apart from a trio of bad Tennysonian poems, I published nothing during my undergraduate years.

Primarily because the GI Bill was so generous, I hastened my graduate work, eventually moving through the B.A., the M.A., and to the Ph.D. in six calendar years. My senior professor at Wisconsin, Jerome Buckley, urged me to take shortcuts, and I have always been grateful. I was anxious to make up for time lost in the army. In 1950 I married Jean Powell, a lady of much charm and talent who was also a teaching assistant, as I was. She had recently published a short story in *Harper's,* which earned many brownie points with me, and owned a temperamental Hudson coupe.

Our eldest son, Robert, now a biologist (via Stanford) with the North American Wildlife Foundation in Washington, D.C., was born the next September. A year later my daughter Meredith arrived. She is today a successful painter and a specialist librarian at the United Nations Library in Geneva, Switzerland. On earning my Ph.D. in 1952 with a dissertation on the "Interrelationship of the Various Arts in the English 1890s," I landed an instructorship at the University of Idaho. I typed out 250 letters that year, to colleges all over the country, for a job. This was the only opening, and luckily I managed to get it. Idaho was a disaster. I taught four sections of Freshman Comp, with around thirty students per class. The department was run by a pseudofascist who required that we keep nine-to-five hours on weekdays, and nine-to-noon on Saturdays. We could go to the faculty club for coffee, if we didn't stay too long. He hated poetry, so had abolished all foreign-language courses in same, as well as courses in English and American literature devoted to poetry. I found myself actively involved with the American Association of University Professors in trying to demote him—and found myself either having to move on or be fired. Again I wrote 250 letters, managing to secure the only possibility, at Boston University's College of General Education.

After two years in Boston, I was informed by the chairman that I would be fired because I "did not practice enough language of social cohesion," a bit of jargon he picked up from Hayakawa's *Language in Action,* in which he saw himself as an expert. My wife, knowing how sensitive this boob was to student criticism, wrote letters in different hands, etc., pretending they came from students threatening to strike if I were fired. This saved my job—and not until after our divorce years later did I realize what she had done.

Realizing that Boston was a dead end, we moved to Ohio Wesleyan, in Delaware, Ohio, a better school than Boston University, I felt, because of the reputations of Ohio liberal-arts colleges. As a young, naive instructor, I did not sense the feuds whirling through the years among the older faculty. I made friends with some of the outcasts among these warring, scarred folk, with the result that I was fired, much to my shock. The very person I was confiding in, a woman in charge of the comparative-literature program, a collector of swords and knives, turned out to be my nemesis. Further, I had helped to found a Unitarian group, and was informed by the president that letters had been received by townspeople and alumni protesting their paying "Christian" money to Unitarian "atheists." Didn't I know, I was asked, that there were four Methodist churches in Delaware, a town of ten thousand people; couldn't I find one of those churches to suit my tastes? As a teacher I was intolerant of slow students and confused teaching with preaching. We were encouraged by the scimitar-collecting lady professor above, who supervised us, to suspect all students. We became detectives sniffing out plagiarisms. When we found any overt examples, she quivered with joy and proceeded with the élan of a barbarian slaughtering a Roman.

After my first year at Wesleyan I decided to write novels, and imagined a long teaching life at Wesleyan teaching rote courses in literature and composition, freeing me to write long novels. I actually wrote one, ambitiously modelling it after *Moby-Dick,* on my dismal experiences at the University of Idaho. Since then I've rewritten the book a number of times, most recently this past year when I showed it to my agent, who was kind but not optimistic. "Joseph Lord" gathers dust in one of my obscure filing cabinets.

As a way of maintaining sanity, I took advantage of liberal faculty travel funds to attend summer writing workshops at Indiana University. I had been encouraged by Robert K. Marshall, a superb iconoclast and fine novelist teaching at Wesleyan. Apart from Marshall's friendship, no one else there was interested in creative work, and certainly not in talking about it. Gossip and conflict ruled almost every social gathering, and since my wife and I empathized with liberal voices fighting the religious conservatives running the school, we were always in trouble. There was no way I would have gotten tenure there.

John Selby taught the Indiana fiction workshops the first summer and actually gave a chunk of my "Joseph Lord" a prize. The following summer Jessamyn West was visitor, and she was most encouraging about a new novel I was writing about northern Wisconsin. I remember my outrage when the director of the session refused to give my new work an award since I had earned one the year before.

One of my lingering regrets is my inability over the years to write a successful novel. I have finished five, not one of them published. I can write good nature description and passable dialogue, but am out of touch with plot intricacies, pace. Still, someday . . . though I turn sixty-four in a few months, there may still be time.

When I knew I was to be fired at Wesleyan, I set about writing scholarly articles to get a job teaching in my field, Victorian literature. I managed to publish an essay on James McNeill Whistler and the poets of the 1890s in *Modern Language Quarterly.* Partly as a result of this essay, and the generosity of a splendid chairman, the musicologist, aesthetician, and critic Herbert M. Schueller, I was hired at Wayne State University and shortly given tenure. I was now a thorough academic. I wrote and published *The Crowns of Apollo,* a prize-winning book on A. C. Swinburne's critical theories; numerous essays and reviews, primarily on nineteenth-century figures; and at Herb Schueller's suggestion, coedited with him *The Letters of John Addington Symonds,* a project that grew out of Schueller's earlier critical study of the Victorian historian, poet, and sexologist. We spent some eight years seeing these massive three volumes into print. I was elected a trustee of the American Society for Aesthetics. At Wayne State I first received respect for my academic achievements, and remain grateful to the school, and particularly to Herb Schueller, a lifelong friend.

On February 10, 1960, my life changed drastically both personally and professionally. My second son, Richard, aged four and a half years, died suddenly of a one-day meningitis. He had attended nursery school in the morning. I fetched him home, and his only complaint was of a bellyache. My wife had a sixth sense that something was drastically wrong, despite there being no frightening symptoms. When she phoned Dr. Snyder he told her that she was being hysterical, that she should bring him in after the weekend, if he was still sick. Under the weather myself with a mild flu, I spent the day with him in bed, both of us reading. I was reading, of all things, Thomas Mann's *Magic Mountain,* a book I have never finished. At six o'clock I went downstairs to supper, leaving him asleep, so I thought. A strange noise. I hurried up to find white clots at his mouth and a series of blue crazes under his skin. Despite efforts by a resuscitation team (they whipped out his heart for massage) Richard was dead by the time we reached the hospital. Of my four children, he was the one with a body build exactly like mine, and had the coal black hair I had had as a child.

Unable to resolve my grief by any conventional religious or philosophical means, I began the very next day to write poems in so simple an idiom a child his age would understand them. The rhythms I heard

*Children Meredith, Robert II, and Richard at a wildlife
refuge near East Lansing a week before Richard's death*

were of my own anguish, punctuated by the Salvation
Army drumbeats I had heard in a pop song, "Waterloo," sung by Stonewall Jackson. I wrote a dozen or
more poems that day, weeping most of the time, the
hi-fi music so loud I could barely stand it. Nine
months later I retrieved the poems, read them, and
wrote more. I heard that W. W. Norton was now
publishing a series of poetry books, edited by Denise
Levertov. The result was my first published book of
poems, *Songs for a Son*, 1967. The splendid news, I
remember, arrived from Levertov on a postal card.
One critic saw the book as predicting a substantial
career as an academic poet—the poems are all well
formed and lyrical. My primary inspiration was Theodore Roethke; in fact, the original title was *Songs for a
Lost Son*.

We investigated a malpractice suit against Dr.
Snyder for his dismissing Richard's illness so summa-
rily, but after months of trying to find another
physician to testify against him we gave up. The
doctor at the hospital said that the only hope would
have been that if Richard had still been alive when he
came to Emergency, and if the doctor had suspected
what was wrong, he might have given Richard a
transfusion of his own blood, since it might have

contained effective antibodies. My wife's solutions to
the loss were these: have another child and/or adopt
one. When she became convinced that I was sterile
(I'd produced three children with no problems) I
agreed to adopt. The Detroit agency was not san-
guine, unless we were willing to take an older, abused
child. A fertility clinic found nothing wrong with me;
and on September 19, 1961, the very day we brought
a year-old daughter home for adoption, our third son,
Jefferson, was born. Issues were most complex; and
Amity (we'd changed her name from Cathy) never fit
in with our natural children. We did not now have a
happy family, and after our separation and divorce,
Amity was adopted by a surgeon and his wife, to be
eventually readopted by my former wife and a second
husband. Jefferson is now twenty-five, married to a
wonderful woman from Nagoya, Japan, and is writing
his Ph.D. dissertation on fantasy and science fiction at
the University of Michigan. Amity has married and
has a daughter of her own.

In 1963 I had moved from Wayne State to a
tenured position at the University of California,
Riverside, specializing in Victorian literature. My last
act on leaving Detroit was to bury Richard's ashes,
which I had kept in my study, under a beech sapling
(now an enormous tree) in the Birmingham Unitarian
Church yard. The minister assisted me, and one of my
strongest and, I think, best poems, "The Burial of the
Ashes," in *Songs for a Son*, records that experience.

My success with *Songs for a Son* led me to think that
perhaps I could write poems on other topics
and themes. Important also was John Ridland's
including me in his *Little Square Review* series. Fourteen of my poems were featured. In the meantime, I
was absorbed by rock music, experimented with
dope, and generally felt crazy, as many liberated folk
of the late sixties did. Furthermore, my marriage was
disintegrating, and I began to write in veiled terms of
my sexual frustration and anguish. The second book,
The Sow's Head and Other Poems (Wayne State University Press, 1968), was a mix of Wisconsin boyhood
visceral farm matters and more surrealist pieces
inspired by Rolling Stones lyrics and rhythms, the
latter style most prominent in *Holy Cow: Parable Poems*
(Red Hill Press, 1974). I was also rifting poems with
messages hoping to attract a male lover.

I now affected black cowboy boots, tight jeans,
and a leather jacket purchased at a gay department
store in San Francisco. I wore my hair long. One
evening in Los Angeles I was stopped by three police
cars on returning from Santa Monica, where I had
dropped off a professor friend who had gone to a film
with me. I was on my way to the San Fernando Valley

Jean and Robert Peters with Robert II (top), Amity, Meredith, and Jefferson, 1962

to spend the weekend with a student and his wife. I was handcuffed and taken by the police to a house in the neighborhood, floodlit, and identified by the inhabitant as the prowler who had tried to steal his car. The police would neither phone the professor (his name was Rousseau, as I recall) nor the student expecting me to verify my innocence. I was thrown into the tank at the Van Nuys jail on a felony charge. The filth was incredible, and I realized at once that you are indeed treated as a criminal the minute you are arrested, and that your guilt or innocence depends on how strong the case is against you. Rousseau, fearing for his reputation, I gather, refused to be "involved" or to testify for me if a trial were to occur. My own chair, Hazard Adams, generously bailed me out, and a lawyer eventually advised me to plead guilty. I had hired a special detective, who took a series of photos to the owner of the property accusing me of trespass; unfortunately, he picked my shot from the set, saying that he had spoken to me face-to-face across his fence for five minutes. Because I was a professor and had enough money to hire a lawyer, the attorney managed a "deal" with the judge: I pled guilty and received ten days probation. I was utterly innocent, but because of my now flamboyant life-style and the rampant homophobia during these months of student campus riots and late-gener-

ation flower children, I took the advice of my lawyer and did not go to trial. Needlessly to say, the experience was an omen, a warning, and I took fewer risks from that time on.

At California, Riverside, much of my energy was absorbed by department squabbles, many of them incredibly vicious and divisive, thanks to the neurotic, bullying temperament of the then mighty but now forgotten critic Frederick J. Hoffman. Hoffman, we found, was persecuting both students and faculty who disagreed with him in faculty meetings and in seminars. I was of the small band of professors demanding that he be removed from all positions of power in the department. We succeeded, and a livid Hoffman moved about the state to other campuses trying to destroy our professional reputations for having deposed him. The department divided between his supporters and the rest of us. Caucuses, presided over mainly by involved faculty wives, occurred almost daily, sometimes far into the night, examining the latest moves and gossiping. Hoffman "punished" us, so he maintained, by accepting a new position at the University of Wisconsin at Milwaukee. He was not there long, dropping dead of a heart attack the evening before his favorite organization, the Modern Language Association, met for its yearly meetings. Much of my residue of idealism about professors, what had not been lost through older faculty machinations at Boston University and Ohio Wesleyan, now disappeared. And yet I greatly admired the courageous stands taken by Herbert Lindenberger and Donald Howard during these painful months.

Among the bright spots were my friendships with Lindenberger and Howard, both of whom eventually moved to Stanford University, Howard as a major Chaucerian, Lindenberger in comparative literature. During the UCR days, Howard was writing poetry, as I was, and he met with me weekly to read and talk over what we had written the preceding week. Lindenberger was writing plays, and we shared long talks and mountain climbs regaling one another with our creative plans. Ben Stoltzfus, of the French department, was writing novels, and shared enthusiasms; our two families went on diving and fishing trips to Mexico.

Also, Christopher Isherwood taught for a full year as a Distinguished Visiting Professor, and I got to know him well. He seemed to love the endless round of parties hosted by the more ambitious faculty wives, avid to capture such a literary giant. The generally homophobic atmosphere at Riverside did not interfere at all with such lionizing. On one occasion, he invited me to dinner in Santa Monica and, while never proselytizing for a gay life-style, enabled me to see that normalcy in male partnerships was possible. I am one of many men whose lives were so touched and strengthened by that generous, gentle, and courageous man.

Also, at UCR a group of us met weekly in one another's homes to share writing. Kathy Kranidas, Ada Schmidt, and my wife were the prime movers. Milton Miller, who for years almost alone among senior professors had fought for poets and fiction writers, was generally in disfavor with his colleagues; yet, he was an inspiration to hosts of students, and was seen as our best undergraduate teacher, something, again, that Hoffman and cohorts dismissed as irrelevant to their own pursuit of what they referred to as UCR's "national visibility." One benighted academic proclaimed that to have a poet or fiction writer on the staff would demean that professional image. Much of the *Sow's Head* was written and first tested at Riverside.

My long years of teaching lead me to conclude that the more stifling and horrid the school you teach in, the greater the efforts of the few gifted people there to try to breathe and live; UCR was one of the worst. There I first met James Dickey, who, then relatively unknown, was teaching at San Fernando Valley State College and appeared for a reading. I was to introduce him. He was the first real profession-

al to see any of my work. I had shown him the Wisconsin farm poems and a few from the elegy for Richard. He embraced me, saying that I didn't know how original I was. That sparked me, and I decided more than ever to devote myself seriously to poetry. I began also to publish poems in literary magazines; among the first were the *Fiddlehead*, *Ante*, and *Prairie Schooner*.

About this time, 1967, Herb Schueller sent me Charles Bukowski's beautiful Loujon Press volumes, now much-prized collector's items. I recall taking *Crucifix in a Deathhand* to a string-quartet concert. As I read, my brain seemed to fly. I had never imagined such liberating poetry—a style seemingly so casual, yet containing so much profundity and beauty. That book, and Robert Creeley's *For Love*, more than any others at the time changed my writing. I now heard cadences quite other than those I had absorbed from Roethke.

I had first heard of Bukowski on a visit to Carl Weissner in Heidelberg, Germany. Carl was then beginning to translate and to represent American Beat writers. One morning a sizeable cardboard box arrived from Charles Bukowski, much of it containing Buk's early books and numerous racing forms with pictures by the author scribbled over them. Carl had purchased these for a German dentist who was assembling an archive of Happening and Experimental art. I accompanied Carl when he delivered the trove. I did not then read Bukowski, but the name registered, and Herb Schueller's gift of the Loujon Press books seemed like an omen for my own work. At the dentist's I first saw Diter Rot's work, and was amused by a collection of "book sausages" hanging from the archive ceiling. The collector had shredded novels by leading German novelists (I remember one by Günter Grass) and stuffed them into sausage casings, pasting the title page on the outside, and hanging the book-sausages as you might find them in a butcher-shop window.

After a Guggenheim spent in Cambridge, England, in 1966–67, where I went to finish a second book on Swinburne, this time on his poetry, I developed friendships with an assortment of young British poets: Peter Jay, Douglas Oliver, Andrew Crozier, John James, and a group of undergraduate poets influenced by Ezra Pound and William Carlos Williams. I walked in the Lake District with Douglas Oliver, later publishing *Connections: In the English Lake District* (Anvil Press, London, 1972), about a harrowing afternoon above Lake Windermere when we were caught in an incredible lightning and hail storm. My study of Swinburne, an *explication de texte* fashionable then, has not been published, except for a small portion on the poet's Impressionism. Swinburne is one of those rare poets in whom there is no real development; he was as good at the end of his career as he was at the beginning. By taking half a dozen major poems from different portions of his long career, and by considering them in detail and writing about their similarities and differences, I could illuminate his entire career. Readers for various presses not only opined that the fashion for explication had passed, but that after my well-received *Crowns of Apollo* they expected me to write about more of the poetry. I still feel the book is good, although I have long since stopped trying to find a publisher.

My most influential English friendships were with Andrew Crozier and John James. Crozier invited me with him to his family place in Hastings for several days, which fascinated me, for this was the city in which John Addington Symonds married. I visited the church and explored other parts of the city frequented by Symonds. I spent many hours with James, who resembled a hunky, incredibly handsome Welsh teddy boy, on long walks from Cambridge to Ely and environs. He was writing a lot, and we shared work. I was in love with him, and behaved in silly fashion, eventually finding my conflicting feelings almost unbearable. I'm sure James felt I was a dope. During one particularly harrowing day, on which we had planned to go on a camping tour of the Highlands in my VW bus, he failed to show up at the appointed time. I found out later that his wife had had to be hospitalized. I felt I was cracking up, and walked Cambridge from one end to the other, passing his favorite pubs, reading *Paterson* at the top of my voice. These lines I chanted over and over: "Love is no comforter, rather a nail in the skull." The process of reading helped, and by the time I returned home I felt better; the crisis passed. Something, though, had drastically changed; on returning to the States, I knew I would have to pursue the freer professional and sexual life I had fantasized and ached for.

The following summer, a former student of mine, Gary D., accompanied me to Europe, where I had gone to give a series of lectures at various German universities and America Houses. Gary was a lanky, strange, handsome youth who was meditating suicide as a way out of homosexual struggles. Like many in his generation, he was steeped in pot and LSD. He fascinated me, and I guess I saw in him much that was positive and free that I should have experienced when I was his age but didn't. When my wife returned to England that May to pursue a friendship with an Englishman she had met during

Peters, on a trip with Gary, boarding a canal boat in Amsterdam, 1968

the Guggenheim year, Gary moved in with me. Just after my wife's return, I took Gary to Europe.

His presence in Europe aroused distaste in the American directors of a couple of America Houses: their report to the Germans in charge was that I had lectured well but they wished I hadn't brought my "young friend" with me. This guaranteed, so I found out from the Germans in charge of the visitors' program, that I would never again go abroad sponsored by the U.S. State Department. My primary goof on that elaborate lecture tour was to mistake the day of the lecture on Williams and Whitman at the University of Berlin. I had the appointment clearly in mind for the next morning, so decided to visit East Berlin. When the professor in charge phoned my hotel and found out where I was, he assumed I had been kidnapped or otherwise detained by the Communist authorities. Needless to say, I was incredibly embarrassed, and my hosts acted with great style. Though regretting that the nearly three hundred students assembled for the seminar were not fed, they insisted on paying my substantial fee. Rarely does my mental time clock so let me down. I've learned since to reinforce it by keeping a meticulous calendar.

During a two-week interlude in the Eifel mountains, I managed to write a pop play, *Fuck Mother,* inspired by *Zap Comix*, Warhol films, and Mick Jagger's lyrics. The work was actually produced by the Cubiculo theater in New York during March and April 1970, directed by Philip Meister, with plans to take it uptown to a larger theater. This was one of those frustrated dreams which might have transpired had I lived in New York and not on the West Coast. Because of the title, only the *East Village Other* would take an ad, using asterisks for "Fuck." One reviewer said I should have my mouth washed out with soap.

After the excursion with Gary to Europe, I knew that my marriage was over, and on returning I moved from home and waited for a legal separation to finalize as a divorce. By selling my sizeable collection of Victorian criticism (I was planning a book on the subject) I managed a down payment on a house and a pair of rental units in Laguna Beach. *Cool Zebras of Light* (Christopher's Books, 1975) celebrated that summer, and is long out-of-print, the remainder of the books destroyed in a Santa Barbara fire that burned out the publisher. Gary had some ability as a poet. His problems with alcohol and drugs, I realized, would prevent us from ever living together. We agreed that we would still see one another, but would live our lives independent and free. One afternoon I drove to Riverside, where he was living, to take him to the Angelus mountains. When he failed to appear as agreed, I phoned the library at the university, where he had been working, and learned that he had shot himself the preceding Sunday. He chose a nearly inaccessible part of the mountains above March Air Force Base, and directed that a unit of young servicemen go up to retrieve him, which is what happened. When, by his direction, a trunk full of his letters and other objects were delivered, I found many letters filled with frustration and pain written to me but never sent.

After the publication of *Songs for a Son* and *The Sow's Head* I sought as many public readings as possible, particularly in the East, to make my work better known. My first break came shortly after *Songs for a Son* appeared, when I was invited to share an evening in the prestigious Guggenheim series with Galway Kinnell, on October 10, 1967. Betty Kray's audio system did not work that night, so my reading was not taped. She said she'd have me return to make the tape, but she never did. Asked what poet I would most like to read with, I had named Dickey and Kinnell. Kinnell was available, and his *Body Rags* was an influence on me at the time.

I went on reading tours whenever I was asked. The energy was worth expending, for a number of publishers heard my work and published some of it.

Among the host of small presses I have had, only two have let me down, the West Coast Poetry Review and Jazz Press. I eventually had to take George Fuller, proprietor of the latter, to small-claims court to recover over five hundred dollars he failed to return to me after reneging on a joint publishing venture. The judgment was in my favor, but Fuller still refuses to repay me. Some publishers, like Peter Schneidre's Illuminati, are months, or even years behind time. Others, like Unicorn Press and Cherry Valley Editions, keep their promises and meet their deadlines.

Readings now are more difficult to arrange than they were then, the readers now most in demand being in their forties or younger, and having credentials from some visible MFA writing program or such conservative journals as the *American Poetry Review*, the Wesleyan Series, or the trade presses. Like the reading circuits, most of today's anthologies are shamelessly ageist.

A major event in my life occurred on Sunday, November 1, 1970, with the appearance of Paul Trachtenberg. I had walked from my Laguna house to the beach early that morning, and near the boardwalk, wearing ripped jeans and no shirt, sat this copper-haired, smiling Anaheim youth. We talked, and he came back to my house. With the exception of a couple of weeks shortly after that first visit, and when he and a friend, Dennis Huston, were living in one of my back rental units, Paul has been with me. We have travelled back and forth across the country to Yaddo, the MacDowell Colony, and the Ossabaw Island Project—driving the whole route four times. We have visited England five times, and Australia and the Continent once. We have gone together on most of my readings and performances.

A few days after he moved in with me in Laguna, he started reading Marguerite Yourcenar's *Memoirs of Hadrian* aloud, underlining and later looking up all the words he didn't know. From that point he became an inveterate student of words, building a large vocabulary, and has come to write highly original poems. On one of our cross-country trips he memorized five hundred basic English vocabulary cards. He also read (and continues to read) philosophy and encyclopedias. His discovery of a brief encyclopedia entry for Elizabeth Bathory led to my writing *The Blood Countess*, reworking the poems as a play in which I have performed throughout the country. The latest of Trachtenberg's discoveries is John D. Lee, the Mormon martyr, who intrigues me, and who will probably figure in my next voice poems.

Paul has brought order and sanity into my life, and to date my eighteen-year "marriage" with him has outlasted my formal one with Jean Powell. With him I no longer feel driven to pursue anonymous lovers, and he has taught me how to be less smothering and possessive than I had been with other people. From the outset, he has had special insights, and is generally smarter on human behavior than I am. Over the years, he has developed into a fine poet. His intensive programs of self-study have resulted in some rare and original books: *Short Changes for Loretta* and *Making Waves,* from Cherry Valley Editions; and *Mercury Tea,* which is about to appear from Latitudes Press. And he has developed talents for the theater, working closely with me on the technical aspects of *Ludwig* and on *The Blood Countess,* directing the latter. He has helped considerably in coaching me in my acting.

Paul Trachtenberg, 1988

Paul's loving patience resolved much of the personal pain I wrote of in *Songs for a Son, The Sow's Head,* and *The Drowned Man to the Fish* (New Rivers Press, 1978). On my first fellowships to Yaddo and MacDowell, in the fall of 1973, I decided that I would write no more of suffering. Since I was no longer in pain, to keep writing as though I were was phony. I would celebrate life or stop writing. Therapy sessions also helped, and one encounter group, attended with

Paul, searingly let me know that I selfishly had held Richard's death to me as a badge of life's maltreatment. In the depths of yelling and kicking on that encounter-group mattress, I talked to Richard, finally letting go, feeling great release and loving him even more than I had hitherto. While this may sound too easy from the vantage point of these cool eighties, it did work, and I have maintained much healthier feelings for my dead son ever since.

One of my ideas for a new poetry was to write a book with the scope of a novel. The only problem: I had not yet found my subject.

Arriving a day early on our way to the MacDowell Colony, in trying to locate an overnight spot for our camper, we visited the Shaker Museum in Old Chatham. After a couple of hours I realized that here was the subject I needed—a verse life of Mother Ann Lee, the eighteenth-century illiterate English mystic and founder of the Shaker religion in America. I bought a life of the Shakers, which I carried to Peterborough. I started writing poems the very next day, and when a month was up, was amazed to find that I had written exactly a hundred poems, most of them in Mother Ann's voice. I took this as a good omen—and decided to keep the poems at that number. I had been able to psych myself into feeling the mystic woman's presence, and whenever I was written out, I took walks through the New Hampshire woods, revivifying her presence for new poems. These, of course, became *The Gift to Be Simple,* published by Liveright, under the editorship of Shaker enthusiast Ned Arnold, in 1975.

The book sold well, assisted by a positive review by M. L. Rosenthal in the *New York Times.* But, alas, Liveright was shortly bought by W. W. Norton, before my second book, continuing the Shaker experiment in America, could be published, a book I wrote the following year, at Yaddo, within a few minutes of Mother Ann's humble grave adjoining the Albany airport. I meditated often at the site.

Good things seemed about to happen. One of the Norton editors hosted me at lunch, saying they would publish *Shaker Light* plus the newest manuscript of all, *The Picnic in the Snow: Ludwig of Bavaria,* which he claimed to like even better than he did the Shaker books. He asked also if I would like to see the two Shaker volumes as a boxed set! Certainly! When, after a few months, no contract arrived, I phoned him. He asked me not to discuss our arrangements with George Brockway, the president of Norton, for fear he would lose his job. The bad news was that he must renege on the contract: they had apparently filled early orders for the paper *Gift* with cloth copies, and as a result, while the book broke even, it did little to contribute to the overhead—so that dream fizzled. It has taken several years, plus another reneging publisher, this time a small press, before the Unicorn Press, bless them, finally published *Shaker Light* this year. I am most grateful to Teo Savory and Alan Brilliant, devoted editors and publishers for the Unicorn Press, who have stayed with me longer than any other publisher; they will soon publish my fifth and sixth titles with them, *Haydon* and a new *Selected Poems.*

The Gift to Be Simple (1975) was my first ambitious treatment of a genre of verse biography and history that I have, I think, made my own. In addition to *Shaker Light* (1988), other voice books include *Hawker* (Unicorn Press, 1984), one hundred poems in the voice of an eccentric Cornish vicar, poet Robert Stephen Hawker, who was obsessed with dredging drowned sailors from the sea and burying them in his churchyard. He was also a poet, loved having animals attend his services, and played mermaid for his parishioners. *Kane* (Unicorn Press, 1985) is a voice portrait of the American explorer Elisha Kent Kane, who reached the Arctic in 1852. His ship froze fast in the ice off Greenland and never thawed free. Based on the explorer's journals, *Kane* delineates the experiences of that harrowing year and the return of the handful of survivors. An earlier edition, entitled *Ikagnak: The North Wind: With Dr. Kane in the Arctic,* appeared from Kenmore Press in 1978 in a limited, hand-set edition of one hundred copies, printed on imported paper and with aluminum-block prints designed by the publisher. *The Picnic in the Snow* (New Rivers Press, 1982; revised edition called *Ludwig of Bavaria: Poems and a Play,* Cherry Valley Editions, 1987), on the life of the pacifist, homosexual Bavarian monarch Ludwig II, who ruled Bavaria from 1864 to 1886, appears both as a book of poems and as a play. *The Blood Countess: Elizabeth Bathory of Hungary: Poems and a Play* (Cherry Valley Editions, 1987) recreates the life and psyche of the notorious Hungarian mass murderer who killed over seven hundred virgins and bathed in their blood as a way of preserving her youth. She was walled up in her castle in 1609. *Haydon,* based on the life of the gifted and eccentric early Victorian painter Benjamin Robert Haydon will be published by Unicorn Press in 1988.

Earlier works of mine anticipated these ambitious voice works: *Connections: In the English Lake District,* never published in America, is made up of collage poems, lyrics, and narrative pieces, juxtaposing some of Wordsworth's experiences in the Lake District with some of my own. *Byron Exhumed* (included in *The Poet As Ice-Skater,* Manroot Books, 1976)

employs parody and satire in monologues by persons who have just heard of Byron's death. In the title poem for my *Gauguin's Chair: Selected Poems* (The Crossing Press, 1977, out-of-print), Van Gogh confronts his agony over the violent rupture of his friendship with Gauguin.

Since 1968 I have been a professor of English at the University of California at Irvine, where I teach courses in contemporary poetry and Victorian literature. My current life divides into these primary areas: teaching; the writing of poetry, criticism, and reviews; and performing and acting.

I have written much criticism of contemporary poets, probably more than any critic writing today. My series of *Great American Poetry Bake-offs,* published by the Scarecrow Press, now run to four. To date I have written on over three hundred poets, some of them well known; most, however, are scarcely known in the mainstream literary world. It is these latter poets I most enjoy writing about and using whatever authority my critical writing has to call attention to their work. My other critical effort is my monthly column, "The Peters Black and Blue Guide," appearing in Len Fulton's *Small Press Review.* These pieces are collected, expanded, added to, and published as the *Peters Black and Blue Guides to Current Literary Journals.* The first two were published by Cherry Valley Editions; the third by Dustbooks. A fourth will appear shortly from Dustbooks. While I have offended some poets, I am sure, I would like to think that I have pleased and nourished more. Certainly, no contemporary critic seems as controversial as I am.

I began to write literary criticism in 1973, when Tom Montag invited me to contribute to his journal *Margins,* at the time the only periodical of its kind devoted primarily to reviewing small-press and little-magazine publications. Montag was a special editor, and once he approved of your writing, awarded you a free hand in choosing poets and saying what you wished to say about them. He once explained to me his editorial function as that of a collector and assembler. As a one-man publication, *Margins* eventually grew too all-consuming for even a man of Montag's energy and dedication. He remains an unsung saint of the small-press and little-magazine world.

I began writing critical essays primarily because of James Dickey, a poet and critic I have much admired for going it alone, without the blessing of coteries or conservative journal powerhouses. Before his seminal *Suspect in Poetry* appeared, published by Robert Bly's Sixties Press, Dickey's verse was little known. His *Suspect* contained brilliant criticisms, and I had the feeling that poets fearing he might review them found his poetry (in the Wesleyan Series) and read it, hoping that might avert his gaze from handling them roughly in his essays. In other words, his reviews and criticisms focused attention on the poetry. I have hoped for my critical writing to function similarly.

There is a danger, of course, that a poet can write too much criticism, that his readers may regard poetry as ancillary to the prose. With me, quite the opposite is true, and has been all along. I have belonged to no coteries, and see myself as an iconoclastic writer who has assumed that the prose would assist the poetry to make its way. I am no longer as certain of this as I once was, and I have now wound down my critical activity, in order to concentrate more on my own poetry and also on my performing and acting. I am also currently working on a series of memoirs. Well-meaning literary friends, thinking to be helpful, advise that if I were to trim my sails a bit and subdue my frank judgments, my poetry might be better known than it is. While it is true that I have received a Guggenheim, a National Endowment for the Arts fellowship, and the Poetry Society of America Di Castagnola Award (for *Hawker*), my work has seldom been represented in the anthologies and critical surveys of American poetry since World War II.

Since 1982 I have performed my chamber-theater version of *Ludwig of Bavaria* over a hundred times, presenting it before audiences in art galleries, coffeehouses, living rooms, and legitimate theaters both on campuses and off, throughout the country. This venture began as a lark, when editor and fellow poet Paul Vangelisti suggested we get a costume, fashion the poems as a stage piece, get a small theater, and see what would happen. Vangelisti had directed a prize-winning series of Pacifica Radio theater productions. I knew little or nothing about acting, beyond the dream that many of us have of being a stage and screen star; I had always wanted to be Clark Gable. I was too shy in college to proceed with an acting career. When, at last, at that initial performance in Los Angeles, at the Fifth Street Studio Theatre, I stepped onto the boards, I was pretty dreadful. Fortunately no critics were there. I did not know, though, that I was awful. My idea of acting the Bavarian king was to clump about the stage as though I had no knees, spouting my lines stridently.

Slowly the piece improved, and the staging three years later on my own university campus, freshly directed by Robert Cohen, head of the theater

department, was a breakthrough. He taught me how to project, how to limber up, and the importance of good costumes. Most recently, after three weeks of daily, intensive rehearsals with a new director, John Traub, I performed for a month in the Works Gallery, Long Beach. I had no idea that as much could still come through the work as Traub managed to elicit. And he hired a professional costumer, makeup person, and lighting man. These performances seemed to cap our long devotion to the piece.

My idea was to find a fresh way, short of performance art (which I see mainly as a form of stand-up comedy), to take my poetry to a larger audience than usually attends readings. I think the efforts have been worth it, for whenever I stage *Ludwig* or the *Countess* we get sizeable and enthusiastic audiences. And my poetry sells well at those events. The compliments I most enjoy are from experienced theater people who like the acting and the direction.

Far more controversial than *Ludwig* is a second stage work, *The Blood Countess*, first performed in February 1985. Here, I confront issues of mass murder and violence, which, through the seventeenth-century mass murderess Elizabeth Bathory, I declare have become "the religion" of our time. She gloats over the omnipresence of serial murder in the

David Brown

Robert Peters as The Blood Countess, *1987*

1980s, and says that in her time, the seventeenth century, they "had more style." To emphasize the outrageousness of the character's actions, I assume female garb and long, flowing black wig, paint my face, and perform the role to appropriate music. I am a very substantial man, over six feet tall and weighing about 230 pounds, with a massive chest and a weightlifter's arms. The bizarreness of my appearance seems to add to the symbolism and power of the piece. Some viewers, though, are upset by it; and curiously they are most often male. I suppose the fact that Bathory sought to behave as she found men behaving, abusing power and torturing their menials, is the primary reason. The theater piece is vibrantly antimale, or anti the destructive, macho elements we prize in males.

The Blood Countess is poetry as theater very much on the edge. Occasional theater groups have refused to sponsor it because of the subject matter; and critics, I am told, who have received the book containing both the complete poems and the play have returned it to the publisher. Some readers and viewers have complained that the work simply projects my own desires to torture women! I loathe such a confusion of the author with his work. Recently, I testified as an expert witness in a murder trial where poems of violence written by the accused were introduced to the jury as proof of guilt. Although the victim was an innocent gay man stabbed through the heart with a "buck knife," I agreed to appear bringing examples of violent material from Homer, Shakespeare, Milton, Browning, Shelley, and some contemporary poets, including myself, to warn the jury against assuming that what a poet writes reflects what he means to do. The accused was found guilty of voluntary manslaughter rather than first-degree murder. One newspaper reported that my testimony resulted in the reduced sentence; another, and the defense lawyer also, said that it had no effect, since by definition a first-degree conviction would have meant that the murderer intended to kill the specific person he did, with malice aforethought. If I had not myself felt victimized by the autobiographical heresy I would not have testified, especially since a gay brother was murdered.

I have faith that *The Blood Countess* will eventually be seen as a seminal confrontation of issues deep in our culture, issues most of us try to avoid, and a literary work of art very much of the 1980s. The world is far too sick, I think, for ignoring issues of violence, murder, and the abuse of power any longer.

I have been supported throughout all of these performances by my friend Paul Trachtenberg, who has been involved from the start. Much of the nuances I have developed in my acting are due to him; and the direction and blocking of the *Countess* reflect his talent and commitment. On several occasions, he has served as stage manager, dresser, lighting designer and lighting operator, and sound technician. He's even managed the door at a small forty-seat theater we occupied for a month and a half in Los Angeles and worked diligently on publicity. Another friend, Larry Elkins, assisted me materially in writing the stage adaptation of *Ludwig;* his acumen for what was stageworthy saved me hours of fumblings with what would otherwise have been inept scripts.

None of my other five voice books seem suited to theater adaptation, something brought home by our failure at staging *Hawker,* the poems on the eccentric Cornish vicar and poet. We engaged actor-poet Robert Crosson for the role. *Hawker* and *Ludwig* were scheduled for a week's run in a 350-seat theater in Los Angeles; alas, hardly anyone came, and we closed after three performances. On the last evening, there were four people in the audience, Christopher Isherwood, Don Bachardy, a woman with a flower basket who walked out early, and a friend of Crosson's.

As my sixty-fourth birthday nears, I feel that I have accomplished far more than I ever imagined, and I am grateful for the many good things, among the disasters, that have occurred. Recent energies have gone into the memoirs. A first book of reminiscences, *Crunching Gravel,* has just appeared, published by Mercury House, to enthusiastic reviews in *Publishers Weekly, Kirkus Reviews, Booklist,* and the *New York Times Book Review.* The work covers the year 1936, when I am twelve and go to high school for the first time. The design is the seasons—I open with winter and return to winter at the end.

I am currently giving a number of book signings and readings in California, and shall shortly be leaving for Australia, a guest of *Poetry Australia,* to judge literary contests and to read my work.

My final scholarly project, a series of letters written by the Tennyson family to their tutor Henry Graham Dakyns, edited by me with the special assistance of Dr. Janine Dakyns of the University of East Anglia, Norwich (HGD was her grandfather), is just out from the Scarecrow Press.

I anticipate, barring unforeseen disasters of health and family, that my life will proceed much as it has over these past few years and months, with more writing, and, I sincerely hope, increasing recognition for my creative work. Critics, via essays and interviews, are beginning to assess the overall sweep of my writing. Most recently, Diane Wakoski, Edward

Robert Peters and Paul Trachtenberg in a pub in Stow-on-the-Wold, England, 1987

Butscher, Philip Jason, Billy Collins, and Ben Bennani have made important contributions. I am most grateful.

BIBLIOGRAPHY

Poetry:

Fourteen Poems. Santa Barbara, Calif.: Little Square Review, 1967.

Songs for a Son. New York: Norton, 1967.

The Sow's Head and Other Poems. Detroit: Wayne State University Press, 1968.

Connections: In the English Lake District: A Verse Suite. London: Anvil Press Poetry, 1972.

Byron Exhumed: A Verse Suite. Fort Wayne, Ind.: Windless Orchard, 1973.

Eighteen Poems. N.p., 1973.

Red Midnight Moon. San Francisco: Empty Elevator Shaft, 1973.

Holy Cow: Parable Poems. Los Angeles: Red Hill, 1974.

Bronchial Tangle, Heart System. Hanover, N.H.: Granite Publications, 1975.

Cool Zebras of Light. Santa Barbara, Calif.: Christopher's Books, 1975.

The Gift to Be Simple: A Garland for Ann Lee. New York: Liveright, 1975.

The Poet as Ice-Skater. San Francisco: Manroot Books, 1976.

Shaker Light (broadside; illustrated by Harley Elliott). Milwaukee: Pentagram, 1975.

Gauguin's Chair: Selected Poems, 1967–1974. Trumansburg, N.Y.: The Crossing Press, 1977.

Hawthorne: Poems Adapted from the American Notebooks (illustrated by Carol Yeh). Fairfax, Calif.: Red Hill, 1977.

The Drowned Man to the Fish (illustrated by Meredith Peters). St. Paul, Minn.: New Rivers Press, 1978.

Ikagnak: The North Wind: With Dr. Kane in the Arctic (illustrated by Steven S. Chayt). Pasadena, Calif.: Kenmore Press, 1978; revised edition published as *Kane.* Greensboro, N.C.: Unicorn Press, 1985.

Celebrities: In Memory of Margaret Dumont, Dowager of the Marx Brothers Movies (1890–1965). Berkeley, Calif.: Sombre Reptiles, 1981.

The Picnic in the Snow: Ludwig of Bavaria. St. Paul, Minn.: New Rivers Press, 1982; revised edition published as *Ludwig of Bavaria: Poems and a Play.* Silver Spring, Md.: Cherry Valley, 1987.

What Dillinger Meant to Me. New York: Sea Horse, 1983.

Hawker. Greensboro, N.C.: Unicorn Press, 1984.

The Blood Countess: Elizabeth Bathory of Hungary: Poems and a

Play. Silver Spring, Md.: Cherry Valley, 1987.

Shaker Light: Mother Ann Lee in America. Greensboro, N.C.: Unicorn Press, 1987.

Haydon. Greensboro, N.C.: Unicorn Press, 1988.

Selected Poems. Forthcoming.

Nonfiction:

The Crowns of Apollo: Swinburne's Principles of Literature and Art: A Study in Victorian Criticism and Aesthetics. Detroit: Wayne State University Press, 1965.

Pioneers of Modern Poetry, with George Hitchcock. San Francisco: Kayak, 1967.

The Great American Poetry Bake-Off (criticism). First Series. Metuchen, N.J., and London: Scarecrow, 1979. Second Series. Metuchen, N.J., and London: Scarecrow, 1982. Third Series. Metuchen, N.J., and London: Scarecrow, 1987. Fourth Series. Forthcoming.

The Peters Black and Blue Guide to Current Literary Journals (illustrated by Meredith Peters). First Series. Silver Spring, Md.: Cherry Valley, 1983. Second Series. Silver Spring, Md.: Cherry Valley, 1985. Third Series. Paradise, Calif.: Dustbooks, 1987.

Crunching Gravel: Growing Up in the Thirties (memoir). San Francisco: Mercury House, 1988.

The Turquoise Lake: A Memoir of World War II. Forthcoming.

Editor of:

Victorians on Literature and Art. New York: Appleton-Century-Crofts, 1961; London: P. Owen, 1964.

America: The Diary of a Visit, Winter 1884–1885, by Edmund Gosse, edited with David G. Halliburton. Lafayette, Ind.: Purdue University, 1966.

The Letters of John Addington Symonds, with Herbert M. Schueller. 3 vols. Detroit: Wayne State University Press, 1967–69.

Gabriel: A Poem, by John Addington Symonds, edited with Timothy D'Arch Smith. London: Hartington, 1974.

Letters to a Tutor: The Tennyson Family Letters to Henry Graham Dakyns. Metuchen, N.J., and London: Scarecrow, 1988.

Plays—Selected Productions:

Fuck Mother, first produced at the Cubiculo in New York, 1970.

The Blood Countess, first produced in 1985.

Ludwig, first produced at the Fifth Street Studio Theatre in Los Angeles, 1982.

A. L. Rowse

1903-

A CORNISH-AMERICAN STORY

A. L. Rowse in the garden of All Souls College, Oxford

My unexpectedly long life has covered most of the too exciting twentieth century, appalling in its events, which I have thus seen from close at hand and, as a historian, can estimate in some perspective. From several points of view, at least from Britain, the story may even have something representative about it.

I was born at St. Austell in Cornwall 4 December 1903. Cornwall is a little land on its own, the peninsula at the south-west extremity of Britain, jutting out into the Atlantic at our nearest point to America. Almost surrounded by water, in shape Cornwall is very like the Upper Peninsula of Michigan, into which a great number of Cornish folk immigrated.

My father's sister immigrated there at the begin-

ning of the century; my own sister raised her family in California, eventually settling in British Columbia, and I have relations elsewhere in the United States. In fact the bulk of the Cornish people are to be found in America—I guess perhaps six or eight times the number of us in Britain. My friend the historian Allan Nevins used to say that if only the Cornish had produced a poet like Robert Burns, Americans would be more conscious of us. Well, I have done my best to bring home our existence among the other elements that have created the greatest of modern nations.

We are, like the Welsh, the remnant of the ancient British stock whom the invading Anglo-Saxons—a very expansive people everywhere—pushed into the western recesses of our island when they came across the North Sea from Germany. (It was just like the western drive of the Americans across their continent later.)

The Cornish have been a great emigrating folk, just as much as the Scots or Irish, proportionately for a little people. Their genius has been for mining, according to the old saying: "Wherever there is a hole in the earth, you will find a Cornishman at the bottom of it." As a researcher, I often think of myself as a miner, mining away in the Huntington Library in California or the Bodleian Library at Oxford, bringing up valuable nuggets of information, for it was in those two places that I found and worked out my epoch-making discoveries about Shakespeare.

Wherever there was hard-rock mining—copper, lead, gold (not coal or slate)—you will find little Cornish communities in the United States, and I have visited most of them for my book *The Cousin Jacks: The Cornish in America.* From Butte, Montana, to Globe, Arizona—where some of my mother's family were miners—and from Pennsylvania through Illinois and Wisconsin to Grass Valley and on to San Diego, California.

After a brief spell in South Africa my father came back home to work all his life as a china-clay worker. This is a form of open-cast mining for china-clay, of which the highlands above St. Austell have the finest quality in the world. So I was reared in the china-clay village of Tregonissey, where we also had a little shop to help out. As a boy I was fascinated to hear stories of the past, and kept a note-book into which I wrote what I could learn about the village life from my parents and my great-uncle, whose memory went back to the Russo-Turkish war of the 1870s and before. This provided the foundation for my book *A Cornish Childhood*, which began not as an autobiography but as a social history of the village. Anyway, it proved a best-seller, and has sold over half-a-million.

We did not think of ourselves as poor people, but in fact we had no money. I do not know what I should have done for an education, if my boyhood and youth had not coincided with the remarkable expansion of education in Britain at the beginning of this century. My parents had had practically no schooling and could hardly read and write, not a book in the house. Perhaps I have rather over-compensated that with, today, a library of twelve thousand, and over forty books to my name.

There was a real enthusiasm for education when I was young, and I was very well taught by an excellent woman teacher at my primary school. From that I won a scholarship to the recently started grammar school, where I embarked on new subjects, Latin and French, which opened up an unknown world to me. I loved school—so much more interesting than a working-class home, no books or pictures, little furniture and no taste. Again I have rather over-compensated that, living in a large country house (but in my native parish) full of antiques, Oriental rugs, and a picture gallery. For the fact was that I was a sport in my simple working-class family, by nature an aesthete.

This side of my nature was provided for by the good old Church of England, to which I owe a great debt. For our parish church—to which I later dedicated a long poem, "The Old Churchyard at St. Austell"—had excellent music, and I became a choirboy, with a remarkable solo-voice. Then there was the inspiration of the services, the ritual, the beauty of the Tudor language of the Prayer Book, roughly contemporary with Shakespeare, who quotes it a lot. Most of all, I owed to the Church the sense of history, the sense of the past as living, continuous in the present.

As a boy I was always more interested in the past than in the present, so here was the making of a historian: the past has always been living for me, and people find that in my books. But there was also poetry, in the language and liturgy of the church, in the architecture of ancient churches, the sculpture, the stained glass. All this spoke to the artistic side of my nature, encouraged the poetry.

I was already writing poetry as a schoolboy, many years before I was equipped at the university for historical research. Naturally, from my remote Cornish school I had no idea of publishing my poems, or how. Here my headmaster took a hand and got my poems published in *Public School Verse*, along with the grandees from famous schools, some of whom became friends and competitors later at Oxford and in literary life: Lord David Cecil, Graham Greene, Peter Quennell, Auden, Isherwood—most of them having fallen, however, by the wayside since.

Bu how to get to the university then?

My people hadn't a bean, damn it—this made me very resentful. And there was only one single scholarship to the university for the whole county of Cornwall! I had to get it, or go down the drain. This doubled resentment, and strain, anxiety and worry. My parents could be little help: they never knew what I was up to—this had the advantage that I pleased myself in what I did, though I felt terribly on my own. I suppose it helped to confirm the solitariness which Henry James regarded as the necessary condition of the real writer.

Winning that scholarship was only a first step. Then my headmaster propelled me towards Oxford, where I won the Open Scholarship in English Literature at Christ Church, first college in the university. There needed yet another scholarship—in those unreformed days—before I could raise the magnificent sum of two hundred pounds a year to pay my way at Oxford. This I managed with a third scholarship from the beneficent Drapers' Company of the City of London. It was scholarships and examinations, worry and anxiety, all the way: no wonder I had started a duodenal ulcer before I got to Oxford.

This blighted, nearly wrecked, the first half of my life, what with peritonitis (twice), four operations, hospitals, nursing homes—right up to the Second World War. Illness was a further condition of my life, gave it another, deeper dimension, enabled me to see the underside of things, and again reinforced the individualism, the necessary egoism in the struggle to survive—for it was a fearful struggle, though I never once thought of giving up or giving in. Never give up, never give in, has been my motto all through life.

Here I have a point to make for the benefit of those who have to struggle with ill health. Paradoxically I owe to illness my long life: I have had to be careful all the way along—no smoking, no drinking, and my strongest drug is tea (Barbara Pym's favourite Earl Grey, in which T. S. Eliot's widow keeps me supplied).

One becomes acclimatised to being careful. Strong toughs who have never had a day's illness are apt at the first attack to be laid low, while we valetudinarians survive by acclimatising ourselves and taking no risks. I am always astonished by the alcoholism and drugging of so many American writers—males, the females are more sensible: I think it adolescent of them, and anyway women regard most men as kids.

One personal point: underneath everything I had a strong proletarian constitution; for I had so much mental energy that, if I had had normal health, I should have killed myself with work long ago. And a general point: William Shakespeare enforces this—that often when you get a bad blow, a set-back, or a stroke of ill-luck, it may turn to nothing but good. He says that three times over, so it must have meant something personal to him.

Getting to Oxford was the grandest stroke of good fortune in my life, my years there the source of great happiness (and naturally some unhappiness). Going to Christ Church with all its grandeur, cathedral, tradition, etc., from the restricted background of working-class village life, was paradise to me. Or rather, seriously, what I found was that *this was my nature*—not the other, any more than Eastwood was D. H. Lawrence's, who had had much the same beginnings and a similar struggle to emancipate himself from it. On the other hand, Lawrence completely cut himself off from the roots of his early life; I have never done that, I have always had a home in Cornwall, returned to it every year of my life. A writer must never pull up his roots. My work has gained strength, kept its vitality, from that and a lot of it is dedicated to Cornwall, history, stories, literary essays, *A Cornish Anthology,* and *A. L. Rowse's Cornwall,* an illustrated book; above all, my poetry, which I set most store by, for it contains my inner life and its secrets, as against the outer life in all the rest.

At Christ Church the dons made me do the History School instead of English Literature as I had expected. I was insufficiently grateful, for the History School was a stronger and more strenuous affair—I found it rather a strain. However, the dons were right: History provided far better intellectual training, uphill work, and the proper background for eventual research; schools of English Literature whether at Oxford or elsewhere are inferior to it, as the dons thought.

This did not mean that I gave up on literature—far from it. I contributed to the literary papers, to successive volumes of *Oxford Poetry* along with Harold Acton, Graham Greene, and others, and even broadcast poems with them in the early days of the BBC. Oddly enough, some who subsequently became writers took no part in this—Evelyn Waugh, Brian Howard, John Betjeman, were up to their eyes in the social and drunken life rendered famously, and fatuously, in *Brideshead Revisited.*

My main outside interest was political. It may be thought natural that a young working-class fellow should join the Labour Party. More to the point: pride is a prime motive with a Celt, I was 100 percent Celt, and would not have it said that, just because I had got to Oxford and the most aristocratic of colleges, I had become a Conservative. Actually all my instincts were conservative; I loved the past and hated change, but became an active Labour man, Chairman of the University Labour Club, proselytiser and propagandist. Here was another source of tension, more strain, for this line of country was neither comfortable nor altogether congenial.

In the continual effort to think things out for myself I was much influenced intellectually by Marxism; this was then rather *avant-garde,* for I was very well read in Marxist literature before it became fashionable in the 1930s. Not that I was ever tempted to become a Communist—too much working-class horse-sense for that; in fact I tried to head-off middle-class types, such as Stephen Spender, from doing so. Our Labour Club at Oxford was a solid middle-of-the-road body following Attlee and Ernest Bevin. At Cambridge there was no such strong, moderate Labour Club; that is why our opposite numbers—people like Maclean, Burgess, Blunt, Philby—were drawn in to the Communist Party. They were more ingenuous politically, all middle class with no proletarian commonsense, and so got caught.

All this mental activity—academic, working for Schools, reading history (which seemed endless to me, as it is); reading the wonderful literature pouring out in the 1920s both in English and in French, writing poetry, essays, articles; all the discussion that went with it was part of one's education. In fact the most important was not the formal lectures and tutorials, but the constant discussion with one's contemporaries, the cleverest boys in England, from the most famous Public Schools. (All my life subsequently I have found myself competing with Etonians and Wykehamists, promoting each other's interests, all middle- or upper-class; since they are much sharper and more sophisticated I have had to work all the harder to keep up.)

The value of such a race-course, such a mutual education, at Oxford (and Cambridge), is immeasurable. A young American student once diagnosed it: he singled out the closeness of the process of reading, talking, and writing, the way they were interwoven in our daily life. He was quite right: we used to discuss everything: David Cecil would read me what he had written for me to criticise, and vice versa; Wystan

The author at Trerice, an Elizabethan house in Cornwall, 1982

Auden used to read me his early poems.

One advantage of having no money was that I came home to Cornwall every vacation for solid reading and writing, solitary long walks and reflection. Not for me winter sports at St. Moritz, or the sight-seeing expeditions on the Continent so brilliantly written up in Cyril Connolly's Letters. In one of these vacations I wrote a long poem on Byron, competing for the celebrated Newdigate Prize. I was furious that it was awarded *proxime accessit* to a more conventional poem by a Canadian Rhodes scholar, years older, who has never been heard of since. Graham Greene complains that his poem didn't even rate a mention.

These vacations gave me the chance to get ahead with heavy historical reading, which I feared would get me down—historical text books are not good for one's prose style: Prayer Book and Bible are better. Academic historians are apt to have little sense of literature, and *no* visual sense; literary folk, little knowledge of history and less historical sense. It is an enormous advantage to be ambivalent between history and literature: literature came first with me, but I should never have made the discoveries I have made in the Elizabethan age without historical research, or in Shakespeare's life and work without both.

Why don't people see that it is a very rare

combination to be both historian *and* poet? Macaulay was both, so was the Elizabethan Samuel Daniel. It is allowable to be poet and critic, or dramatist and poet, but such is the specialisation today that it is not allowed for one to be both historian and poet. In an age besotted with the idea of everybody being equal—as if they ever were!—perhaps it is thought to be somehow unfair, and invites brickbats from critics, who are good at neither. Disraeli deliberately provoked them: "You know who the critics are?—the men who have failed in literature and art." It is more important to understand the indispensability of both history and literature for understanding an Elizabethan like Shakespeare.

After the three-year course I emerged, after all, with my head above water and one of the best Firsts of the year in the History School (reading in French literature actually helped). This was followed, not by a holiday abroad but by yet another long vacation's intensive reading to compete for a Prize Fellowship at All Souls, then the "blue-ribbon" of an Oxford career.

All Souls is a senior college of Fellows without undergraduates. Americans can derive some idea of this distinguished institution from the fact that Abraham Flexner planned the Institute for Advanced Study at Princeton after our model. Its distinction arose from the fact that it was only half-academic; the rest of the Fellows were out in the world in public life, in the Foreign Office, diplomats and ambassadors, in politics, ministers and members of the Cabinet, Viceroys and Governors in the benign days of empire; or in the Church, deans, bishops, archbishops. I was elected along with Roger Makins, who was to become ambassador in Washington.

The tone of this famous college, and its conversation, were of public life, political problems and concerns, not sport and who should win the University boat-race. Though I was by nature an academic, bent on research and writing, and took a hand in teaching undergraduates from other colleges, my interest in politics was reinforced. The younger generation then was inspired by the hope of a better world after the appalling holocaust of 1914–18, and we thought that social democracy offered the way to that better world. Optimistically, ingenuously, I wrote my first book, *Politics and the Younger Generation.*

That book was no sooner out than the time proved a false dawn and buried it. The year 1931 saw the ganging-up of our upper classes, both Conservative and Liberal Parties, against the Labour Movement, which was reduced to a mere remnant of fifty-five in Parliament. Under the fraud of a "National Government" they retained an immense majority throughout that decade, in a position to do whatever was necessary in the country's best interests and even to give a lead in the right direction in Europe.

In 1933 came Hitler's capture of power in Germany, followed in 1934 by the murder of some 1,250 of his opponents both within and without his Nazi following. That should have alerted Europe. Instead, it inspired the British governing class to follow a policy of Appeasement, virtually collusion—as also with Mussolini in Italy and Franco in Spain, which undermined the democracies and exposed Britain to the gravest danger in her history.

I can claim to have seen what was coming: I claim no credit for that, for anyone of moderate intelligence could have seen that Hitler meant war for the domination of Europe. I had at least read *Mein Kampf,* in which his malign genius and his plans were made clear. As a historian I saw that Britain's safety lay in a Grand Alliance of all those threatened by him—as throughout Britain's history, against Philip II of Spain, against Louis XIV and Napoleon, against the Kaiser's Germany. Churchill saw this too, from his reading of history. I made the argument clear in an open correspondence with the arch-Appeaser, Lord Lothian, in the *Times,* which I did not hesitate to republish in *The End of an Epoch.* Nor did I hesitate,

when the folly of Appeasement led to the war in almost hopeless circumstances, to bring the lesson home in a little *aide-mémoire, All Souls and Appeasement;* for some of the most influential Appeasers were senior Fellows of All Souls, Halifax and Simon, Somervell and Geoffrey Dawson, responsible as editor for the appalling record of the *Times.*

This useful tract had no success in Britain—too many were involved in the folly, not to say guilt. Abraham Flexner was able to inform us what was happening to the Jews in Germany: nobody would take warning. In the U.S.A., under the title *Appeasement: A Study in Political Decline, 1933–1939,* people took notice of it: perhaps all the more because the upshot of that appalling decade was the eventual disintegration of the British Empire—if the consequences in Africa and India have made any improvement in the world-picture!

In all this, in the controversies in which I engaged, I had the advantage of a knowledge of European history, some knowledge of Germany, its language and literature. Above all there was my intense friendship with Adam von Trott (a descendant of Chief Justice John Jay, by the way), now regarded as a hero of the Resistance, executed for his part in the generals' plot against Hitler in 1944. My intimacy with him gave me a window into the German soul, and a pretty despairing glimpse I got. Most British had no conception of it, though Europeans, especially Slavs, know well enough. In the enormous archive I have accumulated over the years—historical, political, literary—von Trott's letters have an honoured place.

It is extraordinary to think what we went through. His family had been officials in the Kaiser's time, his uncle had an apartment in the huge Imperial *Schloss* in Berlin. Adam and I would spend evenings alone there: I have a vivid memory of the Kaiser's study, the big desk formed from the timbers of Nelson's *Victory,* the telephone wires cut at the Armistice, 11 November 1918 (it proved indeed only an armistice). One can tell a man from his books: the Kaiser's were half-German, half-English, half-theology, half-politics. Among them was the very copy of Churchill's biography of his father, Lord Randolph (Jenny Jerome of New York's husband), which Winston gave the Kaiser at the Military Manoeuvres of 1909. Nothing left of it all now, the immense palace just rubble.

That ghastly decade of the thirties, which led to such disaster, the poets of the time have attached their name to—some of them friends of mine, like Auden and Spender. Naturally, as writers, they were much to the fore in the public prints, and specially good at publicising each other. In truth they were on the margin, except for the Spanish Civil War. They were not involved in practical politics, and as such suffered the usual illusions, the lack of a sense of realities, of intellectuals about politics.

I took an active part: for the whole of that decade I was a working Labour Party candidate for Parliament, for my home constituency. Cornwall, like most of the country, was dominated by the "National" government, engaged—as I considered—in betraying the interests of the nation. It was an uphill struggle trying to bring this home to a complacent people. I used to console myself with thinking that, if they wouldn't listen to Churchill—as they absolutely would not—it was hardly to be expected that they would listen to me.

I worked hard at it, giving up all my vacations to Party-work, meetings, speaking, often in the open air—sometimes at the quayside of our little harbours, more often in the uplands of the china-clay area. I went the dreary rounds, sometimes with Ernest Bevin, Clem Attlee, or Herbert Morrison: Labour leaders who were to make their mark in Churchill's wartime government, and thereafter in the historic Labour government of 1945–51, which initiated egalitarian Britain with its attendant disillusionments.

In term-time I was occupied with academic work, teaching, examining, researching; my post at All Souls was convenient for lecturing for the Workers' Educational Association, attending Labour Conferences, and speaking engagements around the country. Though I was on the Left as a young man, I never heard Ernest Bevin speak but I was *intellectually* convinced that he was right. At home, along with a good journalist friend, I started the *Cornish Labour News* (of which I have kept a file); so there was regular monthly writing for that too.

By this time my research into the sixteenth century required my moving to London to work at original manuscripts in the Public Record Office and the British Museum (now Library). This I was able to combine with a temporary lectureship at the London School of Economics. Though I did not find this at all enjoyable it opened up a new acquaintance—mostly Left-inclined professors like R. H. Tawney (much too venerated by everybody), Harold Laski, a friendly spirit, beautiful Eileen Power, intolerable Lancelot Hogben of *Mathematics for the Million.* I did not much care for the celebrated Director, Beveridge (not my beverage), nor for the bombinating Lionel Robbins, though candour compels me to confess that his views on economics proved more durable than mine. Always struggling to think out a position for myself, I was more in line with Keynes—then regarded as

heterodox—who encouraged my political reviews in his *Economic Journal.* For the life of me I could not understand why Keynes wouldn't see that, if he was to make his views effective, he should join up with the Labour Movement as the fulcrum for them. I wrote articles urging this in the *Political Quarterly;* he was sympathetic, but would not take the step. After all, hadn't Lenin said that "politics begins with the masses"? Keynes and Ernest Bevin were in rough agreement on the important Macmillan Committee on Finance and Industry at the time.

So I perpetrated another tract for the times, *Mr. Keynes and the Labour Movement.* Victor Gollancz, foremost publisher for the Left at the time, rejected it as insufficiently Leftist; so I took the book to Macmillan, who were more open-minded. That proved my introduction to that famous firm, who were to publish many subsequent volumes: the whole quartet on the Elizabethan Age, those on Shakespeare, and more on other Elizabethans, *Shakespeare's Southampton: Patron of Virginia, Christopher Marlowe, Raleigh and the Throckmortons, Eminent Elizabethans,* and *The Elizabethans and America,* which had been the first G. M. Trevelyan Lectures to be given on their foundation at Cambridge.

My greatest debt, however, was to T. S. Eliot, my relations with whom form too long a story to do justice to here, though some of it will appear in the Correspondence his widow is editing, to which I am contributing some seventy letters of his which I preserve. I owe my first being published in London to him. He recruited me to review and write for his *Criterion* in its early days. He allowed me a free hand to review the history books I wanted, but was always urging me to write on political subjects from my Leftist point of view. I realise now that he wanted me to fill this gap in the *Criterion*—he would not have wanted the more eligible, but more run-of-the-mill socialists like Laski or G. D. H. Cole. Somehow I did not find this easy, churning out essays on Marxism, Communism, etc. and I can only pay tribute now to Eliot's encouragement and forbearance as an editor. He was extraordinarily patient and courteous (the greatest gentleman I have ever known, along with Q.—Quiller Couch), and how good it was of him to print so much stuff he cannot possibly have agreed with. I think now that he was more right about politics than his fanatical young contributor was.

He took any amount of trouble with my youthful *Politics and the Younger Generation,* took his sharp-pointed pencil to the manuscript with his comments, not all of which the self-assured young tyro agreed with. He came down to All Souls to go through it with me: I

With Dr. Mildred R. Bennett, a creator of the
Willa Cather Museum at Red Cloud, Nebraska,
in front of Cather's house

can see him now, sitting on the sofa in our smoking-room—just as in the poem I wrote in America on hearing of his death: lines quoted by the poet Kathleen Raine as so true of him:

Look once more into your eye, limpid and sad,
Note the old expression at once austere and gay,
Diffidence and kindness in your anxious smile.

In those years, after the sad breakdown of his first marriage, he was lonely, willing to be friendly, would press me to come up to London, or to attend the regular *Criterion* dinners. John Crowe Ransom, whom I had controverted, was "anxious to meet" me, then Herbert Read: would I come up? I would not; I never once attended a *Criterion* dinner, though regularly writing for the journal. Dinners, social occasions, had no allure for a worsening member of the duodenal club, and I didn't much want to meet anybody: All Souls provided all the social life I fancied. (H. G. Wells was the President of the Diabetic Society; after lunching with him once at the Reform Club I gave him the go-by. Though I didn't want to know him, I became a great friend of his

ebullient mistress, Rebecca West. In later years, much better in health, I became a reformed character.)

Eliot, himself not strong in health and less well off then than even I was, with my Fellowship to fall back on, proposed that we should share a flat together. I went so far as to explore an inexpensive area, and found charming Georgian Lloyd-Baker Square (which, I gather, survived the German Blitz; No. 1 Brunswick Square, where I lived, was totally obliterated). Eliot needed someone to look after him, but by that time, more and more ill, I was incapable of looking after myself. I returned to the refuge of All Souls, a home to me.

For another reason, too, I had to let him down. After years of incarceration in the Public Record Office I had at length, belatedly, completed my first work of historical research, *Sir Richard Grenville of the "Revenge."* For this I needed the criticism of Professor J. E. Neale, then the top scholar in the Elizabethan field. Never have I been put through a more strenuous exercise: he made me cut 10,000 redundant words out of my typescript and gave me three months' more work on it. I went back to All Souls to do it, have never profited so much from a set-back, and never looked back since. Neale was a reader for Cape, and Jonathan Cape, the old buccaneer, claimed the book; Geoffrey Faber reproached me, Eliot uttered never a word of complaint. But the decision had been right.

The book was an offshoot from my researches into Tudor Cornwall, for which I was gathering an immense mass of material. In the course of it I noticed that there had been no biography of the Elizabethan hero of the *Revenge.* Shortly I understood why: all the personal letters had disappeared, when I went down to his home-port, Bideford, all the town documents had been destroyed. What was I to do to relieve the picture and make it live?

I decided to take a leaf out of Macaulay's notebook, visit the places and scenes Grenville had known, look upon his contemporaries as they appeared in portraits and on their tombs, make the book more visual and thus bring it alive. Most academic historians lack *visual* sense. The famous last fight of the *Revenge* in the Azores had been reported only indirectly from the English side, in Raleigh's pamphlet. There must have been a Spanish account—and, learning Spanish (ill, on the beaches at home), I found that there was. I was just in time to get the reports from Madrid before everything closed down in the Spanish Civil War. Putting the two accounts together, English and Spanish, gave for the first time the complete story of that Azores operation: a new contribution to our knowledge of the Elizabethan age.

Having seen the book through the press I was headed for further tests—two fearful operations, gastro-enterostomy, in University College Hospital, London. I could not have lived without them, the duodenal passage had been blocked by continual growth of scar-tissue, and for years I had endured periods of agony. (Members of the expensive Duodenal Club, and most surgeons, will recognise the symptoms.)

When I emerged, by a very narrow squeak, from these operations the doctors laid down that I was to give up all thought of an active life, accept the condition of a semi-invalid existence, above all no more politics, wasting my energy on a constituency for Parliament. This sentence I had to accept—and was happy, more or less, ever after. It turned out to be a stroke of luck; for after all the work I had put into it my constituency went Labour after the war. If I had got into Parliament it would have killed me in no time—besides the waste of time, in Carlyle's "talking-shop."

For some years I felt sad at deserting faithful friends and supporters, but at last I was free, free to follow my own nature, which was for writing, not for politics. Fortunately, I had never given up on writing, but continued, even with poetry, along with all the rest of it. Of course, I had been putting an intolerable strain on myself; and to that there was added the anguish of the Hitler era. People who did not live through it in Europe can hardly realise the agony it was, the despair and grief. In some ways, like my Jewish friends, I have never got over it, or forgiven it; I still dream about Hitler. I suppose that on top of the physical trouble there was mental and spiritual ulceration too. Something of that is expressed in my *Poems of a Decade, 1931–1941,* and in the autobiographies I was now free to write: *A Cornishman at Oxford, A Cornishman Abroad* (which contains some of the correspondence with Adam von Trott), and *A Man of the Thirties.*

My friends think that my entanglement with politics—I was fanatically engaged against Appeasement, in which I was wholly right—was a mistake. I dare say that they were mostly correct. On the other hand I learned greatly from the intolerable experience. I got to know some of the leaders in political life—Attlee, Bevin, Morrison, Stafford Cripps, and later Churchill, Macmillan, R. A. B. Butler; and I learned something of the operations of politics, as few arm-chair academics do. History and politics are closely related, both historians and politicians *need* to know something of each other. Gibbon claimed that "the captain of the Hampshire grenadiers has not

been useless to the historian of the Roman Empire." I claim that the candidature for Parliament throughout that evil decade was not entirely useless to the historian, though it may more have been for the poet.

Above all, it taught me the bottomless folly of mankind *in the mass;* individuals may or may not be intelligent, but multiply by thousands, let alone millions, and you arrive at the lowest common denominator. Hence, with the masses emerging into the foreground of politics, the horrors of the twentieth century—released and led by Communist, Nazi, Fascist, and religious revolutions alike. This means that my outlook has been much influenced by Swift; from early years I always meant to write a biography of him, and eventually, when free, I did: *Jonathan Swift: Major Prophet.*

The war which Hitler unleashed upon us—which anyone could have foreseen and which would have overwhelmed Britain if it had not been for the United States—was a dividing line. To speak personally, with my medical record I was useless, and was in fact rejected from service, military or civil. What was best to do? Evidently—the only thing I was any good at, was properly meant for: Writing, and on both fronts, historical and literary.

When I wrote *Sir Richard Grenville* historical biography was out of fashion, apt to be decried by academics. Never mind them: if I had not tackled a biography first I should never have been able to tackle the portrait of a society, which I accomplished with *Tudor Cornwall* (1941). Again, if I had not tackled a portrait of a society on a small scale in that, I should never have been able to attempt a portrait of Shakespeare's England, on a large scale in four volumes, *The England of Elizabeth, The Expansion of Elizabethan England, The Elizabethan Renaissance,* part 1: *The Life of the Society,* and part 2: *The Cultural Achievement.*

There you are: my advice to young people setting out on their work is Never to listen to the discouraging advice of the small-minded. First-class minds are encouraging to good work: I have had nothing but encouragement and appreciation from historians of the calibre of G. M. Trevelyan and Samuel Eliot Morison, as in my literary work from Quiller Couch, Rebecca West, Elizabeth Bowen, the Sitwells.

Above all again from Eliot over my poetry. All through those despairing years I had never given up on writing poems, and publishing them under the (then) good literary editors of the *Listener,* the *New Statesman,* the *Times Literary Supplement,* even occasionally the *New Yorker.* But I had a complex against publishing a whole volume of my poems—too near the bone, too revealing of anguish, physical and mental; I felt it was exposing myself.

With the emotional release and inspiration of wartime, Eliot came to the rescue and published my first, belated, volume. Everything with me has been belated, on account of my early hard struggle, then held up by illness. G. M. Trevelyan once said, "We thought you were never going to begin; but, my goodness, once started there's no stopping you." Well, I have had to make up in later years for the shortcomings of the earlier.

Eliot went through that first volume of poems, with sharp pencil, threw out only two pieces, and wrote the blurb; it recognisably contained a French word, *envergure,* we didn't know the meaning of—so like him. Of the six or seven volumes published he wrote the blurbs for five. My work as a poet is overlooked for that of the historian, and in the utter confusion of poetic standards today it is depreciated both by versifiers and critics in the modern fashion. However, if my poetry was good enough for Eliot, it is certainly good enough for *them.* Actually, they are beginning to depreciate him now. I agree with Spender's questioning whether the poets of the past would recognise current "verse" as poetry at all. And a historian knows that fashions change, as they are already changing from the New Brutalism in architecture and the denigration of British and American painting, seeing everything through Parisian eyes.

One aspect of my poetry I was particularly proud of. In my time hardly any English poets had responded to American landscapes in verse. Robert Lowell once said to me that somehow English poets found the climate (spiritually speaking) inclement. One whole section of my Collected Poems is devoted to American landscapes: New York, New England, Mid-West, California mainly; other sections cover Cornwall, Oxford, some English scenes, Wartime.

As in those other ways I was very belated in getting to America, not until middle age. If one is to understand the modern world one must know the United States. My Oxford friends managed to visit it when young (David Cecil actually stayed with the legendary William Randolph Hearst and Marion Davies at San Simeon). But these were usually short visits. For obvious reasons, health and overwork, I could never get over when young; then came the war, and for years after it we had no dollars, no means of going. However, once started, I managed as usual to out-stay the short visits of my friends; eventually, for many years, I came to spend half the year in the U.S., have been in practically every state, and got a knowledge and appreciation of the United States

Rowse in Virginia with a Cather fan

wider, and rather deeper, than most of them.

Because of our common language most English people think that they understand America after a short visit, and write about it accordingly. How wrong they are! They have no idea how complex America is—a whole continent, instead of a normal small European country. To judge from their writers and their books, Americans have difficulty in understanding themselves. I had at any rate the sense to be baffled by the United States: it took me years to come to grips with the Enormous Country and to appreciate it properly, i.e., with sympathy and understanding. Europeans, on the whole, simply do not understand the United States; if they understood the inherent goodness, the generosity and good will within the American people, they would not be so misled by the outward manifestations of American life—on films, TV, Television evangelists, drugging, crime-rate, etc.: all at a higher rate with ethnic minorities, i.e., not "good Americans." I sometimes think that Americans show their worst side to the outer world.

I was not taken in by this: I am not interested in the surface phenomena of modern society. It is the business of the historian to look deeper. Here my double avocation as historian and poet helped me greatly. I was already well read in American literature. As a boy a favourite was Nathaniel Hawthorne; in my primary school the prime poet was Longfellow. Later at Oxford I graduated to Henry James and Henry

Adams, Willa Cather and Eudora Welty; while Eliot's poetry dominated my whole generation.

So I saw the United States, not like the hit-and-run journalists, but historically and poetically; taking it in extremely slowly and diffidently, often baffled and wondering, even after years, whether I should ever get the hang of it all. I came to have a large number of friends, some of them very eminent in their contributions to American life; but, strangely enough, even they didn't, perhaps couldn't, *explain* it. I learned much more intuitively, pragmatically, by watching their goodness of heart, their welcoming spirit, their generosity of *mind*. I think they understood that I was out to learn, not to criticise: any fool can criticise, it is much more difficult to understand, to seek out the positive values within.

I learned much from my oldest American friend, the historian Allan Nevins, a mid-Westerner by birth, New Yorker by career. Then from J. M. Steadman, the leading Milton scholar, who could interpret the Old South for me; also from discussions with Andrew Rolle, historian of California; from my friends out of the Willa Cather circle in Nebraska; New England friends like Orville Prescott and Eleanor Brewster, cousin of Longfellow (who had a trickle of Cornish descent from the Bonythons); latterly from my dear friends in Virginia.

Seven winter semesters I spent as a Research Associate at the Huntington Library in San Marino, California. Thus I fell in love with the Hispanic South-West, all of it—California, Arizona, New Mexico, the Pacific Coast up through Oregon to Washington, Montana, the lovely Cascades. No space to do justice here to my experience of it all, the historic missions all the way up the Camino Real from Mexico to San Francisco, the beauty of mountains and coast; Robert Louis Stevenson's Monterey and Carmel, Bret Harte's mining country; the charm of a Cornish settlement at Grass Valley; stopping with Admiral Nimitz to be shown Drake's Bay; the spectacular view from Irving Stone's hospitable house in Beverly Hills, visits and talks with Rouben Mamoulian there, mostly about Shakespeare.

The Huntington was an ideal library for my research, for it combined history with literature, and that combination—one might almost say, fusion—is indispensable for understanding an Elizabethan writer of four hundred years ago. Here I began on my twenty-year-long stint of tackling the problems of Shakespeare's life and work, and clearing up "the mess they have made of it," as Harold Macmillan described previous work on it. To my astonishment I found that, on the basis of the

historian's settling the dating of the Sonnets, from their topical references (as only an Elizabethan historian could do), all the problems that had confused scholars for so long worked out consistently, firmly, and unanswerably. If these findings had not been absolutely correct—though new, they were also conservative and traditional—I should never have been able to make the further discoveries that have transformed our knowledge of Shakespeare.

These were made from the Bodleian Library at Oxford, to which I regularly returned for the spring and summer semester. It was from Simon Forman's voluminous papers there that I was able to identify the Dark Lady, the discarded mistress of Lord Chamberlain Hunsdon, Patron of Shakespeare's Company—Emilia Bassano, half-Italian Jewish, like the famous Florio, tutor to Southampton, Shakespeare's young patron.

This was not the end of my discoveries: only quite recently have I established the autobiographical character of *The Two Gentlemen of Verona*. No one had noticed what an autobiographical writer William Shakespeare was: the only Elizabethan dramatist to write his autobiography—in the Sonnets. The eventual upshot of this is the firm three-dimensional figure we now have, in place of the confused and unfirm two-dimensional figure that had hitherto prevailed and led to so much mystification and nonsense. Nor should it be surprising that this revolution should have been accomplished by the welding together of literature and history, an intimate knowledge of Shakespeare's time by the leading authority on his age.

The success of my original biography should not have occasioned heart-burn, for no-one has ever been able to fault it, much as some would like to have done. Its exceptional success with the public (occasion of much envy) enabled me to pay visits to universities all over the country I longed to see—from the source of the Missouri in Montana to lovely Charleston in spring, from New Orleans in camellia-time to the numerous colleges of Pennsylvania, Ohio, New England, up to Maine and over the border to deliver the Bailey Lectures at McGill, under the aegis of my friend Hugh MacLennan, first of Canadian novelists.

I chose to spend one winter semester at the University of Wisconsin–Madison, between those two lakes—because I wanted to research into the collections in the two libraries there relating to the Cornish miners and the remarkable early Socialist leader John Spargo, the Cornishman (well known early this century) who had known Karl Marx's brilliant daughter, Eleanor. Not far from Madison is charming Mineral

A. L. Rowse in the library of Trenarren House, his home in Cornwall

Point, almost a museum piece with its old miners' stone cottages, and now a resort area. Here I met a good many of the third and fourth generation settlers, and entertained my colleagues for a day's outing, a proper meal of Cornish pasty (not Cornish hen, which comes from Cornwall, Connecticut), "beef Truro," and saffron cake. Similar folk fare I have enjoyed in Grass Valley and the Upper Peninsula. The substance of my researches, rather than the food, provided the fare for *The Cousin Jacks: The Cornish in America*. But I have followed their tracks in many states, though not, alas, Colorado where there are many descendants of our miners.

In the last decade I have spent half-a-dozen springs—Spring in Virginia!—on the delightful campus of Lynchburg College, prunus, cherries in flower, in full view of the Blue Ridge Mountains. This was the nearby girlhood town of my old friend Lady Astor's family: the Langhornes came over from Cornwall

some time in the seventeenth century.

Here I devoted time to my final literary project: *The Contemporary Shakespeare*. I learned from various sources that the younger generation were put off him by the archaic language. Elizabethan grammar is sometimes ungrammatical to us, and vastly more is moribund: all those subjunctives we no longer use, double negatives, the second personal singular "thou's" and "thee's," the many words of which we no longer know the meaning. Why not clear superfluous difficulties out of the way, instead of burying the text in footnotes?

All over the world people use Shakespeare in learning English. Why tease them with a lot of archaic usage we no longer use? Note that the gap between Shakespeare's language and ours widens with every decade. So I have gone through all the plays just removing superfluous difficulties, very conservatively, sticking to every line and half-line of Shakespeare's text: (though a reactionary, I am an open-minded reactionary).

It was to be expected that Americans would be more open-minded, ready to experiment, than the fuddy-duddies in the Old Country. And that theatre people would be more open to something new than fogies in classrooms—though that is precisely where the *Contemporary Shakespeare* is most helpful. So it has proved. When we produced *Romeo and Juliet* at Lynchburg one of the audience came up to me and said, "I have enjoyed the performance all the more because I could understand every word of it." He could not have pleased me more: that is precisely the end I have in mind.

Since then there have been productions of several more plays in my edition—edition, *not* version: in California, Florida, O'Neill's old theatre in Greenwich Village, and a wonderful production, by a brilliant producer, Zoe Caldwell, at Stratford, Connecticut, leaving Old Stratford high and dry by the banks of the Avon. This was of *The Taming of the Shrew*, in modern American idiom, clothes, etc., to which this play, with its modern theme, is specially adapted—as Richard Burton recognised on his last appearance (with me) on the "Today Show" in New York.

I fear that all this is about my outer life rather than the inner (to be found in the poetry), and perhaps more about my work than about me. But, then, my writing has been my life: I do not write in order to live, I live in order to write.

BIBLIOGRAPHY

Poetry:

Poems of a Decade, 1931–1941. London: Faber, 1941.

Poems Chiefly Cornish. London: Faber, 1944.

Poems of Deliverance. London: Faber, 1946.

Poems, Partly American. London: Faber, 1959.

Poems of Cornwall and America. London: Faber, 1967.

Strange Encounter. London: J. Cape, 1972.

The Road to Oxford. London: J. Cape, 1978.

A Life: Collected Poems. Edinburgh: W. Blackwood, 1981.

Transatlantic: Later Poems. Padstow, Cornwall: Tabb House, 1988.

Nonfiction:

On History: A Study of Present Tendencies. London: Kegan Paul, Trench, Trubner, 1927; also published as *Science and History: A New View of History*. New York: Norton, 1928.

Politics and the Younger Generation. London: Faber, 1931.

Queen Elizabeth and Her Subjects, with G. B. Harrison. London: Allen & Unwin, 1935; Salem, N.Y.: Ayer Co., 1987.

Mr. Keynes and the Labour Movement. London: Macmillan, 1936.

Sir Richard Grenville of the "Revenge": An Elizabethan Hero. London: J. Cape, 1937; Boston: Houghton, 1937.

Tudor Cornwall: Portrait of a Society. London: J. Cape, 1941; revised edition. New York: Scribner, 1969.

A Cornish Childhood: Autobiography of a Cornishman. London: J. Cape, 1942; New York: Macmillan, 1947.

The Spirit of English History. London and New York: Longmans, Green, 1943.

The English Spirit: Essays in History and Literature. London: Macmillan, 1944; revised edition. New York: Funk, 1967.

The Use of History. London: Hodder & Stoughton, 1946; New York: Macmillan, 1948.

The End of an Epoch: Reflections on Contemporary History. London: Macmillan, 1947.

The England of Elizabeth: The Structure of Society. London: Macmillan, 1950; New York: Macmillan, 1951.

The English Past: Evocations of Persons and Places. London: Macmillan, 1951; New York: Macmillan, 1952; revised edition published as *Times, Persons, Places: Essays in Literature*. London: Macmillan, 1965.

An Elizabethan Garland. London: Macmillan, 1953; New York: St. Martin's, 1953.

Royal Homes Illustrated. London: Odhams, 1953.

The Expansion of Elizabethan England. London: Macmillan, 1955; New York: St. Martin's, 1955.

The Early Churchills: An English Family. London: Macmillan, 1956; New York: Harper, 1956.

The Later Churchills. London: Macmillan, 1958.

The Churchills: From the Death of Marlborough to the Present (contains abridged versions of *The Early Churchills: An English Family* and *The Later Churchills*). New York: Harper, 1958.

The Elizabethans and America. London: Macmillan, 1959; New York: Harper, 1959.

St. Austell: Church, Town, Parish (photographs by Charles Woolf). St. Austell, England: H. E. Warne, 1960.

All Souls and Appeasement: A Contribution to Contemporary History. London: Macmillan, 1961; New York: St. Martin's, 1961; augmented edition published as *Appeasement: A Study in Political Decline, 1933–1939*. New York: Norton, 1961.

Ralegh and the Throckmortons. London: Macmillan, 1962; New York: St. Martin's, 1962; also published as *Sir Walter Ralegh: His Family and Private Life*. New York: Harper, 1962.

William Shakespeare: A Biography. London: Macmillan, 1963; New York: Harper, 1963.

Christopher Marlowe: A Biography. London: Macmillan, 1964; New York: Harper, 1964; also published as *Christopher Marlowe: His Life and Work*. New York: Harper, 1965.

A Cornishman at Oxford: The Education of a Cornishman (autobiography). London: J. Cape, 1965; Dover, N.H.: Longwood, 1982.

Shakespeare's Southampton: Patron of Virginia. London: Macmillan, 1965; New York: Harper, 1965.

Bosworth Field and the Wars of the Roses. London: Macmillan, 1966; also published as *Bosworth Field, from Medieval to Tudor England*. Garden City, N.Y.: Doubleday, 1966.

The Cornish in America. London: Macmillan, 1969; also published as *The Cousin Jacks: The Cornish in America*. New York: Scribner, 1969.

Queen Elizabeth and Her Subjects, with G. B. Harrison. Freeport, N.Y.: Books for Libraries Press, 1970.

The Elizabethan Renaissance. Vol. 1: *The Life of the Society*. London: Macmillan, 1971; New York: Scribner, 1972. Vol. 2: *The Cultural Achievement*. London: Macmillan, 1972; New York: Scribner, 1972.

The Tower of London in the History of the Nation. London: Weidenfeld & Nicolson, 1972; also published as *The Tower of London in the History of England*, New York: Putnam, 1972.

Westminster Abbey in the History of the Nation. London: Weidenfeld & Nicolson, 1972.

Shakespeare the Man. London: Macmillan, 1973; New York: Harper, 1973; revised edition. London: Macmillan, 1988.

Simon Forman: Sex and Society in Shakespeare's Age. London: Weidenfeld & Nicolson, 1974; also published as *Sex and Society in Shakespeare's Age: Simon Forman the Astrologer*. New York: Scribner, 1974; also published as *The Case Books of Simon Forman: Sex and Society in Shakespeare's Age*. London: Pan Books, 1976.

Windsor Castle in the History of the Nation. London: Weidenfeld & Nicolson, 1974; also published as *Windsor Castle in the History of England*. New York: Putnam, 1974.

Discoveries and Reviews from Renaissance to Restoration. London: Macmillan, 1975; New York: Barnes & Noble, 1975.

Jonathan Swift: Major Prophet. London: Thames & Hudson, 1975; New York: Scribner, 1975.

Oxford in the History of the Nation. London: Weidenfeld & Nicolson, 1975; also published as *Oxford in the History of England*. New York: Putnam, 1975.

Robert Stephen Hawker of Morwenstow: A Belated Mediaeval (essay). St. Germans, England: The Elephant Press, 1975.

A Cornishman Abroad (autobiography). London: J. Cape, 1976.

Matthew Arnold: Poet and Prophet. London: Thames & Hudson, 1976; Lanham, Md.: University Press of America, 1986.

Heritage of Britain. London: Artus Publishing Co., 1977; New York: Putnam, 1977.

Homosexuals in History: A Study of Ambivalence in Society, Literature, and the Arts. London: Weidenfeld & Nicolson, 1977; New York: Macmillan, 1977.

Milton the Puritan: Portrait of a Mind. London: Macmillan, 1977; Lanham, Md.: University Press of America, 1985.

Shakespeare the Elizabethan. London: Weidenfeld & Nicolson, 1977; New York: Putnam, 1977.

The Tower of London. London: Michael Joseph, 1977.

The Byrons and Trevanions. London: Weidenfeld & Nicolson, 1978; New York: St. Martin's, 1979.

The Illustrated History of Britain. New York: Crescent Books/Crown, 1979.

A Man of the Thirties (autobiography). London: Weidenfeld & Nicolson, 1979.

Portraits and Views, Literary and Historical. London: Macmillan, 1979; New York: Barnes & Noble, 1979.

The Story of Britain. London: Treasure Press, 1979; New York: Putnam, 1979.

Memories of Men and Women. London: Eyre Methuen, 1980.

Shakespeare's Globe: His Intellectual and Moral Outlook. London: Weidenfeld & Nicolson, 1981; also published as *What Shakespeare Read—and Thought*. New York: Coward, McCann & Geoghegan, 1981.

Eminent Elizabethans. London: Macmillan, 1983; Athens: University of Georgia Press, 1983.

Memories of Men and Women, American and British. London: Methuen, 1983; Lanham, Md.: University Press of America, 1983.

Prefaces to Shakespeare's Plays (first appeared in *The Annotated Shakespeare*). London: Orbis Publishing, 1984; Topsfield, Mass.: Salem House, 1986.

Shakespeare's Characters: A Complete Guide. London: Methuen, 1984.

Glimpses of the Great. London: Methuen, 1985; Lanham, Md.: University Press of America, 1986.

In Shakespeare's Land. London: Weidenfeld & Nicolson, 1986; also published as *Shakespeare's Land: A Journey through the Landscape of Elizabethan England*. San Francisco: Chronicle Books, 1987.

The Little Land of Cornwall. Gloucester, England: Alan Sutton, 1986; New York: Hippocrene, 1986.

Reflections on the Puritan Revolution. London: Methuen, 1986.

Court and Country: Studies in Tudor Social History. Brighton, England: Harvester Press, 1987; Athens: University of Georgia Press, 1987.

Froude the Historian: Victorian Man of Letters. Gloucester, England: Alan Sutton, 1987.

The Poet Auden: A Personal Memoir. London: Methuen, 1987.

Quiller Couch: A Portrait of "Q." London: Methuen, 1988.

Friends and Contemporaries. London: Methuen, 1989.

Fiction:

West-Country Stories. London: Macmillan, 1945; New York: Macmillan, 1947.

Cornish Stories. London: Macmillan, 1967.

Peter, the White Cat of Trenarren. London: Michael Joseph, 1974.

Brown Buck: A Californian Fantasy (for children). London: Michael Joseph, 1976.

Chalky Jenkins: A Little Cat Lost. London: Weidenfeld & Nicolson, 1978.

Three Cornish Cats (includes *Peter, the White Cat of Trenarren, Chalky Jenkins,* and *Tommer, the Black Farm-Cat;* illustrated by William Geldart). London: Weidenfeld & Nicolson, 1978.

Night at the Carn and Other Stories. London: Kimber & Co., 1984.

A Quartet of Cornish Cats. London: Weidenfeld & Nicolson, 1986.

Stories from Trenarren. London: Kimber & Co., 1986.

Editor of:

Essays in Cornish History, by Charles Henderson, edited with M. I. Henderson. London: Oxford University Press, 1935.

The West in English History (essays). London: Hodder & Stoughton, 1949.

A History of France, by Lucien Romier, translated and completed by A. L. Rowse. London: Macmillan, 1953; New York: St. Martin's, 1953.

Sonnets, by William Shakespeare. London: Macmillan, 1964; New York: Harper, 1964; revised edition published as *Shakespeare's Sonnets: The Problems Solved.* London: Macmillan, 1973; New York: Harper, 1973.

A Cornish Anthology. London: Macmillan, 1968.

The Two Chiefs of Dunboy: A Story of Eighteenth-Century Ireland, by James Anthony Froude. London: Chatto & Windus, 1969.

Victorian and Edwardian Cornwall from Old Photographs, with John Betjeman. London: Batsford, 1974.

The Annotated Shakespeare. Vol. 1: *The Comedies.* Vol. 2: *The Histories, Sonnets and Other Poems.* Vol. 3: *The Tragedies and Romances.* London: Orbis Publishing, 1978; New York: C. N. Potter Books/Crown, 1978.

The Poems of Shakespeare's Dark Lady, by Emilia Lanier. London: J. Cape, 1978; New York: C. N. Potter Books/Crown, 1979.

A Man of Singular Virtue: Being a Life of Sir Thomas More by His Son-in-law William Roper, and a Selection of More's Letters. London: Folio Society, 1980.

Shakespeare's Self-Portrait: Passages from His Work. London: Macmillan, 1985; Lanham, Md.: Madison Books/ University Press of America, 1985.

The First Colonists: Hakluyt's Voyages to North America. London: Folio Society, 1986.

The Spanish Story of the Armada, by James Anthony Froude. Gloucester, England: Alan Sutton, 1988.

Margaret St. Clair

1911-

THE LACK OF TEDDY BEARS

Margaret St. Clair, about 1980

*For Susan and Hugh Leddy,
who knew us both*

A reviewer once called me an "elusive" writer. I am not quite sure what he meant, but I have always disliked writing about myself. If I write fully and frankly, I sound whiney; if I make omissions, I feel evasive and disingenuous. I can only try to do my best.

I was born February 17, 1911, at home, in Hutchinson, Kansas. My mother had been a schoolteacher, my father was an attorney, brilliant and able, a self-made man. They had lost a child, a boy, in the first year of their marriage. Perhaps that is why—according to family legend—when told that I was a girl, Mother said, "Take her away. I don't want to look at her." She told me, many years later, that no woman ever really wants children: they are always forced upon her, adding hastily that of course she

loves them after they are born.

However that may be, I seem to have experienced a considerable degree of maternal rejection early in life. Mother had many fine qualities, but warmth and cuddliness were not among them. I remember her as boney, rigid, clutching, remote, and withdrawn.

The people around me had trouble finding a feeding formula I would accept, and—obviously this is hearsay—I learned to drink from a cup at the age of a few weeks. Before that, I almost starved.

I survived. I saw the world around me as basically a hostile one, a place where serious threats were invoked for trivial faults, but still a place that offered many small enjoyments. I remember an all-day sucker, butterscotch flavored and imprinted with the image of a duck, that I considered delicious; the taste of a mild vanilla soda; the smell of lilacs and lily of the valley; the soft, sweet coolness of peonies.

Somebody read Hawthorne's *Tanglewood Tales* to me; the book had strange, rich pictures. My father, who always thought I was older than I was, gave me a set of *The Book of Knowledge* when I was three. I was too young for it, but I loved it. It was one of the best things in my life.

I had my share of childish illnesses. I had a bout with typhoid fever in Washington, where my father was in the congress, when I was two or three. I remember being tangled in the folds of a wet sheet that was supposed to reduce my fever, and how I got hotter rather than cooler from my contact with it.

The other recollections of the stay in D.C. involve lobster, which I learned to like, and hominy, which I hated from the start. I remember riding my tricycle around the hotel lobby, and being kissed by some bigwig, I think President Taft. There was a trip down the Atlantic coast by steamer: I saw the Statue of Liberty through a snowstorm and, somewhat later, a broad stretch of brown water that I was told was the Gulf Stream. There were pralines in New Orleans.

Back home in Kansas, I had a tonsilectomy at the age of three or so—rather young—and had an awful sore throat afterwards. Mother used to recount, with fascinated horror, that I had leaped from my hospital

Brother, Newland Neeley, who died in infancy

bed and drunk water from a vase of flowers in the room "before I could stop her." Poor woman, she saw me as a wild, dangerous, uncontrollable force, not as a small child.

Scarlet fever came next, with a printed pink quarantine notice and a trained nurse. I had limewater, which was wonderfully comforting to the stomach. The illness was supposed to have left me with a kidney weakness, which I don't think was true.

Somewhere in here I had chicken pox and measles, but they didn't impress me much. Like a lot of children, I had a lot of colds. One thing I learned early was that Mentholatum, inserted in one nostril, clears that side of the head but stops the other side up. My parents took care of me, even good care. But I wish somebody had just cuddled me up and made me comfortable.

I was a clumsy child, not so much from any real awkwardness as from a deep alienation from my own body: I felt forbidden to use it effectively and enjoyably. I was always falling down, scraping my knees, tearing holes in my stockings. A scraped knee oozes a sticky liquid that glues the stocking to the wound. It's a sort of pattern for neurotic suffering.

When I was seven or so, I wanted a coaster wagon. Roller skates I had, and was always falling down with, but I felt a coaster wagon would be within my limited range of motor competence. One put a cushion in the body of the wagon and knelt on it, while propelling the wagon with the other foot. All simple and straightforward, you see, and with no risk of falling down.

I told my parents about this, and my father agreed it was a reasonable wish. He was doing well in his law practice and could afford it.

He went to the store to buy the wagon, and came back with a bicycle—I suppose in his eyes it was a much better toy than a coaster wagon. Mother objected to the bicycle, on the ground that I might get hurt riding the bike in the street.

A battle followed, and in the end the bicycle was returned to the store.

I hadn't wanted the bike. I was far too clumsy for it to seem like anything except a threat. My father would have insisted that I learn to ride it, and I wouldn't have been able to. But the upshot was that I didn't get anything, not even the bike.

I got blood poisoning from a rusty nail when I was between seven and eight. I was treated with something called toxin-antitoxin. Medicine was just beginning to attain something like real healing power in those years: I imagine that if I'd been born ten years earlier, I'd have died from tetanus.

I don't suppose, actually, that I had any more

illnesses than most children do. I was cautious and conservative in playing, and never broke any bones. But I hated being sick, and was afraid of it. I suppose I was afraid that if I were sick too much, became too much of a nuisance, my parents might simply abandon me.

I could have handled the problems and lacks in my life better if I had had a teddy bear. A teddy bear is a happiness and security blanket raised to a number of powers. To have something warm, soft, reassuring to touch is a basic mammalian need. There was little in my childhood that felt good or was comforting to touch. Thumb sucking was most strictly forbidden; I remember having my fingers dipped in iodine and being told that I would die if I sucked them. I used to pat a lock of my own hair; this infuriated my father, and I remember him standing over me with raised hand, ready to strike. But a teddy bear . . .

My little girlfriend (another Margaret) had a teddy, an electric marvel with eyes that lit up when he was touched. How I coveted that teddy bear! My favorite game with her was to pretend that it was Christmas, that she was my mother, and that she was giving me all her toys. (She had wonderful toys.) She was not as fond of this game as I was.

Christmas was usually a time of bitter disappointment for me. Sometimes I got books, which I liked; occasionally I got an Oz book, which was expensive but wonderful. One of my aunts gave me a pretty little ring, and another year she gave me a hand-painted pitcher and bowl from which I could eat my mush. But usually I got a doll—another rigid, cold, hard, faintly sneering doll, who had to be taken care of, when I could hardly take care of myself.

I don't know why, really, nobody ever gave me a teddy bear. I had a rabbit; it was kept in a cage, and some dogs broke in and killed it. Mother thought cats carried ringworm. I had a duck, called Peter, that was kept with the chickens and eventually killed and eaten. I cried, but in the end I ate some of Peter. My father gave me a .22 rifle when I was seven or so, though I don't remember ever firing it.

This part of my life, the years in the little house on Sherman East, came to an abrupt end when my father died. The flu epidemic in 1919 killed mainly young adults. Quite a number of my contemporaries lost one or both parents in it. My father was only forty. He was dead within five days of the time he first complained of a chest cold.

With his death, a shadow passed from my life. I think he loved me: Mother, who had a gift for these things, said, "Why, your father loved you so much! He loved you just as much as if you'd been a boy!"

There was *The Book of Knowledge*, for one thing, and his financial arrangements.

But I was uneasy in his presence. I perceived him as savage, unpredictable, seductive, punitive. Had I been able to see him with the eyes of maturity, I am sure I would have had kinder memories of him. As it was, I fear Mother's hateful but perceptive comment must stand: "You're not sorry he's dead. You don't cry." I seemed to have perceived him as an inveterate opponent of teddy bears.

Fortunately, he had left some life insurance, and Mother and I were modestly comfortable. We travelled—from Kansas to California, where an aunt and uncle were, and to Colorado for one or two vacations. I remember the Pullman trips with great pleasure—the observation car, with its array of magazines and views from the arch of windows, the ladies' room, with its strange-smelling soap and wonderful silvery washbasins, the steady motion and click and clatter of the train. There was the thrill of waking early and looking out the little window at a strange new scene. And best of all, there was the wonderful Pullman food.

Amtrak has nothing to compare with this.

Another pleasure, while we were still living in Kansas, was visits to the grand house my aunt (the one who gave me the ring) and uncle lived in.

Uncle Ross was a Quaker who had prospered. Most Quakers are honest, hard working, and friendly; since these qualities are strongly conducive to success, many Quakers end up blessed with a considerable portion of the world's goods.

Uncle Ross was in the cattle business. He and Aunt Stella made trips "abroad" (to Europe), and were always a source of gratification and interest. Uncle Ross was governor of Kansas for a while. They climaxed it all by building a grand house, a mansion by any standards, on their twenty-acre farm in Lawrence, where the University of Kansas is.

The house had everything. There was a porte cochere, a noble baronial hall, front and back stairs, a sewing room, a laundry room in the basement, even a ballroom on the third floor. There was a library, where I first encountered the Elsie Dinsmore books. (Elsie was a priggish child who fainted at the piano rather than obey her cruel stepmother's order to defile the Sabbath by obliging the family with some little tune on the piano.)

I don't have a clear picture of the outside of the house, but I think there were pillars and a pediment. The only flowers I remember were marvellous lilac bushes, purple and white, and "flags" (irises) growing near the pond where people went skating in the winter. There was a telescope on the third floor.

Father, George A. Neeley

*Margaret with her mother, Eva M. Neeley,
Hutchinson, Kansas, 1911*

There was a music room, with a beautiful big golden harp. And—final touch of poshness—there were chutes in the bathrooms, down which used towels were dispatched to the laundry room below.

It was incredible. Such splendor, at that time, in Kansas, might well arouse the envy of the gods.

There came a terrible winter, with snowstorm after snowstorm and much cold. Cattle died by the hundreds. And at the end of everything, Uncle Ross was still solvent, but he was no longer a millionaire.

The big house was impossible to heat on a stinted budget. It was sold to some fraternity. I suppose it was pulled down long ago.

I had my first menstrual period a little before my twelfth birthday. I had known about it—Mother had told me, which was unusual of her, but kind—and I was not afraid. In fact, I was as proud as punch of my new condition—I thought, "I'm a woman now. I'm as good as any of them." Mother, however, considered that a terrible misfortune had befallen me. For the record, be it observed that I almost never had menstrual cramps. I don't know whether this means that I simply had a good pelvis, or that I hadn't been close enough to Mother to pick up all the conventional ideas about "the curse."

I don't remember how old I was when somebody noticed that I didn't see very well; I was given glasses, and called Harold Lloyd by my peers. (Harold Lloyd was a famous comic star of the silent screen, who wore horn-rimmed glasses.) My contact with the world improved slightly after that.

In school I hated, loathed, physical education. To this day I am wobbly about the multiplication table. (I have a private rule for remembering the nines.) But I did well in English, and earlier skipped grades.

I read a lot—lots of Kipling, and *Kim* in particular, the Lang fairy books, George MacDonald's magisterial Curdie books, a collection of other works by Andrew Lang called *My Own Fairy Book*. This last contained a sequel to Thackeray's *Rose and the Ring*, and a strange, haunting fairy story by Lang about two children who annointed their eyes with tears from a Roman lachrymatory. My reading, foreseeably, earned me Mother's reproach for always having my nose stuck in a book.

The influence of Greek literature, which has been one of the strongest and most lasting things in my life, began when I read Euripides' *Electra* in translation. I was enormously impressed by it. The play came to me as a small blue pamphlet, issued as one of the Haldeman-Julius Little Blue Books, which sold for five cents.

I began reading Homer in translation about this

time. I was studying Latin in high school—high schools taught Latin in those days—and was impressed with how many of the epithets in the *Aeneid* were direct translations into Latin of the Greek originals.

I had little social life in high school. I was painfully shy and, since I had been reared alone, simply didn't know how to get along with other young people. This was a great disappointment to Mother, who wanted me to be popular—"Why are you so different? So queer? Why don't you try to be a little more normal? More like other girls?" They were all questions to which I knew no easy answer.

I got a crush on a boy a year ahead of me, and went to the church he attended for the thrill of seeing him. I wrote poems to him and, in general, worshipped from afar. More important than the boy was a statue of Athena—Minerva—that stood in one of the high-school halls. I looked at it with immediate comprehension. This was it, what I had been looking for. From that time on I was a Goddess-worshipper.

I had been silently disaffected toward Christianity as far back as I can remember. Later on, I used to sing the customary hymns with the substitution of "her" for "him" when it was appropriate. I don't know why I reacted this way, exactly. I was sent to church, and went to Sunday school—where we always seemed to be hearing about the Israelites crossing the Red Sea—in quite the usual manner. But I had listened to the teaching with complete incredulity. One of the few things that have happened in the world during my lifetime that give me any satisfaction is the return of the Goddess. Who would have thought, seventy years ago, that it would ever be possible to say "the Goddess" seriously? I suppose I found in her the most cogent of teddy bears.

When I was about seventeen, Mother and I moved to California, to Long Beach. She had a brother in Santa Ana, and it hardly seemed reasonable for us to stay on in the harsh Kansas climate when we didn't have to. We were not there very long before Mother developed some sort of functional heart disorder; it made her take to her bed, where she stayed, with one short break, for the rest of her life, about twenty-three years.

It seemed such a terrible waste. I asked her once why she stayed in bed, and she answered, "Because of my blood pressure."

"I know," I said, "but is staying in bed the usual treatment for high blood pressure?"

Rather doubtfully she said, "No . . ."

"Then why stay there?"

"I don't know," she answered almost desperate-

Margaret Neeley, Washington, D.C.

ly, "but I feel safer here."

I always felt sorry for her. When I tried to tell her this, she became quite annoyed and told me sharply, "Why, I've had a happy life." I'm glad she could say that.

Somewhere along in here I decided to learn Greek. I had time. I wasn't gainfully employed, and we had somebody come in to help with Mother's care. My first text was a small, ridged volume called *A First Greek Book*, and from there I went on to a school edition of Xenophon's *Anabasis*. Greek texts were a lot easier to get then than they are now. I got a Greek grammar from the Long Beach public library.

Mother and I had moved to Santa Ana, where her brother John lived, and I was going to Santa Ana Junior College. Uncle John was a lovely man. Both he and Uncle Ross—who was dead by then—were always sweet and kind to a shy and difficult young girl. I had good luck with my uncles. I will always remember them, and wish them well, wherever they are. I don't know if they knew, while they were still alive, how much I valued them.

At the end of the year in Santa Ana, I won a prize for poetry, and persuaded the Greek department of the University of California at Berkeley to accept me as a person qualified to take third-year courses in Greek. I entered the university as a junior.

I loved the university. I used to look up at the beautiful bronze head of Athena over the library entrance and feel that I had come home. I applied for and got a scholarship, and in 1931 I was elected to Phi Beta Kappa, the scholastic honor society.

I was graduated *cum laude* from the university in May 1932. A few days after my graduation I was married to Eric St. Clair—Ray at that time—whom I had met at a friend's house the year before.

A description of Eric might be in order here. He was a few inches taller than I, stocky and sturdily built, with bright blue eyes, abundant very dark brown curly hair, a massive jaw, and high coloring. He tended to bluster and be truculent. It took me many years to realize that his blustering and vehemence hid a deep insecurity. He was prone to oddly abstract outbursts of rage, to loud self-righteous denunciations of just about anything. Yet with all this he had enormous charm. He was in himself a teddy bear of high quality. It is certainly significant that his pet names were Wum-wum, Bear-bear, and Poochie boy. (I hope I am not nauseating you.)

The marriage turned out to be an extraordinarily close one. Certainly we were not always happy. But we were together constantly for almost fifty-four years. On most levels we were extraordinarily compatible.

He was a graduate of Cal Tech, from which, in the late twenties, he had obtained a degree in physical science and economics. He had been a statistician until the investment firm for which he had been working had gone out of business, and, not long after we met, he was once more employed as a statistician with the California State Unemployment Commission, whose findings were the base of the state relief system.

We were married on May 25, 1932. It was the bottom of the Depression; we didn't even dream of a honeymoon. When the fall semester at the university began, we both went back to school, I in the Greek department and he in the economics.

I got a master's degree in Greek early in 1934; Eric refused to work for a higher degree in economics, though the subject for a master's thesis suggested to him by one of his teachers ("The Effect of the Corn Laws on the Condition of the English Poor") seemed to me to be right up his alley. He denounced it as the damnedest silly idea he'd ever heard of, and I kept my trap shut.

The New Deal was in the works. Eric could probably have been in on it from the beginning, but he had never been crazy about statistics, and we wanted to do something where we could be together. We decided to start a nursery specializing in rare bulbs.

It was a remarkably boneheaded idea. Neither of us had any business experience or background, and while we were fairly good in abstract botany, we knew nothing about practical gardening.

What might have been foreseen happened. We imported bulbs, didn't sell many of them, wasted time and money. The nursery went downhill. About the only good thing that did come out of the mess was that we got to grow a lot of interesting bulbs.

World War II coming along made it impossible for us to get gas for our car. The nursery was moribund anyhow. Eric went into the shipyards—El Sobrante, where we were living, was near Richmond, where the Liberty ships were being built—and I tried to cope with what was diagnosed as arthritis, though I was only twenty-eight.

Eric became a shipfitter. It never occurred to either of us that he might get back into statistics. Though his background had been academic, he had always liked working with his hands, and I think he liked his work in the shipyards the best of everything he ever did. As for myself, I had an operation for a deviated nasal septum, my arthritis subsided, and I went into the shipyards too, as a welder.

I was not a success. I burned holes in the metal I was supposed to be welding, and finally, after about two months of failure, I opted out of welding and began taking a course in writing from a now-defunct magazine, *Author and Journalist*.

I was not one of the people who had "always wanted to be a writer," though I had done a fair amount of writing. I wrote one complete mystery novel—it was punk—before I enrolled in *Author and Journalist*'s course. In short, I had some literary aspirations, and wanted to see what I could do.

The course must have been a pretty good one. Of the stories I wrote as assignments, I sold two ("Letter from the Deceased," in *Detective Story Magazine*, my first published story, and "The Perfectionist," in *Mystery Book Magazine*, my most successful single story), and won a prize with the third, "And Tells It Twice as Plain," which appeared in the *New Mexico Quarterly Review*.

Mother was pleased with my writing. It was one of the few times when she really seemed to approve of me. She had opposed my marriage, for reasons which seemed good to her, and I think she felt I was holding a grudge against her for this. I wasn't, but it was nice to have done something of which she really approved.

As you can see, my first published work was

Lawrence, Kansas, about 1920

detective fiction. I wrote more, sold a few, and decided to indulge myself with a try at science fiction.

I had read science fiction and fantasy from quite an early age. The first book I remember reading by myself, *Sugar Loaf Mountain*, was a fantasy. I read Verne's *Journey to the Center of the Earth* at recess when I was in the fifth grade, and the teacher chewed me out for not playing with the other children. Later I read some of the Gernsback magazines, and *Weird Tales*. I remember Eric's reading "The Monster of the Prophecy," by C. A. Smith, from the latter magazine, aloud to me before we were married.

Science fiction at first was pure delight. It was wonderful to write easily and enjoyably, after the hard work of plotting and writing mystery fiction.

My first published science fiction yarn was something called "Rocket to Limbo"; it appeared in *Fantastic Adventures* for November 1946. After that, I began to sell science fiction fairly regularly. I sold a lot to *Startling Stories* and *Thrilling Wonder Stories*, both publications of Standard Magazines, where Sam Merwin was editor. I particularly remember "Hathor's Pets," "The Gardener," the Jick and Oona stories, and *Vulcan's Dolls*.

My experiences with *Vulcan's Dolls* illustrate

something worth knowing about editors: they want to EDIT. Unless they change something, how do they know they're editors? When Ace decided to reprint *Vulcan's Dolls* as one of their double books, they changed the title to *Agent of the Unknown*. I think it's a terrible title, but the change did give somebody an opportunity to edit.

Over the years, I've found that titles with the word "of" in them rarely get changed, and that editors, in changing titles, tend to go for the word "of."

While I was getting established in the science fiction market, Eric had begun to write short fiction for children. He was a natural storyteller; almost from the first days of our marriage, he had told me stories, wonderful stories. The germ of the "bear stories" of which he sold so many to Pflaum Publishing Company could be found in the stories of those early days. They were always about bears—again, the teddy bear motif. Now he was putting them down on paper and sending them out.

He sold several stories to *Story Parade*, and one or two to various church publications. He had a few slick sales—*Esquire*, the *Saturday Evening Post*, and *Redbook* —but didn't have places where he sold consistently. Then he made contact with Pflaum, as I said above, and sold them lots and lots of things. He particularly liked writing the continuity of comic strips for *Treasure Chest*, one of Pflaum's educational comic format books for older children. He had a most happy relationship with them.

He proposed to radio station KPFA, Pacifica Radio, in Berkeley, that he read some of his bear stories for them. They accepted, and he soon had a devoted following.

His recorded voice dismayed him. "Is that how I sound?" he demanded after he first heard one of his tapes. "Like a cross between Calvin Coolidge and a duck?" To which I answered, "That's *exactly* how you do sound."

I kept on writing short science-fiction and fantasy stories. I began to sell to the *Magazine of Fantasy and Science Fiction*. The first story I sold them, "World of Arlesia," was an almost exact transcription of a dream I had had—the first and only time I've done this.

Anthony Boucher, the editor there, insisted that I come up with a pseudonym, and I settled on Idris Seabright. *Fantasy and Science Fiction* published a lot of my really good stories, but certainly not all of them. *Galaxy* did a lot, *Weird Tales* did pretty well by me, and there were odd sales to things like *If* and *Beyond*. I made a few sales to *Dude* and *Gent*, where they always put me on the cover. It was an attention for which I was grateful.

I have wondered sometimes why nobody has wanted to do a collection of the stories I sold *Fantasy and Science Fiction* under the Seabright alias. It would make a slim volume, but it would be good.

Somewhere in here I did some psychotherapy and changed agents, moving to McIntosh and Otis, where I still am.

I started writing longer fiction. *Vulcan's Dolls,* about whose name change I spoke earlier, was the first of novella length. Then I did *The Green Queen* and *The Games of Neith.* All three of these were published by Ace as halves in their double-book series.

I was still writing short fiction, of course. In 1961 Eric and I took a long, happy trip through the South Pacific. We went to Tahiti, the two Samoas, Fiji, and even Australia (where, since it was December, the weather was dreadfully hot).

I believe I had signed a contract for *Sign of the Labrys* before we went. This was my first novel-length piece of fiction. My title for this had been *The Fungus Hunters,* but this is a rather lackluster title, and I do not blame the editor at Bantam for changing it.

It had been written under the influence of the late Gerald Gardner's book *The Meaning of Witchcraft.* I drew heavily on this book for atmosphere and ideas. It is interesting to reflect that Gardner and Robert Graves, the poet and novelist, were, between them, largely responsible for the current vogue of neopaganism, or of what people conceive of as neopaganism.

My novel did not make much of a splash, though somebody called it "A classic of occultism." Sometime after its publication I made contact with two self-styled witches, of the Gardnerian persuasion, and corresponded with them off and on for years.

Back from the luxurious warmth of the South Pacific, I set to work on another piece of novel-length fiction, *The Dolphins of Altair.* I don't remember exactly where I got the basic ideas for this. Some of it, certainly, came from reports of mutated sea life near sites where radioactive wastes had been dumped in the ocean.

The third novel was *The Shadow People.* (My title for this was *World under Berkeley,* which the editor objected to, on the grounds that it would hurt sales. This was at the time of the student unrest in Berkeley and elsewhere, and I suppose the word "Berkeley" frightened him. Personally, I think it would have *helped* sales.)

Much of the background for this came from a book by L. C. Wimberly, *Folklore in English and Scottish Ballads.* The general feel of the book, of constant misery and distress, came from a dreadful attack of shingles I had had a number of years before. The pain

of shingles is something one never forgets. But I always liked this book, probably because it did have so much atmosphere.

In between *Sign of the Labrys* and *The Dolphins* I wrote another novella, *Message from the Eocene.* As I remember, some of the atmosphere for this one came from a book about poltergeists.

Eric, who had been working as a laboratory technician in the physics department of the University at Berkeley, decided to retire about this time. There was not much to keep us in the house in El Sobrante where we had been living for so many years. El Sobrante (this is Spanish for "leftover") had built up enormously during our stay there, and we had the disadvantages of both the country and the town—we had to drive through miles of heavy traffic to buy a loaf of bread. We decided to look for a pleasant place to retire to.

Of course, we felt some regret at leaving the house on Skyline Drive. We had lived there for over thirty years. We had seen the collapse of our nursery business there, lived through World War II, seen the rise and fall of McCarthyism, rejoiced at the landing of the first man on the moon. I had raised five or six

St. Clair with dog "Bottles-the-beloved"

litters of dachshund puppies there, lost my beloved Bottles (golden Labrador crossed with German shepherd), and seen the roof blow off three separate times. Eric and I had done a lot of writing there. We had trapped gophers and shot rattlesnakes. We had almost lost the house to one of the recurrent brushfires. It had been a place of pleasures, pains, and memories. My name for it had been Waelsungen-Haus, but a visitor had described it more accurately by calling it Fortress St. Clair.

But the place, for all its beauty (it had a matchless view of San Pablo and Suisun bays, through 180 degrees), was impossible to heat, wind-lashed, hard-soiled. Camellias throve there, but not much else. I had habitually done my writing in the bedroom, muffled in blankets, with books and papers around me on the bed. I began to feel I was too old for more discomfort.

Despite our long residence there, we had not put out many roots. We weren't churchgoers, and, since we had no children, we had no contacts with other people through the schools.

Here I may say that our lack of children was deliberate. By the time I was in my forties I had begun to think that it might be nice to have a child, but the feeling was not a strong one, not enough for me to make an issue of it with Eric. He tended to be possessive, and would, in any case, I think, have been a poor father.

There was nothing to keep us in El Sobrante any longer.

On the advice of a friend, we drove down the coast to a little settlement called Cambria Pines. They were having serious trouble with their water supply when we got there, and it didn't seem a very good bet. Then we drove up to Ukiah, in Mendocino County, but inland. Somehow I had been expecting high, clean mountain air and redwoods. There may have been redwoods, but Ukiah was muggy and hot. "We came, we saw, we turned around again."

A few days later we got in the little Sunbeam again and went up the Mendocino coast.

We were greatly taken with Point Arena, an old-fashioned, gently mildewed little place. We couldn't find any suitable real estate there. We drove on north, to Manchester, where we heard of a new development, Irish Beach.

It was a place of wonderful white-water views, astonishingly good to find only a hundred and forty miles north of San Francisco. We sold our house in El Sobrante and, in due course, built a new house in Irish Beach.

It is a lovely little house, carefully tailored to our needs. I told the architect that I wanted sea views

from every room, and that is what I got. I still love my little house, though, like me, it is getting old and needs repairs.

The last of my long fictions, *The Dancers of Noyo*, was finished here. As usual, it didn't create much of a stir, even in Mendocino County, where much of the action takes place, though I understand that odd copies have taken on the aspect of a classic with a few readers.

My work has been much more successful and accepted abroad than it ever has here. I still get royalty checks for *Sign of the Labrys* (*Il segno della doppia ascia*) in the Italian edition, and *The Dancers of Noyo* (*I danzatori di Noyo*) has also been reprinted there. The Japanese have reprinted *Change the Sky*, my short-story collection published by Ace, and *The Dolphins of Altair* is still in print in Japan. (I have no idea what the Japanese titles of these are.)

On the other hand, the English barely tolerate me. Only *Sign of the Labrys* has had English publication. I have a hunch they think my work is in bad taste, though I'm not sure.

Change the Sky did come out in French, and several of my novellas appeared in German. But the Japanese and the Italians really like me. I don't know what the reason is. But I'm grateful.

After the move to Mendocino, I neither wrote nor sold much. A story in *Fantasy and Science Fiction*, another in *Isaac Asimov's Science Fiction Magazine*, two stories in *Chrysalis*—that's about it. I kept working on longer fiction and trying to get publishing contracts for one or another of these. I remember *The Once and Future Queen*, about a world in which the higher forms of combustion could no longer occur and in which the North American continent had been divided into duchies, ruled by women (the Duchess of Manchester was the chief character); another abortive novel was *The Euthanasiasts*, in which a group of quixotic people go through time helping timorous would-be suicides to kill themselves. I dimly remember another, *The Earthquake Mistress*, in which the Japanese had become the number one world power.

I worked hard on all of these. But when I reread the first few chapters of *The Once and Future Queen*, I found that despite all the care I had lavished on it, something was wrong. The breath of life was missing. There were exciting incidents, carefully described, but the thing was static, dead.

The first few years at Irish Beach, while we were finishing our house and doing a good deal of gardening, were happy ones. I remember thinking that my life had come out a good deal better than I had any reason to expect. Eric and I had always been together a lot; now we were together almost constantly. Yet I had times of depression and fear; I felt we were getting dangerously isolated, with nobody at all close to us except ourselves. I was considerably more sociable than Eric, and while this didn't cause friction, it made it hard for me to make other friends. Eric didn't welcome visitors.

By now we were getting into early old age—I in my mid sixties, Eric seventy or so. Eric had a mysterious heart ailment and what was finally diagnosed as gout. I had recurrent attacks of bronchitis, which finally settled into chronic asthma. It took quite a while to get it under control.

Two pleasant things happened in 1981: we got our first cat, and Eric started telling me stories again.

We got the cat by advertising. Our garden was full of snakes—snakes and rodents. Serpents slithered back and forth over the garden paths; moles, gophers, shrews, and rabbits constantly menaced our vegetables. A cat seemed the obvious solution.

We put an ad in a local weekly paper: "Gardeners offer affectionate home to cat to help in rodent control. Must be kitten-proof." And in due time Chessie-cat appeared.

I had always had dogs, one or two dachsies in residence most of my married life. When old age took the last little dog from me, I swore never to go through that again. But a cat . . . We wouldn't get so attached to a cat.

Chessie was a small cat, tiger-marked, with coloring of black, gray, rufous, and cream. Her eyes were slanting, big and green, with white and black penciling around them, as if she had used eye makeup. She had an unusually long tail. All in all, she was quite a handsome cat.

She went to work immediately. On her first day with us she plunged into the shrubbery and came out with a mouse in her face. On the second day she climbed up on the deck carrying a dead rabbit slightly more than half as big as she was.

She was a demon toward rabbits, gophers, and moles. As the rodents disappeared, so did the snakes. We could enjoy our garden again. And Chessie, who had been supposed to know her place and sleep in a box in the living room, began showing up at bedtime in the space between our two pillows on the bed. Any cat owner can fill in the rest of the scenario.

Eric's storytelling began again at the time of the 1980 Olympics, when the Soviets (and their enchanting mascot, Misha) were boycotted by the Carter administration. Eric gave me a Misha bear for Yule, just before the boycott was announced, and the stories began.

The chief characters were David and Diana

Eric St. Clair, about 1950

Darling (also known as Dearest), who lived in Berkeley on Penny Lane at the end of the streetcar line (there hasn't been a streetcar line in Berkeley for a long, long time, and there never has been a Penny Lane); their cat, K B; and Misha, the magical stuffed bear. Other characters were the cat guru, who is the friend and protector of cats and cat lovers everywhere, the slightly sinister sea fairies (always trying to kidnap Misha, because they wanted him so), the Singing Goldfish, and an assortment of evil magicians and enchanters, who were evil just for the heck of it.

The house on Penny Lane had four stories, the uppermost of which housed a Senior Center, and the next lowest a bunch of homeless ghosts. Access to these upper stories was provided by a surly and bad-tempered elevator, verbally abusive and in chronic need of oil. Somehow the house got more compact as the narration continued, though the elevator lasted a long while.

Other machines in the Darlings' world were the catmobile, a cycle on which K B rode, pedalling with all four feet and wearing dark glasses (he could go like the wind), and the catapult, which K B used to project himself to the cat guru's residence in the high

Sierras.

After the Darling household got on better terms with the cat guru, he used to come and visit them. The cat guru was a large and stately cat, of an even, medium gray, who always wore a pinkish orange turban and was attended everywhere by an entourage of forty cats. Dearest was always glad to have them come for a visit, and always glad to have them leave, since the noise made by forty purring cats was deafening.

Diana Darling—Dearest—was a huntress, like her eponymous divinity. Riding a bright red bicycle, a bow slung over her back, and with Misha and K B perched on her shoulders, she would bike down to the river that ran at some distance from the house. Here she would find a large cluster of dried weeds and grasses that would turn into a smart little motor cruiser when she and the animals boarded it.

Once on the river's other side, Diana would begin looking for something to shoot. A sort of shimmer in the air overhead would alert her to the proximity of prey. She took careful aim—drew the bowstring back to her ear—let fly—and would bring down comestibles as diverse as a whole roast turkey, a bowl of Crab Louis, or a *Sacher Torte mit Schlagobers.*

Once she got tired of always shooting food, and for quite a period all her booty was wonderful French perfumes and lotions.

Diana went into business once or twice, with fair success, but most of the time she was president of the Penny Lane Ladies' Archery and Meditation Society. The girls did not usually shoot much in the way of food.

Another character appeared at the house at Penny Lane after Yule 1984—a little stuffed lion with a braided tail whose name was Cousin Tangle. He was magic, of course, but in quite a different way from Misha. Cousin Tangle could draw the moon.

Eric told me one of these stories night after night for years. I am permanently regretful that I did not get some of them, at least, down on tape. As it is, all that amazing invention and fertility are lost forever in the night.

Sometime in 1984 I realized I was going to have to have extensive eye surgery. My corneas had been growing increasingly cloudy for years; now they were so opaque that I could hardly see to drive.

The prospects were not very good. The corneal transplant in those days had a lower success rate than the operation for cataracts (though I was told I must have cataract and lens-implant surgery at the same time), and was, in fact, considered the most difficult of all eye operations. The surgeons told me it would be at least nine months after the surgery before I could expect any improvement in my vision. But the operations seemed to be the thing to do, and in June I put my name on the waiting list for a nice fresh cornea from the Eye Bank.

Eric and I spent the rest of the year waiting for a call from the surgeon. It didn't come until November 28. Meantime, since I was legally blind, I had got a record player and a cassette deck on loan from the Library of Congress, and was listening to tapes and records from the library at Sacramento.

The arrangement was only moderately successful. The library sent me stuff I hadn't ordered, and was terribly slow with what I had. The record albums were often short a record, and I had trouble with the tapes. The readers, however, were excellent, and I had, over and over again, the feeling of having read, rather than of having listened to, a book.

The surgery didn't frighten me. There was very little pain, and I seemed to be making a good recovery. But on December 31 I developed a crack in the retina of the operated eye. There wasn't any waiting this time. I went into the hospital on New Year's Eve.

Eric's sterling qualities never came out better than in my eye operations. Euphoria usually made him nervous; he was afraid people would go too far. But he was a tower of strength in adversity. I will never forget how glad I was to see him entering my room at the hospital. Always, when I needed him, he was so blessedly *there.*

I had been writing a few poems and submitting them to local publications. One of them, written about the time of my first eye surgery, I cite here:

Another Name

In a difficult bed, waiting for dubious surgery,
not yet in pain, but wakeful
I turn over my memories, like a sad child
Who empties his small toy chest, hoping for comfort
From a wind-up mouse, a rubber ball.

There's not much solace in my thoughts—triumphs that turned sour, mistakes, loves that got lost, mistakes, mistakes.

But at the bottom, shining like a star, a piece of pagan wisdom, learned twenty years or more ago from the Locrian tablets:
Aphrodite is called Persephone in the underworld.

You don't see—? Oh, it's not like that sure and certain hope they speak of. But the bright and joyous power we felt in our best moments, strong and joyous, that same power, Aphrodite,
Will still be with us, only a little more sober and more

steadfast, in the endless shadows,
Still with us, still ours.
Still the same warm beauty of the foam-born body,
the same drifting hair.
Herself, herself! The muted glory of the triple queen.

Whether she's gateway or finality? I don't know.
But the shadows are full of the scent of her roses,
The cold waters of death hide her welcoming arms.

The poem is about dying, of course. The source of some of the ideas is *Persephone,* a book by Günther Zuntz.

Nineteen eighty-five was a singularly wormy year for us. The transplant gave trouble: I developed simple glaucoma in the operated eye, for which I had a laser treatment, and later, and more seriously, I had an episode of tissue rejection which required me to use eye drops every half hour all day long. Eric had root-canal surgery and two cataract extractions. The operations were successful, but his coordination seemed impaired. He would bang into curbs when he drove, or run into telephone poles. Also, I really suffered from an increasing feeling of alienation from Eric. This was partly his growing deafness; more seriously it came from a feeling that I had *lost* him somehow. The relationship had been dear to me; now I almost felt that he was already dead. Perhaps some myth that was vital to the marriage had failed, perhaps it was an attempt on my part to prepare myself for what did happen, since he was eight years older than I.

The Best of Margaret St. Clair, a short-story collection, came out in 1985. The *Thoughts from My Seventies*, which I wrote as a preface, is the best part of this book. It says some of the things that I am really serious about.

I had written a dedication to Eric; it was supposed to be a surprise for him. But when the copies of the book reached me, the dedication had been omitted. I wish he could have seen it and realized how much he meant to me.

We had had a nice Christmas, despite all the troubles of the year. I began to hope that 1986 would be a better year for us. But on December 28 we were playing dominoes lying opposite each other on the bed when Eric stopped dead, with a domino in his hand. He didn't move, he didn't speak. He had turned into a cardboard cutout.

I couldn't imagine what had happened. I spoke to him, telling him to go on with the game. He didn't move. I thought perhaps he had gone suddenly deaf. I wrote on a writing pad, "What's wrong? What is this?" He picked up the pen and made a few scratches

on the pad. At this point I called 911, the emergency number.

It took the ambulance a long time to get here. He had begun to move and talk a little when it finally arrived. He even tied his own shoelaces while he was being helped with his shoes. The ambulance took him up the coast to the nearest hospital, the hospital at Fort Bragg, about thirty-five miles.

"New Dress," 1964

By now it was about ten o'clock at night. I slept here and there at the hospital; I had, of course, gone up in the ambulance with him. It was determined that he had had a medium severe stroke. They did a lot of tests and gave him a halter monitor. He was released on December 31, and we spent New Year's Eve at home.

He seemed to be making a fair recovery. He was taking an assortment of medications. He still had some verbal confusion; he called Elk, the next town up the coast from us, Eric; once he tried to tell me one of his wonderful stories, but he plainly was having trouble with it. He was badly depressed, and wrote "suicide" several times on the log of activities and thoughts the doctor had him keep while he was wearing the halter monitor. Once, while taking out the garbage, he slipped and fell, and had to crawl to the front steps before he could get up.

He kept calling me "Poor Margaret." I didn't feel sorry for myself, only for him. I was always nervous when he was out of my sight for more than a few minutes. The doctor thought he might need a pacemaker, and kept testing. It seemed Eric was a borderline case.

On the morning of January 28 Eric got up looking tired and confused. He said he had had terrible dreams, nightmares, all night long—about trying and trying to get to his eye doctor in Ukiah. I said that of course I'd be with him when he went in for his next appointment. I called his internist, who said to try his current medication, a new one, for one more day.

He went shopping in the local store; he kissed me in the aisle when nobody was looking. He seemed to feel a little better as the day wore on.

We had supper, washed the dishes together. Eric was in our bedroom, getting undressed for his shower, when I heard a banging crash coming from where he was. I didn't go in for two or three minutes. I was not really alarmed. When I did go in, he was lying out flat on the floor. It was as if some gigantic hand had struck him down full length. He had fallen so hard he had knocked the closet door off its roller.

I called 911 at once. I think this was really the worst night of my life. Things are confused in my mind, but I remember that a couple of local physicians, people who lived at Irish Beach, got here before the ambulance did. They took him up the coast to Fort Bragg again. When they were wheeling him into the hospital I kept saying, "My poor little bear, my poor little bear."

I remember asking one of the doctors that night if he believed personality survived bodily death.

Eric never regained consciousness. There was never any real hope for him—about one chance in five hundred thousand, the doctors said—and that hope got fainter and fainter the longer he lived. It was a really massive stroke: all he had left were excretion and breathing. Once he opened his eyes. I had them do what they could; he lasted longer than anyone had thought he would. Finally he got pneumonia, which is what people get when they can't move about and keep their lungs clean. I had him given antibiotics and morphine, so I know he didn't suffer. I think he had first-rate care. But my poor little bear.

He died on March 10, about ten o'clock. I kissed him good-bye and reminded him of the passwords. Then I called one of my neighbors, one of the doctors who lived in Irish Beach, and he came up to the hospital for me and drove me home.

One thing that helped me greatly was that, before Eric had had even the first stroke, an extraordinarily persistent and intelligent young woman, who had got a degree in Greek from Harvard before she became a doctor of medicine, had tried me out on quite a variety of mood elevators and antianxiety drugs, and had finally found a combination I could tolerate. Things like Elavil, for example, dry me out so much that I can hardly talk or urinate. Dr. Huff persevered. It seemed the very mercy of God that during all that terrible time I was usually able to sleep when I went to bed. I don't think I could have stood it if I had had to stay awake all night.

My neighbors, too, helped me wonderfully. They were the kindest, most helpful people in the whole world. I was supported, too, by a kind of incredulity, a belief that Eric wasn't really dead, couldn't possibly be really dead. I'd find myself hurrying home expecting he'd be there waiting for me. Or I'd start to put a magazine away and then think, "You mustn't do that. Eric hasn't read it yet."

In May a friend from Alaska, who had known him well, helped me scatter his ashes off Mussel Rock, where we used to go to hunt mussels. It was extraordinary how heavy his ashes were.

But I miss him dreadfully—sometimes it seems more and more, not less and less. Of the poems I wrote at that time, the two I cite here express it pretty well:

The Nurse with Does' Eyes

The nurse with does' eyes—half-Cherokee, beautiful, a gazelle—told me gently, "When there's no urine in the bag, it's almost over." So I must have known.

All the same, I was asleep on the other bed when somebody touched my wrist lightly. "Mrs. St. Clair . . ."
He was perfectly warm when I kissed him. He didn't look dead.
His skin looked so young.

But what really happened? Did the long wave in which he'd rolled like a stone for so many weeks Desert him at last, strand him, nothing on nothing, in the dark common lot of the dead,
Or did that power that in the end I think he trusted, strong, feminine, did she, that same power—
Blankness of dying over—begin to lead him gently toward the light,
And now, as the light grows, is he re-learning, under her hand, the laws of the endless dance?
Oh, I hope so. He trusted her, she must have loved him.
He had such pretty hair.

Porch Light

Almost two years, and still foot's hard on pedal,
Eyes hunt me-welcoming light ahead, as always,
Looking for rainbow halo in the coastal
     fog-drift.
Surely the light'd be on now.

No, never. Never the fog-diluted glow,
Never the opening door, and never you,
Welcoming me with a hug, and asking,
"Why were you so late? Where have you been?"

But now you're late, not I.
You-welcoming light might burn forever.
You'd not come.

Rolled in the long swell, mixing with the sand,
You-heavy ashes, you shut in a heavy cardboard
     box
Released to mingle with the salt, around our
     rock,
The place where we found mussels.

Perhaps it's only a sad dream
That lasts too long, and hurts, and hurts, and
     still's only a dream,
Only a long sad illusion, even the ashes in the
     box, and some night soon,
Foot hard on pedal, hurrying through the fog,
I'll see the light ahead, and know you turned it
     on.

It seems strange that I have dreamed about him
so little—only four times in more than two years.
Certainly my relationship with my mother was ambivalent, but after she died I dreamed over and over
that she was not really dead. I'd like to dream about
him.

My biggest regret is that I wasn't kinder and
more loving to him. I wish he could know how sorry I
am.

There were a lot of things that were wrong with
the marriage. But there were a lot more that were
right.

In time of grief, people look for solace in
unlikely places. Somebody recommended a book by
C. S. Lewis, *A Grief Observed.* I read it, but without any
particular reaction except to think that the wife the
loss of whom Lewis was expressing sounded like a
thoroughly unpleasant person. The hospital gave me
some mimeographed sheets—about the stages of
grief, and what to expect—that really were helpful. I
got a small amount of wound-licking consolation
from the verses of Propertius, about how a lover
". . . *revocaverit aura puellae / Concessum nulla lege*

Eric, 1985

redibit iter." ("If a lover hears the faint voice of his
mistress, even when he sits at the oar of the Stygian
boat, he will retrace the road that no law allows.")

Commonsense consolations were no use at all. I
suppose it *was* "better" that Eric predeceased me.
With his great deafness and his unsociability, his life
without me would, I think, have been literally terrible.
But I always thought, somehow, that I would die first.

He wasn't, by present standards, awfully old—
though eighty-two can't be considered precisely dying young. But I feel resentful when I see men
considerably older than he was walking around
briskly and apparently enjoying life. Actually, anytime
he died it would have been a dreadful loss for me.
And, of course, the older we both were, the harder it
would have been for me to pick up the pieces.

And with all this, I wish I still had him. I want
him back.

Widows of my acquaintance tell me that one
never really gets over this loss—it recedes into
the background, but it's always there. In the years
since his death I've tried to make a new life for myself.
I've had accidents and illnesses—a broken thigh,
pneumonia, more eye surgery, an operation for a
hernia—as well as troubles with social security, including one rather amusing episode where the Medi-
care people kept insisting that I was dead and wanting
a death certificate from the funeral director. I seem to
be above average in physical resilience, since I've

made quick recoveries from my physical woes.

I'd like to start writing again, but I lack incentive and confidence. My greatest auctorial asset was my exuberance and that, I feel, I have in large measure lost. Perhaps it will come back. I'd like to take a good course in writing poetry.

People sometimes ask me about working habits, idea sources, and so on. When I was writing on a regular schedule I always wrote lying on the bed, propped up with pillows, and with the typewriter, a portable, resting on my lap. (Try this with a word processor!) The ideas came from all sorts of places. I usually kept a notebook, and jotted down what seemed promising.

I am sometimes asked which of my works I like the best. In short stories, it would unquestionably be the funny ones—stories like "An Old-Fashioned Bird Christmas," "Short in the Chest," "Prott," or "The Marriage Manual." I like them because I had so much fun writing them. Next to the funny ones, I favor the horrid scary yarns, stories like "Hathor's Pets," "The Gardener," or "Brenda." Down at the bottom I'd put what I call "uplift." Any fool can be profound.

Of my two short-story collections, I prefer the first one, *Change the Sky,* to *The Best of Margaret St. Clair.* There are more funny stories in *Change the Sky.*

I've done a good deal of unpublished writing. Besides the mystery novel I mentioned earlier, there was a short, funny thing, a lightweight novel, called *Pidgintoe Island,* and a raft of short stories that never quite made it into print. I had two dud projects for nonfantasy novels, one about Giovanni Boccaccio, and another about Kepler, the laws-of-planetary-motion man.

I don't remember what drew me to Kepler as the subject of a novel—he had a short, agitated life, caught up in the religious wars of his century, and isn't particularly well known.

The choice of Boccaccio as the subject of a novelized biography is easier to explain. I have always liked the *Decameron* (Boccaccio isn't good at characterization, but boy, does he know how to tell a story!), and everybody knows who he was.

The novels never got written. Kepler I abandoned early, and Boccaccio, though a much better subject, did not have a life that conformed to the ideas that people would have about the author of such a famous piece of light erotica. His life was certainly not filled with amorous adventures; he had one known mistress, a married woman named Maria d'Aquino, a collateral relative of Saint Thomas Aquinas, and a child by . . . somebody. His life was full of hard, rather dull literary work.

But did you know that Boccaccio was half French? He was born at Paris, the illegitimate son of a Frenchwoman named Jeanne de la Roche. Boccaccio was a pioneer in Dantean studies; he gave a course of lectures on that poet at Florence, and was scolded by the censors for having "displayed the private parts of poetry" to the vulgar crowd. He was great pals with Petrarch, whose influence on him was deplorable. Boccaccio himself never really esteemed the *Decameron*; he said that he wrote it in youth and blushed for it in middle age. He had wanted to be a poet, a serious poet, like Petrarch. (How many people have read the *Decameron* compared to the readers of Petrarch?) It was another case of a writer despising his best work.

Besides the unpublished novels, I wrote two three-act plays. One of them, *Rudolph,* was about a dog who drank, and I am ashamed to say that I had him drinking Grands Échézeaux, a marvellous Burgundy, far too good for most human beings, let alone a dog. The other play, *The Courier,* was based on the thesis that Jack the Ripper was a courier for the Second International whose brain had been rotted by tertiary syphilis. I believe that one of Jack's victims actually was found near a hall where members of the Workingmen's Association met. Karl Marx's daughter Eleanor was one of the characters, and as somebody said, what will these writers think of next?

Neither of these plays ever got anywhere near production. The theatre isn't something one can take up on a part-time, trifling basis.

Of my published novels, my favorites are probably *Sign of the Labrys* and *The Shadow People,* I suppose because there is a lot of atmosphere in them. Oddly enough, in both novels a large part of the action takes place underground.

I have often wondered why I was not more successful as a science fiction writer. Besides the obvious reason, so wounding to a writer's pride, that maybe my work just wasn't all that good, I used to think that perhaps the fans intuited a certain lack of seriousness toward science fiction in me. While I take writing very seriously indeed, and work hard at it, science fiction itself has never been a sacred cause to me. I saw it as another of the genres, like mystery fiction and westerns, whose freedom and range I found stimulating (but see my remarks about science fiction in *Thoughts from My Seventies* in the introduction to *The Best of Margaret St. Clair.*) Perhaps, somehow, this lack of seriousness leaked through and repelled people who might otherwise have liked my work. It is also possible that most of my work was done at a time when women writers were not very welcome in the field.

Lately, however, I have come to feel that the fans of the day didn't much like me because I wanted to have, and to give, a good time. I think the fans felt I was making fun of them; the storm of hostility the Jick and Oona stories aroused can only be understood as coming from that source.

I have always written *amusing* stories, even when they were horrid. As I take it, the fans then didn't *want* to be amused. They wanted to be tha-rilled, astonished, scared shitless, even entertained sometimes (if entertainment means reading about huge actions and big ideas). Empires and epics are an extension of swords and sorcery, but neither category is particularly *amusing.* Sometimes I think the fans wanted the psychological equivalent of being goosed.

I can't logically feel injured if somebody doesn't like me as a writer. That's certainly his privilege. But it's possible that as science fiction and fantasy have grown more widely popular, readers have grown less touchy. Perhaps they would have less objection to being amused now than they used to. I wish some publisher would reprint one or two of my better novels. I'd like a second chance.

Looking over these pages, I see I have omitted two things that seemed important at the time—a short space in the sixties when Eric and I were nudists, and an earlier flirtation with Marxism during the hungry thirties. Nudism was *dull,* and Marxism was too doctrinaire. Neither has been a durable influence.

BIBLIOGRAPHY

Fiction:

Agent of the Unknown (bound with *The World Jones Made,* by Philip K. Dick). New York: Ace, 1956.

The Green Queen (bound with *Three Thousand Years,* by Thomas Calvert McClary). New York: Ace, 1956.

The Games of Neith (bound with *The Earth Gods Are Coming,* by Kenneth Bulmer). New York: Ace, 1960.

Sign of the Labrys. New York: Bantam, 1963; London: Corgi, 1963.

Message from the Eocene [and] *Three Worlds of Futurity* (short stories). New York: Ace, 1964.

The Dolphins of Altair. New York: Dell, 1967.

The Shadow People. New York: Dell, 1969.

The Dancers of Noyo. New York: Ace, 1973.

Change the Sky and Other Stories. New York: Ace, 1974.

The Best of Margaret St. Clair (short stories), edited by Martin H. Greenberg. Chicago: Academy Chicago, 1985.

Ronald Sukenick

1932-

AUTOGYRO: MY LIFE IN FICTION

Ronald Sukenick at Grand Army Plaza, New York City,
at the time of publication of his first book, Up, *1968*

Richard Baron

Unfortunately my life is not very interesting, even to me. However, what is even less interesting is certain accounts of my life and work that are sloppy or inaccurate if not downright false. I'm thinking in particular about the account in the *Dictionary of Literary Biography,* which those interested in the subject at hand, i.e., me, should ignore. It is the impulse to correct such accounts that is the chief motive in this exercise.

My first novel, *Up,* to begin at the beginning of the confusion, was a way of relating my Brooklyn past to my underground present. In order to do it I invented a new genre, which I call pseudo-autobiography. Novelists have always used their own lives, more or less disguised, as the main source of data for their fictions. Why not do away with the subterfuge and frankly use one's own identity? On the other hand, fiction does not aspire to the factuality of history. Fiction is *recreation*—in both senses. The distinction between Ronald Sukenick and "Ronald Sukenick," one of the "real" characters who appear in many of my works, has confounded some naive critics, though I've never had any complaints from common readers, who seem to assume, correctly, that fiction is an extension of fact. This mode derived basically from Henry Miller, but there was a lot of iconoclastic Laurence Sterne influence in *Up* that challenged the by-then overly literary artifice of the dominant realistic novel. From the beginning my major effort was entirely in the mainstream of the novel in its effort to pierce the veil of conventional artifice that has become so familiar we don't even realize that it's artifice anymore, don't realize that it's not real or even interestingly "real"—to break through the artificial to the actualities of experience.

Ironically, the label for this effort bestowed by some reviewers and book marketeers interested in maintaining a standard literary product was "experimental."

If you call me an experimental writer, you assume that I disdain the wider audience for writing. You can call me anything you want but let me set the record straight. The question of audience is always a painful question for American writers in a way that it is not for writers in other countries. In other countries you either have an educated class for whom you write, or you have a popular tradition of respect for and interest in the well-written word, as in Eastern Europe. In either case, you know for whom—and for what taste—you are writing. In this country the case is much more complicated. We have a large and half-educated audience that prefers cheap, simplistic writing, or the electronic media, but, not to underestimate it, will on capricious occasion take to its heart in large numbers some of the best writing around. So, for the American writer, the problem is always to find that elusive formula for communication that will satisfy his sense of quality as well as the audience's mysterious imaginative needs. Needless to say, you avoid the debased formulas favored and encouraged by the merchandising system. If you're actually getting rich, you're probably doing something wrong. Though you, no doubt, will be the exception.

This is essentially a rhetorical problem, though I have always contended that no real distinction can be made between what is said and how it is said. Of course, in the equation expressing the relation between author and reader, the author is the more important term. He has to be. People ask me whether I write for myself, as if, in a democratic country, that were some sort of sin. Of course I write for myself. What do you think I'm in it for? I could make more bucks in any number of other professions, not to mention businesses. But since I'm in it for the kicks, the kicks I get out of the writing itself, if you deny me that then I'm left with nothing.

And yet, besides that, there's nothing I'd like better than to reach the large, general audience. Not merely the professionals of the book—the critics, editors, and academics—but, much more important to me, the common reader and especially those on the fringe of the reading public. In fact, it's always been certain of the book pros who've given me most trouble, probably because those who pretend to know what good writing is are often precisely those who are stuck with an idea of good writing they learned about in their sophomore English classes from professors who are themselves often forty years behind what's going on in contemporary writing. Or they are class-bound, Ivy League white males with corresponding attitudes and a usually nonconscious reflex to defend their turf. Or they belong to the ex-socialist elite, loosely defined as intellectuals, who used to wear jackets and ties to demonstrations and still wear them when reading fiction. So that in many ways I prefer an audience that is innocent, open, and unspoiled by preconceived notions. If I can reach it through the distribution monopoly the book pros exercise.

To illustrate the problem let me tell you a story. A true story, since this is autobiography. Once upon a time, when I was a young writer, a well-known editor agreed to publish a section of my soon-to-appear first novel, *Up*, in a well-known magazine he was starting. This editor was widely known as one of the quality saints in the publishing establishment. By quality saint I mean those editors known to favor quality at all costs as against the tide of shlock that always threatens to overwhelm the industry, editors known for their willingness to make a stand for integrity, editors who are willing to take risks and go out on a limb for literature by, say, giving Philip Roth a million-dollar advance on a new novel. Such editors are few and far between and when you meet one you can sometimes actually see a halo hovering over his head in dim light.

Anyway, this editor called me in to talk about my piece before finally agreeing to print it. Turned out he wanted me to change the punctuation. It's true my punctuation in that book is quirky, though not as quirky as in some of my books. I was using punctuation as a kind of scoring, as in music, rather than as an adjunct to grammar. The editor was bugged by this, and I couldn't quite figure out why. I guess it was too experimental. Despite the fact that I was terribly intimidated by my first meeting with a big-time editor, I had no intention of changing my punctuation. But we went back and forth for a while and finally the reason for his wanting the change came out. It was the first issue of the magazine and this editor was afraid the readers would think he didn't know correct grammar. Smart, smart. He chose the one argument that would bring me over to his way of seeing things. My piece was threatening his literary integrity. Of course, I agreed to change the punctuation.

I left his office, nevertheless, feeling that I had sold my soul. After lying awake all night, I called him in the morning and told him I was sorry, but I'd changed my mind about the punctuation. Much to my amazement he published the damn thing anyway, but I'm sure that to this day there are people out there in the reading public who are convinced this guy doesn't know a comma from a coma.

I have to say that I think it's preferable to write for people who have no attitudes about the placement of commas and colons than for people with the knee-jerk conventionality that shores up Proper English Usage. If nothing else, punctuation illiterates are at least likely to know their colons from their elbows.

Which brings me to my childhood. And this is the point. Which is that, though I eventually blundered onto Ivy League turf, I grew up outside the great middle class. Proper English Usage we didn't know from. We were too experimental. And when as a college-bound adolescent I finally found myself in the middle of the great middle class I didn't think it was so great. In fact, I thought it was absolutely loony. The only thing that made sense to me about the great middle class was that it liked to make a great deal of money. Okay, that's what it was supposed to do. But that everything else should be so geared to that seemed to me a little, frankly, sick. This made me even more experimental.

If you've read Malamud's *Assistant* then you know where I grew up. And if you know where I grew up you begin to understand why I ain't got no. Satisfaction. I ain't got, I ain't got, I ain't got, I ain't got. I ain't got no. Not in the great middle class. And why whatever it was that I did I did it—my way. I did it my way. I did it my w-a-a-a-y.

They used to make me go to Malamud's depressing delicatessen, my parents, down the block and around the corner under the El. I hated going there because it was such a down, empty shelves and a herring or two in the refrigerator case, the glum old guy behind the counter always looking like he was about to go out of business. This was the deli of *The Assistant,* a moralistic, if not Pollyannish, book I'm not crazy about, but interesting to me because my father used to give me the lowdown on who was who in what seemed in fact to be a neighborhood *roman à clef.* My parents made me go there because, number one, the Malamuds were poor, number two, my father was

their dentist, and number three, they were among the few other Jews in the neighborhood. My father used to fix their teeth at very cut rates, even after Bernie started making money on teaching and his books—I remember that in later days he even had to urge my father to charge more to make false teeth for Bernie's brother, who was, according to my father, not "quite right." My father was very experimental with money. When I told Malamud that my father had died he reacted with the kind of regret you have over the death of a good man. This should be said, so I say it.

I wrote bluntly about this Malamudian scene in *Up.* When my father sent Malamud the book, he wrote back a note saying it was "an interesting experiment that doesn't quite come off."

My playing fields were the streets, East Second Street between Avenues I and J in Brooklyn, to be specific, my companions were kids who probably found it easier to imagine going to jail than to college, and my discipline was stickball and stoopball. Not that life was all that rosy. I was a Christ killer among the Christians, a clumsy kid among energetic athletes, and my family was New Deal liberal while the neighbors literally ran through the streets cheering the day the news spread that FDR had died. These kids had no ambitions. They never thought about their "future." Instead they were very experimental. They improvised a present. They played hard at sports because they enjoyed it. The kid next door raised chickens and rabbits with his father in their backyard. They plodded through school, learning little, because education was minimally relevant to their concerns. They didn't have to know a hell of a lot to be cops, postmen, factory workers.

We lived halfway between Ebbets Field and Coney Island, where we used to play hookey. The big thing for all of us, for the whole community, the thing that even created community, was the Dodgers. The most exciting thing in my life was going to Ebbets Field. On the radio, Red Barber's anomalously soothing southern voice serenaded the neighborhood with the play-by-play. If a game was on you could hear it in the streets, out the windows, in the shops. Little kids who pronounced oil like erl and Earl like oil, including me, would talk about eatin' high on the hog and sittin' in the catbird seat. Probably because we were experimental. None of us had ever seen a hog, and I used to imagine a catbird as something like an alley cat with furry wings. Instead of saying, Hello, you said, What's the score? Malamud's best novel (if you subtract the mythy modernist *Golden Bough* bullshit), *The Natural,* is about the old Dodgers.

The other big community amusements were betting on the horses and the numbers, small-time

"In Pasadena, 1952, after breaking an ankle falling off a cliff at Bryce Canyon, Utah"

rackets run by the local Mafia types, though the neighborhood Mafia wasn't all that local. The brick house where all the Murder Incorporated killings were planned under the supervision of Louis "Lepke" Buchalter was a few blocks away. But nobody talked about this stuff. Mysterious gestures were exchanged, small wads of paper were passed in the local barbershop.

It was a vestigially bucolic world in some ways. People grew grapes and a few other things in their yards, raked and burned their leaves in the autumn. We played in the numerous empty lots and in the tall grass and bushes of the Long Island railroad "cut" a block away. There also we hopped freights when the frequent steam locomotives chuffed ferociously through. As a result of which a thumb would be mangled here, a leg amputated there, sometimes an entire child sent to the netherworld either by the steel wheels or the high-tension electric wires they put up when they modernized the locomotives. Death was literally all around us in the form of the giant cemeteries that bordered the neighborhood on two sides and my grammar school, P.S. 121, on three. The

main drag was called Gravesend Avenue, though it was later renamed McDonald. The vegetable man, the milkman, the coal and ice man would come around on horse-drawn carts. Later the milkman and the baker got these little trucks, but I still remember the sparrows pecking at the horse shit in the streets, and there was a stable across the avenue and halfway down the block. I've written about this scene, particularly in my novel *Out*. It was, of course, experimental.

Not so many people had cars early on. My uncle Benny was one of the first in our family—we never got one—and his was a beauty, a bright red coupe with a glorious rumble seat that everyone in the neighborhood loved to ride in. He kept it for years. It was probably from him that I developed my respect for durable old cars, like the '37 Ford I used to crisscross the country in during the early fifties and which may have been, I figured out later, the same '37 Ford immortalized in Kerouac's *On the Road* (see my book *Down and In*). Or the Deux Chevaux I travelled all over Europe in. Or the '68 Dodge Dart my ex-wife still drives. Or the '66 Volvo P1800 I've driven for the last fifteen years. By the way, if anyone knows where I can get a piece of side trim for a '66 Volvo P1800, please let me know.

Anyway, my uncle Benny, an exceedingly humble mechanic who in some ways resembled Dostoyevsky's idiot, had a romantic streak which expressed itself in gestures like suddenly showing up with a spectacular red coupe or, later, dropping out and living in Mexico for some years. He was a role model. While almost everybody else in the family was out grubbing money his attitude seemed to be why not do something magnificent?—though he would never, in his timidity, have put it that way. I have to say that my father never cared much about money either, much to the aggravation of my mother. He was something like a playboy jock without the bucks. Benny and my father were both very experimental.

Benny was my first literary influence, having more or less taught me how to read with comic books and the Sunday funnies. I think a lot of kids in my generation would still be illiterate if it weren't for comic books. And I suspect that comic books are still the most experimental influence on my style, an influence that separates me unbridgeably from the classics. While I'm at it, let me say that, contrary to a lot of well-meaning commentary on my work, Wallace Stevens was not a major influence on my writing, though I did write the first, and some say still best, extensive explication of his poetry. (Published by New York University Press in 1967, it's still available from Small Press Distribution in Berkeley.) Rather, the case is that I chose to work on Stevens because I

*Ronald with Lynn Luria-Sukenick at their home in
Ben Lomond, California, in the mid-seventies*

felt he was close to my already formed, if not totally
crystallized, literary posture. The really crucial influences, the ones that got me going finally, were
Laurence Sterne and Henry Miller. Some smart critic
could probably trace my whole evolution on the basis
of those two. Sterne, Miller, and the experimental
rhythm of the Gravesend Local rumbling over the
nearby El when I was a kid going to sleep at night.
Clickety-clack, take me back, clickety-clack, take me
back.

Arthur Miller partially catches the quality of the
family life I grew up in, especially in *Death of a
Salesman.* In fact, Miller is in a vague, in-law way
related to my mother's family through the Mendelwitz family, in some complicated manner that only my
mother and Sadie Mendelwitz can figure out. One of
my mother's most radiant memories is of going to the
funeral of Miller's father and exchanging a few words
with Marilyn Monroe. ("Excuse me," said Marilyn as
she passed my mother. "Of course," answered my
mother. Just so the immortal conversation doesn't go
unrecorded.) Miller and Monroe had already been
divorced. "He wouldn't even look at her," says my
mother. "And she was so timid." But the Brooklyn
tone that Miller gets is one of pathos—the pathos of
uprooted first and second immigrant generations
with no values but money—or, rather, nothing to
measure their innate values by except money. In this,
Miller is quite experimental.

In my mid-teens my life took a new turn because my
sister married a guy who was taking a doctorate at
Columbia. This guy, who had a European background, was openly contemptuous of Brooklyn culture. One day he showed up at the door with dollar
bills sticking out of his ears, nose, and mouth. He
never missed an issue of the *New Yorker.* He papered
his walls with old *New Yorker* covers. I mean, sophisticated. I'd never even heard of the *New Yorker.* But
there were kids in Brooklyn who had never seen the
ocean. Certainly a lot of them had never been to
Manhattan, except maybe to go to Times Square to
see a movie. Anyway, my brother-in-law opened up
new vistas. The snide *New Yorker* comments on
snippets from the media were a revelation. I discovered the possibility of irony.

When the time came for me to go to college
there was trouble. My parents didn't know from
college—my father had gone to dental school before
it was necessary to go to undergraduate school first—
though they understood it was important to go if you
were a boy. I had already in effect dropped out of the
mad grade grind in middle-class Midwood High (see
Down and In) and my grades were no match for the
median 99.8 average of most of my classmates. I was
hardly considered precocious, or even interested, and
students and teachers alike were always surprised that
someone who did not want to go to Harvard Medical
School or Yale Law School would show occasional
signs of intelligence. My main claim to fame in the
community was in writing a sports column for a local
paper.

I didn't even know where to apply to college, and
my school advisers told me the application limit was
three. Actually, nobody could stop you from applying
to as many schools as you wanted to, and kids who
knew the ropes applied to as many as ten colleges, I
discovered too late. My only criterion was that the
school not be in Brooklyn, and I applied to some
unlikely places, one of which I got into. Then I won a
New York State Scholarship as the result of an exam,
but it could only be used in-state and the school I got
into was not. This vexed my father, who was very—
shall we say—thrifty. So he asked a lawyer friend who
sent his kid to prep school and on to the Ivy League
how to do such things. The answer—as I discovered
years later—was bribe somebody. As naive as this
may seem, it worked. The quid pro quo was a gift
certificate for a suit to an admissions dean at Colgate.

So there I was at Colgate, mid-America, 1950.
There were three Jews there, including me, all with
complicated, unpronounceable names, and all three
were the smartest kids in the school. There was one
"Negro." His name was Laff. He did. All the time. Or

The author in the Berkshires, Connecticut, 1967

Lynn Luria-Sukenick

else. There were no girls. Everyone had to belong to a fraternity, and you were beaten out into the snow to learn the football songs. The school elite were the guys on the cheerleading squad. Turned out they were all secretly gay and would seduce freshmen in their frat rooms. I left after a term.

I got a scholarship to a crazy place in L.A. called Pasadena Branch of the Telluride Association. Nothing could have been more different from Colgate. Though Telluride is nationally a conservative and boring organization that pretends to turn out "leaders"—it actually turns out boring and conservative liberals—Pasadena Branch was run by a radical Quaker pacifist and was full of dissident New York intellectuals and West Coast kids in the Wobbly tradition. My roommate, Norman Rush, was taken off by the FBI for refusing to register for the draft during the Korean War. Recently he's published an acclaimed collection of stories about his experiences in the Peace Corps in Africa.

Pasadena Branch was in some ways a mini Black Mountain, chaotic but challenging. I remember meeting there Richard Feynman, the famous physicist, the one who torpedoed NASA by dipping a piece of O-ring into a glass of ice water at the congressional hearings on the Challenger disaster. When he came over to Pasadena Branch, he started talking about how he drove the authorities crazy at Los Alamos during the A-bomb project by cracking safes and leaving notes inside for the security people, about

bongo-drum rhythms—he was about to go down to the Amazon to study drum rhythms—and I don't remember what else, all very funny, nonstop, very fast, and in a glorious Brooklyn accent (Far Rockaway branch). It was the speed and complexity of connection that fascinated me. No plod. This was the opposite of the kind of education that had been pushed on me since P.S. 121. His discourse was a perfect model for good writing, though I didn't know it at the time, nor did I know that I was observing one of the major geniuses of his generation.

Not to make a whole short story out of it, what was going on with me at this period was the discovery of thinking. The best way I can describe what that felt like is through an erotic analogy. I remember, long ago, making love to a virgin (I say long ago not because I'm so old but because I have the impression that there are no longer any virgins—or I should say virgins as a distinct class—as there were then). At first it was like trying to make love to something inert, self-contained, and impossible—like trying to kiss a statue. Then at a certain point there was a sudden awakening, I could feel it in her body, an opening, a flowing, a coming to life, desire, and possibility. This is what I began to feel in myself—the possibility of and the desire for the worlds within worlds, and worlds within words, that thinking opens up. The discovery of thinking was for me like the discovery of the fifth dimension—oh, this is what it's all about.

The discovery of sex, never mind analogies, was another dimension evolving in my life at the time. My own experience persuades me that evolution in the sexual dimension is connected with evolution in the intellectual dimension, especially during times of rapid development (and I'm not speaking only of youth). Any suppression of the sex glands suppresses the intellectual glands. The mind is part of the body and is part of its economy. But just as an unbalanced mind can repress sexuality, so can an unbalanced sexuality repress the mind. Like the *Playboy* mentality. However in the fifties the imbalance was tipped way over toward the mind. Forget sex, anything to do with the body was taboo. I was almost kicked out of Cornell for using the word "birdshit" in a story (see *Down and In*). Girls at the time were American as apple pie—frozen apple pie. Luckily for me there was a community of European women on campus, emigrés or children of emigrés, very sophisticated in the academic context, and these were the women I hung out with. Thanks, ladies.

It was at Cornell that I first stumbled across the swine factor in American life. I had met rich people before, I had met ambitious people before, I had met unprincipled people before. But this was a genteel set that you ran across in the wealthier fraternities that combined these charming traits with an element of supercilious callousness that they seemed to consider the key to success. And you have to think that maybe they were right when you look at the Reagan administration. I have a heavy streak of Jewish moralism and I find the domestic swine offensive. Foreign swine are usually more up front—the American equivalent would be somebody like Roy Cohn or maybe Jimmy Hoffa, but these types ultimately enrage the domestic swine. The essential trait of the American Swine is a certain nasty smugness. Plus all of the above. Add a dash of hypocrisy where necessary. The Ivy League schools are full of this type, some are even famous for it. Despite William Buckley's title, I doubt that you can find either God *or* Man at Yale. Or Cornell or you name it. But you can find a lot of *Swinus americanus.* And these people end up controlling most of our institutions, the swine factor going off the scale in corporate and bureaucratic circles. These are the people I don't write for. I wouldn't be caught dead writing anything they could understand or, worse, like.

"Probably the orangutan cage of the San Diego Zoo,"
early seventies

California, to get back to California, was also the opening of a new life: the discovery of the possibility of life beyond New York. Some of my novels show the impact of California on me, especially *Out*, *98.6*, and *Blown Away*. Again there was an opening out, a relaxation, a discovery of new possibilities. California, where I have lived on and off for a considerable time, was a place that immediately felt both strange and familiar. Strange compared to Brooklyn but, yes, this was the way one should live, in a supportive harmony with one's physical environment, as opposed to the mean puritan attitude of life as struggle and survival. My new California attitudes brought me into some comic conflicts with people back east. I remember flying in from California and arriving at the door of a New York friend in my comfortable Mexican shirt. He opened the door, blinked, and said, "Why are you wearing your nightgown?" There is still a big difference between the East and the West in the U.S., despite the same fast-food restaurants, and the two cultures still have a lot of trouble understanding one another. There aren't too many fiction writers around who can take in both without animosity, contempt, or paranoia. I guess it's appropriate that I now spend most of my time in Colorado (when I'm not in New York or Paris), practically on top of the Continental Divide, so I can look both ways.

I owe my academic career to the U.S. Army. I created my own GI Bill of Rights—the right not to be drafted. Every time I was about to drop out of college the swine started some new war to stay out of. That's how I got a Ph.D. at Brandeis. There I studied with J. V. Cunningham, the poet, and Irving Howe, the critic, and it was a study in contrasts. Howe is one of the more respectable New York Jewish Intellectuals and Cunningham was basically a cowboy from Montana. I didn't agree with either of them about anything. But, much more important to me, they were both very smart. They both provided me with effective new thought weapons to use against them. I think that's the best thing a teacher can do for a student.

Somewhere during that period I went to France on a Fulbright, thanks to Howe. The fellowship was about to be cancelled at the last minute because the French-language reference had come in and it was apparently devastating. I had requested it from an old French teacher of mine who also, it happened, had been a lover. How was I supposed to know she was mad at me, mad enough to be vindictive? But she was older, and French, and her rules were different from the ones I was so far familiar with. Of course she was right, my spoken French was lousy, but why did that skin her teeth? I figured after a year in France it

Lynn Luria-Sukenick

would be a lot better, and it was. Anyway, Howe persuaded poet Claude Vigée, then head of the French Department, to right the injustice, and so began my long and ambivalent relation with French culture. That was my first chance to see French culture on the hoof. I loved it. And I hated it. I still do. Not only that, I had the chance to do the Grand Tour, which gave me my first inkling that Pound, Eliot, and that bunch were basically culture tourists creating an intellectual Baedeker for the deprived American intelligentsia.

Many years later, in Paris, I invited Vigée over to my apartment. At that time I was renting an apartment on Place St.-Michel, spectacular in its way, black walls, mirrors, I think it must have been decorated by a hooker. I had published several books, one of them translated into French, I had been the subject of articles in French journals, I had participated in Paris symposia, and I spoke fluent French. A grey-haired Vigée walked in, looked at me in disbelief, and said, I quote: "This is little Ronnie?"

When I finally left the shelter of graduate school for good I thought I was home free because the army wasn't supposed to be drafting anyone over twenty-five. But I hadn't counted on the antiwar movement. I had been protesting. I had been photographed at the famous Justice Department–Pentagon demonstrations of *The Armies of the Night.* I had signed petitions. I had contributed money. Suddenly, at the age of thirty-four and a half, I got a draft notice. The legal cutoff was thirty-five. Anyone who thinks the government doesn't keep secret lists for illegal purposes, baloney. I investigated every possibility, physical and mental, but none of my recorded maladies would get me a 4-F. I went to my physical with a sense of doom, but for once being from Brooklyn turned out to be helpful. The physical was at an army base in Brooklyn. At the very end of the physical, last stop, there was this very Brooklyn sergeant who was supposed to gather all the papers and give you your final rating. Here was a guy I knew how to talk to. He looked at me, he looked at the papers, he looked back at me.

"You're thirty-four and a half?" he asked.

"Yeah."

"And they're drafting you?"

"Yeah." I shrugged. "So what can I do?"

He looked back through my papers.

Finally he said, "You had a collapsed lung once."

"Yeah," I said. "But I already checked it out. It was too long ago. And besides, it doesn't keep you out."

He looked at me. He didn't say it but I knew what he was thinking: *Shmuck.* "So you use it for an appeal," he added.

"What good does that do?"

"They have to process it," he says, exasperated.

"So?"

"So it takes six months and by that time you're thirty-five."

Wherever you are, buddy, here's to you. I would have fought in World War Two. I would have enlisted. If it's true as they say that FDR manipulated us into it, he was right. But the wars since then have been bullshit, basically swine wars tragic for those fooled or flogged into them. That's the truth and you know it. Ask a Viet vet.

By this time I had pretty much dropped out of academe. I was living on New York's lower east side in an apartment that cost thirty-three dollars a month. For the next fifteen years I would live basically on academic odd jobs and free-lance writing. A lot of people couldn't figure out why I lit out for the underground at this point, but the answer is simple: freedom. In America, freedom for an artist means freedom from money, and there are only two ways of getting it—having money, or not needing it, i.e., low overhead. So I retired to the lower east side to begin my campaign against Literature with my first novel, *Up.*

Literature is both the friend and the enemy of the novelist. The novel is a way of salvaging experience from the flux of time and the impositions of official history and the media. It is inherently experimental. By the point some form has become certified as Literature it has become a formula useable in prefabricated repetitions. But experience is never prefab. It is immediate, metamorphic, and unpredictable. Writing that tries to package experience can only falsify it. Literature is packaged experience. You can and must learn a lot from the best Literature but you don't learn anything new from it, unless it happens to be new to you. So half the fight when you're writing is to avoid Literature. The other half is to find forms that accommodate, discover, and even create your particular experience.

When I started writing there had already been some breakthroughs. Burroughs was a good model, though his collage technique was still the tail end of the exhausted Modern tradition. Beckett had utterly broken down the convention of verisimilitude, and Genet had shown how fiction could be used to invent rather than imitate reality. Borges I always thought of as a secondary figure, Kafka without anguish. The best of the modern Latin American tradition comes from Faulkner, whom I had long since absorbed. Of the best contemporary examples Barth was inventive but bookish, in his attempt to exhaust the literary

Sukenick in the Colorado mountains, 1986

tradition of its treasures exhausting to read; Brautigan was brilliant at transferring techniques of poetry to fiction, but a little facile; Gass knew how to use the medium as medium but was a little too heavy with ideas to be useful to me; Hawkes was splendid but had been doing the same thing for years; Barthelme wrote wonderful sentences and used language as language, broken away from reference to create new reference, but seemed to have no sense of longer form. Besides, his style was too much of the world he was out to subvert, the consumer world, which may be why he had such a successful relation with the *New Yorker*. Coover was lively, but just getting started.

While I'm at it, let me spike a cliche that went around for years, that Barthelme was America's most imitated writer. *N*obody, but *no*body ever imitated Barthelme. First of all he's inimitable. His particular stylistic fingerprint is so characteristic anyone trying to imitate him would immediately be run out of town as a copycat. I was teaching hundreds of creative-writing students all over the country during those years and I never ran across one who was imitating Barthelme. There was some character actually writing Barthelme stories and getting them published under Barthelme's name, but that's a different story. Though maybe that's what they meant—that Barthelme was America's most *completely* imitated writer, by this particular counterfeiter.

What I did, following the success of *Up*, was I

started working with the tape recorder. My idea was, all right, you want to get an accurate description of reality into fiction, let's find out what reality really sounds like. Hey, very experimental. It was in a way a challenge both to "realistic" fiction and the formalist tradition out of Modernism and especially Joyce and Gertrude Stein. The result was the stories in *The Death of the Novel and Other Stories.* Immediately, of course, the intellocrats, confronting a kind of writing beyond their narrow ideological categories, labeled me an experimentalist, a formalist, and even worse, an elitist. Masturbatory, academic, pretentious, and art-for-art's-sake were also pulled out of the old epithet bag. What, me, a kid from Brooklyn, an experimentalist? a formalist? I was almost flattered.

Some of the New York Intelligentsia got absolutely hysterical in their criticism of the work I and friends like Steve Katz and Raymond Federman were doing. Whether I liked it or not, I became part of a movement, but it was better than being part of a stasis. I suppose it is no accident, as they say, that many of these same critics turned out to be among the worst Reaganite neoconservatives. Since there's no arguing with people of hardened understanding, there was nothing to do but bait them, which I did in a *Partisan Review* essay called "The New Tradition," in which I made light of every literary term I could think of in the social(ist) realism that these people held up as the one valid model for fiction. I suppose it's partly my fault, then, that the label "experimentalist" stuck, just as later the label "postmodernist" stuck. I wonder what the next one will be. But of course movements are often labeled by their enemies, derisively in intention, though the derisive label often turns into a term with the cachet of prestige. The label "surfiction," invented by Raymond Federman, would have been a much more accurate one to apply to those of us who published with the early Fiction Collective, the writer-controlled publishing house, writers such as Clarence Major, Russell Banks, Jonathan Baumbach, or to others like Walter Abish, Rudolfo Anaya, Steve Dixon, Harry Mathews, and Ishmael Reed.

But though there were critics who were hostile, there were also those who were friendly. One who never gets the credit he deserves, and is practically boycotted by the old-boy academic establishment, is Jerome Klinkowitz. Klinkowitz's voluminous commentary on writers like myself and Clarence Major has been of great importance in bringing us into the public eye. His criticism is sometimes put down as naive and inadequately bedded in contemporary theory. But those critics interested in contemporary theory are usually not interested in contemporary writing, unless it illustrates their theory, so there's a sort of catch-22 operative here. I think the crude fact of it is that Klinkowitz, out there in Iowa, just isn't part of the Ivy League old-boy network. Klinkowitz is what I would call an advocacy critic. He actually reads contemporary fiction, he actually tries to explicate it and so create a bridge to the general reading public, and he actually takes the writers seriously enough to ask them what it is they're trying to do. This, I believe, is an old and honorable and critical critical role, one only recently surrendered by theory-oriented academics. Okay, Jerry?

As to the neocon intelligentsia, let's not pretend they're not influential. They're more influential than I would like to believe. They grasp the connection between culture and politics in a country where that connection is beyond the civic imagination of most people. What? police dramas on TV? what has that got to do with politics? Social realism? what has that got to do with distributing a standardized commodity to the maximum number of people? what has that got to do with using your imagination only in prescribed ways that don't conjure up any visions of any oppositional flies in any establishment ointments? The

ointments of the establishment, its facilities, its networks, and its rewards to dispose, thus flow oleaginously into the neocon troughs, where the swine lap gratefully and become strong. I won't even bother to go into the effect of similar influences on the grunt reviewer out in the journalistic trenches. Do you think it was purely coincidental, amigo, that cultural conservatism began to establish its hold the year, the very year, after Nixon was elected? that certain films were discouraged by the studios (I was writing one of them) and others soft-pedaled in distribution? that music with lyrics about social issues began to disappear? that some writers, especially those from Eastern Europe with certified anti-red attitudes were promoted, while domestic "experimentalists" were tabooed as elitists?—even as their foreign experimentalist clones, writing of course about strictly elsewhere, were welcomed? Ay, ay, ay, amigo! We live in the real world, where we are nothing but cucarachas on the levers of power. La cucaracha, la cucaracha. Allan Bloom is culture czar. La cucaracha, la cucaracha. Irving Howe is commissar.

And now I have a startling announcement to make. I am actually Tom Pynchon, and it's me who's

"With my companion, Julia Frey, in the Colorado mountains," 1987

written all his books. If Jerzy Kosinski could do it why can't Pynchon? All right, just kidding. Just trying to get your attention for the next episode, which is titled—The Resistance.

Besides cultural conservatism, by the early seventies the economics of the publishing industry, which were changing, made it doubly hard for the kind of writing that needs a certain amount of economic support because it takes time to be absorbed by the culture.

The first step in the direction of an organized resistance to the difficult cultural situation had been the establishment of the Coordinating Council of Literary Magazines, which had wrested money from federal and state governments to subsidize the country's literary magazines—an important development since just about all such magazines run at a permanent deficit. CCLM was started by William Phillips of *Partisan Review*, and editors of some other, similar magazines. These magazines were mostly East Coast, intellectually oriented, and had substantial budgets, but as the organization grew into a genuinely national one, the membership tipped in the direction of small-budget West Coast poetry journals with distinctly different tastes. This created an organizational strain that eventually helped to tear CCLM apart. I was brought onto the board of CCLM, I believe, to mediate between the East and West Coast contingents, since I was one of the few who had allegiances to both.

At my first meeting in San Francisco, organized to conciliate the two groups, the strains were symbolized by Phillips's misguided attempts to extend friendly hospitality to the Frisco underground poetry scene. He made the mistake of holding the meeting in a well-appointed hotel room instead of somebody's pad, and served whisky instead of jug wine. This confirmed all of the poets' worst suspicions about the New York Establishment.

When Phillips retired as chairman of CCLM, he was replaced by Michael Anania, and then by myself. I had to deal with the political situation created by the minorities moving into CCLM, trying to mediate among different interest groups. Middlemen in such situations always get caught in the middle, and I was no exception, almost losing some good minority friends like Ishmael Reed (who succeeded me as chairman) and Rudy Anaya, as well as friends from Phillips's East Coast faction and Anania's Midwest bunch. In fact, probably the greatest benefit of CCLM was in the network of underground literary people it generated, a network I would draw on in future organizational projects. However, the grants function

of CCLM should not be underestimated: during my time as chairman, its budget reached the one-million-dollar mark, and its grant support changed the underground literary scene enormously, some say for the better, some say for the worse. Both are right, but those who opt for the better are righter, in that it represented a first significant step by writers (and editors) to take their economic fate into their own hands.

I helped start the Fiction Collective during my CCLM days, aiding the main movers, Peter Spielberg and Jon Baumbach, from the West Coast, where I was living, while B. H. Friedman also provided considerable help. The Collective was a very visible success, and perhaps for that very reason aroused animosity in certain quarters of the publishing industry. The attitude of many editors, as expressed in a *Partisan Review* symposium I participated in, was basically that, yes, it's a shame we can't publish more good fiction, but don't worry, if anything good comes along, we'll publish it. Speaking of logic. The resentment lingered. Many years later, critics Larry McCaffery and Tom LeClair presented a manuscript of interviews with eminent contemporary novelists to Knopf. The manuscript was accepted on the condition that it contain no Fiction Collective writers. Since the book contained three Collective authors out of fifteen, and the editors refused to take them out, McCaffery and LeClair took the book to the University of Illinois Press, which published it under the title *Anything Can Happen*. There are other stories of this sort. For example, Knopf later published Tom Glynn's second novel as his first, ignoring the one published by the Collective.

The next link in the chain was *American Book Review*. Actually, a review magazine that would give a fair shake to non-publishing-industry presses was first suggested to me by Ishmael Reed in a cab to the airport from a CCLM meeting in Louisville, Kentucky, only he wanted me to do it and I wanted him to do it. Both of us were already doing too many things. Still are. Somehow I ended up doing it, largely because one year I had a big income-tax refund, and someone pointed out that if I spent it that would be that, but that if I used it to start a book-review magazine, I might end up with something important and durable. So we plunged in, Clarence Major, Suzanne Zavrian, and Charles Russell—the original editors—and myself, with some help from the University of Colorado (where by then I was organizing and directing the creative-writing program), and some other writers. As I write this, *ABR*, under myself and editors Rochelle Ratner and John Tytell, has just put out its tenth-anniversary issue.

Lynn Luria-Sukenick

"With The Captain, model for a character in
Blown Away," *late seventies*

Meanwhile I was still writing steadily. *Out,* which later became a movie starring Peter Coyote, was a novel about the hope generated by the era called the sixties, despite all its conflict and insanity, and *98.6* was about the failure of the sixties. In both books I used techniques—very different in each—to break down standard form in fiction in order to reach beyond literary artifice to actual experience (don't think I'm not aware of the contradictions involved). In general, I think this is the misunderstood thrust of the "Postmodern" in fiction: an attempt to get at the truth of experience beyond our fossilizing formulas of discourse, to get at a new and more inclusive "reality," if you will. This is a reality that includes what the conventional novel tends to exclude and that encompasses the vagaries of unofficial experience, the cryptic trivia of the quotidian that help shape our fate, and the tabooed details of life—class, ethnic, sexual—beyond sanctioned descriptions of life. It is an orientation that is distinctly democratic in tendency, which may explain some of the hostility it meets. What is currently called "Minimalism" seems to be a subgenre of this mode that does some of the same things. Maybe that's why some critics are down on it lately.

In *Long Talking Bad Conditions Blues* I pushed the narrative form as far in the direction of poetry as I could, using the symmetries of poetic form, albeit idiosyncratic, within which to improvise the rhythms that most accurately express the unpredictable flow of experience. *Blown Away* explores my idea of the novel as related to suppressed traditions of magic, shamanism, prophecy, and the functions of the holy book, all this based on an interpretation of Prospero, our tradition's most eminent literary wizard. My idea is that narrative is or can be a mediumistic form, rather than the empirical form that positivism has delineated for it. The interconnected pieces in *The Endless Short Story* represent a variety of formal improvisations, reflecting my conviction that improvisation is at the heart of art in the American mode.

Down and In, though nonfiction, goes back to my interest in the use of tape recorder as technique for writing, and presents the same narrative considerations as any of my fictions. It looks back to a little-known electronic novel I did for the Berkeley Pacifica station, using recorded voices, which I consider unsuccessful because it got so complicated sonically that it became impossible to reproduce it on the page. Warning! Technique as such is baloney. Lately I've seen any number of techniques out of James Joyce, Laurence Sterne, or Nabokov used to produce slick, tricky novels that are the fictive equivalent of fast food. Give me Theodore Dreiser. In a way, *Down and In* is continuous with *Up* in its interest in autobiography. There is one major difference, however, in that it is not pseudo-autobiography. "My wife, Lynn," for example, in *Up* is not Lynn, my ex-wife, but a character in a novel, just as "Ronald Sukenick" in that book, or in any of my fictions, is not Ronald Sukenick.

But of course, as soon as a real-life character is inscribed on the page, even the page of history, s/he becomes a construct of words. And that includes this page. And, curiously, the character "Ronald Sukenick," initially unleashed in the pages of my own fiction, has since become a persona in a number of novels by other writers—Steve Katz, E. L. Doctorow, Raymond Federman, to name some. He has also become a character in a plenitude of critical works, one who has attained an independent existence to the point where he is sometimes unrecognizable, at least to me. But what the hell, we continually make one another up, we make ourselves up, we make our lives up, do we not? That's not experimental, that's experiential. All I'm trying to do is keep fiction as close as possible to the available data, despite the often profitable make-believe of that Romantic concept Coleridge and Walt Disney call Imagination. What can you say about Imagination? Imagination is . . . funny. It makes a cloudy day sunny. It gave us the Easter Bunny. It brings in a lot of money. But aside from that it's irrelevant to the real business of writing, which is to tell it like, to use a cliche, it is. That's not as easy as it looks and you get it only in the greatest, yes, Literature.

The author at home in Boulder, Colorado, 1988

BIBLIOGRAPHY

Fiction:

Up. New York: Dial, 1968.

The Death of the Novel and Other Stories. New York: Dial, 1969.

Out. Chicago: Swallow Press, 1973.

98.6. New York: Fiction Collective, 1975.

Long Talking Bad Conditions Blues. New York: Fiction Collective, 1979.

Blown Away. College Park, Md.: Sun & Moon, 1986.

The Endless Short Story. New York: Fiction Collective, 1986.

Nonfiction:

Wallace Stevens: Musing the Obscure. New York: New York University Press, 1967.

In Form: Digressions on the Act of Fiction. Carbondale: Southern Illinois University Press, 1985.

Down and In: Life in the Underground. New York: William Morrow/Beech Tree Books, 1987.

Reed Whittemore

1919-

Reed Whittemore, nine months old

And now he is in his high chair in the kitchen. His porridge is in his porridge bowl before him. He eats his porridge with his little silver spoon. He picks up the porridge bowl, shouts, "All gone," and throws the bowl over his shoulder.

And now he is in his high chair not eating but reading. He has a large book in front of him and is turning the pages slowly, saying, "Bararum bararum bararum." Lottie the cook is watching and listening. She says, "Look, Reed is reading."

Do I remember these events? The memories I am sure of come later; what I can vouch for is in the yellowing snapshots. I was chubby and round-faced. I was overdressed, and in winter I was invisible behind coats, caps, mittens, blankets. There was often a dog beside me, a white Samoyede. Once there were two half-brothers—twins—beside me, in knickers, with their slicked-back hair. And there was always Mother holding me, smiling at me, Mother in a *cloche* standing, looking down at me, perhaps beside a Wills Sainte Claire with a metal goose flying on the radiator.

But now I think I remember the Wills Sainte Claire directly. I am in the backseat alone. Mother is in the front, driving and talking endlessly with a friend. I am bored. I am bouncing on the backseat. I am fooling with the door handle. And now, surprise, I am out on the dirt road with scuffed knees watching the car drive on without me. I am running after it, crying.

Where was Father in all this? He could have been at the office for all the early years, except for one day when he had his picture taken holding me on his shoulder. Those years were at 175 East Rock Road in New Haven. The house was an ugly stucco affair with a square, pillared porch sitting in front of a square, two-story facade, but sometime before school began in earnest we moved from that house to Grandmother's more elegant one, up the street at 193.

Grandmother was Nangma. She was long silk and velvet dresses. She was an old, stiff body sealed to the chin with "chokers." She was white hair with a bun, a tortoise comb, and pince-nez glasses with a silver chain. She was wrinkled hands with ringed fingers that stroked heads and gave electric shocks.

H e is in his crib and the crib is in a wallpapered corner. It is nap time but he is not napping. He is standing in his crib, wetting his fingers on his tongue, and rubbing the fingers on the wallpaper. Bits of wallpaper are beginning to come off in little rolls. He is rubbing harder, and now there is a blank place where there is no wallpaper. But Mother is coming. He hears her, lies down in the little rolls, and pretends to sleep.

And she was an inhabitant of two rooms, upstairs front, that were off-limits. There is no more of her except the hearsay, the bad words about her from Mother.

And Lottie? Lottie was round and black, dressed in blue with a white apron and black, patent-leather shoes with one strap across the instep. She was at the big black stove, or sitting in the kitchen rocking chair. She laughed, she scolded.

And sometimes John, tall and black in a white coat, was in the kitchen with her. Or he was in the pantry cleaning silverware with paste in a copper sink. Or he was outside sweeping the front walk. Or he was smoking in the cellar. He told me about railroads and winning at the numbers.

So Nangma and Lottie and John were at 193 with Mother and Father and me, and there was Cat too, and Bulldog Bobbie, who had asthma. Brothers Frank and Dick were not there, but at school. Their empty rooms had banners on the walls: Taft, Choate, Lehigh (which was taken down), and For God, for Country, and for Yale.

It was a large house with rhododendrons under the front windows and a heavy brass doorknocker that John made shine. Beyond the doorknocker was a front hall with a tall blue Chinese vase on a long dark table with a silver tray. To the right of the hall was the dining room, with a heavy sideboard and another dark table with a silver tray. To the left of the hall was the living room, with a gas-heater fireplace, book-cases holding uncut books, two stiff couches, and a big blue leather rocking chair next to a table covered with *Saturday Evening Post*s. In a corner was a grand piano with a player mechanism hidden in a drawer under the keyboard. Next to the piano was a case for piano rolls. "The Blue Danube" had a small, neatly pencilled circle on it, as guide for a prereader.

To the rear of the hall the staircase rose to a landing with a grandfather clock. When I climbed the fourteen stairs, passed the slow pendulum, and walked around the landing, I came to my room, three more steps up, front right. In the hall I did nothing except stroke Cat, who slept on the heat register under the silver tray. In the dining room I ate quietly, though I once dropped a butterball on the floor, and many times tried to refuse Bartlett pears. When I had finished my meal and the others were still gabbing, I was to say, "Ihavehadagreatsufficiencymaylbeexcused." I did. Then in the living room I lay on my neck in the leather chair looking at *Post*s, or perhaps sat at the piano pretending to play "The Blue Danube." But it was in my own room—with clocks, tools, gadgets, and Japanese waltzing mice—that I lived.

My brother gave me the mice for Christmas. They waltzed in a goldfish bowl. In the middle of the bowl was a square cardboard house filled with cotton. During the day the mice slept in the cotton, with just their little red noses showing, and perhaps a skinny tail. At night they waltzed. They spun around chasing their tails for hours, or they raced around the bowl for hours, higher and higher on its banked side. They seemed to go faster in the dark than when the light was on, and when they were really on the move they sounded like heavy beasts, until they squeaked. They were white and clean. My mother hated them, which must have been why Dick bought them for me.

There were radios in the room too. First there was one that Father, who had as a hobby actually making radios, helped me put together. He drew a plan and gave me the parts to fit it. I found a board, screwed the parts into the board, and attached a hard-rubber panel, with holes for knobs, to the front of the board. I strung striped copper wire to each of the parts, put pronged vacuum tubes into the four sockets, fitted tuning knobs, a rheostat knob, and a toggle switch to the panel, hooked up to big round "C" batteries, plugged in earphones. I turned the radio on and the tubes lit up.

But the radio did not play, not even static, and Father was at his office. I jiggled and punched, punched and jiggled. Nothing. Then, looking for the plan that Father had drawn (though it would have done me no good), I lifted one end of the radio perhaps an inch. Lo, static!

I put a screwdriver under that end of the radio, and soon I had WTIC, Hartford.

Father never found out why the radio only worked with a screwdriver under it, so soon he bought me a Philco.

Resumé (part I)
(Edward) Reed Whittemore (Jr)
1919–

Father: Edward Reed Whittemore, physician, New Haven
Mother: Margaret Carr, North Adams
Schooling: Mrs. Weiss's kindergarten, Canner Street Elementary, Hopkins Grammar School, Phillips Academy Andover, Yale
Events and hobbies: white mice, radios, electric trains, jigsaw puzzles, and finally a black 1937 Ford V8 Roadster, followed by Furioso *and World War II*
First book: Heroes and Heroines, *1946*

At a political party in Washington when I was fifty-five, a young sociologist tricked me into talking about the past in *her* terms. She led me to say that my past had been an ordinary middle-class business, at which point she averred it had not been. Had not father been a prominent New Haven medico from a prominent "old" family up there? Was I not a Yale man from a stable of same?—then I had not been a middle-class business, but something patrician.

I spent the rest of the party drinking and trying to be admitted to my class. To be an old New England WASP is to be driven into the role of last Puritan, and does not stop with remarks about what snobs and racists Puritans are. It goes to the quick, saying what the *first* last Puritan, Henry Adams, said of himself long ago in his *Education*. He described himself as an eighteenth-century relic, unable to keep up with the raw immigrant blood around him. He said he had an energy deficiency, and was afraid of it. He kept walking up to the new forces around him, then backing away.

And thirty years later George Santayana described *his* last Puritan similarly, as a spent force in a changed world.

And fifty years after that?

My own writings have shown plenty of spent force, and as if the writings themselves were not enough, I contracted, at age fifty, a muscle disease that made me unable to close fist, lift arm, even walk. It plagued me intermittently for several years, and is even now only in remission. One can easily see a connection between last Puritans and myasthenia.

Yet young social-science persons who tell last Puritans that they are what they are should at least be told how complicated they can be. There may still exist old Puritan families in the country whose hormones have not been eroded, but mostly the last Puritans have been *forced* into ordinary middle-class business. Not many have been rich enough to fade away ideologically like Adams and Santayana; myasthenia remains a rarity. Usually eating has come first.

Eating came first, even in Nangma's big house, and surrounded by big houses filled with professors (*those* were the professorial days with private incomes). The Depression hit, and soon the hall with the Chinese vase was replaced by a hall-less, two-bedroom apartment into which the player piano fit poorly, so was disposed of, like everything else except the sideboard, the blue leather chair, and three beds. A young sociologist might be driven to compare my father and me with the impoverished lesser nobility in Spain and Poland in the eighteenth century, the ones who starved rather than soil their hands by labour, but she would be wrong. We were quite willing to soil our hands with labour; we simply had strange patrician notions about what to labour *at*. Father, a stiff Republican reading the *New York Herald Tribune* and cursing Franklin Roosevelt, knew in his bones that we

should never be "in trade," yet making money in the stock market was permissable labour, so he lost our money there.

Thereby making Mother's role in Nangma's house even less tenable.

Mother was a little unmonied girl who had been teaching school in the Palisades across from Manhattan when Father met her, after the death of his first wife. The first wife had died of ptomaine poisoning from lobster at a fashionable dinner party on St. Ronan Street, died while the party was still in progress, in an upstairs room with Father beside her. The death was so scandalous that I was in the dark about it until after both Mother and Father were long dead and I was told the tale by an old family friend. Father married Mother within a year of the poisoning, and Mother entered Whittemore-land as an outsider under suspicion. The sad move to Nangma's house had been made because Nangma said she needed to be taken care of, but of course after the move Nangma had asserted her rule there to her last breath. She allowed Mother to order the meals but little else. Lottie and John were Nangma's servants, the dead living room was Nangma's living room, the Chinese vase her vase, the house her house. Mother's domain became two and a half bedrooms on the second floor—one was mine—plus a small room called the den in the rear on the first floor where bridge was played once or twice a week with just two other couples. When Father lost his capital in a radio stock, Nangma knew what to do. She set up a trust for *her* money that bypassed Father and Mother, leaving, after her own losses in the Crash, and after several years of gifts to Frank and Dick as they finished college (and Frank law school), a small amount to be divided among Frank, Dick, and myself. Mother went to drinking.

Father lived with her drinking for fifteen years. She died in 1943 when I was overseas in the war; and when Father died in 1946 I found in his papers a long letter to me about drinking. It was a hard letter to live with, a letter about his love for Mother, and about "the complete loyalty of her affections," followed by a close account of what and how much "dear Margaret" drank, followed by reassertions of love. Of course the letter was meant as a warning, but included with it, among his papers, was a pencilled statement by Mother, an informal will, in which she made *her* position clear:

In case my husband should not be living at the time of my death, all my possessions [she had few] *will go to my own son—E. Reed Whittemore Jr. The twins have been given from time to time a great many things and have had the advantage of money which rightly belonged to their father, so I am sure they will not feel slighted if their younger brother is left the remainder. He—ERW Jr—was deliberately left out of his grandmother's will.*

What did Father talk about in all those young years? He had words of wisdom on jigsaws and radios, and occasionally he would take me to his office to look at one-celled life under his brass microscope, and to learn how to focus the microscope and keep eyelashes clear. Also, on a long trip to camp he once lectured me, literally, about the birds and the bees, blushing to the tops of his prominent ears when he arrived at humans.

But we were both New England. In New England there is never much to say, or if there is it is not much that is searchingly intimate. Father could recite lovingly the name of a twenty-syllabled lake in New Hampshire (it began "Chugaugugaug, munchauga-gaug"). He could also talk about the universe like a Deist, believing that the whole thing was a large Erector Set, but he could not talk about sex, birth, and death except as a medico, and he could not talk of himself, the sadness of his own lost life, what had happened to it, and why the fine medical practice that had been *his* father's had dwindled to nothing. (I still don't know.) He let his feelings show about matters off in the distance like FDR, not about 193 East Rock Road.

Yet he was affectionate, dependable, unswerving, whole in his New Englandness. And in *my* own New Englandness I was closer to him than to Mother, who had, though from North Adams, a streak of anti–New England in her. The streak was partly just anti-Whittemore, but anyway she would say to Father, "You are just like your mother," or, "You won't face up to things." And Father wouldn't.

So I was sent off to Andover at fifteen to develop my New Englandness while escaping some of its gloom. It must have been Mother's hope that at Andover I would turn into a rare bloom that would dazzle East Rock Road, but I didn't dazzle. I listened to my now illegal Philco late at night (keeping it locked in the day in a strongbox). I also listened, on a windup phonograph, to records of Louis Armstrong, Bing Crosby, Ray Noble, Glen Gray, Fred Waring, Red Nichols, Jimmy Lunceford, and, at the end, Benny Goodman.

In my first year I was billeted in the attic of an old frame house with two other boys, each of us with a separate low-ceilinged room. The housemaster was a little moustached man who tried to catch us smoking or listening to the radio, but since he didn't catch us he may have been more on our side than we knew. On weekends that year it always rained, and we were always disconsolate in our crow's nest. One of the boys, Dave Jones, was a good tennis player, but in our rooms there was no room for tennis. When we bounced a ball against the wall the noise brought the little moustache upstairs, so we resigned ourselves just to bouncing the ball up a foot or two from the racket. We did the same thing with Ping-Pong balls and paddles, our scores soaring into the thousands. Eventually the year was over.

In the second year we were all moved to a dormitory where I had a fat chemist-roommate whom I seldom saw. Dave roomed alone, and that year both of us learned to drink. I would go to Boston on Saturday afternoons, consume beer in dives near North Station, then come back to school with a pint of whiskey. One Saturday night Dave drank about half a bottle in the sudden way that the young begin by doing. He was giggly at midnight when our new housemaster, the school chaplain, knocked. I shoved Dave in my closet with the laundry, told him to shut up, closed the door, and we passed inspection. When the chaplain was clearly gone I opened the closet door and found Dave asleep in the dirty shirts. It was a good night, but there were few others.

Nangma died in my last and worst Andover year, which was also perhaps the first year of my education. What did I learn? (At this point *The Education of Henry Adams* enters my brain and I am tempted to switch to the third person.) During the dismal fall I went AWOL to New York on an overnight bus, thinking to join the world, but learning that joining the world was not easy. Two days later I came back to school, via home, in embarrassment, and learned, as a further part of education, to finish the Andover year. The unexpected reward for my misery was that I wrote two chapters of a novel about being miserable, then destroyed them and switched to writing poems of misery. The poems somehow arranged for me to be put in a seminar conducted by Alan Blackmur in an elegant, leathery room in Bulfinch Hall, and it was there that I had sudden dim insights into my future. Blackmur was the first teacher in my experience to try a bit of positive reinforcement.

Travel is a trick I learned
From my betters
For trifling with the troubles that attend
All that matters.

The pains, the wear and tear
Of living in the closenesses and loving

By the year I forswear
By simply leaving.

The regions in the distance are my homelands.
The cities with the shimmering walls and
  steeples
House my gibbering friends,
My peoples.

The whole world I inhabit except the bit
Where I at the moment sit.

The author of that eccentric sonnet (who was then more than a decade out of Andover, but his "travel trick" had started at Andover) is mixed up. The words are and are not speaking for him. He does not mean "betters" except ironically (and the irony is wasted), nor does he believe what he says, that staying home is all that matters. He flogs himself for fourteen lines for his love of homelessness, his failure to settle down, but in the process he shows himself rather pleased about the failure. He is thematically mixed up, for all his irony, but he is aesthetically very very neat. He must have written every line ten times, and been bowled over by such technical triumphs as his *tr* tetralogy in stanza one, and his long line–short line balancings throughout. For weeks, he remembers, he lacerated himself deciding whether or not to put "chosen" before "peoples" in stanza three. The poem has finish if not wisdom, and is one of the few poems of his own that he has been able to recite without a trot for thirty years. Why?

A little late-life psychoanalysis suggests that though he professed to be scornful of his escapism he really loved it. He learned early the joys of loner projects like cutting an intricate, thousand-piece jigsaw puzzle (he produced several of these before he was shipped to Andover) or a well-made poem. The genre didn't matter as much as the solitude, so that when a disliked godfather amazingly provided $760 for a car, he was sure he had reached maturity (he was sixteen) and heaven too. The car was a mobile one-man workshop. He could travel anywhere in it, yet be more at home in it than at home. He could be a genius with a pencil and pad of paper on top of East Rock.

Aside from my sweet escapism I had, starting at Andover but blossoming at Yale, something of a social conscience. I grew into it naturally with the Depression, the money troubles at home, the Spanish War, the Moscow trials, the Russo-German Pact, Archibald MacLeish's attack on the "irresponsibles" and much else, including the *Daily Worker* (to which I subscribed for some months) and all the crosscur-

Reed Whittemore

rents between Stalinists, Trotskyites, and homegrown hawks and isolationists. Four years at Yale helped me into literature and little magazines—especially the magazine *Furioso,* which I will describe later—but they were issue-ridden years too, ending with the grand graduation-present issue, in 1941, of World War II—together with my 1-A draft card. World War II often provided exotically lonely places to park in a jeep and write, but other times it provided engagement, whether one liked it or not. In Sicily, where we stayed only two wild months, it provided so much that I went up to my colonel one afternoon and told him I couldn't hack it any more and was resigning from our honorable and distinguished Twelfth Air Force Service Command. The colonel was amused but I was not. I hadn't slept for a couple of days and could see that I was personally losing the war for everybody. Out with me.

Ah, but when the war proved not to be lost, our honorable XII AFSC regularized its pace and moved into the sort of quarters that supply officers normally find for themselves, an apartment in Naples with marble tables and a grand piano. For a year I could ignore 100-octane gasoline two or three afternoons a week, and sit in the sun on a sixth-floor balcony looking out over the great bay and Vesuvius, as if I were not only a genuine but a well-paid poet. I wrote several escapist travel poems on that balcony but I also wrote the skeptical lines printed below about the Isle of Capri. (Capri had become an air-force rest camp immediately after our occupation of Naples, and I visited it several times.) Note my heavy suspicion that all is not well in the world's Capris:

Capri

There are hells under every mountain, hill and rock, and under every plain and valley.
—Emanuel Swedenborg

It is good you are here as you are
And will stay for only a day or two, and will see
Only the worthwhile sights, olives and grapes
And a lovely old *Mare.* Ships
And clouds and stars in the close of an eye
Will beckon as far and as deep as you'd best
    wander.
For were you to linger and let the elegant vision
Work, as it were, of a garden scene,
You of a sameness season on season
Fathoms would fathom there sown,
And plumb not so much as a honeycomb hewn
Out of alien stone.

Travel was not, though, my main topic while the war went on. Except for the Naples year the XII AFSC travelled too much for me to like travel, so much that when I couldn't sleep at night I was in the habit of conjuring up all the beds or floors or grounds I had slept on since leaving New Haven—and counting them over and over. So instead of travel I became busy writing about the heroic. Not in *my* war, mostly, but in all the literary wars. I had in my barracks bag, or could pick up when the culture shipments from the States came in, all that anybody needed in the way of heroic models, ancient and modern. I read novels mostly, and wrote poems about their heroes and heroines. Then I mailed the results to my most resilient teacher at Yale, Arthur Mizener.

I had bothered Arthur steadily for my last two college years, especially on Sunday mornings when he was trying to be alone in his Pearson College office. After the war came and I left the country (he had to leave Yale, but he kept teaching), he was officially liberated from me but continued to accept my intrusions by mail and cope with them. He not only wrote back (he and my father were my chief correspondents for three years overseas) but sometimes he even wrote back to say he liked the stuff. I had despised much that was Yale, but Arthur

had been there to make it habitable, as well as Andrews Wanning and a couple of other instructors who taught me what a teacher was for. (The ones I was indebted to were kicked out by Yale my graduation year.) Arthur and I could argue endlessly about a single word in a young sonnet without thinking the "issue" trivial. Precisions of tone and feeling were our game, with Arthur, about ten years older, backing off from his days as an ideological Trotskyite, and with me struggling to establish, on paper, some connection or other with the world that seemed worldly. Partly because of Arthur the time overseas became for me one of constant mental shuffling, while I physically shuffled air-force supplies. Especially I shuffled between the great big war and the little, but indecently noisy, me.

I suppose that in any memorable private experience there is always a kind of San Andreas Fault lying underneath, to the presence of which the young learner must accustom himself as the Fault intermittently shakes him up, telling him, Watch it, kid, the ground you walk on is not yours. I know that in my own wartime life, even on sunny days on the Neapolitan balcony, the Fault kept speaking to the frivolity of my being where I was, doing what I was doing. And in retrospect it seems clear that if there was one subject that Arthur and I were really working at in our many long letters, it *was* the Fault: what it did, what it meant, how one reckoned with it. What the War and the Fault kept telling us was that though our correspondence was in some ways ridiculous—who cared about an infelicitous word in the first line of a tiny tiny sonnet?—still, the word was what we had and what we *could* intelligently care about. Furthermore it was *good* to care so long as we didn't care too much.

With Arthur's help I scribbled myself through many useful carings. And Arthur? He wasted more time on his ex-student than he could sometimes afford, but perhaps the correspondence helped him live with that larger talent, but not larger ego, than mine, Scott Fitzgerald. He took on a biography of Fitzgerald right after the war, and when he did he brought to the job our wartime assumptions about the self and the Fault underneath. He did not abide by the rising fashions of psychobiography, but moved as diligently *out* from Fitzgerald as he bored *in*.

Probably what I chiefly learned as soldier-scribbler was a little about the *deceptions* of self. For instance I learned that just settling in to study self-deception needs to be a core subject, in our time, in any curriculum devoted to understanding rather than doing. A tangled subject it is. Thus, in the sciences the professional focus is on the obstacles keeping an experimenter's self from making experimental objectivity possible. In psychobiography the focus is on how a biographee leads himself and his disciples astray by mythologizing his own being. And in literary criticism the focus is on the slipperiness of textual meaning, with much heavy argument proceeding out of those who tell us that no literary text has meaning independent of its readers' meaning for it. Tell away. I feel lucky that as a young critic I wrestled with the deceptions of self not in academia but by V-letter, and in the sun in Naples.

Not that I was so lucky as to be an *undeceived* self. My mind was a smorgasbord of amateurish speculations—a bit of my father's Darwinism, a bit of Marxism, a bit of Mizener, and a large bit of New England me. The me learned to disapprove of American self-glorification generally, but remained a me through all the disapproval, yearning, as a me always does, for glorification.

At least my confusion made me an amateur scholar of self-understanding. Most of my war poems were little studies of it. In a series of sonnets, for instance, I summarized what Emma Woodhouse, Hester Prynne, Lady Ashley, and a number of other well-known fictions learned, or failed to learn, about themselves as they progressed through the lives that their authors had provided. My analyst, if I had one, might tell me that I was not escaping *my* self by summarizing theirs, but while he wouldn't be wrong, there was more, I think, to the poems than that. All in all they were little verse tentacles reaching out for general truths from their self-cave, doing so in the long tradition of such reaching in poetry (though I did work hard to keep from sounding like Arthur Hugh Clough). I wanted to express the general rather than, or in addition to, the local and private, and being in the war helped; the military is not to be scorned as a self-chastener. I accommodated to it well, and it taught me duties, loyalty. It taught living for something beside a dollar (except when playing poker on payday). And it brought me the difficulties of democracy at a new, telling angle, starting with the first lineup, nude, at the reception center in Fort Devens, Massachusetts, for short-arm inspection. The army had great educational merit, and was cheap too.

But of all the lessons in self-understanding that I had, none was more critical than that of coming home to my lonely father *after* the war. Sharply I can remember, as I entered, his old bathrobe, his old voice, his telling me to sit in the old leather rocker amid the neat clutter (the neatness was his, the clutter had been Mother's). And as in a deep dream I can remember discovering that *his* self was no longer a depth to reach for. Four years earlier he had had

"interests," but in the leather chair I learned he was now someone else. So there he was, and there I was, and as we sat together producing long silences I could see that I was the only full self in the room.

Now I can say, as if with wisdom, that I was in the process of finding myself, while Father was in the process of losing his self; but that is glibness. So is saying that I had to make decisions, that he did not, and that I had to go on with my life, while he had no further imperatives. What is cleanest to say is that neither of us seems to have been greatly deceived by our respective states. He lay in bed much of the time doing crossword puzzles and reading detective stories. I sat in my room or up on East Rock with books and pads, becoming intense. We both knew we were as we were.

My intensities were indiscriminate but made a kind of sense, at least on paper. In the first few months at home I moved (tentatively) from sonnets to several verse dramas, none of which advanced past a scene or two. I was a nut about Joseph Conrad at the time, and as I struggled to revive, single-handedly, verse drama (I had decided that Eliot had simply been routed by the genre), my main efforts were aimed at converting *Heart of Darkness* and *Lord Jim* to the stage. I even became scholarly and wandered off to Sterling Library to see how Conrad (and Henry James too) had fared when they attempted conversion. I found that they had both been routed too by the process, neither being able to do anything, even in prose, but butcher stage dialogue. I marched on undeterred for about a month, but then my labors on *Heart of Darkness* suddenly emerged as merely more sonnets, and my *Lord Jim* added up to just a few unrelated soliloquies.

So the experiment did not work but was a useful failure. Half a century later I still know the immensities involved. And aside from the virtue of trying, there was the wisdom gained from simply reckoning with Conrad's characters' complicated selves, especially Jim's.

Two fragments of my work with Jim crept into my first book, one being a sonnet soliloquy by Jim, in which I had ship officer Jim talking tensely about the nasty little fix he had put himself into by abandoning his ship, the sinking *Patna,* in the middle of the Gulf of Aden (only to find out later that it *didn't,* with its boatload of Mecca-bound pilgrims, sink). I had personally abandoned no ship, had not even been able to abandon the XII AFSC, yet the heroic chatter I supplied Jim with in the sonnet must have had *something* to do with me, a modest supply-officer hero from the war who now lay abed, unshaven, feeling like a comic-strip derelict. The sonnet began with Jim crying, "Why this?" and came back to the same tough question at the end. "Why this? / Why are all my bravest plans amiss?"

But the other, longer monologue went further than to have its speaker fret. The speaker was a narrator like Conrad's narrator, Marlow, and he told Jim at some length to stop moping around and *do* something. Do what? Do something escapist, but do it. Do what Conrad's Jim did in the last half of the novel: go to Patusan (a remote, primitive, Eastern country in the novel, where Jim recovered his self-respect and became the head man). The connection with me seems to have been that I was arranging to go to a Patusan of my own at the time. My Patusan was the Princeton Graduate College, behind the golf course and flanked by bankers. The poem began like this:

Jim, there's a land within this land
(Of parakeets and palms)
Where a man may partly live;
Live and partly die; a land of whispers.
Jungles of greenest wonder crowd the clouds.
Creatures of zoos, flowers for fabulous gardens
Creep to a lush and lazy end. A man,
A man of garden talents
(Looking for long-tailed monkeys, flying frogs)
Might, might, might there, at last
Find peace.

That poem doesn't sound much like Princeton, though the golf course—like the poem—is lush. Anyway I went to Princeton, and went history. For a year and a half I sat on an inflated rubber pillow (the graduate student's balm) in the history-seminar room of the old Witherspoon Library (the Firestone Library was being built next door). Princeton and history were not nearly as educational as the war, but I did learn about the French Revolution, the Haymarket riot in Chicago, and drinking in Colonial New England. Also, from the chairman of the history department, Joseph Strayer, I learned how to read a scholarly book without reading it, a necessity for graduate students and a dubious luxury for reviewers. Princeton was good, in the sense of useful at the time, but its role in my life was pretty well destroyed by the news, after I'd been there three months, of my father's death.

He had wanted me to go, or had said he did. He knew I had to do something. But there it was.

After the funeral and the settlements (my two married brothers and I dealt with the burial of our past with customary New England familial frigidity and communed little), and after sitting in the New Haven apartment (now to be abandoned) for a few days feeling like an empty burlap sack, I went back to Princeton and was instantly invited to lunch, at the old French restaurant just off Nassau Street, by an apparently sane editor, and asked for the manuscript

The author with his wife, Helen, and his daughter Cate, Christmas, 1955

of my first book. It was like a children's game I think I remember called upsy downsy.

The editor's name I forget. The publisher's name was Reynal and Hitchcock, a firm briefly in chips from a best-seller during the war. The name of my book was *Heroes and Heroines,* and it had in it all the poems that Arthur and I had argued about. I dedicated it to Arthur. Meanwhile he had been called west to be chairman of the English department at Carleton College in Northfield, Minnesota, and fate was arranging for me to fill in for an ailing teacher out there, for one term only. Way out there in nowhere.

Resumé (continued)
Schooling: One and a half years Princeton Graduate School, interrupted by Carleton offer. Moved to Minnesota. Stayed nineteen years.
Events: Furioso *continued. Learned to fly. Married Helen Lundeen of Fergus Falls, Minnesota. Stopped flying. Taught, wrote. Family grew to three children (and to four in the late sixties when we moved to Washington). Furioso was replaced by the* Carleton Miscellany.
Books: Two more volumes of poems: An American Takes a Walk, The Self-made Man. *They were followed by two books mixing poetry and prose:* The Boy from Iowa, The Fascination of the Abomination. *There was also a pamphlet on little magazines.*

The war was one kind of education, teaching another, adjusting to the open spaces of Minnesota another, and magazining still another. And marrying, the education I delayed longest, was the most important other, as well as the one I had most trouble with. Helen was younger, and from the Minnesota I didn't know. She was, and is, fine. She had to put up with what she thought of as a colossal ego, but what she didn't understand was that he was trying to put up with the ego too, busily hating the strident complaints and false impieties he kept trapping himself with. Much later in life he discovered of himself, while seriously ill, that he was really a simpler organism than he had led himself to believe, and could naively struggle for simple survival. But he didn't, then, feel illuminated. He was no D. H. Lawrence, and spent much of his creative breath protesting the easy illuminators. As a poet he had, of course, a steady, sneaky feeling that he *ought* to be an illuminator, and as a family man he had feelings like that too, but mostly he would sit quiet in his study until the feelings went away. He was a New Englander, and when, once, he wrote the beginnings of a rather "straight" novel of family life, they were rotten.

Still, the family was there, and he knew they were there, and Helen knew that he knew. From Helen—and then from Cate, Ned, Jack, and Daisy—he learned something bigger than the war and the writing, and

The Whittemore children on the shore of Ottertail Lake, Minnesota:
Ned, Jack, Daisy, and Cate

he is grateful for the learning. But will not report on it.

Northfield, Minnesota, was where Jesse James had his comeuppance, and where all the Jesse James movies came first, to be jeered at by the students of Northfield's two colleges. I learned more about English departments there, and higher education there, than I ever wanted to know, yet the place was a good place and, for me, a good choice, ending the gap that had been Princeton. Princeton was useful but Northfield was a commitment.

It certainly didn't seem so, first term. I taught one course (Arthur told me I shouted in class so that I was heard in neighboring offices) and made six hundred dollars. I was full of the French Revolution when I should have been teaching Wordsworth—cool it, said my elders—and I was most melancholy in the presence of student themes. But I settled in, and cooled it. Soon academia, together with student themes, became my home.

And little magazines became my home too. At Yale *Furioso*—which my roomate Jim Angleton and I started as sophomores—had been a bright idea full of surprises, like playing host to Ezra Pound in my parents' apartment for a night, and paying E. E. Cummings off in neckties. After the war Jim, who had joined the OSS while I squandered 100-octane in Africa and Italy, stayed with the "Agency," so *Furioso* fell to me; but certainly the original impulse was heavily his. He had searched out Pound in Rapallo, had played tennis with him, taken pictures of him, and talked Dante with him. Pound in return, in his grand cultural way, had decided that Jim was one of those who were going to save American literature. So Pound visited us in New Haven for twenty-four hours,[1] and then let us print in our first issue— Summer, 1939—a one-page economics textbook he had composed consisting of four quotations opposing usury—from John Adams, Thomas Jefferson, Abraham Lincoln, and George Washington (could there have been better evidence that he was, though eccentrically, a patriot?), followed by a bibliographical Pound note telling the reader what to read on the subject. Then, for later issues, he let us have a few light poems, plus a fine prose obituary for Ford Madox Ford.

With Pound came, as part of our earlier-generation stable, William Carlos Williams (who let us print an elegy of his to Ford in the same issue), Cummings, Archibald MacLeish, Wallace Stevens, Marianne Moore, and a number of others who were uncommonly kind in letting two undergraduates publish them. Little magazines were different then, partly because there were not so many, and partly because a mystique hovered about them that the contributors in our stable—especially Pound himself—believed in and helped promote.

There have been other magazines, but absolutely none as good as *Furioso*. Yes indeed, there never was . . . but as I say this I feel my nose growing longer, for I remember that sometime after the war we *Furioso* editors, now numbering about a dozen, actually received in the mail somebody else's *Furioso*. From Australia. An inferior product. Jim, with his partly Italian upbringing, originally chose the name, and Jim was the main driving force behind the early issues. Also, if Jim had not stayed in intelligence he might have made a far better magazine of it, after the war, than we did (though it almost certainly would not have come out regularly). Yet even without Jim it was good, and it certainly was an education. Every poet should have his own magazine. (Perhaps I should withdraw that remark. Too many have!)

In starting the magazine up again in 1947, without Jim (one intervening wartime issue had been turned out by Jim's sister Carmen in 1942), I changed the magazine's focus from our elders to my contemporaries and me. The shift was natural enough, since by then we had a few credentials other than having passed Shakespeare and the Romantics. The shift was also necessary psychologically—for me anyway. I wanted to be *in* the magazine, and have the other editors in it. We printed our own work mercilessly.[2]

But we also became more portentously editorial, and with our large, loose, unpaid staff tried to be objective and judicious about what should be accepted, what not. We passed manuscripts around in grocery-store bags, and argued, and took votes, and argued more. Sometimes we agreed, but what impressed us most was how much disagreement we could arrive at. Put an innocent poem in front of us and we would come up with three yes's, three no's, and a maybe. A wilful mind like Pound's may move in and start a culture-saving movement, and may write angry letters to opponents, and make fine critical copy for scholars, but he won't live long with an editorial board. The mystique of little magazines that bred *Furioso* in Jim's head and mine originally could

---

[1] This was during EP's short 1939 visit to America, when he tried to persuade several senators in Washington to keep America out of the war.

[2] The "we" consisted of two complete sets of editors—this was 1946 to 1953. The roll call: Howard Nemerov, John Pauker, William R. Johnson, Ambrose Gordon, Jr., Irwin Touster (art editor), Scott Elledge, John Lucas, Arthur Mizener, Rosemary Mizener, Charles Shain, Edwin Pettet, Liane Elledge.

not survive editorial boards long in any culture or country, and in *Furioso's* case the mystique did slowly fade into the light of common day. Probably a good change, all in all.

I gave the magazine up in 1953, partly because of the fading but partly also because of money, and when in 1960 Carleton saw its way to backing it—the earlier money had been mine—we started it up again as the *Carleton Miscellany*. By then I had clearly become an old institutional type, being forty-one and a professor and *not* represented in an anthology of the *new* American poetry; and the magazine's new name signalled the shift. Still, we at least managed to be noisy in its pages. We attacked the *New York Times Book Review*, we had a feminist issue, we bombed the atom bomb, and we printed a socialist-realist diatribe that provoked more diatribes. Perhaps the project most indicative of what my own little magazining had come to by then was an attempt to form a combine, a collective, a *harmonious* association of little magazines.[3] "Wrong from the start," Pound would certainly have said of it, but fifteen years later it even became something of a success. It was an organizational event, a money event, something of a non-little-magazine event, but, as the first meeting to organize it showed, it was still spiritually attuned to the old mystique.

The project began at a two-week writers' conference in Salt Lake City, where my teacher-colleagues were two other editors, Andrew Lytle of the *Sewanee Review* and Robie Macauley of the *Kenyon Review*. For me the Utah conference was a fine extended editorial meeting, and the immediate result was the promoting of a gathering of editors in St. Paul the following winter. Twenty or so magazines sent representatives, about half aged and half fiery. The gathering became formalized as the proceedings of the Association of Literary Magazines of America (ALMA), and the extensive minutes were soon printed in the *Miscellany*. (Later, after several more meetings in New York and Washington, ALMA changed its name and became an official nonprofit corporation known as the Coordinating Council of Literary Magazines: CCLM.) With the snow piling up around us in St. Paul, Allen Tate chaired the two-day event, during which we made speeches to each other that steadily invoked the wonders of the little-magazine tradition. Then we put on paper, aside from minutes and bylaws, a mighty

Reed Whittemore

© Hartley Alley

preamble to the bylaws in which the wonders were again flaunted. In effect we said that *no* great living American writers would have gone *any*where or been *any*thing if they hadn't first been printed in some *Blast* or *Little Review* or *Furioso*.

After loud arguments the assemblage approved the extravagance, and since we approved little else it seemed to have been written in gold. Yet I can remember the cynical hours or so that the preamble committee—Tate, Whit Burnett, and I—spent in a hotel room away from the general meeting, putting it together. Sentence by sentence we found ourselves hovering on the edge where principle becomes propaganda. Worse, the principle itself kept turning sour. At least for me the trouble with the preamble was that there was nothing in it touching on all those honesties that Arthur and I had wrestled with, nothing, for instance, about how the geniuses created by little magazines coped with the great Fault, what they did with their talents except show them, literarily, off. More and more my own talent, such as it was, had been battling for some time the phenomenon of "self-expression," as so fashionably promoted for health, education, and welfare, or just for its own lovely sake, yet there I was in a hotel room promoting it. There was further confusion to come.

---

[3] The new board was smaller, less cumbersome, consisting of Wayne Carver, Erling Larsen, and myself, with help from Wayne Booth in Chicago, and Helen Lundeen (my wife) and Ruth MacKenzie (her sister)—but many of the projects were group projects.

Resumé (continued)
*Events: Poetry Consultantship at Library of Congress. Perma-
nent move to Washington. Humanities consultant in urban
affairs think tank. Professorship at University of Maryland. Back-pages editor of* New Republic. *Then the call
to be a biographer. Retirement and more biography.*
Books: Four more books of poems: Poems, New and
Selected, Fifty Poems Fifty, The Mother's Breast
and the Father's House, *and* The Feel of Rock. *Also
a book of lectures,* From Zero to the Absolute; *writings
from the* New Republic, The Poet as Journalist; *and*
William Carlos Williams: Poet From Jersey.

From its infancy in the early 1940s the Poetry
Consultantship at the Library of Congress par-
took of the early little-magazine mystique, but because the library was not little, and was a public
institution, it did so in a suitably complicated way. In
effect it mixed the notion of a poet's responsibility to
his society, as announced by Archibald MacLeish in
The Irresponsibles, and the notion of his private responsibility, as announced by Allen Tate, "to his conscience, in the French sense of the word: the joint
action of knowledge and judgment" (in "To Whom Is
the Poet Responsible?"). It mixed them as I think no
other conspicuous literary appointment in our country does, but the mixture may have been inevitable at
the library, with both MacLeish and Tate originally
behind the Consultantship's conception.

Before MacLeish became the Librarian of
Congress (in 1939), there had been a less loftily
principled poetry consultant on the library's regular
staff, a working consultant looking up quotations and
sources for congressmen. But when MacLeish came
to his duties the time was wartime, MacLeish had
been damning the social irresponsibility of American
writers and scholars across the board, and was
anxious to persuade the literary community of which
he had been a part to become engagé. Meanwhile
Tate, who had been engagé about being désengagé,
decided to disagree publicly with MacLeish in the
quarterlies, with the result that they made excellent
combatants, seemingly opposed but actually "lean-
ers," each in the direction of the other. It was they
who concocted the *non*working, privately funded
Consultantship we still have (in the last few years it
has merely been *supplemented* by the laureateship role).
And it was they too who stirred up the private money
for it, and put Allen himself in as the first Consultant
of the new dispensation.

The dispensation gave the Poetry Consultant the
right to continue to be irresponsible in the way that
Tate insisted a responsible poet sometimes had to be,
but it also put him in the middle of our whole federal

machine. Tate, being full of the engagement principle
despite himself, delighted in the position, or, rather,
in the problems of the position, the challenges of
having for a poetic office an elegant third-floor room
with a balcony looking straight at the Capitol across
the street. The poets who came after him varied in
their opinions of those delights, but when the appointment came to me I agreed with Tate.

I got the appointment because Howard Nemerov
was my predecessor, and probably because Tate put
in a plug too. I trafficked in public poetry that year—
poetry from platforms, poetry saying social things—
and I also pushed ALMA hard, gathering together
eighty editors for two days of mayhem in the Coolidge Auditorium. Also I became absorbed by the
MacLeishian issue of a poet's role in a big bureaucracy, if he had one. One noon in the cafeteria of the
Department of Agriculture, for instance, I fired a few
salvos at that helpless, hopeless target, bureaucratic
prose, to the applause of about fifty paper-pushers.
And I had similar, short-lived success at the Department of Interior when I rewrote (and was allowed to
sign—a big issue) a government pamphlet describing,
for tourists, the Jefferson Memorial. These were
indeed delights, and the year at the library was a
delight, but as far as my relationship to the literary
community was concerned a dangerous one. Soon,
serving on literary committees and writing magazine
pieces, I began to look like an enemy of *all* that
confused dissidence to which the literary community
was committed, or like the unqualified enemy of self-
expression, or perhaps like the unqualified enemy of
just forgetting social affairs. I wasn't an enemy of that
magnitude, but I was certainly becoming an enemy of
the inward, isolate, Neapolitan-balcony excesses of
the poetry being published around me, so much so
that I even wrote a piece that Tate himself delighted
in refuting, just as he had MacLeish. It was called
"The Poet in the Bank" and made reference to T. S.
Eliot's early position in a London bank, one that
Pound started a one-man fund-raising campaign just
to spring him *from.* In it I said that a bank might even
be good for a poet, which, aside from being heresy,
was almost as bad as saying that Washington might be
good for a poet. And I believed what I said, mostly.
And soon my family and I—having already enjoyed a
year of Washington's bright lights and returned for a
year of Northfield's dim ones—took the big step of
leaving Minnesota permanently.

The step was especially big because when we did
it I had only a temporary job to make the switch
possible, and the job was in Princeton at that. For one
term I commuted to Princeton weekly for a visiting
professorship. Then I settled into Washington as a

The author

temporary thinker about bureaucracy in a temporarily well-endowed entity called the National Institute of Public Affairs. There, for more than a year, I concocted wild educational proposals, and told visiting mayors and other urban officials how the humanities would help them at their trade, though I was not sure they would. Soon the University of Maryland came along and I was able to go back to ordinary teaching again—but this time near the bright lights.

I thought the College Park campus would be a good place to play my socially dutiful role, it being a big, sprawling phenomenon supported by state money and in need of reform. But what mattered most about it for me was that I was coming on fifty and needed something permanent. The English department there was not as a whole respectful of my reformist ambitions for it (many colleagues thought I was becoming unhealthily interdisciplinary), but it had enough other problems not to be bothered by me, as did Maryland's diffuse faculty generally. An open institution collecting, loosely, many good minds, it had no center at all, no sense of community; it could hardly get quorums for small committee meetings. So I could see plenty before my eyes to reform, and I suppose that I might well have become more of a campus disturbance than I proved to be if I had not, my very first year, contracted myasthenia gravis: an excellently symbolic disease.

First there was double vision and droopy eyelids,

then muscular weakness in hands and feet, then lung trouble—so it added up to no-see, then no-write, then no-walk, then no-breathe: a thorough no-can-do syndrome. I was spread too thin. Everything was becoming too much, financially, parentally, professionally, so the disease came along to diagnose my ailment.

Several years of hospitals and futile experiments followed, out of which finally came an unexpected cure in the form of the common hormone drug prednisone, which had been "contraindicated." I emerged nearly whole, and am still on prednisone (every *other* day), but there were psychic scars that naturally showed up in my poetry. I was led away from the platform poems that the Washington experience, not to mention my dramatic efforts, had encouraged, though the poems of my own that I like best still include some of those—a few narrative poems, a few polemics (especially "Ode to New York"), and a number of fables. But the long-term effect of the disease—or perhaps of aging itself—was to drive me back toward quieter, more introspective verse, like this one reaching back to the darknesses in my father.

When Father Left in the Morning

When father left in the morning
He had the mark of evening
On him, and at evening the evening
Was wholly evening.
He lay with forever
After supper.

Mother watched him
From the other bed,
Brushing her hair back, looking for slippers,
Smoking.
Somewhere out in the hall
Were the living. She was ill.

The moon revolved
Over East Rock Road.
The Packard sat by the curb.
I lay in my bed in the next room
Listening,
Waiting for news.

But the news in the evening
Was always the same news,
And in the morning
The drift was to evening.
I was grown
Before morning came.

In the early stages of the disease I crazily took on

a second job, a marvelous job, as editor of the back pages of the *New Republic.* Nancy and Gilbert Harrison were our neighbors in Cleveland Park, and Gil was an extraordinarily kind employer as I became erratically incapacitated. The *New Republic* was a fine antidote to the casualness of little quarterlies, for though it had been going so long that we could joke about its coming out by itself every week even if we all went elsewhere, it was basically relentless in its weekly discipline, differing from any other writing-editing role I had ever played. Then too, in running the reviews and writing a good many myself, I found it relentless as a maker, for me, of enemies—but at least enmity can be broadening.

And as a dividend, being in hospitals and at the same time trying to function as an editor, I picked up a new profession while just pushing buttons. I lay in bed staring at the tube, and became *NR*'s TV critic. Gil gave me an alias: Sedulus.

Where would the world now be if Sedulus had persisted? Could his reformism have taken hold of the media as a whole, and moved them sullenly away from inanity and Alka-Seltzer? Would they have *been,* suddenly, a new message? Ho ho. But Sedulus did not persist; he got better.

He also received at that time a different kind of opportunity. He was sitting at home minding his business when a publishing-house editor he did not know called him, and within a week he had a contract to write a biography of William Carlos Williams. The contract loosely coincided with the end of Gil's ownership and editing of *NR,* and it was also the kind of assignment the Guggenheim people liked. Soon Sedulus was not only not Sedulus any more, but he was not an editor and, for a year, not a teacher either. He was an explorer in the unknown seas of a new genre.

If ever there was a genre in which a practitioner needs to display professional and personal modesty, it is biography. Its obligations are only incidentally to the forms and graces native to other literary struggles, and only minimally to the art of self-expression and salesmanship. Always there is the biographee to reckon with, and even if the biographee is Attila the Hun, he comes first. Nor is he apt to *be* Attila the Hun. Biographees who are deserving victims of a biographer's scorn are not many; the tradition of biography is largely commemorative, and though our age is one of muckrakers looking for muck, a biographee is not usually chosen if he does not have a few qualities worth honoring. Ignorant though I was, I knew this about biography before I entered upon it, and I also knew that I would not have been approached to "do" Williams if I had looked unfriendly.

Soon I learned that I was an approved or authorized biographer. Williams's widow, Flossie, had blessed me via James Laughlin, who had been Williams's publisher, with the result that the Williams private papers were open to me, as well as the resources, memories, and friendship of the Williams family. Assets, obligations. I was aware of both when I settled in, and thought I understood both my freedoms, which the Williamses insisted on, and the limits to the freedoms. Now, long after the event, I can say that I misjudged those limits, and I sometimes wish I'd been commissioned to write a biography of someone *long* dead.

Yet I say that, oddly, without reference to the Williams clan itself. The clan itself was fine. It was not the clan but the literary community with a professional stake in Williams that went after me when the book appeared. The community was, I think, wrong, but from Allen Tate (who had never much liked Williams) I at least learned how I had erred, tactically. Tate wrote me a postcard with the simple, courteous intent of praising the book. So he said he liked it, and that was good news, but then he added that the trouble with Williams was that he had no brains. That was, inadvertently on his part, the bad news. The trouble with Williams. I had not meant to describe a trouble so much as a quality. I had meant to reinforce Ezra Pound's comic comment about him that he was the most incoherent bloke who ever gargled. I had thought that if *Pound* could dwell on the impressionistic urgencies of the man's writings and speech, while still respecting him, *I* could. I was wrong. For the professionals it was clear I had not shown respect: their kind. So: lesson number one about biography came my way expensively. The book was praised but in the places without clout. It did not make it to paperback.

So I was ready for biography lesson number two, and received that quickly in the form of rejections from several publishers of a partly completed manuscript of six short biographies. What was wrong with *it?* Everything. In the first place *nobody* was doing short biographies, they hadn't been done since Plutarch. In the second place my scheme for tying the six biographees together was ridiculous; I was working on social rather than literary connections between them, and was not suitably attuned to the critical infelicity of putting Henry Adams and Jack London in the same room (along with Upton Sinclair, John Dos Passos, Allen Tate, and of course Williams). And thirdly the focus of the biographies was wrong. In them I kept worrying about what my subjects were saying and thinking about their times, their world, their culture, when anybody with half a brain knew that literary people and literary biographers had more important private things to worry about. In other words lesson number two was that biography, though probably the fuzziest of literary genres, was not fuzzy for its merchandisers. *They* knew its dimensions and purpose.

So with my six-subject manuscript in a drawer I was ready for lesson number three.

But I was also ready to retire from teaching, and did so at age sixty-five, a financial error (there are no golden parachutes in academia, despite all the complaints about tenure). Retirement was also, however, an educational opportunity, since by putting aside my forty English-department years I was an instant free intellect. And by now I was even relatively free of family obligations, with all the children out of the nest and doing strange adult things. Nor was I yet, so far as I could determine, senile. So I entered retirement in 1984 and managed to tie myself up all over again.

Tying myself up seems to be my fate, though the first tying after retirement was not my doing. In June of 1984 Robert Fitzgerald had been asked to be Poetry Consultant at the Library of Congress, and having accepted had almost instantly learned he had cancer. I was asked to fill in—he died during the year—and so renewed my affair with the library and the Consultantship. Neither, I found, had changed much in twenty years, except that in the interval the *Washington Post,* that sole arbiter of Washington thought and culture, seemed to have decided that neither existed. My second stint at the library was quieter, but still rewarding, and it was followed by lesson number three, a happier one, in biography.

Lesson number three involved becoming a student of the history of the genre and discovering, among many other things, that my manuscript in the drawer was not intellectually alien to it. Lesson number three also involved writing yet another book, *Pure Lives,* which is now out in the world and waiting to be accompanied by its sequel, *Whole Lives. Pure Lives* rushed the history of biography up to Johnson and Boswell. *Whole Lives* takes the genre up to the here and now. Both books are small. At age seventy one favors small books, especially when tied up with still other affairs.

Yes, in 1987—as if I had not had enough editing—I started another magazine: *Delos.* Why? I believe that Chaucer's Nun's Priest explained its appearance in my life precisely a few centuries before I existed, when, describing Chanticleer's foolishness in flying down from the beam, he cried, "O Destinee, that mayst not be eschewed!"

Reed Whittemore

© H. Lundeen-Whittemore

BIBLIOGRAPHY

Poetry:

Heroes and Heroines (illustrated by Irwin Touster). New York: Reynal, 1946.

An American Takes a Walk and Other Poems. Minneapolis: University of Minnesota Press, 1956; London: Oxford University Press, 1956.

The Self-made Man and Other Poems. New York: Macmillan, 1959.

The Boy from Iowa: Poems and Essays. New York: Macmillan, 1962.

The Fascination of the Abomination: Poems, Stories, and Essays. New York: Macmillan, 1963; London: Collier-Macmillan, 1963.

Return, Alpheus: A Poem for the Literary Elders of Phi Beta Kappa. Williamsburg, Va.: King & Queen Press, 1965.

Poems, New and Selected. Minneapolis: University of Minnesota Press, 1967.

Fifty Poems Fifty. Minneapolis: University of Minnesota Press, 1970; London: Oxford University Press, 1970.

The Mother's Breast and the Father's House. Boston: Houghton, 1974.

The Feel of Rock: Poems of Three Decades. Washington, D.C.: Dryad, 1982.

Nonfiction:

Little Magazines (pamphlet). Minneapolis: University of Minnesota Press, 1963; London: Oxford University Press, 1963.

From Zero to the Absolute (lectures). New York: Crown, 1967.

William Carlos Williams: Poet from Jersey. Boston: Houghton, 1975.

The Poet as Journalist: Life at the New Republic. Washington, D.C.: New Republic, 1976.

Pure Lives: The Early Biographers. Baltimore: Johns Hopkins University Press, 1988.

Whole Lives. Forthcoming.

Editor of:

Robert Browning. New York: Dell, 1960.

Sound Recordings:

A Whittemore Miscellany. Washington, D.C.: Watershed Intermedia, 1977.

Jack Williamson

1908-

FRONTIERS OF WONDER

Paternal grandparents, Peter and Joanna Williamson (seated at center), with their children, about 1895:
(clockwise from front left) Hattie, Albert, Asa (the author's father),
Jimmie, Frank, John, George, Almira

What makes a writer? That's hard to say. Traits are inborn, but reshaped by living. Skills can be learned, though the best of them aren't even half the answer. Writing can be therapy: good medicine for tormenting discontents that are sometimes hard to cope with.

In my own case, it has been a sort of obsession, an addiction as hard to break as the craving for drugs must be. One wellspring must be the lonely childhood that left me pretty much to my own resources. Alone in an empty land, trapped behind some farm implement or a little herd of cattle, I learned to escape into imagination, dreaming through endless epics of impossible adventure, or, between such tedious chores, inventing elaborate games that I played with my younger siblings.

I write science fiction. At its best, that tries to explore the frontiers of what we know, or think we know. Some of that bent toward the unknown may have come down from my pioneering forebears who spent their generations pushing west against the wilderness. Most of them got here before the Revolution.

What I know of my father's family comes mostly from a memoir written in 1932 by his younger sister, Hattie. For my mother's people, there is nothing quite so formal. Most of their records were lost, I suppose, when the Civil War ruined and scattered them, and most of what I know came orally in the nostalgic legends handed down through elderly aunts. I have the fragmentary notes my mother left, and her collection of family photographs and correspondence, some of the letters written in beautiful copperplate script before the war.

To aid my own uncertain memories of more recent times, I have the diary I kept for a few months in the South Pacific and, best of all, the names and notes and photos in the book Blanche asked guests to sign while the candle burned at our house for nearly forty years.

On both sides, my family roots were Scotch, though the last ancestor to arrive seems to have been Christina Schaffer, who came with her family from Württemberg in 1819, moving because her brothers wanted to escape military conscription. Beginning at the age of twelve, she served four years as a bond servant to help pay for their passage.

The first John Williamson in the record left Fife in 1691 with his wife on a leaky ship that had to put into Lisbon for repair. The voyage took seven weeks, and his wife died at sea. He settled in New Jersey, married again, and fathered Williamsons who migrated west, generation after generation, through Ohio and Indiana and Minnesota, clearing land and building homes and rearing families of sternly righteous Methodists to marry and load the wagon or the ox cart and move west again.

Peter and Joanna Williamson came south to Texas after the Civil War. My father, Asa Lee Williamson, was born in 1868 on a farm in central Texas. A seventh son, he was dedicated to the Lord at birth. Brought up for the ministry, he graduated from the University of Texas in 1900 with Latin and Greek enough to enjoy reciting Virgil and retelling the epic of Xenophon's *Anabasis.*

With too much education for the narrow fundamentalism of his childhood, he never preached or even joined a church, and his silent skepticism must have been a handicap. Yet I see him as a born frontiersman, frustrated because the empty lands were gone. He became a teacher; he was principal of the small school where he met my mother. Yet he always preferred physical toil and life in the open.

Pushing farther south and west, he went to Arizona with my mother and joined her brothers in a ranching venture south of the border. Forced out of that by the Mexican Revolution, he bought an irrigated farm in Texas, just west of the Pecos. When that failed, we moved by covered wagon to the arid Llano Estacado, in eastern New Mexico. My childhood was spent on the almost worthless sandhill homestead there.

My father was something of a misfit, respected for his learning but always a little suspect for his failure to profess any specific religious faith. He fought drought and disaster to wring a living from soil unwilling to yield it. Too late for better land, we were sharecroppers for earlier comers. He was a stern parent, seldom openly loving. Though I sometimes bitterly resented his discipline, it was fair and just. I loved him.

My mother's people were pioneers of a different sort, who had arrived farther south and done well there, as family legends told it. The wistful tales of great families and their spacious ways of life, of all the hardships of the war, of lost wealth and status, I later found echoed in William Faulkner.

She was born Lucy Betty Hunt, but her mother had been a Stewart, the name said to come from the royal Stuarts of Scotland. The family names I used to hear were Bedford and Ruffin and Clay and Dandridge; Martha Washington was a Dandridge. Such legends were cherished long after war had driven them west again to Texas and beyond, the old myths a last weapon against the grinding pinch of poverty.

They had rationalized slavery as a benign institution, and fled from its collapse. Better educated than most of my father's people, they had never learned to work and save for the glory of the Lord. Yet my grandmother Hunt was a woman of admirable spirit, making the best of adversity with guts and good cheer. She used to spend summers with us, doing her bit in the household and generous with the small gifts she could make. Her, too, I loved.

My mother had met the frontier even before she knew my father, cooking for her brother when he was starting a stage line in Mexico and again for a Bedford cousin when he was building a railroad there. The ranch in Mexico was a last lonely outpost against time and change.

Named La Loba, "the She-Wolf," it was high in the Sierra Madre, beyond any road wheels could travel. My parents had been waiting in Bisbee, Arizona, for my birth, my father shoveling ore as a "mucker" in the Copper Queen mine. When six weeks old, I was taken to the ranch by rail and stage and, the last day, riding a pillow in front of my father on a horse.

The house was rough stone laid up with mud and roofed with grass, rawhide curtains hung across the doorways, the furniture roughly made of rawhide and axe-hewn wood. My mother lived in fear of renegade Apaches, of mountain lions, of bears or even fighting bulls that might invade the unfenced house, of scorpions whose sting might kill me.

Her life there seems grim enough when I look back, yet she and my father used to speak of those years as a romantic adventure. He enjoyed hunting deer for venison to feed the hounds the hunters had brought to rid the range of mountain lions, enjoyed his horseback trading trips to Mexican towns below the mountains. Both enjoyed life on that last frontier;

"My first home, on El Rancho La Loba"

they always carried fond recollections of the colorful Americans they knew, most of them refugees from difficulties on this side of the line, yet loyal friends, tenderly concerned for my mother and her baby.

Stewart, my mother's elder brother, became a storybook hero in my own imagination. His life might have made a dozen Western dramas. Aged twelve, he left their Texas home to wrangle horses for a cattle herd bound for Wichita. He worked on ranches and leased them and owned them, lost fortunes and made them back again in Mexico and Arizona and Mexico. He learned Spanish, bought and imported Mexican cattle, fathered a son by the widow of one of his cowboys killed, he believed, by renegade Apaches, married a Mexican woman, died a sort of feudal baron surrounded by retainers. He deserves a book, and I wish I had written it.

We left La Loba before I was three. Though I can't be sure of any actual recollections, the tales I used to hear about it lived in my mind with the force of actual memory. Northern Mexico was almost empty then, a last wilderness where life was spiced with alluring unknowns, possible perils, possible wealth, the illusion of escape from everything. The first story I sold was set there.

Back in Arizona, I nearly died of a diarrhea called *cholera infantum.* But yet my first clear memories are of crawling over a splintery pine floor after we had moved to Pecos, Texas, rolling a big glass marble and learning to walk again. We lived nearly five years

on that farm; my sister Joan and my brother, Jim, were born there.

My early recollections are generally pleasant: lying on my belly to drink out of the irrigation ditch the way my father did; my own tiny farm by the pump, where I cultivated a single plant I called an oat; the mysterious thicket of brush around the pond my father called the *laguna;* the hammer Grandma gave me, complete with nails to drive in the ground; my heroic doll, Felix Eaton, who broke his head falling off my well drill.

The farm failed. The year I was seven, we moved by covered wagon to the Llano Estacado, "the Staked Plains." The *llano* is an enormous plateau, high and flat and dry, rimmed with the caprock and the "breaks." Grassland, with little permanent water, it was almost empty of humanity until the late 1800s, when the windmills came. Parts of it are farmed now, sometimes under irrigation. Crops can be abundant in good seasons, but drought is always a threat.

We were seventeen days on the road, a few chickens in a coop on an old hack that trailed behind the wagon and a few milk cows we herded with us. That must have been a desperate time for my parents;

Jack at age seven, Pecos, Texas: "It was a blazing summer day, but the overcoat had just come in a gift package from some relative, and I was proud of it."

315

nearly penniless, they were fighting for survival. I remember my mother's frantic pursuit of little Jim when he got lost and ran off down an unknown road, crying too loud to hear her own calls.

For me it was endless adventure, though I recall one painful incident when I was riding the old roan mare behind the cows. Unused to children, she ran with me until I picked a landing place and jumped off. Each day we crossed wide new country and camped each night in a strange new place, and I was waiting anxiously to see our new home ahead.

That was the homestead. A small pine shack, until my father built a second room. We hauled water a mile and a half to fill a dug cistern. The barren flats and drifting dunes were empty all around us, the nearest neighbors my grandmother Williamson and my father's brother Frank, who had bought the farm where the well was, out on better land. We lived three years there, "proving up" to get title to the homestead.

During those years of hardship for my parents, I was sometimes aware of all we didn't have, sometimes envious of those who had. Not so keenly, though, as my mother must have been. Even from her, I heard little complaint, but I know now that she must have been bitterly hurt by that stark isolation. For myself, I knew no better.

My mother had Katie there, my younger sister.

"My parents, Asa and Lucy Williamson, sometime in the 1950s"

Now we were four. I knew no other children. My parents taught us at home, at least when they had time to teach. Out of narrow means, they subscribed to a few magazines. My mother read aloud to us with a good deal of skill. I learned to read—and learned to live in my own dreamlands.

We worked Frank's land on the shares and later rented other places where water didn't have to be hauled. My father taught school again, earning what he could to keep us alive, riding that old mare to the job. I rode behind him to attend my first school, one where he was principal; I was ten by then and in the fourth grade. With no social skills, I was a victim of bullies, and except in the classroom I had a pretty miserable time.

After two more years at home, I went back to school in the seventh grade. I used to spend recesses reading at my desk unless the teacher sent me outside, because the playground required arts I had never learned. I remember admiring a blonde, athletic girl named Blanche Slaten. Admiration at a distance; I had no skills for any close approach.

At the end of the year I passed a state test that promoted me into a country high school which no longer exists. My father had bought a Ford truck. I learned to drive. When he equipped it as a school bus, I was the driver. With no driver training, in those less formal days when no license was required, I began learning the art with the bus full of passengers.

I finished high school in 1925—with nowhere to go.

Science had always fascinated me, the dated and scattered bits of it I could learn from popular magazines and a box of outdated textbooks and an old two-volume encyclopedia a friendly teacher had given me. It was close to magic in my mind, a way to wonder and power. Vaguely, I hoped to become some sort of scientist, but there was no money for college.

I had dreamed of writing for money, ever since I had heard that Mark Twain got a dollar a word. Even for the shortest words! Perhaps I caught the contagion from my mother; she had bought a little mail-order writing course and got a few small items into print. I had even made a few fumbling efforts; once I wrote away to ask for a sample copy of a Western pulp and scrawled a story on the back of a sheet of wallpaper.

That dismal world suddenly brightened in 1926, when Hugo Gernsback launched a new magazine called *Amazing Stories.* All reprints at first, put out on cheap pulp paper, it was filled with the great science fiction classics, the best of H. G. Wells and Jules

The author, the year he turned twenty-one:
"Hugo Gernsback used to run this picture with my stories.
(One of the ego-pleasing rewards of authorship!)"

Verne and A. Merritt and Edgar Rice Burroughs. A friend gave me a sample copy. I wrote for a sample copy of my own. With help from my older sister, I subscribed.

The impact on me is hard to imagine today. Those stone-age years in Mexico were still not far behind me. Radio was still a marvel, TV still to come. We had never had electric lights or running water. I had never been beyond Portales, our county seat town, never ridden a train or seen an airplane close up or even spoken on the telephone.

Amazing opened wide worlds of wonder. The covers, by artist Frank R. Paul, may look crude today, but they were dazzling then. On the breathtaking issue for March 1926, he showed a light-propelled spacecraft with a crew of green-blooded creatures taking off for Jupiter. There was travel in time as well as space, invisible men, new inventions, a whole glittering future universe.

Science fiction comes in many kinds. Often the sheerest fantasy, it is sometimes a serious attempt to extrapolate a possible future from the visible present. I prefer that "hard" sort. In cold reality, technology is changing everything. There is a sense in which fiction that accepts that fact, that sets out upon plausible explorations of those widening frontiers of possibility, is closer to reality than most "realistic" fiction.

With no real preparation for it, I started writing my own stories, pounding them out on an old basket-model Remington typewriter borrowed from my uncle John. I mailed a few of them off, one with a misspelled word in the title. They came back with rejection slips until the summer of 1928, when one was not returned. The title was "The Metal Man."

My father had a little money from selling oil rights to the homestead. He sent Joan and me away to school that fall at Canyon, Texas. Walking by a newsstand, I recognized my metal man on the cover of the December *Amazing.* A moment I'll never forget. Suddenly, improbably enough, I was a published writer!

The secret, of course, was that science fiction was still something new—not even named "science fiction" until 1929. The pay was too low to interest the pros. When the reprints ran out, the editors began filling their columns with stories by such eager newcomers as I was. For a few of us, getting into print mattered more than the pay.

I stayed two years at Canyon, majoring in chemistry and writing desperately. Still a social oddball, I had nothing else to do. By the second year, I was selling fiction enough to pay my expenses. At the end of the year, the chemistry professor offered me a student assistantship. My life might have been different if I had accepted it, but I declined.

What I wanted was to write science fiction. It's still what I want. A habit now, rooted back in those early years when dreams kept me alive. I left Canyon to write, yet with still everything to learn. That fall I rode a bus to California, got up Mount Wilson to see the big telescope, and took an actual airplane flight, a trip from Los Angeles to San Francisco on a four-engine Fokker that cost twenty-four precious dollars.

I tried to enter the University of California at Berkeley to study astronomy. An academic adviser kept me out, because I stubbornly and not very wisely refused to take a Shakespeare course. I stayed, however, through most of the fall, auditing astronomy and seeing San Francisco, which was another wonderland. I came back to New Mexico before Christmas to write another novel.

I set out to model a career on such great pulp professionals as Max Brand (Frederick Faust), who is said to have produced forty million words during his lifetime, pounding out four thousand words every day to be published under twenty-odd names. I wrote my words at white heat and mailed them out, commonly in first draft. Often they were bought. Two days to hammer out eight thousand words at two cents a word could pay me $160, a fabulous income for a young farm kid in the depths of the Great Depression.

Sometimes, of course, the stories came back. The shorts more often; short stories have always been hard for me to do, I like the freedom of the longer forms. As my own standards grew, along with those of the field, I learned to rewrite. Slowly, over the years, I came to feel that I was something of a pro. Just as slowly, I discovered that my early goals had been too narrow. For a time, however, I had a heady sense of success.

Though my trips east were rare and brief, I came to know most of the science fiction editors. I am grateful to Hugo Gernsback for putting me into print. He was the pioneer. An able and aggressive publisher as well as editor, he christened science fiction. The Hugo awards are aptly named in his honor. I was sadly disillusioned, however, by his reluctance to pay for published work except on threat of legal action.

The man who paid me that dazzling two cents a word was Harry Bates, the editor on the Clayton chain who launched *Astounding Stories of Super-Science* (which evolved over the years into *Analog*). I never met him, but I recall him warmly for that quick two cents, paid without threat of lawsuit. He cared more about story values than Gernsback did, if less about science.

When you look back at the biographies of writers who learned their craft during those years, you find that most of them made their first sales to the pulps. They served as a training ground that, sadly, ceased to exist when they disappeared. For my own part, I certainly learned the basics of fiction from the pulps, and I think such pulp editors as Harry Bates did good things for early science fiction.

A greater editor was Farnsworth Wright at *Weird Tales*. Great in spite of heavy handicaps. His life was a heroic battle against the Parkinson's disease that finally killed him. His magazine was never far above the ragged edge, but he was devoted to it and to the genre, and he had more ability and better literary tastes than were common in the pulps. The most he could pay was one cent a word on publication, but he liked my work. I came to love him and the best of his magazine—some of the stuff he published was pretty bad, which is what gave me the nerve to submit anything in the first place.

I wrote, too, for Mort Weisinger, who was on the staff of the Thrilling group under Leo Margulies. That was less fun, but story orders from *Thrilling Wonder* and *Startling Stories* and *Thrilling Mystery* were hard to resist, because the pay was quick and nearly

sure. The problem was that the stories had to fit a rigid formula. Mort was clever in inventing story gimmicks to fill out the formula, but it stifled any real creation. He told me once that he didn't object to good writing, but the formula was what Leo wanted. Follow it well, and you would get the check.

John W. Campbell was the ablest and most notable early editor of science fiction, and far more fun to work for. He took over *Astounding* in 1938, a few years after the Clayton chain failed and the magazine was bought by Street and Smith. He gathered and inspired such new writers as Heinlein and Asimov and van Vogt and Sturgeon and del Rey, and recruited a few older hands to make his first dozen years the fabulous "golden age of science fiction," a phrase that has some justice. After H. G. Wells, Campbell was the most influential shaper of modern science fiction.

He had a science degree, a remarkable gift for creation, and a magnificent dream of the human future in the universe. He was optimistic about the future of technology—back before the A-bomb exploded to shatter such rose-colored glasses—though willing enough to publish and praise a strong pessimistic story when it came in. A successful writer before he took the editorship, he was an unceasing source of story ideas, at least until he became involved with L. Ron Hubbard's "dianetics."

Uncomfortable with my own fumbling career, I went back to college for another year in the early 1930s. Transferring to the University of New Mexico at Albuquerque, I changed my major to psychology, hoping the courses would help me understand my story characters and myself and make a better adjustment to the world.

I made good friends and enjoyed the year, but I came away still unhappy with myself. I had gained no social skills. Although I admired girls, I never found anything to say or do with them. Looking for ways toward some better life, I had read a book about psychoanalysis by a Dr. Sumner Ives. When I wanted to go to Boston for analysis, he referred me to Dr. Karl Menninger at Topeka, Kansas.

In the spring of 1936, I went there. After a series of interviews and examinations, I began analysis with Dr. Charles W. Tidd, five days a week. I had very little money, and the process of analysis itself came to interfere in a perverse way with earning more, but the clinic was generous with me. I was able to stay a year before my funds ran out. The analysis is described in a little article I wrote while I was there.

Five times a week I go for the fifty-minute

"hour." I always start a little early, lest I be delayed. . . . Walking lightly and hastily, a little breathless, sometimes with a pounding heart, I climb the stairs and walk across the hall and enter the office of the analyst. He has laid a paper napkin for me across the pillow on the couch. He stands and bows to meet me, a handsome man with an easy, friendly smile—and yet I feel confused and afraid.

Quickly, feeling a self-conscious restraint, I lie supine on the couch. It is difficult for me to begin speaking. I delay: my hands ball into fists; my body tenses; I make aimless striking motions.

"Just say what you feel," the analyst prompts me quietly. He is sitting relaxed in a chair behind my head. His manner is always easy, unsurprised. His low voice is sympathetic, encouraging. "Just tell me all your thoughts."

With a convulsive effort, I begin. I try to talk rapidly, because there is so much to say; because the time is so costly and I do not wish to waste it; perhaps because I wish to hurry over some painful, shameful thing; also because the talk eases tensions and sometimes I become relaxed and comfortable toward the end of the hour.

My hurried voice is low—all through life I have spoken softly, as I have stooped, to make myself inconspicuous and avoid aggression and danger. Sometimes I become inaudible. The analyst asks me to repeat, and I make a brief effort to speak distinctly.

Continually, too, he must urge me to go on. For when I come to a difficult matter, my voice checks and stops. To speak each word takes a desperate new effort. I catch a deep breath or make convulsive body movements to delay the need to speak. I search for painless asides and diversions. Often the thoughts flee and leave my mind a blank. Hopefully, I inquire if the hour isn't already gone.

The analyst says little, except for his continual, sometimes tormenting pressure to "go on. . . . Yes. . . . Yes. . . . Just tell me all about it." But his few questions, his suggestions and disarmingly tentative explanations tear the veil from many a disguised expression. Slowly I have come to understand myself.

[Or anyhow at least a little of myself.]

[Quoting from a later journal, it was] a year of cramping limits in what now looks like painful poverty. . . . With less money than ever, no car and no confidence, I could only envy men with female friends. Yet with the moral support of my analyst, I made uneasy effort against the old dread of sex. Prostitution was still wide open in Topeka, and I was lucky enough to find a friendly-seeming girl already familiar with the quirks of Menninger patients. . . .

A lonely year. I remember walking the river bridge many times that dry summer, when low water wandered between red mud banks, and again on bitter winter days when the river lay frozen under drifting snow, and in the spring when it ran high, choked with drifting rafts of dirty ice.

A year of little human contact, except those analytic hours. If I made few friends, perhaps I didn't really want them. Everything I did, all those uncertain meetings, even my own penny-pinching, became matter for more analysis. More than anywhere, I lived inside myself. But there, with Dr. Tidd for a guide, I was making those bits of self-discovery.

A difficult year, but good for me.

The analysis broken off, I felt a liberating sense of escape. Suddenly I was able to write again. I went east, to visit Farnsworth Wright and my friend Edmond Hamilton, another *Weird Tales* writer. I went with Ed to New York and visited John W. Campbell, the new editor at *Astounding,* as well as Margulies and Weisinger at the Thrilling Magazines group, and Julius Schwartz, later best known as a *Superman* editor.

At home again, I kept on writing with some success, though a journal entry reports that I was "increasingly dissatisfied with my life." Still I had no car. Still I felt exiled from society. Yet things were better than they had been. My health was better. I had been remodeling the little shack I built for a writing workshop. I had begun spending the fall seasons in Santa Fe, at first to escape the hay fever I got from the weeds at home.

In May of 1939, I went back to New York and stayed several months in a tiny studio apartment just off Riverside Drive. Campbell had brought out *Unknown,* a new fantasy magazine. I proposed a new serial for him and began research for it, exploring the museums for the archaeology and artifacts of Minoan Crete. I wrote another half-cent-a-word novel for *Startling* and met a good many other writers at their weekly gatherings at Stuben's Tavern. I saw the World's Fair on Long Island and had my first glimpse of TV.

In July I attended the first World Science Fiction Convention. Only a modest affair, with a couple of hundred members in contrast to the thousands in recent times, it stands out in my memory for the new friends I found there. The best of them the Futurians, their organization locked out of the convention hall because of a fan feud. Such future notables as Fred Pohl, Don Wollheim, Isaac Asimov, Cyril Kornbluth were among them. Fred and I have since collaborated on half a score of novels.

I returned with Ed Hamilton to his home in New Castle, Pennsylvania, and went on to Detroit to buy that long longed-for car. A new Ford V-8 sedan, it cost six hundred forty pre-inflation dollars. I drove it home to New Mexico. When hay fever struck again, I went back to Santa Fe and found new doors opened by the car and the new social self that Dr. Tidd had helped me uncover.

Campbell bought the serial "The Reign of Wizardry." Weisinger bought a novelette for *Thrilling Wonder.* I explored old Santa Fe, which was still a small town. The state capital and the nerve center of the old Spanish and Pueblo cultures, it was not yet congested with retirees and tourists. I met anthropologists and archaeologists and artists and writers, among them Brian Boru Dunn. He was an old friend of H. G. Wells's, with a gift for Irish gab. He used to hold court at La Fonda as a sort of civic host. I bought skis that winter and learned to use them, though not with much skill. But I enjoyed the year—and found my fiction output lagging again.

One welcome distraction was Jean Cady, an eastern girl with a museum job. I fell far enough in

"At work with Fred Pohl in my office at home on my birthday, April 29, 1971"

love with her to consider marriage. She had a dim opinion of science fiction, however, and when the choice came I loved it more. Troubled again by my working difficulties and my own unresolved conflicts, I left Santa Fe to resume the interrupted analysis.

Dr. Tidd had set up a practice by then in Beverly Hills. His schedule was full when I first inquired, but he wrote in May that I might come out to talk things over. When that happened, he agreed to let me come in twice a week. Generously, he set the fee at only five dollars an hour.

California was nicer then. The automobile had not yet overwhelmed the fine old streetcar and interurban transit system. Smog yet to come, the air smelled good. After I had begun to make friends, we could drive along the point below Redondo Beach and climb down the cliffs and build a driftwood fire, feeling as isolated as if we were on a desert island.

The analysis was useful again, if never magical. At only two sessions a week, it was less intensive than Topeka. I don't recall it so vividly, but I later realized that a story I wrote that year is a sort of allegory of my analytic experience. The story is *Darker than You Think,* published in Campbell's *Unknown* and later expanded into a full-length novel.

It is a fantasy, set in a familiar contemporary Midwest, but given a science-fictional gloss. The hero is Will Barbee, a newspaper reporter whose old friends and associates have just returned from an archaeological expedition to the Gobi. Attempting to interview them, he meets April Bell, an alluring redhead who is gradually revealed to be a witch.

In the course of the story, Barbee discovers paranormal gifts in himself and learns that the expedition had brought back evidences of *Homo lycanthropus.* That was a race of prehistoric witch-folk exterminated in old wars with mankind, but still alive in the human genes because the two races interbred. Human beings carry witch genes. Now, by selective breeding, the witch race is recreating itself. The best genes, it turns out, are now carried by April Bell and Barbee himself. Their child is to be the messiah of the reborn witch-folk.

Long afterwards, I came to see that Barbee's self-discovery is my own, under the analysis. He recoils at first with fear and horror from what he learns about himself, but comes slowly to accept his reborn self. At the end of the novel he has become a flying saurian and April is a slim she-wolf. The novel ends:

> With a silent red laugh she ran from him, up the dark wooded slope where his wings couldn't follow. The change, however, was easy now. Barbee let the saurian's body flow

into the shape of a huge gray wolf. He picked up her exciting scent and followed her into the shadows.

That story was successful enough, but after it my writing slowed to a crawl. Another *Startling* novel took a long time to do and even then was only indifferently done. The problem may have been "unconscious resistance to the analysis," or perhaps it was only the lamentable fact that I had not been born a better writer. Yet I had the car and at least a little more money than in Topeka. Certainly I had a better time.

Ed Hamilton came out to Los Angeles, with Julie Schwartz and Mort Weisinger. I met Leigh Brackett at their motel; an attractive, athletic young woman, she was just beginning her fine career. I drove up the coast with Ed to visit two old *Weird Tales* hands, E. Hoffmann Price and Clark Ashton Smith, memorable if vastly different characters.

I met more fans and writers at the Los Angeles Science Fantasy Society. The young Ray Bradbury among them. And John Parsons, a rocket engineer who dabbled in the occult. He took me and Cleve Cartmill to a meeting of the Order of the Oriental Templars (OTO), an underground order that seems to have been founded by the satanist Aleister Crowley. A little to my disappointment, no actual witch or Satan appeared at the ceremony, but the people were interesting. Parsons, I have heard, inspired some of the mystical revelations of L. Ron Hubbard's Scientology.

The most notable new friend was Robert Heinlein. The brightest new star in our little constellation of science fiction writers, he was living then on Laurel Canyon in Hollywood with Leslyn, his first wife. I was delighted when he invited me to the little Saturday-night gatherings he called the Mañana Literary Society. A very remarkable group, usually small, the membership shifted from evening to evening. It included Cartmill, a sardonic but likeable newspaperman; Anthony Boucher (William Anthony Parker White) and his wife, Phyllis—Tony wrote mystery fiction as H. H. Holmes and, with J. Francis (Mick) McComas, was a founding editor of the *Magazine of Fantasy and Science Fiction,* still a leader in the pack; sometimes Bradbury, who was still very eagerly learning his craft; Art Barnes and Henry Kuttner and C. L. Moore. I remember a vivacious redhead named Marda Brown.

Sometimes Hubbard. I'm not sure I recall him from there, but I recall a long talk with him at a later party of Heinlein's, when I listened to his tales and evasive hints of half-secret adventure with no more credulity than I could later give to the claims of his new religion.

I liked and admired Heinlein. He was setting new directions in science fiction. I learned a good deal from him and the others in the Society, but nothing was reflected in my own output. My sales had slowed to a trickle. Even at that bargain price, I could no longer pay Dr. Tidd. At the end of a year, we agreed to suspend the analysis and I returned to New Mexico.

This second break, sadly, brought me no second burst of creativity. I worked for months on an ambitious project I called *Star of Empire*, based on the notion of Arnold Toynbee's that societies are great organisms that are born, grow, age, and die like live creatures. The idea is probably a fallacy, and I ran into problems with the manuscript. It was successfully completed a dozen years later as *Star Bridge*, in collaboration with Jim Gunn, but then I had to put it on the shelf.

John Campbell came to my rescue. He wrote me that he had recently adopted a new pen name, Don A. Stuart, to fit a new literary personality and a new writing style. He wanted me to follow suit, and I felt desperate enough to try. I picked syllables out of my own name to become Will Stewart, and proposed to do a series of stories about the planetary engineers who "terraform," or transform, new worlds to fit them for human use.

Campbell suggested that some of those new planets might be antimatter, which we then called "contraterrene." That is hazardous stuff, matter inside out, with positrons instead of electrons orbiting negative instead of positive nuclei. In contact with common terrene matter, it flashes into pure energy with a thousand times the force of any nuclear explosion. Campbell wrote me long letters outlining what was known about it. Not much, then; it was still more theory than reality.

I spelled out the abbreviation, "CT," to call the stuff "seetee," and wrote two novelettes and a serial, all rewritten after the war into a couple of novels, *Seetee Ship* and *Seetee Shock*. Pearl Harbor had come by then. Dr. Tidd had arranged a medical deferment for me but my brother was in the service and I wanted to go. In the summer of 1942, I volunteered for the draft.

Lucky enough to get into army weather, I went through the schools for observers and forecasters at Chanute Field, spent a couple of years doing weather for pilot-training schools in New Mexico, and finally got overseas in the spring of 1945 to forecast tropical weather for the marine air groups harassing the Japanese bypassed in the Northern Solomons.

By August 7, the day of the bomb, I was stationed on Emirau, "the Isle of Storms," north of Rabaul. Another science fiction fan brought me the news that an atomic bomb had been dropped on Japan. So far as I could tell, nobody else on the island had any notion what it meant, but he and I knew something about the atom; we had even read prophetic stories about atomic war in the science fiction magazines, as early as H. G. Wells's *War in the Air*, published in 1913.

I wrote in a diary that "atomic power threatens to upset the old world in unpredictable ways. . . . Man must increase his stature somewhat, as the alternative to self-destruction." The upset, of course, has happened. As for the alternative, at least we are still alive.

Certainly, the bomb changed science fiction. Before the war, people had been generally optimistic about the promises of science and continued human progress toward a brighter future, in spite of the dark forecasts of such seers as Wells. Suddenly, all such confidence was shattered. Campbell's "golden age" had been inspired by his grand vision of an unlimited human future; after the war, such great hopes were hard to keep alive. Though Campbell carried stoutly on at *Analog* for another quarter-century, other brilliant editors appeared to challenge him with darker but distinguished fiction in great new magazines.

In the urgency of war, I had been taken by air out to the islands; the return trip was not so hurried. I came back from Manila on a troop ship, twenty-eight days aboard. We landed at Portland; I was discharged a few days later at Fort McArthur, in California.

The war had been more good than bad for me. Meteorology is an interesting science; forecasting weather was a challenging and responsible job. A different sort of challenge then, before we had cameras on space satellites. Tropical islands had always fascinated me, and I had touched a dozen of them. The best part of it, I think, was the new faith I had found in my fellow Americans. Transferred a good many times from unit to unit, I had always soon found loyal new friends.

Getting adjusted to peace again proved harder than getting adjusted to the army. Writing is a lonely enterprise, every new story a set of new problems, and not every idea works. I missed those army friends, and keeping alive was suddenly a very different, if still familiar problem.

In Los Angeles, I looked up Leigh Brackett. We had a good visit, but she was now a busy and successful film writer, doing scripts for Howard Hawks, working with the likes of William Faulkner and John Wayne and Bogart and Bacall. Her career, I felt, had moved far ahead of mine.

I tried and failed to find Dr. Tidd, whom I

recalled as a good friend as well as a physician. His name was gone from the phone books, and forty years had gone by before an inquiry to Menningers got us back in touch. He was retired by then, after a rewarding career. We had a cordial correspondence, but he died before I was able to see him again.

Back at the typewriter in New Mexico, my first project was a story about the humanoids, little black man-shaped robots designed in the aftermath of a terrible war "to serve and obey and guard men from harm." Doing that too well, they suffocate their creators with too much care. The best invention, they have become the worst invention.

That was bleak pessimism about our technology and ourselves. A bleaker pessimism, in fact, than I wanted to admit. In the beginning, I planned for my heroes to stop or destroy the too-efficient robots. I soon realized that they were here forever, self-protected against all tampering. In despair, I left the story to plot "The Equalizer," about another paradoxically benign invention, a simple new weapon that liberates all mankind from any tyranny because no owner of it can be coerced.

Cheered by the success of that, I returned to replot the story of my rebel humanoids as another novelette, "With Folded Hands." Optimist that he had been, Campbell liked its tragic tone and asked for a sequel, which became *The Humanoids*, my most often translated and reprinted novel.

I have come since to see it as another unconscious allegory. The humanoids, I think, can be read as symbolic of society. By restraining my rebel individualists, they can stand for the massed social forces of the family, the school, the church, the company, the law, and even the opinions of our peers, which all act in unison to trim our impulsive wings and drive us into our various refuges of compromise and conformity.

Those stories had gone rather well, but I wanted to escape the isolation of my little shack on the ranch. When the novel was finished, I moved into town to take a new job as wire editor on the *Portales News-Tribune*. The editor, Gordon Greaves, was an old college friend sympathetic to my need for a change.

The change in lifestyle came faster than I had expected. In Portales, I found Blanche Harp, once the Blanche Slaten I had known and admired long ago, during my second year at that rural school. Married and divorced some years before, she had raised two children on the small income from a children's clothing shop. Our first date was July 8, 1947; on August 15 we were married in her mother's home.

"Blanche, from her passport picture when we went overseas," 1965

We were together thirty-seven years, until her death on January 5, 1985, after a car accident. A good marriage, and certainly a welcome and rewarding change in my life. I got on well with the children, Adele, recently married and soon to be a mother, and her athletic younger brother, Keigm. I came to love them both.

The half a lifetime since I rediscovered Blanche is not easy to sum up, but I must make some attempt. Her family was large and convivial. I got used to huge family gatherings, commonly with a feast. We lived in a small house her parents owned until we could build a new house of our own, still my home after nearly forty years. I helped with the housework and lent a hand at the shop when I could. A life of mutual aid and trust.

I stayed at the paper for the rest of the year, until the old allure of science fiction grew too strong to resist. Though I had enjoyed the job and was offered a raise in pay, I quit and went back to writing, working at home.

Science fiction had been confined to the low-paying pulp magazines, but that had begun to change as young fans grew up, went to school, earned money of their own. Science fiction was suddenly in the movies and on TV. Book markets at last were

"Our daughter, Adele Lovorn"

opening. Small presses began asking to reprint my old pulp serials. Simon and Schuster brought out *The Humanoids.* I wrote another "seetee" novel, and then *Dragon's Island.* I still recall that with some pride because of the phrase "genetic engineering," which I invented for the epigraph. Prophetic in a sense, the story was published in 1951, a couple of years before Watson and Crick announced that they had decoded the double helix.

Yet, for me, writing has seldom been easy. I worked for months on a project called *Mindsmith* that I sold to Simon and Schuster but finally had to abandon. I began to feel that change was leaving me behind. Still at home with Campbell's *Analog,* I saw no place for me in the important new magazines, Horace Gold's *Galaxy* and Tony Boucher's *Magazine of Fantasy and Science Fiction.* Gold was presenting darker and more enigmatic futures than Campbell; Boucher cared more for wit and polish than for science.

Feeling uneasy about my own future in science fiction, I was sitting at the typewriter one day in the fall of 1951, grappling with some story problem. The phone rang. Ama Barker was on the line. She was the editor, she told me, of the Sunday edition of the *New York Daily News.* She asked if I would come to New York to create a comic strip. I had never considered

writing a comic strip, or even read many of them, but I caught my breath and said I would.

The call had come from an ironic set of circumstances. That was back at the dawn of TV. The circulation of the Sunday *News* had been close to three million, but people were suddenly turning on the tube instead of buying the paper. Reviewing one of my "seetee" novels, the *New York Times* had rather snidely said that it read like a space-adventure strip. Somebody at the *News* thought a new comic strip might repair that ailing circulation. The editors, searching for somebody to write a space-adventure strip, happened to read the review. Instead of searching through the twenty-five thousand unsolicited submissions coming in every year, they called me.

The check for expenses arrived. I went to New York to meet my new associates: Ama Barker, John Gardner, her assistant who was to edit the project, and Lee Elias, the selected artist. Working with Milt Caniff on "Terry and the Pirates," Elias had developed a sure hand for character and action. I was allowed to call Chester Gould, the creator of "Dick Tracy," for advice on plots. We spent seven weeks in the huge city room of the *News,* working out space settings and story lines. Before Christmas I was back at home again, to write the weekly strips for Gardner to pass along to Elias.

We called the strip "Beyond Mars." It ran for three years on the back page of the color wraparound that had "Dick Tracy" on the front. The pay was a hundred dollars a week. The dollar not yet much inflated, that was comfortably more than I had ever earned. I enjoyed the money and the work, even though I often had to compromise my own ideas to fit what Elias wanted to draw and what John Gardner wanted to print.

Blanche and I met exciting new people when she came with me on another trip to New York. We attended her first science fiction convention, a startling new experience for her. Science fiction, confined so long to its own narrow literary ghetto, had become a sort of subculture, a little world apart with its own loyalties and friendships, its own traditions and songs and slang. A world where I had found a welcome, but strange to her.

I had cherished giddy notions that writing the strip had become my lifetime career. Sadly, however, at least for the *News,* "Beyond Mars" turned out to be no answer to TV. After three years, the syndicate killed it. A hard blow for me, because it had let me drift farther than ever out of the new currents of science fiction. Writing it, I had found little undivided time for anything else, though I had done successful collaborations with Jim Gunn and Fred Pohl. More

Jack Williamson, Jim Gunn, and Fred Pohl on the campus of Eastern New Mexico University: "Jim and Fred were here as the first speakers at the Williamson Lectureship, established when I retired from the faculty in 1977."

than ever, I felt that the science fiction field had run away from me.

Anxious to replace those regular checks, I returned to academe. While the strip was running, I had begun taking a few courses in electronics and math at Eastern New Mexico University, my hometown school. With credit for my army weather courses, I enrolled for the master's degree, taught for a year as a graduate assistant, received the degree, and taught again for two years at New Mexico Military Institute.

During the summers, I began work toward the doctorate at the University of Colorado at Boulder. Loyally, Blanche stayed at home to keep the shop alive while I spent another year in graduate school there. Teaching a class to help pay expenses, I thoroughly enjoyed everything: the Colorado landscape, my fellow students and the professors I knew, the great literature we read.

At the end of that year, I was lucky enough to get a place on the English faculty at Eastern. I taught there until the crowding years caught up with me in 1977. A good career; far richer, in fact, than a lifetime of grinding out a comic strip might have been. Since Eastern is small, I got to teach a wide variety of courses, ranging all the way from the inevitable freshman English to James Joyce and linguistics and the history of literary criticism.

One good course was science fiction. Creeping out of that pulp ghetto, it had begun to win a narrow beachhead in college offerings. There are still snob-bish critics who look down on it, even though the great works of Wells and Huxley and a few others are still acceptable from the days before it fell into its scorned estate. Able new writers keep emerging; the best science fiction written today, I think, is as good as the best of anything else.

My own science fiction course, begun in 1964, was one of the first. A three-hour course at the junior level, I taught it almost every semester for a dozen years, every now and then later. Students like it. To offer a helping hand to other teachers who meet resistance from reluctant curriculum committees, I gathered and published descriptions of similar courses in other schools. The movement has grown. The Science Fiction Research Association, founded twenty years ago, now has four or five hundred members, most of them teaching science fiction. It's a new literary genre, most of us feel, vital to today's education because it accepts and illuminates the fact that technology is changing all our world.

Those were good times for Blanche and me. She kept the shop a good many years, but we still made long trips overseas during the summers, finally reaching all the continents. When the grandchildren came, and great-grandchildren, we enjoyed them. Retired from teaching, I found a new literary agent and went back to full-time writing: new collaborations with Frederik Pohl; another novel about my first popular heroes, the defenders of mankind in the Legion of Space; another novel about those too-zealous little robots, the humanoids, who demonstrated once again that their excessive protection of future humanity cannot be curbed.

I began judging stories for the Writers of the Future contest. It is a controversial thing, because it was funded by L. Ron Hubbard, founder of the Church of Scientology, which has as many critics as adherents. I am no scientologist myself. I regard Hubbard as a brilliantly successful con artist, and I suspect that the contest was set up in an effort to polish his clouded image. Yet I have found his followers generally dedicated and sincere. The contest is fairly run and the prizes are generous. I know a good many young writers whom it has launched into promising careers. On balance, I think it is worth support.

Time seemed kind enough to Blanche and me until that tragic accident in 1985. We were driving to the airport that morning to begin a cruise to Brazil. I was at the wheel. To me, the accident was a dazing blow from nowhere. I still don't know just how it happened. I must have been at fault. Blanche and I were wearing seat belts. I didn't know at first that we were badly hurt, but she died that afternoon of internal injuries.

It seemed then like the end of my own life. The emotional wound will never heal, but physically I had been merely battered. In a wheelchair for a week and half-disabled for months, I made a slow recovery, now more complete than I had any right to expect. Though I live alone, I have kind friends and loving relatives. Our daughter, Adele, lives near, and she tries to look after me.

Though the years have slowed me down, I keep busy. I am writing steadily, now on a new computer. Fred Pohl and I have just published a new collaboration and have planned yet another. I have a novel of my own, too long in progress. Still doing a bit of travel, I spent part of last summer in central Europe.

I am still teaching occasional classes at the university, and my friends there have been generous to me. The science fiction collection, which began with the donation of my own library and working papers, has been christened the Jack Williamson Science Fiction Library.

I am eighty in 1988, as these words are written,

Jack Williamson, 1986

and *Amazing Stories* has bought a new story to be published on the sixtieth anniversary of my first. The university is observing those occasions with a "Williamson Year," a more elaborate celebration than I feel entitled to.

Ever since childhood, I have wanted to write. Since I discovered science fiction, that has been what I wanted to write. As well as I could, I have written it. I can wish that I had been born a better writer, yet I feel lucky. In spite of hard knocks, life has been good. In the nature of the case, it can't go on forever. Yet, however and whenever it may end, I have few regrets.

What more is there to say?

BIBLIOGRAPHY

Fiction:

The Girl from Mars, with Miles J. Breuer. New York: Stellar, 1929.

Lady in Danger. London: Utopian, 1945.

The Legion of Space (illustrated by A. J. Donnell). Reading, Pa.: Fantasy Press, 1947; London: Sphere, 1977.

Darker than You Think. (Illustrated by Edd Cartier) Reading, Pa.: Fantasy Press, 1948; London: Sphere, 1976; (illustrated by David J. Klein) New York: Bluejay, 1984.

The Humanoids. New York: Simon & Schuster, 1949; London: Museum Press, 1953.

The Cometeers [and] *One against the Legion* (illustrated by E. Cartier). Reading, Pa.: Fantasy Press, 1950.

The Green Girl. New York: Avon, 1950.

Seetee Shock, under pseudonym Will Stewart. New York: Simon & Schuster, 1950; also published under name Jack Williamson. New York: Lancer, 1968; London: Mayflower, 1969.

Dragon's Island. New York: Simon & Schuster, 1951; London: Museum Press, 1954; also published as *The Not-Men.* New York: Tower Publications, 1968.

Seetee Ship, under pseudonym Will Stewart. New York: Gnome, 1951; also published under name Jack Williamson. New York: Lancer, 1968; London: Mayflower, 1969.

The Legion of Time [and] *After World's End.* Reading, Pa.: Fantasy Press, 1952; also published as *Two Complete Novels: The Legion of Time; After World's End.* New York: Galaxy, 1963.

The Crucible of Power: Three Science Fiction Novels, with Norman L. Knight and Norvell W. Page, edited by Martin Greenberg. London: Bodley Head, 1953.

Undersea Quest, with Frederik Pohl. New York: Gnome, 1954; London: Dobson, 1966.

Dome around America. New York: Ace Books, 1955.

Star Bridge, with James E. Gunn. New York: Gnome, 1955; London: Sidgwick & Jackson, 1978.

Undersea Fleet, with F. Pohl. New York: Gnome, 1956; London: Dobson, 1967.

Undersea City, with F. Pohl. New York: Gnome, 1958; London: Dobson, 1968.

After World's End. London: Brown, Watson, 1961.

The Legion of Time. London: Brown, Watson, 1961.

The Trial of Terra. New York: Ace Books, 1962.

The Reefs of Space, with F. Pohl. New York: Ballantine, 1963; London: Dobson, 1965.

Golden Blood. New York: Lancer, 1964; (illustrated by Steve Fabian and J. Allen St. John) Edgewater, Md.: Tamerlane, 1978.

The Reign of Wizardry. New York: Lancer, 1964; London: Sphere, 1981.

The Cometeers. New York: Pyramid, 1967; London: Sphere, 1967.

One against the Legion. New York: Pyramid, 1967; London: Sphere, 1967.

Starchild, with F. Pohl. New York: Ballantine, 1965; London: Dobson, 1966.

Bright New Universe. New York: Ace Books, 1967; London: Sidgwick & Jackson, 1969.

One against the Legion [and] *Nowhere Near.* New York: Pyramid, 1967.

Three Stories, by Murray Leinster, Jack Williamson, and John Wyndham. Garden City, N.Y.: Doubleday, 1967; also published as *A Sense of Wonder: Three Science Fiction Stories.* London: Sidgwick & Jackson, 1967; also published as *The Moon Era: Three Stories by Murray Leinster, Jack Williamson, and John Wyndham.* New York: Modern Literary Editions, 1979.

Trapped in Space (illustrated by Robert Amundsen). Garden City, N.Y.: Doubleday, 1968.

The Pandora Effect (short stories). New York: Ace Books, 1969.

Rogue Star, with F. Pohl. New York: Ballantine, 1969; London: Dobson, 1972.

People Machines (short stories). New York: Ace Books, 1969.

The Moon Children. New York: Putnam, 1972; Yorkshire, England: Elmfield Press, 1972.

The Early Williamson (short stories). Garden City, N.Y.: Doubleday, 1975; London: Sphere, 1978.

Farthest Star: The Saga of Cuckoo, with F. Pohl. New York: Ballantine, 1975; also published as *The Saga of Cuckoo.* Garden City, N.Y.: Doubleday, 1983; also published as *Wall around a Star: The Saga of Cuckoo.* New York: Ballantine, 1983.

The Power of Blackness. New York: Berkley Publishing, 1976; London: Sphere, 1978.

Dreadful Sleep. Chicago: R. Weinberg, 1977.

One against the Legion. London: Sphere, 1977.

The Starchild Trilogy, with F. Pohl (contains *Starchild, The Reefs of Space,* and *Rogue Star*). Garden City, N.Y.: Doubleday, 1977; Harmondsworth, England: Penguin, 1980.

The Best of Jack Williamson (short stories). New York: Ballantine, 1978.

Brother to Demons, Brother to Gods. Indianapolis: Bobbs-Merrill, 1979; London: Sphere, 1981.

The Alien Intelligence (illustrated by Paul Morey and Kenneth Hafer). New Orleans: P. D. A. Enterprises, 1980.

The Humanoid Touch. New York: Holt, 1980; London: Sphere, 1982.

Three from the Legion (contains *The Cometeers, The Legion of Space,* and *One Against the Legion*). Garden City, N.Y.: Doubleday, 1981.

Manseed. New York: Ballantine, 1982; London: Sphere, 1986.

The Queen of the Legion. New York: Pocket Books, 1983; London: Sphere, 1984.

Lifeburst. New York: Ballantine, 1984; London: Sphere, 1987.

Firechild. New York: Bluejay, 1986; London: Methuen, 1988.

Land's End, with F. Pohl. New York: Tor Books, 1988.

Nonfiction:

H. G. Wells: Critic of Progress. Baltimore: Mirage Press, 1973.

Talking, Listening, and Learning: The Development of Children's Language, with Janet Ede. London: Longman, 1980.

Wonder's Child: My Life in Science Fiction (autobiography). New York: Bluejay, 1984.

Editor of:

Teaching Science Fiction: Education for Tomorrow. Philadelphia: Owlswick, 1980.

Cumulative Index

CUMULATIVE INDEX

For every reference that appears *in more than one essay,*
the name of the essayist is given before the volume and page number(s).

INDEX

INDEX

INDEX

INDEX